MANAGING AND USING INFORMATION SYSTEMS

EIGHTH EDITION

A STRATEGIC APPROACH

Keri E. Pearlson
MIT Sloan School of Management and KP Partners

Carol S. Saunders
University of Central Florida
University of Pretoria

Dennis F. Galletta
Katz Graduate School of Business
University of Pittsburgh, Pittsburgh, PA

WILEY

VICE PRESIDENT, CONTENT	Kristin Ford
DIRECTOR	Lise Johnson
EDITOR	Jennifer Manias
EDITORIAL ASSISTANT	Campbell McDonald
SENIOR MANAGING EDITOR	Judy Howarth
PRODUCTION EDITOR	Vijay Amirtha Raj David
MARKETING COORDINATOR	Jessica Spettoli
COVER PHOTO CREDIT	© lukpedclub/Getty Images

This book was set in 10/12 Times LT Std by Straive™.

Founded in 1807, John Wiley & Sons, Inc. has been a valued source of knowledge and understanding for more than 200 years, helping people around the world meet their needs and fulfill their aspirations. Our company is built on a foundation of principles that include responsibility to the communities we serve and where we live and work. In 2008, we launched a Corporate Citizenship Initiative, a global effort to address the environmental, social, economic, and ethical challenges we face in our business. Among the issues we are addressing are carbon impact, paper specifications and procurement, ethical conduct within our business and among our vendors, and community and charitable support. For more information, please visit our website: www.wiley.com/go/citizenship.

ISBN: 978-1-394-21544-7 (PBK)

Library of Congress Cataloging-in-Publication Data

LCCN 2023047402

The inside back cover will contain printing identification and country of origin if omitted from this page. In addition, if the ISBN on the back cover differs from the ISBN on this page, the one on the back cover is correct.

SKY10070749_032124

Philip Russell Saunders
March 16, 1977 – August 9, 2021

Russell Saunders had many loves. His greatest love, the love of his life, is his wife, Janel. He also loved family and friends, summiting Colorado 14ers, trying a new IPA with friends, and watching team ball games—especially basketball. His favorite holiday was March Madness. Russell helped us in researching the fourth edition of this textbook and he has a contribution in this, the 8th edition, which is dedicated to him.

PREFACE

Information technology and business are becoming inextricably interwoven. I don't think anybody can talk meaningfully about one without the talking about the other.

Bill Gates
Microsoft[1]

I'm not hiring MBA students for the technology you learn while in school, but for your ability to learn about, use and subsequently manage new technologies when you get out.

IT Executive
Federal Express[2]

Give me a fish and I eat for a day; teach me to fish and I eat for a lifetime.

Proverb

Managers do not have the luxury of abdicating participation in decisions regarding information systems (IS). Managers who choose to do so risk limiting their future business options. IS are at the heart of virtually every business interaction, process, and decision, especially when the vast penetration of the web over the last 25 years is considered. Mobile and social technologies, the Internet of Things, cloud computing, big data, generative artificial intelligence (AI), and business analytics have brought IS to an entirely new level within firms and between individuals in their personal lives. Managers who let someone else make decisions about their IS are abdicating responsibilities that concern the very foundation of their business. This is a textbook about managing and using information. It is written for current and future managers to introduce the broader implications of the impact of IS.

The first edition of this book was published over a quarter of a century ago. Information systems and technologies have changed significantly since the first edition, but the principles for managing and using information systems have, remarkably, stayed relatively constant. As with that initial book, the goal of this book continues to be assisting managers in becoming knowledgeable participants in IS decisions. Becoming a knowledgeable participant means learning the basics about information systems and feeling comfortable enough with information technology to ask questions. It does not mean having all the answers or having a deep understanding of all the technologies out in the world today. No text will provide managers everything they need to know to make important IS decisions. Some texts instruct on the basic technical background of IS. Others discuss applications and their life cycles. Some take a comprehensive view of the information systems (IS) [formerly called management information systems (MIS)] field and offer readers snapshots of current systems along with chapters describing how those technologies are designed, used, and integrated into business life.

This book takes a different approach. It is intended to provide the reader a foundation of basic concepts relevant to using and managing information and taking advantage of the tremendous opportunities that information technology is unlocking. This text is not intended to provide a comprehensive treatment on any one aspect of IS, for certainly each aspect is itself a topic of many books. This text is not intended to provide readers enough technological knowledge to make them IS experts. It is not intended to be a source of discussion of any particular technology. This text is written to help managers begin to form a point of view of how IS will help or hinder their organizations and create opportunities for them.

[1] Bill Gates, *Business @ the Speed of Thought* (New York: Warner Books, Inc. 1999).

[2] Private conversation with one of the authors.

The idea for this text grew out of discussions with colleagues in the IS area. Many instructors use a series of case studies, trade and popular press readings, and websites to teach their IS courses. Others simply rely on one of the classic texts, which include dozens of pages of diagrams, frameworks, and technologies. The initial idea for this text emerged from a core IS course taught at the business school at the University of Texas at Austin in 1999. That course was considered an "appetizer" course—a brief introduction into the world of IS for MBA students. The course had two main topics: using information and managing information. At the time, there was no text like this one; instead, students had to purchase thick reading packets made up of articles and case studies to provide the basic concepts. The course was structured to provide general MBA students enough knowledge of the IS field so that they could recognize opportunities to use the rapidly changing technologies available to them. The course was an appetizer to the menu of specialty courses, each of which went much more deeply into the various topics. But completion of the appetizer course meant that students were able to feel comfortable listening to, contributing to, and ultimately participating in IS decisions. Those needs still exist.

Today, many students are digital natives—people who have grown up using information technologies (IT) all their lives. They have never lived in a world without IT. Many have never had to function without a smartphone, and hence have instant access to information, in their pocket. That means that students come to their courses with significantly more knowledge about things such as tablets, apps, personal computers, smartphones, texting, the web, social networking, online purchasing, chatbots, embedded AI, and social media than their counterparts in school just a few years ago. This is a significant trend, and it will continue; students will be increasingly knowledgeable about the personal use of technologies. That knowledge has begun to change the corporate environment. Today's digital natives expect to find at least the functionality they have at home everywhere they go, but especially in their work locations. At the same time, these users expect to be able to work in ways that take advantage of the technologies they have grown to depend on for social interaction, collaboration, and innovation. We believe that a foundation is still needed for managing and using IS, but we understand that the assumptions and knowledge base of today's students is significantly different than those of previous generations.

Also, different today is the vast amount of information amassed by firms, sometimes called the "big data" problem. Organizations have figured out that there is an enormous amount of data around their processes, their interactions with customers, their products, and their suppliers. These organizations also recognize that with the increase in communities and social interactions on the web, there is additional pressure to collect and analyze vast amounts of unstructured information contained in these conversations to train generative AI apps and identify trends, needs and projections. We believe that today's managers face an increasing amount of pressure to understand what is being said by those inside and outside their corporations and to join those conversations reasonably and responsibly. That is significantly different from just a few years ago.

Each chapter of this book begins with a navigational guide, a short case study, and the basic language for a set of important management issues. These are followed by a set of managerial concerns related to the topic. Each chapter concludes with a summary, key terms, a set of discussion questions, and case studies.

The introduction to this text explores the argument presented in this preface: managers must be knowledgeable participants in making IS decisions. The first few chapters build a basic framework of relationships among business strategy, IS strategy, and organizational strategy and explore the links among them. The strategy chapters are followed by ones on work design and business processes that discuss the use of IS. General managers also need some foundation on how IT is managed if they are to successfully discuss their business needs with IT professionals who can help them. Therefore, the remaining chapters describe the basics of information architecture and infrastructure, IT security, the business of IT, the governance of the IS organization and platforms, IS sourcing, project management, business analytics/AI, and relevant ethical issues.

Given the acceleration of new technologies available to managers and accompanying increase in security vulnerabilities, readers will find a focus on digital transformation throughout and four chapters with major revisions in this eighth edition of the text. In particular, this edition offers a significantly updated chapter on IS security with two new end of chapter cases, as well as a new introductory case on the Colonial Pipeline ransomware cyberattack. Second, the material on analytics, big data, and AI (especially generative AI) has been extensively updated to reflect the growing importance of these topics. A third chapter that has undergone a major revision is the one on the design of work, which now reflects the tremendous changes in the workplace created by the COVID-19 pandemic, algorithmic management, robots, AI and generative AI. The end of chapter case explores remote work before, during, and after the COVID-19 pandemic at Colorado Division of Banking. Fourth, the architecture and infrastructure chapter has undergone a major overhaul and now offers architectural and infrastructure happenings at Lego and a new Australian bank, Judo, as intriguing enticements to read and use to understand the chapter.

As with every edition of this text, it's the cases that seem to get out of date most quickly, and new examples are needed to put theory into context. This edition has new or significantly updated cases in every chapter. They have contemporary contexts, raise current issues, and discuss new concepts. And like the seventh edition, every chapter begins with a navigation guide to help readers understand the flow of key topics in the chapter.

No text in the field of IS is completely current. The process of writing the text coupled with the publication process makes a book somewhat out-of-date prior to delivery to its audience. With that in mind, this text is written to provide the "timeless" elements of using and managing information. Looking back at the success of our earlier editions of this text, we have seen that our frameworks and approaches support our initial vision that there are key foundational ideas in this area to assist managers.

A Book Companion Site accompanies this text and provides teaching and learning resources, including the Instructor Manual, Test Bank, and PowerPoint presentations. Visit www.wiley.com/go/pearlson/informationsystems8e. A multitude of additional resources are available on the author-created community hub at http://pearlsonandsaunders.com. The Hub provides faculty members who adopt the text additional resources organized by chapter, including recent news items with teaching suggestions, videos with usage suggestions, blog posts and discussions from the community, class activities, additional cases, cartoons, and more. Supplemental materials, including longer cases from all over the globe, can be found on the web.

Although this text is complete in and of itself, learning is enhanced by combining the chapters with the even more current articles and cases. Faculty are encouraged to read the news items on the faculty Hub before each class in case one might be relevant to the topic of the day. Students are encouraged to search the web for examples related to topics and current events, experience new technologies like generative AI and bring them into the discussions of the issues at hand.

Who should read this book? IS students will be able to use the book's readings and concepts at the beginning of their journey to become informed and successful businesspeople. General managers interested in participating in IS decisions will find this a good reference resource for the language and concepts of IS. Managers in the IS field will find the book a good resource for beginning to understand the general manager's view of how IS affect business decisions.

The information revolution is here. Where do you fit in?

KERI E. PEARLSON, CAROL S. SAUNDERS, AND DENNIS F. GALLETTA

ACKNOWLEDGMENTS

As we come up on the 25th anniversary of the first edition of this text, we are reminded of the many people who have helped us with this book and all the previous editions. Books of this nature are written only with the support of many individuals. We would like to personally thank everyone who helped with this text. Although we've made every attempt to include everyone who helped make this book a reality, there is always the possibility of unintentionally leaving some out. We apologize in advance if that is the case here.

We have been blessed with the help of our colleagues in this and in previous editions of the book. They helped us by writing cases and reviewing the text. Thank you to Kara Hunter and Ricardo Giardiello, who contributed to the case on remote work at the Colorado Division of Banking in the design of work chapter of this edition. Our thanks continue to go out to many who helped us with this and earlier editions including Rajiv Kohli, Jonathan Trower, Espen Andersen, Janis Gogan, Ashok Rho, Yvonne Lederer Antonucci, E. Jose Proenca, Bruce Rollier, Dave Oliver, Celia Romm, Ed Watson, D. Guiter, S. Vaught, Kala Saravanamuthu, Ron Murch, John Greenwod, Tom Rohleder, Sam Lubbe, Thomas Kern, Mark Dekker, Anne Rutkowski, Kathy Hurtt, Kay Nelson, Janice Sipior, Craig Tidwell, Russell Saunders, and John Butler. The book would not have been started were it not for the initial suggestion of a wonderful editor in 1999 at John Wiley & Sons, Beth Lang Golub. Also, although we cannot thank them by name, we greatly appreciate the comments of the anonymous reviewers who have made a mark on this and previous editions.

We also appreciate the help of our current editor, Jennifer Manias. Special thanks go to Judy Howarth who helped us with the revision process and who was always there to ably work out the kinks. We also appreciate the help of all the staff at Wiley who have made this edition a reality.

We would be remiss if we did not also thank Lars Linden for the work he did in building the Pearlson and Saunders Faculty Hub for this book. Our vision included a web-based community for discussing teaching ideas and posting current articles that supplement this text. Lars made that vision into a reality. Thank you, Lars!

We also want to acknowledge and thank pbwiki.com. Without its incredible and free wiki, we would have been relegated to e-mailing drafts of chapters back and forth, or saving countless files in an external drop box without any opportunity to include explanations or status messages. We found that having used the wiki for our previous editions, we were able to get up and running much faster than if we had to start over without the platform.

From Keri: Thank you to my daughter, Hana, a graduate of Tulane University with an emphasis in finance, data science, and analytics, and now a consultant at EY. Over the years, she has watched and encouraged my professional endeavors in so many ways. But now she's also a professional in this area and her comments and suggestions for this edition were even more insightful. She was particularly helpful and provided guidance for the analytics chapter! Thank you also to Dr. Alan Gustman, who provided daily support and a very insightful sounding board throughout this project. Writing a book like this happens in the white space of our lives—the time in between everything else going on. My family and friends listened to ideas, made suggestions, and celebrated the book's completion. I am very lucky to have each of them in my life.

From Carol: I would like to thank my co-authors and friends, Keri Pearlson and Dennis Galletta, for making this edition something special. Rusty, thank you for putting your excellent editing skills to work on this book. Thank you also being my compass and my release valve. I couldn't do it without you. Paraphrasing the words of an Alan Jackson song ("Work in Progress"): I may not be what you want me to be, but I'm trying really hard. Just be patient because I'm *still* a work in progress. I love you, Kristin, Russell, and Janel very much!

From Dennis: I'd like to acknowledge my family, who lacked my presence during several months while writing new material for this 8th edition. I'd like to thank my wife Carole, daughters Christy and Lauren, and sons-in-law Matt and Jacob. Of course, deserving special mention are my four grandkids Grace,

Matthew, Claire, and Emma, for whom I promise to do more babysitting now that this project is complete for this next cycle. My dear Grace, I won't need to babysit you, but very soon I'll be watching you look for your car keys and worrying sick about your safe return. I would also like to thank Keri Pearlson and Carol Saunders for allowing me to participate in the authorship of my favorite book on Information Systems starting from the 6th edition. I used this book in my core IS course in our Executive MBA program for many years and several expressions of praise from students over the years reinforced my passion for the book's approach. Thanks to all the adopters of 8e, and when technology turns the world upside down again sooner than we can imagine, we hope you will stick with us through 9e and beyond!

About the Authors

Dr. Keri E. Pearlson is the Executive Director of the Cybersecurity at MIT Sloan (CAMS) research consortium and President of KP Partners, an advisory services firm working with business leaders on issues related to the strategic use of information systems (IS) and organizational design. She is an entrepreneur, teacher, researcher, consultant, and thought leader. Dr. Pearlson has held various positions in academia and industry. She has been a member of the faculty at the Graduate School of Business at the University of Texas at Austin where she taught management IS courses to MBAs and executives and at Babson College where she helped design the popular IS course for the Fast Track MBA program. Dr. Pearlson has held positions at the Harvard Business School, International Institute of Analytics (IIA), CSC, nGenera (formerly the Concours Group), AT&T, and Hughes Aircraft Company. She was named the Leader of the Year by the national Society of Information Management (SIM) in 2014. Dr. Pearlson is coauthor of *Zero Time: Providing Instant Customer Value—Every Time, All the Time* (John Wiley, 2000). Her work has been published in numerous places including *Harvard Business Review, Sloan Management Review, Wall Street Journal, Academy of Management Executive*, and *Information Resources Management Journal*. Many of her case studies have been published by Harvard Business Publishing and are used all over the world. Dr. Pearlson holds a Doctorate in Business Administration (DBA) in Management Information Systems from the Harvard Business School and both a Master's Degree in Industrial Engineering Management and a Bachelor's Degree in Applied Mathematics from Stanford University.

Dr. Carol S. Saunders is Professor Emerita at the University of Central Florida, a Schoeller Senior Fellow at the Friedrich-Alexander University of Erlangen-Nuremberg, Germany, and Extraordinary Professor at the University of Pretoria, South Africa. She served as General Conference Chair of the International Conference on Information Systems (ICIS) in 1999, Program Co-Chair of the Americas Conference on Information Systems (AMCIS) in 2015, and the Association for Information Systems (AIS) Vice President of Publications from 2016 to 2019. Dr. Saunders was the Chair of the ICIS Executive Committee in 2000. For three years, she served as Editor-in-Chief of *MIS Quarterly*. Dr. Saunders has been recognized for her lifetime achievements by the AIS with a LEO award and by the Communication, Digital Technology and Organization (previously OCIS) Division of the Academy of Management. She is a Fellow of the AIS. Dr. Saunders' research interests include the impact of IS on power and communication, overload, virtual teams, time, sourcing, control, algorithmic management, digital business models, co-opetition, and interorganizational linkages. Her research is published in a number of journals including *MIS Quarterly, Information Systems Research, Journal of the AIS, Journal of MIS, Communications of the ACM, Journal of Strategic Information Systems, European Journal of Information Systems, Journal of Information Technology, Information & Organization, Academy of Management Journal, Academy of Management Review, Communications Research*, and *Organization Science*. In 2019, she and A-F Rutkowski co-authored the book entitled *Emotional and Cognitive Overload: The Dark Side of Information Technology*.

Dr. Dennis F. Galletta is Thomas H. O'Brien Professor of Information Systems at the Katz Graduate School of Business, University of Pittsburgh, where he directs the PhD and DBA programs. He also won a Provost's mentoring award for working with doctoral students. He taught summer IS Management graduate courses in Harvard's College of Arts and Sciences (2009-2019). He obtained his doctorate from the University of Minnesota and is a CPA. For the Association of Information Systems (AIS), he served as president and, like Dr. Saunders, is a Fellow and won an AIS LEO lifetime achievement award. He also served in leadership roles for the International Conference (ICIS): Program Co-Chair (Las Vegas) and Conference Co-Chair (Shanghai); and for the Americas Conference (AMCIS), as Program Co-Chair (Tampa) and Inaugural Conference Chair (Pittsburgh), with several paperless "firsts" in the field back in 1995, including online registration, submissions, reviews, payment, placement, and website storage of all papers in advance. He served as ICIS Treasurer and Chair of the Executive Committee. He taught IS courses on the Fall 1999 Semester at Sea voyage. He established the concept of Special Interest Groups in AIS. In 2014, he won an Emerald Citation of Excellence for a coauthored article that reached the top 50 in the fields of management, business, and economics. His current research addresses usability and behavioral security issues such as phishing, protection motivation, and antecedents of security-related decision making. He has published his research in *Management Science, MIS Quarterly (MISQ), Information Systems Research (ISR), Journal of MIS (JMIS), European Journal of Information Systems, Journal of the AIS, Communications of the ACM, Information and Organization, DataBase,* and *Decision Sciences* and in proceedings of conferences such as ICIS, AMCIS, and the Hawaii International Conference on Systems Sciences. He was recently a senior editor at *MISQ* and is an editorial board member at *JMIS; and was* founding Co-editor in Chief for *AIS Transactions on HCI*, senior editor at *Journal of AIS*, and associate editor for *MISQ* and *ISR*. He won an *MISQ* Developmental Associate Editor Award and is currently on the Pre-eminent Scholars Board of *DataBase*.

CONTENTS

Introduction

We live in a world that has undergone a phenomenal amount of transformation, much of which has been induced by information technology (IT). Every organization today is dependent on information technology. Computers ushered in a new age, following the agricultural and industrial revolutions. The impact was primarily felt by business and governments because these organizations were able to afford them. The Internet was started in 1969 when the first message was sent over the United States (US) Department of Defense's Advance Research Projects Agency Network (ARPANET). But use of the Internet didn't really take off until the turn of the millennium when a number of technologies were combined to bring immense capabilities to people in their homes around the globe: personal computers with easy-to-use interfaces, the world wide web (www) and Web browsers. When the US government lifted restrictions on the commercial use of the Internet, the floodgates opened and companies like the nascent Amazon perceived—and grasped—the tremendous potential of e-commerce.

Another truly astounding societal transformation came with the introduction of Apple's iPhone in 2006. The iPhone was not just a phone; It made it possible to get to the Internet, take pictures, access social media sites, and do thousands of other functions using applications loaded onto the iPhone (and soon other smartphones) around the globe. In addition to that, iPhones and other smartphones are mobile, easy to take virtually everywhere, and don't require shutting down and restarting between sessions. Now owners can even give their commands verbally to their smartphones, which will answer them verbally. Just look around and it's obvious how smartphones truly have transformed the way people live.

Businesses have been caught up in these waves of transformation and are now undergoing their own **digital transformation** by using IT to redefine (and not just support) their business strategies and identify themselves in a new way. Digitalization (another word for digital transformation) is changing the way businesses operate to the very core. It has become imperative for managers to understand how IT and Information Systems (IS) are at the heart of digital transformation. Even if their companies aren't undergoing a transformation, others around them are. Managers need to understand and participate in the IS decisions of their organizations.

Why do managers need to understand and participate in the IS decisions of their organizations? After all, most corporations maintain entire departments dedicated to the management of IS. These departments are staffed by highly skilled professionals devoted to the field of technology. Shouldn't managers rely on experts to analyze all aspects of IS and to make the best decisions for the organization, especially those involving digitalization? The answer to that question is an emphatic "no."

Managing information is a critical skill for success in today's business environment. In the past, making better management decisions was the major focus of IT; Management Information Systems (MIS) departments worked within well-defined, rather static boundaries with rather well-defined roles; IS strategy was often seen as supporting business strategy. Today IS strategy is often THE business strategy, and if not, every business must at least consider developing a digital business strategy. For example, it is no longer an issue for organizations to decide *whether* they want to collect and manage large amounts of information, develop websites and platforms, and engage in social networks and ecosystems; but rather *how* to initiate, manage, and nurture all those evolving channels—and more, such as sensors in equipment, wearable health fitness devices, and other systems and things in which IT is embedded. A successful manager continuously re-evaluates the company's vision in light of new opportunities and threats from IT. A successful manager realizes that customers, colleagues, trading partners, and platform partners have ubiquitous access to sophisticated technologies, and all, perhaps unreasonably, expect nearly instant responses in a business world that is more dynamic and complex than ever before.

Most importantly, change can come from unforeseen directions. New information-based products have emerged that have endangered businesses that were managed as if they were going to last forever. One needs to only examine how Uber and Lyft suddenly led to sharp reductions in taxicab use, how Amazon has shrunk the number of brick-and-mortar stores such as Sears and K-Mart, how music streaming has all but eliminated music stores, and how online video streaming has challenged cable television companies.[1] **Generative AI** (i.e., a type of AI using machine learning that can produce new content in response to prompts), such as embodied by OpenAI's ChatGPT, Google's Bard, and Microsoft's Bing AI, appears to be on the crest of another wave of transformation so massive that some claim it will be the Artificial Intelligence Revolution. Generative AI promises untold opportunities and threats. Hence, understanding how to manage and use IS is no longer a luxury; it is a necessity to understand how to take advantage of IT, rather than to become a victim of IT.

The use of SMACIT (social media, mobile, analytics, cloud, and Internet of Things) implies that individuals now manage a "personal IS" and make decisions about usage, data, and applications. Many even manage their own wireless network at home. Doesn't that give them insight into managing IS in corporations? Students often think they are experts in corporate IS because of their personal experience with consumer technology. Although there is a glimmer of truth in that perspective, it's a very dangerous perspective for managers to take. Certainly, knowing about interesting apps, being able to use a variety of technologies for different personal purposes, and being familiar with the ups and downs of networking for their personal IS provide some experience that is useful in the corporate setting. But in a corporate setting, IS must be ready for use by an enterprise and beyond. These systems must be scalable for a large number of employees and customers, often simultaneously; they must be delivered in an appropriate manner for the enterprise; and they must be managed with corporate guidelines and appropriate governmental regulations in mind. Issues such as security, privacy, risk, support, and architecture take on new meaning within an enterprise, and someone has to manage them. Enterprise-level management and use of IS require a unique perspective and a different skill set.

At the time of this writing, four of the five world's most innovative[2] and largest companies in terms of market capitalization are technology companies (in order of market capitalization): Apple, Inc., Microsoft, Alphabet, Inc. (parent company of Google), and Amazon.com, Inc.[3] Two (Alphabet and Amazon.com) began as small online startups less than three decades ago.

Google (now listed as its holding company "Alphabet") built a business that has revolutionized the way information is found. Google began in 1999 as a basic search company but its managers quickly learned that its unique business model could be leveraged for future success in seemingly unrelated areas. The company changed the way people think about web content by making it available in a searchable format with incredibly fast response time and in a host of languages. Further, Google's AdWords keyword-targeted advertising program and Google Analytics revolutionized the way companies advertise and track their progress in reaching customers. Then Google expanded, offering a suite of web-based applications, such as calendaring, office tools, e-mail, collaboration, shopping, and maps. Google Drive is one of the most popular file-sharing tools and Gmail one of the most popular e-mail services. As of June 2023, Google is offering its customers very inexpensive fiber connections in 22 cities.[4] Finally, Google is heavily invested in generative AI to stave off competitive threats to its crown jewel, its search engine, which at one time was thought to be invincible. In so doing, Google has further expanded into infrastructure, on-demand services, and AI, and shows no signs of slowing its progress.[5]

Likewise, Amazon.com's rise is meteoric. It began as an online bookseller and expanded rapidly by leveraging its business model into other marketplaces, such as music, electronics, health and beauty

[1] Robert Hof, "How Amazon Cleared the Profitability Hurdle," February 4, 2002, http://www.bloomberg.com/bw/stories/2002-02-03/how-amazon-cleared-the-profitability-hurdle (accessed October 29, 2015).

[2] Boston Consulting Group, "The Most Innovative Companies in 2023" https://www.visualcapitalist.com/most-innovative-companies-2023/ (accessed June 14, 2023) The top 5 in order are Apple, Tesla, Amazon, Alphabet, and Microsoft.

[3] Statistica, "The 100 Largest Companies in the World by Market Capitalization," https://www.statista.com/statistics/263264/top-companies-in-the-world-by-market-capitalization/ The third largest and the only non-technology company is Saudia Arabian Oil Company (Saudia ARAMCO). (accessed June 12, 2023).

[4] Google.com, https://fiber.google.com// (accessed June 14, 2023).

[5] For more information on the latest services by these two companies, see http://aws.amazon.com/ec2 and http://www.google.com/enterprise/cloud/

products, lawn and garden products, auctions, tools and hardware, groceries, and more. It succeeded by achieving a good mix of IS and business basics: capitalizing on operational efficiencies derived from inventory software and smarter storage, cost cutting, and effectively partnering with companies ranging from suppliers (such as the US Postal Service) to competitors (such as Target) to customers (who can sell their used goods on its platform). More recently, Amazon.com changed the basis of competition in another market, but this time it was the web services business. Amazon.com web services offer clients the extensive technology platform used for Amazon.com but in an on-demand fashion for developing and running the client's own applications. Its cloud platforms offer advanced technology to support generative AI, such as the built-in generative AI tool, CodeWhisperer, designed to facilitate coding. Amazon is also heavily involved in robotics. Over half a million robotic units now "staff" its global warehouses and distribution centers.

These and other online businesses were able to succeed where traditional companies have not, in part because their management understood the power of information, IS, and the web. These exemplary online businesses aren't succeeding because their managers can build web pages or assemble an IS network. Rather, the executives in these new businesses understand the fundamentals of managing and using information and can marry that knowledge with a sound, unique business vision to dominate their intended market spaces.

The goal of this book is to provide the foundation to help the general business manager become a knowledgeable participant in IS decisions because any IS decision in which the manager doesn't participate can greatly affect the organization's ability to succeed in the future. This introduction outlines the fundamental reasons for taking the initiative to participate in IS decisions. Moreover, because effective participation requires a unique set of managerial skills, this introduction identifies the most important ones. These skills are helpful for making both IS decisions and all business decisions. We describe how managers should participate in the decision-making process. Finally, this introduction presents relevant models for understanding the nature of business and IS. These models provide a framework for the discussions that follow in subsequent chapters.

The Case for Participating in Decisions about Information Systems

In today's business environment, maintaining a back-office view of technology is certain to cost market share and could ultimately lead to the failure of the organization. Managers who claim ignorance of IS can damage their reputation. Technology has become entwined with all the classic functions of business—operations, marketing, accounting, finance—to such an extent that understanding its role is necessary for making intelligent and effective decisions about any of them. Furthermore, as firms find digital business models at the core of just about every business today, failing to align IT decisions between business and technology leaders can cause a firm to fail to meet corporate objectives. As is covered in Chapter 9 on Governance, many decisions historically made by the IS group are increasingly being made by individuals outside that group. Envisioning new or enhanced digital business models requires an understanding of technologies and their capabilities and impacts on firms.

Therefore, understanding the fundamentals about using and managing information is worth the investment of time. These fundamentals include: a business view of IT as a critical resource; considering how people and technology work together; integrating business with information systems; and realizing opportunities and new strategies that can be derived from rapid changes in technology.

A Business View of Critical Resources

IT is a critical resource for today's businesses. It both supports and consumes a significant amount of an organization's resources. Just like the other three major types of business resources—people, money, and machines—it needs to be managed wisely. Chapter 3 describes how information resources can be managed and used as strategic tools.

IT spending represents a significant portion of corporate budgets. Worldwide IT spending is projected to top US $5 trillion by the end of 2024.[6] While the COVID-19 pandemic dampened IT spending, IT budgets rebounded after it ended. Resources must return value, or they will be invested elsewhere. The business manager, not the IS specialist, decides which activities receive funding, estimates the risk associated with the investment, and develops metrics for evaluating the investment's performance. Therefore, the business manager needs a basic grounding in managing and using information. On the flip side, IS managers need a business view to be able to explain how technology impacts the business and what its trade-offs are.

People and Technology Work Together

In addition to financial issues, managers must know how to mesh technology and people to create effective work processes. Collaboration is increasingly common, especially with the rise of social networking. Companies are reaching out to individual customers using social technologies such as Facebook, Instagram, Reddit, Renren, YouTube, and numerous other tools. Platform-based systems are generating widespread contributions, as well as use, across organizational boundaries. Analytics, Artificial Intelligence (AI), and machine learning are able to complement human decision-making and are being embedded in many organizational processes. Robots and robotic units embedded with AI are working alongside humans on assembly lines and in warehouses and distribution centers. Technology is facilitating the work that people do and the way they interact with each other and with machines. Appropriately incorporating IS into the design of a business model enables managers to focus their time and resources on issues that bear directly on customer satisfaction and other revenue- and profit-generating activities.

Adding a new information system to an existing organization, however, requires the ability to manage change.[7] Skilled business managers must balance the benefits of introducing new technology with the costs associated with changing the existing behaviors of people in the workplace. There are many choices of technological solutions, each with a different impact. Managers' decisions must incorporate a clear understanding of the consequences. Making this assessment doesn't require detailed technical knowledge. It does require an understanding of short-term and long-term consequences, risk mitigation, and why adopting new technology may be more appropriate in some instances than in others. Understanding these issues also helps managers know when it may prove effective to replace people with technology at certain steps in a process.

Integrating Business with Information Systems

Jeremy King, former Vice President Chief Technology Officer of US Walmart and US e-Commerce, led Walmart's transition into a technology company from just a retailer, albeit a very large one. According to King, to achieve success, companies must realize that they are becoming technology companies. As King wrote in a blog that in the past, there was a way to distinguish between companies, because some develop the technologies for enterprises, and some depended on those technologies. However, King went on to state:

> *". . . that distinction is now diminishing for this simple reason: every global company is becoming a tech company. . . . we're seeing technology as a critical component for business success."*[8]

---

[6] Statistica, "Information Technology (IT) Worldwide Spending from 2004–2024," https://www.statista.com/statistics/203935/overall-it-spending-worldwide/ (accessed June 12, 2023).

[7] Chapter 5 deals with the changes organizations face and provides suggestions for the acceptance of change.

[8] Jeremy King, "Why Every Company Is a Tech Company," November 21, 2013, http://www.walmartlabs.com/2013/11/21/why-every-company-is-a-tech-company-by-jeremy-king-cto-of-walmartlabs (accessed August 18, 2015) and Lauren Thomas and Christina Farr, "Walmart's Chief Technology Officer is Leaving the Company," *CNBC*, March 20, 2019, https://www.cnbc.com/2019/03/20/walmarts-chief-technology-officer-jeremy-king-is-leaving-the-company.html (accessed June 12, 2023).

Walmart, to counter a threat from Amazon, built platforms to support all its ecommerce and digital shopping experiences around the world. Walmart's teams created a new search engine to enable engaging and efficient ways for online customers to find items in inventory. IS placed information in the hands of Walmart associates so that decisions could be made closer to the customer. IS simplified organizational activities and processes such as moving goods, stocking shelves, and communicating with suppliers. For example, handheld scanners provide floor associates with immediate and real-time access to inventory in their store and the ability to locate items in surrounding stores, if necessary.

Opportunities and New Strategies Derived from Rapid Changes in Technology

The proliferation of new technologies creates a business environment filled with opportunities. The rate of adoption of these new technologies has increased due in part to the changing demographics of the workforce and the integration of "**digital natives**," individuals whose entire lives have been lived in an era with Internet availability through the web. Therefore, digital natives are completely fluent in the use of personal technologies and the Internet, whereas "**digital immigrants**," or people born before the 1990s, weren't always around computers when they were young. Even today, innovative uses of the Internet produce new types of online businesses that keep every manager and executive on alert. New business opportunities spring up with little advance warning. The manager's role is to frame these opportunities so that others can understand them, evaluate them against existing business needs and choices, and then pursue those that fit with an articulated business strategy. The quality of the information at hand affects the quality of both decisions and their implementation. Managers must develop an understanding of what information is crucial to the decisions, how to get it, and how to use it. They must lead the changes driven by IS.

IS can be useful in helping general managers anticipate and respond to ever-changing competitive challenges. They are in the best position to see emerging opportunities and threats and utilize IS effectively in response. It is the general managers who are often called on to demonstrate a clear understanding of how their own technology programs and products compare with those of their competitors. Further, they can see how IS can provide competitive advantage and change the competitive landscape for the entire industry. Managers and executives are now trying to interpret what might be the next big wave—such as generative AI—and its likely impact on their own business.

Managers are increasingly using evidence-based management to make decisions based on data gathered from experiments, internal files, customer sales data, and other relevant sources. Data-driven decision making, based on new techniques for analytics, data management, and business intelligence, has taken on increased importance. Social media and the sensors associated with the **Internet of Things (IoT)** (i.e., machines and sensors talking to each other over the network) have created rich streams of real-time data that give managers increased insights into the impact of decisions much faster than traditional systems. Midcourse corrections are much easier to make. Predictive and prescriptive analytics are eerily close to what eventually happens. Big data stores can be mined for insights that were unavailable with traditional IS, creating competitive advantage for companies with the right tools and techniques.

With the emergence of SMACIT, social networks such as Facebook, microblogs such as Twitter (renamed X), and myriad web and mobile applications, businesses have had to redesign their existing business models to respond to the increase in power now wielded by customers and others in their ecosystems. Redesigning the customer experience when interacting with a company is paramount for many managers and the key driver is IS. And it's not just customers who are using SMACIT. Employees are increasingly bringing their own devices to work (i.e., BYOD) and creating a trend called IT consumerization. **IT consumerization** means that technologies such as social tools, smartphones, and web/mobile applications targeted at individual, personal users are creating pressures for companies in new and unexpected ways. At the same time, technologies initially intended for the corporation, such as cloud computing, are being retooled and "consumerized" to appeal to individuals outside the corporation.

What If a Manager Doesn't Participate?

Decisions about IS directly affect the profits of a business. The basic formula Profit = Revenue – Expenses can be used to evaluate the impact of these decisions, from the purchase of large-scale software to the adoption of a new digital business model. Choosing the wrong digital business model can cause a company to miss business opportunities and any revenues those opportunities would generate. Inadequate IS can cause a breakdown in servicing customers, which hurts sales. Poorly deployed social IT resources can badly damage the reputation of a strong brand. On the expense side, a miscalculated investment in technology can lead to overspending and excess capacity or underspending and restricted opportunity. Inefficient business processes sustained by ill-fitting IS also increase expenses. Lags in implementation or poor process adaptation reduce profits and therefore growth. All these situations demonstrate that IS decisions can dramatically affect the bottom line.

Failure to consider IS strategy when planning business strategy and organizational strategy leads to one of three business consequences: (1) IS that fail to support business goals, (2) IS that fail to support organizational systems, and (3) a misalignment between business goals and organizational capabilities. These consequences are discussed briefly in the following section and in more detail in later chapters. The driving questions to consider are the potential effects on an organization's ability to achieve its business goals. How will the consequences impact the way people work? Will the organization still be able to implement its business strategy?

Information Systems, Business Goals and Organizational Systems

IS represent a major investment for any firm in today's business environment. Yet poorly chosen IS can actually become an obstacle to achieving business goals. The results can be disastrous if the systems do not align IS with business goals and organizational systems. When IS lack the capacity needed to collect, store, and transfer critical information for the business, decisions can be impacted and options limited. Customers will be dissatisfied or even lost. Production and operation costs may be excessive. Worst of all, management may not be able to pursue desired business directions that are blocked by inappropriate IS. Southwest Airlines learned only too well in a recent holiday meltdown that ignoring investments in IT can lead to a catastrophic grounding of planes, stranding of customers and flight personnel, and halting of operations. (See the case introducing Chapter 1 for more details.)

Organizational systems represent the fundamental elements of a business—its people, work processes, tasks, structure, and control systems—and the plan that enables them to work efficiently to achieve business goals. It might seem odd to think that a manager might add functionality to a corporate website without providing the training employees need to use the tool effectively. Yet, this mistake—and many more costly ones—occur in businesses every day. Managers make major IS decisions without informing all the staff of resulting changes in their daily work. Deploying technology, from an individual's desktop to enterprise-wide systems, requires careful planning about how it actually will be used in the organization—who will use it, how they will use it, and how to make sure the applications chosen will actually accomplish what is intended.

The general manager, who, after all, is charged with ensuring that company resources are used effectively, must guarantee that the company's IS will support its organizational systems and that changes made in one system are reflected in the other. For example, a company with traveling employees needs an IS strategy compatible with its organizational strategy. Purchasing smartphones and/or connected tablets would only be a superficial solution. Those employees need a careful analysis of information needs while on the road. Factors that make it difficult to close a sale should be anticipated and apps on their smartphones or connected tablets need to be able to respond to those information needs in real time. Sometimes it involves pulling up product comparisons that highlight their strengths. In other situations, it requires displaying seasonal fluctuations in local, regional, national, or international sales. Analytics detailing the impact of product improvements on customer satisfaction might just be what is needed. If the organization tries to adopt traditional information retrieval systems that mirror those used in the past, the technologies are doomed to fail.

Increasingly, IS strategy propels an organization's digital transformation. In that case business strategy and IS strategy are one and the same. They must both be aligned with organizational strategy.

Managerial Role	Skills
Visionary	Creativity Curiosity Confidence Focus on business solutions Flexibility
Informational and interpersonal	Listening Information gathering Interpersonal skills
Structural	Project management Analytical Organizational Planning Leading Controlling

FIGURE I-1 Skills for successful IT use by managerial role.

Skills Needed to Participate Effectively in Information Technology Decisions

Participating in IT decisions means bringing a clear set of skills to the table. All managers are asked to take on tasks that require different skills at different times. Those tasks can be divided into three types: visionary tasks that provide leadership and direction for the group; informational/interpersonal tasks that provide information and knowledge the group needs to be successful; and structural tasks that organize the group. Figure I-1 lists basic skills required of managers who wish to participate successfully in key IT decisions. Not only does this list emphasize understanding, organizing, planning, and solving the business needs of the organization but also it is an excellent checklist for all managers' professional growth.

These skills may not look much different from those required of any successful manager, which is the main point of this book: General managers can be successful participants in IS decisions without an extensive technical background. General managers who understand a basic set of IS concepts and who have outstanding managerial skills, such as those listed in Figure I-1, are ready for the digital economy.

How to Participate in Information Systems Decisions

Technical wizardry isn't required to become a knowledgeable participant in the IS decisions of a business. Managers need curiosity, creativity, and the confidence to ask questions in order to learn and understand. A solid framework that identifies key management issues and relates them to aspects of IS provides the background needed to participate in business IS decisions.

The goal of this book is to provide that framework. The way in which managers manage and use information is directly linked to business goals and the business strategy driving both organizational and IS decisions. Aligning business and IS decisions is critical. Business, organizational, and IS strategies are fundamentally linked in what is called the *Information Systems Strategy Triangle*, discussed in the next chapter. Failing to understand this relationship is detrimental to a business. Failing to plan for the consequences in all three areas can cost managers their jobs. This book provides a foundation for understanding business issues related to IS from a managerial perspective.

Organization of the Book

To be knowledgeable participants, managers must know about both managing and using information. The first five chapters offer basic frameworks to make this understanding easier. Chapter 1 introduces the Information Systems Strategy Triangle framework to discuss alignment of IS and the business. It describes how digital transformations that we are seeing increasingly are propelled by business strategy that is IS strategy. This chapter also provides a brief overview of relevant frameworks for business strategy and organizational strategy. It is provided as background for those who have not formally studied organization theory or business strategy. For those who have studied these areas, this chapter is a brief refresher of major concepts used throughout the remaining chapters of the book. Subsequent chapters provide frameworks and sets of examples for understanding the links between IS and business strategy (Chapter 2), links between IS and organizational strategy, notably information resources (Chapter 3), the design of work, collaboration, and individual work (Chapter 4), and business processes, change and digital transformation (Chapter 5).

The rest of the text covers issues related to the business manager's role in managing IS itself. These chapters are the building blocks of an IS strategy. Chapter 6 provides a framework for understanding the four components of IS architecture: platforms, applications, networks, and data. Chapter 7 discusses how managers might participate in decisions about cybersecurity. Chapter 8 focuses on the business of IT with a look at the IS organization, funding models, portfolios, and monitoring options. Chapter 9 describes the governance of IS resources and platforms. Chapter 10 explores sourcing and how companies provision IS resources. Chapter 11 focuses on project and change management. Chapter 12 concerns business intelligence, knowledge management, artificial intelligence, and analytics and provides an overview of how companies manage knowledge and create a competitive advantage using them. And finally, Chapter 13 discusses privacy and the ethical use of information.

Basic Assumptions

Every book is based on certain assumptions, and understanding those assumptions makes a difference in interpreting the text. The first assumption made by this text is that managers must be knowledgeable participants in the IS decisions made within and affecting their organizations. That means that the general manager must develop a basic understanding of the business and technology issues related to IS. Second, because technology changes rapidly, this text also assumes that today's technology is different from yesterday's technology. In fact, the technology available to readers of this text today might even differ significantly from that available when the text was being written. Therefore, this text focuses on generic concepts that are, to the extent possible, technology-independent. It provides frameworks on which to hang more up-to-the-minute technological evolutions and revolutions, such as new uses of the web, big data, business analytics, new social tools, platform-based systems, or new cloud-based services. We assume that the reader will supplement the discussions of this text with current case studies and up-to-date information about the latest technology.

A third, perhaps controversial, assumption is that the roles of a general manager and of an IS manager require different skill sets and levels of technical competency. General managers must have a basic understanding of IS in order to be a knowledgeable participant in business decisions. Without that level of understanding, their decisions may have serious negative implications for the business. On the other hand, IS managers must have more in-depth knowledge of technology so they can partner with general managers who will use the IS. As digital natives take on increasingly more managerial roles in corporations, this assumption may change—all managers may need deeper technical understanding. But for this text, we assume a different, more technical skill set for the IS manager and we do not attempt to provide that here.

Assumptions about Management

Although many books have been written describing the activities of managers, organizational theorist Henry Mintzberg offers a view that works especially well with a perspective relevant to IS management. Mintzberg's model describes management in behavioral terms by categorizing the three major roles a manager fills: interpersonal, informational, and decisional (see Figure I-2). This model is useful because it considers the chaotic nature of the environment in which managers actually work. Managers rarely have time to be reflective in their approaches to problems. They work at an unrelenting pace, and their activities are brief and often interrupted. Thus, quality information becomes even more crucial to effective decision making. The classic view, described below, is often seen as a tactical approach to management, whereas some regard Mintzberg's view as more strategic.

Type of Roles	Manager's Roles	IS Examples
Interpersonal	Figurehead	CIO greets touring dignitaries.
	Leader	IS manager puts in long hours to help motivate project team to complete project on schedule in an environment of heavy budget cuts.
	Liaison	CIO works with the president and with marketing, operations, and human resource vice presidents to ensure that IT is effectively leveraged to create a planned business transformation.
Informational	Monitor	Division manager compares progress on IS project for the division with milestones developed during the project's initiation and feasibility phase.
	Disseminator	CIO conveys organization's business strategy to IS department and demonstrates how IS strategy supports the business strategy.
	Spokesperson	IS manager represents IS department at organization's recruiting fair.
Decisional	Entrepreneur	IS division manager suggests an application of a new technology that improves the division's operational efficiency.
	Disturbance handler	IS division manager, as project team leader, helps resolve design disagreements between division personnel who will be using the system and systems analysts who are designing it.
	Resource allocator	CIO allocates additional personnel positions to various departments based upon the business strategy.
	Negotiator	IS manager negotiates for additional personnel needed to respond to recent user requests for enhanced functionality in a system that is being implemented.

FIGURE I-2 Managers' roles.
Source: Adapted from H. Mintzberg, *The Nature of Managerial Work* (New York: Harper & Row, 1973).

Assumptions about Business

Everyone has an internal understanding of what constitutes a business, which is based on readings and experiences with different firms. This understanding forms a model that provides the basis for comprehending actions, interpreting decisions, and communicating ideas. Managers use their internal model to make sense of otherwise chaotic and random activities. This book uses several conceptual models of business. Some take a functional view and others take a process view.

The classical view of a business is based on the functions that people perform, such as accounting, finance, marketing, operations, and human resources. The business organizes around these functions to coordinate them and to gain economies of scale within specialized sets of tasks.

The process view takes into account the activities in each functional area that are needed to complete a process and assumes that any organization can be described by the processes it performs. Michael Porter defines a business in terms of the primary and support activities that are performed to create, deliver, and support a product or service. The primary activities are not limited to specific functions, but rather are cross-functional processes. For example, the product creation process might begin with an idea from R&D, which is transferred to an operations organization that builds the actual product and involves marketing to get the word out, sales to sell and deliver the product, and support to provide customer assistance as and when needed. Improving coordination among activities increases business profit. Organizations that effectively manage core processes across functional boundaries are often the industry leaders because they have made efficiencies that are not visible from the functional viewpoint. IS are often the key to process improvement and cross-functional coordination.

Both the process and functional views provide insights for understanding IS. The functional view is useful when similar activities must be explained, coordinated, executed, or communicated. For example, understanding a marketing information system means understanding the functional approach to business in general and the marketing function in particular. The process view, on the other hand, is useful when examining the flow of information throughout a business. For example, understanding the information associated with order fulfillment, product development, or customer service means taking a process view of the business. This text assumes that both views are important for participating in IS decisions, and the plethora of enterprise-wide systems and platforms further emphasize that every portion of a business needs access to that information.

Assumptions about Information Systems

Consider the components of an information system from the manager's viewpoint rather than from the technologist's viewpoint. Both the nature of information (hierarchy and economics) and the context of an information system must be examined to understand the basic assumptions of this text.

Information Hierarchy

The terms *data*, *information*, and *knowledge* are often used interchangeably, but have significant and discrete meanings within the knowledge management domain (and are more fully explored in Chapter 12). Tom Davenport, in his book *Information Ecology*, pointed out that getting everyone in any given organization to agree on common definitions is difficult. However, his work (more fully explored in Chapter 12) provides a nice starting point for understanding the subtle but important differences.

Briefly, the information hierarchy begins at the bottom of Figure I.3 with **data**, or simple, specific observations, such as "inventory contains 45 units." In isolation, such facts have no intrinsic meaning but can be easily captured, transmitted, and stored electronically. **Information** is data endowed with relevance and purpose.[9] A simple example would be "The inventory of 45 units is the lowest we've had this year."

Knowledge has greater context and provides more value. Values, beliefs, and timing help in interpreting and organizing knowledge. Tom Davenport and Larry Prusak, experts who have written about this relationship, say, "The power of knowledge to organize, select, learn, and judge comes from values and beliefs as much as, and probably more than, from information and logic."[10] Knowledge also involves the synthesis of multiple sources of information over time.[11] It often addresses causal reasons to answer "*why*," such as, "After running three online coupon promotions, sales increased as is typical, and therefore, our inventory is the lowest we've had this year."

Some people attribute high importance to a fourth level in the information hierarchy: wisdom. **Wisdom** is knowledge fused with intuition, judgment, insights, and empathy that facilitates decision making, often with a long-term perspective. Wisdom is that level of the information hierarchy used by subject matter experts, gurus, and individuals with a high degree of experience who seem to "just know" what to do and how to apply the knowledge they gain. This is consistent with Aristotle's view of wisdom as the ability to

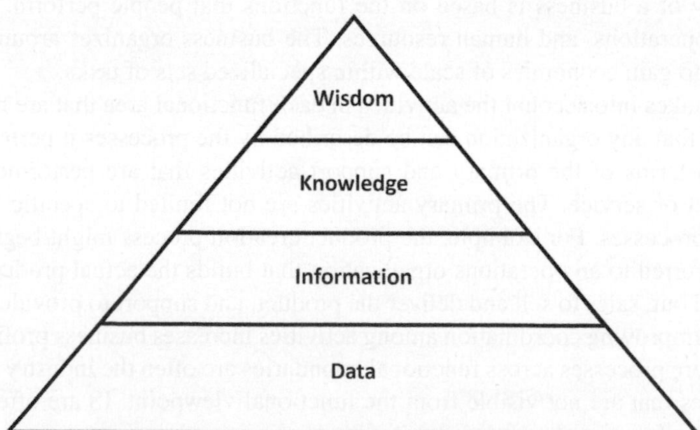

FIGURE I.3 Hierarchy of data, information, knowledge, and wisdom.

---

[9] Peter F. Drucker, "The Coming of the New Organization," *Harvard Business Review* (January–February 1988), 45–53.

[10] Thomas H. Davenport and Laurence Prusak, *Working Knowledge* (Boston, MA: Harvard Business School Press, 1998), 12.

[11] Thomas H. Davenport, *Information Ecology* (New York: Oxford University Press, 1997), 9–10.

	Top Management	Middle Management	Supervisory and Lower-level Management
Time horizon	Long: years	Medium: weeks, months, years	Short: day to day
Level of detail	Highly aggregated Less accurate More predictive	Summarized Integrated Often financial	Very detailed Very accurate Often nonfinancial
Source	Primarily external	Primarily internal with limited external	Internal
Decision	Extremely judgmental Uses creativity and analytical skills	Relatively judgmental	Heavily reliant on rules

FIGURE I-4 Information characteristics across hierarchical levels.
Source: Adapted from Anthony Gorry and Michael S. Scott Morton, "A Framework for Management Information Systems," *Sloan Management Review* 13, no. 1 (1971): 55–70.

appreciate and balance different and conflicting elements together in ways that are only learned through experience. Wisdom, therefore, enables us to make the best use of knowledge. An example of wisdom could be "Should we save energy and materials by allowing, or even requiring, consumers to redeem the online promotions in stores?"

This book has a heavy focus on the information needs of managers. To be relevant and have a purpose for managers, information must be considered within the context in which it is received and used. Because of differences in context, information needs vary across functions and hierarchical levels. For example, when considering functional differences related to a sales transaction, a marketing department manager may be interested in the demographic characteristics of buyers, such as their age, gender, and home address. A manager in the accounting department probably won't be interested in any of these details, but instead wants to know details about the transaction itself, such as method of payment and date of payment. Similarly, information needs may vary across hierarchical levels. These needs are summarized in Figure I-4 and reflect the different activities performed at each level. As managers move up the hierarchy, their information needs broaden in scope and become more oriented toward the long-term.

System Hierarchy

IS are composed of three main elements: technology, people, and process (see Figure I-5). When most people use the term "information system", they actually refer only to the technology element as defined by the organization's infrastructure. In this text, the term **infrastructure** refers to everything that supports the flow and processing of information in an organization, including platforms, applications, and network

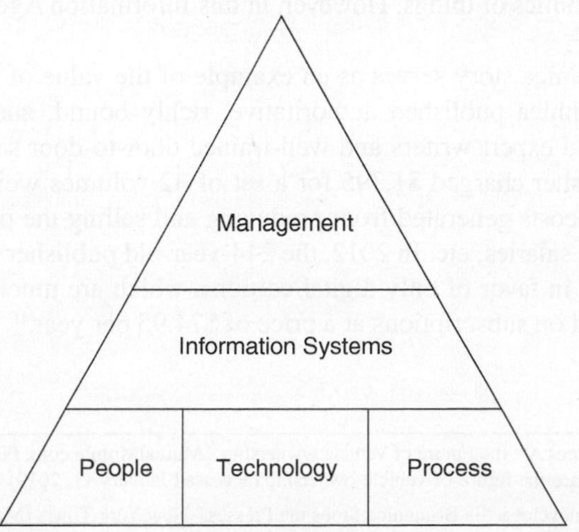

FIGURE I-5 System hierarchy.

components, whereas **architecture** refers to the blueprint that reflects strategy implicit in combining these components. **IS (Information systems)** are defined more broadly as the *combination* of technology (the "what"), people (the "who"), and process (the "how") that an organization uses to produce and manage information. In contrast, IT focuses only on the technical devices and tools used in the system. We define **information technology** as all forms of technology used to create, store, exchange, and use information. Many people use the terms IS and IT interchangeably. In recent years, "IT" has become more fashionable, but terminology in IS can change quickly when new important technologies are introduced.

Economics of Information vs. Economics of Things

In their groundbreaking book, *Blown to Bits*, Evans and Wurster argue that every business is in the information business. Even those businesses not typically considered information businesses have business strategies in which information plays a critical role. The physical world of manufacturing is shaped by information that dominates products as well as processes. For example, a conventional automobile contains as much computing power as a personal computer, with specialized processors and sensors alerting the driver to its malfunctions. Autonomous (self-driving) vehicles have extended that power to another order of magnitude, merging location awareness (through GPS data) with visual input (using cameras). Several of the current manufacturers see a future market for automobiles as a "subscription" or "sharing" model rather than a "purchase" model. Made possible only by IT, most notably platforms and artificial intelligence, such a model would eliminate the need to search, negotiate, own, and maintain a vehicle.[12] Perhaps in the future a user will be able to signal for a car on a watch or smartphone to autonomously drive to her location, ride to the proper destination, and then dismiss the car to return to its "home base." The car can make its own appointment at the repair shop when it senses that maintenance is needed, and then can navigate to the facility by itself. Making the "sharing" or "subscription" models a reality would require information and IT to be leveraged across information-intensive industries.

As our world is reshaped by information-intensive industries, it becomes even more important for business strategies to differentiate the timeworn economics of things from the evolving economics of information. Things wear out; things can be replicated at the expense of the manufacturer; things exist in a tangible location. When sold, the seller no longer owns the thing. The price of a thing is typically based on production costs. In contrast, information never wears out, although it can become obsolete or untrue. Information can be replicated at virtually no cost without limit; information exists in the ether. When sold, the seller still retains the information, but this ownership provides little value if others have no legal limit in their ability to copy it. Finally, information is often costly to produce but cheap to reproduce. Rather than pricing it to recover the sunk cost of its initial production, its price is typically based on its value to the consumer. Figure I-6 summarizes the major differences between the economics of goods and the economics of information. Evans and Wurster suggest that traditionally the economics of information has been bundled with the economics of things. However, in this Information Age, firms are vulnerable if they do not separate the two.

The Encyclopedia Britannica story serves as an example of the value of separating information from things. Encyclopedia Britannica published authoritative, richly bound, and colorful physical volumes every several years and used expert writers and well-trained door-to-door salespeople. In its last year of print publication, the publisher charged $1,395 for a set of 32 volumes weighing 129 lb. in total.[13] The price was based on myriad costs generated from producing and selling the physical thing: printing costs, binding costs, salesperson's salaries, etc. In 2012, the 244-year-old publisher announced that the print edition would be discontinued in favor of only digital editions, which are much less costly to produce.[14] Its revenue model is now based on subscriptions at a price of $74.95 per year.[15]

[12] Rhinehart, "Car Subscription Services Are the Future of Vehicle Ownership," MutualMobile.com, February 26, 2018, https://mutualmobile.com/blog/car-subscription-services-are-the-future-of-vehicle-ownership (accessed January 11, 2019).

[13] Julie Bosman, "After 244 Years, Encyclopaedia Britannica Stops the Presses," New York Times (March 13, 2012), https://archive.nytimes.com/mediadecoder.blogs.nytimes.com/2012/03/13/after-244-years-encyclopaedia-britannica-stops-the-presses/ (accessed January 26, 2019).

[14] Ibid.

[15] According to the Britannica.com signup page at Subscription (britannica.com) (accessed June 11, 2023).

Things	Information
Wear out	Doesn't wear out but can become obsolete or untrue
Are replicated at the expense of the manufacturer	Is replicated at almost zero cost without limit
Exist in a tangible location	Does not physically exist
When sold, possession changes hands	When sold, seller may still possess and sell again
Price based on production costs	Price based on value to consumer
Are based on a physical infrastructure	Is based on a digital infrastructure
Are fixed units, each needing physical handling	Can be repackaged/customized/generated on demand
Usually, cannot be combined to operate with other physical units	Requires only translation software to be combined with, or augmented by, other data

FIGURE I-6 Comparison of the economics of things with the economics of information.

So, are people rushing to buy an annual subscription to the Encyclopedia? Probably not when information is freely available to all on Wikipedia and updated on a nearly real-time basis continuously by thousands of volunteers. Currently, Wikipedia reports that it has articles written in 333 different languages,[16] receives over 2 edits per second globally, and boasts an average of 550 new articles each day.[17] A paid publication that is updated every three years is no match for a free resource that is updated constantly and almost instantly. In fact, a free search on Google revealed: "Encyclopedia Britannica has a rating of 1.89 stars from 9 reviews, indicating that most customers are generally dissatisfied with their purchases."[18]

A strong two-century-old tradition of bundling the economics of things with the economics of information made it difficult for Encyclopedia Britannica to envision the threats looming against it. Only when it was threatened with its very survival by a surge of networked computers accessing Wikipedia did Encyclopedia Britannica grasp the need to separate the economics of information from economics of things and sell bits of information online. Clearly, Encyclopedia Britannica's business strategy, like that of many other companies, needed to reflect the difference between the economics of things from the economics of information.

SUMMARY

Aligning IS and business decisions is no longer an option; it's imperative for business. Every business operates as an information-based enterprise. In addition, the explosive growth of smart phones, tablets, social tools, and web-based businesses provides all managers with some experience in IS and some idea of the complexity involved in providing enterprise-level systems. This highlights the need for all managers to be skilled in managing and using IS.

It is no longer acceptable to delegate IS decisions to the management information systems (MIS) department alone. In fact, digital transformations, IT consumerization, platforms used by customers and external partners, the IoT, and myriad other changes have drastically altered the role of MIS departments since the turn of the millennium. The general manager must be involved in both executing business plans and protecting options for future business vision. IS and business maturity must be aligned to provide the right level of information resources to the business.

This chapter makes the case for general managers' full participation in strategic business decisions concerning IS. It outlines the skills required for such participation, and it makes explicit certain key assumptions about the nature of business, management, and IS that will underlie the remaining discussions. Subsequent chapters are designed to build on these concepts by addressing the following questions.

[16] Wikipedia, https://meta.wikimedia.org/wiki/List_of_Wikipedias (accessed June 12, 2023).

[17] Wikipedia Statistics, https://en.wikipedia.org/wiki/Wikipedia:Statistics (accessed June 12, 2023).

[18] Google search, Price of Encyclopedia Britannica subscription - Google Search, https://www.google.com/search?q=Price+of+Encyclopedia+Britannica+subscription&rlz=1C1GCEB_enIN1031IN1031&oq=Price+of+Encyclopedia+Britannica+subscription&gs_lcrp=EgZjaHJvbWUyBggAEEUYOTIHCAEQIRigATIHCAIQIRigATIKCAMQIRgWGB0YHtIBCDMxOTBqMGo3qAIAsAIA&sourceid=chrome&ie=UTF-8 (accessed June 11, 2023).

Frameworks and Foundations

- How should information strategy be aligned with business and organizational strategies? (Chapter 1)
- How can a business achieve competitive advantages using its IS? (Chapter 2)
- How do organizational decisions and design impact and are impacted by IS decisions? (Chapter 3)
- How is the work of the individual in an organization and society affected by IS? (Chapter 4)
- How are information systems integrated with business processes? (Chapter 5)

IS Management Issues

- What are the components of an IS architecture? (Chapter 6)
- How are IS kept secure? (Chapter 7)
- How is the IT organization managed and funded? (Chapter 8)
- How are IS decisions made and the IT organization and platforms governed? (Chapter 9)
- What source should provide IS services/products and how and where should they be provided? (Chapter 10)
- How are IS projects managed and risks from change management mitigated? (Chapter 11)
- How is knowledge enhanced by artificial intelligence tools and analytics business intelligence managed within an organization? (Chapter 12)
- What ethical and moral considerations bind the uses of information in business? (Chapter 13)

KEY TERMS

architecture, 12
data, 10
digital immigrants, 5
digital natives, 5
digital transformation, 1
generative AI, 2
Information Technology (IT) consumerization, 5
information technology, 12
information, 10
infrastructure, 11
internet of things (IoT), 5
IS (information systems), 12
knowledge, 10
wisdom, 10

FOUNDATIONAL READINGS

Davenport, Thomas. *Information Ecology*. New York: Oxford University Press, 1997.

Drucker, Peter F. "The Coming of the New Organization." *Harvard Business Review* (January–February 1988): 45–53.

Evans, Philip and Wurster, Thomas. *Blown to Bits*. Boston, MA: Harvard Business School Press, 2000.

Gorry, Anthony and Morton, Michael S. Scott. "A Framework for Management Information Systems." *Sloan Management Review* 13, no. 1 (1971): 55–70.

Mintzberg, Henry. *The Nature of Managerial Work*. New York: Harper & Row, 1973.

Porter, Michael. *Competitive Strategy*. New York: The Free Press, 1998.

The Information Systems Strategy Triangle

1

The Information Systems Strategy Triangle highlights the alignment necessary between decisions regarding business strategy, information systems, and organizational design. This chapter describes the role of business models and introduces frameworks pertaining to business strategy, organizational strategy and design, and information systems strategy.

On December 22, 2022, a "perfect storm" created a meltdown of epic proportions at Southwest Airlines, the largest domestic carrier in the United States. The meltdown was precipitated by a brutal winter storm that pummeled many U.S. states on December 21, 2022. Between December 22 and 29, Southwest had to cancel more than 16,700 flights, leaving more than a million holiday travelers—and their displaced bags—stranded in airports across the country. During this chaotic period, the carrier flew more than 500 flights without any paying customers. It was using the flights to reconnect lost luggage with their owners and to reposition flight crews. The cost of the meltdown in terms of lost ticket revenues, overtime, compensation, and goodwill gestures to placate irate customers is estimated to be a whopping $1 billion, though this number is likely to grow when the damage to customer trust is manifested in lower sales.[1] In March 2023, Southwest announced a Technical Action Plan that detailed how it would spend another whopping $1.3 billion improving its technology and tools for supporting a greater volume and pace of flights, cross-team collaboration, and winter operations.[2]

Southwest Airlines' meltdown was so extraordinary that it garnered the scrutiny of the U.S. President, Congress, and Department of Transportation (DOT). Pete Buttigieg, the Secretary of the U.S. DOT, labelled the carrier's handling of its massive cancellations and the disruption they created to be "unacceptable" and met with its CEO Bob Jordan to convey the need for Southwest to provide refunds for cancelled flights, meals, hotel rooms, and other forms of compensation to the stranded customers, many of whom voiced their anger by filing a record number of complaints with the DOT in December 2022 and January 2023.[3]

CEO Jordan apologized profusely, and on December 27, he laid heavy blame for the meltdown on the winter storm, along with not having flight crews where they needed to be. Southwest senior executives added that the storm also left airplanes unable to function in extreme cold and that it had hit particularly hard in two large operation centers, Denver and Chicago, where more than a quarter of the Southwest crew members start or end their assigned flights. Secretary Buttigieg was quick to point out in a TV interview that "Where most airlines saw their performance start to improve, Southwest has actually moved in the

---

[1] Lori Aratani, Ian Duncan, and Michael Laris, "As Southwest, FAA probes begin, fallout could shape flying for years, *Washington Post,* https://www.washingtonpost.com/transportation/2023/02/07/faa-southwest-airlines-travel-investigations/ (accessed February 15, 2023).

[2] Joe Kunzler, "Southwest Airlines Formulates Tactical Action Plan to Increase Operational Resiliency," Simple Flying, March 15, 2023, Southwest Airlines Formulates Tactical Action Plan To Increase Operational Resiliency (simpleflying.com) (accessed April 10, 2023).

[3] Justin George, Rachel Lerman, and Hannah Sampson, "Southwest draws regulatory scrutiny as thousands more flights canceled. *Washington Post,* https://www.washingtonpost.com/transportation/2022/12/27/southwest-airlines-cancellations-holiday-travel/ (accessed February 15, 2023); Over 110 complaints were filed with the D.O.T. Dawn Gilbertson, Travel Math, *Wall Street Journal Travel Journal mobile*, May 24, 2023.

other direction."[4] So, the meltdown wasn't just weather-related! In another TV interview, Buttigieg added: "Cancellation rates across the system for all of the other airlines together are averaging about 5%. With Southwest, it's more in the neighborhood of 60% or 70%."[5]

It is now obvious that in the 2022 holiday period Southwest Airlines did have its very own "Perfect Storm." Many things converged to create it. One of the biggest issues was obsolete technology—most notably the crew scheduling system. A chorus of knowledgeable people confirmed this: Southwest executives, Lyn Montgomery (President of TWU Local 556, a union representing about 18,000 flight attendants), Robert Mann (an aviation analyst), and two members of the U.S. Senate Commerce Committee blamed the meltdown on Southwest's archaic internal scheduling system. Employee unions had complained for years about the scheduling system, and although the reservation system was upgraded in 2017, the software used for staff scheduling still had uncorrected problems. Andrew Watterson, Southwest's Chief Operating Officer clarified: "the software was not designed to solve something that was that large. And therefore, we had to revert back to manual mode for a lot of tasks." That's right. The backup system was volunteers who notified the crew of flight changes and also manually entered the latest information about crew locations and time remaining to fly within a period.[6] However, a problem with the manual process was that Southwest flight attendants (at least those that weren't out sick with COVID, flu or RSV) were stuck on hold when trying to reach the scheduling desk.[7] Not surprisingly, the manual backup system couldn't come close to handling massive flight cancellations.

Another issue that contributed to the "Perfect Storm" was Southwest's business strategy based on a point-to-point network vs. the hub and spoke system used by most major airlines. As a consequence, Southwest crews are spread over dozens of locations and they often catch a ride on a Southwest flight to get to one of Southwest's 121 locations for their own assigned flights. The strategy worked well when there weren't as many locations and when the weather was good. Casey A. Murray, President of Southwest Airlines Pilots Association (SWAPA) summarized the problem with this strategy: "Once one card falls, the whole house falls here at Southwest."[8]

As if that weren't enough, SWAPA wrote a scathing letter, signed by Capt. Tom Nekauei on December 31, 2022, blaming the leadership of CEO Jordan and past CEO Gary Kelly for the meltdown and saying that it was "not a Southwest Airlines problem. This is not an employees of Southwest Airlines problem. This is not an unprecedented weather problem. This is a Gary Kelly problem." The letter argues that the previous and current systemwide breakdowns "were all results of conscious operational, manpower, or tech infrastructure investment decisions made at the senior levels of our Company. . . .As CEO, Gary Kelly made a conscious decision to make the less than necessary investments in tech upgrades in favor of maximizing shareholder return because, well, "our tech's been working OK for 20 years." The letter adds that Kelly focused on generating "revenue without the commensurate investment in tech infrastructure necessary to support that explosive growth" in the network.[9]

The SWAPA letter quotes Kelly as saying: "Arguably, our shareholders have suffered for a long time when it comes to getting a return and our employees have been very well taken care of." Kelly's focus was in marked contrast to that of the first Southwest CEO, Herb Kelleher: "You put your employees first." It looks as if the Southwest pilots don't like the change.

[4] Isabella Simonetti and Peter Eavis's "Southwest's Debacle, Which Stranded Thousands, to be Felt for Days" *New York Times*, December 27, 2022 Updated December 29, 2022 https://www.nytimes.com/2022/12/27/business/southwest-flights-canceled-travel.html (accessed February 15, 2023).

[5] Teddy Grant, Sam Sweeney, Peter Charalambous, Kiara Alfonseca, and Will McDuffie, "Southwest CEO apologizes to passengers, staff after flight cancellation chaos," December 28, 2022, ABC News, https://abcnews.go.com/US/airlines-cancel-thousands-flights-amid-winter-storm-chaos/story?id=95834221.

[6] Ian Duncan, Justin George, and Andrea Sachs, "After Meltdown, Southwest Airlines Prepares for Near-Normal Operations," *Washington Post*, December 29, 2022, https://www.washingtonpost.com/transportation/2022/12/29/southwest-airlines-flight-cancellations/?utm_campaign=wp_the7&utm_medium=email&utm_source=newsletter&wpisrc=nl_the7&carta-url=https%3A%2F%2Fs2.washingtonpost.com%2Fcar-ln-tr%2F38b0ee2%2F63aed3e1ef9bf67b233f82c3%2F63ac47f5c5a38f5037ff5fe4%2F11%2F59%2F63aed3e1ef9bf67b233f82c3&wp_cu=2913637b76e5788d43f59932568073a4%7C801847b1-e85f-4fbc-8e4d-db5ecba66a85 (accessed February 15, 2023).

[7] Aratani, Duncan, and Laris, 2022; Duncan, George, and Sachs, 2022.

[8] Lyle Niedens, "Southwest CEO at Center of Storm After Thousands of Canceled Flights," Investopedia, December 29, 2022, https://www.investopedia.com/southwest-airlines-critics-zero-in-on-ceo-jordan-7090274 (accessed February 15, 2023).

[9] Rob Wile, "Southwest Airlines Pilots Union Write Scathing Open Letter to Company Executives," NBC News, January 3, 2023, https://www.nbcnews.com/business/business-news/southwest-airlines-pilots-union-slams-company-executives-open-letter-rcna64121 (accessed February 15, 2023); Also see letter at: Two Legacies https://www.swapa.org/news/2022/two-legacies/ (accessed September 22, 2023).

The IS department is not an island within a firm. Rather, IS manages an infrastructure that is essential to the firm's functioning. Further, the Southwest Airlines case illustrates that a firm's IS must be aligned with the way it manages its employees and processes. For Southwest Airlines, a scheduling system overload precipitated by an especially bad winter storm created an epic meltdown. The company employees had long complained about the system, but the company chose to concentrate on keeping the stockholders happy instead of investing in updated systems and an adequate technology infrastructure to support an explosively-growing network. Other contributing factors to the meltdown were a business strategy of point-to-point flights, flight crews that weren't living close to their assigned flights, and a change in focus from taking care of employees to taking care of shareholders.

This chapter introduces a simple framework for describing the alignment necessary with business systems and for understanding the impact of IS on organizations. This framework is called the **Information Systems Strategy Triangle** because it relates business strategy with IS strategy and organizational strategy. This chapter also presents key frameworks from organization theory that describe the context in which IS operate as well as the business imperatives that IS support. The Information Systems Strategy Triangle presented in Figure 1.1 suggests three key points about strategy.

1. Successful firms have an overriding business strategy that drives both organizational strategy and IS strategy. The decisions made regarding the structure, hiring practices, vendor policies, and other organizational design components, as well as decisions regarding applications, platforms, and other IS components, are all driven by the firm's business objectives, strategies, and tactics. Successful firms carefully align these three strategies—they purposely design their organizational and IS strategies to complement their business strategy.

2. IS strategy can itself affect and is affected by changes in a firm's business and organizational design. To perpetuate the alignment needed for successful operation, changes in the IS strategy must be accompanied by changes in the organizational strategy and must accommodate the overall business strategy. If a firm designs its business strategy to use IS to gain strategic advantage, it can only sustain that advantage by constant innovation. The business, IS, and organizational strategies must constantly be adjusted.

3. IS strategy always involves consequences—intended or not—within business and organizational strategies. Avoiding harmful unintended consequences means remembering to consider business and organizational strategies when designing IS implementation. For example, deploying tablets to employees without an accompanying set of changes to job expectations, process design, compensation plans, and business tactics will fail to achieve expected productivity improvements. Success can be achieved only by specifically designing all three components of the strategy triangle so they properly complement each other.

At Southwest Airlines' the IT strategy was not aligned with the business strategy of point-to-point networks. Southwest needed to modernize its technology and have better IT support. In the case of its catastrophic meltdown, it was very clear that a better reservation system (and backup) was needed. The carrier's organizational strategy in terms of the distributed nature of its staffing did not align well with the growth of locations in its business strategy. Its employees, notably the flight attendants and pilots, were not on board with the business strategy and were displeased with the inadequate investments in technology (IS strategy). In this case the lack of alignment helped create a disastrous "Perfect Storm."

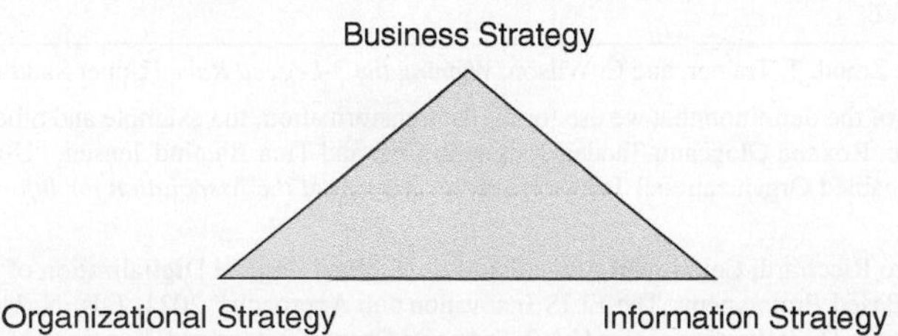

FIGURE 1.1 The information systems strategy triangle.

What does *alignment* mean? The book *Winning the 3-Legged Race* defines **alignment** as the situation in which a company's current and emerging business strategy is enabled and supported, yet unconstrained, by technology. The authors suggest that although alignment is good, there are higher goals, namely, synchronization and convergence, toward which companies should strive. With synchronization, technology not only enables current business strategy but also anticipates and shapes future business strategy. In the case of Southwest Airlines, technology hindered business strategy and neither the organizational strategy nor IS strategy were adjusted (synchronized) so that they could effectively support Southwest's growth business strategy with its rapidly expanding point-to-point network. If the IS strategy had been synchronized with the business strategy, a large investment would have been made to update the IS infrastructure, as well as to support technology and IT-enabled processes. Convergence goes one step further by exhibiting a state in which business strategy and technology strategy are "intertwined" or fused. *Alignment* in this text means any of these states.[10]

To date in practice and research, IS strategy has been viewed as a functional-level strategy that is subordinate to the chosen business strategy. In other words, business strategy directs IS strategy. However, as IS becomes more embedded within organizations and organizations turn to digital technologies to enhance their products, expand the number and nature of their service offerings, fundamentally change their business processes, and support customer and interfirm relationships, then there is a fusion (i.e., convergence) of IS strategy and business strategy. This is definitely the case in digital transformations.

You may have been hearing about digital transformations. The term is often used to broadly describe a situation when an organization undertakes a big change that is enabled by digital technologies. Such IT-enabled change is not new. However, we are using the term digital transformation in a specific way to highlight a phenomenon that is relatively new and increasingly widespread. We define **digital transformation** (also called digitalization) as the use of digital technology by an organization to redefine (and not just support) its value proposition and which leads the organization to identify itself in a new way. An example would be when a firm known for selling customized, top-quality manufacturing equipment became the provider of control software systems for manufacturing companies instead. In so doing, it redefined its corporate identity. The company used digital technologies (e.g., Internet of Things, control systems) to change the way it provided value to its customers, as well as its own value creating processes. Its business strategy was fused with the IS strategy. At the same time, its business strategy directed changes to its organizational strategy including its organizational structure, the role and compensation system for its salesmen, the composition of its workforce, its Human Resources training program, and its pricing models.[11]

Digital transformation is about exchanging bricks for bits. . . not just in the products/services but in many of the processes, too. For example, consider the attempts that are underway to digitize the entire insurance claims management process for car insurance. Currently the process is semi-automated in many insurance companies.[12] However, to date, parts of the process have resisted digitalization: fraud detection and claims settlement where images must abide by the European Union's rigid General Data Protection Regulation (GDPR) and other legal requirements. AI-based prototypes have been developed to demonstrate that these processes can be digitized. Once photos of an accident damage have been uploaded by the customer or insurance agent, they are anonymized using data science/AI tools with deep learning so that identifying objects such as faces and license plates don't go into the claims database. As part of the claims management processing, AI tools also determine if the claim is fraudulent. When the digital claims management system is implemented, insurance personnel to process the claims will be entirely out of the picture. End-to-end automation of the claims management process by an insurance company may be considered an example of digital transformation.

[10] F. Hogue, V. Sambamurthy, R. Zmud, T. Trainer, and C. Wilson, *Winning the 3-Legged Race* (Upper Saddle River, NJ: Prentice Hall, 2005).

[11] This article provides the basis of the definition that we use for digital transformation, the example and other related concepts in the chapter: Wessel, Lauri, Abayomi Baiyere, Roxana Ologeanu-Taddei, Jonghyuk Cha, and Tina Blegind-Jensen. "Unpacking the Difference Between Digital Transformation and IT-enabled Organizational Transformation," *Journal of the Association for Information Systems* 22, no. 1 (2021), 102–129.

[12] Alessandra Andreozzi, Lorenzo Riccirardi Celesi, and Antonella Martini, "Enabling the Digitalization of Claim Management in the Insurance Value Chain Through AI-Based Prototypeps: The ELIS Innovation Jub Approach," 2021, Eds. N. Urbach, M. Roeglinger, K. Kautz, R. Alias, C. Saunders, M. Wiener in *Digitalization Cases Vol. 2*, Springer: Cham, Switzerland. See Case 11.1 for more details.

A word of explanation is needed here. Studying IS alone does not provide general managers with the appropriate perspective. This chapter and subsequent chapters address questions of IS strategy squarely within the context of business strategy. Although this is not a textbook of business strategy, a foundation for IS discussions is built on some basic business strategy frameworks and organizational theories presented in this and the next chapter. To be effective, managers need a solid sense of how IS are used and managed within the organization. Studying details of technologies is also outside the scope of this text. Details of technologies are relevant, of course, and it is important that in any organization a sufficient knowledge base to plan for and adequately align with business priorities. However, because technologies change so rapidly, keeping a textbook current is impossible. Instead, this text takes the perspective that understanding what questions to ask and having a framework for interpreting the answers are skills more fundamental to the general manager than understanding any particular technology. That understanding must be constantly refreshed using the most current articles and information from experts. This text provides readers with an appreciation of the need to ask questions, a framework from which to derive the questions to ask, and a foundation sufficient to understand the answers received. The remaining chapters build on the foundation provided in the Information Systems Strategy Triangle.

Brief Overview of Business Strategy Frameworks

A **strategy** is a coordinated set of actions to fulfill objectives, purposes, and goals. The essence of a strategy is setting limits on what the business will seek to accomplish. Strategy starts with a mission. A **mission** is a clear and compelling statement that unifies an organization's effort and describes what the firm is all about (i.e., its purpose).

In a few words, the mission statement sums up what is unique about the firm. The information in Figure 1.2 indicates that even though Zappos, Amazon, and L.L. Bean are all in the retail industry, they view their missions quite differently. For example, Zappos' focus is on WOW-worthy customer service and a culture of happiness; Amazon is about a virtuous cycle (flywheel) that includes lower prices, selection, customer experience, traffic, and sellers; and L.L. Bean is about the outdoors. When Amazon purchased Zappos in 2009, the acquisition agreement specified that Zappos would continue to run independently of its new parent. It is interesting to note that both companies now (but not earlier) claim on their websites to be customer-centric. However, the Zappos culture of creating "fun and a little weirdness" was slowly dismantled by Amazon, most notably after the departure of its visionary founder, Tony Hsieh, in 2020. Mr. Hsieh worried about "Amazon creep" and the growing intrusion of Amazon executives into Zappos' management. As part of the 18,000 layoffs announced in February 2023 at Amazon, Zappos had to let go 300 employees, or 20% of its workforce. Many of these layoffs were in the area critical for "WOWing" customers, the customer service division. Amazon has been demanding that Zappos meet the growth targets that Amazon establishes, and some Zappos departments (e.g., logistics, fulfillment and information

Company	Mission Statement
Zappos	Since our humble beginnings, Zappos has been a customer-obsessed company that focuses on **delivering a WOW experience**. We aim to inspire the world by showing it's possible to simultaneously deliver happiness to customers, as well as employees, vendors, shareholders, and the community, in a long-term, sustainable way.[a]
Amazon	**"being Earth's most customer-centric company, best employer, and safest place to work."**[b]
L.L. Bean	Being outside brings out the best in us. That's why we design products that make it easier to take longer walks, have deeper talks, and never worry about the weather.[c]

[a] http://www.inboundmarketingagents.com/inbound-marketing-agents-blog/bid/361859/Zappos-WOW-Philosophy-Tips-for-Fostering-Customer-Delight (accessed February 12, 2019).

[b] https://www.aboutamazon.com/about-us/leadership-principles Mission Statement on Amazon Leadership Principles page (accessed July 27, 2023).

[c] https://www.llbean.com/llb/shop/516917?lndrNbr=516884&nav=leftnav-cust (accessed February 12, 2019).

FIGURE 1.2 Mission statements of three retail businesses.

technology) have been integrated into Amazon departments in order to reduce duplication. Even Zappos' branded signature white boxes have been replaced with Amazon's recognizable brown ones.[13]

A **business strategy** is a plan articulating where a business seeks to go and how it expects to get there. It is the means by which a business plans to achieve its goals. Management constructs this plan in response to market forces, customer demands, and organizational capabilities. Market forces create the competitive context for the business. Some markets, such as those faced by package delivery firms, laptop computer manufacturers, and credit card issuers, face many competitors and a high level of competition, such that product differentiation becomes increasingly difficult. Other markets, such as those for airlines and automobiles, are similarly characterized by high competition, but product differentiation is better established. Customer demands comprise the wants and needs of the individuals and companies who purchase the products and services available in the marketplace. Organizational capabilities include the skills and experience that give the corporation a currency that can add value in the marketplace.

A type of business strategy existing companies that face a dynamic and increasingly digital environment might choose is a digital business strategy. A **digital business strategy** is defined as "a business strategy inspired by the capabilities of powerful, readily accessible digital technologies (**SMACIT** like social media, mobile, analytics, cloud, and Internet of Things), intent on delivering unique, integrated business capabilities in ways that are responsive to constantly changing market conditions" (p. 198).[14] This means that business strategy is formulated and implemented by using digital technologies to create value. The opportunity to strategically leverage a digital technology or technologies is made possible by fusing the organization's business strategy with its IS strategy. Thus, a digital business strategy is broader and more embedded than a more functional IS strategy. In order to execute a digital business strategy, a company must have an *operational backbone* (or the technology and business capability to deliver efficient and reliable core operations) and a *digital service platform* (or the technology and business capability to pave the way for developing and implementing digital innovations). Digital transformations require a digital business strategy.

Over time, as companies change their business strategy, we can expect to see changes in their mission statements. Mark Zuckerberg's reflection on the mission of Facebook and subsequent changes in business strategy at Facebook (now Meta) provide an interesting example. Originally conceived as a product rather than a service, the CEO of Facebook commented: "after we started hiring more people and building out the team, I began to get an appreciation that a company is a great way to get a lot of people involved in a mission you're trying to push forward. Our mission is getting people to connect."[15] Facebook was on the forefront of connecting people via Facebook and apps like Messenger, Instagram, WhatsApp, and Threads. In fact, Facebook was the most downloaded mobile app in the 2010s. Back in 2004 when Facebook was founded, Facebook's business strategy focused on connecting with 2-dimensional screens. At that time, Zuckerberg had not anticipated how his creation could be used for spreading fake news, cyberbullying, political manipulation (as in the 2016 U.S. elections) and facilitating major security breaches like that perpetrated by Cambridge Analytica. Because of the privacy and security concerns, Facebook adopted this mission statement: "to give people the power to share and make the world more open and connected."[16] To reflect its new business strategy emphasizing advanced technologies such as augmented and virtual reality in the metaverse, Facebook was branded as Meta Platforms Inc. in 2021 and a new mission statement was written: "giving people the power to build community and bring the world closer together." Meta indicates that it intends to build community and connectivity while serving everyone, giving them a voice, keeping them secure, and protecting their privacy. Meta keeps the social networking aspect of its previous Facebook mission statements, while also pointing toward a global market with activities in the **metaverse**, or a 3-D enabled digital world that is accessed through technologies such as virtual reality, augmented reality, and other advanced Internet technologies, and where users can interact with others via simulated shared experiences.

---

[13] Kirsten Grind, "Amazon Changes at Zappos Slowly Dismantle Tony Hsieh's Legacy," *Wall Street Journal*, February 11, 2023, https://www.wsj.com/articles/amazon-changes-at-zappos-slowly-dismantle-tony-hsiehs-legacy-5d393647 (accessed February 17, 2023).

[14] I. M. Sebastian, J. W. Ross, C. Beath, M. Mocker, K. G. Moloney, and N. O. Fonstad, "How Big Old Companies Navigate Digital Transformation," *MIS Quarterly Executive* 16, no. 3 (2017): 197–213.

[15] Shayndi Raice, "Is Facebook Ready for the Big Time?" *The Wall Street Journal*, January 14–15, 2012, B1.

[16] To read more about Meta see: Business Mavericks, Meta Mission Statement and Vision Statement in 2022 (Formerly Facebook), Maverick, October 2022, https://businessmavericks.org/meta-mission-statement/ (accessed February 20, 2023) and https://about.meta.com/company-info/ (accessed February 17, 2023).

Business Models vs. Business Strategy

Some new managers confuse the concept of a business model with the concept of a business strategy. The business strategy, as discussed in this chapter, is the coordinated set of actions used to meet the business goals and objectives. It is the path a company takes to achieve its goals. According to Osterwalder and Pigneur, one component of the business strategy is the **business model**, or the "blueprint of how a company does business." The business model can be used to create new products and services that add value to its customers and partners (value creation) and to describe how it will make money from that value it has created (value capture). Some might argue that a business model is the outcome of strategy.

In this chapter we talk a lot about value. Al-Debei and Avison suggest that four major dimensions of a business model—all of which are concerned with value: (1) **value proposition** is focused on a firm's market offerings and targeted customer group(s); (2) **value architecture** describes the configuration of core resources and capabilities that a firm needs to create its market offerings; (3) **value network** involves interfirm relationships and interactions with key external partners and stakeholders; (4) **value finance** primarily focuses on a firms revenue model, pricing strategies, and cost structure.

The value proposition dimension makes it really clear to targeted customers how a firm's product, service, or innovation can benefit them. For instance, L.L. Bean's value proposition is that its products are good for outdoor activities—they won't let you down even when it is raining. In describing digital transformations we explain that they change a firm's value proposition, such as when the firm that had sold expensive, customized machinery started charging for data-driven services that offered value to its customers. By the way, this type of business model involving the shift from selling products to selling product-service systems is called *servitization* and is becoming increasingly popular in the manufacturing industry.

The value architecture dimension often includes the IS infrastructure that a firm needs to create value and make its value proposition a reality. The basic premise of the value network dimension is that every individual or organization in the network can benefit from it. Probably the best example is the enjoyment, connections, and other benefits that people derive from using social media such as Facebook or Renren.

The value finance dimension focuses on the value captured by implementing the business model. This dimension includes a *revenue model*, which generates revenue for the company. Pricing strategies such as those examples listed below represent different types of revenue models:

- *Selling products or services:* Customers make purchases.
- *Subscription:* Customers pay a recurring fee for the product or service.
- *Advertising:* Customers access the product or service for "free," and sponsors or vendors pay fees for advertising that goes with the product or service.
- *Renting/Licensing:* Customers pay a fee to use the product or service for a specified period or number of times. They can also pay one fee for access to as much of the product or service as they want to consume, usually over a specific period of time (i.e., all-you-can-eat).
- *Freemium:* Customers get something for "free," and the company makes money from selling customers something after they get the giveaway. This is similar to a business model used in brick-and-mortar businesses that give away something or sell something for a very low price, but the customer has to pay for refills or upgrades such as giving razors away but making money from selling razor blades or practically giving away printers, but charging a lot for ink.

In 2023, large tech firms, facing a down market, devised new revenue streams or modifications of current ones. One approach implemented by Twitter (rebranded as "X") and Meta, Facebook's and Instagram's parent company, is a verification system service in which subscriber accounts receive a famed "blue check" to confirm their authenticity. Time will tell if this approach works to generate revenue.[17] It didn't work on the New York Times (NYT) that lost its gold verification badge on April 1, 2023. The NYT said it wouldn't pay the $1,000 monthly subscription fee because the purchasable symbol no longer represents authenticity.

A business model can create value without bringing in new revenue from customers. A business model might, instead, use *cost displacement*, in which case a firm funds a project or creates a new service by cost savings, such as replacing personnel by adding new customer self-service options. A striking example is that of Federal Express, which is said to deliver 14 million packages a day.[18] A simple analysis reveals the importance of FedEx's PowerShip (a hardware system to automate a firm's shipping process and expedite large volume shipping). If only 10% of those shipments are tracked, and only 10% of those would have resulted in a 10-minute phone call to FedEx, there would need to be enough operators to handle 1.4 million minutes of phone calls daily. If the business day covered only 8 hours (480 minutes), then FedEx would need to employ almost 3,000 phone operators to cover the calls. If a phone operator is paid a salary of $30,000 (including benefits), the total annual savings PowerShip provides to FedEx is $90 million. This is clearly value creation derived from an information system.

Data-driven business models are equally powerful and relatively new. They are enabled by business analytics tools and big data. **Big data** is a term used to describe exceptionally large data sets of structured, semi-structured, and unstructured data used in computational analysis. In data-driven business models, customers benefit directly or indirectly from how a company employs big data. There are three types of data-driven business models: (1) *data users*, companies that leverage big data for internal purposes to improve their operations or develop new products and services for its customers; (2) *data suppliers*, companies that sell big data that they have harvested, and (3) *data facilitators*, companies that supply data users and suppliers with big data infrastructure solutions (e.g., platforms and apps) and services (e.g., consulting and outsourced analytics services).[19]

Firms need their processes to be aligned with their strategy. FedEx provides access to their PowerShip platform to customers to provide better service, and as demonstrated above, with substantial efficiency. Connecting that platform electronically to merchants, such as Nordstrom's or Walmart, is an additional link in the chain. Providing web-based tools to the merchants completes the circle and enables information to flow without any manual intervention. The end customer provides digital data with minimal effort, and the merchant transmits the data from the order to the shipper almost instantaneously. Adding any manual steps at this volume would be silly. Not as silly, though, as Southwest Airlines reverting back to a manual scheduling system staffed by volunteer employees during the nine-day period when it cancelled over 16,000 flights.

A classic, widely used model developed by Michael Porter still frames most discussions of business strategy. In the next section, we review Porter's Competitive Advantage Strategies framework as well as dynamic environment strategies. We then share questions that a general manager must answer to understand the business strategy.

The Competitive Advantage Strategies Framework

Companies sell their products and services in a marketplace populated with competitors. Michael Porter's framework helps managers understand the strategies they may choose to build a competitive advantage. In his book, *Competitive Advantage*, Porter claims that the "fundamental basis of above-average performance in the long run is sustainable competitive advantage." Porter identifies three primary strategies for achieving competitive advantage: (1) cost leadership, (2) differentiation, and (3) focus. These advantages derive from the company's relative position in the marketplace, and they depend on the strategies and tactics used by competitors. **Cost leadership** results when the organization aims to be the lowest-cost producer in the marketplace. The organization enjoys above-average performance by minimizing costs. The product or service offered must be comparable in quality to those offered by others in the industry so that customers perceive its relative value. Typically, only one cost leader exists within an industry. If more than one organization seeks an advantage with this strategy, a price war ensues, which eventually may drive the organization with the higher cost structure out of the marketplace.

[17] Joseph Pisani, "Facebook, Instagram Roll Out New System for User Verification," *Wall Street Journal*, March 18–19, 2023, pg. B3; Kate Conger and Ryan Mack, "Twitter's Logo Changes to Doge as Users Await Blue Check-Mark Removal," *New York Times*, April 3, 2023, https://www.nytimes.com/2023/04/03/technology/twitter-blue-check-elon-musk.html (accessed April 6, 2023).

[18] Andra Picincu, "How to Find a FedEx Tracking Number," Bizfluent.com, January 22, 2019, https://bizfluent.com/how-8077705-fedex-tracking-number.html (accessed March 6, 2019).

[19] R. Schroeder, "Big Data Business Models: Challenges and Opportunities," *Cogent Social Sciences* 2 (2016): 1166924.

Aldi, a German grocery store chain that has gained a strong foothold in the United States, recently placed first on a list of the cheapest grocery store chains in the United States.[20] Aldi claims: "With our smaller selection of high-quality foods, along with wider aisles and smaller stores, our shoppers can save time and money."[21] The small (but high-quality) selection is touted as an advantage because its customers are "not overwhelmed by choice." Aldi achieves its cost leadership position by removing "unnecessary and costly aspects of grocery shopping." This translates into policies such as minimizing store personnel, predominately selling its own branded products, providing mostly self-service checkouts, not providing bags for groceries, not providing curbside delivery, and renting out shopping carts for a quarter (so the staff don't need to roam its parking lots collecting them.)[22] One of this book's authors noticed that many Aldi shoppers don't rent the carts, but rather (like her) try to stuff the items they purchase on a shopping trip into the few reusable grocery bags that they have brought.

Through **differentiation**, the organization offers its product or service in a way that appears unique in the marketplace. The organization identifies which qualitative dimensions are most important to its customers and then finds ways to add value along one or more of those dimensions. For this strategy to work, the price charged to customers for the differentiator must seem fair relative to the price charged by competitors. Typically, multiple firms in any given market employ this strategy.

Whole Foods Market is an example of a company that uses the differentiation strategy. It views itself as a mission-driven company that seeks out "the finest natural and organic foods available, maintain the strictest quality standards in the industry, and have an unshakeable commitment to sustainable agriculture." It claims to be "world's leader in natural and organic foods, with 500+ stores in North America and the UK."[23] Other grocery chains in this market space include Sprouts and Fresh Market. Unlike these competitors, Whole Foods is owned by Amazon.com that provides it with the added advantage of making it possible to shop on the Amazon website for groceries or return the goods ordered on Amazon.com at Whole Foods stores.

Focus allows an organization to limit its scope to a narrower segment of the market and tailor its offerings to that group of customers. This strategy has two variants: (1) *cost focus*, in which the organization seeks a cost advantage within its segment, and (2) *differentiation focus*, in which it seeks to distinguish its products or services within the segment. This strategy allows the organization to achieve a local competitive advantage even if it does not achieve competitive advantage in the marketplace overall. Porter explains how the focuser can achieve competitive advantage by focusing exclusively on certain market segments:

> *"Breadth of target is clearly a matter of degree, but the essence of focus is the exploitation of a narrow target's differences from the balance of the industry. Narrow focus in and of itself is not sufficient for above-average performance."*

Trader Joe's has a focus strategy. Trader Joe's is known for its unique, often international, gourmet product offerings such as white truffle potato chips, honey-roasted pumpkin ravioli and sweet cinnamon-filled Korean pancakes. Its website claims: "We are committed to providing our customers outstanding value in the form of the best quality products at the best everyday prices."[24] Its employees, called "crew members," dress in colorful t-shirts or Hawaiian shirts, and they are tasked with providing adventure, or at least a great shopping experience, for the customers. Trader Joe's comes in fifth on a list of low-cost grocery stores; It offers lower prices than even Costco (6th place), Walmart (7th place), and Sam's Club (10th place)—companies long-known for their low prices.[25] Of course, Trader Joe's doesn't have as many offerings as these other stores. Trader Joe's makes its low prices possible by providing its own more affordable brand products and not offering any coupons, discounts, online special promotions, or curbside delivery. It gets products that aren't its own brands at a discount because it buys in volume directly from its suppliers,

[20] For an overview of cheapest U.S. grocery stores, and Aldi and Trader Joe's in particular, see: Rachel Cruze, "What Is the Cheapest Grocery Store? Ramsey, December 13, 2022, https://www.ramseysolutions.com/budgeting/cheapest-grocery-store (accessed February 18, 2023).

[21] Aldi, "Our Purpose and Core Values," https://corporate.aldi.us/en/about-us/our-purpose-and-core-values/ (accessed February 18, 2023).

[22] R. Cruze, "What is the Cheapest Grocery Store?".

[23] Whole Foods Market, "Company Information," https://www.wholefoodsmarket.com/company-info, (accessed February 19, 2023).

[24] Trader Joe's "About Us" https://www.traderjoes.com/home/about-us (accessed February 19, 2023).

[25] R. Cruze, "What is the cheapest grocery store?".

it contracts early for the products, and its crew members put them on the shelves, consequently saving their suppliers shelving costs which are passed on to Trader Joe's customers. Trader Joe's has stores throughout the United States and is owned by the same family that also owns Aldi (Nord).

Dynamic Environment Strategies

Porter's Competitive Advantage Strategies model is useful for diagnostics, for understanding how a business seeks to profit in its chosen marketplace, and for prescriptions about building new opportunities for advantage. It reflects a careful balancing of countervailing competitive forces posed by buyers, suppliers, competitors, new entrants, and substitute products and services within an industry. As is the case with many models, dynamic environment strategies offer managers useful tools for thinking about strategy.

However, the Porter model was developed at a time when competitive advantage was sustainable because the rate of change in any given industry was relatively slow and manageable. Since the late 1980s, when this framework was at the height of its popularity, newer models were developed to take into account the increasing turbulence, complexity, and velocity of the marketplace. Organizations need to be able to respond instantly and change rapidly, which requires dynamic structures and processes. One example of this type of approach is D'Aveni's hyper competition framework. Discussions of hyper competition take a perspective different from that of the previous framework. Porter's framework focuses on creating competitive advantage in relatively stable markets, whereas D'Aveni's and subsequent **hyper competition** frameworks suggest that the speed and aggressiveness of the moves and countermoves in a highly competitive and turbulent market create an environment in which advantages are rapidly created and eroded. In a hypercompetitive market, trying to sustain a specific competitive advantage can be a deadly distraction because the environment and the marketplace change rapidly. To manage the rapid speed of change, firms value agility and focus on quickly adjusting their organizational resources to gain competitive advantage. Successful concepts in hypercompetitive markets include dynamic capabilities and creative destruction.

Dynamic capabilities allow a firm to orchestrate its resources in the face of turbulent environments. According to Teece and colleagues, the dynamic capabilities view focuses on the ways a firm can integrate, build, and reconfigure resources using internal capabilities, or abilities, to adjust to rapidly changing environments. These dynamic capabilities are built rather than bought. They are embedded in firm-specific routines, processes, and asset positions. Thus, they are difficult for rivals to imitate. In sum, they help determine the speed and degree to which the firm can marshal and align its resources and competences to match the opportunities and requirements of the business environment. The clusters of dynamic capabilities for *sensing* opportunities and environmental change in the environment, *seizing* resources to take advantage of the opportunities and changes, and consequently *transforming* (including reconfiguring) resources, as well as the organizational structure and culture as needed, are especially important in designing and implementing coherent business models. Thus, good business strategy evolves along with the shifting business environment and dynamic capabilities. Dynamic capabilities are discussed in greater detail in Chapter 2.

Since the 1990s, a competitive practice, called **creative destruction**, emerged. First predicted over 60 years ago by the economist Joseph Schumpeter, it was made popular more recently by Harvard Professor Clay Christensen. Coincidentally (or maybe not), the accelerated competition has occurred concomitantly with sharp increases in the quality and quantity of information technology (IT) investment. The changes in competitive dynamics are particularly striking in sectors that spend the most on IT. An example of creative destruction is provided in Apple's cannibalizing its own products. Steve Jobs, Apple's founder and former CEO, felt strongly that if a company was not willing to cannibalize its own products, someone else would come along and do it for them. That was evident in the way Apple introduced the iPhone while iPod sales were brisk and the iPad while its Macintosh sales were strong. Apple continues to exhibit this strategy with subsequent releases of new models for all its products. It's even generating revenues from sales of services to older models that others have refurbished. In fact, Apple generates higher margins from its sales of services for these phones than from the sale of the phones themselves.[26]

[26] Christopher Mim, "Apple's Smartphone Dominance," *Wall Street Journal*, April 15–16, 2023, p. b2.

Strategic Approach	Key Idea	Application to Information Systems
Porter's competitive advantage strategies	Firms achieve competitive advantage through cost leadership, differentiation, or focus.	Understanding which strategy is chosen by a firm is critical to choosing IS to complement the strategy.
Dynamic environment strategies	Speed, agility, and aggressive moves and countermoves by a firm create and sustain competitive advantage.	The speed of change is too fast for manual response, making IS critical to achieving business goals.

FIGURE 1.3 Summary of strategic approaches and IT applications.

Why Are Strategic Advantage Models Essential to Planning for Information Systems?

A general manager who relies solely on IS personnel to make all IS decisions not only gives up authority over IS strategy but also hampers crucial future business decisions. In fact, business strategy should drive IS decision making, and changes in business strategy should entail reassessments of IS. Moreover, changes in IS capabilities or potential should trigger reassessments of business strategy—as in the case of the Social IT when companies that understood or even considered its implications for the marketplace quickly outpaced their competitors who failed to do so. For the purposes of our model, the Information Systems Strategy Triangle, understanding business strategy means answering the following questions:

1. What is the business goal or objective?
2. What is the plan for achieving it? What is the role of IS in this plan?
3. Who are the crucial competitors and partners, and what is required of a successful player in this marketplace?
4. What are the industry forces in this marketplace?
5. How can dynamic capabilities be developed and used in a rapidly changing business environment?

Porter's Competitive Advantage Strategies framework and the dynamic environment frameworks (summarized in Figure 1.3) are revisited in the next few chapters. They are especially helpful in discussing the role of IS in building and sustaining competitive advantages (Chapter 2) and for incorporating IS into business strategy. The next section of this chapter establishes a foundation for understanding organizational strategies.

Brief Overview of Organizational Strategies

Organizational strategy includes the organization's design as well as the choices it makes to define, set up, coordinate, and control its work processes. How a manager designs the organization impacts every aspect of operations from dealing with innovation to relationships with customers, suppliers, and employees. The organizational strategy is a plan that answers the question: "How will the company organize to achieve its goals and implement its business strategy?"

A useful framework for organizational design can be found in the book *Building the Information Age Organization* by Cash, Eccles, Nohria, and Nolan. This framework (Figure 1.4) suggests that the successful execution of a company's organizational strategy comprises the best combination of organizational, control, and cultural variables. Organizational variables include decision rights, business processes, formal reporting relationships, and informal networks. Control variables include the availability of data, nature and quality of planning, effectiveness of performance measurement and evaluation systems, and incentives to do good work. Cultural variables comprise the values of the organization. These organizational, control, and cultural variables are **managerial levers** used by decision makers to effect changes in their organizations. These managerial levers are discussed in detail in Chapter 3.

Our objective is to give the manager a framework to use in evaluating various aspects of organizational design. In this way, the manager can review the current organization and assess which components may

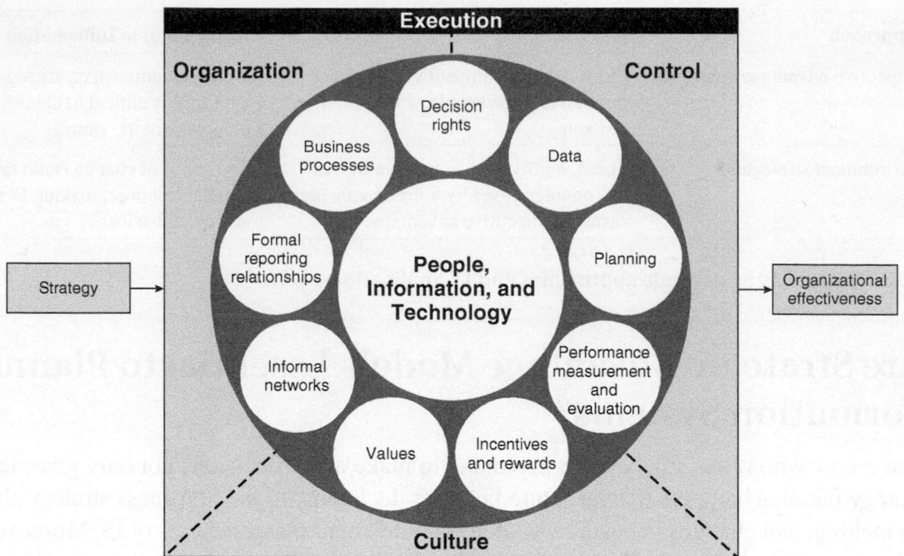

FIGURE 1.4 Managerial levers model.
Source: J. Cash, R. G. Eccles, N. Nohria, and R. L. Nolan, *Building the Information Age Organization* (Homewood, IL: Richard D. Irwin, 1994).

be missing and what future options are available. Understanding organizational design means answering the following questions:

1. What are the important structures and reporting relationships within the organization?
2. Who holds the decision rights to critical decisions?
3. What are the important people-based networks (social and informational), and how can we use them to get work done better?
4. What control systems (management and measurement systems) are in place?
5. What are the culture, values, and beliefs of the organization?
6. What is the work that is performed in organizations, who performs it, and where and when is it performed?
7. What are the key business processes?

The answers to these questions inform the assessment of the organization's use of IS. Chapters 3, 4, and 5 use the managerial levers model to assess the impact of IS on the firm. Chapters 8 and 9 use this same list to understand the business and governance of the IS organization.

Brief Overview of Information Systems Strategy

IS strategy is a plan an organization uses to provide information services. IS allow a company to implement its business strategy. JetBlue's former Vice President for People explained it nicely: "We define what the business needs and then go find the technology to support that."[27]

Business strategy is a function of competition (What does the customer want and what does the competition do?), positioning (In what way does the firm want to compete?), and capabilities (What can the firm do?). IS help determine the company's capabilities. An entire chapter is devoted to understanding key issues facing general managers concerning IT architecture, but for now a more basic framework is used to understand the decisions related to IS that an organization must make.

[27] Hogue et al., *Winning the 3-Legged Race*, 111.

	What	Who	Where
Platforms	The "orchestrator" that calls into action apps that record, report, or transform data.	System users and managers; vendors; platform partners	Physical location of devices (cloud, data center, etc.)
Applications (apps)	The components that generally work on a particular platform. They request data for recording or reporting, and also transform data by performing calculations and making updates as needed.	System users and managers; app providers and developers	The platform it resides on and physical location of that platform
Networks	Platform and app components for local or long-distance networking.	System users and managers; company that provides the service	Where the nodes, the wires, and other transport media are located
Data	Electronic representation of facts or observations.	Owners of data; data administrators	Where the information resides

FIGURE 1.5 IS strategy matrix.

The purpose of the matrix in Figure 1.5 is to give the manager a high-level view of the relation between the four IS infrastructure components and the other resource considerations that are keys to IS strategy. Infrastructure used to be discussed in terms of hardware and software but today we talk about platforms and applications (or apps). Platforms are technically any set of technologies upon which other technologies or applications run. Often they are a combination of hardware and operating system software. Microsoft Windows and Apple's Macintosh with its latest operating system are two examples of platforms. Also common are mobile platforms such as the iPhone and Samsung/Android phone. **Applications** or **apps**, on the other hand, are self-contained software programs that fulfill a specific purpose and run on a platform. The term "apps" became popular from the smartphone industry, beginning when Apple introduced the App Store. But more recently, because all platforms have applications that run on them, the term *apps* has taken on a broader meaning; some use the term to describe almost any software that users encounter. Business activities are supported by, and in some cases support, platforms and apps. For example, a bank deploys an app for a PC, smartphone, or tablet. The app sits on top of a platform (the PC running windows, for example).

The third component of IS infrastructure is the network, which is the physical means by which information is exchanged among system components. Examples include fiber networks such as Google Fiber; cable networks such as those provided by Time Warner, AT&T, and Comcast; Wi-Fi provided by many local services; and 4G/5G/WiMax technologies (which are actually Internet communication standards, but some phone companies adopt those terms as the name of networks they offer). Some communications are conducted through a private digital network, managed by an internal unit.

Finally, the fourth component of IS infrastructure is the data. Data are the bits and bytes stored in the system. In current systems, data are not necessarily stored alongside the programs that use them; hence, it is important to understand what data are in the system and where they are stored. Many more detailed models of IS infrastructure exist, and interested readers may refer to any of the dozens of books that describe them. For the purposes of this text, the IS strategy matrix provides sufficient information to allow the general manager to assess the critical issues in information management.

SUMMARY

The Information Systems Strategy Triangle represents a simple framework for understanding the impact of IS on businesses. It relates business strategy with IS strategy and organizational strategy and implies the alignment that must be maintained in business planning. The Information Systems Strategy Triangle suggests the following management principles.

Business Strategy

Business strategy drives organizational strategy and IS strategy. Sometimes the IS strategy is the Business strategy. The organization and its IS should clearly support defined business goals and objectives.

- Definition: A well-articulated vision of where a business seeks to go and how it expects to get there
- Example Models: Porter's Competitive Advantage Strategies framework; dynamic environment frameworks

Organizational Strategy

Organizational strategy must complement business strategy. The way a business is organized either supports the implementation of its business strategy or it gets in the way.

- Definition: The organization's design, as well as the choices it makes to define, set up, coordinate, and control its work processes
- Example Model: Managerial levers

IS Strategy

IS strategy must complement or serve as business strategy. When IS support business goals, the business appears to be working well. IS strategy can itself affect and is affected by changes in a firm's business and organizational strategies. Moreover, IS strategy always has consequences—intended or not—on business and organizational strategies.

- Definition: The plan the organization uses in providing IS and services
- Models: A basic framework for understanding IS decisions for platform, applications, network, and data that relate architecture (the "what"), and the other resource considerations ("who" and "where") representing. important planning constraints

Strategic Relationships

Organizational strategy and information strategy must complement each other. They must be designed so that they support, rather than hinder, each other. If a decision is made to change one corner of the triangle, it is necessary to evaluate the other two corners to ensure that alignment is preserved. Changing business strategy without thinking through the effects on the organization and IS strategies will cause the business to struggle until alignment is restored. Likewise, changing IS or the organization alone will cause problems with alignment.

KEY TERMS

FOUNDATIONAL READINGS

Business Models: A. Osterwalder, Y. Pigneur, and colleagues have written prolifically about business models. This award-winning book is considered by many as a key source for business model concepts: Osterwalder, Alexander, and Yves Pigneur. *Business Model Generation: A Handbook for Visionaries, Game Changers, and Challengers*. Vol. 1. John Wiley & Sons, 2010. Our definition of a business model and business model concepts as they relate to IS comes from: A. Osterwalder, Y. Pigneur, and C. L. Tucci, "Clarifying Business Models: Origins, Present, and Future of the Concept," *Communications of the Association for Information Systems* 16, no. 1 (2005), Article 1, page 2; An influential piece for IS-related business models and their dimensions is Al-Debei, M. M., & Avison, D. (2010). Developing a unified framework of the business model concept. *European Journal of Information Systems*, 19, no. 3: 359–376.

Competitive Advantage Strategies Framework: M. Porter, *Competitive Advantage*, 1st ed. (New York: The Free Press, 1985). M. Porter, *Competitive Advantage: Creating and Sustaining Superior Performance*, 2nd ed. (New York: The Free Press, 1998). This book (multiple editions) presented the Competitive Advantages Strategies Model.

Dynamic Capabilities: D.J. Teece and various colleagues have written extensively about Dynamic Capabilities for decades. See, for example: D. J. Teece, G. Pisano, and A. Shuen, "Dynamic Capabilities and Strategic Management," *Strategic Management Journal* 18 (1997), 509–533; David Teece, "Dynamic Capabilities," *vol. 1 of The Encyclopedia of Management Theory*, ed. Eric Kessler (Los Angeles, CA: Sage, 2013), 221–24; Teece, David J. "Business models and dynamic capabilities." *Long Range Planning* 51, no. 1 (2018): 40–49.

Hypercompetition: R. A. D'aveni, *Hypercompetition*. Simon and Schuster, 2010. For a summary, see: D. Goeltz, "Hypercompetition," vol. 1 of *The Encyclopedia of Management Theory*, ed. Eric Kessler (Los Angeles, CA: Sage, 2013), 359–360.

Managerial Levers: James I. Cash, Robert G. Eccles, Nitin Nohria, and Richard L. Nolan, *Building the Information Age Organization* (Homewood, IL: Richard D. Irwin, 1994).

DISCUSSION QUESTIONS

1. Why is it typically important for business strategy to drive organizational strategy and IS strategy? What might happen if the business strategy is not the driver?
2. Consider a traditional manufacturing company that wants to undergo a digital transformation. What might be a reasonable business strategy, and how would it relate to IS strategy? How would organizational strategy need to change? How would this differ for a restaurant chain? A consumer products company? A nonprofit?
3. This chapter describes key components of an IS strategy. Describe the IS strategy of a consulting firm using the matrix framework (Figure 1.5).
4. What are the challenges Meta and Twitter (which has been renamed "X") face in implementing a verification system service revenue model described in this chapter after they have used an advertising-based revenue model for so long? How does Meta's Threads complicate these challenges for Meta and Twitter ("X")? (Note: Meta's Threads, a direct competitor of Twitter, started off without any revenue model at all, but with blue checks obtained without cost from its Instagram customers.) Devise and describe an alternative revenue model for social networking companies. What are the strengths and weaknesses of the revenue model you are proposing?

Case Study 1-1 Judo Bank: Business Strategy

In 2016, an Australian bank was established that assumed the name of its business strategy. The bank was named Judo Bank and it adopted two Judo principles as its business strategy: (1) Go where your opponent isn't and (2) Use your opponent's size and strength against them. In a nutshell: "Judo Strategy is the art of using size and agility to outwit larger opponents."

It was a tumultuous time for Australian banks when Judo Bank was founded, and a martial art strategy seemed especially appropriate. The competition among the four biggest Australian (Big Four) banks populating the lending market space was fierce. They had been quite profitable in the 1980s when they were provided with preferred access to domestic and international payment systems. After the global financial crisis in 2007–2008, they struggled to be profitable. They focused on residential mortgage lending. Various scandals related to money laundering, lax lending standards, and abusing their customers brought down the ire of the Australian Government's Royal Commission into Misconduct in the banking industry. It became clear to the chief banking regulator, the Australian Prudential Regulation Authority (ARPA), that something needed to be done to lower entry barriers and make the industry more competitive and respected. However, a subsequent study by the Australian Competition and Consumer Commission (ACCC) in 2018 concluded that the Big Four still acted like an oligopoly and that some of ARPA's regulations actually hurt the smaller banks. For example, meeting some of ARPA's accreditation requirements was termed "prohibitive" for the smaller Authorized Deposit-taking Institutions (ADIs) and the limits on the monthly allowable growth of the Big Four was much larger than that of the other banks (i.e., $A1.1 billion vs. $A100 million, respectively).

One helpful pathway APRA pursued to make industry healthier was to grant new ADI banking licenses to four fintech startups. Judo Bank was one of the four. It had acquired a license from APRA in 2019 as an ADI and within a year it was privately valued at A$1 billion. But that wasn't enough funding to purchase IT to rival the big Australian banks.

Judo Bank focused on servicing small and medium-sized enterprises (SMEs), an underserved market. Its mission is "to be Australia's most trusted SME business bank." Judo Bank determined that to serve SMEs successfully as their business bank, it needed to hone its relationship management skills and not its IT skills. It created a culture based on the values of trust, teamwork with the customers, and accountability—values that the larger banks could not easily brag about. In fact, because they were so large, the big banks used self-service technologies to be efficient and profitable, and they were not known for establishing personal relationships with their customers. Judo Bank automated its back-office tasks while allowing its frontline employees to invest their time in developing interpersonal relationships and trust with its employees.

What Judo Bank didn't do was invest in IT. Yet, on its website Judo claims that it is a "high-touch, high-tech" business model. How can that be if it didn't invest in IT? Judo Bank did it by adopting an IT strategy that complemented the capabilities of its employees by allowing them to engage directly with their customers; Judo Bank relied on something called Everything.as.a.Service (X.a.a.S), which allows the bank the ability to get best-of-breed technology for the flexibility and speed that it needs. It doesn't own IT; rather it acquires what it needs as an operational expense. For example, Judo paid a subscription for each employee's computer, it used the Customer Relationship Management system Sales.force (S.a.a.S), and it employed a security solution in the cloud (Authentication.a.a.S). By using an array of X.a.a.S, Judo didn't have to invest in technology. However, the bank was and continues to be faced with the especially challenging task of managing an orchestra of suppliers. Its IT strategy seems to have worked because Judo Bank is the only one of the four challenger ADI banks to survive and thrive.

Sources: This case is primarily based upon a 2022 case in MISQ Executive: Breidbach, Christoph F., Amol M. Joshi, Paul P. Maglio, Frederik von Briel, Alex Twigg, Graham Dickens, and Nancy V. Wünderlich. "How Everything-as-a-Service Enabled Judo to Become a Billion-Dollar Bank Without Owning IT." *MISQ Executive,* 21, no. 3 (2022): 185–203; See also Judo Bank, https://www.judo.bank/about-judo/ (accessed February 21, 2023); Australian Competition & Consumer Commission, Residential Mortgage Inquiry: Final Report, November 2018, "Residential mortgage price inquiry—Final report", November 2018, https://apo.org.au/node/210046 (accessed March 20, 2023).

Case Study 1-1 (Continued)

Discussion Questions

1. Based on the description of Judo Bank provided above, describe its business, IS, and organizational strategies.
2, Does Judo Bank have a digital business strategy? Please provide a rationale for your response.
3. Explain the extent to which you consider Judo Bank's business, IT, and organizational strategies to be aligned.
4. What is the purpose of a mission statement? Does Judo Bank's mission statement seem to be satisfying the purpose of a mission statement? Please explain your response.
5. Describe Judo Bank's value proposition, value architecture, and value network.
6. Which of the Competitive Advantage Strategies does Judo Bank appear to be using based on this case? Provide support for your choice.

Case Study 1-2 Amazon in 2023

The horror of the COVID-19 pandemic cannot be overstated. Yet during that time when people were isolated in their houses, there was an exponential increase in requests for goods to be delivered to people, and Amazon rose to the challenge. Amazon was able to deliver the goods they needed in a timely manner. It was able to scale up its operations to meet demand. Fortuitously, just prior to the pandemic it had planned to build its own product delivery network and in February 2019 it let FedEX, UPS, and USPS know of its intentions to deliver products to its own customers. The network now is also used as a shipping service by its selling partners. This product delivery network helped Amazon when it changed its promised delivery time from two days to one day in the United States to Prime customers in many locations.

Amazon's far-flung logistics network includes a fleet of aircraft to speedily deliver a wide selection of goods to its customers and a fleet of delivery trucks for last mile delivery to homes, offices, and lockers. Amazon has also invested in the latest technology to make deliveries. Prime Air is a fleet of "safe" drones that can make deliveries of packages weighing under 5 pounds in a radius of 15 miles within 30 minutes. Service with the drones was piloted in Lockeford, California in June 2022. Amazon also started a field test in Snohomish County, Washington of a fully-electric autonomous delivery vehicle called Amazon Scout in January, 2019. However, that project was halted in October 2022 in response to Amazon's lower sales growth. It is easy to consider Amazon as a firm having instant success, but it began by targeting bookstores as "Cadabra" in 1994 in a Seattle basement, with initial funding from the parents of then 30-year-old CEO Jeffrey Bezos. Within a year, Bezos decided he had to rename the site due to some confusion about the name, and also because of his desire to reflect a strategic vision of Amazon.com becoming "Earth's Biggest Bookstore," just as Amazon is the Earth's biggest river. By the end of 1996, Amazon tallied almost $16 million in sales. After an IPO in 1997, Amazon shipped its 1 millionth order.

While this might not seem to dispel the "instant success," myth mentioned above, a deeper look is quite interesting. You might be surprised to learn that Amazon operated at a loss for just over 9 years. In fact, the losses increased as revenue increased, which was contrary to expectations at first glance. A deeper look reveals that the losses resulted from Amazon's reinvestment that focused on expansion and growth. But how did it eventually recover from what seemed at the time to be losses that appeared to be spiraling out of control? Is there a secret to its eventual success?

In 2012, Bezos was reported to have changed the vision from "Earth's Biggest Bookstore" to the "Biggest Store on Earth." Currently, Amazon boasts a more ambitious strategic vision of having "Earth's biggest selection and being the Earth's most customer-centric company."

Bezos has ascribed its success to using a "flywheel" strategy where lower prices stimulate sales, which allows fixed costs to be spread over more items, lowering costs in the long run. A flywheel is a heavy object, which takes great force to move it, but once it moves, it is difficult to slow or stop it.

Case Study 1-2 **(Continued)**

Bezos explains that feeding the movement of the flywheel can occur in many different ways besides merely lowering prices. Procuring the Whole Foods chain not only builds revenues but also provides potential for online grocery sales because the widely dispersed inventories in those stores can enable them to serve as additional distribution centers.

Sources: Alyssa Newcomb, "Amazon Delivers Its Shipping Intentions to FedEx, UPS, USPS via Regulatory Filing," February 6, 2019, https://finance.yahoo.com/news/amazon-delivers-shipping-intentions-fedex-002643430.html (accessed July 27, 2023); Amazon, Amazon Delivery & Logistics https://www.aboutamazon.com/what-we-do/delivery-logistics (accessed February 22, 2023) and A drone program taking flight (aboutamazon.com) and https://www.aboutamazon.com/news/transportation/amazon-prime-air-prepares-for-drone-deliveries (accessed July 27, 2023); Sean Scott, Meet Scout, About amazon, January 23, 2019, https://www.aboutamazon.com/news/transportation/meet-scout (accessed July 27, 2023); Spencer Soper and Matt Day, Amazon Abandons Home Delivery Robot Tests in Latest Cost Cuts, Bloomberg, October 6, 2022 https://www.bloomberg.com/news/articles/2022-10-06/amazon-abandons-autonomous-home-delivery-robot-in-latest-cut (accessed February 22, 2023); Fundable.com, "Amazon Startup Story," https://www.fundable.com/learn/startup-stories/amazon (accessed February 9, 2019); Juan Carlos Perez, "Amazon Records First Profitable Year in Its History," *Computerworld*, January 28, 2004, https://www.computerworld.com/article/2575106/amazon-records-first-profitable-year-in-its-history.html (accessed February 8, 2019); Robin Lewis, *The Robin Report*, January 24, 2012, https://www.therobinreport.com/amazon-from-earths-biggest-bookstore-to-the-biggest-store-on-earth (accessed February 11, 2019); Scott Davis, "How Amazon's Brand and Customer Experience Became Synonymous," *Forbes.com*, July 14, 2016, https://www.forbes.com/sites/scottdavis/2016/07/14/how-amazons-brand-and-customer-experience-became-synonymous/#1a4b9d643cd5 (accessed February 11, 2019); Jeff Haden, "The 1 Principle Jeff Bezos and Amazon Follow to Fuel Incredible Growth," *Inc.*, June 28, 2017, https://www.inc.com/jeff-haden/the-1-principle-jeff-bezos-and-amazon-follow-to-fuel-incredible-growth.html (accessed February 9, 2019).

Discussion Questions

1. How does Amazon's Flywheel strategy fit with its evolving vision statements over the years?
2. Focusing on online product sales, which of the Competitive Advantage Strategies does Amazon appear to be using based on this case? Provide support for your choice.
3. How far could Bezos have gone in Amazon's evolution without using information technology?
4. Assume that there is hypercompetition in product sales. How is Amazon responding to that environment?
5. Are Amazon's endeavors in shipping services consistent with Amazon's mission (see Figure 1.2)? Defend your position.

Strategic Use of Information Resources

2

This chapter introduces the concept of building competitive advantage using information systems-based applications. It begins with a discussion of a set of eras that describe the use of information resources historically. It then presents information resources as strategic tools, discussing information technology (IT) assets and IT capabilities. Michael Porter's Five Competitive Forces model provides a framework for discussing strategic advantage, and his Value Chain model addresses tactical ways organizations link their business processes to create strategic partnerships. We then introduce the Piccoli and Ives model to show how strategic advantage may be sustained in light of competitive barriers while the Resource-Based View (RBV) focuses on gaining and maintaining strategic advantage through information and other resources of the firm. We complement our perspective of strategic advantage from the RBV by considering the Dynamic Capabilities View. The chapter offers insights about the risks of strategic use of IT and a description of external relationships including strategic alliances, business ecosystems and co-opetitive relationships. The chapter concludes with a brief discussion about co-creating IT and business strategy. Just as a note: This chapter uses the terms *competitive advantage* and *strategic advantage* interchangeably.

Zara, a global retail and apparel manufacturer based in Arteixo, Spain, needed a dynamic business model to keep up with the ever-changing demands of its customers and industry. At the heart of its model was a set of business processes and an information system that linked demand to manufacturing and manufacturing to distribution. The strategy at Zara stores was simply to have a continuous flow of new products that were typically in limited supply. As a result, regular customers visited their stores often—an average of 17 times a year, whereas many retail stores averaged only four times a year. When customers saw something they liked, they bought it on the spot because they knew it would probably be gone the next time they visited the store. The result was a very loyal and satisfied customer base and a wildly profitable business model.

How did Zara do it? It was possible in part because the company aligned its information system strategy with its business strategy. An early version of its corporate website gives some insight:

> *"Zara's approach to design is closely linked to our customers. A non-stop flow of information from stores conveys shoppers' desires and demands, inspiring our 200-person strong creative team."*[1]

Inditex, Zara's parent company, states on its corporate website that it wants to bring "beautiful, consciously-crafted fashion to everyone, everywhere." It sees itself as a "family of brands that celebrate style, self-expression and the power to make a change."[2] However, accomplishing this is not so simple. Martin Roll shows in an extensive analysis of Zara that such a strategy is accomplished only through an amazing orchestration of information systems (IS), employing two important rules: "To give customers

[1] Inditex website, http://www.inditex.com/en/who_we_are/concepts/zara (accessed February 20, 2012). Much information in the case was derived from the Inditex website.

[2] Inditex Home Page, https://www.inditex.com/itxcomweb/en/home (accessed March 6, 2023).

what they want" and "get it to them faster than anyone else."[3] While other brands can take six months to get their new designs into stores, Zara can get a new design created and in stores within two weeks. Producing about 12,000 new designs each year and manufacturing over 450 million items in runs of no more than 8,000 pieces for any particular design requires a well-oiled supply chain coupled with more than simple daily sales reports.

Zara is constantly vigilant, on the lookout for new design trends, so its stores can stock their shelves with items that are still likely to be top-of-mind for customers. Those trends often come from fashion influencers including actors, actresses, and social-media celebrities worldwide. For example, an influencer on WhoWhatWear.com based in the UK frequently talks about looking at new Zara arrivals to see what's trending.[4] Zara also captures comments from customers, visits college campuses and nightclubs, and even notes what their customers are wearing in their stores, to find new fashion ideas. In short, customers help co-create fashions that will appear in Zara stores.

An interesting illustration of Zara's rapid response is when four women visited separate Zara stores in Tokyo, Toronto, San Francisco, and Frankfurt, asking for pink scarves. Over the next few days, this story was repeated in other stores globally. One week later, Zara sent 500,000 pink scarves to 2,000 stores globally, which sold out in three days. This story illustrates how trends begin on a small scale but develop rapidly. Thanks to meticulous use of IS, Zara is equipped to handle that rapid development and reach the fashion market before the inevitable decline of a trend.[5]

The entire process from factory to shop floor is coordinated from Zara's headquarters by using IS. The point-of-sale (POS) system on the shop floor records the information from each sale, and the information is transmitted to headquarters at the end of each business day. Using a proprietary smartphone app, the Zara shop managers also report daily to the designers at headquarters to let them know what has sold and what the customers wanted but couldn't find. Real-time analysis of the sales information is used to determine which product lines and colors should be kept and which should be altered or dropped. Further, the analysis of sales information derives the average weight of residents in each store's neighborhood and thus predicts the demand for every neighborhood.[6] The designers communicate directly with the production staff to plan for the incredible number of designs that are manufactured every year.

Shop managers have the option to order new designs twice a week using the smartphone app. Before ordering, they can use the smartphone app to check out the new designs. Once an order is received at the manufacturing plant at headquarters, a large computer-controlled piece of equipment calculates how to position patterns to minimize scrap and cut up to 100 layers of fabric at a time. The cut fabric is then sent from Zara factories to external workshops for sewing. The completed products are sent to distribution centers where miles of automated conveyor belts are used to sort the garments and recombine them into shipments for each store. Zara's IS department wrote the applications controlling the conveyors, often in collaboration with vendors of the conveyor equipment.

Zara recognizes that the proximity of its suppliers and small batches help make it possible to get new designs quickly to its stores. Over 50% of its final product is manufactured by suppliers close to its headquarters.[7] However, new entrants not encumbered with a large inventory of stores are making inroads in Zara's market. For example, the British firm, Boohoo.com, headquartered in Manchester, saw its sales of fashion products growing rapidly; like Zara, more than half of its designs are manufactured in Britain near its headquarters and its lead times are as short as two weeks.[8]

As the Zara example illustrates, innovative use of a firm's information resources can provide substantial and sustainable advantages over competitors. Every business depends on IS, making its use a necessary

---

[3] Martin Roll, "The Secret of Zara's Success: A Culture of Customer Co-creation," March 2018, https://martinroll.com/resources/articles/strategy/the-secret-of-zaras-success-a-culture-of-customer-co-creation/ (accessed February 17, 2019). Also see IE Insights, "Zara: Technology and User Experience as Drivers of Business, December 15, 2017, https://www.ie.edu/insights/articles/zara-technology-and-user-experience-as-drivers-of-business/ (accessed March 6, 2023).

[4] For example, see Yushra Siddiqui, "I've Noted Every Winter It Trend at Zara—Take Note of these 9," WhoWhat Wear, December 14, 2022, https://www.whowhatwear.co.uk/2022-zara-trends (accessed March 6, 2023).

[5] Yushra Siddiqui, 2022.

[6] IE insights, "Zara: Technology and User Experience as Drivers of Business," December 15, 2017, https://www.ie.edu/insights/articles/zara-technology-and-user-experience-as-drivers-of-business/ (accessed March 6, 2023).

[7] Inditex, "Our Approach," https://www.inditex.com/itxcomweb/en/group/our-approach (accessed March 6, 2023).

[8] Sonya Dowsett, "Zara Looks to Technology to Keep Up with Faster Fashion," *Reuters*, June 15, 2018, Zara looks to technology to keep up with faster fashion | Reuters (accessed March 6, 2023).

resource every manager must consider. IS can also create a strategic advantage for firms that bring creativity, vision, and innovation to their IS use. The Zara case is an example. The Zara case also points out that general managers constantly need to work to maintain competitive advantage. This chapter uses the business strategy foundation from Chapter 1 to help general managers visualize how to use information resources to gain and maintain competitive advantage. This chapter highlights the difference between simply using IS and using IS strategically. It also explores the use of information resources (IS assets and capabilities) to support the strategic goals of an organization.

The material in this chapter can enable a general manager to understand the linkages between business strategy and information strategy on the Information Systems Strategy Triangle. General managers want to find answers to questions such as: Does using information resources provide a sustainable and defendable competitive advantage? What tools are available to help shape strategic use of information? What are the risks of using information resources to gain strategic advantage?

Evolution of Information Resources

The Eras model (Figure 2.1) summarizes the evolution of information resources over the past six decades. To think strategically about how to use information resources now and in the future, a manager must understand how the company arrived at where it is today. This model provides a good overview of trends and uses that have gotten the company from simple automation of tasks to extending relationships and managing their business ecosystems to where it is today.

IS strategy from the 1960s to the 1990s was driven by internal organizational needs. First came the need to lower existing transaction costs. Next was the need to provide support for managers by collecting and distributing information followed by the need to redesign business processes. As competitors built similar systems, organizations lost any advantage they had derived from their IS, and competition within a given industry once again was driven by forces that existed prior to the new technology. Most recently, enterprises have found that IT platforms and digital capabilities drive a new evolution of applications, processes, and strategic opportunities that often involve an ecosystem of partners rather than a list of suppliers. **Business ecosystems** are collections of interacting participants, including vendors, customers, and other related parties, acting in concert to do business.[9]

In Eras I through III, the value of information was tied to physical delivery mechanisms. In these eras, value was derived from scarcity reflected in the cost to produce the information. Information, like diamonds, gold, and MBA degrees, was more valuable because it was found in limited quantities. However, the networked economy beginning in Era IV drove a new model of value—value from plenitude. **Network effects** offered a reason for value derived from plenitude; the value of a network node to a person or organization in the network increased when others joined the network. For example, an e-mail account has no value without at least one other e-mail account with which to communicate. As e-mail accounts become relatively ubiquitous, the value of having an e-mail account increases as its potential for use increases. Further, copying additional people on an e-mail is done at a very low cost (virtually zero), and the information does not wear out (although it can become obsolete). As the cost of producing an additional copy of an information product within a network becomes trivial, the value of that network increases. Therefore, rather than using production *costs* to guide the determination of price, information products might be priced to reflect their *value* to the buyer. A more recent example of the value from plentitude is blockchain. Many firms in the financial services industry are holding off their adoption of the blockchain technology until other firms in their network adopt.[10]

As each era begins, organizations adopting a strategic role for IS must consider not only the firm's internal circumstances but also its external circumstances. Thus, in the value-creation era (Era V), companies sought those applications that again provided them an advantage over their competition and kept them from being outgunned by start-ups with innovative business models or traditional companies entering new markets. For example, companies such as Microsoft, Google, Apple, and Facebook created and continue

[9] For further discussion of business ecosystems, refer to Nicholas Vitalari and Hayden Shaughnessy, *The Elastic Enterprise* (Longboat Key, FL: Telemachus Press, 2012).

[10] Dozier, P., & Saunders, C. (2020). The Inter-organizational Perspective in Blockchain Adoption within an Ecosystem. Presented virtually at ECIS, 2020.

	Era I 1960s	Era II 1970s	Era III 1980s	Era IV 1990s	Era V 2000s	Era VI 2010s	Era VII 2020+
Primary role of IT	Efficiency	Effectiveness	Strategy	Strategy	Value creation	Value extension	Value capture and co-creation
	Automate existing paper-based processes	Solve problems and create opportunities	Increase individual and group effectiveness	Transform industry/organization	Create collaborative partnerships	Create community and social business	Connect intelligent devices; establish platforms; Harness big data
Justify IT expenditures	Return on investment	Increase in productivity and better decision quality	Competitive position	Competitive position	Added value	Creation of relationships	New revenue models and digital transformation
Target of systems	Organization	Organization/group	Individual manager/group	Business processes	Customer/supplier relationships	Customer/employee/supplier ecosystem	Platforms, Ecosystems
Information models	Application specific	Data driven	User driven	Business driven	Knowledge driven	People driven (or relationship driven)	Big data driven
Dominant technology	Mainframe, "centralized intelligence"	Minicomputer, mostly "centralized intelligence"	Microcomputer, "decentralized intelligence"	Client server, "distributed intelligence"	Internet, global "ubiquitous intelligence"	Social platforms, social networks, mobile, cloud	Intelligent devices, sensors, IoT, platforms, analytics, AI, machine learning, generative AI
Basis of value	Scarcity	Scarcity	Scarcity	Plenitude	Plenitude	Hyper plenitude	
Underlying economics	Economics of information bundled with economics of things	Economics of information bundled with economics of things	Economics of information bundled with economics of things	Economics of information separated from economics of things	Economics of information separated from economics of things	Economics of relationships bundled with economics of information	Economics of information and data bundled with economics of things

FIGURE 2.1 Eras of information usage in organizations.

to maintain a competitive advantage by building technical platforms and organizational competencies that allowed them to bring in partners as necessary to create new products and services for their customers. Their business ecosystems give them agility as well as access to talent and knowledge, extending the capabilities of their internal staff. Other firms simply try to solve all customer requests themselves.

Eras VI and VII have brought another paradigm shift in the use of information with an era of hyper plentitude: seemingly unlimited availability of information resources as the Internet and processing and storage through cloud computing sparked new value sources such as community and social business, the Internet of Things (connecting intelligent devices, sensors, and other electronics), analytics, AI, machine learning and generative AI (i.e., a type of AI that can produce new content in response to prompts).

The Information System Strategy Triangle introduced in Chapter 1 reflects the linkages between a firm's IS strategy, organizational strategy, and business strategy. Maximizing the effectiveness of the firm's business strategy requires that the general manager be able both to identify and use information resources, for either enhancing revenues or cutting costs. Many managers are fond of cost cutting because it enhances the "bottom line" (net income) results directly. Increasing sales, on the other hand, usually has costs that need to be deducted first. For instance, in the FedEx example in Chapter 1, cutting costs by $90 million would increase the bottom line by $90 million. However, selling $90 million of services will require staffing, wear and tear on trucks, and supplies such as gasoline. The net bottom line result will only increase after deducting those expenses.

This chapter describes how information resources can be used strategically by general managers, in searching for opportunities to fulfill both internal and external requirements of the firm.

Information Resources as Strategic Tools

Crafting a strategic advantage requires the general manager to cleverly combine all the firm's resources, including financial, production, human, and information, and to consider external resources such as the Internet, platform contributors outside the firm, and cloud computing providers. Information resources are more than just the infrastructure. This generic term, **information resources**, is defined as the available data, technology, people, and processes within an organization to be used by the manager to perform business processes and tasks. Piccoli and Ives state that information resources can either be assets or capabilities. An **IT asset** is anything, tangible or intangible, that can be used by a firm to create, produce, and/or offer its products (goods or services). Examples of IT assets include a firm's website, data files, or computer equipment. An **IT capability** is something that is learned or developed over time for the firm to create, produce, or offer its products. An IT capability makes it possible for a firm to use its IT assets effectively. The ability and knowledge to create a website, work with data files, and build apps are examples of capabilities.

An *IS infrastructure* (a concept that is discussed in detail in Chapter 6) is an IT asset. The infrastructure provides the foundation for the delivery of a firm's products or services. Another IT asset is an *information repository*, which is logically related data captured, organized, and retrieved by the firm. Information repositories can be filled with internally-oriented information designed to improve the firm's efficiency or with externally-oriented information about the industry, competitors, partners, and customers. Although most firms have these types of information repositories, not all firms use them effectively.

The view of IT assets is continually broadening to include potential resources that are available to the firm but that are not necessarily owned by it. These additional information resources are often available as a service rather than as a system to be procured and implemented internally. For example, cloud-based software (also called *software as a service, or SAAS*), such as SalesForce.com's CRM, offers managers the opportunity to find new ways to manage their customer information with an externally-based IT resource. Social networking systems such as Facebook, Renren, and LinkedIn offer managers the opportunity to find expertise or an entire network of individuals ready to participate in the corporate innovation processes using relatively little capital or expense.

The three major categories of IT capabilities are technical skills, IT management skills, and relationship skills. *Technical skills* are applied to designing, developing, and implementing IS. *IT management skills* are critical for managing the IS department and IS projects. They include an understanding of business processes, the ability to oversee the development and maintenance of systems to support these processes effectively, and the ability to plan and work with the business units in undertaking change. *Relationship*

IT Assets	IT Capabilities
IT Infrastructure	Technical Skills
• Platforms	• Proficiency in systems analysis
• Company apps	• Programming and web design skills
• Network	• Developing apps and integrating them with platforms
• Data	• Data analysis/data scientist skills
• Website	• Network design and implementation skills
Information Repository	IT Management Skills
• Customer information	• Business process knowledge
• Employee information	• Ability to evaluate technology options
• Marketplace information	• Project management skills
• Vendor information	• Envisioning innovative IT solutions
• Platform partner information	Relationship Skills
	• *Spanning* skills such as business-IT relationship management
	• *External* skills such as vendor and platform management

FIGURE 2.2 Information resources.

Source: Adapted from G. Piccoli and B. Ives, "IT-Dependent Strategic Initiatives and Sustained Competitive Advantage: A Review and Synthesis of the Literature," *MIS Quarterly* 29, no. 4 (2005): 755.

skills can be focused either externally or internally. An externally-focused relationship skill includes the ability to respond to the firm's market, to collaborate with platform partners, and to work with customers and suppliers. An internally-focused relationship between a firm's IS managers and its business managers is a spanning relationship skill and includes the ability of IS to manage partnerships with the business units. Even though it focuses on relationships in the firm, it requires spanning beyond the IS department. Relationship skills develop over time and require mutual respect and trust. They, like the other information resources, can create a unique advantage for a firm. Figure 2.2 summarizes the different types of information resources and provides examples of each.

Information resources exist in a company alongside other resources. The general manager is responsible for organizing all resources so that business goals are met. Understanding the nature of the resources at hand is a prerequisite to using them effectively. By aligning IS strategy with business strategy (or even making the IS strategy the business strategy), the general manager maximizes the company's profit potential. To ensure that information resources being deployed for strategic advantage are used wisely, the general manager must identify what makes the information resource valuable (and the Eras model may provide some direction) and sustainable. Meanwhile, the firm's competitors are working to do the same. In this competitive environment, how should the information resources be organized and applied to enable the organization to compete most effectively?

How Can Information Resources Be Used Strategically?

The general manager confronts many elements that influence the competitive environment of his or her enterprise. Overlooking a single element can bring about disastrous results for the firm. This slim tolerance for error requires the manager to take multiple views of the strategic landscape. Three such views can help a general manager align IS strategy with business strategy. The first view uses the *five competitive forces model* by Michael Porter to look at the major influences on a firm's competitive environment. Information resources should be directed strategically to alter the competitive forces to benefit the firm's position in its industry. The second view uses Porter's *value chain model* to assess the organization's internal operations and partners in its supply chain. Information resources should be directed at altering the value-creating or value-supporting activities of the firm. We extend this view further to consider the value chain of an entire industry to identify opportunities for the organization to gain competitive advantage. The third view specifically focuses on the types of *IS resources* needed to gain and sustain competitive advantage. These three views provide a general manager with varied perspectives from which to identify strategic opportunities to apply the firm's information resources.

Using Information Resources to Influence Competitive Forces

Porter provides the general manager a classic view of the major forces that shape the competitive environment of an industry, which affects firms within the industry. These five competitive forces result from more than just the actions of direct competitors. We explore each force from an IS perspective.

Potential Threat of New Entrants

Existing firms within an industry often try to reduce the threat of new entrants to the marketplace by erecting barriers to entry. New entrants seem to come out of nowhere; established firms can diversify their business models and begin to compete in the space occupied by existing firms, or an enterprising entrepreneur can create a new business that changes the game for existing firms. Barriers to entry—including a firm's controlled access to limited distribution channels, public image of a firm, unique relationships with customers, and an understanding of their industry's governmental regulations—help the firm create a stronghold by offering products or services that are difficult to displace in the eyes of customers based on apparently unique features. Information resources also can be used to build barriers that discourage competitors from entering an industry. For example, Google's search algorithm is a source of competitive advantage for the search company, and it's a barrier of entry for new entrants that would have to create something better to compete against Google. So far, new entrants have failed to erode Google's market share, which continues to fulfill about 89% of all desktop searches in the United States,[11] over 95% of mobile searches, and over 85% of all searches worldwide.[12] Search engine optimization (actions that a firm can take to improve its prominence in search results) has served as a barrier to entry for some businesses. Consider the website that has the number one position in a user's search. There is only one number one position, making it an advantage for the company enjoying that position and a barrier for all other websites seeking that position.

Bargaining Power of Buyers

Customers often have substantial power to affect the competitive environment. This power can take the form of easy consumer access to several retail outlets to purchase the same product or the opportunity to purchase in large volumes at superstores such as Walmart. Information resources can be used to build switching costs that make it less attractive for customers to purchase from competitors. Switching costs can be any aspect of a buyer's purchasing decision that decreases the likelihood of "switching" his or her purchase to a competitor. Such an approach requires a deep understanding of how a customer obtains the product or service. For example, Amazon.com's "Prime" subscription provides access to fast (one day in the United States) and free shipping as well as an expanding library of original and third-party digital content. Amazon.com also stores buyer information, including a default credit card number, shipping method, and "ship-to" address, so that purchases can be made with one click, saving consumers the effort of data reentry and further repetitive choices.

Bargaining Power of Suppliers

Suppliers' bargaining power can reduce a firm's options and ultimately its profitability. Suppliers often strive to "lock in" customers through the use of systems (and other mechanisms). For example, there are many options for individuals to back up their laptop data, including many "cloud" options. The power of

[11] Statista, "Worldwide Desktop Market Share of Leading Search Engines from January 2015 to January 2023," https://www.statista.com/statistics/216573/worldwide-market-share-of-search-engines/ (accessed March 4, 2023).

[12] Statcounter Global Counts, "Search Engine Market Share in the United States of America: February 2022–February, 2023," https://gs.statcounter.com/search-engine-market-share/all/united-states-of-america (accessed March 4, 2023); Statcounter Global Stats, "Mobile Search Engine Market Share in United States of America: February 2022–February 2023," https://gs.statcounter.com/search-engine-market-share/mobile/united-states-of-america (accessed March 4, 2023).

any one supplier is low because there are a number of options. But Apple's operating system enables easy creation of backups and increases Apple's bargaining power. Millions of customers find it easy to use iCloud, and they do.

The force of bargaining power is strongest when a firm has few suppliers from which to choose, the quality of supplier inputs is crucial to the finished product, or the volume of purchases is insignificant to the supplier. For example, steel firms lost some of their bargaining power over the automobile industry because car manufacturers developed technologically advanced quality control systems for evaluating the steel they purchase. Manufacturers can now reject steel from suppliers when it does not meet the required quality levels.

Threat of Substitute Products

The potential of a substitute product in the marketplace depends on the buyers' willingness to substitute, the relative price-to-performance ratio of the substitute, and the level of switching costs a buyer faces. Information resources can create advantages by reducing the threat of substitution. Substitutes that cause a threat come from many sources. Internal innovations can cannibalize existing revenue streams for a firm. For example, new iPhones motivate current customers to upgrade, essentially cannibalizing the older product line's revenue. Of course, this is also a preemptive move to keep customers in the iPhone product family rather than to switch to another competitor's product. The threat might come from potentially new innovations that make the previous product obsolete. Tablets and smartphones have reduced the market for laptops and personal computers. GPSs have become substitutes for paper maps. Most interesting is the way digital cameras made film and film cameras obsolete, and then more recently, smartphones are replacing digital cameras. Similarly, digital music sharply reduced the market for vinyl records, record players, CDs, and CD players, and now paid streaming is replacing the purchase of digital songs. Revolutions of many kinds and levels of maturity seem to be lurking everywhere. Cloud services are a substitute for data centers. Uber offers a substitute for taxicabs. Online news sites have reduced the size of the physical newspaper market. Managers must watch for potential substitutes, over and over again, from many different sources to fully manage competitive threats.

Industry Competitors

Rivalry among the firms competing within an industry is high when it is expensive for a firm to leave the industry, the growth rate of the industry is declining, or products have lost differentiation. Under these circumstances, the firm must focus on the competitive actions of rivals to protect its own market share. Intense rivalry in an industry ensures that competitors respond quickly to any strategic actions.

When launched in November of 2022, OpenAI's ChatGPT became the first generative AI tool of its kind in the marketplace as well as the "fastest growing app in history".[13] It was backed by Microsoft in July 2019 to the tune of one billion dollars and then with a couple more billion dollars over the next few years. It was rumored that Microsoft invested up to another ten billion dollars in OpenAI in January 2023[14] in return for Microsoft's Azure being the exclusive provider of cloud computing services to OpenAI. Microsoft integrated ChatGPT technology (e.g., GPT-4) into its Bing search engine, which in April 2023 was being considered by Samsung as the replacement to Google's as the default search engine on its devices.[15] OpenAI's partnership with Microsoft appears to be a good one since only a few companies have the cloud power to support the generative AI tool with large language modeling like ChatGPT.

Google is another company that has massive cloud power. In response to ChatGPT's viral reception, it launched its own chatbot, Bard—but the launch was premature. Bard gave an incorrect answer to a factual question about NASA's James Webb telescope, precipitating a 9% drop in the stock price of Google's

---

[13] Tristan Bove, "Noam Chomsky Says A.I. Is Far from 'True Intelligence' and ChatGPT Is the 'Banality of Evil', Fortune, March 8, 2023, Noam Chomsky says A.I. is far from 'true intelligence' and ChatGPT is the 'banality of evil' (msn.com).

[14] Capoot, Ashley, "Microsoft Announces Multibillion-dollar Investment in ChatGPT-maker the OpenAI," CNBC. Archived from the original on January 23, 2023 (accessed March 7, 2023); also Cade Metz and Karen Weise, "Microsoft said to invest $10 billion in OpenAI, the Creator of ChatGPT," *The New York Times*, January 23, 2023, https://www.nytimes.com/2023/01/23/business/microsoft-chatgpt-artificial-intelligence.html (accessed March 10, 2023).

[15] Times Digest, "Google Promises Radical Changes to Keep Up with Bing's AI," Monday, April 17, 2023, pg. 4.

parent company, Alphabet.[16] Google restricted the access to Bard immediately and subsequently made it available only on a limited basis as an experiment. While experimentation is part of the Google culture (see Chapter 3), it may not be impressive that users of Bard were asked to take the time to inform Google of mistakes Bard made when responding to them. Now Google has to weigh the risk of another problematic launch against value of maintaining its position as a technology leader, especially in the search engine arena.[17]

The processes that firms use to manage their operations and to lower costs or increase efficiencies can provide an advantage for cost-focused firms. However, as firms within an industry begin to implement standard business processes and technologies—often using enterprise-wide systems such as those of SAP and Oracle—the industry becomes more attractive to consolidation through acquisition. Standardizing IS lowers the coordination costs of merging two enterprises and can result in a less competitive environment in the industry.

One way competitors differentiate themselves with an otherwise undifferentiated product is through creative use of IS. Information provides advantages in such competition when added to an existing product. For example, the iPod, iPhone, iPad, and iWatch are differentiated in part because of the iTunes store and the applications available only to users of these devices. Competitors offer some of the same information services, but Apple was able to take an early lead by using IS to differentiate their products. Notably, the iTunes store was the first digital music sales platform and Apple's digital rights management software (FairPlay) implemented usage rights and controls that were of great importance to content owners.[18]

Each force identified by Porter's model acts on firms at all times, but perhaps to a greater or lesser degree. See Figure 2.3 for a summary of these five forces working simultaneously at Zara, the case discussed at the beginning of this chapter.

The five competitive forces model has been a game changer for strategic thinking for managers. It provides a language for discussing strategic decisions. General managers can use the five competitive forces model to identify the key forces currently affecting competition, to recognize uses of information resources to influence the forces, and to consider likely changes in these forces over time. The changing forces drive both the business strategy and IS strategy, and this model provides a way to think about how information resources can create competitive advantage for a business unit and, even more broadly, for the firm. The forces also can reshape an entire industry—compelling general managers to take actions to help their firm gain or sustain competitive advantage.

Competitive Force	IT Influence on Competitive Force
Threat of new entrants	Zara's rich information repository about customers is hard for new entrants to replicate.
Bargaining power of buyers	Zara's augmented reality app helps customers see virtual fashion models showcasing its products and Zara's AI tool helps customers navigate its products. Thus, Zara gains control over buyers.
Bargaining power of suppliers	Zara's computer-controlled cutting machine cuts up to 1,000 layers at a time. Sewing together the pieces is a simple task that can be done by many sewing suppliers from which it chooses. Thus, Zara gains bargaining power over its suppliers.
Industry competitors	To achieve its sustainability goals and transform the industry, Zara is reducing the use of energy in its operations so that it can achieve Net Zero Emissions and making its stores more efficient using renewable energy.
Threat of substitute products	IT helps Zara offer extremely fashionable lines at hard-to-beat prices making substitutes difficult.

FIGURE 2.3 Applying the five competitive forces model to Zara.

[16] Theara Coleman, "Google Didn't Believe Bard AI Was 'Really Ready' for a Product Yet," The Week, February 14, 2023, https://theweek.com/google/1020969/google-didnt-believe-bard-ai-was-really-ready-for-a-product-yet (accessed July 29, 2023).

[17] Miles Kruppa and Sam Schechner, "How Google Became Cautious of AI and Gave Microsoft an Opening," *Wall Street Journal*, March 7, 2023, https://www.wsj.com/articles/google-ai-chatbot-bard-chatgpt-rival-bing-a4c2d2ad (accessed March 10, 2023).

[18] Schoemaker, Paul JH, Sohvi Heaton, and David Teece, "Innovation, Dynamic Capabilities, and Leadership," *California Management Review* 61, no. 1 (2018): 15–42.

Using Information Resources to Alter the Value Chain

A second lens for describing the strategic use of IS is Porter's value chain. The value chain model addresses the activities that create, deliver, and support a company's product or service. Porter divided these activities into two broad categories (Figure 2.4): support and primary activities. Primary activities relate directly to the value created in a product or service, whereas support activities make it possible for the primary activities to exist and remain coordinated. Each activity may affect how other activities are performed, suggesting that information resources should not be applied in isolation. For example, more efficient IS for repairing a product may increase the possible number of repairs per week, but the customer does not receive any value unless his or her product is repaired, which requires that the spare parts be available. Changing the rate of repair also affects the rate of spare parts ordering. If information resources are focused too narrowly on a specific activity, then the expected value may not be realized because other parts of the chain have not adjusted.

The value chain framework suggests that competition stems from two sources: lowering the cost to perform activities and adding value to a product or service so that buyers will pay more. To achieve true competitive advantage, a firm requires accurate information on elements outside itself. Lowering activity costs achieves an advantage only if the firm possesses information about its competitors' cost structures. Even though reducing isolated costs can improve profits temporarily, it does not provide a clear competitive advantage unless the firm can lower its costs below a competitor's. Doing so enables the firm to lower its prices as a way to grow its market share.

For example, many websites sell memory to upgrade laptops. But some sites, such as crucial.com, have an option that automates the process prior to the sales process. The "Crucial System Scanner Tool" scans the customer's laptop, identifies the current configuration and the capacity, and then suggests compatible memory upgrade kits. The scanner then automatically opens a web page with the appropriate memory upgrades, enabling an immediate purchase. The customer does not have to figure out the configuration or requirements; it's done automatically. By combining a software program like its configurator with the sales process, crucial.com has added value to the customer's experience by automating and eliminating most of the inconvenience of a key process.

Although the value chain framework emphasizes the activities of the individual firm, it can be extended, as in Figure 2.5, to include the firm in a larger value system. This value system is a collection of firm value chains connected through a business relationship and through technology. From this perspective, various strategic opportunities exist to use information resources to gain a competitive advantage. Understanding how information is used within each value chain of the system can lead to new opportunities to change the information component of value-added activities. It can also lead to shakeouts within the industry as firms that fail to provide value are forced out and as surviving firms adopt new business models.

Opportunity also exists in the transfer of information across value chains. For example, sales forecasts generated by a manufacturer, such as a computer or automotive company, and linked to supplier systems

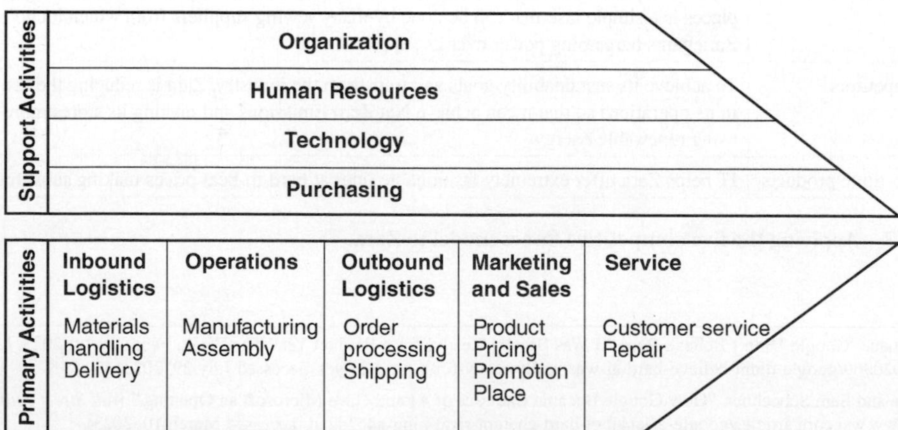

FIGURE 2.4 Firm value chain.

Source: Adapted from Michael Porter and Victor Millar, "How Information Gives You Competitive Advantage," *Harvard Business Review* (July–August 1985), reprint no. 85415.

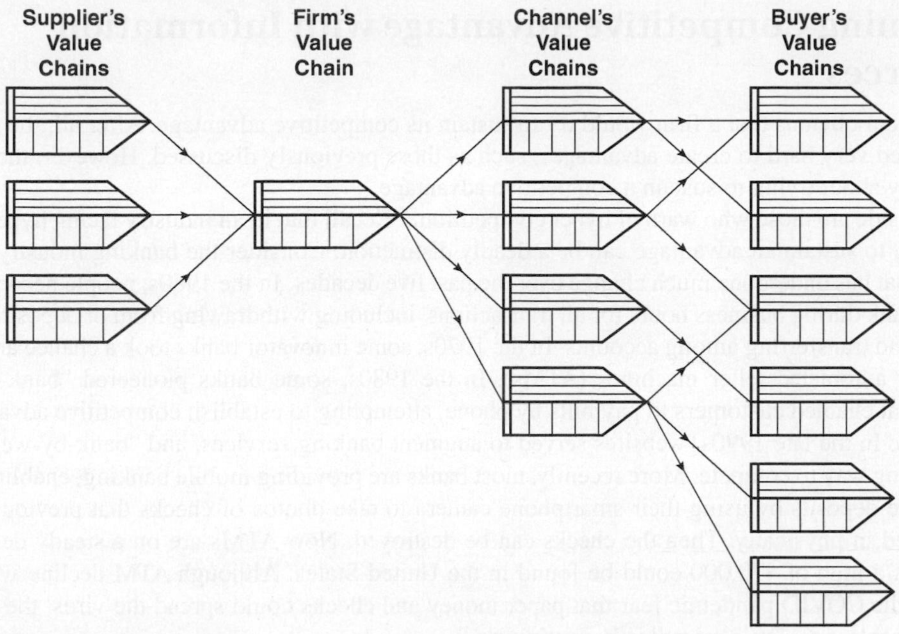

FIGURE 2.5 The value system: interconnecting relationships between organizations.

create orders for the manufacture of the necessary components for the computer or vehicle. Often this coupling is repeated from manufacturing company to vendor/supplier for several layers, linking the value chains of multiple organizations. In this way, each member of the supply chain adds value by directly linking the elements of its value chains to others.

Optimizing a company's internal processes, such as its supply chain, operations, and customer relationship processes, can be another source of competitive advantage. Tools are routinely used to automate the internal operations of a firm's value chain, such as **supply chain management (SCM)** to source materials for operations, **enterprise resource planning (ERP)** systems to automate functions of the operations activities of the value chain, and **customer relationship management (CRM)** systems to optimize the processing of customer information. These systems are discussed in more detail in Chapter 5.

The value chain model can also be applied to the Zara example discussed earlier. Here we focus on the value added by IS to Zara's primary and support activities. For example, IS supports a number of primary activities: To speed up Operations, fabric is cut and dyed by robots in 12 highly automated factories located proximally in Spain, Portugal, Turkey, and Morocco; To support Outbound Logistics, clothes are transported on miles of automated conveyor belts at distribution centers and reach stores within 48 hours of the order; Marketing and Sales are supported by POS that allow store managers to communicate daily with headquarters about how items are selling. IS also add value to support activities at Zara: In terms of Organization activities, IT supports tightly knit collaboration among designers, store managers, market specialists, production managers, and production planners; In terms of Technology, IT is integrated to support all primary activities and Zara's IT staff works with vendors to develop automated conveyors to support distribution activities. While these examples primarily demonstrate the IS-enabled value added to Zara's processes, the suppliers and customers in its supply chain also realize the value added by IS. Most notably, the customer is better served as a result of IS that support store communications, demand analyses, production and inventory management.[19] In this way, Zara can be very timely in responding to customer preferences.

Unlike the competitive forces model, which explores industry dynamics, the value chain focuses on the firm's activities as well as value chains of other firms in its supply chain. Yet, using the value chain as a lens for understanding strategic use of information resources affects competitive forces. For example, Zara's miles of automated conveyor belts and automated factories enable it to deal effectively with industry competitors.

[19] Vishal Patel, "Zara—a Master Class in Supplier Relationships and Supply Chain Management, Ivalua, May 6, 2020; Zara's Supply Chain Management Model (ivalua.com); Also the Inditex website discusses its sustainability goals and manufacturing locations, Inditex.com (accessed March 10, 2023).

Sustaining Competitive Advantage with Information Resources

It might seem obvious that a firm would try to sustain its competitive advantage. After all, the firm might have worked very hard to create advantages, such as those previously discussed. However, there is some controversy about trying to sustain a competitive advantage.

On one side are those who warn of hyper competition.[20] Recall that in an industry facing hyper competition, trying to sustain an advantage can be a deadly distraction. Consider the banking industry as a good example that has undergone much change over the past five decades. In the 1960s, people needed to visit a physical bank during business hours for all transactions, including withdrawing from or depositing to their accounts and transferring among accounts. In the 1970s, some innovator banks took a chance and invested in 24-hour automated teller machines (ATMs). In the 1980s, some banks pioneered "bank-by-phone" services that enabled customers to pay bills by phone, attempting to establish competitive advantage with technology. In the late 1990s, websites served to augment banking services, and "bank-by-web" was the new, exciting way to compete. More recently, most banks are providing mobile banking, enabling customers to make deposits by using their smartphone camera to take photos of checks that previously needed to be turned in physically. Then the checks can be destroyed. Now ATMs are on a steady decline since 2019 when a high of 470,000 could be found in the United States. Although ATM decline was initially fueled by the COVID pandemic fear that paper money and checks could spread the virus, the movement toward a cashless society is steadfastly continuing.[21]

The obvious picture to paint here is that competitors caught up with the leaders very quickly, and competitive advantage was fleeting. When ATMs were introduced, it did not take long for others to adopt the same technology—a technology that is now going out of style. Even small banks found that they could band together with competitors and invest in the same technologies. The same imitation game took place with "bank-by-phone," "bank-by-web," and mobile banking.

Rather than arguing that sustaining a competitive advantage is a deadly distraction, Piccoli and Ives provided a framework that outlines the ways in which a firm can provide barriers to competitors, which would build sustainability. The framework outlines four types of barriers: IT project barrier, IT resources and capabilities barrier, complementary resources barrier, and preemption barrier. See Figure 2.6 for a brief definition and a few examples of each.

So, should a firm focus attention on building barriers to the competition, or should it just give up on the established competitive advantage and focus on seeking a way to start the next revolution? Given that some technologies can be copied quickly, or even just purchased from the same well-known vendor who

Barrier	Definition	Examples
IT project barrier	It would be a large undertaking for a competitor to build the system to copy the capability.	• Requires a large investment • Requires a long time to build • Complicated to build
IT assets and capabilities barrier	Competitors might lack the IT resources to copy the capability.	• Database of customers that cannot be copied • Expert developers or project managers
Complementary resources barrier	The firm has other resources that create a synergy with the IT that provides competitive advantage.	• Respected brand • Partnership agreements • Exclusivity arrangements • Good location
Preemption barrier	The firm "got there first."	• Loyal customer base built at the beginning • Firm known as "the" source

FIGURE 2.6 Barriers to competition and building sustainability.

[20] See Chapter 1 and Foundational Readings at the end of this chapter.

[21] Jim Carlton, "The Number of ATMs Has Declined as People Rely Less on Cash," *Wall Street Journal*, March 4, 2023, https://www.wsj.com/articles/the-number-of-atms-has-declined-as-people-rely-less-on-cash-81268fa2?page=1 (accessed March 10, 2023).

supplied it to the leader in the first place, it seems prudent to spend some time exploring each technological option in the Piccoli and Ives' framework and determining where the firm can increase sustainability. Some might even argue that since technologies can be replicated or improved, competitive advantages derived from technologies are always limited and the only real competitive advantage comes from the relationships a company has with those in its ecosystem, particularly their customers and suppliers. Those are much more difficult to replicate. If the firm can build loyalty with customers who appreciate innovation, a two-month competitive advantage might turn into a two-year or longer advantage, thus building a valuable preemption barrier that could sustain them well toward making the next innovation. If a firm can capture valuable data right at the beginning, a copycat firm may fall further behind. Also, building partnerships or securing exclusive rights to some of the technologies can further delay a competitor from catching up.

It would not be wise to stop there, however. The firm should continue to seek ways in which IT can improve offerings or service to customers. Consider some of Amazon's many strategic initiatives. It moved from its initially innovative strategy of selling books online to selling a range of goods online by buying and integrating firms known for selling various products such as Zappos with its shoes and Whole Foods with its health foods. Amazon also provided a platform on which other companies could sell their products. As a result, when you ask someone in the United States where they got something that you admire, a typical response is "Amazon."

Amazon also developed a distribution system that allows it to fulfill its promise of a speedy delivery. It has 175 fulfillment centers around the globe and a fleet of delivery vehicles including airplanes, delivery trucks, and even drivers in their own cars.[22] Consider how this recent, actual Amazon sales experience differs from a typical buying experience fifteen years ago: Two friends were at a tailgate party for a Saturday afternoon college football game in Orlando, Florida. One friend noticed the other had a new Fitbit and asked if it was possible to see the statistics (i.e., time, steps, miles traveled, etc.) better with the Fitbit's new face. As is often the case in this city, it was a sunny day, and it was possible to actually see the statistics (unlike with the old Fitbit face). So, the inquiring friend went to the Amazon site on her phone, placed the order, paid for the order and shortly thereafter the tailgaters went to the game. The buyer went straight home after the game and found the Fitbit that she had ordered on her doorstep.

In summary, a firm might simultaneously (1) seek ways to build sustainability by looking into each of the four potential barriers to identify promising ways to block the competition, and at the same time (2) continue to innovate and change the industry. Amazon has done both by building a dependable and efficient global retail platform and delivery network, as well as constantly creating new business models focused on new technologies such as streaming, cloud computing, AI, and delivery drones. Focusing only on building sustainability has the potential effect of fighting a losing battle, and focusing only on new business models might be too risky and striking gold too infrequent as the sole source of growth. The next strategic frameworks, the resource-based view, and its complement, the dynamic capabilities view, are more general and emphasize ways in which to exploit potential resources. The frameworks, described next, can be helpful for managers in understanding how their firms can leverage their IT resources to create and sustain competitive advantage.

Using the Resource-Based View (RBV)

The **resource-based view (RBV)**, first proposed by Jay Barney, is useful for determining whether a firm's strategy has created value by using IT. Like the value chain model, the RBV concentrates on areas that add value to the firm. Whereas the value chain model focuses on a firm's activities, the resource-based view focuses on the resources that it can manage strategically in a rapidly changing competitive environment. Like the Piccoli and Ives framework, the RBV focuses on sustaining competitive advantage but by using resources rather than by raising competitive barriers.

The RBV has been applied to IS as a way of identifying two types of information resources: those that enable a firm to *attain* competitive advantage and those that enable a firm to *sustain* the advantage over the long term. From the IS perspective, some types of resources are better than others for creating attributes that enable a firm to attain competitive advantage (i.e., value, rarity), whereas other resources are better for creating attributes to sustain competitive value (e.g., low substitutability, low mobility, low imitability).

[22] Amazon website, https://www.aboutamazon.com/workplace/tours (accessed March 10, 2023).

Resources to Attain Competitive Advantage

Valuable and rare resources that firms must leverage to establish a superior resource position help companies attain competitive advantage. A resource is considered valuable when it enables the firm to become more efficient, effective, or innovative. It is a rare resource when other firms do not possess it. For example, no bank today would think of doing business without a mobile banking app. Mobile banking apps are very valuable to the banks in terms of their operations. A bank's customers expect it to provide a mobile banking app that can be used on any mobile device. However, because many other banks also have mobile banking apps, they are not a rare resource, and they do not offer a strategic advantage. Some call them *table stakes* or resources required just to be in the business. Many systems in Eras I and II, and especially Era III, were justified on their ability to provide a rare and valuable resource. In some cases, these very systems have become table stakes.

Resources to Sustain Competitive Advantage

Many firms that invested in systems learned that gaining a competitive advantage does not automatically mean that they could sustain it over the long term. The only way to do that is to continue to innovate and to protect against resource imitation, substitution, or transfer. For example, Walmart's complex logistics management is deeply embedded in both its own and its suppliers' operations so that imitations by other firms are unlikely. Another relatively inimitable, value-adding initiative is the digital platform Walmart now uses to hire drivers as needed as a way of ensuring that its deliveries to customers are timely and cost-efficient.[23] Perhaps Walmart's main competitor, Amazon, is one of the few firms that can imitate the driver platform. Yet, Amazon likely can't imitate Walmart's more recent initiative: fast-charging electric vehicle stations at its stores. With 90% of Americans living within 10 miles of a Walmart or Sam's Club store, heavily virtual Amazon can't compete on this dimension.[24] The Oakland Athletics' use of IS propelled it to victory, as depicted in the movie *Moneyball*, but as soon as other teams learned about the secret behind the success Oakland was having with analytics and IS, they, too began to use similar techniques, reducing the advantage Oakland initially enjoyed. Finally, to sustain competitive advantage, resources must be difficult to transfer or replicate, or relatively immobile. Some information resources can be easily bought. However, technical knowledge, especially that which relates to a firm's operation—reputation for quality products or services, deep relationships with customers, and managerial experience in the firm's environment—is less easy to obtain and, hence, considered harder to transfer to other firms.

Some IT management skills are general enough in nature to make them easier to transfer and imitate. Although it clearly is important for IS executives to manage internally-oriented resources such as IS infrastructure, systems development, and running cost-effective IS operations, these skills can be acquired in many different forms. They are basic IT management skills possessed by virtually all good IS managers. Other skills, however, are unique to a firm and require considerable time and resources to develop. For example, it takes time to learn how the firm operates and to understand its critical processes and socially complex working relationships. However, the message suggested by the RBV is that IS executives must look beyond their own IS shop and concentrate on cultivating resources that help the firm understand changing business environments and allow it to work well with all its external stakeholders. Even when considering internally-oriented information resources, there are differences in the extent to which these resources add value. Many argue that IS personnel are willing to move, especially when offered higher salaries by firms needing these skills. Yet, some technical skills, such as knowledge of a firm's use of technology to support business processes and technology integration skills, are not easily exported to, or imported from, another firm. Further, hardware and many software apps can be purchased or outsourced, making them highly imitable and transferrable. Because it is unlikely that two firms have exactly the same strategic alternatives, resources at one firm might have only moderate substitutability in the other firm.

Figure 2.7 indicates the extent to which the attributes of each information resource create and sustain value for Zara. Zara's advantage did not come from the specific hardware or software technologies it employed. Its management spent five to ten times less on technology than its rivals. In contrast, Zara created considerable value from its information repository with customers' preferences and body types and from its IT management and relationship skills.

[23] Böttcher, Timo Phillip, Jörg Weking, Andreas Hein, Markus Böhm, and Helmut Krcmar. "Pathways to Digital Business Models: The Connection of Sensing and Seizing in Business Model Innovation." *The Journal of Strategic Information Systems* 31, no. 4 (2022): 101742.

[24] Sarah Jean Callahan, "Walmart Makes a Surprise Move Amazon Can't Copy," The Street, April 9, 2023, (accessed October 4, 2023).

	Value Creation		Value Sustainability		
Resource/Attribute	**Value**	**Rarity**	**Imitation**	**Substitution**	**Transfer**
IT Asset					
IT infrastructure	**Moderate** value/rarity; skillful use of POS equipment, proprietary smartphone app, automated conveyors, and computer-controlled equipment to cut patterns, but similar technology could be purchased and used by competitors		**Easy** to imitate and transfer its infrastructure **Moderate** for substitution of infrastructure (automated conveyers)		
Information repository	**High** value/rarity; information about customers' preferences and body types, which Zara leverages strategically to identify and design new products		**Difficult** to imitate and transfer **Extremely difficult** to substitute; massive volume and contextual nature of the data		
IT Capability					
Technical skills	**Low** value/rarity; IS professionals could be hired relatively easily to perform the technical work		**Moderately difficult** to imitate, substitute, or transfer; integration of technical skills across Zara's operations		
IT management skills	**High** value/rarity; acquired over time		**Difficult** to imitate, substitute, or transfer; resources leveraged well		
Relationship skills—*Externally focused*	**High** value from relationships with proximally-located manufacturers **Moderate** rarity; other companies also have relationships with manufacturers although required time to develop the deeper relationship		**Difficult** to imitate, substitute, or transfer; turnaround time of under 2 weeks from conception to distribution		
Relationship skills—*Spanning*	**High** value/rarity of spanning; Good relationships across buyers, designers and operations acquired over time		**Difficult** to imitate, substitute, or transfer spanning; unusual tight-knit teams at headquarters not easy to imitate or purchase in the marketplace, allowing the ability to correctly interpret and quickly respond to customer needs		

FIGURE 2.7 Information resources at Zara, by attribute.
Source: Based on M. Wade and J. Hulland, "The Resource-Based View and Information Systems Research: Review, Extension and Suggestions for Future Research," *MIS Quarterly* 28, no. 1 (2004): 107–42.

The resource-based view, although highly cited, has received its share of criticism. The major criticism is that it doesn't clearly distinguish between value and strategic competitive advantage. Another criticism of the original theory is that it doesn't consider different types of resources. However, IS researchers addressed this concern when they categorized resources into assets and capabilities and then provided examples of each. In applying the theory, it is important to recognize that it is focused on internal sources of a firm's competitive advantage and, thus, does not thoroughly take into account the environment in which the firm is embedded, especially when the environment is quite dynamic.

Using Dynamic Capabilities

A view that is considered an alternative or complement to RBV is the Dynamic Capabilities view (DCV), which does take into account the firm's dynamic environment. DCV considers two types of capabilities: ordinary and dynamic. *Ordinary capabilities* are those abilities that are necessary for a firm to operate, but which do not propel change or offer competitive advantage. They typically focus on internal (operational) processes and tend to be widely available. They may include IT skills such as maintaining networks, building and installing systems and keeping platforms up and running. In contrast, dynamic capabilities are those that allow the firm to attain and sustain strategic advantage. **Dynamic capabilities (DCs)** are the firm's ability to create, extend, and alter the firm's resources to respond to its rapidly changing environment.[25] They are hard to acquire and hold on to.

[25] Steininger, Dennis M., Patrick Mikalef, Adamantia Pateli, and Ana Ortiz-de-Guinea, "Dynamic capabilities in information systems research: A critical review, synthesis of current knowledge, and recommendations for future research," *Journal of the Association for Information Systems* 23, no. 2 (2022): 447–90.

	Zara's Capabilities
Type	
Ordinary	IT skills to keep equipment running
Dynamic	Analytics to maximize sales by sending the most appropriate sizes and customer-centric trends to neighborhood (mirror) stores
Capacities	
Sensing	Daily report of sales managers to designers to identify new trends; Training of sales managers to listen to what customers want
Seizing	Strategic agility of collaborative teams to act on the latest trends.
Transforming	Proximal manufacturing plants to get latest trends to stores within 48 hours; Agile supply chain

FIGURE 2.8 Applying dynamic capabilities to Zara.

Dynamic capabilities must encompass one or more of these three capacities: Sensing, Seizing, and Transforming. A *sensing* capacity allows firms to see signs of change in their environment and ferret out opportunities. The firm needs a *seizing* capacity to take advantage of those opportunities by making decisions to support action and commitment such as laying the groundwork for change and mobilizing resources. Firms use their *transforming* capacities to change their resource configurations in such a way as to take advantage of the sensed opportunity. Ordinary capabilities may be changed, enhanced or recombined into dynamic ones and new resources may be created or built. These capacities must be orchestrated so that they can work together well, and over time they are called on to adjust to the constantly changing dynamic environment.

The DCV, which originated in the strategic management literature, is particularly salient for understanding the many ways in which firms can use IT to renew their value-creating mechanisms and to strategically leverage change in dynamic environments. For example, IT assets such as a flexible infrastructure or rich customer information can *enable* the capacities of sensing, seizing, and transforming. Sometimes IT assets and capabilities are viewed as dynamic capabilities that are *embedded* in the firm's digital strategy—that is you can't implement a digital strategy without them. Sometimes dynamic capabilities are used to *create IT-related outcomes* such as digital transformations or IT such as enterprise platforms and customer relationship management systems. Figure 2.8 illustrates the application of the DCV to Zara. Zara's IT assets and capabilities primarily *enable* their dynamic capability capacities.

Risks

As demonstrated throughout this chapter, information resources may be used to gain strategic advantage even if that advantage is fleeting. When IS are chosen as a tool to outpace a firm's competitors, executives should be aware of the many risks that may surface. Some of these risks include:

- *Awakening a sleeping giant:* A firm can implement IS to gain competitive advantage only to find that it nudged a larger competitor with deeper pockets into implementing an IS with even better features. FedEx offered its customers the ability to trace the transit and delivery of their packages online. FedEx's much larger competitor, UPS, rose to the challenge. UPS not only implemented the same services but also added a new set of features eroding some of the advantages FedEx enjoyed, causing FedEx to update its offerings. Both the UPS and FedEx sites passed through multiple website iterations as the dueling delivery companies are continuing to struggle for competitive advantage.
- *Encountering bad timing:* Sometimes customers are not ready to use the technology designed to gain strategic advantage. For example, Grid Systems created the GRiDPAD in 1989. It was a tablet computer designed for businesses to use in the field and was well reviewed at that time. But it didn't get traction. Three decades later, in 2010, Apple introduced the iPad, and tablet computing took off.
- *Implementing IS poorly:* Stories abound of IS that fail because they are poorly implemented. Typically, these systems are complex and often global in their reach. An implementation fiasco took place at Hershey Foods when it attempted to implement its supply and inventory system. Hershey developers

brought the complex system up too quickly and then failed to test it adequately. Related systems problems crippled shipments during the critical Halloween shopping season, resulting in large declines in sales and net income.

- *Failing to deliver what users want:* Systems that do not meet the needs of the firm's target market are likely to fail. For example, in 2011, Netflix leadership divided the company into two, calling the DVD-rental business Qwikster and keeping the streaming business under Netflix. But customers complained, and worse, closed their accounts. Less than a month later, Qwikster was gone. Netflix reunited both businesses under the Netflix name, though it continued to ship DVDs to subscribers until September 2023, at which time it had shipped over 5 billion.[26]
- *Creating predatory partnerships:* Attempting to gain competitive advantage by "partnering" that is camouflaged as collaboration doesn't always work in dynamic business environments. Uber created a strategic partnership in 2017 with the Chinese mobile transportation and ride-sharing company, Didi Chuxing, only to find that Didi started servicing the Mexican market a year later and within two years captured a 30% share of the Mexican ride-sharing market.[27]
- *Running afoul of the law:* Using IS strategically may promote litigation if the IS result in the violation of laws or regulations. Years ago, American Airlines' reservation system, Sabre, was challenged by the airline's competitors on the grounds that it violated antitrust laws. Google also has been embroiled in numerous antitrust suits filed by the U.S. government and the European Union (EU).[28] Now that appeals have been exhausted on several suits, Google and its parent company, Alphabet, has received fines by the EU of over €5.5 billion—and there are still some suits in play.[29] Google faced another type of legal risk in 2010, when it said it was no longer willing to adhere to Chinese censorship. The Chinese government responded by banning searching via all Google search sites (not only google.cn but all language versions, e.g., google.co.jp, google.com.au). To keep its profitable license to operate in China, Google caved in and resumed its compliance with the Chinese government's censorship laws, resulting in Chinese users of Google.cn seeing filtered results as before. Later, in 2019, the discovery of a secret "Dragonfly" project, a mobile search engine for the Chinese market that complies with China's censorship laws, resulted in resistance by Google employees and the project's shutdown later that year.[30] Similarly, the U.S. government is considering legislation to ban the download of the TikTok app onto U.S. devices out of fear that the Chinese government is spying on U.S. citizens and that the app represents a threat to national security.[31]

Every business decision has risks associated with it. However, with the large expenditure of IT resources needed to create sustainable, strategic advantages, the manager should carefully identify and then design a mitigation strategy to manage the associated risks.

---

[26] Todd Olmstead and Dave Cole, "The End of Netflix's DVD Service: A Look Back at the Red Envelope Era," *Wall Street Journal*, April 19, 2023, https://www.wsj.com/story/the-end-of-netflixs-dvd-service-a-look-back-at-the-red-envelope-era-acd031c7?page=1 (accessed April 20, 2023).

[27] Ting LI, Yolande Chan, Nadege Levallet, "How Instacart Leveraged Digital Resources for Strategic Advantage," *MIS Quarterly Executive* 21, no. 3 (2022): 227–39.

[28] The U.S. Department of Justice, "Justice Department Sues Google for Monopolizing Digital Advertising Technologies," January 24, 2023, https://www.justice.gov/opa/pr/justice-department-sues-google-monopolizing-digital-advertising-technologies#:~:text=In%202020%2C%20the%20Justice%20Department,for%20trial%20in%20September%202023 (accessed March 11, 2023).

[29] European Commission, "Antitrust: Commission Fines Google €2.42 Billion for Abusing Its Dominance as Search Engine by Giving Illegal Advantage to Its Own Comparison Shopping Service—Factsheet," https://ec.europa.eu/commission/presscorner/detail/es/MEMO_17_1785 (accessed March 11, 2023); Silvia Amaro, "Google Loses Battle with EU as Court Upholds 2017 Order to Pay $2.8 Billion Fine," CNBC, September 10, 2021, https://www.cnbc.com/2021/11/10/google-loses-battle-with-eu-as-court-upholds-2017-order.html (accessed March 11, 2023); Jenni Reid, "Google Loses Appeal over EU Antitrust Ruling but Fine Cut to $4.12 Billion," CNBC, November 22, 2022, https://www.cnbc.com/2022/09/14/eu-court-backs-antitrust-ruling-against-google-but-reduces-fine.html (accessed March 11, 2023).

[30] Kate Conger and Daisuke Wakabayashi, "Google Employees Protest Secret Work on Censored Search Engine for China," *The New York Times*, August 16, 2018, https://www.nytimes.com/2018/08/16/technology/google-employees-protest-search-censored-china.html?hp&action=click&pgtype=Homepage&clickSource=story-heading&module=first-column-region®ion=top-news&WT.nav=top-news (accessed March 2, 2019); The U.S. Department of Justice, "Justice Department Sues Google for Monopolizing Digital Advertising Technologies," January 24, 2023, https://www.justice.gov/opa/pr/justice-department-sues-google-monopolizing-digital-advertising-technologies#:~:text=In%202020%2C%20the%20Justice%20Department,for%20trial%20in%20September%202023 (accessed March 11, 2023).

[31] Josh Hawley, " Hawley, Buck Introduce New Bill to Ban Tiktok in U.S.," January 25, 2023, https://www.hawley.senate.gov/hawley-buck-introduce-new-bill-ban-tiktok-us#:~:text=The%20No%20TikTok%20on%20United%20States%20Devices%20Act%20would%3A,attempt%20to%20evade%20these%20sanctions (accessed March 11, 2023).

External Relationships

Firms can participate in a wide range of external relationships. Strategic alliances, business ecosystems and co-opetitive relationships are just a few. Below we discuss some ways in which they can become strategic.

Strategic Alliance

A **strategic alliance** is an interorganizational relationship that affords one or more companies in the relationship a strategic advantage. An example of a strategic alliance is the alliance between Microsoft and OpenAI which was mentioned earlier in this chapter. Microsoft's sizeable investment in OpenAI and its provision of much-needed cloud services enabled OpenAI to thrive. In return, Microsoft is receiving benefits from the strategic alliance, including 49% ownership of the for-profit part of OpenAI, profits from the sale of subscriptions of ChatGPT and the opportunity to use ChatGPT's underlying technology (GPT-4) for its own search engine, Bing.

Externally-oriented relationships can take many forms, including joint ventures, joint projects, trade associations, buyer–supplier partnerships, or cartels. Often such relationships use information technologies to support strategic alliances and integrate data across partners' IS. Platforms are a technology that is increasingly used to support these externally-oriented relationships and share information resources. Platforms support customers in developing products (as LEGO discovered), as well as other companies (i.e., partners) in creating and providing services and products to jointly benefit those in the strategic alliance.

Business Ecosystems

A business ecosystem is a group of strategic alliances in which a number of partners provide important services to each other and jointly create value for customers. Platform ecosystems are a very important type of business ecosystem. For example, the Facebook ecosystem includes the many companies that use that platform to deliver their apps, allow customers to post directly on their Facebook page from the app, or allow customers to log on to their site using their Facebook account. This adds value for customers by providing greater convenience, and by offering the ability to automatically update their activity stream with information from the app. Both Facebook and the app provider benefit from their alliance. Facebook's ecosystem also includes those companies that buy the data Facebook harvests from its customers' use.

IS often provide the platform upon which a strategic alliance functions. Technology can help create the product developed by the alliance, share information resources across the partners' existing systems, or facilitate communication and coordination among the partners. Because many services are information based today, an IS platform is used to deliver these services to customers. For instance, OpenAI's ChatGPT was developed and is hosted on Microsoft's Azure cloud platform.

Co-opetitive Relationships

Clearly, not all strategic alliances are formed with suppliers or customers as partners. Rather, co-opetition is an increasingly popular alternative model. As defined by Brandenburg and Nalebuff in their book of the same name, **co-opetition** is a strategy whereby companies cooperate and compete at the same time with companies in their value net. The value net includes a company and its competitors and complementors, as well as its customers and suppliers, and the interactions among all of them. A *complementor* is a company whose product or service is used in conjunction with a particular product or service to make a more useful set for the customer. For example, Goodyear is a complementor to Ford and GM because tires are a complementary product to vehicles. Likewise, Amazon is a complementor to Apple in part because the Amazon reading application, the Kindle, is one of the most popular apps for the iPad. Finally, a cellular service is a complementor to Google's search engine because the service allows more consumers to use Google's search function.

Co-opetition, then, is the strategy for creating the best possible outcome for a business by optimally combining competition and cooperation. It can also be used as a strategy for sourcing as discussed in Chapter 10. It frequently creates competitive advantage by giving power in the form of information to other organizations or groups. For example, Covisint.com was created to host the auto industry's e-marketplace, which grew out of a consortium of competitors, including General Motors, Ford, DaimlerChrysler, Nissan, and Renault. By addressing multiple automotive functional needs across the entire product life cycle, Covisint offered support for collaboration, SCM, procurement, and quality management. Covisint.com extended this business-to-partner platform to other industries including health care, manufacturing, life sciences, food and beverage, and oil and gas. Thus, co-opetition as demonstrated by Covisint not only streamlined the internal operations of its backers but also had the potential to transform an industry. Covisint was purchased by the Canadian company OpenText in 2017,[32] but such a system has forever made competitors realize that they could gain mutual advantage through cooperation.

Co-creating IT and Business Strategy

This chapter has discussed the alignment of IT strategy with business strategy. Certainly, the two strategies must be carefully choreographed to ensure receiving maximum value from IT investments and obtaining the maximum opportunity to achieve the business strategy. However, in the fast-paced business environment where information is increasingly a core component of the product or service offered by the firm, managers must co-create IT and business strategy. That is, one cannot be created independently of the other. In many cases, most notably in digital transformations, they are now one and the same.

For companies whose main product is information, such as financial services companies, it's clear that information management is the core of the business strategy itself. A financial services company must co-create business and IT strategy. But consider a company such as FedEx, most well known as the package delivery company. Are customers paying to have a package delivered or to have information about that package's delivery route and timetable? One could argue that they are one and the same, and that increasingly the company's business strategy *is* its IS strategy. Certainly, there are components of the operation that are more than just information. There are physical packages to be loaded on actual trucks and planes, which are then flown and/or driven to their destinations. However, to make it all work, the company must rely on IS. Should the IS stop working or have a serious failure, FedEx would be unable to do business. A company like this must co-create IT strategy and business strategy.

This was not true a few years ago. Companies could often separate IS strategy from business strategy in part because their products or services did not have a large information component. For example, a few years ago, should the IS of a trucking company stop working, the trucks would still be able to take their shipments to their destination and pick up new ones. It might be slower or a bit more chaotic, but the business wouldn't stop. Today, that's not the case. Complicated logistics are the norm, and IS are often the foundation of the business as seen at FedEx.

With the increasing number of IS applications on platforms, firms increasingly co-create value with their platform partners. Take the iTunes platform as an example. Value is co-created when content providers put their music on Apple's platform, and both Apple and the content providers benefit financially with the downloading of that content. In such cases IT and business strategy is co-created and the process depends on the external relationships critical for co-creating value. Managers who think they can build a business model without considering the opportunities and impact of IS, using both the resources owned by the firm and those available through external partners, will find they have significant difficulties creating business opportunities as well as sustainable advantage in their marketplace.

SUMMARY

- Information resources include data, technology, people, and processes within an organization. Information resources can be either IT assets or IT capabilities.
- IT infrastructure and information repositories are IT assets. Three major categories of IT capabilities are technical skills, IT management skills, and relationship skills.
- Using IS for strategic advantage requires an awareness of the many relationships that affect both competitive business and information strategies.

[32] Joann Muller, "Covisint Didn't Die; It Just Went to the Cloud," Forbes, June 27, 2012, https://www.forbes.com/sites/joannmuller/2012/06/27/covisint-detroits-failed-internet-venture-is-alive-and-well-and-about-to-go-public/#8cd24a737acb (accessed March 6, 2019); OpenText Blog, July 26, 2017, www.opentext.com (accessed March 10, 2023).

- Analyzing the five competitive forces—threat of new entrants, buyers' bargaining power, suppliers' bargaining power, industry competitors, and threat of substitute products—from both a business view and an IS view helps general managers use information resources to minimize the effect of these forces on the organization.
- The value chain highlights how IS add value to the primary and support activities of a firm's internal operations as well as to the activities of its customers and of other components of its supply chain.
- The resource-based view (RBV) helps a firm understand the value created by its strategy. RBV maintains that competitive advantage comes from a firm's information resources. Resources enable a firm to attain and sustain competitive advantage.
- The dynamic capabilities view (DCV) can be used to create innovative business models that adjust to create strategic advantage. Clusters of dynamic capabilities can sense opportunities and market changes, seize opportunities by mobilizing resources and making decisions about actions to take, and transform the opportunities into strategic advantage.
- Numerous risks are associated with using IS to gain strategic advantage: awaking a sleeping giant, encountering bad timing, implementing poorly, failing to deliver what customers want, creating predatory partnerships, and running afoul of the law.
- IT can facilitate strategic alliances. Business ecosystems are groups of strategic alliances working together to deliver goods and services.
- Co-opetition is the complex arrangement through which companies cooperate and compete at the same time with other companies in their value net.

KEY TERMS

business ecosystems, 35
co-opetition, 50
customer relationship management (CRM), 43
dynamic capabilities, 47
enterprise resource planning (ERP), 43
information resources, 37
IT asset, 37
IT capability, 37
network effects, 35
resource-based view (RBV), 45
strategic alliance, 50
supply chain management (SCM), 43

FOUNDATIONAL READINGS

Competitive Strategy: Five Competitive Forces Model, Value Chain: Michael Porter, *Competitive Strategy* (New York: The Free Press, 1998)

Co-opetition: A. Brandenburg and B. Nalebuff, *Co-opetition* (New York: Doubleday, 1996).

Dynamic Capabilities: D.J. Teece and various colleagues have written extensively about Dynamic Capabilities for decades. See, for example: D. J. Teece, G. Pisano, and A. Shuen, "Dynamic Capabilities and Strategic Management," *Strategic Management Journal* 18 (1997), 509–33; Teece, David J. "Business models and dynamic capabilities." *Long Range Planning* 51, no. 1 (2018): 40–49.

Hypercompetition: R. A. D'aveni, *Hypercompetition*. Simon and Schuster, 2010. For a summary, see: D. Goeltz, "Hypercompetition," vol. 1 of *The Encyclopedia of Management Theory*, ed. Eric Kessler (Los Angeles, CA: Sage, 2013), 359–60.

Information Resources: G. Piccoli and B. Ives, "IT-Dependent Strategic Initiatives and Sustained Competitive Advantage: A Review and Synthesis of the Literature," *MIS Quarterly* 29, no. 4 (2003), 747–76. Much of the discussion of Information Resources is based on this article.

Resource-Based View: The resource-based view was originally proposed by management researchers, most prominently Jay Barney, "Firm Resources and Sustained Competitive Advantage," *Journal of Management* 17, no. 1 (1991), 99–120 and "Is the Resource-Based 'View' a Useful Perspective for Strategic Management Research? Yes," *Academy of Management Review* 26, no. 1 (2001), 41–56. For an excellent discussion of criticisms of the resource-based view, see J. Kraaijenbrink, J-C. Spender, and A. J. Groen, "The Resource-Based View: A Review and Assessment of Its Critiques," *Journal of Management*, 36, no. 1 (2010), 349–72.

For an IS-related article see: M. Wade and J. Hulland, "Review: The Resource-Based View and Information Systems Research: Review, Extension and Suggestions for Future Research," *MIS Quarterly* 28, no. 1 (2004), 107–42.

DISCUSSION QUESTIONS

1. What do you think the next era will be for Figure 2.1? Please explain.
2. How can data itself provide a competitive advantage to an organization? Give two or three examples. For each example, describe its associated risks.
3. Use the five competitive forces model as described in this chapter to describe how information technology might be used to provide a winning position for each of these businesses:
   (a) A global advertising agency
   (b) A local restaurant
   (c) A mobile applications provider
   (d) An insurance company
   (e) A local clothing store
4. Using the value chain model, describe how information technology might be used to provide a winning position for each of these businesses:
   (a) A global advertising agency
   (b) A local restaurant
   (c) A mobile applications provider
   (d) An insurance company
   (e) A local clothing store
5. Use the resource-based view as described in this chapter to describe how information technology might be used to provide and sustain a winning position for each of these businesses:
   (a) A global advertising agency
   (b) A local restaurant
   (c) A mobile applications provider
   (d) An insurance company
   (e) A local clothing store
6. Use dynamic capabilities as described in this chapter to describe how information technology might be used to provide and sustain a winning position for each of these businesses:
   (a) A global advertising agency
   (b) A local restaurant
   (c) A mobile applications provider
   (d) An insurance company
   (e) A local clothing store
7. At what point does having the top position in the marketplace become a disadvantage?
8. Some claim that the only sustainable competitive advantage for an organization is its relationships with its customers. All other advantages eventually erode. Do you agree or disagree? How can IS play a role in maintaining the organization's relationship with its customers? Defend your position.

Case Study 2-1 Instacart: Gaining Strategic Advantage During a Pandemic

Instacart, founded in 2012, is a platform-based delivery company that operates in North America. It originally focused on delivering food and pharmaceuticals to customers in their homes from stores such as Sam's Club, Kroger, Aldi, Costco, and CVS. During the COVID-19 pandemic Instacart added non-grocery retailers such as Sephora and H&M to its network of stores. It has aggressively expanded the shopping opportunities for its customers and now delivers over 500 million grocery and non-grocery products purchased from over 40,000 stores. Instacart's sales have continued to grow since the start of the COVID-19 pandemic, though not as aggressively.

The heart of Instacart is its web-based and mobile app and the platform on which they reside. Customers must download the app and use it to place orders for products in the stores of their choice near them and then make online payments for items in their shopping cart. Shoppers receive and pick the orders at the specified stores and deliver them to the customer at the customer-specified address within two hours. Customers may tip the shoppers if they so desire.

Instacart was premised on the concept of timely deliveries and customer convenience—saving customers from the unpleasantries of grocery shopping. Customer convenience took on a whole new meaning during the COVID-19 pandemic. Customers under lockdown measures were urged to stay home to protect themselves and others from the virus. Instacart became a way for customers to get necessary groceries and pharmaceuticals without leaving their homes—once they downloaded the app. There was a dramatic spike of 1.7 and 2.7 million downloads of the Instacart app in the United States in March and April 2020, respectively. This translated into 85% of U.S. households in March 2020 who had downloaded the app. Downloads were also strong in Canada where Instacart captured 60% of the market. Instacart's rapid growth led to doubling its valuation to $39 billion from late 2020 to April 2021—a valuation which dropped by 40% 18 months later as the threat of the virus dwindled.

There are three major groups serviced by the Instacart app and platform:

Customers who order and pay for the goods on the app. They can order goods simultaneously from multiple stores or make recurring orders.

Shoppers who then fulfill the orders placed by the customers on the app. The app uses analytics to match shoppers who are near in real time to where the order is to be delivered. The app also has a store map to make the picking more efficient. The shoppers may or may not deliver the goods depending upon whether they are a full-service shopper or an in-store shopper. Instacart has adopted an Uber-like approach by not hiring the full-service shoppers fulltime, but rather by using the Instacart app to pay them a commission based on the total amount of the order, plus 100% of the tips. The in-store shoppers pick and pack the goods. They are paid by the store and by Instacart on a commission basis. Shoppers have autonomy in selecting their hours of work.

Stores that advertise and vend their goods through the app. The app allows stores to reach a wider audience, have their goods delivered by a reliable third party, and advertise. However, the data about their customers and practices that they share with Instacart may be used strategically against them. Instacart may use the data to get helpful insights for its own business.

Instacart generates revenues from a monthly or yearly customer membership fee. For those customers who haven't paid a membership fee, a 5% service fee and a delivery fee both are charged depending upon the amount of the order and if it is an express delivery (i.e., made in an hour or less from the time of the order). Instacart also may charge customers a surcharge on the store's price of the goods. Instacart generates revenues from an advertising and fulfillment platform on which brands, retailers, and advertising agencies may promote their products. As much as 30% of Instacart sales are of products advertised on its advertising platform.

Instacart monitors its environment to spot new technology trends, and it is constantly updating its digital infrastructure to stay competitive. It can easily add new stores to the platform. It uses machine learning and data science to identify opportunities for improving its service. Some examples are providing new ordering options such as "fast & flexible" or "order ahead," and adjusting the app to deactivate customers who often deleted the tip after the order was delivered. Instacart also monitors its relationships in terms of their strategic advantages and threats. For example, Instacart recently teamed up with Aldi to launch Aldi Express, which, with the Instacart app and infrastructure, makes

Case Study 2-1 **(Continued)**

it possible for Instacart to get about 2,000 of Aldi's most popular products to customers quickly—sometimes in as little as 30 minutes. A little further back in time, when Amazon bought Whole Foods which had been its major store partner and investor, Instacart ended its relationship with Whole Foods and established a relationship with Walmart that touted same day delivery. The strategic move was designed to mitigate the threat of Amazon as a competitor, since Amazon has its own grocery delivery company, Amazon Fresh. Ironically, Instacart surpassed Amazon's online grocery market share in 2021—but Walmart has been the clear front runner in the online grocery market since 2020 and Walmart now has its own grocery delivery service.

Sources: This case is primarily adapted from Ting Li, Yolande Chan, Nadege Levallet, "How Instacart Leveraged Digital Resources for Strategic Advantage," *MIS Quarterly Executive*, 2022, 21, no. 3, pg. 227–39 and Anurag Jain, "Instacart Business Model: How the App works & Why it is Successful," Oyelabs, May 25, 2022, How Instacart Works - Business & Revenue Model (oyelabs.com) (accessed March 11, 2023); See also Statistica.com, "Instacart Overview", https://www.statista.com/topics/9357/instacart/#topicOverview; Instacart homepage, Instacart | Grocery Delivery or Pickup from Local Stores Near You (accessed March 12, 2023); Instacart, "Aldi Launches 30-Minute Delivery with New Instacart-Powered Virtual Convenience Store," June 1, 2023, Instacart.com (accessed July 29, 2023); Heard on the Street, "Why Amazon Isn't Checking Out of Groceries," *Wall Street Journal,* May 13–14, 2023, B12.

Discussion Questions

1. Describe Instacart's platform ecosystem? What value is added to each component in Instacart's platform ecosystem?
2. How can the Resource Based View be applied to understanding how and to what extent Instacart gained and sustained competitive advantage?
3. Describe Instacart's dynamic capabilities. Why have you described them as dynamic capabilities?
4. To what extent should the stores be concerned about predatory risk or the risk from a sleeping giant. Explain your answer.

Case Study 2-2 Amazon Go: How Far Can It Go?

Amazon has many lines of business in its bid to be the largest and most customer-centric company. One unexpected area in which it has publicized a new vision is in-store shopping.

On January 22, 2018, Amazon announced a new concept in physical shopping, called "Amazon Go." In short, imagine walking into a convenience store after identifying yourself using an app just like those at the airport scanning a bar code on their mobile device instead of a paper boarding pass. As you walk through the store, you take items from the shelf, put some back after looking them over, put some in your basket, and even return some to the shelf from your basket after finding a more desirable item elsewhere in the store. Then you put everything in your bag, your pockets, or your mouth, and next leave the store without stopping by any cash registers. The receipt can be found in the app.

This feat is accomplished with the help of hundreds of cameras pointing down from the ceiling that carefully watch you, your items, and your basket all the while you are in the store. Weight sensors and shelf cameras reveal products removed or replaced. The monitoring process is managed by image recognition, artificial intelligence, and machine learning. A 3-D representation of each customer is built and tracked. Amazon assures us that after the checkout process is complete, nearly all data are discarded.

Shoplifting is virtually impossible with such technology, Amazon states. Matt McFarland, a CNN reporter, tried in vain to fool the system for almost an hour, by pointing closely at items, covering up scanning symbols used by the cameras scanners, and grabbing products from behind his back. Amazon told him that errors are highly infrequent.

Of course, a major benefit of Amazon Go includes reducing or eliminating the need to hire cashiers. McFarland reported that there currently is no research to suggest whether the personnel savings will cover losses in sales of convenience items strategically placed near the cash register while customers wait several minutes in line, or for a potential loss in "social proof"; that a long line

***Case Study 2-2* (Continued)**

signals that the store must be pretty great. However, there could be other new opportunities to upsell and cross-sell customers. The AI, through the app, can suggest complementary goods such as side dishes, special deals on foods that the customer tends to buy often, and new items that are likely to be desirable to that particular customer. A physical store cannot do this without a shopping concierge who knows a customer well and follows the person around. This is analogous to the Amazon.com site that suggests other products that each online shopper might like.

The future indeed seems to hold many opportunities for the concept. Amazon has secured patents for several technologies (e.g., Just Walk Out, Amazon One, and Dash Cart—a smart shopping cart) that enable the stores to operate. Amazon originally had planned to open 3,000 cashless stores in the United States using these technologies. However, Jim Kenney, Mayor of Philadelphia, signed off on a bill passed by city council by a wide margin to ban cashless stores because low-income customers without credit cards would not be able to shop in them. That bill would have essentially prevented Amazon Go from operating in the city that is plagued by a 25% poverty rate. Other cities might take note of such a move and follow suit. To keep this from happening, Amazon later acquiesced and agreed to accept cash in its Amazon Go stores after all.

Sources: Adapted from Matt McFarland, "I Spent 53 Minutes in Amazon Go and Saw the Future of Retail," *CNN Business*, October 3, 2018, https://www.cnn.com/2018/10/03/tech/amazon-go/index.html (accessed February 20, 2019); Alan Boyle, "Fresh Patents Served Up for the Smart Shelf Technologies Seen in Amazon Go Stores," September 4, 2018, https://www.geekwire.com/2018/fresh-patents-served-smart-shelf-technologies-seen-amazon-go-stores/ (accessed February 20, 2018); Christian Hetrick, "Amazon Warns It May Rethink Plans to Open a Philly Store If the City Bans Cashless Retailers," *Philly.com*, February 15, 2019, https://www.philly.com/business/retail/amazon-go-philadelphia-cashless-store-ban-20190215.html (accessed February 20, 2019); Christian Hetrick, "Philadelphia Passes Ban on Cashless Stores; Amazon Go Plans Said to Be in Jeopardy," *The Morning Call* (March 4, 2019), https://www.mcall.com/news/nationworld/pennsylvania/mc-nws-philadelphia-cashless-stores-bill-20190304-story.html (accessed March 6, 2019); and "Amazon Says Go Stores Will Soon Accept Cash, One Month After Philly Passes Cashless Store Ban," *Phillyvoice.com*, April 10, 2019, https://www.phillyvoice.com/amazon-go-accept-cash-cashless-store-ban-philly/ (accessed June 23, 2019); "Introducing Amazon Go and the World's Most Advanced Shopping Technology," December 5, 2016, https://www.youtube.com/watch?v=NrmMk1Myrxc (accessed February 20, 2019).

Discussion Questions

1. Assess the time savings of not having to cope with a line in a convenience store. How would it impact your life? Stated another way, does Amazon Go have a genuine competitive advantage, or is it simply a gimmick that will likely fade after it loses its novelty? If it has a genuine competitive advantage, which of the three types described in Chapter 1 does it represent?
2. Describe how Amazon Go is positioned (or not positioned) to resist each of the Five Competitive Forces.
3. Which of the four sustainability factors are positioned to help Amazon Go? Describe how.
4. Consider the world in 20 years. Argue (a) for and (b) against the proposition that most stores will be just like Amazon Go.
5. Are there opportunities for improving the efficiency of the value chain of a typical retail store? Support your answer.
6. How closely aligned are the business strategy and IT strategy for Amazon Go? Support your answer.
7. Several risks of rolling out technologies that yield a competitive advantage are identified in the chapter. Which of these risks do you believe should be of greatest concern for Amazon Go?
8. If you were the CEO of Amazon, to what extent would you expand Amazon Go? In your answer, consider the positioning of Amazon's Whole Foods chain.
9. Amazon has made it profitable to adopt a two-sided platform, where third-party vendors can also sell on Amazon, and where Amazon receives a commission on every sale. If Amazon Go decided to license the enabling technologies to firms such as Walmart and Target, do you believe the net impact would be positive or negative to Amazon Go? Why?

3

Organizational Strategy and Information Systems

In order for information systems (IS) to support an organization in achieving its goals, the organization must reflect the business strategy and be coordinated with the organizational strategy. This chapter focuses on linking and coordinating the IS strategy with the three components of organizational strategy:

- Organizational design (decision rights, formal reporting relationships and structure, informal networks)
- Management control systems (planning, data collection, performance measurement, evaluation, and incentives)
- Internal culture (values, beliefs, and levels of culture)

Managers need to make decisions about how their organizations are going to work. Often decisions about structuring their organizations, controlling organizational operations and employees, and putting in place the desired culture are made early on in their organization's life. However, these decisions are not set in stone. They need to be revisited and revised as the environment changes over time.

When Larry Page and Sergey Brin founded Google in 1998 on a shoestring, they made decisions about the firm's internal culture. According to Larry Page: "it's important that the company be a family, that people feel that they're part of the company, and that the company is like a family to them. When you treat people that way, you get better productivity."[1]

Google's co-founders worked to establish a place where Googlers (i.e., Google's term for its employees) are happy to work and where creativity thrives. Given the nature of Google's core product, it had to be data driven and any potential innovation to be implemented needed to be supported with cold, hard facts. As is the case with many start-ups, Page and Brin adopted a flat structure, and to this day, the structure is relatively flat with a relatively minimal number of layers.

Google's massive Silicon Valley headquarters, called Googleplex, manifests a motivating, fun-to-work culture.[2] Each Googler's office is self-decorated and Googlers can bring their dogs to work. Googlers have free access to excellent on-site gyms and pools, as well as various game options scattered throughout the campus such as table tennis, foosball, ping pong, and video game stations. Googlers can "live" in the office. They don't need to leave the campus to get haircuts, dental or health checkups, professional massages, meals or snacks, or a snooze in an in-house nap pod.

But, it's not all play at Google. Googlers are expected to be productive and innovative—and they are well rewarded when they are. Google, recognizing that innovations may not always succeed, has created a culture that nurtures experimentation. VP of Sales and U.S. Operations, Jon Kaplan states that, "We do

[1] Avin Kline, "What Every Company Can Learn From Google's Company Culture," Success Agency, January 19, 2023.

[2] Lori Li, "10 Reasons Why Google's Company Culture Works," *Tiny Pulse*, April 21, 2020.

dozens of tests and experiments every single quarter."[3] For example, Google runs tests on only one percent of its core product, its prodigious search engine, and if it's successful it's scaled up. "We can start very small and test a theory, and if it doesn't work, we can very quickly pull that back. That's a really important part of what we do every day." Similarly, Googlers are expected to learn from their failures and they receive feedback about their performance to help them improve. Thus, it's not surprising that Google's Bard, the generative AI rival of OpenAir's ChatGPT, was released on a limited basis as an experiment. Google, knowing that Bard would generate bad answers, asked Bard users to let it know when such errors occurred so that Bard could learn from its mistakes (using machine learning technology).

Google is known for its open culture where ideas and information are freely exchanged. Camaraderie and social interactions are important and Google's warm work environment encourages them. To ensure the culture is open and innovative and the Googlers are satisfied with their managers, compensation and other aspects of their jobs, an internal survey called Googlegeist is conducted annually. If the survey uncovers areas needing improvement, they are each addressed. Thus, there is much to consider in creating and maintaining a desired internal culture.

Google has been much lauded for its exemplary culture. Why then did Google, a company that had worked so hard to create a culture focused on keeping its employees happy, lay off 12,000 of them with an email in January 2023?[4] To make matters worse, the laid-off employees weren't allowed to pack up their self-decorated cubicles or bid farewell to the comrades that Google's culture had nurtured and deemed so important. It has been suggested that the change had been gradual since 2015, when Google was restructured into a subsidiary of Alphabet. That was when company started basing decisions less on co-founder vision and more on the Chief Executives Officer's (Sundar Pichai) and Chief Financial Officer's (Ruth Porat) focus on profit and corporate wisdom. The company became more answerable to investors, stockholders, and Wall Street and far less answerable to the employees who had helped build it into a tech giant. The new focus was accompanied by a new physical workspace designed to foster creativity and productivity. With its new Bay View campus planned for 2,000 Googlers, the live-at-work concept was traded for a building with well-designed collaboration areas on an upper floor and sound-buffered deep-focus workspaces on the ground floor.[5] This Google case helps illustrate the many factors that go into building a culture and the importance of managers making decisions about that culture over time.

Chapter 1 introduces a simple framework for understanding the role of IS in organizations. The Information Systems Strategy Triangle relates business strategy with IS strategy and organizational strategy. In an organization that operates successfully, either an overriding business strategy drives both organizational strategy and IS strategy, or the IS and business strategy are co-created. Either way, the most effective businesses optimize the interrelationships between the organization and its IS, maximizing efficiency and productivity.

Organizational strategy includes the organization's design, as well as the managerial choices that define, set up, coordinate, and control its work processes. As discussed in Chapter 1, many models of organizational strategy are available. One is the managerial levers framework that includes the complementary design variables shown in Figure 3.1. Optimized organizational designs support optimal business processes, and they, in turn, reflect the firm's values and culture. **Organizational strategy** may be considered as the coordinated set of actions that leverages the use of organizational design, management control systems, and organizational culture to make the organization effective by achieving its objectives. The organizational strategy works best when it meshes well with the IS strategy.

This chapter builds on the managerial levers framework. Of primary concern is how IS impact the three types of managerial levers: organizational, control, and cultural. This chapter looks at organizational designs that incorporate IS to define the flow of information throughout the organization, explores how IS can facilitate management control at the organizational and individual levels, and concludes with some

[3] Barr Seitz, "Learning from Google's Digital Culture," *McKinsey*, June 1, 2015, https://www.mckinsey.com/~/media/McKinsey/Industries/Technology%20Media%20and%20Telecommunications/High%20Tech/Our%20Insights/Learning%20from%20Googles%20digital%20culture/Learning%20from%20Googles%20digital%20culture.ashx (accessed March 28, 2023).

[4] Ryan Clancy, "Google Lays Off Largest Number of Workers in Company History via Email," March 21, 2023, https://www.msn.com/en-us/money/companies/google-lays-off-largest-number-of-workers-in-company-history-via-email/ar-AA18UbbZ (accessed March 22, 2023).

[5] David Radcliffe, Bay View is open—the first campus built by Google, *Life at Google website*, May 17, 2022, https://blog.google/inside-google/life-at-google/bay-view-campus-grand-opening/ (accessed August 2, 2023). If you would like to see what the Bay View campus looks like, see the Washington Post video: Google aims to reimagine the office with new Bay View campus (washingtonpost.com) (accessed August 2, 2023).

Variable	Description
Organizational Variables	
Decision rights	The authority to initiate, approve, implement, and control various types of decisions necessary to plan and run the business
Business processes	The set of ordered tasks needed to complete key objectives of the business
Formal reporting relationships	The structure set up to ensure coordination among all units within the organization; reflects allocation of decision rights
Informal networks	Mechanisms, such as ad hoc groups, which work to coordinate and transfer information outside the formal reporting relationships
Control Variables	
Data	The facts collected, stored, and used by the organization
Planning	The processes by which future direction is established, communicated, and implemented
Performance measurement and evaluation	The set of measures that are used to assess success in the execution of plans and the processes by which such measures are used to improve the quality of work
Incentives	The monetary and nonmonetary devices used to motivate behavior within an organization
Cultural Variables	
Values	The set of implicit and explicit beliefs that underlies decisions made and actions taken; reflects aspirations about the way things should be done
Locus	The level or span of the culture, i.e., local, national, regional

FIGURE 3.1 Organizational design variables based on managerial levers.

Source: Adapted from James I. Cash, Robert G. Eccles, Nitin Nohria, and Richard L. Nolan, *Building the Information Age Organization* (Homewood, IL: Richard D. Irwin, 1994).

ideas about how culture impacts IS and organizational performance. It primarily focuses on organizational-level issues related to strategy. The next two chapters complement these concepts with a discussion of new approaches to work and organizational processes in Chapters 4 and 5, respectively.

Information Systems and Organizational Design

Organizations must be designed in a way that enables them to perform effectively. Different designs accomplish different goals. This section examines organizational variables. It focuses on how IS are designed in conjunction with an organization's structure. Ideally, an organizational structure is designed to facilitate the communication and work processes necessary for it to accomplish the organization's goals, and IS can help managers coordinate and control the workflows they are responsible for. Perhaps intuitively, organizational designers at those companies used organizational variables described in Figure 3.1 to build their structures. Those variables include decision rights that underlie formal structures, formal reporting relationships, and informal networks.

Decision Rights

Decision rights indicate who in the organization has the responsibility to initiate, supply information for, approve, implement, and control various types of decisions. Ideally, the individual who has the most information about a decision and who is in the best position to understand all the relevant issues should be the person who has its decision rights. But this may not happen, especially in organizations in which senior leaders make most of the important decisions. Much of the discussion of IT governance and accountability in Chapter 9 is based upon who has the decision rights for critical IS decisions. When talking about accountability, one must start with the person who is responsible for the decision—that is, the person who has the decision rights. Organizational design is all about making sure that decision rights are properly assigned—and reflected in the structure of formal reporting relationships. IS support decision rights by getting the right information to the decision maker at the right time and then transmitting the decision to those who are affected. In some cases, IS enable a centralized decision maker to pass information that has been gathered from operations and stored centrally down through the organization. If IS fail to deliver the right information, or worse, deliver the wrong information to the decision maker, poor decisions are bound to be made.

Consider the case of Zara from the last chapter. Each of its 5800+ stores orders clothes in the same way, using sophisticated technology-driven systems and follows a rigid weekly timetable for ordering, which provides the headquarters commercial team with the information needed to manage fulfillment. Many other large retailers make the decision centrally about what to send to their stores, using forecasting and inventory control models. However, at Zara, store managers have decision rights for ordering, enabling each store to reflect the tastes and preferences of customers in its localized area. But the store managers do not have decision rights for order fulfillment because they have no way of knowing the consolidated demand of stores in their area. The decision rights for order fulfillment lie with the commercial team in headquarters because it is the team that knows about overall demand, overall supply, and store performance in their assigned areas. The information from the commercial team then flows directly to designers and production, allowing them to respond quickly to customer preferences.[6]

Formal Reporting Relationships and Organizational Structures

Organizational structure is the design element that ensures that decision rights are correctly allocated. The structure of reporting relationships typically reflects the flow of communication and decision making throughout the organization. Traditional organizational structures are hierarchical, flat, matrix, and networked. A comparison of these four types of organizational structures may be found in Figure 3.2.

Hierarchical Organizational Structure

As business organizations entered the 20th century, their growth prompted a need for systems for processing and storing information. A new class of worker—the clerical worker—flourished and went to work in offices. From 1870 to 1920 alone, the number of U.S. clerical workers mushroomed from 74,200 to more than a quarter of a million.[7] Offices and factories alike structured themselves using the model that

	Hierarchical	Flat	Matrix	Networked
Description	Bureaucratic form with defined levels of management	Decision making pushed down to the lowest level in the organization	Workers assigned to multiple supervisors so as to promote integration	Formal and informal communication networks that connect all parts of the company
Characteristics	Division of labor, specialization, span of control, unity of command, formalization	Informal roles, planning, and control; often small and young organizations	Dual reporting relationships often based on function and purpose	Creativity, flexibility, and adaptiveness,
Type of environment best supported	Stable, certain	Dynamic, uncertain	Dynamic, uncertain	Dynamic, uncertain
Basis of structuring	Primarily by function	Very loose	By function and purpose (i.e., location, product, customer)	Through networks
Power structure	Centralized	Decentralized	Distributed (matrix managers)	Distributed (network)

FIGURE 3.2 Comparison of organizational structures.

[6] Martin Roll, "The Secret of Zara's Success: A Culture of Customer Co-Creation," March 2018, https://martinroll.com/resources/articles/strategy/the-secret-of-zaras-success-a-culture-of-customer-co-creation/ (accessed February 17, 2019).

[7] Frances Cairncross, *The Company of the Future* (London: Profile Books, 2002).

Max Weber observed when studying the Catholic Church and the German army. This model, called a **bureaucracy**, was based on a hierarchical organizational structure.

Hierarchical organizational structure is an organizational form based on the concepts of division of labor, specialization, span of control, and unity of command. Decision rights are highly specified and centralized. When work needs to be done, orders typically come from the top and work is subjected to the division of labor. That means it is segmented into smaller and smaller pieces until it reaches the level of the business in which it will be done. Middle managers do the primary information processing and communicating, telling their subordinates what to do and telling senior managers the outcome of what was done. Jobs within the enterprise are specialized and often organized around particular functions, such as marketing, accounting, and manufacturing. **Span of control** indicates the number of direct reports. **Unity of command** means that each person has a single supervisor. Rules and policies are established to handle the routine work performed by employees of the organization. When in doubt about how to complete a task, employees turn to the rules. If a rule doesn't exist to handle the situation, employees turn to a supervisor in the hierarchy for the decision. Key decisions are made at the top and filter down through the organization in a centralized fashion. Hierarchical structures, which are sometimes called *vertical structures*, are most suited to relatively stable, certain environments in which the top-level executives are in command of the information needed to make critical decisions. This allows them to make decisions quickly.

IS are typically used to store and communicate information and to support the information needs of managers throughout the hierarchy. IS convey the decisions of top managers downward, and data from operations are sent upward through the hierarchy using IS. Hierarchical structures are also very compatible with efforts to organize and manage data centrally. The data from operations that have been captured at lower levels and conveyed through IS increasingly need to be consolidated, managed, and made secure at a high level.

Flat Organizational Structure

In contrast to the hierarchical structure, the *flat, or horizontal, organizational structure* has a less well-defined chain of command. You seldom see an organization chart for a flat organization because the relationships are fluid and the jobs are loosely defined. That is, drawing an organization chart for a flat organization is like trying to tie a ribbon around a puddle. In flat organizations, everyone does whatever needs to be done to conduct business. There are very few "middle managers." For this reason, flat organizations can respond quickly to dynamic, uncertain environments. Entrepreneurial organizations, as well as smaller organizations, often use this structure because they typically have fewer employees, and even when they grow, they initially build on the premise that everyone must do whatever is needed. Teamwork is important in flat organizations. To increase flexibility and innovation, decision rights may not be clearly defined. Hence, decision making is often decentralized because decisions are made across the organization. It is also time-consuming. As the work grows, new individuals are added to the organization, and eventually a hierarchy is formed where divisions are responsible for segments of the work processes. Many companies strive to keep the "entrepreneurial spirit," but in reality, work is done in much the same way as with the hierarchy described previously. Flat organizations often use IS to off-load certain routine work in order to avoid hiring additional employees. As a hierarchy develops, the IS become the glue tying together parts of the organization that otherwise would not communicate. IS also enable flat organizations to respond quickly to their environment.

An example of an organization with a flat organizational structure is Zara. Zara claims on its website that "The new facilities, which stand out for the simplicity of their lines, broad open spaces, energy efficiency and sustainability credentials, have been designed to reinforce the brand's essence and support its flat organizational structure."[8]

Matrix Organizational Structure

The third form is the **matrix organizational structure**. It typically assigns employees to two or more supervisors to make sure multiple dimensions of the business are integrated. Each supervisor directs a different aspect of the employee's work. For example, a member of a matrix team from marketing would have

[8] Inditex, "A New 170,000 m^2 Building to House the Zara Sales and Design Teams Within Inditex's Complex in Arteixo," December 21, 2021, News Detail https://www.inditex.com/itxcomweb/en/press/news-detail?contentId=d6a11054-f905-4f0f-8593-96097bc21f37 (accessed March 23, 2023).

a supervisor for marketing decisions and a different supervisor for a specific product line. The team member would report to both, and both theoretically would be responsible in some measure for that member's performance and development. That is, the marketing manager would oversee the employee's development of marketing skills and the product manager would make sure that the employee develops skills related to the product. Thus, decision rights are shared between the managers. The matrix structure allows organizations to concentrate on both functions and purpose. The matrix structure allows the flexible sharing of human resources and achieves the coordination necessary to meet dual sets of organizational demands, especially on a temporary basis. It is suited for complex decision making and dynamic and uncertain environments. IS reduce the operating complexity of matrix organizations by allowing information sharing among the different managerial functions. For example, a saleswoman's sales would be entered into the information system and appear in the results of all managers to whom she reports.

Cognizant, one of the largest IT services company in the world, grew at such a breakneck speed that it had to reinvent its organizational structure many times to make sure that it successfully facilitated the flow of necessary information to support organizational processes and decisions. Initially, its India-centric structure located project managers in India along with software engineers. Employees at customer locations worldwide reported to the India-based managers. As the company grew and its projects shifted from simple, cost-based solutions to complex, relationship-based solutions, this structure changed to become more customer oriented. Under the redesigned reporting structure, managers were moved to customer locations, but software engineers remained in India. This change improved customer relations, but new headaches appeared on the technical side. Managers unexpectedly had to spend their days with customers and spend their nights with software engineers to clarify customer requirements and fix bugs. This slowed the system development process and created a tremendous strain on managers, who threatened to quit. Thus, neither of these organizational structures worked well nor were they well aligned with the business strategy and the IS strategy.[9]

Cognizant solved the problem by implementing a better structure for complex projects—a matrix structure in which each project has two managers equally responsible for outcomes such as customer satisfaction, project deadlines, and group revenue. A technical manager (typically a software engineer) in India and the business manager at the customer site resolve project-related problems and issues among themselves. The matrix structure enabled Cognizant to work more closely with its customers on improving their operations and meeting their needs. However, not all employees were happy with the structure as noted by one disgruntled employee who claimed that the functional manager: "most of the time doesn't know what you are working on but still evaluates your performance, and then the project manager/lead who closely works with you but can't assess you [because] you don't report to him. It's [a] complicated structure and can get you [ticked] off."[10]

As suggested in the quote above, the matrix organizational structure possesses its own downsides. Although theoretically each boss has a well-defined area of authority, employees often find the matrix organizational structure frustrating and confusing because they are frequently subjected to two authorities with conflicting opinions. Consequently, working in a matrix organizational structure can be time-consuming because confusion must be dealt with through frequent meetings and conflict resolution sessions.

Networked Organizational Structure

Made possible by advances in IT, a fourth type of organizational structure emerged: the networked organizational structure. **Networked organizational structures** are those that rely on highly decentralized decision rights and utilize distributed information and communication systems to replace inflexible hierarchical controls with controls based in IS. They are particularly well suited to dynamic, unstable environments. Networked organizations are defined by their ability to promote creativity, adaptiveness, and flexibility while maintaining operational process control. Because networked structures are distributed, many employees throughout the organization can share their knowledge and experience and participate in making key organizational decisions. Data are gathered and stored in centralized data warehouses for use

[9] Cognizant Computer Goods Technology, "Creating a Culture of Innovation: 10 Steps to Transform the Consumer Goods Enterprise," October 6, 2009.

[10] Cognizant website, August 4, 2015, https://www.glassdoor.com/Reviews/Employee-Review-Cognizant-Technology-Solutions-RVW 7459726.htm (accessed February 18, 2019).

in analysis and decision making. In theory at least, decision making is more timely and accurate because data are collected and stored when generated. The extensive use of communication technologies and networks also renders it easier to coordinate across functional boundaries. In short, the networked organization is one in which IT ties together people and processes.

Other Organizational Structures

An organization is seldom a pure form of one of the four structures described here. It is much more common to see a hybrid structure in which different parts of the organization use different structures depending on the information needs and desired work processes. For example, the IS department may use a hierarchical structure that allows more control over data warehouses and centrally-located hardware, whereas the research and development (R&D) department may employ a networked structure to capitalize on knowledge sharing. In the hierarchical IS department, information flows from top to bottom, whereas in the networked R&D department, all researchers may be connected to one another. Google has a different type of hybrid structure: A matrix structure supports cross-functional teams focusing on both its wide range of products (e.g., cloud services, AI, Search, etc.) and its critical functions (e.g., marketing, finance, etc.)—while keeping the structure relatively flat to allow the company to be flexible and respond quickly to innovation.[11]

Further, IS are enabling even more advanced organizational forms such as the adaptive organization and zero time organization.[12] Common to these advanced forms is the idea of agile, responsive organizations that can configure resources and people quickly to adapt to changing demands. Building in the capability to respond instantly means designing the organization so that each of the key structural elements is able to respond instantly. Dynamic capabilities discussed in Chapter 2 are especially good in helping organizations sense and adapt successfully to change.

In 2018, Tata Consultancy Services (TCS), India's largest exporter of IT services implemented a new vertical organizational structure under the direction of its new CEO at the time, Rajesh Gopinathan.[13] The structure was intended to focus on long-term strategies and was designed along industry service group lines (e.g., Banking and Financial Services, Healthcare, Communications, Healthcare, etc.). Then in 2022, TCS implemented a novel structure that is clearly focused on innovation and adaptation. Only four people report directly to TCS's CEO Gopinathan. This means that Gopinathan's span of control of TCS's new organizational structure is quite small for such a large organization (i.e., 4). The new groups are named for future-oriented activities: acquisition, relationship incubation, enterprise growth and business transformation. The announcement of the change in the organizational structure on the TCS website claims: "the new structure further deepens the customer-centricity that TCS was always known for and is expected to help make TCS the preferred growth and transformation partner to more of its clientele."[14]

Why the Differences in Organizational Structures?

While both Cognizant and TCS are large Indian IT services companies that found they often needed to reorganize to respond to various problems resulting from growth, their problems were profoundly different at different points in time. In the example above, Cognizant's main problem at the time was its lack of necessary information flows between the software engineers in India and the customer service managers on the client location. Its complex problems resulted in a correspondingly complex matrix structure. It focused on the delivery of IS that reflect refined technical solutions to their problems to its customers. The matrix organizational structure allows it to improve both customer responsiveness and necessary information flows. The matrix organizational structure can zero in on system development and delivery and addresses the information flow problem that Cognizant was experiencing.

---

[11] Nathaniel Smithson, "Google's Organizational Structure & Its Characteristics (An analysis)," September 8, 2018, https://panmore.com/google-organizational-structure-characteristics-analysis (accessed September 19, 2023).

[12] For more information on zero-time organizations, see R. Yeh, K. Pearlson, and G. Kozmetsky, *ZeroTime: Providing Instant Customer Value Every Time, All the Time* (Hoboken, NJ: John Wiley, 2000).

[13] ET Now Digital, "TCS Shifts to a New Operational Structure, Creates 4 Distinct Business Groups," March 1, 2022, https://www.timesnownews.com/business-economy/companies/tcs-shifts-to-a-new-operational-structure-creates-4-distinct-business-groups-article-89921721 (accessed March 23, 2023).

[14] Tata Consultancy Services, https://www.tata.com/business/tcs (accessed March 23, 2023).

In contrast, TCS's latest organization chart reflects a focus on change and innovation as a way of growing its revenues. It is moving away from the more traditional focus on industry service groups. The new focus is on acquisition, relationship incubation, enterprise growth, and business transformation.

Cognizant and TCS are both in the same business but chose different organizational structures to carry out their objectives. The point is that different organizational structures reflect different organizational strategies that are used to implement business strategies and accomplish organizational goals. These organizational strategies need to be aligned with IS strategies. When used appropriately, IS leverage human resources, capital, and materials to create an organization that optimizes performance. Companies that design organizational strategy without considering IS strategies run into problems like those Cognizant experienced. A synergy results from designing organizations with IS strategy in mind—a synergy that cannot be achieved when IS strategy is just added on.

Informal Networks

The organization chart reflects the authority derived from formal reporting relationships in the organization's formal structure. However, informal relationships also exist and can play an important role in an organization's functioning. Informal networks, in addition to formal structures, are important for alignment with the organization's business strategy.

Occasionally, management designs some of the informal relationships or networks. For example, when working on a special project, an employee might be asked to let the manager in another department know what is going on. This is considered an informal reporting relationship. Or a company may have a job rotation program that provides employees with broad-based training by allowing them to work a short time in a variety of areas. Long after they have moved on to another job, employees on job rotations may keep in touch informally with former colleagues or call upon their past coworkers when a situation arises that their input may be helpful. Hewlett Packard's Decision Support and Analytics Services unit encouraged the development of work-related informal networks when it established focused interest group/forums known as Domain Excellence Platforms (DEPs). An IT-enabled DEP allows at least five people who hold a common interest related to the business to form a team to share their knowledge on a topic (e.g., cloud computing, web analytics). For nonbusiness-related topics, the employees can join conferences to talk about the topic and get to know one another better. The hope is that they will start thinking beyond their work silos.[15]

However, not all informal relationships are a consequence of a plan by management. Some networks unintended by management develop for a variety of other factors including work proximity, friendship, shared interests, family ties, and so on. The employees can make friends with employees in another department when they play together on the company softball team, share the same lunch period in the company cafeteria, or see one another at social gatherings. Informal networks can also arise for political reasons. Employees can cross over departmental, functional, or divisional lines to create political coalitions that further their goals. Some informal networks even cross organizational boundaries. As computer and information technologies facilitate collaboration across distances, social networks and virtual communities are formed. Many of these prove useful in getting a job done, even if not all members of the network belong to the same organization. LinkedIn is an example of a tool that enables large, global, informal networks.

One type of informal network is a social network, or a network of social interactions and personal relationships. Alternatively, and more commonly, a social network in organizations provides an IT backbone linking all individuals in the enterprise, regardless of their formal title or position. Social networks can be established, structured, and managed by social networking sites. A **social networking site (SNS)** is a "networked communication platform in which participants (1) have uniquely identifiable profiles that consist of user-supplied content, content provided by other users, and/or system-provided data; (2) can publicly articulate connections that can be viewed and traversed by others; and (3) can consume, produce, and/or interact with streams of user-generated content."[16]

[15] T. S. H. Teo, R. Nishant, M. Goh, and S. Agarwal, "Leveraging Collaborative Technologies to Build a Knowledge Sharing Culture at HP Analytics," *MIS Quarterly Executive* 10, no. 1 (March 2011): 1–18.

[16] N. B. Ellison and D. Boyd, "Sociality Through Social Network Sites," in *The Oxford Handbook of Internet Studies*, ed. W. H. Dutton (Oxford, UK: Oxford University Press, 2013), 158.

Within the organizational context, enterprise social network sites are becoming increasingly common. An **enterprise social network (ESN)** is basically a social networking site that is used within an organization, that is formally sanctioned by management, and that can restrict membership and interactions to the organization's employees. For example, the ESN Yammer limits an individual's network to other users who share the same corporate email domain. Though ESNs are platforms that are technically similar to SNSs, their focus is on forming and maintaining connections and knowledge sharing internal to the organization. An ESN can support individual blogs, internal wikis and websites, and file shares. An ESN links individuals together in ways that enable them to find experts, get to know colleagues, and see who has relevant experience for projects across traditional organization lines. At the financial services firm USAA, one social network on the company's ESN was created to help new hires assimilate better into the organization by enabling them to connect with one another.

Some might regard an ESN as a "super-directory" that provides not only the names of the individuals but also their role in the company, their title, their contact information, and their location. It might even list details such as their supervisor (and their direct reports and peers), the project(s) they are currently working on, and personal information specific to the enterprise. What differentiates an ESN from previous IT solutions to connect individuals is that it is integrated with the work processes themselves. Conversations can take place, work activities can be recorded, and information repositories can be linked or merely represented within the structure of the social network.

Information Systems and Management Control Systems

Controls are the second type of managerial lever. Not only does IS change the way organizations are structured but also it profoundly affects the way managers control their organizations. Management control is concerned with the process of control: how planning is performed in organizations and how people and processes are monitored, evaluated, and compensated or rewarded. Ultimately, it means that senior leaders make sure the things that are supposed to happen actually happen—when they are supposed to happen. There are many different types of control (e.g., formal, informal, and through clans). Below we contrast two: control that is likened to a thermostat and control that is associated with algorithms.

Control Like a Thermostat

Management control systems can be compared to room thermostats. Thermostats register the desired temperature. A sensing device within the thermostat determines whether the temperature in the room is within a specified range of the one desired. If the temperature is beyond the desired range, a mechanism is activated to adjust the temperature. For instance, if the thermostat is set at 70 degrees and the temperature in the room is 69, then the heater can be activated (if it is winter) or the air conditioning can be turned off (if it is summer). Similarly, management control systems must respond to the goals established through planning. Measurements are taken periodically and if the variance is too great, adjustments are made to organizational processes or practices. For example, operating processes might need to be changed to achieve the desired goals.

IS offer new opportunities for collecting and organizing data for three management control processes:

1. *Data collection:* IS enable the collection of information that helps managers determine whether they are satisfactorily progressing toward realizing the organization's mission as reflected in its stated goals.
2. *Evaluation:* IS facilitate the comparison of actual performance with the desired performance that is established as a result of planning.
3. *Communication:* IS speed the flow of information from where it is generated to where it is needed. This allows an analysis of the situation and a determination about what can be done to correct problematic situations. It also allows for coordination.

When managers need to control work, IS can play a crucial role. IS provide decision models for scenario planning and evaluation. For example, the airlines routinely use decision models to study the effects of changing routes or schedules. IS collect and analyze information from automated processes, and they can make automatic adjustments to the processes. For example, a paper mill uses IS to monitor the mixing of ingredients in a batch of paper and to add more ingredients or change the temperature of the boiler as necessary. IS collect, evaluate, and communicate information, leaving managers with time to make more strategic decisions.

Management control can also be focused on individuals who have objectives in line with organizational goals. In the case of thermostat-like controls, the individual or the organization may set standards or targets based on performance. For example, a sales person may have a target stating the amount of sales to be made in a month or an Emergency Room doctor may have a target of the number of patients to see in a day or the average response time for treating them. Sometimes it may be difficult to have specific behavioral targets, so the thermostat may measure how close the individual's behavior is to a standard behavior. For instance, an individual may be evaluated on her time in front of a computer terminal. If the individual is working on a team, the manager may consider if the employee is collaborative, or a social worker's manager may assess how empathetic the employee is when working with clients. Until recently, the assessment of such behaviors was hard to measure and, consequently, often subjective—or at least more so than when a specific performance goal is set. However, now programs such as Google's OXYGEN analyze collaborative behaviors by tabulating the number of interactions an employee has with other members of the team (engagement) or by counting caring expressions in their written communications.[17]

Control Through Algorithms

Of course, the implicit assumption in this section on Management Control Systems is that both the controller (i.e., manager) and controllee (i.e., employee) are human. But what if, in fact, the controller is a form of technology? As organizations hire more remote workers, use ubiquitous technologies, and become more reliant on mobile technologies, there is a possibility that technology may serve as a proxy for a manager when it comes to measuring, monitoring, evaluating, and compensating or rewarding employee performance. This is the case with **technology-mediated control**, or the use of technology in management control. A specific type of technology-mediated control is **algorithmic control**, or the "use of algorithms to monitor platform workers' behavior and ensure its alignment with the platform organization's goals."[18] Sometimes the algorithms act like a "boss" to the extent that they establish and impose common standards and rules. The "boss" actively controls workers' behaviors and sanctions them when they deviate from the standards and rules. For example, if Uber drivers don't accept three trips in a row, their app is automatically deactivated. The algorithms also use lots of data about workers to analyze their behavior. The Uber app gathers multiple data points to figure out what drivers are doing when they don't accept a trip. Further, the algorithms "learn" from the process data to subtly and informally "nudge" their workers to make specific behavioral choices. For example, Uber drivers may be nudged into working longer and harder with text messages, alerts, pop-ups, and other algorithmically-derived strategies.

Other well-known companies besides Uber use algorithmic control to monitor employee behavior and manage their performance in numerous ways. For example, UPS tracks employees' driving behaviors (e.g., speed and seatbelt use) with sensors embedded in their delivery trucks, and compares their performance against an established standard, stops-per-on-road hour. Further, UPS uses analytics, GPS tracking and sensors to optimize the routing of their delivery trucks, which is reported to have saved the company 8.5 million gallons of fuel and cut CO_2 emissions by 85,000 metric tons annually.[19]

Algorithmic control is an important part of **algorithmic management**, which has been defined as "a platform's large scale data collection and use of data to develop and improve learning algorithms that carry out coordination and control functions traditionally performed by managers in a highly automated

[17] Schafheitle, Simon, Antoinette Weibel, Isabel Ebert, Gabriel Kasper, Christoph Schank, and Ulrich Leicht-Deobald, "No Stone Left Unturned? Toward a Framework for the Impact of Datafication Technologies on Organizational Control," *Academy of Management Discoveries* 6, no. 3 (2020): 455–487.

[18] Möhlmann, Mareike, Lior Zalmanson, Ola Henfridsson, and Robert Wayne Gregory, "Algorithmic Management of Work on Online Labor Platforms: When Matching Meets Control," *MIS Quarterly* 45, no. 4 (2021): pg. 2006; And for TMC: W. A. Cram and M. Wiener, "Technology-Mediated Control: Case Examples and Research Directions for the Future of Organizational Control," *Communications of the Association for Information Systems*, 46, no. 1 (2020): 4.

[19] Schafheitle et al. (2020), "No Stone Left Unturned."

and data-driven fashion."[20] Algorithmic management also involves algorithmic matching, such as finding workers who are best able to complete a task such as with Uber and Amazon's Mechanical Turk.

Planning and Information Systems

In the first chapter, the importance of aligning organizational strategy with the business strategy is discussed. An output of the strategizing process is a plan to guide in achieving the strategic objectives. IS can play a role in planning in four ways:

- IS can provide the necessary data to develop the strategic plan. They can be especially useful in collecting data from organizational units and integrating the data to transform those data into information for the strategic decision makers.
- IS can provide scenario and sensitivity analysis through simulation and data analysis.
- IS can be a major component of the planning process.
- In some instances, an information system is a major component of a strategic plan. That is, as discussed in Chapters 1 and 2, IS can be used to gain and maintain strategic advantage or enable a digital transformation.

Data and Information Systems

Planning systems and both organizational- and individual-level control systems rely on lots of data gathered from a wide range of sources including IS, sensors, social media posts, smart ID badges, wearable GPS devices, or bio radio-frequency ID (bio RFID chips). Algorithms, data mining, and machine learning used for management control typically require Big Data. The volume (e.g., petabytes, tens of millions of observations) and variety (e.g., audio, video, image, text) of the Big Data that are collected by organizations is increasing exponentially. Two other aspects of Big Data to consider are velocity (e.g., data collected instantaneously, over long periods of time) and veracity (e.g., accuracy, non-obsolescence, completeness).[21] IS can collect, store, and process all types of data.

Data-driven technologies can support the management control of individual employees when managers set individual and group goals for them, monitor the process of achieving those goals, evaluate performance and compensate them through salaries, incentives, and rewards. IS can streamline the process of data collection and analysis of the collected data.

Monitoring work can take on a completely new meaning with the use of information technologies. IS make it possible to collect such data as the precise time spent on a task, exactly who was contacted, and the specific data that passed through the process. The data collected from operations create large data stores that can be analyzed for trends, assessments of employee potential, predictions of turnover intent, and more. For example, a call center that handles customer service telephone calls is typically monitored by an information system that collects data on the number of calls each representative received and the length of time each representative took to answer each call and then respond to the question or request for service. Managers at call centers can easily and non-intrusively collect data on virtually any part of the process. The organizational design challenge in data collection is twofold: (1) to embed monitoring tasks within everyday work and (2) to reduce the negative impacts to employees being monitored. Workers perceive their regular tasks as value adding but have difficulty in seeing how value is added by tasks designed to provide information for management control. Research has found that monitoring does not always increase stress of the employee, especially when it fits the task and is automatic and nonintrusive.[22] But, employees often avoid activities aimed at monitoring their work or worse, find ways to ensure that data

[20] Möhlmann et al. (2021), "Algorithmic Management of Work on Online Platforms," pg. 2005.

[21] Katherine C. Kellogg, Melissa A. Valentine, and Angele Christin. "Algorithms at Work: The New Contested Terrain of Control." *Academy of Management Annals* 14, no. 1 (2020): 366–410.

[22] D. Galletta and R. Grant, "Silicon Supervisors and Stress: Merging New Evidence from the Field," *Accounting, Management and Information Technology* 5, no. 3 (1995): 163–183.

recorded are inaccurate, falsified, or untimely. Collecting monitoring data directly from work tasks—or embedding the creation and storage of performance information into software used to perform work—renders the data more reliable.

Many software products are available for companies to monitor employees. Software monitoring products are installed by companies to get specific data about what employees are doing. This information can help ensure that work is being performed correctly. It can also be used to avoid barriers to employee productivity from "cyberslacking" and "cyberslouching." The intention may seem both ethical and in the best interest of business, but in practice, the reverse actually may be true. In many cases, employees are not informed that they are being monitored or that the information gleaned is being used to measure their productivity. In these cases, monitoring violates both privacy and personal freedoms. Managers need to take into account employee privacy rights and try to balance their right to privacy against the needs of the business to have surveillance mechanisms in place.

Performance Measurement, Evaluation, and Information Systems

IS make it possible to evaluate actual performance data against reams of standard and historical data, often by using models and simulations. Algorithms, analytics, and big data tools have changed the way many companies use data to make decisions. Managers can more easily and completely understand work progress and performance. In fact, the ready availability of so much information catches some managers in "analysis paralysis": analyzing too much or too long. In our example of the call center, a manager can compare an employee's output to that of colleagues, to earlier output, and to historical outputs reflecting similar work conditions at other times. Even though evaluation constitutes an important use of IS, how the information is used has significant organizational consequences. Information collected for evaluation may be used to provide feedback so that the employee can improve personal performance; it also can be used to determine rewards and compensation. The former use—for improvement in performance—is nonthreatening and generally welcomed.

Using the same information for determining compensation or rewards, however, can be threatening. Suppose that a call center's goal is to ensure all calls are answered quickly, and the manager communicates that goal to his or her staff. Then the call center manager may evaluate the number and duration of calls that service representatives answer on a given day to make sure that those goals are met. If the manager simply provides the employees with information, then the evaluation is not threatening. If handled this way, employees might respond by improving their call numbers and duration. A discussion may even occur in which the service representative highlights other important considerations or extenuating circumstances. On the other hand, some managers use the same information to rank employees so that top-ranked employees are rewarded and those lower ranked are, in some way, punished, reprimanded, or even fired. This may cause employees to feel threatened and respond in ways that are detrimental to the performance and morale of the call center.

How feedback is communicated in the organization plays a role in affecting behavior. Some feedback can be communicated via IS and mobile apps themselves. A simple example is the feedback built into an electronic form that will not allow it to be submitted until it is properly filled out. Algorithmic control often provides instantaneous feedback, typically from customers. For more complex feedback, IS may not be the appropriate vehicle. For example, no one would want to be told she or he was doing a poor job via e-mail or voice mail. Negative feedback of significant consequence is best delivered in person.

IS can allow for feedback from a variety of participants who otherwise could not be involved. Many companies provide "360-degree" feedback in which the individual's supervisors, subordinates, and coworkers all provide formal input. Social tools are making inroads in evaluation, too. For example, a "thumbs up" or "1–5 stars" evaluation system makes it easy and fast to provide informal feedback and evaluate activities. Because that feedback is received more quickly, improvements can be made faster.

Incentives and Rewards and Information Systems

Incentives and rewards are the ways organizations encourage good performance. A clever reward system can make employees feel good without paying them more money. IS can affect these processes too. Some organizations use their websites to recognize high performers, giving them electronic badges that are displayed on the social network to identify them as award recipients. Others reward them with new technology. At one organization, top performers get new computers every year, while lower performers get the "hand-me-downs."

IS make it easier to design complex incentive systems, such as shared or team-based incentives. IS make it easier to keep track of contributions of team members and, in conjunction with qualitative inputs, allocate rewards according to complex formulas. For example, in a call center, agents can be motivated to perform better by providing rewards based on tracking metrics, such as average time per call, number of calls answered, and customer satisfaction. IS can provide measures of all of these on a real-time basis—even customer satisfaction through automated audio or website questionnaires after a customer interaction.

When specifying reward metrics, managers must be careful because they tend to drive the behavior they specify. For example, call center agents who know they will be evaluated only by the volume of calls they process may rush callers and provide poorer service in order to maximize their performance according to the narrow metric. Those measured only by customer satisfaction might spend more time than necessary on each call and perhaps try endlessly to solve problems that should be routed to more technical personnel. The lesson for managers is to pay attention to what is monitored and how the information is used. Metrics for performance must be meaningful and balanced in terms of the organization's broader goals and measured, managed, and communicated appropriately.

Information Systems and Culture

The third managerial lever of organizational strategy is culture. Culture plays an increasingly important role in IS management and use. Because IS management and use are complicated by human factors, it is important to consider culture's impact. **Culture** is defined as a set of shared attitudes, values, and beliefs held by a group that determines how the group perceives, thinks about, and appropriately reacts to its various environments.

A "collective programming of the mind" distinguishes not only societies (or nations) but also industries, professions, and organizations. **Beliefs** are the perceptions that people hold about how things are done in their community, whereas **values** reflect the community's aspirations about the way things should be done. Culture is something of a moving target because it evolves over time as the group solves problems adapting to the environment and internal operations.

Culture has been compared to an iceberg because, like an iceberg, only part of the culture is visible from the surface. In fact, it is necessary to look below the surface to understand the deep-rooted aspects of culture that are not visible. Edgar Schein suggests that culture may be thought of in terms of layers: observable artifacts, values, and assumptions. **Observable artifacts** are the most visible level. They include such physical manifestations as type of dress, symbols in art, acronyms, awards, myths and stories told about the group, rituals, and ceremonies. For instance, Google, out of respect for its global workforce, allows employees to wear the traditional clothes of their country. **Espoused values** are the explicitly stated preferred organizational values. Google has a webpage, "Ten Things We Know to be True" which lists espoused values such as "There is always more information out there." and "Great just isn't good enough."[23] Ideally, espoused values should be consistent with the **enacted values**, which are the values and norms that are actually exhibited or displayed in employee behavior. For example, if an organization says that it believes in a good work–life balance for its employees but actually requires them to work 12-hour days and on weekends, the enacted values don't match with the espoused ones. Google's co-founders did not appear to be worried about a work–life balance. Rather they wanted Google's enacted values to reflect a family atmosphere and encourage its workers to spend more time working, playing, and even sleeping at its Googleplex. The deepest layer of culture is the underlying assumption layer, or the fundamental part of every culture that helps discern what is real and important to the group. **Assumptions** are unobservable because they reflect organizational values that have become taken for granted to such an extent that they guide organizational behavior without any group members thinking about them. At Google, one underlying assumption appears to be that a happy, smart employee is a productive and creative one.

[23] Google, "Ten Things We Know To Be True," https://about.google/philosophy/ (accessed August 2, 2023).

Levels of Culture and IT

Culture can vary depending upon which group you are studying. Countries, organizations, and subgroups in organizations all have a culture. IS management and use can be impacted by culture at all these levels. IS can even play a role in promoting it. With the growth of analytics and the availability of large stores of data, many organizations are adopting a data-driven culture in which virtually all decisions are made with the support of analytics. In a data-driven culture, managers are typically expected to provide data to support their recommendations and to back up decisions. Information is often freely shared in this culture, and IS take on the important role of collecting, storing, analyzing, and delivering data and information to all levels of the organization. Dell, Procter and Gamble, Google, and Facebook are examples of companies that are known to have a data-driven culture. Sometimes the employees in these companies are said to "speak the language of data" as part of their culture.

When IS developers have values that differ from the clients in the same organization for whom they are developing systems, cultures, or more specifically, subcultures can clash. For example, clients may favor computer-based development practices that encourage reusability of components to enable flexibility and fast turnaround. Developers, on the other hand, may prefer a development approach that favors stability and control but tends to be slower. Both national and organizational cultures can affect IT management and usage and vice versa. National culture may affect IT in a variety of ways, impacting IS development, technology adoption and diffusion, system use and outcomes, and management and strategy. These relationships are shown in Figure 3.3 and described next. The model and the discussion of the impact of culture on IT issues draws heavily from the foundational work of Leidner and Kayworth on levels of culture. At the broadest (highest) level are national values. At the next level are organizational values that are held by the entire organization. Within the organization are subcultures with their own subgroup values such as those held by the IT department.

Information Systems Development

Variation across national cultures may lead to differing perceptions and approaches to IS development. In particular, systems designers may have different perceptions of the end users and how the systems would be used. For example, Danish designers who had more socialist values were more concerned about people-related issues compared to Canadian designers with more capitalist values. The Canadian designers were more interested in technical issues. National culture may also affect the perceptions of project risk and risk management behaviors. At the organizational level, cultural values can affect the features of new software and the way it is implemented.

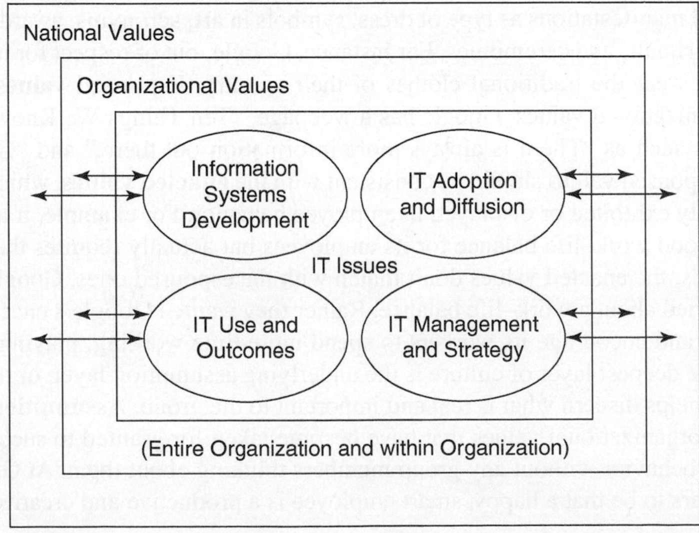

FIGURE 3.3 Levels of culture.

Source: Adapted from D. Leidner and T. Kayworth, "A Review of Culture in Information Systems Research: Toward a Theory of Information Technology Culture Conflict," *MIS Quarterly* 30, no. 2 (2006), 372, Figure 1.

Information Technology Adoption and Diffusion

National cultures that are more willing to accept risk appear to be more likely to adopt new technologies. Those cultures that are less concerned about power differences among people (i.e., have low power distance) are more likely to adopt technologies that help promote equality. People are more likely to adopt a new technology if they think that the technology's embedded values match those of their national culture. Further, if a technology is to be successfully implemented into an organization, either the technology must fit with the organization's culture or the culture must be shaped to fit the behavioral requirements of the technology. For example, a dashboard that shares analytics and Key Performance Indicators (KPIs) with all employees would reduce the "power" of leaders in a hierarchical organization in which only the senior managers have access to the data. In such organizations, implementation of such an information system would likely be very slow or rejected altogether because the culture would not support broad information sharing.

Information Technology Use and Outcomes

Research has shown that differences in culture result in differences in the use and outcomes of IT. At the organizational level, cultural values are often related to satisfied users, successful IS implementations, or knowledge management successes. At the national level, e-mail adoption was much slower in Japan than in the United States. Japanese prefer richer forms of communication such as meeting face-to-face. The lean e-mail can't accommodate the symbols in their language as easily as a fax. Further, in countries that are more likely to avoid uncertainty, such as Japan and Brazil, IT is used often for planning and forecasting, whereas in countries that are less concerned about risk and uncertainty, IT is more often used for maintaining flexibility. Furthermore, some things are acceptable in one country but not another. For example, Ditch Witch could not use its logo globally because a witch is offensive in some countries.

Information Technology Management and Strategy

National and organizational cultures affect planning, governance, and perceptions of service quality. For example, having planning cultures at the top levels of an organization typically signal that strategic systems investment is important. At Adidas, a multinational sports apparel company headquartered in Germany, national culture played a role in its multisourcing strategy. Adidas' managers selected an Eastern European vendor because they were looking for a provider whose culture was similar to their own. They thought that vendor's employees were more likely to question system requirements and to make creative, innovative contributions than the Indian vendors they had hired previously.[24]

National Cultural Dimensions and Their Application

One of the best-known (and prolific) researchers in the area of differences in the values across national cultures is Geert Hofstede. Most studies about the impact of national cultures on IS have used Hofstede's dimensions of national culture. Hofstede originally identified four major dimensions of national culture: power distance, uncertainty avoidance, individualism/collectivism, and masculinity/femininity. To correct for a possible bias toward Western values, another dimension, Confucian work dynamism, also referred to "short-term vs. long-term orientation," was added. More recently, a sixth dimension, indulgence/restraint, was added to capture the extent to which a national culture is fun-loving vs. one that suppresses gratification of needs. Many others have used, built upon, or tried to correct problems related to Hofstede's dimensions. One notable project is the Global Leadership and Organizational Behavior Effectiveness (GLOBE) research program, which is a team of 150 researchers who have collected data on cultural values and practices and leadership attributes from over 18,000 managers in 62 countries. The GLOBE project has uncovered nine cultural dimensions, six of which have their origins in Hofstede's pioneering work. The Hofstede dimensions and their relationship to the GLOBE dimensions are summarized in Figure 3.4.

Even though the world may be becoming "flatter," the research of Hofstede and the GLOBE researchers demonstrates that cultural differences have not totally disappeared. But some leadership traits, such

[24] Martin Wiener and Carol Saunders, "Forced Coopetition in IT Multi-Sourcing," *Journal of Strategic Information Systems* 23, no. 3 (2014): 210–25.

Hofstede Dimensions (Related GLOBE Dimensions)	Description[a]	Examples of Effect on IT[b]
Uncertainty avoidance (*uncertainty avoidance*)	Extent to which a society tolerates uncertainty and ambiguity; extent to which members of an organization or society strive to avoid uncertainty by reliance on social norms, rituals, and bureaucratic practices to alleviate the unpredictability of future events.	Countries with high uncertainty avoidance are less likely to adopt new IT and have higher perceptions of project risk than countries with low uncertainty avoidance.
Power distance (*power distance*)	Degree to which members of an organization or society expect and agree that power should be equally shared.	Individuals from high power distance countries are found to be less innovative and less trusting of technology than individuals from low power distance countries.
Individualism/collectivism (*societal and in-group collectivism*)	Degree to which individuals are integrated into groups; extent to which organizational and societal institutional practices encourage and reward collective distribution of resources and collective action.	Individualistic cultures are more predisposed than collectivistic cultures to report bad news about troubled IT projects; companies in collectivist societies are more likely than individualistic societies to fill an IS position from within the company.
Masculinity/femininity (*general egalitarianism and assertiveness*)	Degree to which emotional roles are distributed between the genders; extent to which an organization or society minimizes gender role differences and gender discrimination; often focuses on caring and assertive behaviors.	Australian groups (high masculinity) are found to generate more conflict and rely less on conflict resolution strategies than Singaporean groups (low masculinity).
Confucian work dynamism (*future orientation*)	Extent to which society rewards behaviors related to long- or short-term orientations; degree to which individuals in organizations or societies engage in future-oriented behaviors such as planning, investing in the future, and delaying gratification.	When considering future orientation, differences are found in the use of Executive Information Systems and the evaluation of service quality across countries.
Indulgence/restraint	Degree to which individuals are encouraged to satisfy their basic and natural drives and have fun vs. to suppress the gratification of their needs by following strict social norms.	Indulgent societies purchase more on the Internet.

[a] Adapted from R. House, M. Javidan, P. Hanges, and P. Dorfman, "Understanding Cultures and Implicit Leadership Theories across the Globe: An Introduction to Project GLOBE," *Journal of World Business* 37, no. 1 (2002): 3–10 and G. Hofstede and G. J. Hofstede, "Dimensions of National Culture," http://www.geerthofstede.nl/dimensions-of-national-cultures.aspx (accessed August 20, 2015).

[b] All examples except the last one were provided in D. Leidner and T. Kayworth, "A Review of Culture in Information Systems Research: Toward a Theory of Information Technology Culture Conflict," *MIS Quarterly* 30, no. 2 (2006): 357–99. Last example was found in E. Yıldırım, Y. Arslan, and M. Türkmen Barutçu, "The Role of Uncertainty Avoidance and Indulgence as Cultural Dimensions on Online Shopping Expenditure," *Eurasian Business and Economics Journal* 4 (2016): 42–51.

FIGURE 3.4 National cultural dimensions.

as being trustworthy, just, and honest; having foresight and planning ahead; being positive, dynamic, encouraging, and motivational; and being communicative and informed, are seen as universally acceptable across cultures.

The generally accepted view is that the national culture predisposes citizens of a nation to act in a certain way along a Hofstede or GLOBE dimension, such as in an individualistic way in England or in a collectivist way in China. Yet, the extent of the influence of a national culture may vary among individuals, and culturally based idiosyncrasies may surface based upon the experiences that shape each person's ultimate orientation on a dimension. Having an understanding and appreciation for cultural values, practices, and subtleties can help in smoothing the challenges that occur in dealing with these idiosyncrasies. An awareness of the Hofstede or GLOBE dimensions may help to improve communications and reduce conflict.

Effective communication means listening, framing the message in a way that is understandable to the receiver, and responding to feedback. Effective cross-cultural communication involves each of these plus searching for an integrated solution that can be accepted and implemented by members of diverse cultures. This may not be as simple as it sounds. For instance, typical American managers, noted for their high-performance orientation, prefer direct and explicit language full of facts and figures. However, managers in lower-performance-oriented countries such as Russia or Greece tend to prefer indirect and vague language that encourages the exploration of ideas. Communication differences surfaced when one of this book's authors was designing a database in an Asian country. She asked questions that required a "yes" or "no" response. In trying to reconcile the strange set of responses she received, the author learned that people in that country are hesitant to ever say "no." Communication in meetings is also subject to cultural differences. In countries with high levels of uncertainty avoidance such as Switzerland and Austria, meetings should be planned in advance with a clear agenda. The managers in Greece or Russia who come from a low uncertainty avoidance culture often shy away from agendas or planned meetings.

Knowing that a society tends to score high or low on certain dimensions helps a manager anticipate how a person from that society might react. However, this provides only a starting point because each person is different. Importantly, without being aware of cultural differences, a company is unlikely to successfully develop IS or to use it effectively.

SUMMARY

- Organizational strategy reflects the use of the managerial levers of an organization's design, organizational culture, and management control systems that coordinate and control work processes.
- Organizational designers today must have a working knowledge of what IS can do and how the choice of an information system will affect the organization itself.
- Organizational structures can facilitate or inhibit information flows and processes.
- Organizational design should take into account decision rights, organizational structure, and informal networks.
- Structures such as flat, hierarchical, matrix, and networked organizations are being enhanced by information technology.
- Information technology affects managerial control mechanisms: planning, data, performance measurement and evaluation, incentives, and rewards.
- A more traditional model of management control compares control to a thermostat. Another more recent model associates control with algorithms.
- Management control at the individual level is concerned with monitoring (i.e., data collection), evaluating, providing feedback, compensating, and rewarding. It is the job of the manager to ensure that the proper control mechanisms are in place, and the interactions between the organization and the IS do not undermine the managerial objectives.
- Culture is the shared values, attitudes and beliefs held by individuals in an organization. Organizational and national culture impact the success of an IS, and should be taken into account when designing, managing, and using IS.

KEY TERMS

algorithmic control, 66
algorithmic management, 66
assumptions, 69
beliefs, 69
bureaucracy, 61
culture, 69
decision rights, 59
enacted values, 69
enterprise social network (ESN), 65
espoused values, 69
hierarchical organizational structure, 61
matrix organizational structure, 61
networked organizational structure, 62
observable artifacts, 69
organizational strategy, 58
social networking site (SNS), 64
span of control, 61
technology-mediated control, 66
unity of command, 61
values, 69

FOUNDATIONAL READINGS

Culture: E. Schein, *Organizational Change and Leadership*, 4th ed. (San Francisco, CA: Jossey-Bass, 2010); In terms of a framework that focuses on culture in IS see: D. Leidner and T. Kayworth, "A Review of Culture in Information Systems Research: Toward a Theory of Information Technology Culture Conflict," *MIS Quarterly* 30, no. 2 (2006), 357–99.

Culture and Leaders: Hofstede's work on the cultural values of leaders is highly cited: G. Hofstede, *Culture's Consequences: International Differences in Work-Related Values* (London: Sage, 1980); G. J. Hofstede, *Culture's Consequences: Comparing Values, Behaviors, Institutions, and Organizations across Nations*, 2nd ed. (Thousand Oaks, CA: Sage Publications, 2001); G. Hofstede and M. H. Bond, "The Confucius Connection: From Cultural Roots to Economic Growth," *Organizational Dynamics* 16 (1988), 4021; https://www.hofstede-insights.com/models/national-culture/ (accessed February 17, 2019); The GLOBE project is also well-known: Mansour Javidan and R. J. House, "Cultural Acumen for the Global Manager," *Organizational Dynamics* 29, no. 4 (2001), 289–305.

Managerial Levers: James I. Cash, Robert G. Eccles, Nitin Nohria, and Richard L. Nolan, *Building the Information Age Organization* (Homewood, IL: Richard D. Irwin, 1994).

DISCUSSION QUESTIONS

1. How might IS change a manager's job?
2. Is monitoring an employee's work on a computer a desirable or undesirable activity from a manager's perspective? From the employee's perspective? How does the organization's culture impact your position? Defend your position.
3. Do you think it was a good idea strategically for Google to launch Bard the way it did (see description in chapter introduction)? Please discuss the pros and cons.
4. Encana Oil & Gas Inc. is a natural gas firm. It enacted a digital transformation in what is considered a latecomer industry.[1] To do so, Encana's senior management team and CIO worked together to establish ten IS guiding principles that were intended to provide an adequate level of IT support for capitalizing on data for cost cutting and business agility. To support the guiding principles, Encana restructured its IS Organization. The structure was designed to allow IS managers to work closely with business unit (BU) managers in BU-IS Groups and to provide local solutions to meet the needs of the BUs. The IS professionals were encouraged to learn the business and find ways to create efficiencies in the BUs. Based on this information, what type of organizational structure would be most suitable for Encana? Please explain.

Source:

[1] R. Kohli and S. Johnson, "Digital Transformation in Latecomer Industries: CIO and CEO Leadership Lessons from Encana Oil & Gas (USA) Inc.," *MIS Quarterly Executive*, 10, no. 4, (2011).

Case Study 3-1 [24]7.ai

[24]7.ai is a conversational AI company that pledges to improve the customer experience of its customers' customers. Its AI tools can be used to support customer interactions with agents working in contact centers. [24]7.ai also provides expertise on running contact centers. Customers can choose to use the company's agents, its cloud platform, or managed services.

[24]7.ai's website claims that it is "the only platform that combines behavioral, transactional, and historical data to anticipate intent, [24]7.ai understands what your customers mean—not just what they say." [24]7.ai blends machine learning from its huge database of customer-agent interactions with human insights and its contact center expertise. It manages human and bot interactions across digital and voice channels.

[24]7.ai boasts over 250 enterprises as customers in 12 different industries, including, banks, education, utilities, technology, services and healthcare. It has managed customer service campaigns for companies like Verizon, AT&T, Walmart and Target. IT was recognized with a CCW Excellence Award as the Business Process Outsourcing (BPO) of the year in 2022.

This all sounds very good! However, the results weren't as laudatory when [24]7.ai used its AI technology designed to monitor customer service agents on its own employees who worked remotely. [24]7.ai used webcam photographs captured by the "Orange Eye" in intervals from 5 to 30 minutes. Unfortunately, the system reported that employees weren't working when they actually were, which negatively impacted their pay and performance productivity.

In addition to detecting when employees were away from their desk, the AI software was also supposed to detect when they were on their phones or when unauthorized people were in the room. Orange Eye clearly needs more machine learning since it mistook faces on posters and t-shirts, and even dogs, for unauthorized people. One former [24]7.ai manager claimed "Despite the fact that 'AI' is in the company's name, and that's actually their main business, the AI behind that software taking photos and everything was junk. It was absolutely terrible."

Although employees were supposed to have breaks and time off for lunch, Orange Eye continued monitoring them after they locked their computers so that they could step away. The AI software would then make it impossible for them to get back into their computers until a manager signed them back in. During the time that they were unable to get into their own computers, their pay was docked.

Employees were extremely stressed mentally because of system errors, being locked out of their computer, and feeling that they were constantly being monitored. As one employee explained "Because of Orange Eye lockouts, I had to remain on call pretty much basically the entire time of our hours of operation."

The timekeeping system developed by [24]7.ai, "Time On," was also subject to numerous technical errors and crashes. Because Time On couldn't keep time correctly, it didn't always correctly log when employees were working, and it sometimes incorrectly deducted time for breaks. Because of timekeeping problems, the supervisors needed to spend extra time checking employee-completed manual timecards with the login system to ensure that their employees would be paid correctly. The manual timecard backup was used so often that employees' supervisors were reprimanded for submitting so many of them.

[24]7.ai management responded to concerns about Time On with this statement: "Time On is a dashboard but it is not specifically used to track time for payroll purposes. Payroll uses reports from the agent workspace consoles." Too bad the [24]7.ai supervisors don't seem to know this.

Sources: Adapted from Grace Stanley, "'By the time I left, I was broken': Workers speak out against company after remote workers' video on being monitored through webcam goes viral," *Daily Dot*, July 20, 2022, https://www.dailydot.com/irl/workers-speak-out-against-247ai/ (accessed March 29, 2023); See also [24]7.ai website, https://www.247.ai/company; Corporate Fact Sheet: Redefining Customer Experiences with Conversational AI, chrome-extension://efaidnbmnnnibpcajpcglclefindmkaj/https://www.247.ai/resources/brochures/br-corporate-fact-sheet.pdf (accessed March 29, 2023).

Discussion Questions

1. Describe the positive and negative consequences of [24]7.ai using its Orange Eye on its employees.
2. Describe the positive and negative organizational consequences of [24]7.ai using Orange Eye as it does.
3. Do you think that the way [24]7.ai uses Orange Eye is an invasion of employee privacy? Please explain your response.
4. What could [24]7.ai do to improve the surveillance and compensation of its employees?

Case Study 3-2 Uber's Use of Algorithmic Management

Uber Technologies, founded in 2009, is a ride-hailing company that leverages the cars and time of millions of drivers who are independent contractors in countries around the globe. One estimate by Uber Group Manager, Yuhki Yamashita, is that Uber drivers globally spend 8.5 million hours on the road—daily. As independent contractors, Uber tells its drivers "you can be your own boss" and set your own hours. Yet, Uber wants to control how they behave. Uber exerts this control not through human managers, but through a "ride-hail platform on a system of algorithms that serves as a virtual 'algorithmic boss.'" Drivers' work experiences are entirely mediated through a mobile app and drivers are constantly under surveillance.

Uber's mobile app collects data and guides the behavior of the drivers in such a way that in reality they aren't as much their own boss as they might like to be. For example, while they can work when they want, Uber's surge fare structure of charging riders more during high-volume periods motivates them to work during times that they might not otherwise choose. The app even sends algorithmically derived push notifications like: "Are you sure you want to go offline? Demand is very high in your area. Make more money, don't stop now!" Hence, Uber uses technology to exert "soft control" over its drivers.

Uber employs a host of social scientists and data scientists to devise ways to encourage drivers to work longer and harder, even when it isn't financially beneficial for them to do so. Using its mobile app, it has experimented with video game techniques, graphics and badges and other noncash rewards of little monetary value. The mobile app employs psychologically influenced interventions to encourage various driver behaviors. For example, the mobile app will alert drivers that they are close to achieving an algorithmically generated income target when they try to log off. Like Netflix does when it automatically loads the next program in order to encourage binge-watching, Uber sends drivers their next fare opportunity before their current ride is over. New drivers are enticed with signing bonuses when they meet initial ride targets (e.g., completing 25 rides). To motivate drivers to complete enough rides to earn bonuses, the app periodically sends them words of encouragement ("You're almost halfway there, congratulations!"). The mobile app also monitors their rides to ensure that they accept a minimum percentage of ride requests, complete a minimum number of trips, and are available for a minimum period of time in order to qualify to earn profitable hourly rates during specified periods. Uber has a blind acceptance rate policy, where drivers do not get information about the destination and pay rate for calls until after they accept them. This can mean that drivers might end up accepting rates that are unprofitable for them. On the other hand, drivers risk being "deactivated" (i.e., be suspended or removed permanently from the system) should they cancel unprofitable fares. The system keeps track of the routes taken to ensure that the driver selected the most efficient route. The system knows what they are doing, but the drivers don't know how the system that is directing them works.

The mobile app also captures passenger ratings of the driver on a scale of one to five stars. Since the drivers don't have human managers *per se*, the passenger satisfaction ratings serve as their most significant performance metric, along with various "excellent-service" and "great-conversation" badges. But how satisfied are the drivers themselves? Well, the drivers have negative feelings about customer ratings being used to calculate their earnings or allocate rides to them. And their turnover rates suggest that the Uber drivers aren't all that happy. Uber's driver turnover rate is high—reportedly closing in on 50% within the first year that the drivers sign up. One senior Uber official said: "We've underinvested in the driver experience. We are now re-examining everything we do in order to rebuild that love."

Sources: JC, "How Many Uber Drivers Are There?" Ridester, January 29, 2019, https://www.ridester.com/how-many-uber-drivers-are-there/ (accessed February 18, 2019); Wiener and Cram AMCIS 2017 and Cram and Wiener 2020 *Communications of the Association for Information Systems*, 46 no. 1 (2020); Möhlmann, Mareike, Lior Zalmanson, Ola Henfridsson, and Robert Wayne Gregory. "Algorithmic Management of Work on Online Labor Platforms: When Matching Meets Control," *MIS Quarterly* 45, no. 4 (2021); and N. Scheiber, "How Uber Uses Psychological Tricks to Push Its Drivers' Buttons," *New York Times*, 2017, https://www.nytimes.com/interactive/2017/04/02/technology/uber-drivers-psychological-tricks.html (accessed February 18, 2019); and A. Rosenblat, *Uberland: How Algorithms Are Rewriting the Rules of Work* (Oakland, CA: University of California Press, 2018).

Case Study 3-2 **(Continued)**

Discussion Questions

1. Uber is faced with the monumental challenge of controlling and motivating millions of drivers who are important to its business, but who aren't on its payroll. How effective do you think Uber's "algorithmic boss" is as a managerial control system for Uber drivers? Please explain.
2. What are the benefits to Uber of using algorithmic control through its mobile app? What are the downsides?
3. What impact, if any, do you think Uber's use of algorithmic control has on its organizational culture?
4. Do you think the Uber digital business model is a sustainable one? Please provide a rationale for your response.

4 Information Technology and the Design of Work

Flexible work arrangements made possible by remote work combined with collaboration, social, mobile, cloud, robotic, and analytic technologies have opened up dramatically different ways to work. This chapter explores the impact technology has on the nature and design of work. A Work Design Framework is used to explore how digital technology can be used effectively to support these changes and help make employees more effective. In particular, this chapter discusses technologies to support communication and collaboration, new types of work, new ways of doing traditional work, new challenges in managing employees, and issues in working remotely, on virtual teams, and with robots and AI. It concludes with a section on the future of work.

COVID-19 turned the whole way of thinking about work on its head. Working from home became the new norm—and not the exception. But working from home was not a new concept to consumer financial services powerhouse American Express. Amex had viewed workplace flexibility as a strategic lever since 2014 when it had initiated its award-winning BlueWork program and integrated it into the company's human resource policies. In addition to receiving the Chairman's Award for Innovation (i.e., the Top Innovators Prize), the BlueWork program enabled increased employee productivity and more than $10 million in annual savings from reduced office space costs.[1] BlueWork was Amex's term for workplace flexibility which included staggered working hours, off-site work areas such as home/virtual office arrangements, shared office space, touch-down (laptop-focused, temporary) space, and telecommuting. The corporate focus was on results rather than on hours clocked in the office and face-to-face time.

Amex employees were assigned to a type of work arrangement based on their role: Hub employees worked from a fixed desk every day because they held down the office or performed on-site security or technology services; Club employees shared time between the office and other locations because their roles involved both face-to-face and virtual meetings; Home employees worked from home at least three days a week; Roam employees were on the road or at customer sites. Susan Chapman-Hughes, then Senior Vice President at Amex, commented on the importance of technology's role in alternative work arrangements: "Technology drives workplace flexibility. . . . Technology has become a strategic competency that drives revenue growth. It's not just about enabling productivity."[2]

How did BlueWork impact the staff? In addition to the productivity improvements and savings in office expenses, overall employee satisfaction was up. American Express managers were happy with these arrangements too. They found employees to be more engaged while working, more committed to the company, and better able to drive-needed results.[3]

---

[1] Christopher Palafax, "American Express's New Design Team," *American Builders Quarterly*, April/May/June 2014, http://americanbuildersquarterly.com/2014/american-express/ (accessed August 25, 2015); Monak Mitra, "Best Companies to Work for 2012," *The Economic Times*, http://articles.economictimes.indiatimes.com/2012-07-16/news/32698433_1_employee-benefits-jyoti-rai-american-express-india (accessed August 25, 2015).

[2] Gensler, Dialog 22, https://www.gensler.com/doc/dialogue-22-pdf.pdf (accessed August 25, 2015).

[3] Jeanne Meister, "Flexible Workspaces: Employee Perk Or Business Tool To Recruit Top Talent?" *Forbes*, April 1, 2013, http://www.forbes.com/sites/jeannemeister/2013/04/01/flexible-workspaces-another-workplace-perk-or-a-must-have-to-attract-top-talent/ (accessed June 9, 2019).

Just prior to the start of the pandemic, 20% of Amex's employees worked virtually.[4] The percentage of virtual workers skyrocketed when the COVID-19 pandemic lockdowns were put into place. During the pandemic, Amex proved that working remotely allowed its workforce to become more agile, more efficient, and better able to handle their personal and professional lives. In early 2021, as a prelude to developing a new way of working after COVID-19, a survey was administered that showed nearly 80% of Amex workers wanted to come back to the office at least some of the time. The CEO and Chairman, Stephen Squeri, announced a program, Amex Flex, designed "to achieve the best of both worlds—recapturing the creativity, connections, collaboration and relationship building of working together in person, while also retaining the flexibility and progress we have made together in this virtual world."[5]

Amex Flex went into effect on March 15, 2022, with a blended approach. Depending upon their job, Amex workers could work On-site 4–5 days a week (notably if they are Hub workers), Hybrid 1–3 days a week on average, or Fully Virtual with zero days in the office. There are some stipulations: For instance, leaders can set "team days" for workers on the Hybrid plan; New workers must start out on On-site plan until they completed their training and orientation; Workers who had not worked virtually prior to the pandemic needed to formally request virtual work options; Those who were not on-site workers could apply annually to work up to four calendar weeks from a location other than their primary work location.

American Express has been at the forefront of providing flexible work arrangements to its employees. Thanks to COVID-19, many other companies quickly learned how to be more accommodating about when and where their employees work.

When the pandemic officially ended, many workers wanted to continue working remotely, especially those with long and/or stressful commutes. Consequently, public transportation was not returning to pre-pandemic ridership numbers. Furthermore, commercial real estate took a nosedive because office space wasn't being used fully. One 2023 survey of 350 of the world's biggest companies (those with more than 50,000 employes) reported that half of them intended to downsize their office space by 10%–20% by 2026.[6] Even the Federal Government didn't need all of the office space it had leased. As of Fall 2022, only 5% of its pre-pandemic workforce had shown up to work in their offices in federally leased buildings in Washington DC. By Spring 2023, a concerned President Biden prodded federal workers to return to their offices and asked their agencies to evaluate the effectiveness of remote work.[7]

After COVID-19, Eric Adams, the mayor of New York City, wanted workers back in their offices and using public transportation to get them there. In June 2023, he ceded to cries for remote work by allowing some employees to work at home for up to two days a week. However, he put a blended program into place by requiring some employees who are providing "core services" (e.g., police patrols and metro workers) to come into work when their roles can't be performed remotely. He is sweetening the requirement by allowing these "core service" workers to build flexibility in their schedules in terms of the particular hours that they work.[8]

It's hard for companies, federal agencies, and city governments to ignore how much employees enjoy working remotely, at least part-time, once they had the opportunity to do so during the pandemic. Many employees questioned whether they needed to return to the office. But executives aren't always so convinced that remote work is a panacea because of their concerns about its negative impacts on creativity, collaboration, productivity, and company culture. They are evaluating whether to have all, or some employees (i.e., a blended workforce), working remotely all of the time or in a hybrid arrangement where they work remotely less than five days a week. The hybrid arrangement is the most popular remote work option to date.

---

[4] Newsroom, "American Express Officially Launches Amex Flex, Our New Way of Working," March 18, 2022, https://about.americanexpress.com/newsroom/press-releases/news-details/2022/American-Express-Officially-Launches-Amex-Flex-Our-New-Way-of-Working/default.aspx (accessed April 30, 2023).

[5] Newsroom, "American Express, Introducing Amex Flex – Our New Way of Working," October 21, 2021, https://about.americanexpress.com/newsroom/press-releases/news-details/2021/American-Express-Introducing-Amex-Flex--Our-New-Way-Of-Working-10-18-2021/default.aspx#:~:text=Work%20From%20Anywhere%20Component,into%20the%20office%20at%20all (accessed April 24, 2023).

[6] Pete Syme, "Half the World's Biggest Companies are Downsizing Office Space Amid Hybrid Working," June 8, 2023, https://www.msn.com/en-us/money/companies/half-the-world-s-biggest-companies-are-downsizing-office-space-amid-hybrid-working/ar-AA1chqWb (accessed June 9, 2023).

[7] Annie Linsky and Paul Kierman, "Biden Administration Nudges Federal Workers Back to the Office," *Wall Street Journal*, April 13, 2023, https://www.wsj.com/articles/biden-administration-nudges-federal-workers-back-to-the-office-f145d923?mod=Searchresults_pos4&page=1 (accessed April 24, 2023).

[8] Jimmy Vielkind, "NYC Mayor Eric Adams, a Critic of Remote Work, Cedes Some Ground," June 1, 2023, *Wall Street Journal*, https://www.wsj.com/articles/nyc-mayor-eric-adams-a-critic-of-remote-work-cedes-some-ground-fec4f80e (accessed June 9, 2023).

The American Express example illustrates how the nature of work has changed—and information technology (IT) is supporting, if not propelling, the changes. In preindustrial societies, work was seamlessly interwoven into everyday life. Activities all revolved around nature's cyclical rhythms (i.e., the season, day, and night; the pangs of hunger) and the necessities of living. The Industrial Revolution changed this. With the practice of dividing time into measurable, homogeneous units for which they could be paid, people started to separate work from other spheres of life. Their workday was distinguished from family, community, and leisure time by punching a time clock or responding to the blast of a factory whistle. Work was also separated into space as well as time as people went to a particular place to work.[9]

Technology and new work arrangements have once again enabled an integration of work activities into everyday life—even during a pandemic. Technologies have made it possible for employees to do their work in their own homes, on the road, or at an alternative workspace at times that accommodate home life and leisure activities.[10] Paradoxically, however, employees often want to create a sense of belonging within the space where they work. That is, they wish to create a sense of "place," which is a bounded domain in a space that structures their experiences and interactions with objects that they use and other people that they meet in their work "place." People learn to identify with these "places," or locations in a space, based on a personal sharing of experiences with others within the space. Over time, visitors to the place associate it with a set of appropriate behaviors.[11] Increasingly "places" are being constructed in virtual space with IT tools (including the metaverse and Apple's Vision Pro) that encourage collaboration, allowing people to easily communicate on an ongoing basis, once again changing the nature of where work is done.

This chapter focuses on the way IT is changing the nature of work, the rise of new work environments, and IT's impact on different types of employees, where and when they do their work, and how they collaborate. It explores how IT enables and facilitates a shift toward collaborative and virtual work. The terms *IS* and *IT* are used interchangeably in this chapter, and only basic details are provided on technologies used. The point of this chapter is to look at the impact of IT on the way work is done by individuals and teams. This chapter can help managers understand the challenges in designing technology-intensive work, develop a sense of how to address these challenges, and anticipate what work will look like in the future.

Work Design Framework

As the place and time of work becomes less distinguishable from other aspects of people's lives, the concept of "jobs" changes and is replaced by the concept of "work." Prior to the Industrial Revolution, a job meant a discrete task of a short duration with a clear beginning and end.[12] By the mid-20th century, the concept of a job evolved into an ongoing, often unending stream of meaningful activities that allowed the worker to fulfill a distinct role. More recently, organizations are moving away from organization structures built around particular jobs to a setting in which a person's work is defined in terms of what needs to be done, with changes over time. In many organizations, it is no longer appropriate for people to establish their turfs and narrowly define their jobs to address only specific functions. Yet, as jobs "disappear," IT can enable employees to better perform their roles in tomorrow's workplace; that is, IT can help employees function and collaborate in accomplishing work that more broadly encompasses all the tasks that need to be done.

In this chapter, a simple framework is used to assess how emerging technologies may affect work. As is suggested by the Information Systems Strategy Triangle (in Chapter 1), this framework links the organizational strategy with IS. Significant changes in IS and the work environments in which they function are bound to coincide with significant changes in the way that companies are structured and how people experience work in their daily lives. This framework is useful in designing characteristics of work by asking key questions and helping identify where IS can affect how the work is done.

---

[9] S. Barley and G. Kunda, "Bringing Work Back In," *Organizational Science* 12, no. 1 (2001): 76–95.

[10] S. Harrison and P. Dourish, "Re-Place-ing Space: The Roles of Place and Space in Collaborative Systems," *Proceedings of the 1996 ACM Conference on Computer Supported Cooperative Work* (1996), 67–76.

[11] C. Saunders, A. F. Rutkowski, M. Genuchten, D. Vogel, and J. M. Orrega, "Virtual Space and Place: Theory and Test," *MIS Quarterly* 35, no. 4 (2011): 1079–98.

[12] William Bridges, *JobShift: How to Prosper in a Workplace without Jobs* (New York: Addison-Wesley, 1995).

Consider the following questions:

- *What work will be performed?* Understanding what tasks are needed to complete the process being done by the employee requires an assessment of the transformation needed to turn inputs into specific, desired outcomes. Many types of work are based upon recurring operations and involve managing knowledge, information, or data. Most work has a unique set of characteristics and tasks that need to be supported by IT.
- *Who is going to do the work?* Sometimes the work can be automated, or even performed by a robot or artificially intelligent system. However, if a person is going to do the work, who should that person be? What skills are needed? From what part of the organization should that person come? If a team is going to do the work, many of these same questions need to be asked—within the context of the team: Who should be on the team? What skills do the team members need? What parts of the organization need to be represented by the team members? Will the team members be dispersed?
- *Where will the work be performed?* With the increasing availability of networks, web tools, social media, videoconferencing, apps, mobile devices, cloud-based computing, and the Internet, in general, managers can now design work for employees who come to the office or who work remotely. Does the work need to be performed locally at a company office? Can it be done remotely at home? On the road?
- *When will the work be performed?* Traditionally, work was done during "normal business hours," which meant 9 a.m. to 5 p.m. In many parts of the world, a job between the hours of 9 and 5 is an anomaly. Technologies make it easier to work whenever necessary. The reality of modern technologies is that they often tether employees to a schedule of 24 hours a day, seven days a week (24/7) when they are always accessible to calls or other communications through their mobile devices.

Figure 4.1 shows how these questions can be used in a framework to incorporate technologies into the design of work. Although it is outside the scope of this chapter to discuss the current research on either work or job design, you are encouraged to read these rich literatures.

What Types of Work Are Impacted by Information Technology

When the United States was founded, two/thirds of the workers were farmers.[13] Thanks to the Agricultural (i.e., First Industrial) Revolution at the end of the 18th century, mechanization fueled by coal propelled the replacement of agriculture with industry as the backbone of the economy. The percentage of farmers

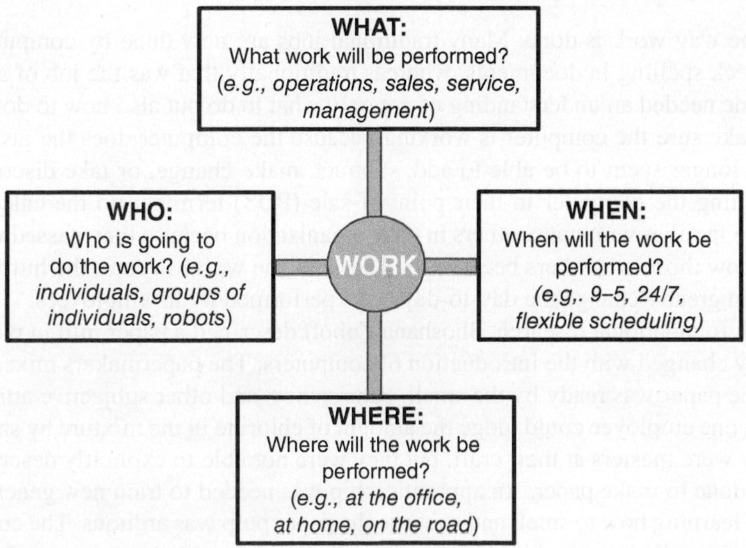

FIGURE 4.1 Framework for work design.

[13] Christopher Mims, "Amazon's Quest for the 'Holy Grail' of Robotics," *Wall Street Journal*, December 3, 2022, https://www.wsj.com/articles/amazon-robots-workers-11670022563 (accessed May 1, 2023).

decreased further as the Second Industrial Revolution at the end of the 19th century and beginning of the 20th century introduced myriad technological advancements such as internal combustion engines, telephones, the telegraph, automobiles, and planes. The workers in the electrified factories with complex machinery needed a higher level of skills (i.e., "middle-skills") to work the complex equipment, and a middle class blossomed.[14] The Digital (i.e., Third) Industrial Revolution at the end of the 20th century saw the dawn of nuclear energy, electronics, telecommunications, and computers. Typically, a much higher level of skill and a college education were required to support the information processing required by the technology in this revolution. The middle-skilled assembly plant and office workers were increasingly replaced by technology. Technological advancements have led to massive increases in agricultural yields and produce quality, enabling the percentage of farmers in the United States to drop to only 2%. Other traditional work has been similarly transformed, replaced by new types of work—or totally eliminated.

Advances in IT provide an expanding set of tools that make individual employees more productive and broaden their capabilities. They transform the way work is performed—and the nature of the work itself. This section examines three ways in which new IT alters employee life: by creating new types of work, by enabling new ways to do traditional work, and by supporting new ways to manage people.

Creating New Types of Work

IT often leads to the creation of new jobs or redefines existing ones. The high-tech field has emerged in its entirety over the past 70 years and has created a wide range of positions in the IT sector. IS departments employ individuals who create and manage technologies, such as systems analysts, user experience designers, database administrators, support specialists, IT managers, network engineers and administrators, and IT security advisors. The web has given rise to many other types of jobs, such as web masters and website designers. Even within traditional non-IT organizations, the growing reliance on IS creates new types of jobs, such as data scientists who mine for insights in the company's data, community managers who manage the firm's online communities and communications managers who manage the use of communication technologies for the business. Virtually, every department in every business has someone who "knows the information systems" as part of his or her job. With the increased capabilities of AI, new types of work are emerging.

Changing the Way Traditional Work Is Done

IT has changed the way work is done. Many traditional jobs are now done by computers. For example, computers can check spelling in documents, whereas traditionally that was the job of an editor or writer. Workers at one time needed an understanding of not only what to do but also how to do it; now their main task often is to make sure the computer is working because the computer does the task for them. Sadly, many cashiers no longer seem to be able to add, subtract, make change, or take discounts because they have grown up letting the computer in their point-of-sale (POS) terminal do the calculations for them. Workers once were familiar with many others in their organization because they passed work to them; now they may never know those coworkers because the IT routes the work. In sum, the introduction of IT into an organization can greatly change the day-to-day tasks performed by its employees.

In her landmark foundational research, Shoshana Zuboff described a paper mill in which papermakers' jobs were radically changed with the introduction of computers. The papermakers mixed big vats of paper and knew when the paper was ready by the smell, consistency, and other subjective attributes of the mixture. For example, one employee could judge the amount of chlorine in the mixture by sniffing and squeezing the pulp. They were masters at their craft, but they were not able to explicitly describe to anyone else exactly what was done to make paper. An apprenticeship was needed to train new generations of masters, and the process of learning how to smell and squeeze the paper pulp was arduous. The company, seeking to increase productivity in the papermaking process, installed an information and control system. Instead of

[14] Greg Rosalsky, "What if AI Could Rebuild the Middle Class," National Public Radio, May 9, 2023, https://www.npr.org/sections/money/2023/05/09/1174933574/what-if-ai-could-rebuild-the-middle-class (accessed June 10, 2023).

employees looking at and personally testing the vats of paper, the system continuously tested parameters and displayed the results on a panel located in the control room. The papermakers sat in the control room, reading the numbers, and making decisions on how to make paper. Many found it much more difficult, if not impossible, to make the same high-quality paper when watching the control panel instead of personally testing, smelling, and looking at the vats. The new information system required a different set of skills to make paper. Abstracting the entire process and displaying the results on electronic readouts required skills to interpret the measurements, conditions, and data generated by the new computer system.

Now the IoT, cloud computing, analytics, AI, and machine learning (ML) are enabling change of such a magnitude in factories and production facilities that it is considered to be the Fourth Industrial Revolution, or Industry 4.0. Industry 4.0 builds on the computerization and automation of manufacturing facilities that were started in the Third Industrial Revolution. **Industry 4.0** pertains to smart factories with advanced technologies such as embedded software, sensors, robotics, and connected machines that are transforming manufacturing. It capitalizes on large amounts of data gathered from sensors on machines and the IoT to inform predictive maintenance and self-optimization of processes.[15] For example, operational data from an Enterprise Resource Planning system can be merged with data about customers and supply chain partners and their activities to make better decisions, sometimes without involving any humans.[16]

An example of the use of the IoT, machine sensors, the cloud and analytics is a German compressor manufacturer that had sold customized air compressors to its customers and now sells product services,[17] a strategy call *servitization*. This company adopted a non-ownership business model in which it leases its compressors to companies in a wide range of industries. It generates revenue from the leases and by charging for maintenance services. Its customers like this arrangement because they don't have to invest large sums in the equipment and instead pay a flexible service fee based on compressed air consumed and an additional fee for add-on services. The customers thus can shift uncertainties about equipment breakdowns and service costs to the compressor company. Meanwhile the compressor company can service its equipment better and more efficiently than its customers because it relies on large amounts of data from the IoT and all of its machines that are aggregated in a central cloud database, as well as analytics that mine the data to provide information to support remote monitoring, preventive maintenance, and machine optimization. The compressor company works with its customers to make their operations more energy efficient and passes along some of the energy savings back to them in the form of an outcome-based bonus.

Changing Communication Patterns

All one has to do is observe people on subways, elevators, busy downtown streets, or college campuses to note changes in communication patterns over the last decade. Some people are talking on their cell phones, but even more are texting, instant messaging, or using apps for all kinds of reasons, such as watching short videos, buying something in stores or on Amazon, or checking out game scores, movie schedules, specials at nearby restaurants, the weather, and so on. Consider meeting a friend at a busy subway station in Hong Kong. It is virtually impossible without the aid of a cell phone to locate each other. Some may say that we are addicted to our mobile technologies, unable to put them away even when driving or walking, which unfortunately sometimes leads to dangerous behaviors.

The value of IT for communication was discovered by many during the global pandemic. When COVID-19 reared its ugly head, billions of meetings were held on Zoom, Teams, and other video conferencing tools. To demonstrate the phenomenal change, consider that in December 2019, Zoom had 10 million meeting participants; Four months later as COVID-19 lockdowns went into effect, it had over 300 million. Video conferencing made it possible to conduct work, learn online, see a doctor, or stay in touch with loved ones and friends. Of course, back-to-back meetings often created "Zoom fatigue," as manifested in "zoombies" with glazed eyes. Zoom etiquette started to emerge, such as angling the camera so a person's head is at the top of the screen, keeping the camera on to demonstrate high engagement in the meeting

[15] IBM, "How Industry 4.0 Technologies are Changing Manufacturing," IBM, https://www.ibm.com/topics/industry-4-0 (accessed April 29, 2023).

[16] Bernard Marr, "What is Industry 4.0? Here's A Super Easy Explanation for Anyone," Forbes, Sept 2, 2018, https://www.forbes.com/sites/bernardmarr/2018/09/02/what-is-industry-4-0-heres-a-super-easy-explanation-for-anyone/?sh=38ee8fd69788 (accessed July 9, 2023).

[17] Maximilian Bock, Martin Wiener and Carol Saunders, "Non-ownership Business Models in the Manufacturing Industry: Uncertainty-exploiting Versus Uncertainty-mitigating Design and the Role of Context," *Electronic Markets,* 33. no.16 (2023). https://doi.org/10.1007/s12525-023-00630-x.

(or that the meeting participant is actually still in the room), arriving on time to the meeting, and not doing emailing or other tasks during the meeting.[18] Spontaneous video conferencing calls are even becoming the norm.[19] Now, although the threat of COVID-19 is gone, video conferencing, with updated software and a whole new set of mores, is here to stay!

Today, people have an array of communications technologies that they use. Some rely on texting, others on one-to-one video chatting such as FaceTime, and still others on social networks such as Facebook or Renren, for their primary communications channel. The challenge created by the large number of choices is that individuals now must have a presence on numerous platforms to ensure that they can be contacted. Further, one must know how not only to contact someone but also to recognize that the person's preferred medium might change during the day, week, or month. For example, during normal business hours, an employee might prefer to receive e-mail or a phone call. But after hours, he or she might prefer a text, and late at night, while surfing the web, may prefer a message on Instagram. Without knowledge of a recipient's preferences for how to receive the message, the sender is likely to be unsuccessful in communicating with the recipient over the proper channel. A sender who doesn't know which medium the recipient prefers might use one medium (e.g., e-mail) to see whether the recipient is open to using another medium (e.g., phone).

Similarly, IT is changing the communication patterns of employees. Consider how data scientists use social media. A recent study by Vaast and Pinsonneault found that data scientists use social media in various contexts to connect with others, share knowledge, advance their careers, and socialize.[20] They might use Stack Overflow to exchange technical knowledge, GitHub to learn about data science fundamentals and newer developments, Twitter (rebranded X) to thank colleagues or recount a workday, special Facebook features to adjust the content and recipients of their postings, and Slack to control tiers of connections for sharing more or less data publicly. These different contexts have different norms and procedures, and the data scientists had to develop tactics for dealing with the many contexts. Further, the researchers found that the social media tactics varied across career stages. In particular, early-career data scientists used self-monitoring in the sense that they carefully constructed their postings to showcase their knowledge so as to enhance their image and reputation in their social media engagements; In contrast, senior data scientists used self-monitoring as a way of preventing knowledge leakages that would be harmful to their companies. Senior data scientists also totally disengaged from social media when they were really busy.

Changing Decision Making and Information Processing

IT changes organizational decision-making processes in part by changing the information used in making those decisions. Data processed to create more accurate and timely information are being captured earlier in a process. This data is then stored in large comprehensive data warehouses that are mined by using tools to analyze patterns, trends, and relationships. These tools include analytics[21] which have made it possible to identify insights, make predictions, and even suggest decisions. Some systems even have a feedback loop so the suggestions improve over time, helping managers make better decisions. Through IT, information that employees need to do their job can be pushed to them in real time or saved and made available when they need it.

AI is frequently viewed as a form of **Intelligent Augmentation** or expanding human knowledge and expertise by combining human strengths with machine-generated analysis, often using large data sets, to assist humans in performing a task or job. With Intelligent Augmentation, the human is kept "in the loop" and human intelligence is complemented or enhanced by "machine intelligence," enabling improvements in human capabilities and performance.[22] For example, sensor technologies often can complement human information processing by sensing far more or far faster than humans can sense, and technologies such as AI and ML combined with big data can help improve one aspect of intelligence—prediction.

[18] Katherine Karl, Joy Peluchette, and Navid Aghakhani, "Virtual Work Meetings During the COVID-19 Pandemic: The Good, Bad and Ugly," *Small Group Research* 53, no. 3, (2022), 343–65.

[19] Christopher Mims, "The Pandemic Habits That Won't Die," *Wall Street Journal*, June 17–18, 2023, B2.

[20] Emmanuelle Vaast and Alain Pinsonneault, "Dealing with the Social Media Polycontextuality of Work," *Information Systems Research* 33, no. 4, (2022), 1428–51.

[21] See Chapter 12.

[22] Paul, Souren, Lingyao Yuan, Hemant K. Jain, Lionel P. Robert Jr, Jim Spohrer, and Hila Lifshitz-Assaf. "Intelligence Augmentation: Human Factors in AI and Future of Work." *AIS Transactions on Human-Computer Interaction* 14, no. 3 (2022): 426–45.

In the case of human-AI augmentation in critical decision making, it is important for human decision makers to relate the results and predictions generated by AI with their own initial judgments and knowledge and work to resolve any differences between the two. For example, when radiologists use an AI tool to improve the accuracy of a lung cancer diagnosis, they need to investigate why there are differences in the AI tool's results and their own initial diagnosis. One study has shown how radiologists probe to understand the differences, not totally unlike how they would question human colleagues holding differing diagnoses. Only after they have tried to understand the differences would they use the AI tool's results to modify their original diagnosis.[23]

Intelligent Augmentation can also be used to help humans (and not replace them) when the information processing needs or decisions are not as critical as diagnosing lung cancer. A recent study reports the use of generative AI (the technology behind OpenAI's ChatGPT) by 5000 customer support representatives in the Philippine customer support center of an administrative software company. The customer center reps in this company communicated with customers via online chats averaging 40 minutes. Based on a huge number of conversations between support center reps and customers (many of whom were quite irate), ChatGPT was able to generate a real-time chat, which could be viewed alongside the employee's actual chat, with suggestions for the employees about how to respond and with links to internal company documentation to help them more quickly find solutions to their customers' technical problems. New employees quickly learned how to deal with a variety of situations that otherwise would have taken them months to master. Customers rated their interactions better and asked to talk with supervisors less; Employee productivity improved by 14%, on average in the center; Employees were happier; The problematic turnover decreased. Interestingly, it was the productivity of low performers and new employees that improved, and not that of the high-skilled customer support reps who already knew how to come up with good responses.[24]

Changing Collaboration

IT helps make work more team oriented and collaborative and supports remote collaboration. A recent survey of 669 CEOs found that 78% of them endorsed the importance of remote collaboration as a long-term business strategy.[25] Technologies such as texting (SMS), instant messaging (IM), microblogs (e.g., Threads), meeting room technologies (e.g., groupware), document sharing systems (e.g., wikis, Google Drive, Dropbox), video teleconferencing (e.g., Zoom, Teams), and team collaboration software suites (e.g., Basecamp, Slack, Cisco Webex) are at the heart of collaboration today. Groups form and share documents with less effort using these platforms. Group members can seek or provide information from or to each other much more easily than ever before. And groups can connect by voice or with voice and video using these platforms.

Changing the Ways to Connect

Probably one of the biggest impacts of new technologies is that people are always connected. In fact, many feel tethered to their mobile phones, tablets, or laptops to such a large extent that they must be available at all times so that they can respond to requests from their supervisors, colleagues, customers, friends, and family. As a result, the boundaries between work and play have become increasingly blurred, causing people to struggle even more with work–life balance.

Further, technology is connecting more people and devices than ever before. It has been estimated that 30.9 billion IoT devices and 10.3 billion non-IoT devices (e.g., mobile phones, smartphones, tablets) will soon be connected to the Internet.[26] The problem is trying to figure out with whom or what among those billions of people and devices you want to use to connect.

[23] Lebovitz, Sarah, Hila Lifshitz-Assaf, and Natalia Levina. "To engage or not to engage with AI for critical judgments: How professionals deal with opacity when using AI for medical diagnosis," *Organization Science* 33, no. 1 (2022): 126–48.

[24] Greg Rosalsky, "This Company Adopted AI: Here's What Happened to its Human Workers," May 2, 2023, National Public Radio, https://www.npr.org/sections/money/2023/05/02/1172791281/this-company-adopted-ai-heres-what-happened-to-its-human-workers (accessed June 7, 2023).

[25] Intuition, "Remote working statistics you need to know in 2023," https://www.intuition.com/remote-working-statistics-you-need-to-know-in-2023/ (accessed June 9, 2023).

[26] "Statista Internet of Things (IoT) and non IOT active device connections worldwide from 2010–2025. Global IoT and non-IoT connections 2010–2025," Statista, https://www.statista.com/statistics/1101442/iot-number-of-connected-devices-worldwide/#:~:text=IoT%20and%20non%2DIoT%20connections%20worldwide%202010%2D2025&text=The%20total%20installed%20base%20of,that%20are%20expected%20in%202021 (accessed April 29, 2023).

Many in the workforce prefer to connect with technologies that they use at home rather than those provided at work. For example, while many use social media tools on their tablets, laptops, or smartphones during the weekend at home, on Monday morning, they find themselves working on an older desktop system with slow access to the files and web-based systems they want to use for their work. They find this quite bothersome because they want their work systems to be as flexible and offer as many apps as their personal devices. For that reason, they are pushing for BYOD (Bring Your Own Device). This has ushered in IT consumerization[27] in the companies where they work.[28]

The preceding examples show how technologies have become a key component in the design of work. IT has greatly changed day-to-day tasks, which in turn has changed the skills needed by employees. The examples show how adding IT to a work environment can change the way that work is done.

New Ways to Manage People

New working arrangements create new challenges in supervising, evaluating and compensating workers. Modern organizations often face the challenge of managing a workforce that is spread across the world in isolation from in-person supervision and collaboration. As the work becomes more complex, teams are formed to leverage the expertise of the many individuals who are required to effectively deal with problems.

When supervising work today, managers typically choose between two types of formal controls to ensure that individual employees are properly doing the work they are supposed to do: behavior and outcome.[29] **Behavior controls** involve direct monitoring and supervision of employee actions while the work is being done. The way the work is done is the focus of this type of control. Vivid depictions of behavior controls are provided in road construction projects that have one employee digging and another watching, motionless with arms folded, for example. On the other hand, **outcome controls** involve examining work outcomes rather than the work process itself. Using the above example, the outcome would be the road construction itself and evaluating if the final product of the team is adequate.

It is important for managers to choose the right type of control for each position being supervised. Behavior controls make the most sense for physical labor in which incorrect body movements might be inefficient or even dangerous. Programmers would consider it quite insulting to have a supervisor exercise control and watch every keystroke, whereas transcriptionists might understand the need to track each keystroke. On the other hand, evaluating how the work is done might be something a manager assesses as part of evaluating the worker. Outcome controls make more sense not only for programmers but also for many other personnel, such as engineers, sales managers, and ad writers. It is the actual product produced or service performed, and how well it turned out, that is evaluated.

Traditionally, managers supervised their employees by observing if they were present at the place of work and what they were doing when at work. The employees were evaluated on their manager's subjective evaluation based on their observations of how well the employees did their jobs, using primarily behavior metrics and possibly some outcome metrics. Employee compensation was individually based, often a function of the number of hours worked.

The Digital Revolution introduced technological solutions to supervising. One technological solution, electronic employee monitoring can provide detailed *behavior controls*, automatically listing the websites visited, or even recording the contents of an employee's screen. Technology can also provide *outcome controls* by tracking the number of calls processed, online chats completed, or e-mail responses sent. When output is monitored digitally, pay-for-performance compensation strategies reward employees for deliverables produced or targets met as opposed to vague subjective factors such as "attitude" or "teamwork." The introduction of BlueWork at American Express illustrates the need to change from an approach in which managers watch employees and count the hours they spend at their desks to one that focuses instead on the work they actually do. These changes are summarized in Figure 4.2.

---

[27] See Chapter 9 on Governance for a more complete discussion of IT consumerization.

[28] R. W. Gregory, E. Kaganer, O. Henfridsson, and T. J. Ruch, "IT Consumerization and the Transformation of IT Governance," *MIS Quarterly* 42, no. 4 (2018): 1225–53.

[29] L. J. Kirsch, "Portfolios of Control Modes and IS Project Management," *Information Systems Research* 8, no. 3 (1997): 215–39; W. G. Ouchi, "The Transmission of Control through Organizational Hierarchy," *Academy of Management Journal* 21, no. 2 (1978): 173–92; and K. A. Merchant, *Modern Management Control Systems, Text and Cases* (Upper Saddle River, NJ: Prentice Hall, 1998).

	Traditional Approach	Digitally-Supported Approach	Algorithmic Approach
Supervision	*Human boss.* It is personal and informal. Manager is usually present or relies on others to ensure that the employee is present and seemingly productive.	*Human boss.* It is electronic or assessed by deliverables. As long as the employee is producing value, he or she does not need direct formal supervision and may even work remotely.	*Digital boss.* It is platform-based with well-specified deliverables and sometimes careful monitoring of behaviors.
Evaluation	Behavior controls are predominant. Focus is on process through direct observation. Manager sees how employee performs at work. Subjective (personal) factors are very important.	Outcome controls are predominant. Focus is on output by deliverable (e.g., produce a report by a certain date) or by target (e.g., meet a sales quota). Primarily objective measures are used; Few, if any, subjective measures are used.	Outcome controls are predominant. Focus is on performing well on algorithmically-derived goals and subjective customer ratings.
Compensation and Rewards	It is often individually based.	It is often team based or contractually spelled out.	It is often algorithmically-derived based on the individual performance of tasks or projects as rated by customers; May include bonuses and non-monetary rewards.

FIGURE 4.2 Comparison of changes to supervision, evaluations, and compensation.

Algorithmic control was introduced in Chapter 3 as a new type of automated control that is increasingly used to manage workers. It is an important part of **algorithm management**,[30] which requires a platform that uses massive amounts of data gathered from sensors or apps to improve learning algorithms for carrying out coordination and control functions normally performed by humans. Typically, workers perform a specific task like providing a ride or delivering a dinner; They often are not employees of the firm maintaining the platform or of the firm hiring them using an app to perform a particular task, job, or project. The work they perform is closely supervised with sensor data and other technology captured by the app and platform. Some freelance workers can contract for the fee for their work, but often it is set by an algorithm based on an analysis of work performed by other workers and themselves. Interestingly, many platforms outsource the evaluation of performance to customers who provide subjective ratings and who are in no way accountable to the platform for the ratings.[31] For example, Uber workers use an app to be matched with potential customers based on data gathered from GPS about their location and cumulative customer ratings. They may be paid on the basis of the number of miles driven or an algorithmically-derived fixed amount that considers cumulative customer ratings, demand, and miles to destination. The app gathers data about the driver acceptance rates, cancellation rates, and pickups. Occasionally it will give them a bonus or non-monetary award to "nudge" them to keep working.

Algorithmic management is making possible a whole new type of work—that which is performed on online labor platforms. Labor platforms using algorithmic management promise the workers autonomy in selecting when they work and, often, what tasks they perform. However, the workers often don't earn as much as they think they will because they have to supply and maintain the equipment (i.e., cars, bikes, computers, etc.) or the tasks take longer to complete than they had anticipated. Sometimes workers (such as those on Amazon's M-Turk) agree to perform very brief tasks (microtasks) at low pay so they can gain higher status and qualify for higher-paying tasks. Because the microtasks tend to be simple and require little skill, the customers hiring them at bargain rates have considerably more power in setting a wage. As a result, low-skilled workers may be marginalized and exploited in terms of low pay.[32] Further, workers on

[30] Möhlmann, Mareike, Lior Zalmanson, Ola Henfridsson, and Robert Wayne Gregory, "Algorithmic Management of Work on Online Labor Platforms: When Matching Meets Control," *MIS Quarterly* 45, no. 4 (2021), 1999–2022.

[31] L. Cameron and H. Rahman, "Expanding the Locus of Resistance: Understanding the Co-construction of Control and Resistance in the Gig Economy," *Organization Science* 33, no. 1, (2022), 38–58.

[32] Wagner, Gerit, Julian Prester, and Guy Paré, "Exploring the Boundaries and Processes of Digital Platforms for Knowledge Work: A Review of Information Systems Research," *The Journal of Strategic Information Systems* 30, no. 4 (2021): 101694.

these online labor platforms often complain that they feel like they are working in a panopticon—always being watched. They don't understand the algorithms that guide their work and pay, and they often feel isolated from other workers. Some are concerned about "algorithm cruelty" to the extent that workers can't appeal to the empathy of a human manager when they receive fully automated feedback about their work that they think is unfair. Instead, they have unempathetic "digital bosses."

The design of the work needed by an organization is a function of the skill mix required for its work processes and of the flow of those processes. Thus, a company that infuses technology effectively and employs a workforce with a high level of IT skills designs itself differently from a company that does not. The skill mix required by an IT-savvy firm reflects a high capacity for using the technology itself. For example, because many clerical skills such as spelling and grammar checking are embedded in the technologies staff use, clerical staff often do specialized work that is not easily automated or subsumed by technology, such as exception reporting and problem solving. The staff hired for this type of work would have a different, higher skill set than those hired for spelling and grammar editing.

IT has drastically changed the landscape of work today. As a result of IT, many new jobs have been created. In the next section, we examine how IT can change where work is done, when it is done, and who does it.

Where and When Work Is Done and Who Does It

This section examines another important effect of IT on work: the ability of some employees to work anywhere at any time. The COVID-19 pandemic normalized remote work, and there are some benefits and detriments to this type of work arrangement. With wi-fi virtually ubiquitous, individual employees can connect to the Internet from almost anywhere. Research also suggests that employees—especially those employees who have never known a world without ubiquitous access to personal smart devices and the web—prefer to have the work–life flexibility that remote and mobile work arrangements provide. At the group level, virtual teams have become standard operating mechanisms to bring the best individuals available to work together on a task. We explore remote work from the perspective of both individuals and teams in the next two subsections.

Remote Work and Virtual Teams

Flexible work arrangements enable employees to be "virtually present" for their employers. The terms *telecommuting*, *teleworking*, and remote work *(i.e., working remotely)* are often used to describe flexible work arrangements in terms of location. **Remote workers** (i.e., telecommuters, teleworkers) refers to employees working from home, at a customer site, or from other convenient locations instead of coming into the employing company office. A popular type of remote work is called a **hybrid remote work arrangement** in which people work at home sometimes and at the office the remainder of the time. For example, in some cases employees don't follow fixed schedules and have great control over when they work at home and when they work at the office. In other cases employers require employees to come into the office a certain number of days or on specific days depending on their work roles and responsibilities.

Very often employees working remotely also work with remote members on virtual teams. **Virtual teams** are defined as two or more people who (1) work together interdependently with mutual accountability for achieving common goals, (2) do not work in either the same place and/or at the same time, and (3) must use electronic communication and other digital technologies to communicate, coordinate their activities, and complete their team's tasks. Initially, virtual teams were seen as an alternative to conventional teams that meet face-to-face. However, it is simplistic to view teams as either meeting totally face-to-face or totally virtually. Rather, teams may reflect varying degrees of virtuality. Virtual team members may be in different locations, organizations, time zones, or work shifts (day, evening, or overnight). Further, such as most teams, virtual teams may have distinct, relatively permanent membership, or they may be relatively fluid as they evolve to respond to changing task requirements and as members leave and are replaced by new members.

One advantage of having members in different time zones is that virtual teams can "follow the sun." One classic example of this can be found in software development. London members of a virtual team of software

Phase	Preparation	Launch	Performance Management	Team Development	Disbanding
Key Activities	Mission statement Personnel selection Task design Rewards system Technology selection and installment	Kick-off meetings Getting acquainted Goal clarification Norm development	Leadership Communication Conflict resolution Task accomplishment Motivation Knowledge management Norm enforcement and shaping	Assessment of needs/deficits Individual and/or team training Evaluation of training effects Trust building	Recognition of achievements Reintegration of team members

FIGURE 4.3 Key activities in the life cycle of teams.

Source: Adapted from Guido Hertel, Susanne Geister, and Udo Konradt, "Managing Virtual Teams: A Review of Current Empirical Research," *Human Resource Management Review* 15, no. 1 (2005): 69–95.

developers at Tandem Services Corporation initially code a project and transmit its code each evening to a U.S. team for testing. The U.S. team forwards the tested code to Tokyo for debugging. London team members start their next day with the code debugged by the Japanese team, and another cycle is initiated.[33]

Virtual teams are thought to have a life cycle like most teams.[34] Their life cycle, shown in Figure 4.3, is noteworthy because it consists of the important activities in team development: Teams are formed; their work is completed; and the team is disbanded.

COVID-19 and Remote Work

Remote work has been around since the 1970s, but its popularity skyrocketed during the COVID-19 pandemic when millions of people around the globe worked remotely because of COVID-19-related lockdowns. As the pandemic neared its end, the US Labor Department noted that the percentage of hybrid remote workers decreased in all measured industries in 2022 compared to their peak in 2021, with an average decline of 13.4%. The drop was especially precipitous in the financial sector (including banks and brokerages) where the share of those in hybrid remote working arrangements was cut in half from 44.9% in 2021 to 22% in 2022.[35]

While fewer people currently work in hybrid remote work arrangements, they are still very popular—and likely to stay so, especially for knowledge workers. Now that work is increasingly knowledge-based, employees equipped with the right IT can create, assimilate, and distribute knowledge as effectively from home as they can from an office. Gartner reported that before COVID-19, 10% of all knowledge workers globally always worked remotely and 20% sometimes worked remotely (i.e., 30% working remotely); Shortly after the COVID-19 pandemic they predicted, 19% would always work remotely and 29% would sometimes work remotely (i.e., 48% working remotely).[36]

Even though the percentage of remote workers decreased after COVID-19, a sizeable number of workers liked the flexibility offered by working virtually and did not want to return to work full-time in the office. Consequently, many companies like American Express kept hybrid work arrangements after COVID. Companies that didn't, faced dissatisfied employees and some, like Google, needed to deal with active protests. Companies and governments were forced to reassess the benefits and detrimental aspects of remote work.

Benefits of Remote Work

One benefit of remote work is that employees often find that they are more productive when working in an environment of their choosing without the distractions of the office or around sick coworkers. Many employees can actually gain hours by not commuting to an office. Though some of the time gained from

[33] Marie-Claude Boudreau, Karen Loch, Daniel Robey, and Detmar Straub, "Going Global: Using Information Technology to Advance the Competitiveness of the Virtual Transnational Organization," *Academy of Management Executive* 12, no. 4 (1998): 120–28.

[34] G. Hertel, S. Geister, and U. Konradt, "Managing Virtual Teams: A Review of Current Empirical Research," *Human Resource Management Review* 15, no. 1 (2005): 69–95.

[35] Gwynn Guilford, "Work-From-Home Era Ends for Millions of Americans," Wall Street Journal, March 25, 2023, https://www.wsj.com/articles/work-from-home-era-ends-for-millions-of-americans-8bb75367 (accessed June 15, 2023).

[36] Intuition, "Remote working statistics you need to know in 2023," https://www.intuition.com/remote-working-statistics-you-need-to-know-in-2023/ (accessed June 9, 2023).

not having to commute is used for non-work activities, the additional time typically has also been devoted to work-related activities. Furthermore, impediments to productivity such as traffic delays, canceled flights, bad weather, and mild illnesses become less significant. From the employer's perspective, however, the findings are mixed about increased productivity. Many report that their employees are less productive when they work away from the office, especially when considering employees with fully remote work arrangements. That said, American Express and other large companies have documented increases in productivity from remote workers. Amex workers were so efficient when working from home during the COVID-19 pandemic that the AmexFlex program was initiated.

A second benefit is that remote workers and virtual team members often report less stress due to the ability to shift the time of their work to accommodate their lifestyles. For instance, parents modify their work schedules to allow time to take their children to school and attend extracurricular activities. Working remotely from the home provides an attractive alternative for parents who might otherwise decide to take leaves of absence from work for child rearing.

A third benefit is that remote work provides employees and virtual team members enormous geographic flexibility. The freedom to live where one wishes, even at a location remote from one's corporate office, can boost employee morale and job satisfaction. Companies enjoy this benefit, too. Those who build in remote work as a standard work practice may hire employees from a much larger talent pool than those companies that require geographical presence. It also enables companies to hire capable people who are housebound by illness, disability, or the lack of access to transportation.

Fourth, as a workplace policy, it may also lead to improved employee retention, commitment, trust, and higher job satisfaction. For example, Amex employees used the BlueWork program as part of its recruiting pitch. Further, employee satisfaction, commitment, and engagement for those on the BlueWork program was markedly higher, and voluntary turnover was down.

A fifth benefit is that remote work is responsive to the increasing emphasis on energy conservation. As concerns about greenhouse gases, carbon footprints, and even potential future gasoline price increases, employees are looking for ways to be more responsible and frugal at the same time. Remote work is especially appealing in such a scenario, especially when public transportation is not readily available. Companies can also experience lower energy usage and costs from working remotely. SAP, a globally recognized leader in sustainability management, is reducing its global greenhouse footprint by continuously encouraging employees to shift their commuting behavior. As a result of these ongoing efforts, emissions from employees' commutes have dropped. In addition to working remotely and encouraging the use of mass transit and carpooling while decreasing the use of business travel, SAP provides employees information on their carbon footprint from commuting through an internal dashboard aimed at ensuring greater transparency and accountability. Further, SAP has initiated a target of net zero carbon emissions by 2030 and is measuring its progress using its own internal carbon pricing scheme as well as the current social cost of carbon value set by the Value Balancing Alliance.[37]

Sixth, employers often find that it is less expensive to provide a remote employee the tools needed than to pay for the office space for the employee. Employees no longer need to be tied to official desks. When remote workers do come into the company's office, they might not work in their own permanently assigned office. Rather they might "hotel" by sharing office "flex" space with other remote workers who also aren't in the office every workday. Thus, the real estate needs of their employers are shrinking, and companies such as Amex are saving costs by reducing the office space they own or rent. This reduction lowers their energy needs by no longer needing to heat, cool, or maintain these spaces. Companies are realizing that they can comply with the Clean Air Act and be praised for their "green computing" practices at the same time they are reaping considerable cost savings.

Detriments of Remote Work and Virtual Teams

There are also detriments associated with remote work. Remote employees often report that work–life balance suffers. While many enjoy the flexibility of working around the schedules of children or other family members, they paradoxically find it difficult to separate work from their home life. The technology keeps them tethered to their coworkers and bosses, often on a 24/7 basis. If their co-workers or virtual team

[37] SAP Sustainability Report, Greenhouse Gas Footprint, http://www.sapsustainabilityreport.com/greenhouse-gas-footprint (accessed February 2, 2012) and "SAP Integrated Report 2022", Environmental Performance | SAP Integrated Report 2022 You may download the pdf of this report at this website (accessed June 10, 2023).

members are in different time zones they may be forced to stay up late or work in the middle of the night to communicate with them. Consequently, they may work many more hours than the standard nine-to-five employee and experience the stress of trying to separate work from play.

Remote work challenges managers when it comes to controlling their subordinates, evaluating their performance, and determining their compensation. Managers of remote workers must evaluate employee performance in terms of results or deliverables, and not behaviors. Virtual offices make it more difficult for managers to appreciate the skills and efforts of the people reporting to them, which in turn makes it more difficult to evaluate their performance and reward them fairly. Managers accustomed to traditional work models in which they can exert control more easily may strongly resist remote working. In fact, managers are often the biggest impediment to implementing remote work programs.

Determining compensation for virtual team members may be especially difficult. Compensation for virtual teams must be based heavily on the team's performance and ability to reach its goal rather than on individually measured performance. Compensating team members for individual performance may result in "hot-rodding" or lack of cooperation among team members. Organizational reward systems must be aligned with the accomplishment of desired team goals. This alignment is especially difficult when virtual team members belong to different organizations, each with her or his own unique reward and compensation system, each of which may affect individual performance in a different way. Managers need to be aware of differences and discover ways to provide motivating rewards to all team members.

Self-discipline is a key concern for many remote workers and their managers. Managers must rely heavily on the remote worker's self-discipline to ensure that work is done and that the employees are not intentionally abusing their privileges. Sometimes workers without the structure imposed at the office or from required visits to customer locations may become distracted at home by personal phone calls, visitors, social networking sites, and inconvenient family disruptions. A remote worker must carefully set up a home/work environment and develop strategies to enable quality time for work tasks.

Working remotely can disconnect employees from their company's culture and make them feel isolated. The casual, face-to-face encounters that take place in offices transmit extensive cultural, political, and other organizational information, including those about organizational processes. These "water cooler" encounters are lost to an employee who seldom, if ever, works at the office. Consequently, remote workers need to undertake special efforts to stay connected by using technologies such as instant messaging or participating in telephone calls/conferences, e-mail, social networking, blogs, or even video conferencing. The most successful remote work arrangements typically include regular visits to the office to solidify personal connections. Managers of remote workers need to create opportunities for them to engage in and feel a part of the organization.

When calling Disney employees back to their offices four days a week after they had so enjoyed working from home during COVID-19, CEO Robert Iger explained, "Creativity is the heart and soul of who we are and what we do at Disney. And in a creative business like ours, nothing can replace the ability to connect, observe, and create with peers that comes from being physically together."[38]

Not all jobs are suitable for remote work. Some jobs, such as a server in a restaurant, clerk in a grocery store, worker in an assembly line, and facilities manager in a high-rise building, require the employee to be at the work location. These jobs involve physical activities requiring a physical presence. Further, new employees who need to be socialized into the organization's practices and culture are not good candidates for remote work. Finally, some organizations have cultures that do not support remote workers.

Companies that make managing remote work a competency also open up the opportunity for **offshoring**, or foreign outsourcing of jobs once performed internally in the organization. Once a company establishes an infrastructure for remote work, the work often can be performed abroad as easily as it is done domestically. U.S. immigration laws limit the number of foreigners who may work in the United States. However, no such limitations exist on work performed outside this country by employees who transmit their work to the United States electronically. Because such work is not subject to minimum wage controls, companies may have a strong economic incentive to outsource work abroad. They find it particularly easy to outsource clerical work related to electronic production, such as copy editing and computer programming.[39]

Security is another issue for remote workers. The concern is that they might access office systems from unsecure remote locations or networks, and inadvertently introduce a bug or malware, creating a threat

[38] Times Digest, "Disney Call Employees Into Offices 4 Days a Week," January 10, 2023, *Wall Street Journal*, page 4.

[39] Sourcing is further discussed in Chapter 10.

Benefits	Detriments
Higher personal productivity	Increased stress from inability to separate work life from home life
Reduced stress due to increased ability to meet schedules and to have fewer work-related distractions	Harder for managers to control, evaluate, and reward performance
Geographic flexibility for worker; capitalization on distant expertise for organization and inclusion of housebound individuals	More difficult to exert self-discipline and avoid distractions
Higher morale; lower absenteeism	Greater feelings of isolation and being disconnected from company culture
Energy conservation	Lack of suitability for all jobs or employees
Reduced costs related to office space	More easily replaceable by offshore workers
	Harder to achieve high security

FIGURE 4.4 Some advantages and disadvantages of remote work.

to other office systems. It is impossible for organizations to be immune from breaches and make remote workers totally secure. Nonetheless, general managers need to assess the areas and severity of risk and take appropriate steps, via policies, education, and technology, to reduce the risks and make remote workers as secure as possible. IS leaders must provide many levels of security to sense and respond to threats.[40] Benefits and potential detriments associated with remote working are summarized in Figure 4.4.

Managing the Challenges of Virtual Teams

Managing virtual teams offers its own set of challenges. In addition to management control challenges discussed earlier in the chapter, communication, technology, and diversity challenges need to be managed. These virtual team challenges are included in Figure 4.5 and approaches for managing them are discussed below.

Managing Communication Challenges

Because virtual teams and remote workers communicate differently than workers in the office, managers must plan carefully and continue to ensure that business processes as well as communication policies, practices, and norms support these work arrangements. For example, any presentation slides to be used in the meeting must also be shared with the remote participants, either over a video conference with meeting software or beforehand. When most coworkers are in the office and only one or two are dialing or zooming

Issue	Virtual Teams (VT) Challenges
Communication	• Difficulties in scheduling and conducting meetings and interactions • Infrequent communications • Altered communication dynamics with limited facial expressions, vocal inflections, verbal cues, and gestures
Technology	• Need for proficiency across wide range of technologies • Lack of adequate technology support and equipment • Lack of access to necessary information • Need to align group structure and technology with the task environment
Team Diversity	• Need to establish a group identity • Need to build trust, norms, and shared meanings about roles because team members have fewer cues about their teammates' performance • Different perceptions about time and deadlines

FIGURE 4.5 Challenges facing highly virtual teams.

[40] IT security is discussed more fully in Chapter 7.

in from other locations, the remote participants miss all the nonverbal communication that takes place in the meeting room. Soft-spoken individuals are often difficult to hear. Managers must make sure key messages are being conveyed to the remote participants or the results of the meeting are suboptimal.

If possible, team leaders may decide to initiate or supplement a team's virtual activity with a face-to-face meeting so that the seeds of trust can be planted and team members feel as if they know one another on a more personal basis. Face-to-face meetings indeed appear to contribute to successful global virtual teams. An in-depth, classic study of three global virtual teams found that the two effective teams created a rhythm organized around regularly scheduled face-to-face meetings coupled with *synchronous* (i.e., everyone is present at the same time) virtual meetings as needed. Before each meeting, there was a flurry of communication and activity as team members prepared for the meeting. After the meeting, there were many follow-up messages and tasks. The ineffective team did not demonstrate a similar pattern.[41] Because not all teams can meet face-to-face, well-managed synchronous meetings using video teleconferencing can activate the rhythm and accelerate the workflow.

Because team leaders cannot always see what their team members are doing or whether they are experiencing any problems, frequent communications and feedback are important. If remote employees or team members are quiet, the team leader must reach out to them to identify their participation and ensure that they feel their contributions are appreciated. Further, team leaders can scrutinize the team's *asynchronous* communications (i.e., communications that are sent as time permits rather than when receiver and sender are simultaneously present) to evaluate and give feedback about each team member's contributions. Even when a majority of team members are in one location, the team leader should rotate meeting times to alternate the convenience among team members. The rule of thumb is that "more communication is better than less" because it is very difficult to "overcommunicate." One exception might be when team members are experiencing "zoom fatigue," a common problem during the pandemic because conferences were scheduled one after another (or overlapping one another) and the members did not have time to collect their thoughts or have a moment to relax during the day.

Managing Technology Challenges

Information and communication technologies are at the heart of the success of remote work and virtual team accomplishments. However, managers must ensure that their remote colleagues have access to the compatible technologies and support they need to do their jobs. All team members must have the ability to connect to the information sources and communications pathways used by the group. Managers must make sure meetings over video or audio conference tools are well coordinated and all attendees have the right access codes and meeting times. Time zone differences often confuse this issue, so it is critical to make sure everyone knows the right time for a meeting in their time zone.

Support processes for technologies must also be designed with remote employees in mind. If the only support for them is in the office, they may find it difficult, if not impossible, to access the help they need. Bringing a laptop to the office during normal business hours to get technical support may not be possible if the remote worker is hundreds or thousands of miles away. Processes must be designed from the perspective of both remote and non-remote employees.

Managers must ensure that all employees and team members are provided with seamless telephone transfers, desktop support, compatible equipment, network connectivity, and security support to the remote workers. How and where information is stored and used must be considered because all workers must have access to the files, data sets, electronic repositories, and applications they need to do their work. And, of course, the importance of security for remote work cannot be overstated. A good rule of thumb is to design work processes so they work for remote workers, and consider the office as just another location. If the process works for the remote workers, it most likely will work for someone in the office, but the converse is not necessarily true. Unforeseen problems can develop for those remotely located.

Further, managers must also provide the framework for using the technology. Team roles must be well-defined. Policies and norms or unwritten rules about how all employees should use the technology to work with one another must be established.[42] These include norms about telephone, e-mail, and

[41] M. L. Maznevski and K. Chudoba, "Bridging Space over Time: Global Virtual Team Dynamics and Effectiveness," *Organization Science* 11, no. 5 (2000): 373–92.

[42] C. Saunders, C. van Slyke, and D.R. Vogel, "My Time or Yours? Managing Time Vision in Global Virtual Teams, *Academy of Management Executive*, 18, no. 1, (2004): 19–31.

videoconferencing etiquette (i.e., how often to check for messages, the maximum time to wait to return e-mails, and alerting team members about absences or national holidays), work to be performed, and so on. Such norms are especially important when team members are not in the same office and cannot see when team members are unavailable.

Managing Diversity Challenges

Managers may also seek to provide technologies to support diverse team member characteristics. For example, team members from different parts of the globe may have different views of time. Team members from Anglo-American cultures (i.e., United States, United Kingdom, Canada, Australia, and New Zealand) may view time as a continuum from past to present and future. For such team members, each unit of time is the same. These team members are likely to be concerned with deadlines and often prefer to complete one task before starting another (i.e., they are *monochronic*). For team members who are conscious of deadlines, planning and scheduling software may be especially useful. In contrast, team members from India often have a cyclical view of time. They do not get excited about deadlines, and there is no hurry to make a decision because it is likely to cycle back—at which time the team member may be in a better position to make the decision. Many people from India tend to be *polychronic*, preferring to do several activities at one time. Team members who are polychronic may benefit from having instant messaging or instant video chats available to them so that they can communicate with their teammates and still work on other tasks.[43]

In addition to providing the appropriate technologies, managers with team members who have different views of time need to be aware of the differences and try to develop strategies to motivate those who are not concerned with deadlines to deliver their assigned tasks on time. Or the managers may wish to assign these team members to do tasks that are not sensitive to deadlines and are not on the critical path.

Of course, views of time are only one dimension of diversity. Although team diversity has been demonstrated to lead to more creative solutions, it can also make it harder for team members to learn to communicate, trust one another, and form a single group identity. Through open communications, managers may be able to uncover and deal with other areas of diversity, such as culture, training, gender, personality, position, and language, that positively or negatively affect the team. Managers may establish an expertise directory at the start of the team's life and encourage other ways of getting team members to know more about one another. The rule of thumb here is to not assume that a team will work just because it has been created by management. Specific thought must be given to helping the team members function together and embrace, rather than reject, the differences diversity brings to the table.

The Future of Work

New forms of automation based on AI and ML are going to shape future work. Stationary and mobile robots combined with AI and ML will be able to perform manual tasks and Intelligent Automation will be able to increasingly support (if not replace) humans performing cognitive work tasks. These cognitive tasks include knowledge work, learning, and problem solving that were previously performed only by humans. Intelligent Automation can adapt and improve the performance of cognitive tasks over time. However, work that requires judgment, abstract thinking, creativity, social intelligence, or empathy is not yet a good candidate for Intelligent Automation.

A study by Frey and Osborn examined 702 occupations and noted that 47% of total U.S. employment is at high risk of being automated in the next few years. The most likely employees to be replaced by automation and robots are workers in transportation and logistics occupations who will be replaced by driverless cars, a large number of office and administrative support workers, and an ever-growing number of workers on the production line. Least likely to be automated are those jobs with nonroutine tasks involving complex perception and finger or manual dexterity as well as creative and social intelligence.[44] Though not as likely in the near future, knowledge employees, who once felt safe in their jobs because of the high degree of analysis and diagnosis they perform, are at risk of automation as analytics, generative AI chatbots, and

[43] Saunders et al. (2004), "My Time or Yours?"

[44] C. B. Frey and M. Osborn, "The Future of Employment: How Susceptible Are Jobs to Computerisation?" *Technological Forecasting and Social Change* 114 (2017): 254–80.

cognitive intelligence systems incorporating ML become increasingly accurate in their predictions and diagnoses. Even medical doctors whose work used to be considered sacrosanct from automation now work alongside robots like the DaVinci surgical system during surgeries and are predicted to be replaced by them by 2035.[45] Generative AI tools like ChatGPT will be employed to respond to patients' online questions. In pilot tests, a blind panel of doctors thought ChatGPT responded better than the doctors—though caution is urged since the tool sometimes makes things up and gives incorrect responses.[46]

Intelligent Automation

AI has enabled a new form of automation called **Intelligent Automation**, or the application of AI technologies "to replace human capabilities, particularly those involving cognition such as learning and problem solving, for the execution of work tasks that were previously carried out by a human."[47] Intelligent Automation takes humans "out of the loop"—and possibly out of a job. Fears of job loss have been ignited when employee replacement is the goal. The counter-argument is that employees will be liberated from boring, "mind-numbing" tasks to do more enriched jobs. This has been the case when Intelligent Automation is applied to **Robotic Process Automation (RPA)**, or a "software solution to automate tasks previously performed by humans that uses rules to process structured data to produce deterministic outcomes."[48]

Typically, RPA tasks are "swivel chair" meaning that they are performed at a workstation and involve electronic inputs (e.g., e-mails, faxes, spreadsheets) and rule-based, highly standardized processes that may access data from one or more systems and then input the completed work to other systems. The work is not actually performed by a physical robot, but rather by a software license called a robot. RPAs often lead to happier employees (probably because their jobs are less boring) while also contributing to process improvements in terms of quality and speed. When Intelligent Automation and ML are applied to RPA, entire business processes, and not just discrete tasks, can be automated.

Robots in the Workplace

Up until now, our discussion about the "who" is doing the work has been either individuals or teams of individuals. However, increasingly the work is being done by robots (which are technically "what," though sometimes they are designed to have features that look very human-like). A **robot** is "a reprogrammable, multifunctional manipulator designed to move material, parts, tools, or specialized devices through variable programmed motions for the performance of a task."[49] Though robots have been around since Archytas created a mechanical bird in the third century, they did not become part of the assembly line until General Motors (GM) put them to work in 1961.[50] Since then they continue to be used heavily in automobile manufacturing, though other businesses and organizations use them in myriad ways ranging from executing warehouse functions, serving as companions to occupants of Japanese retirement homes, detonating bombs, working on the International Space Station, inspecting bridges and industrial infrastructures, and even performing minimally invasive laparoscopic surgery.

Robots offer many advantages. They can perform tasks that are "dangerous, dirty, or dull"; they can lift and move heavy objects and place them with an accuracy within minute fractions of a millimeter; they can reliably perform boring tasks over and over again—with enviable consistency. Their capabilities are

[45] K. Grace, J. Salvatier, A. Dafoe, B. Zhang, O. Evans, "Viewpoint: When Will AI Exceed Human Performance? Evidence from AI Experts," *Journal of Artificial Intelligence Research*, 62 (2018): 729–754.

[46] Nidhi Subbaraman, "ChatGPT Doctors Will See You Now," *Wall Street Journal*, April 29–30, pgs 1A, 2A.

[47] Coombs, Crispin, Donald Hislop, Stanimira K. Taneva, and Sarah Barnard. "The Strategic Impacts of Intelligent Automation for Knowledge and Service Work: An Interdisciplinary Review." *The Journal of Strategic Information Systems* 29, no. 4 (2020): 101600. (Definition on page 3).

[48] Asatiani, Aleksandre, Olli Copeland, and Esko Penttinen, "Deciding on the Robotic Process Automation Operating Model: A Checklist for RPA Managers," *Business Horizons* 66, no. 1 (2023): 109–21.

[49] J. E. Hamilton and P. A. Hancock, "Robotics Safety: Exclusion Guarding for Industrial Operations," *Journal of Occupational Accidents* 8, nos. 1–2 (1986): 69–78.

[50] A. F. Rutkowski and C. Saunders, *Emotional and Cognitive Overload: The Dark Side of Information Technology* (Routledge, 2018).

increasing in terms of variability and complexity simultaneously with the drop in their price tag. In the past 30 years, the price of a typical robot has halved both in real terms and in relation to labor costs.[51] Further, the efficiencies, increased storage, labor savings, and other operational improvements that their use engenders often produce considerable cost savings. The CEO of Dynamic Group, a manufacturer of molds for mass producing small plastic and metal parts, reported: "The robot's price tag was $35,000 and within two months it paid for itself by quadrupling the efficiency of the press and eliminating scrap."[52]

As if their capabilities and cost savings are not enough, robots are also becoming smarter, thanks to ML and data-driven analytics. For example, industrial robots can use spectral analysis to check the quality of a weld as it is being made. This increases the accuracy of the weld and decreases the effort spent on post-manufacture inspection.[53]

Robots do have disadvantages, most notably in relation to safety, integration into the workplace, and negative impact on human jobs. While a number of deaths have been attributed to robots, their incidence has dropped drastically as robot manufacturers develop proximity sensing systems to prevent robots from colliding with humans. Further, robots cannot just be placed on factory floors and expected to immediately start generating savings. Rather, employees need to learn to work with and around them, not to mention taking time from their regular jobs to monitor them.

Probably the greatest disadvantage associated with robots is the fear that they will generate massive job losses and contribute to a growing economic divide. "There's never been a worse time to be a worker with only 'ordinary' skills and abilities to offer, because computers, robots and other digital technologies are acquiring these skills and abilities at an extraordinary rate," state Erik Brynjolfsson and Andrew McAfee in their book *The Second Machine Age*.[54] To attach a number to support this statement, a recent study reported that for every robot added per thousand workers, wages declined by 0.42% and the employment-to-population ration declined by 0.2%.[55] Those numbers don't sound massive, but they could be as the use of robots grows exponentially.

Amazon first invested in robotics when it bought the robotics firm, Kiva, in 2012. It is now the proud owner of over 520,000 robotic drive units that work in its facilities worldwide. Robots offer a wide range of skills when considered in toto. Some sort and move the inventory needed to fill customer orders. Others like the mobile, fully-autonomous Proteus robot can lift and move packages weighing up to 800 pounds while maneuvering around employees.[56] One of Amazon's most recent arrivals is a robotic arm, "Sparrow," that can speedily and precisely pick up to 65% of the items in a typical Amazon warehouse and potentially save the company billions of dollars in the future.[57] The Amazon warehouses that use robots have realized a 50% increase in storage efficiency.[58] Robots have also dramatically increased the efficiency of the humans at these warehouses. Despite initial concerns, Amazon had not laid off any workers more than a decade after the robots were introduced (though robots and its automated systems have triggered layoffs in the retail sector). In fact, several high-skilled jobs (e.g., designing and training the robots) and middle-skilled jobs (repairing the robots) have been created. Robots rule the core of the Amazon warehouse while humans have learned to "dance seamlessly" around them on the periphery of the facility. The company's best workers are called "Amabots" since they are so at one with the system.[59] While a spate of early accidents resulted in Amazon being criticized for putting productivity over worker safety,[60] its website

---

[51] Jonathan Tilly, "Automation, Robotics and the Factory of the Future," *McKinsey*, September 2017, https://www.mckinsey.com/business-functions/operations/our-insights/automation-robotics-and-the-factory-of-the-future (accessed March 1, 2019).

[52] Kim Tingley, "Learning to Love Our Robot Co-workers," *New York Times*, February 23, 2017, https://www.nytimes.com/2017/02/23/magazine/learning-to-love-our-robot-co-workers.html (accessed March 1, 2019).

[53] Jonathan Tilly, "Automation, Robotics and the Factory of the Future".

[54] Angel Gonzalez, "Amazon's Robots: Job Destroyers or Dance Partners?" *The Seattle Times*, August 11, 2017, https://www.seattletimes.com/business/amazon/amazons-army-of-robots-job-destroyers-or-dance-partners/ (accessed March 1, 2019).

[55] Peter Funt, "The New Everyday Reality of Service Robots," *Wall Street Journal*, May 20–21, 2023, C5.

[56] Amazon staff, "Ten Years of Amazon Robotics: How Robots Help Sort Packages, Move Products and Improve Safety," June 21, 2022, https://www.aboutamazon.com/news/operations/10-years-of-amazon-robotics-how-robots-help-sort-packages-move-product-and-improve-safety (accessed May 4, 2023).

[57] Christopher Mims, "Amazon's Quest for the 'Holy Grail' of Robotics".

[58] Angel Gonzalez, "Amazon's Robots: Job Destroyers or Dance Partners?" *The Seattle Times*.

[59] Aaron Brown, "Rise of the Machines? Amazon's Army of More Than 100,000 Warehouse Robots Still Can't Replace Humans Because They Lack Common Sense," DailyMail, June 5, 2019, https://www.dailymail.co.uk/sciencetech/article-5808319/Amazon-100-000-warehouse-robots-company-insists-replace-humans.html (accessed March 1, 2019).

[60] Jasper Jolly, "Amazon Robot Sets Off Bear Repellant, Putting 24 Workers in Hospital," *The Guardian*, December 6, 2019, https://www.theguardian.com/technology/2018/dec/06/24-us-amazon-workers-hospitalised-after-robot-sets-off-bear-repellent (accessed March 1, 2019).

now boasts how robots make jobs safer for its workers. Of course, the robots are performing many of the same jobs as humans—only faster, more accurately, with larger loads and at a cheaper cost. Plus, robots don't want to join a union (something Amazon has resisted). Thus, it may only be a matter of time before economics and competition compel Amazon to replace humans with robots throughout their facilities, leading to layoffs in an Amazon workforce that is already bloated with the additional hires made during the COVID-19 pandemic.

Where Do Humans Fit Into This Picture?

As generative AI, robots and Intelligent Automation become more prevalent in factories and other workplaces, the role of humans will need to be re-examined. When it comes to robots, steps must be taken to train humans to work safely and productively with them, and to ensure that they are not too stressed from the technology-based pacing of tasks, loss of autonomy, additional work related to monitoring robots' work and, especially, the loss of a job. For example, Paro, the seal-like Japanese robot that is being used to care for elderly dementia patients, can react to humans automatically. Nonetheless, a healthcare or social worker needs to decide how often and for how long the robot can interact with the patient and then supervise the interaction.[61] So far, Paro is not *sentient*, or able to perceive and feel. Thus, Paro and other such service robots are unable to provide caring on the scale that humans can. That said, enough of them could end up dehumanizing the places where they "work." They also may end up making more work for the humans with whom they "work."[62]

When implementing Intelligent Automation, human workers also may be needed to supervise, control, or correct errors from the AI-based systems. Of course, this is becoming progressively more difficult since AI results are increasingly opaque such that the machines typically cannot explain themselves, especially after ML has changed the original algorithms. That is, they are learning on their own and it seems like they may be "developing their own agency."[63]

Employees have well-founded fears that they will lose their jobs to others who have more technical skills—or to robots. This fear is considered to be a form of *technostress*[64] attributed to job insecurity. It is prevalent and could be dealt with either by complementing the employees' jobs with Intelligent Augmentation or training them for new jobs that require them to be more tech savvy. That is, their technostress needs to be dealt with if the middle class that was displaced by the Digital Revolution were to be rebuilt or if less-skilled workers were to be employed.[65]

Researchers, philosophers and system designers, and developers are starting to ask at what point will robots, Intelligent Automation, and AI systems be responsible for their output and actions. Sherry Turkle, a well-known researcher of the sociology of technology thinks it will be when they are sentient and she predicts, "there is going to be a kind of new category of object relations that will form around the inanimate—new rules and new norms."[66]

Some of this widespread questioning is already leading to new norms and laws. For example, the proposed European Union's A.I. Act places restrictions on the riskiest uses of the technology such as facial recognition software and it requires generative AI applications to show the sources of data used for training the system.[67] Of course, trying to regulate emerging technologies is a moving target. Hopefully, these new laws and norms ultimately will always be "connected to human agency" to ensure that humans (e.g., system and equipment designers, developers, manufacturers, implementers, users) are "responsible and accountable for what the machines do."[68]

---

[61] Coombs et al. (2020), "The Strategic Impacts of Intelligent Automation for Knowledge and Service Work."

[62] Souren Paul et al. (2022), "Intelligent Automation: Human Factors in AI and Future of Work."

[63] Walter Isaacson, "Will AI Help Us or Leave Us Behind? May 13–14, 2023, *Wall Street Journal*, C3.

[64] Monideepa Tarafdar, Qiang Tu, T. S. Ragu-Nathan, and Bhanu S. Ragu-Nathan, "Crossing to the Dark Side: Examining Creators, Outcomes, and Inhibitors of Technostress," *Communications of the ACM*, 54, no. 9 (2011): 113–20.

[65] See Chapter 13 for more details.

[66] Daniel Akst, "Should Robots with Artificial Intelligence Have Moral or Legal Rights?" *Wall Street Journal*, April 10, 2023, https://www.wsj.com/articles/robots-ai-legal-rights-3c47ef40 (accessed June 10, 2023).

[67] Adam Satariano, "Europeans Take a Major Step Toward Regulating A.I.," *The New York Times*, June 14, 2023, https://www.nytimes.com/2023/06/14/technology/europe-ai-regulation.html#:~:text=Under%20the%20latest%20version%20of,tech%20developers%20as%20technically%20infeasible (accessed June 18, 2023).

[68] Isaacson (2023), "Will AI Help Us or Leave Us Behind?" and Satariano (2023).

SUMMARY

- The nature of work is changing, and IT supports, if not propels, these changes.
- Communication and collaboration are vital for today's work. Technology supports communication and collaboration.
- IT affects work by creating new work, creating new working arrangements, and presenting new managerial challenges in employee supervision, evaluation, and compensation.
- Newer approaches to management reflect increased use of computer and IT in supervising employees, a more intense focus on output (compared to behavior), and an increased team orientation.
- The COVID-19 pandemic caused the world to rethink how to work, and it created an appreciation for remote work.
- Building remote work capabilities can be an important tool for attracting and retaining employees, increasing their productivity, providing flexibility to otherwise overworked individuals, reducing office space and associated costs, responding to environmental concerns about energy consumption, and complying with the Clean Air Act. Alternative work arrangements also promise employees potential benefits: schedule flexibility, higher personal productivity, less commuting time and fewer expenses, and increased geographic flexibility.
- Detrimental aspects of remote work include increased stress from trying to maintain work–life balance; difficulties in planning, communicating, supervising, and evaluating performance; increased distractions; feelings of isolation among employees; easier displacement of employees by offshoring; dangers to security; and limitations in terms of the types of jobs and employees that can engage in it.
- Virtual teams are a phenomenon that became more popular during the COVID-19 pandemic. They can be defined as two or more people who (1) work together interdependently with mutual accountability for achieving common goals, (2) do not work in either the same place and/or at the same time, and (3) must use electronic communication technology to communicate, coordinate their activities, and complete their team's tasks.
- Managers of remote workers and highly virtual teams must focus on overcoming the challenges of communication, technology, and diversity of team members.
- Robots are becoming more common in the workplace because of their many advantages such as greater efficiencies and cost savings. Some disadvantages have also surfaced: safety, integration into the workplace, dehumanization, and the negative impact on human jobs.
- Technologies like AI, ML, Intelligent Automation will change the nature of work. They may increasingly support work and make workers more "intelligent." A concern is that they may replace workers in some jobs without opening up opportunities for new jobs for them.

KEY TERMS

algorithm management, 87
behavior controls, 86
hybrid remote work arrangements, 88
Industry 4.0, 83
Intelligent Augmentation, 84
Intelligent Automation, 95
offshoring, 91
outcome controls, 86
remote workers, 88
robot, 95
Robotic Process Automation (RPA), 95
virtual teams, 88

FOUNDATIONAL READING

The Changing Nature of Work: Thomas L. Friedman, *The World Is Flat* (New York: Farrar, Straus, and Giroux, 2005).

Shoshana Zuboff, *In the Age of the Smart Machine: The Future of Work and Power* (New York: Basic Books, 1988), 211.

DISCUSSION QUESTIONS

1. What do you predict will be the impact of artificial intelligence (AI) (including generative AI) on knowledge workers? How can a manager ensure that the impact is positive rather than negative?
2. What currently emerging technologies do you predict will show the most impact on the way work is done? Why?
3. Given the growth in working remotely during the COVID-19 pandemic, how might offices physically change in the coming years? Will offices as we think of them today exist by 2030? Why or why not?
4. How did the COVID-19 pandemic affect your working and/or learning remotely? What, if any, changes in working and learning have become a part of your life now?
5. Would you stay in a hotel room that cleans itself? Copenhagen's Hotel Ottilia has introduced a self-disinfecting technology (CleanCoat) into its rooms and suites.[69] CleanCoat is a Teflon-like spray that breaks down harmful microbes, as well as purifies and deodorizes the air in a room for up to a year. It is undetectable by sight or scent and is activated by sunlight. The main ingredient of CleanCoat is a naturally occurring oxide, titanium dioxide, which is found in sunscreen and food additives. Hotel Ottilia has justified the hefty purchase price ($2,500 per room) on the basis that it reduces the time the housekeeping staff spend cleaning the room (i.e., vacuuming, dusting, and making beds) by 50%. An added benefit is that the housekeeping staff can avoid smelling bleach and disinfectants. Knowing this, would you stay at Hotel Ottilia (or another hotel with this self-cleaning system)? Do you think most travelers will resist this change? Why or why not? A technology that helps hotel customers clean their own rooms is CleanseBot, a packable cleaning robot about the size of a hockey puck that is designed to kill *E. coli* on a hotel room's most germ-ridden surfaces.[70] Would you use CleanseBot in your hotel rooms? Why or why not?
6. How has the power dynamic between employee and employer shifted in your workplace since the COVID-19 pandemic?

[69] Caitlin Morton, "Would You Stay in a Hotel Room That Cleans Itself?" *Conde Nast Traveler*, February 26, 2019, https://www.cntraveler.com/story/would-you-stay-in-a-hotel-room-that-cleans-itself (accessed February 28, 2019).

[70] Nikki Ekstein, "This Hotel Has Rooms That Clean Themselves," February 21, 2019, https://www.bloomberg.com/news/articles/2019-02-21/copenhagen-s-newest-hotel-has-rooms-that-clean-themselves (accessed February 28, 2019).

Case Study 4-1 Conducting Bank Examinations Remotely

The Colorado Division of Banking (DOB) is headquartered in downtown Denver in a high-rise office building that overlooks the gold dome of the Colorado State Capitol. The DOB is responsible for the examination of 50 state-chartered commercial banks on a 5-point scale, which is also used by federal regulators, where 1-rated banks are considered strong performers, 2-rated banks are considered satisfactory, and banks rated 3–5 are considered troubled and hence face greater and more frequent regulatory scrutiny. The number of bank examiners on an examination team varies from approximately 6 up to 25–30 examiners for the largest Colorado State Chartered Banks.

The possibility of working remotely from home to conduct bank examinations was sparked by a report written by Russell Saunders in 2018 as part of the requirements for his graduate degree from the Graduate School of Banking at Colorado. Saunders noted that 26 examinations are typically conducted physically "on-site" at the banks each year. This means that a varying-sized team of bank examiners filling various roles would travel to the city in which the bank is located, work on the examination on-site for a 5-day work week during the day, "stay out" at a hotel in the city at night, either remain in that city or commute home for the weekend, and complete the examination in the second 4-day week consistent with the DOB's flex-scheduling. The examination concludes with a Report of Examination detailing the examination results including a rating and recommendations for improvements. If the bank is located within a 50-mile radius of the DOB office, the examiners commute daily to the bank. Examiners commute during work hours, starting at 8 a.m., which means that the exam could actually start in the afternoon of the first day if it is a 4-hour commute to the bank's physical location.

Saunders recommended that the first week of a bank examination be conducted remotely from examiners' homes, with the second week conducted on-site. His rationale was that there would be savings from fewer travelling expenses and the examiners would be more satisfied because they would not be faced with long commutes. He quoted a report that showed Denver had an average commute of 46.11 minutes, placing it 17th in the nation for the longest commute and 13th in terms of the most stressful. Saunders' proposal would save the examiners a substantial amount of commute time (i.e., 35 hours over a year) to devote to more enjoyable or productive activities. Because they "stay out" for several weeks, the examiners are away from their families which is perceived by many, especially those with young children, as undesirable. Saunders also argued that the banks would have an easier time accommodating the examination team. One downside is that it might take longer to conduct examinations because of delayed responses. Some of Saunders' suggestions from 2018 were adopted prior to the COVID-19 pandemic. In particular, the first week of the exam was conducted off-site at the DOB, and the second week the examiners were at the bank.

When COVID-19 led to forced lockdowns starting in March 2020, the Colorado DOB was prepared to conduct all bank exams remotely from the homes of the individual examiners. The examiners already had access to laptops, dual screens, and mobile Wi-Fi needed to support remote work. Most examiners preferred working from home and were able to conduct thorough exams, though sometimes the communications among examiners were not as frequent or complete as they typically are when exams were conducted face-to-face (ftf). The examiners saved precious time and money by not having to commute to the banks and to the Denver DOB office; their work/life balance improved. The banks managed to supply the needed documentation, though some smaller banks struggled to provide the necessary documents electronically.

Another examiner in Saunders' office, Ricardo Giardiello, said he appreciated the bonus time he had because he no longer needed to commute from and to Longmont, CO (over an hour each way), as well as the savings from parking in downtown Denver. As the IT expert on the team, he was able to conduct the required examination components without any problem. However, he found it better to present technical issues to bank employees ftf.

Kara Hunter, the Deputy Bank Commissioner for the State of Colorado observed: "*We could not be where we are now without the pandemic. We were too rigid to change to more remote work. The pandemic forced us to make changes.*"

For the DOB, the COVID-19 pandemic was not all bad: savings in cost and time were realized, productivity increased, and the Examiners seemed satisfied with the remote work arrangements. Hunter mentioned that the COVID-19 pandemic challenged the DOB in many ways, and the DOB had to rise to this challenge by being flexible and risk-focused, as well as adopting new and more

Case Study 4-1 **(Continued)**

efficient methods to complete its supervisory activities. For example, the examiners immediately started using virtual meetings, such as Google Hangouts and Zoom, and they are still using these tools. However, the DOB lost some efficiency when using virtual meetings and found that it was not always as effective for training new employees or conducting critical conversations with bank management. There was less camaraderie and, therefore, teamwork suffered.

The DOB believes that ftf interactions, both internally and externally, have significant value. Thus, in mid-2022, the DOB resumed some on-site activities including loan reviews, new executive management, and management and Board of Director exit meetings. Examinations are also conducted on-site at banks that cannot accommodate off-site work, such as when hardcopy loan files or other bank records are unavailable electronically. Almost no examiners wanted to go back on-site for the exam: Everyone liked it and was comfortable working remotely. Ricardo reflected, *"It is interesting that companies are now backtracking . . . Why not go hybrid or stay fully remote?"*

Since the pandemic a more flexible remote work model has been adopted by the DOB. For example, on-site examination activities are based upon a defined business need, banker input, training needs, as well as an assessment of the travel time. Who works and what examination areas are completed remotely or on-site at the bank are determined case by case with input from the manager and the Examiner-in-Charge and vary bank to bank. Some examiners might be on-site the first week, and different examiners the second week.

Post-COVID, Hunter is having difficulty filling vacant positions. She adds: *"Now everyone I'm interviewing to hire says that they want to work remotely."* She thinks that while these people think that they want to work remotely, a human connection at work is important. Plus, it helps in socializing new employees and making them feel part of the organization.

Sources: Russell Saunders, "Improving Examinations and Examiner Job Satisfaction: Streamlining Processes in a Way that Could be Mutually Beneficial to Bankers and Examiners," *Report for the Graduate School of Banking at Colorado*, 2018. Personal interviews with Kara Hunter, Deputy State Bank Commissioner and Ricardo Giardiello, former IT Bank Examiner, at the Colorado Division of Banking.

Discussion Questions

1. Conducting bank examinations remotely during the COVID-19 pandemic seemed to have been effective and well-liked by the bank examiners. Should the Colorado Division of Banking return to a totally remote work arrangement? Why or why not?
2. Describe in detail the advantages and disadvantages realized by the Colorado Division of Banking related to working remotely during the COVID-19 pandemic.
3. What type of people are best suited to working remotely? What type of jobs are best suited to working remotely?
4. Suppose Kara Hunter has tasked you to make recommendations about how to improve the hybrid remote work model currently in place at the Colorado Division of Banking. Provide recommendations and detailed support for your recommendations.
5. In the first half of 2023, the failures of three US regional banks (Silicon Valley Bank, First Republic Bank, and Signature Bank) rocked the banking world. Detail how concern about future bank failures might affect the design of policies related to remote work for regulatory banking agencies.

Case Study 4-2 Automation at Southern Glazer's Wine and Spirits LLC

Southern Glazer's Wine and Spirits LLC is the largest alcoholic-beverage distributor in the United States. Its 1.2 million-square-foot facility is the biggest liquor distribution warehouse in the world. Would you believe that it is located in Lakeland in central Florida—a metropolitan area that has been designated as the third most vulnerable to automation in the country? Southern Glazer was enticed to set up in Lakeland because of incentives offered by the state: cheap land in the area, three interstates relatively nearby, and moderately low wages. Prior to the Lakeland facility, it had five warehouses in Florida which it consolidated into the current mega-facility.

Case Study 4-2 **(Continued)**

Much of the work in the facility is highly automated. Technologies include beverage distribution software to support 4-part order wave and automated order routing, pallet and case conveyor systems, voice-directed picking, five-level pick robotic modules, and a Human Machine Interface master control station. The highly automated system makes it possible to process 25.5 million cases a year (12,000 cases an hour), which represents a 22% increase over the number of cases processed before the integrated automation system was introduced.

Southern Glazer has been named a "Most Loved Workplace" by Newsweek. Its workforce is reported to include 368 warehouse workers and 392 delivery drivers. Many jobs require only a high school education. As is the case in automated warehouses around the globe, humans do the knowledge work or physical tasks that robots can't do. Those physical tasks typically require a combination of speed, delicacy, and visual acuity such as when operating machinery in tight spaces.

Even though Southern Glazer laid off 20% of their total workforce when transitioning to the large Lakeland warehouse, it eventually rehired most of these workers as automation fueled the company's growth. However, the jobs changed because of automation, according to Ron Flanary, the Senior Vice President of Southern Glazer's National Operations. Employees now have to use their brains to manage the flow of goods through the system. Since warehouse operations currently are tightly integrated with automated inbound logistics and outbound supply chain systems, warehouse employees must use these advanced systems, for instance, to plan warehouse operations and to "chase the case" internally, which means figuring out where a particular inventory item of interest is sitting. Further, they need to adapt the system to fluctuations in consumer demand. For example, many customers who have limited storage space expect daily deliveries.

One warehouse job that many low-skilled workers are still performing is at the final "pick" station where single bottles are transferred from bins to shipping containers. This job is accomplished by humans but assisted by machines. Ironically, the only thing that keeps the humans from being replaced by machines is their manual dexterity—and not their minds. However, Mr. Flanary opined that "there will be a time when we have a 'lights out' warehouse, and cases will come in off trucks and nobody sees them again until they're ready to be shipped to the customer. The technology is there. It's just not quite cost-effective yet."

Video: The automation is described in 5 minute video at *World's Largest Wine & Spirits Distribution Center Invests in Automation & Software – YouTube, Feb 1, 2019 (accessed April 20, 2023).*

Sources: Christopher Mims, "Where Robots Will Soon Rule," *Wall Street Journal*, February 9–10, 2019, B4; see also Bob Trebilcock, "Southern Glazer's Wine & Spirits: Designed to Last," *Modern Materials Management*, July 14, 2017, https://www.mmh.com/article/southern_glazers_wine_spirits_designed_to_last (accessed February 28, 2019); and Southern Glazer's Wine & Spirits Lakeland, loda https://www.bastiansolutions.com/about/media-library/case-studies/food-beverage/southern-glazers-wine-spirits-lakeland-florida/ (accessed February 28, 2019); Bob Trebilcock, "Transforming Inbound Logistics, in Real Time," Supply Chain Management Review, May 2, 2022, https://www.scmr.com/article/transforming_inbound_logistics_in_real_time (accessed April 24, 2023); Southern Glazer's Wine and Spirits, "Culture," https://southernglazers.com/careers/culture (accessed August 9, 2023).

Discussion Questions

1. What do you think will happen to the low-skilled warehouse workers when the technology becomes more cost effective? What responsibility, if any, do you think that Southern Glazer managers have toward their workers who are displaced by automation and robots? Please explain.
2. What are the advantages and disadvantages of using highly automated systems like those used in Southern Glazer's warehouses?
3. How do you think the workers would react to having robots as "coworkers?" If you think they might resist the robots, describe how you think they would do so.
4. What do you think humans actually do in the warehouses that the robots cannot do? Besides the example in this case of the "final pick," what are the warehouse workers doing? Why don't robots do that work in a cost-effective manner today?

Information Systems and Digital Transformation

5

Transformation requires thinking about things in a revolutionary way—recognizing and shedding outdated rules and fundamental assumptions that underlie the business. Business processes, the cross-functional sets of activities that turn inputs into outputs, are at the heart of how businesses operate and how transformation takes place. **Digital transformation** uses the principles of finding new ways to differentiate a business by offering customers a new and valuable way to meet their needs, often over digital media. This chapter discusses business processes, changes to business processes, gaining acceptance to change, digital transformation, and the systems that support them. The chapter begins with a discussion of a functional (silo) versus a process perspective of a firm, including agile and dynamic business processes. The chapter then focuses on the way managers change business processes, including incremental and radical approaches, and gain acceptance for these changes. Digital transformation is then introduced. Workflow, business process management systems, and enterprise systems that support and automate business processes follow. The chapter concludes by examining when IS drive business transformations and the complexities that arise when companies integrate systems.

Walmart Canada faced high costs in the act of paying invoices at an immense scale, involving 500,000 truckloads of products per year to sell in their stores. The chain has 2,000 of their own trucks on the roads, but that is not enough; they also use 70 third-party freight carriers. Those third-party carriers would quote a price beforehand with a specific agreed-upon delivery date, but any of 200 variables sometimes created billing changes and delays. For example, unanticipated road conditions, weather, or fuel problems could create delays, and changes in tolls, fuel prices, and import tariffs could add costs. These were not isolated incidents, as up to 70% of invoices were under dispute at one time or another, sometimes taking weeks or months to settle. These disputes boosted administrative costs, requiring both the third-party carriers and Walmart Canada to arduously reconcile billing costs back to the quoted pricing before they could be paid. Some carriers would give up and discontinue working with Walmart Canada entirely.[1] The invoicing and payment processes were clearly troubled and required digital transformation.

After some very vocal carriers complained about how long it took for them to be paid, Walmart Canada worked together with the carriers to find a solution to this costly problem. As they studied the system, the 11-step system needed to clear an invoice was based on two different invoices: one maintained by Walmart Canada, and one maintained by each carrier. The carriers added costs and adjusted delivery schedules as they encountered problems along the way, which of course caused the two invoices to disagree, requiring reconciliation.

[1] This case is based on Lacity, Mary C. and Van Hoek, Remko, "How Walmart Canada Used Blockchain Technology to Reimagine Freight Invoice Processing," *MIS Quarterly Executive* 20, no. 3, Article 5; Abhisek Mohanty, "The Evolution of DL Freight," DLTLabs, March 8, 2021, https://www.dltlabs.com/blog/the-evolution-of-dl-freight-933754 (accessed June 11, 2023); and Kate Vitasek, John Bayliss, Loudon Owen, and Neeraj Srivastava, "How Walmart Canada Uses Blockchain to Solve Supply-chain Challenges," *Harvard Business Review*, January 5, 2022, https://hbr.org/2022/01/how-walmart-canada-uses-blockchain-to-solve-supply-chain-challenges (accessed June 11, 2023).

They looked for a way to fix the system but quickly realized the system needed to be completely redesigned and built from scratch. They envisioned a need to split a contract into individual agreements that covered the potential deviations, and to have those agreements stored on a shared resource. They also needed the entries to be permanent, unchangeable after the event, able to display accurate status at all times, updated in real time. One of the team members realized that those three factors were perfectly suited to a blockchain solution.[2]

Walmart Canada engaged DLT Labs, which already had a solution that could be built quickly; DLT promised delivery of the solution within three months. If Walmart Canada would have tried to create a solution in house, the system would have taken an estimated 18 months to create. By March of 2021, the system was rolled out to all their third-party carriers.

The reengineered system was unique because it required buy-in from the carriers, real-time IoT data from trucks, the ability of certain individuals to enter pre-approved charges as they occurred and involved apps available in the cloud[3] to avoid further delays by requiring the various freight haulers to create their side of the systems. Each hauler had specific conditions on their contracts that would be pre-approved. For instance, one hauler might tack on extra charges if the Walmart Canada loading docks were too crowded and required an overnight stay. Others might stipulate added fees if fuel price changes exceed a specified amount.

The impact of the changes was significant. The 11 steps were collapsed to five steps to process invoices. Better yet, the invoices were most often finalized within 24 hours of delivery, and the number of disputes fell from 70% to under 2%. Not only were administrative costs dramatically lowered for Walmart Canada by those improvements, but they could also take advantage of early-payment discounts. On the hauler side, cash flows were greatly improved, making for stronger vendor–client relationships. Greater trust was formed on both sides of the transactions, as invoice changes were always on display and easy to validate using the pre-approved rules. Also, business intelligence was improved, it was now possible to evaluate many practices. For example, they could discover preferred routes and time-of-day schedules with respect to factors such as delivery time, road safety, and fuel consumption.[4]

IS can enable or impede business change. The right design coupled with the right technology can result in substantial benefits such as those experienced by Walmart Canada. The wrong business process design or the wrong technology, however, can force a company into an operational, and sometimes financial, crisis.

To a manager in today's business environment, an understanding of how IS enable business change is essential. The terms *management* and *change management* are used almost synonymously in today's business vocabulary: To manage effectively means to manage change effectively. As IS have become ever more prevalent and more powerful, there are relentless increases in speed and magnitude of the changes that organizations must address to remain competitive. To be a successful manager, one must understand how IS enable change in a business; one must gain a process perspective of the business, and must understand how to transform business processes effectively. This chapter provides managers with a view of business process change. It provides tools for analyzing how a company currently does business and for thinking about how to effectively manage the inevitable changes that result from competition and the availability of IS. This chapter also describes what managers need to know about an IT-based solution commonly known as *enterprise-wide IS*.

A brief word to the reader is needed. The term *process* is used extensively in this chapter. In some instances, it is used to refer to the steps taken to change aspects of the business. At other times, it is used to refer to the part of the business to be changed: the business process. The reader should be sensitive to the potentially confusing use of the term *process, and to consider the context for fully understanding what people are saying about what improvements are proposed.*

---

[2] Briefly, a blockchain works by sharing a cloud document among all vendors, containing a chain of blocks of data. After many transactions are recorded into a block, the contents are processed by adding to the block a special arbitrary number (called a nonce, or number only used once) and subjecting the block to a very strange algorithm to receive a long, random-looking numeric stamp, called a "hash." If the hash does not have a certain characteristic (such as starting with four zeros), the nonce is incremented and tried again and again. When the condition is finally satisfied, the block is accepted, added to the chain, and shared with everyone. The next block receives the hash from the previous block, so if someone tries to fraudulently change data already recorded in a previous block, the hash will no longer work, and the entire chain will be broken for that one vendor's copy of the blockchain. All other parties will have the correct information, so the effort will be revealed quickly, and the culprit easily identified.

[3] Such a scheme involves Software as a Service, covered in more depth in Chapter 6.

[4] Business Intelligence is covered more fully in Chapter 12.

Functional Perspective Versus Business Process Perspective

When effectively linked with improvements to business processes, advances in IS enable changes that make it possible to do business in a new way, one that is better and more competitive than before. On the other hand, IS can also inhibit change, which occurs when managers fail to adapt business processes because they rely on inflexible systems to support those processes. Finally, IS can also drive change for better or for worse. Examples abound of industries that were fundamentally changed by advances in IS and of companies whose success or failure depended on the ability of their managers to adapt. This chapter considers IS as an enabler of business transformation, a partner in transforming business processes to achieve competitive advantages. We begin by comparing a process view of the firm with a functional view.

Transformation requires discontinuous thinking—recognizing and shedding outdated rules and fundamental assumptions that underlie operations. "Unless we change these rules, we are merely rearranging the deck chairs on the *Titanic*. We cannot achieve breakthroughs in performance by cutting fat or automating existing processes. Rather, we must challenge old assumptions and shed the old rules that made the business underperform in the first place."[5]

The old, outdated freight recording rule at Walmart Canada could be summarized as: "Keep the original freight quotes in a private file and then compare to the final bill the shipper sends from its private file. Ask for justification of any additional charges before paying the bill." The new rule would be: "Establish permissible additional charges and empower an agent to approve them. Keep a shared record of the current invoice and only question items outside of the norm or contrary to data found in public sources such as weather and traffic reports. Pay the invoice when the shipment is complete."

Functional Perspective

Many think of business by imagining a hierarchical structure (described in Chapter 3) organized around a set of functions. A traditional organization chart provides an understanding of what the business does to achieve its goals. A typical hierarchical structure, organized by function, results in disconnected silos that might look like the one in Figure 5.1.

In a functional organization, departments are organized on the basis of their core competencies. For example, the operations department focuses on operations, the marketing department focuses on marketing, and so on. This functional structure is widespread in today's organizations and business curricula follow suit with majors in the functions, perhaps becoming predisposed to think in terms of these same functions.

Even when companies use the perspective of the value chain model (as discussed in Chapter 2), they still focus on functions that deliver their portion of the process and "throwing it over the wall" to the next

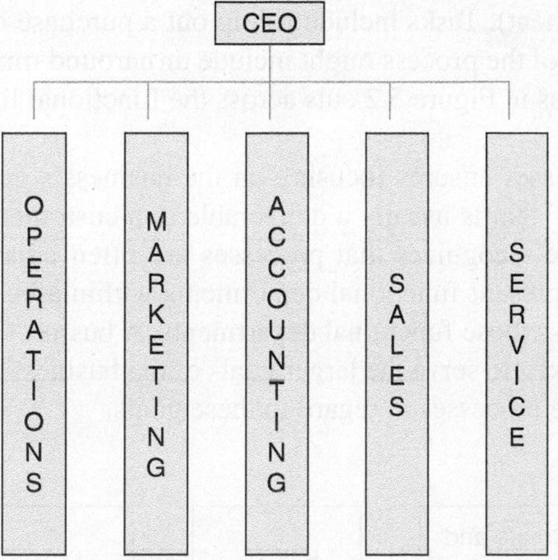

FIGURE 5.1 A simple functional structure.

[5] Michael Hammer, "Reengineering Work: Don't Automate, Obliterate," *Harvard Business Review* 68, no. 4 (July–August 1990): 104–112.

group on the value chain. These areas become self-contained functional units, which can be useful for two main reasons. First, they allow an organization to optimize and improve expertise and training over time. For example, all the marketing people can informally network and learn from each other. Second, the functions allow the organization to avoid redundancy in expertise by hiring one person (such as a web designer) who can be assigned to projects all over the organization.

On the other hand, functional organizations can experience significant suboptimization. First, individual departments often recreate information maintained by other departments. Second, communication gaps between departments are often wide, and information could be lost in translation with departments blaming each other. Finally, functions tend to lose sight of the objective of the overall organization and try to maximize their local goals. The last point is illustrated by a production department that pushes the concept of a limited number of product sizes and options while the marketing department urges management to consider a larger variety or even to engage in customization of those products. Such conflicts can be difficult to resolve in a way that is best, overall, for the firm.

Losing the big picture means losing business effectiveness. After all, a business's main objective is to create as much value as possible for its shareholders and other stakeholders by satisfying its customers to stimulate repeat sales and positive word-of-mouth. When functional groups either duplicate work, or fail to communicate with one another, or lose the big picture and establish suboptimal processes, the customers and stakeholders are not being well served.

Business Process Perspective

A manager can avoid such suboptimization—or begin to "fix" it—by managing from a business process perspective. A **business process perspective**, or more simply a **process perspective**, keeps the big picture in view and allows the manager to concentrate on the work that must be done to ensure the optimal creation of value. A process perspective helps the manager avoid or reduce duplication of work, facilitate cross-functional communication, optimize business processes, and ultimately, best serve the customers and stakeholders.

In business, a **process** is defined as an interrelated, sequential set of activities and tasks that turns inputs into outputs and metrics, to measure effectiveness. Two examples of metrics that are often important for a business process are *throughput,* which is how many outputs can be produced per unit of time, or *cycle time*, which is how long it takes for an entire process to execute. Others include survey outcomes like customer satisfaction as well as internal records of revenue per output, profit per output, and quality of the output.

Business processes often include customer order fulfillment, manufacturing planning and execution, payroll, financial reporting, and procurement. A procurement process might look like the sample in Figure 5.2. The process begins with inputs (requirements for goods or services) and ends with outputs (receipt of goods, vendor payment). Tasks include filling out a purchase order and verifying the invoice. Success metrics of the success of the process might include turnaround time and the number of paperwork errors. The procurement process in Figure 5.2 cuts across the functional lines of a traditionally structured business.

Focusing on business processes ensures focusing on the business's goals (the "big picture") because each process has an "endpoint" that is usually a deliverable to a customer, supplier, or other stakeholder. A business process perspective recognizes that processes are often cross-functional. In the diagram in Figure 5.3, the vertical bars represent functional departments within a business. The horizontal bars represent processes that flow across those functional departments. A business process perspective requires an understanding that processes exist to serve the larger goals of the business and that functional departments must work together to optimize processes in regard to these goals.

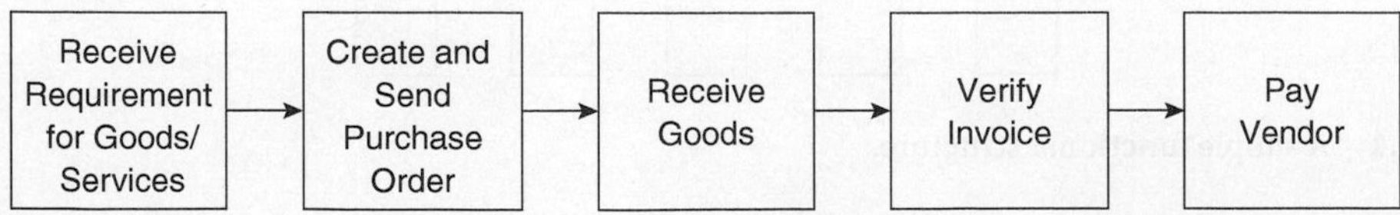

FIGURE 5.2 Sample procurement business process.

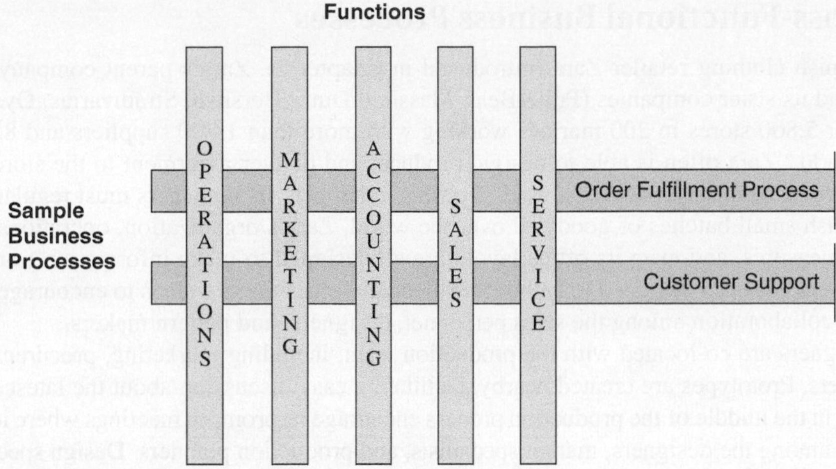

FIGURE 5.3 Cross-functional nature of business processes.

In Figure 5.3, the order-fulfillment process could include tasks that correspond to the functions. They might offer competitive price reductions to customers (marketing), selling (sales) shipping (operations), receipts of payment (accounting), and after-sales service tasks (services). The "sales order" would be the input for this process. One important output would be customer satisfaction, which could be measured by surveys, reviews, or rating scales found on a seller's website. Other important outputs can be found by examining metrics from internal records such as customer repurchases, warranty repairs, or refunds made.

When managers take a business process perspective, they are able to optimize the value that customers and stakeholders receive by managing the flow as well as the tasks. They might identify that offering a special customization for a customer resulted in higher costs that were not covered by the revenue, resulting in a loss. The marketing department's victory turned into the organization's loss.

The differences between the functional and business process perspectives are summarized in Figure 5.4. An example will help illustrate the differences that sometimes are obvious to consumers. Using a functional perspective, a customer with a warranty issue would need to explain the problem to a customer service representative in the service department. If the problem is technical, the call would be transferred to a technical support person (in a different department), and the customer might need to explain the entire problem again. If the technical support representative determined that a part is needed, the customer would be transferred to the sales department and might need to explain the issue yet another time. Because the departments are not talking with one another, the customer might even need to provide proof of purchase several times to avoid having to pay for the service.

In contrast, with a business process perspective, either one representative would work with the customer on all problems, or an enterprise system would enable the representative to take notes of the problem, then transfer both the call and notes with the details to a specialist.

	Functional Perspective	Business Process Perspective
Definition	Self-contained functional units such as marketing, operations, and finance	Interrelated, sequential set of activities and tasks that turns inputs into outputs
Focus	Function	Cross-function
Goal Accomplishment	Goals optimized for the function, which may be suboptimal for the organization	Goals optimized for the organization, or the "big picture"
Benefits	Core competencies highlighted and developed; functional efficiencies	Avoidance of work duplication and cross-functional communication gaps; organizational effectiveness
Problems	Redundancy of information throughout the organization; cross-functional inefficiencies; communication difficulties	Difficulty in finding staff who can be knowledgeable generalists; need for sophisticated software

FIGURE 5.4 Comparison of functional perspective and business process perspective.

Zara's Cross-Functional Business Processes

Consider Spanish clothing retailer Zara (introduced in Chapter 2). Zara's parent company, Inditex, has grown Zara and its sister companies (Pull&Bear, Massimo Dutti, Bershka, Stradivarius, Oysho, and Zara Home) to over 5,800 stores in 200 markets working with more than 1,700 suppliers and 8,200 factories around the world.[6] Zara often is able to design, produce, and deliver a garment to the stores within two weeks and stores get new styles twice a week. For this to happen, its managers must regularly create and rapidly replenish small batches of goods all over the world. Zara's organization, operational procedures, performance measures, and even its office layout are all designed to make information transfer easy. Its new headquarters has been designed to be both aesthetically pleasing as well as to encourage communication and open collaboration among the sales personnel, designers, and pattern makers.

Zara's designers are co-located with the production team, including marketing, procurement, and production planners. Prototypes are created nearby, facilitating easy discussion about the latest design. Large circular tables in the middle of the production process encourage impromptu meetings where ideas are readily exchanged among the designers, market specialists, and production planners. Design speed and quality is greatly enhanced by the cross-functional team's co-location because the designers can quickly check their ideas with others. For example, the market specialists can quickly respond to designs in terms of the style, color, and fabric, whereas the procurement and production planners can update these specialists about manufacturing costs and available capacity. Without this focus on cross-functional process efficiency, the company would not be able to sustain the high velocity of designs that are delivered to the stores.

Logistics at Zara are also designed for speed and efficiency. The 12 logistics centers serve the needs of the stores, making deliveries possible anywhere in the world in no more than two days. The logistics centers are in Spain, Portugal, Turkey, and Morocco—all in close proximity to the head offices and the production facilities, cutting travel time and distance to increase responsiveness. IS manage dispatch time, making the movement, storage, and collection of shipped boxes precise and efficient.

Zara's information technology provides a platform but does not preclude informal face-to-face conversations. Retail store managers are linked to marketing specialists through customized mobile devices but sometimes use the telephone to share order data, sales trends, and customer reactions to a new style. Zara's cross-functional teams enable information sharing among everyone who "needs to know" and therefore creates the opportunity to change directions quickly to respond to new market trends.

Building Agile and Dynamic Business Processes

To stay competitive and consistently meet changing customer demands, organizations build dynamic business processes or agile business processes, processes that repeat through a constant renewal cycle of design, deliver, evaluate, redesign, and so on. **Agile business processes** are designed to simplify redesign and reconfiguration. They are designed to be flexible and easily adaptable to changes in the business environment and can be incrementally changed with little effort. **Dynamic business processes**, on the other hand, reconfigure themselves as they "learn" and the business utilizes them. To be agile or dynamic, a process often has a high degree of IT use. The more the process can be done with software, the easier it is to change, and the more likely it can be designed to be agile or dynamic.

Examples of agile processes are often found in manufacturing operations, where production lines are reconfigured regularly to accommodate new products and technologies. For example, automobile production lines produce large numbers of vehicles, but very few are identical to the ones made before or after it on the production line. Also, vehicles are often built with space and a standard wiring harness that can also accommodate various options (such as a remote starter) that can be added by a dealer quickly and with minimal labor.

Another common example is in software development. Agile software development methodologies are often used to rapidly and collaboratively create working and relevant software.[7] Such an approach uses an incremental and iterative development process to enable the agility they promise.

[6] Inditex, "A new 170,000m² building to house the Zara sales and design teams within Inditex's complex in Arteixo", December 21, 2021, News Detail, https://www.inditex.com/itxcomweb/en/press/news-detail?contentId=d6a11054-f905-4f0f-8593-96097bc21f37 (accessed March 23, 2023); Statistics from Inditex Annual Report 2022. Inditex Group Annual Report 2022, https://static.inditex.com/annual_report_2022/en/ (accessed June 8, 2023).

[7] See Chapter 11.

More recently, with the use of the Internet through "as a service" variants,[8] building agility into business processes is increasingly common. Processes run entirely in the digital world. Some common examples are order management, service/product provisioning, human resource support, and bill payment. The pervasiveness of the digital world has necessitated rethinking many business processes, because customers, employees, and other stakeholders expect to be able to access processes on an app or on the web to perform self-service.

Many processes have been designed as apps. Consider smartphones or tablets. Each app loaded on these devices is, in reality, an automated business process. And because it's an app, it's relatively easy for the developer to update, fix, and enhance. Apps are good examples of software that support agile processes.

An example of a dynamic process is a network with a changing flow of data. The network could have sensors built in to monitor the flow, and when flow is greater than what the current network configuration can handle, the network automatically redistributes or requisitions more capacity to handle the additional data and reconfigures itself to balance the flow over the new channels. As more devices are connected to the Internet, more processes will become dynamic, a direct benefit of the Internet of Things (IoT) trend. For example, thermostats connected to the Internet make it possible to dynamically adjust the temperature in an office building without an individual visiting the space. Another example, with a more physical configuration, would be a call center. Call center systems are designed to monitor the flow of calls coming into a center and record the time it takes for agents to respond to them. These systems can automatically redistribute calls to or from other centers as volume increases or decreases. The system might be sufficiently sophisticated so that it can add additional agents to the schedule or alert a supervisor of an increase and route calls to standby agents, preventing lost calls.

Dynamic IT applications, a component of software defined architecture, are required for dynamic business processes. When the underlying IT is not designed with this goal in mind, the business process itself cannot adapt as necessary to changing requirements of the business environment. The benefits of agile and dynamic business processes are operational efficiency gained by the ease of incrementally improving the process as necessary and the ability to create game-changing innovative processes more quickly.

Changing Business Processes

Often managers realize that they need to redesign their business processes. Two well-known techniques for redesigning business processes are: (1) radical process redesign, which is sometimes called **business process reengineering (BPR)**, or simply **reengineering**, and (2) incremental, continuous process improvement, which includes total quality management (TQM) and Six Sigma. Radical and incremental improvement concepts are important; they continue to be different tools a manager can use to effect change in the way his or her organization does business. The basis of both approaches is viewing the business as a set of business processes rather than using a **functional perspective**.

For example, Facebook in 2021 changed its corporate name to Meta, which for many appeared to emphasize that Facebook was merely one app in their tool kit, alongside Instagram, WhatsApp, and Oculus. The latter was emblematic of Facebook's vision and symbolized their new long-term vision for adopting virtual and augmented reality.

A recent case study about this new vision questioned whether Facebook is undergoing an incremental or radical change, and scanned 153 articles, websites, investor reports, and press releases to seek clues to an answer. Their results indicated that Facebook appears to be setting their sights on incremental innovation, because the new vision mainly has a focus on technology, the core offering remains the same, and their revenue streams remain the same.[9]

On the other hand, Walmart Canada chose one subunit of the firm and changed all of the main rules they previously followed. This example is similar to one followed by Ford in aspiring to achieve the substantial downsizing of their accounts payable in the accounts of Hammer and Champy, in the foundational readings section of this chapter.

---

[8] "As a service" variants and software defined architecture are discussed in Chapter 6.

[9] Sascha Kraus, Dominik K. Kanbach, Peter M. Krysta, Maurice M. Steinhoff, and Nino Tomini, "Facebook and the Creation of the Metaverse: Radical Business Model Innovation or Incremental Transformation?" *Emerald Insights* 28, no. 9 (2022): 52–77.

Incremental Change

At one end of the continuum, managers use incremental change approaches to improve business processes through small, incremental changes. This improvement process generally involves the following activities:

- Choosing a business process to improve.
- Choosing a metric for measuring the business process.
- Enabling personnel to find ways to improve the business process based on the metric.

Personnel often react favorably to incremental change because it gives them control and ownership of improvements and, therefore, renders change less threatening. The improvements grow from their grassroots efforts. **Total quality management (TQM)** is one such approach that incorporates methods of continuous process improvement. At the core of the TQM method is W. Edwards Deming's "14 Points," or key principles to transform business processes. The principles outline a set of activities for increasing quality and improving productivity.[10] TQM has lost some of its luster given that Six Sigma has gained more attention over the years.[11]

Six Sigma is an incremental and data-driven quality management approach for eliminating defects from a process. The term *six sigma* comes from the idea that if the quality of all output from a process were to be mapped on a bell-shaped curve, the tail of the curve, six sigma (standard deviations) from the mean, would represent less than 3.4 defects per million. Such a low rate of defects would be close to perfect. The Six Sigma methodology is carried out by experts known as *Green Belts* and more experienced experts known as *Black Belts*, who have taken special Six Sigma training and worked on numerous Six Sigma projects. Motorola was one of the first companies in the United States to use Six Sigma, but GE made the method such a significant part of its business culture, that it saved $12 billion in the first five years.[12]

An example of incremental change is when the state of Kansas implemented the Kansas Information Technology Architecture (KITA) slowly over numerous years. A small staff (two to three people) made 12 incremental updates to make sure that the KITA stayed relevant and met the needs of the state.[13]

Radical Change

Incremental change approaches work well for tweaking existing processes. However, they tend to be less effective for addressing cross-functional processes. Major changes usually associated with cross-functional processes require a different type of management tool. At the other end of the change continuum, radical change enables the organization to attain aggressive improvement goals (again, as defined by a set of metrics). The goal of radical change is to make a rapid, breakthrough impact on key metrics.

Sloan Valve is an example of a company that set aggressive improvement goals and reached them with a radical change approach. The company set out to dramatically improve new products' time to market and was able to reduce it from 18–24 months to 12 months. Another example of radical change may be seen in the way that the State of California undertook a much-needed major reorganization of its IT environment. It decided to implement an enterprise architecture to standardize the process for designing and implementing e-Government solutions, as well as to address its IT governance crisis. It took ten people from multiple agencies to deliver version 1.0 of the complex enterprise architecture framework in just a little over a year.[14]

The difference in the incremental and radical approaches over time is illustrated by the graph in Figure 5.5. The vertical axis measures, in one sense, how well a business process meets its goals. Improvements are made either incrementally or radically. The horizontal axis measures time.

---

[10] For more information about TQM and Deming's 14 Point approach to quality management, see the ASQ (formerly known as the American Society for Quality), a global community of experts on quality and the administrators of the Malcolm Baldrige National Quality Award program, https://asq.org/quality-resources/total-quality-management/deming-points (accessed June 12, 2023).

[11] Alexander S. Gillis, "Total Quality Management (TQM)," Techtarget, April 2023, https://www.techtarget.com/searchcio/definition/Total-Quality-Management (accessed June 12, 2023).

[12] Admin, "Remembering Jack Welch and His Relation to Six Sigma," SixSigmaDaily, May 2020, https://www.sixsigmadaily.com/remembering-jack-welch-and-his-relation-to-six-sigma/ (accessed June 12, 2023).

[13] Q. Bui, "Increasing the Relevance of Enterprise Architecture Through 'Crisitunities' in US State Governments," *MIS Quarterly Executive* 14, no. 4 (2015): 169–179.

[14] Ibid.

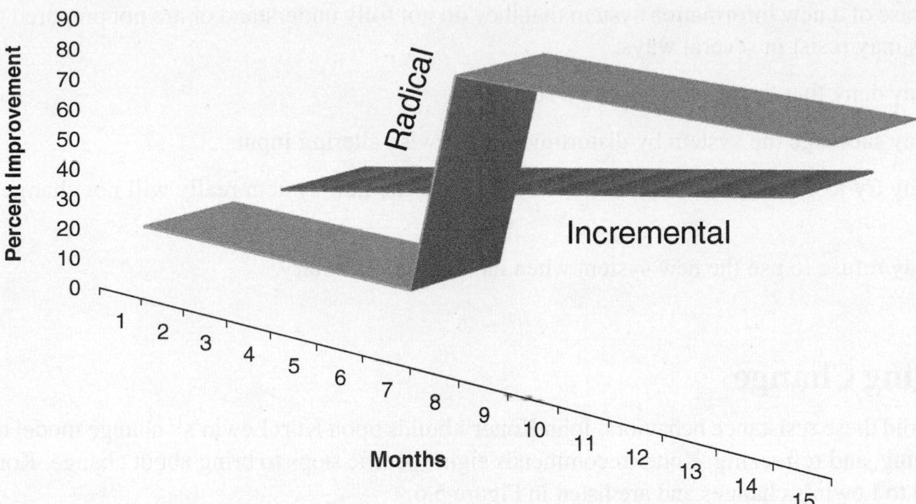

FIGURE 5.5 Comparison of radical and incremental improvement.

Not surprisingly, radical change typically faces greater internal resistance than incremental change. Therefore, radical change processes should be carefully planned and used only when major change is needed in a short time. Some examples of situations requiring radical change are when the company is in trouble, when it faces a major change in its operating environment, or when it must change significantly to outpace its competition. Key aspects of radical change approaches include the following:

- Need for major change in a short amount of time.
- Thinking from a cross-functional process perspective.
- Challenge to old assumptions.
- Networked (cross-functional) organization.
- Empowerment of individuals in the process.
- Measurement of success via metrics tied directly to business goals and the effectiveness of new processes (e.g., production cost, cycle time, scrap and rework rates, customer satisfaction, revenues, and quality).

Gaining Acceptance for IT-Induced Change to Work

The changes described in this chapter no doubt alter the frames of reference of organizational employees and may be a major source of concern for them. Employees may resist the changes if they view the changes as negatively affecting them. For example, in data-driven algorithmic-driven systems that incorporate machine learning (ML), the employees might not understand the opaque, unexplained predictions that the systems produce, or they may notice that new systems (or chatbots like Google's Bard) are "learning" from bad data. Even when AI systems report high performance according to standard AI accuracy measures, they may be resisted. For example, after five ML-based AI diagnostic tools had been purchased by an urban hospital, medical specialists (e.g., pediatric, chest, and neuro-radiologists), didn't have confidence in the caliber of the "experts" providing ML training data, the tools' fit with their own setting or the tools' failure to consider prior images. As a result of careful comparison of the tools' results with the diagnoses of the hospital specialists, two tools were discarded and the other three were studied for ways to improve their diagnoses.[15] Hence, bad results can erode trust in a new system and result in employees resisting the change.

[15] Sarah Lebovitz, Natalia Levina, and Hila Lifshitz-Assaf, "Is AI Ground Truth Really True? The Dangers of Training and Evaluating AI Tools based on Experts' Know-What," *MIS Quarterly* 45, no. 3 (2021): 1501–1525.

In the case of a new information system that they do not fully understand or are not prepared to operate, employees may resist in several ways:

- They may deny that the system is up and running.
- They may sabotage the system by distorting or otherwise altering inputs.
- They may try to convince themselves, and others, that the new system really will not change the status quo.
- They may refuse to use the new system when its usage is voluntary.

Managing Change

To help avoid these resistance behaviors, John Kotter[16] builds upon Kurt Lewin's[17] change model of unfreezing, changing, and refreezing. Kotter recommends eight specific steps to bring about change. Kotter's steps are related to Lewin's changes and are listed in Figure 5.6.

Managers can keep these eight steps in mind as they introduce change into their workplaces. It is important for managers to make clear why the change is being made before it is implemented, and they must follow the change with reinforcement behaviors such as rewarding those employees who have successfully adopted new desired behaviors.

Technology Acceptance Model and Its Variants

To avoid the negative consequences of resistance to change, those implementing change must actively manage the change process and gain acceptance for new IS. To help explain how to gain acceptance for a new technology, Professor Fred Davis and his colleagues developed the Technology Acceptance Model (TAM).

Lewin's Stage	Unfreezing	Changing	Refreezing
Definition	Creating motivation to change	Providing stakeholders with new information, systems, products, or services	Reinforcing change by integrating stakeholders' changed behaviors and attitudes into new operations resulting from change
Kotter's Steps	**1.** Establish a sense of urgency: Create a compelling reason why change is needed. **2.** Create the guiding coalition: Select a team with enough expertise and power to lead the change. **3.** Develop a vision and strategy: Use the vision and strategic plan to guide the change process. **4.** Communicate the change vision: Devise and implement a communication strategy to consistently convey the vision.	**5.** Empower broad-based action: Encourage risk-taking and creative problem solving to overcome barriers to change. **6.** Generate short-term wins: Celebrate short-term improvements and reward contributions to change effort. **7.** Consolidate gains and produce more change: Use credibility from short-term wins to promote more change so that change cascades throughout the organization.	**8.** Anchor new approaches in the culture: Reinforce change by highlighting areas in which new behaviors and processes are linked to success.

FIGURE 5.6 Stages and steps in change management.
Source: Adapted from John Kotter, *Leading Change* (Boston, MA: Harvard Business School Press, 1996).

[16] John Kotter, *Leading Change* (Boston, MA: Harvard Business School Press, 1996).

[17] Kurt Lewin, "Frontiers in Group Dynamics II. Channels of Group Life; Social Planning and Action Research," *Human Relations* 1, no. 22 (1947): 143–153.

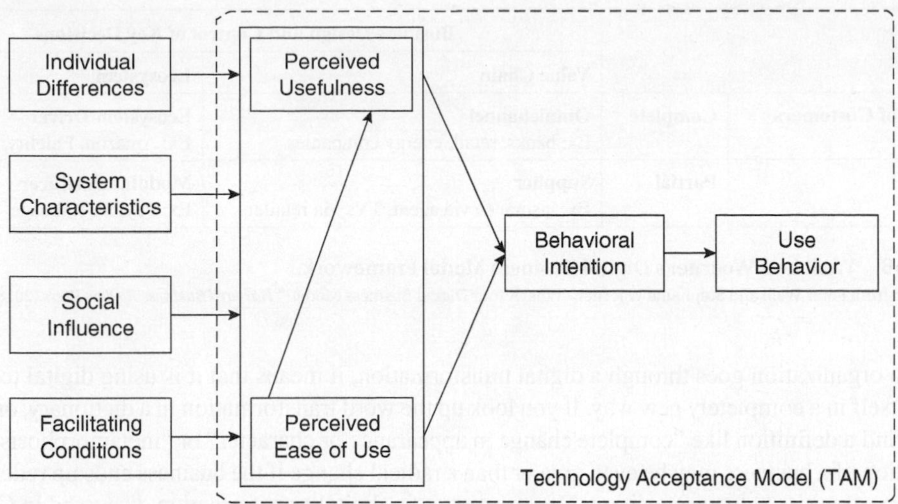

FIGURE 5.7 Simplified technology acceptance model (TAM3).
Source: Viswanath Venkatesh and Hillol Bala, "Technology Acceptance Model 3 and a Research Agenda on Interventions," *Decision Sciences* 39, no. 2 (2008): 276.

Many variations of TAM exist (i.e., TAM2, UTAUT), but its most basic form is displayed on the right-hand side in Figure 5.7. TAM suggests that managers cannot get employees to use a system until they want to use it. To convince employees to want to use the system, managers may need to employ unfreezing tactics to change employee attitudes about the system. Attitudes may change if employees believe that the system will allow them to do more or better work for the same amount of effort (perceived usefulness), and that it is easy to use. Training, documentation, and user support consultants are external variables that may help explain the usefulness of the system and make it easier to use.

The left-hand side of Figure 5.7 provides four categories of determinants of perceived usefulness and perceived ease of use from the point of view of organizational users. Specifically, they are *individual differences* (e.g., gender, age), *system characteristics* (e.g., output quality and job relevance that help individuals develop favorable or unfavorable views about the system), *social influence* (e.g., subjective norms), and *facilitating conditions* (e.g., top management support). TAM assumes that system use is under the control of the individual users. When employees are mandated to use the system, they may use it in the short run, but over the long run, negative consequences of their resistance may surface. Thus, gaining acceptance of the system is important, even in those situations where it is mandated.

Digital Transformation

> *"Digital transformation involves fundamentally rethinking an organization's processes, services, and roles from a technology-enabled perspective. . . The process of how organizations can successfully intertwine their digital and workforce transformations, especially at scale, is far less understood. This is an area where insights from exemplar cases are much needed." (p. 1)*[18]

The quote above is made by part of a research team that scrutinized a digital transformation of a hospital in Australia. The hospital rolled out an electronic medical record system that integrated computerized order entry, prescribing, decision support, analytics, and research, in an ecosystem throughout the state of Queensland. The effort won innovation awards, showing some early evidence of success.[19]

[18] Rebekah Eden, Andrew Burton-Jones, Veronica Casey, and Michael Draheim, "Digital Transformation Requires Workforce Transformation," *MIS Quarterly Executive* 18, no. 1 (March 2019): 1–18.

[19] Eden, R., Burton-Jones, A., Ballantine, C., Donovan, R., McKavanagh, D., Staib, A., and Sullivan, C., The Digital Transformation Journey of a Large Australian Hospital: A Teaching Case. Communications of the Association for Information Systems, 51, 2022, paper 34.

		Business Design and Control of Key Decisions	
		Value Chain	Ecosystem
Knowledge of Customers	Complete	**Omnichannel** Ex: banks, retail, energy companies	**Ecosystem Driver** Ex: Amazon, Fidelity, WeChat
	Partial	**Supplier** Ex: insurance via agent, TVs via retailer	**Modular Producer** Ex: PayPal, Kabbage

FIGURE 5.8 Weill and Woerner's Digital Business Model Framework.
Source: Adapted from Peter Weill and Stephanie Woerner, "What's Your Digital Business Model?" *Harvard Business Review Press* (2018) page 8.

When an organization goes through a digital transformation, it means that it is using digital technologies to identify itself in a completely new way. If you look up the word transformation in a dictionary, or Google it, you might find a definition like "complete change in appearance or character" or "metamorphosis." A digital transformation of a business may be even greater than a radical change if the business ends up redefining (and not just supporting) its value proposition. One example of a digital transformation discussed in Chapter 1 is when the organization's business model changes from a product orientation to a service orientation.[20]

Digital technologies have enabled managers to create entirely new **digital business models**. Research by Peter Weill and Stephanie Woerner[21] suggests that these new business models have changed from value chains to digital ecosystems and enabled managers to have a razor-sharp understanding of customer needs. Their work suggests that digital business models fall into one of four types based on knowledge needed/known of the customer and business design and control of key decisions. Figure 5.8 summarizes these model types.

Omnichannel companies allow diverse methods to serve customers (apps, websites, or face-to-face). *Ecosystem drivers* use digital technologies to collect and use customer data from all interactions with customers, and add complementary products even if they are offered by competitors. In so doing, they become the key company in their space. *Suppliers* sell through others by being the low-cost producer in the value chain of the company who has the primary connection with the customer. *Modular producers* also offer products and services primarily to others who manage the ultimate customers, but they can plug in easily to different value chain models. In sum, digital transformation means understanding where a company is today and where it wants to be as digital technologies force examination of more traditional business models.

A subsequent model by Weill and Woerner focuses on becoming ready for the future, by describing how to transform the user's experience and also transform operational efficiency, to become "future ready." Their 2022 book provides recommendations for various paths from poor experience and efficiency to becoming future ready.[22]

Techniques for Understanding Business Processes

To try and make changes, it's important to begin by understanding the business processes before trying to work with them. Two tools can be used for this task. First, documenting the workflows and processes is an important step, because counting on simple observations will provide only anecdotal evidence, missing the richness of more complete information. Then, there are tools to use for keeping organized and being more thorough about the changes. These next two sections cover those two areas.

Workflow and Mapping Processes

Workflow in its most basic meaning is the series of connected tasks and activities performed by people and computers that together form a business process. Consideration of workflow is a way to assess a cross-functional process. But the term *workflow* has also come to mean software products that document

[20] Markus, M. Lynne, and Frantz Rowe. "The Digital Transformation Conundrum: Labels, Definitions, Phenomena, and Theories," *Journal of the Association for Information Systems* 24, no. 2 (2023), 328–335.

[21] Peter Weill and Stephanie Woerner, "What's Your Digital Business Model?" *Harvard Business Review Press* (2018).

[22] Woerner, S. L., Weill, P., and Sebastian, I. M., *Future Ready: The Four Pathways to Capturing Digital Value* (Harvard Business Press, 2022).

and automate processes. Workflow software facilitates the design of business processes and creates a digital workflow diagram. Workflow software lets the manager diagram answers to questions such as how a process will work, who will do what, what the information system will do, and what decisions will be made and by whom. When combined with business process management (BPM) modules, processes can be managed, monitored, and modified.

The tool used to understand a business process is a **workflow diagram**, which shows a picture, or map, of the sequence and detail of each process step. More than 200 products are available to help managers draw the workflow. The objective of process mapping is to understand and communicate the dimensions of the current process. Typically, process engineers begin the process mapping procedure by defining the scope, mission, and boundaries of the business process. Next, engineers develop a high-level overview flowchart of the process and a detailed flow diagram of everything that happens in the process. The diagram uses active verbs to describe activities and identifies all process actors, inputs, and outputs. The engineers verify the detailed diagram for accuracy with the actors in the process and adjust it accordingly.

A detailed blueprint for proceeding can be found in Ross, Beath, and Mocker's recent book *Designed for Digital*.[23] Their process begins with building an operational IT backbone. Second is to build a digital platform on top of the backbone, with the proper components to make it work. Third, an external developer platform needs to be assembled, which allows an ecosystem of third parties to form. Fourth, collect insights from customers and suppliers that teams can use to find problems and seek solutions, sometimes through experimentation. Last, an accountability framework allows coordination of all the new features and components.

Business Process Management (BPM)

Thinking about a business as a set of processes has become more common, but managing the business as a set of processes is another story. Some claim that to have truly dynamic or agile business processes requires a well-defined and optimized set of IT processes, tools, and skills called *BPM suites*. These systems include process modeling, simulation, code generation, process execution, monitoring, and integration capabilities for both company-based and web-based systems to document and redesign workflow and business processes. The tools allow an organization to actively manage and improve its processes from beginning to end. BPM software automates, executes, and monitors business processes, making it possible for managers and analysts to build and modify processes quickly and without having to know programming languages that historically were necessary to create the code needed to run a process.

Enterprise Rent-A-Car is one of the largest car rental companies in the world with over 65,000 employees at 7,000 locations worldwide. Enterprise uses BPM from Appian to model, manage, and streamline its IT-based processes. Enterprise had used a manual system for IT service requests, which was not scalable and could not be automated. The IT staff developed a model that worked, with very little coding, around the world in local languages.[24] The result was a BPM-based system called Request Online, that provided better management capabilities and created a common platform for rapid change and capacity for future growth. That proved critical when Enterprise acquired National Car Rental and Alamo Rent A Car, creating much more demand for Request Online. Enterprise was able to shift development to less costly IT staff who could make process modifications directly through the BPM. Finally, the usability of the system was increased as the BPM facilitated the creation of customized interfaces based on characteristics of the specific users.

Business process management (BPM) systems provide a way to build, execute, and monitor automated processes that are intelligent, dynamic, and may go across organizational boundaries. BPM systems offer process designers a number of design and management capabilities (see Figure 5.9).

Types of Enterprise Systems

Information technology is a critical component of almost every business process today because information flow is at its core. A class of IT applications called an **enterprise system** is a set of IS tools that many organizations use to enable this information flow within and between processes across the organization.

[23] Ross, J. W., Beath, C. M., and Mocker, M., *Designed for Digital: How to Architect Your Business for Sustained Success* (MIT Press, 2019).

[24] Adapted from https://appian.com/about/explore/customers/all-customers/enterprise-rent-a-car.html (accessed June 12, 2023).

BPM Capability	Description
Business Process Automation	Capabilities to automate the interaction of the people, machines, and other components of the process to create repeatable and predictable task execution
Human Task Management and Collaboration	Capabilities for process stakeholders to initiate tasks and processes as needed and to collaborate with each other
Monitoring and Business Alignment	Capabilities to plan, model, coordinate, govern, and monitor the life cycle of business processes in real time
Business Rules and Decision Management	Capabilities to manage rule engines, recommendation engines, and decision management engines to ensure operational decisions follow company policies
Analytics	Capabilities to use process and business data for insights, predictions, and prescriptions to aid in decisions and trigger automatic responses in applications
Interoperability	Capabilities to connect to external applications that might provide additional features and services (for example, Robotic Processing Automation (RPA) tools)
Process Discovery and Optimization	Capabilities that speed up the time necessary to discover and optimize behaviors needed to improve business processes (for example, analyzing historic information or simulating proposed behaviors of process users)
Context and Behavioral History	Capabilities to manage data about the context and behavior of past versions of the process

FIGURE 5.9 Sample capabilities of BPM.
Source: Adapted from the Gartner Report on BPM: "Magic Quadrant for Intelligent Business Process Management Suites," ID G00345694, published January 30, 2019 by Gartner, Inc.

These tools help ensure integration and coordination across functions such as accounting, production, customer management, and supplier management. Some are designed to support a particular industry such as health care, retail, and manufacturing.

Organizational computing groups faced the challenge of linking and maintaining the patchwork of loosely overlapping, redundant systems. In the 1980s and 1990s, software companies in a number of countries, including the United States, Germany, and the Netherlands, began developing integrated software packages that used a common database and cut across organizational systems. Some of these packages were developed from administrative systems (e.g., finance and human resources), and others evolved from materials resource planning (MRP) in manufacturing. These comprehensive software packages that incorporate all modules needed to run the operations of a business are called **enterprise information systems (EIS)** or simply *enterprise systems.* Enterprise systems include ERP, supply chain management (SCM), CRM, and **product life cycle management (PLM)** systems (see Figure 5.10). Some companies develop proprietary enterprise systems to support mission-critical processes when they believe these processes give them an advantage and using a vendor-supplied system would jeopardize that advantage. Other enterprise systems may be developed specifically to integrate organizational processes. Figure 5.10 describes some examples of the processes supported by an enterprise system.

Two of the largest vendors of enterprise systems are German-based SAP and California-based Oracle. Initially, SAP defined the ERP software space, and Oracle had the database system supporting it. But more

Enterprise System	Sample Processes
Enterprise resource planning (ERP)	Financial management (accounting, financial close, invoice to pay process, receivable management); human capital management (talent management, payrolls, succession planning); operations management (procurement, logistics, requisition invoice payment, parts inventory)
Customer relationship management (CRM)	Marketing (brand management, campaign management); lead management; loyalty program management; sales planning and forecasting; territory and account management; customer service and support (claims, returns, warranties)
Supply chain management (SCM)	Supply chain design; order fulfillment; warehouse management; demand planning, forecasting; sales and operations planning; service parts planning; source-to-pay/procurement process; supplier life cycle management; supply contract management
Product life cycle management (PLM)	Innovation management (strategy and planning, idea capture and management, program/project management); product development and management; product compliance management

FIGURE 5.10 Enterprise systems and examples of processes they support.

recently, SAP has moved to its own database system, and Oracle has acquired many other smaller vendors, creating their own suite of enterprise software solutions.

Enterprise Resource Planning (ERP)

Enterprise resource planning (ERP) was designed to help large companies manage the fragmentation of information stored in hundreds of individual desktop, department, and business unit computers across the organization. These modules offered the IS department in many large organizations an option for switching from underperforming, obsolete mainframe systems to client–server environments designed to handle the changing business demands of their operational counterparts. Many firms moved from their troubled systems in the late 1990s to avoid the year 2000 (Y2K) problem[25] and to standardize processes across their businesses.

The next generation of enterprise system emerged: ERP II systems. Whereas an ERP makes company information immediately available to all departments throughout the company, ERP II also makes company information immediately available to *external stakeholders*, such as customers and partners. ERP II enables e-business by integrating business processes between an enterprise and its trading partners. More recently, a move to better manage IS using the cloud has again called into question the design of some business processes.

ERP III systems include all ERP II functionality plus social and collaboration features (see Figure 5.11). A good example is Chatter from Salesforce.com,[26] which includes an activity stream interface (similar to Facebook) for employees with easy connections to the firm's information in its ERP. An *activity stream* is a flow of information recording all transactions and interactions of people and processes connected to the system. SAP's ERP solution includes SAP ERP Financials, SAP ERP Human Capital Management,

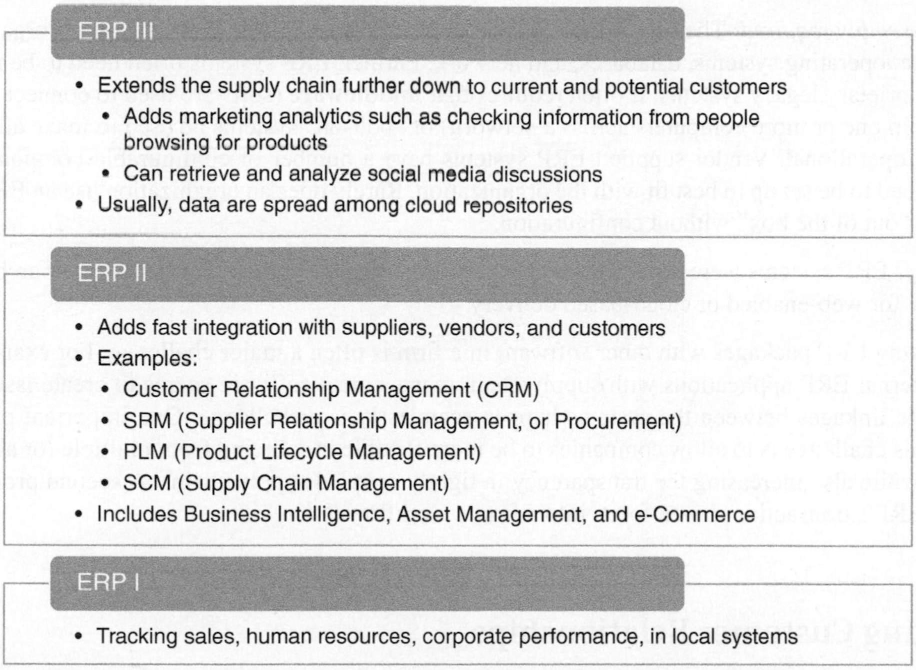

ERP III

- Extends the supply chain further down to current and potential customers
  - Adds marketing analytics such as checking information from people browsing for products
  - Can retrieve and analyze social media discussions
- Usually, data are spread among cloud repositories

ERP II

- Adds fast integration with suppliers, vendors, and customers
- Examples:
  - Customer Relationship Management (CRM)
  - SRM (Supplier Relationship Management, or Procurement)
  - PLM (Product Lifecycle Management)
  - SCM (Supply Chain Management)
- Includes Business Intelligence, Asset Management, and e-Commerce

ERP I

- Tracking sales, human resources, corporate performance, in local systems

FIGURE 5.11 Enterprise systems and the processes they automate.

Sources: Adapted from Shing Hin Yeung, http://commons.wikimedia.org/wiki/File:ERP_Modules.png (accessed June 12, 2023); Luminita Hurbean and Doina Fotache, "ERP III: The Promise of a New Generation," Proceedings of the IE 2014 International Conference, www.conferenceie.ase.ro; Julian Vasilev, "The change from ERP to ERP III systems," 3rd International Conference on Application of Information and Communication Technology and Statistics in Economy and Education, December 6–7th, 2013, 382–384.

---

[25] The Y2K problem was of great concern at the end of the 1990s because many old systems used two digits instead of four digits to represent the year, making it impossible to distinguish between years such as 2025 and 1925.

[26] See http://www.salesforce.com/chatter/overview/ (accessed August 27, 2015).

and SAP ERP Operations. Oracle's ERP solution, EnterpriseOne, offers these same functions. Both vendors have integrated their ERP solutions with their supply chain/logistics solutions, their CRM solutions, and several other modules that make them a one-stop shop for software that provides the backbone of an enterprise.

Characteristics of ERP Systems

ERP systems have several characteristics[27]:

- *Integration:* ERP systems are designed to seamlessly integrate information flows throughout the company. ERP systems are configured by installing various modules, such as:
  - Manufacturing (materials management, inventory, plant maintenance, production planning, routing, shipping, purchasing, etc.)
  - Accounting (general ledger, accounts payable, accounts receivable, cash management, forecasting, cost accounting, profitability analysis, etc.)
  - Human resources (employee data, position management, skills inventory, time accounting, payroll, travel expenses, etc.)
  - Sales (order entry, order management, delivery support, sales planning, pricing, etc.)
- *Packages:* ERP systems are usually commercial packages purchased from software vendors. Unlike many packages, ERP systems usually require long-term relationships with software vendors because the complex systems must typically be modified on a continuing basis to meet the organization's needs.
- *Best practices:* ERP systems reflect an industry's best (or at least "very good") practices for generic business processes. To implement them, businesses often must change their processes in some way to accommodate the software.
- *Some assembly required:* The ERP system is software that needs to be integrated with the organization's hardware, operating systems, databases, and network. Further, ERP systems often need to be integrated with proprietary legacy systems. It often requires that **middleware** (software used to connect processes running in one or more computers across a network) or "bolt-on" systems be used to make all the components operational. Vendor-supplied ERP systems have a number of configurable components, too, which need to be set up to best fit with the organization. Rarely does an organization use an ERP system directly "out of the box" without configuration.
- *Evolving:* ERP systems were designed first for mainframe systems, then for client–server architectures, and now for web-enabled or cloud-based delivery.

Integrating ERP packages with other software in a firm is often a major challenge. For example, integrating internal ERP applications with supply chain management software seems to create issues. Making sure the linkages between the systems happen seamlessly is a challenge. One important problem in meeting this challenge is to allow companies to be more flexible in sourcing from multiple (or alternative) suppliers while also increasing the transparency in tightly coupled supply chains. A second problem is to integrate ERP's transaction-driven focus into a firm's workflow.[28]

Managing Customer Relationships

A type of software package that is increasingly considered an enterprise system is a customer relationship management system. **Customer relationship management (CRM)** is a set of software programs that supports management activities performed to obtain, enhance relationships with, and retain customers. They include sales, support, and service processes. Today, CRM has come to mean the enterprise systems that support these processes, and the term is used interchangeably with the set of activities.

[27] M. Lynne Markus and Cornelis Tanis, "The Enterprise System Experience—From Adoption to Success," *Framing the Domains of IT Management: Projecting the Future through the Past*, ed. R. Zmud (Cincinnati, OH: Pinaflex Educational Resources, 2000): 176–179.

[28] Amit Basu and Akhil Kumar, "Research Commentary: Workflow Management Issues in e-Business," *Information Systems Research* 13, no. 1 (March 2002): 1–14.

CRM processes create ways to learn more about customers' needs and behaviors with the objective of developing stronger relationships. CRM systems consist of technological components as well as many pieces of information about customers, sales, marketing effectiveness, responsiveness, and market trends. Optimized CRM processes and systems can lead to better customer service, more efficient call centers, product cross-selling, simplified sales and marketing efforts, more efficient sales transactions, and increased customer revenues. The goal of CRM is to provide more effective interaction with customers and bring together all information the company has on a customer.

The leading CRM software vendor is Salesforce.com, with almost 24% of the market in 2021, and SAP, Oracle, and Microsoft each have just over 5% market share.[29] The systems have varying levels of features, compatibility with other programs, and user experience. CRM systems usually include modules for pricing, sales force automation, sales order management, support activities, customer self-service, and service management, marketing support such as resource and brand management, campaign management, real-time offer management, loyalty management, and e-marketing. Often there is an e-commerce module that facilitates personalized interface and self-service applications for customers. Managers who seek a CRM system for their organizations should compare the features and integration with other enterprise systems of these and other solutions provided by niche vendors who specialize in systems optimized for specific industry applications.

CRMs capture and store information about customer preferences so as to better meet customer needs and enhance the customer experience. For example, movie site Netflix stores all the streams and product reviews a customer makes in its CRM. Using that information, the site recommends additional films the customer might enjoy based on analysis of the data in the CRM.

Managing Supply Chains

Another type of enterprise system in common use is a **supply chain management (SCM)** system, which manages the integrated supply chain. Business processes are not just internal to a company. With the help of information technologies, many processes are linked across companies with a companion process at a customer or supplier, creating an integrated supply chain. Technology, especially web-based technology, allows the supply chains of a company's customers and suppliers to be linked through a single network that optimizes costs and opportunities for all companies in the supply chain. By sharing information across the network, guesswork about order quantities for raw materials and products can be reduced, and suppliers can make sure they have enough on hand if demand for their products unexpectedly rises.

The supply chain of a business typically includes the procurement of materials or components, the activities to turn these materials into larger subsystems or final products, and the distribution of these final products to warehouses or customers. But with the increase in IS use, the supply chain may also include product design, product planning, contract management, logistics, and sourcing. Globalization of business and ubiquity of communication networks and information technology have enabled businesses to use suppliers from almost anywhere in the world. At the same time, this has created an additional level of complexity for managing the supply chain. *Supply chain integration* is the approach of technically linking supply chains of vendors and customers to streamline the process and to increase efficiency and accuracy.

Without such linking, a temporary increase in demand from a retailer might become interpreted by its suppliers as permanent, and the changes can become magnified by each supplier up the chain when each supplier attempts to add another percent or two just to be "safe." Those erratic and wild changes are called the *bullwhip effect*. Linking synchronizes all suppliers to the same demand increase up and down the chain and prevents that effect.

Integrated supply chains have several challenges, primarily resulting from different degrees of integration and coordination among supply chain members.[30] These challenges make them excellent candidates for CRM. At the most basic level, there is the issue of information integration. Partners must agree on the type of information to share, the format of that information, the technological standards they both

[29] Lionel Sujay Vailshery, "Market share of CRM leading vendors worldwide 2016–2021," Statista, June 13, 2022, https://www-statista-com.pitt.idm.oclc.org/statistics/972598/crm-applications-vendors-market-share-worldwide/ (accessed June 12, 2023).

[30] Hau Lee and Seungjin Whang, "E-Business and Supply Chain Integration," Stanford University Global Supply Chain Management Forum (November 2001).

use to share it, and the security they use to ensure that only authorized partners access it. Trust must be established so the partners can solve higher-level issues that may arise. At the next level is the issue of synchronized planning. At this level, the partners must agree on a joint system of planning, forecasting, and replenishment. The partners, having already agreed on what information to share, now have to agree on what to do with it. The third level can be described as workflow coordination—the coordination, integration, and automation of critical business processes between partners. For some supply chains, this might mean simply using a third party to link the procurement process to the preferred vendors or to communities of vendors who compete virtually for the business. For others, it might be a more complex process of integrating order processing and payment systems.

Another challenge became evident during the COVID-19 pandemic, where supply chains were so tightly integrated and distributed worldwide that firms often found themselves dependent on a small number of partners, leading to shortages in components for many products. The auto industry suffered greatly, as electronic components for cars were difficult to obtain. Auto sales were constrained due to a lack of supply, often with cars 99% built but awaiting some components. Prices of used cars soared and there were long waiting lists for new cars. At the same time, BEVs (battery electric vehicles) and PHEVs (plug-in hybrid electric vehicles) were gaining popularity but were also in short supply. In 2022, the US Inflation Reduction Act created larger incentives for those vehicles, but many buyers were forced to join long waiting lists.

Integrated supply chains are truly global in nature. Tesla Motors, a pioneer in electric powered cars, had originally planned the production of a luxury roadster for the U.S. market based on an integrated global supply chain. The 1,000-pound battery packs for the cars were to be manufactured in Thailand, shipped to Britain for installation, and then shipped to the United States where they would be assembled into cars. However, because of the extensive costs associated with shipping the batteries more than 5,000 miles, and consumer rebates under the Inflation Reduction Act's incentives for domestic sourcing, Tesla decided to make the batteries and assemble the cars near its headquarters in California. Darryl Siry, Tesla's Senior Vice President of Global Sales, Marketing, and Service explains that shipping alone was instrumental in that decision: "It was kind of a no-brain decision for us. A major reason was to avoid the transportation costs, which are terrible." Economists warn managers to expect the "neighborhood effect" in which factories may be built closer to component suppliers and consumers to reduce transportation costs. This effect may apply not only to cars and steel but also to chickens and avocados and a wide range of other items.[31]

Enterprise System Issues

There are several issues that need to be addressed when deciding to use enterprise systems and implementing them. The advantages and disadvantages of enterprise systems should be fully assessed before an organization decides to implement one. Which situations are appropriate for the enterprise system driving a business transformation, as well as the challenges of integrating them across organizations, should also be considered.

Advantages and Disadvantages of Enterprise Systems

One major benefit of enterprise systems is that they represent a set of industry best practices. One story relayed to the authors described a large university that had suffered for years with inconsistent, incomplete, and immature processes. The university's leaders announced in advance that rather than customize a new ERP to fit the old processes, the directive was to replace them with the ones created by the new ERP. As a result, the ERP's best practices dramatically improved the university's ability to provide information services to faculty, staff, and students and also to track the entire "life cycle" of people from initial inquiry to graduation and beyond.

Another major benefit of an enterprise system is that all modules of the information system easily communicate with each other, offering enormous efficiencies over stand-alone systems. In business,

[31] Larry Rohter, "Shipping Costs Start to Crimp Globalization," *The New York Times*, World Business, August 3, 2008, http://www.nytimes.com/2008/08/03/business/worldbusiness/03global.html (accessed June 12, 2023).

information from one functional area is often needed by another area. For example, an inventory system stores information about vendors who supply specific parts. This same information is required by the accounts payable system, which pays vendors for their goods. It makes sense to integrate these two systems to have a single accurate record of vendors and to use an enterprise system to facilitate that integration.

Because of the focus on integration, enterprise systems are useful tools for an organization seeking to centralize operations and decision making. Redundant data entry and duplicate data may be eliminated; standards for numbering, naming, and coding may be enforced; and data and records can be cleaned up through standardization. Further, the enterprise system can reinforce the use of standard procedures across different locations.

The obvious benefits notwithstanding, implementing an enterprise system represents an enormous amount of work. For example, if an organization has allowed both the manufacturing and the accounting departments to keep their own records of vendors, then most likely these records are kept in somewhat different forms (one department may enter the vendor's name as IBM, the other as International Business Machines or even IBM Corp., all of which make it difficult to integrate the databases). Making matters worse, a simple data item's name itself might be stored differently in different systems. In one system, it might be named Phone_No, but in another, it might be simply Phone. Such inconsistencies in data items and values must be recognized and fixed so that the enterprise system can provide optimal advantage.

Moreover, even though enterprise systems are flexible and customizable to a point, most also require business processes to be redesigned to achieve optimal performance of the integrated modules. It is rare that an off-the-shelf system is perfectly harmonious with an existing business process; the software usually requires significant modification or customization to fit with the existing processes, or the processes must change to fit the software. In most installations of enterprise systems, both take place. The system is usually customized when it is installed in a business by setting a number of parameters. Many ERP projects are massive undertakings, requiring formal, structured project management tools.[32]

All systems make assumptions about how the business processes work, and at some level, customization is not possible. For example, one major Fortune 500 company refused to implement a vendor's enterprise system because the company manufactured products in lots of "one," and the vendor's system would not handle the volume this company generated. If the company had decided to use the ERP, a complete overhaul of its manufacturing process in a way that executives were unwilling to do would have been necessary.

Implementing enterprise systems requires organizations to make changes beyond just the processes, but also in their organization structure. Recall from Chapter 1 that the Information Systems Strategy Triangle suggests that implementing an information system must be accompanied with appropriate organizational changes to be effective. Implementing an enterprise system is no different. For example, who will be responsible for entering the vendor information that was formerly kept in two locations? How will that information be entered into the enterprise system? The answer to such simple operational questions often requires managers to modify business processes minimally and more likely to redesign them completely to accommodate the information system.

Enterprise systems are also risky. A number of enterprise system horror stories demonstrates this risk. For example, American LaFrance (ALF), the manufacturer of highly customized emergency vehicles, declared bankruptcy, blaming its IT vendor and its ERP implementation. The problems with the implementation kept ALF from being able to manufacture many preordered vehicles.[33] Two months after the installation of a new ERP system, the Fort Worth Police Officers Association complained that paychecks were not being received correctly or on a timely basis by officers. Some officers had not been paid since the installation, and others were shortchanged in their paychecks because the new system was not able to handle odd hours and shift work.

Furthermore, enterprise systems and the organizational changes they induce tend to come with a hefty price tag. In addition to the initial acquisition and implementation costs of ERP systems, there are also additional hidden costs in the form of technical and business changes likely to be necessary when

[32] See Chapter 11 for a discussion of formal structured project management tools.

[33] For additional examples of IT failures in general and enterprise systems failures in particular, visit the blog written by Michael Krigsman, http://blogs.zdnet.com/projectfailures/.

Advantages	Disadvantages
• Represent "best practices" • Allow modules throughout the organization to communicate with each other • Enable centralized decision making • Eliminate redundant data entry • Enable standardized procedures in different locations	• Require enormous amount of work • Require redesign of business practices for maximum benefit • Require organizational changes • Have high risk of failure • Have very high cost • Are sold as a suite, not individual modules

FIGURE 5.12 Advantages and disadvantages of enterprise systems.

implementing an enterprise system. These included project management, user training, and IT support costs.[34] Some surveys uncovered negative impacts on performance including cost overruns, implementation delays, and disruption in business processes such as shipping products on time.[35]

One reason that ERP systems are so expensive is that they are sold as a suite, such as financials or manufacturing, and not as individual modules. Because buying modules separately is discouraged, companies implementing ERP software often find the price of modules they won't use hidden in the cost of the suite.[36]

A set of advantages and disadvantages of enterprise systems is provided in Figure 5.12.

When the System Drives the Transformation

When is it appropriate to use the enterprise system to drive transformation and business process redesign, and when is it appropriate to redesign the process first and then implement an enterprise system? Although it may seem like the process should be redesigned first and then the information system aligned to the new design, there are times when it is appropriate to let the enterprise system drive business process redesign. First, when an organization is just starting out and processes do not yet exist, it is appropriate to begin with an enterprise system as a way to structure operational business processes. After all, most processes embedded in the "plain vanilla" enterprise system from a top vendor are based on the best practices of corporations that have been in business for years. A 2023 survey revealed that over 34% of organizations implemented ERP software without any customization.[37]

Second, when an organization does not rely on its operational business processes as a source of competitive advantage, then using an enterprise system's standard processes to redesign business processes is appropriate. Third, it is reasonable when the current systems are in crisis and there is not enough time, resources, or knowledge in the firm to fix them. Even though it is not an optimal situation, managers must make tough decisions about how to fix the problems. A business must have working operational processes; therefore, using an enterprise system as the basis for process design may be the only workable plan.

Likewise, it is sometimes inappropriate to let an enterprise system drive business process change. When an organization derives a strategic advantage through its operational business processes, it is usually not advisable for it to buy a vendor's enterprise system without planning on extensive (and perhaps costly) customization. Using a standard, publicly available information system that both the company and its competitors can buy from a vendor may mean that any system-related competitive advantage is lost. For example, consider a major computer manufacturer that relied on its ability to process orders faster than its competitors to gain strategic advantage. Adopting an enterprise system's standard approach would result in a loss of that advantage. Furthermore, the manufacturer might find that relying on a third party as the provider of such a strategic system would be a mistake in the long run because any problems with

[34] T. Wailgum, "Why CEOs and CFOs Hate It: ERP," CIO, April 8, 2009, https://www.cio.com/article/292419/enterprise-software-why-cfos-and-ceos-hate-it-erp.html (accessed June 12, 2023).

[35] Panorama Consulting 2023 Report, "The 2023 ERP Report," undated, https://www.panorama-consulting.com/resource-center/erp-report/ (accessed June 12, 2023); Also the 2014 Report, "Organizational Issues Number One Reason for Extended Durations," https://www.panorama-consulting.com/company/press-releases/panorama-consulting-solutions-releases-2014-erp-report/ (accessed June 12, 2023).

[36] Ibid.

[37] Panorama Consulting, 2023 Report, Ibid.

the system due to bugs or changed business needs would require negotiating with the ERP vendor for the needed changes. With a system designed in-house, the manufacturer was able to ensure complete control over the IS that drives its critical processes.

Another situation in which it would be inappropriate to let an enterprise system drive business process change is when the features of available packages and the needs of the business do not fit. An organization may use specialized processes that cannot be accommodated by the available enterprise systems. For example, many ERPs developed for discrete part manufacturing would not support some processes in paper, food, or other process industries.[38]

A third situation would result from lack of top management support, company growth, a desire for strategic flexibility, or decentralized decision making that render the enterprise system inappropriate. For example, a large manufacturing company stopped the full implementation of an enterprise system after installing the human resources module because the CIO did not think that the software would be able to keep pace with the company's extraordinary growth. Enterprise systems were also viewed as culturally inappropriate at a highly decentralized consumer products company.

Challenges for Integrating Enterprise Systems Between Companies

With the widespread use of enterprise systems, the issue of linking supplier and customer systems to the business's systems brings many challenges. As with integrated supply chains, there are issues of deciding what to share, how to share it, and what to do with it when the sharing takes place. There are also issues of security and agreement on encryption or other measures to protect data integrity as well as to ensure that only authorized parties have access.

Some companies have tried to reduce the complexity of this integration by insisting on standards either at the industry level or at the system level. An example of an industry-level standard is the bar coding used by all who do business in the consumer products industry. An example of a system-level standard is the use of SAP or Oracle to provide the ERP system used by both supplier and customer. And the increasing use of cloud-based systems with standard interfaces makes the integration easier.

SUMMARY

- Most business processes today have a significant IS component to them. Either the process is completely executed through software, or an important information component complements the physical execution of the process. Transforming business, therefore, involves rethinking the IS that support business processes.
- IS can enable or impede business process change. IS enable change by providing both the tools to implement the change and the tools on which the change is based. IS can impede change, particularly when the process flow is mismatched with the capabilities of the IS.
- To understand the role IS plays in digital transformation, one must take a business process rather than a functional (silo) perspective. Business processes are well-defined, ordered sets of tasks characterized by a beginning and an end, sets of associated metrics, and cross-functional boundaries. Most businesses operate business processes even if their organization charts are structured by functions rather than by processes.
- Agile business processes are designed to be easily reconfigurable. Dynamic processes are designed to automatically update themselves as conditions change. Both types of processes require a high degree of IS, which makes the task of changing the process a software activity rather than a physical activity.
- Making changes in business processes typically involves either incremental or radical change. Incremental change with TQM and Six Sigma implies an evolutionary approach. Radical change with a BPR approach, on the other hand, is more sudden. Either approach can be disruptive to the normal flow of the business; hence, strong project management skills are needed.

[38] Markus and Tanis, "The Enterprise System Experience," 176–179.

- To gain acceptance of a new technology, potential users must exhibit a favorable attitude toward the technology. In the case of IS, users' beliefs about its perceived usefulness and perceived ease of use color their attitudes about the system. Kotter provides some suggested steps for change management that are related to Lewin's three stages of change: unfreezing, change, and refreezing.
- A digital transformation is defined as the use of digital technology by an organization to redefine (and not just support) its value proposition and which leads the organization to identify itself in a new way.
- Digital business models disrupt traditional business models by enabling companies to better understand their customers, offer new and innovative products and services, and dynamically leverage ecosystems.
- BPM systems are used to help managers design, control, and document business processes and ultimately the workflow in an organization. There are tools available to understand and modify business processes.
- An enterprise system is a large information system that provides the core functionality needed to run a business. These systems are typically implemented to help organizations share data between divisions. However, in some cases, enterprise systems are used to effect organizational transformation by imposing a set of assumptions on the business processes they manage.
- An ERP system is a type of enterprise system used to manage resources including financial, human resources, and operations.
- A CRM system is a type of enterprise system used to manage the processes related to customers and the relationships developed with customers.
- An integrated supply chain is often managed using an SCM system, an enterprise system that crosses company boundaries and connects vendors and suppliers with organizations to synchronize and streamline planning and deliver products to all members of the supply chain.
- IS are useful as tools to both enable and manage business change and digital transformation. The general manager must take care to ensure that consequences of the tools themselves are well understood and well managed.

KEY TERMS

agile business processes, 108
business process management (BPM), 115
business process perspective, 106
business process reengineering (BPR), 109
customer relationship management (CRM), 118
digital business models, 114
digital transformation, 103
dynamic business processes, 108
enterprise information systems (EIS), 116
enterprise resource planning (ERP), 117
enterprise system, 115
functional perspective, 109
middleware, 118
process perspective, 106
process, 106
product life cycle management (PLM), 116
reengineering, 109
six Sigma, 110
supply chain management (SCM), 119
total quality management (TQM), 110
workflow diagram, 115
workflow, 114

FOUNDATIONAL READINGS

Davenport, T. H., *Process Innovation: Reengineering Work Through Information Technology* (Harvard Business School Press, 1992).

Fred Davis, "Perceived Usefulness, Perceived Ease of Use, and User Acceptance of Information Technology," *MIS Quarterly* 13, no. 3 (1989), 319–339.

Fred Davis, Richard P. Bagozzi, and Paul R. Warshaw, "User Acceptance of Computer Technology: A Comparison of Two Theoretical Models," *Management Science* 35, no. 8 (1989), 982–1003.

Michael Hammer. "Reengineering Work: Don't Automate, Obliterate," *Harvard Business Review* 68, no. 4 (July–August 1990), 104–112.

Michael Hammer and James Champy, *Reengineering the Corporation: A Manifesto for Business Revolution* (Harper Business, 1993).

John Kotter, *Leading Change* (Boston, MA: Harvard Business School Press, 1996).

Kurt Lewin, "Frontiers in Group Dynamics II. Channels of Group Life; Social Planning and Action Research," *Human Relations* 1, no. 22 (1947), 143–153.

Ranganathan, C., Balaji, S. and Coleman, T. "IT-Led Process Reengineering: How Sloan Valve Redesigned Its New Product Development Process," *MIS Quarterly Executive* 10, no. 2 (June 2011), 81–92.

DISCUSSION QUESTIONS

1. Why would a manager prefer radical redesign of business processes over incremental improvement? Why do you think reengineering was so popular when it was first introduced?
2. Off-the-shelf enterprise IS often force an organization to redesign its business processes. What are the critical success factors to make sure the implementation of an enterprise system is successful?
3. ERP systems are usually designed around best practices. But as discussed in this chapter, a Western bias is common, and practices found in North America or Europe are often the foundation. Why do you think this is the case? What might an ERP vendor do to minimize or eliminate this bias?
4. Have you been involved with a company doing a redesign of its business processes? If so, what were the key things that went right? What went wrong? What could have been done better to minimize the risk of failure?
5. What do you think the former CIO of Dell Computers meant when he said, "Don't automate broken business processes"?
6. What might a digital business model look like for a financial services company such as an insurance provider or a bank? What are the critical components of the business model? What would the customer relationship management process look like for this same firm?
7. What do you think are the critical success factors in making a digital transformation successful?

Case Study 5-1 Gnosis Freight: Post-COVID Digital Transformation

Gnosis is an international freight software company, based in Charleston, South Carolina, USA. Their specialty is shipping "visibility," which enables firms to determine where their shipping containers are at any given time. Even large firms have trouble locating their shipments, so the Gnosis software can be quite helpful to shippers of all sizes. They were responsive to user needs, with most of their product features having their origin in customer requests. Gnosis had one important goal: to build an ecosystem that enabled supply chain partners to work together.[1] But, they knew that the process of integrating supply chains is quite challenging.

The shipping containers were quite large, at 20 or 40 feet long, so it might seem unexpected that they could become lost. However, there are about 17 million shipping containers being transported worldwide, and one container ship can contain over 24,000.[2] These containers might travel between two or three destinations in the US, and then back to China for reloading. The complex routes taken to move the merchandise to stores make it difficult to predict when they would arrive and when the container would again be empty and ready to make another trip. The lack of that information makes it difficult for the parties to plan for cooperating with their own supply chain partners. Spreadsheets and emails were too hard to organize and manage.

The vision for an ecosystem was ambitious and would change the nature of their previous products. More importantly, it would change how they developed software. Writing code took weeks and months, and once they completed the code, the customer's specifications changed due to an inability to differentiate features they *wanted* from those they *needed*. Those errors caused long delays in developing apps.

Software to enable tracking can be purchased, but often some important features are left out. Gnosis wanted to be responsive to user needs and a purchased solution was not available to address those needs. A new approach, using "enterprise flexible software," enabled "low-code" development of app features by experts in the shipping domain, rather than relying on programmers' expertise when they might misunderstand what is important for shippers.

Gnosis started by designing and creating the first level of transformation with their basic "Track and Trace." Using a unique tracking number (Master Bill of Lading, or MBL), a real-time report could reveal where all a customer's containers were, as well as arrival/departure times and dates in transit. Estimates of departure and arrival times were also provided. The software allowed a wide variety of charts and graphs, as well as maps, displayed on a desktop or mobile device. The next iteration introduced an ability to look into the container, allowing all parties to see detail down to the purchase order. Other levels permitted all interactions to be traced for a purchase order, and finally, analytics and machine learning were used to optimize how drivers were assigned to routes under due date constraints. As conditions changed, the assignments were updated dynamically.

Discussion Questions

1. Each step in a low-code environment is much quicker than in a traditional programming environment. How is the problem of the fast pace compounded by the confusion of users who are not sure what they want or need in an app?
2. Do you think the features described in the case would be more important during the challenging height of the COVID-19 pandemic or for more "normal" times? For instance, could the system be more helpful for a car manufacturer with a large lot full of 99% assembled SUVs waiting for a computer chip, or for a car manufacturer with equilibrium between supply and demand?
3. It is likely that competitors will be attracted to the container visibility market. What might Gnosis do to raise switching costs for its customers?
4. With these levels possible with little coding, Gnosis faces the issue of branching out to other industries. What industry or industries might make use of some of their newfound skills and experience?

Sources:

[1] This case is based on Olga Biedova, Blake Ives, and Iris Junglas, "Gnosis Freight: Harnessing Data and Low-Code to Shipping Container Visibility and Logistics," March 28, 2023, *Communications of the Association for Information Systems*, Vol. 52, 538–551.

[2] Container FAQs, "How Many Containers on a Container Ship? You'll be amazed!" Containerfaqs.com, undated, https://containerfaqs.com/how-many-containers-cargo-ship/ (accessed June 12, 2023).

Case Study 5-2 Carestream Health

In 2019, Carestream Health employed more than 6,000 employees and operated in 150 countries. It was founded in 2007 when a private equity investment firm, Onex Corporation, purchased Kodak's Health Group. At the time of its acquisition, Kodak's Health Group had three primary businesses: Film, Mental Digital, and Digital Dental. Eileen Wirley, the CIO of Kodak's Health Group, became the first CIO at Carestream Health. The main goal for the business overall, and IT in particular, was to create cost-savings through simplification. In IT this translated into consolidating applications so that every part of the business was standardized in terms of its processes and systems. In 2014, Carestream had a single instance of SAP running across the entire company and several horizontal processes such as HR, ordering, supply chain, and purchasing.

When the Carestream CEO Kevin Hobart asked CIO Bruce Leidal to envision the Film business of the future, Leidal knew mass-scale digitalization was inevitable. He said: "We could either build the bus or get run over by the bus, so I had to figure out ways to free up some funding to explore how our back-end processes could be redesigned for this transformation." In 2014 and 2015, Leidal adopted a customer-centric approach for his group and created a target digital architecture that included a customer portal, e-commerce software, mobile apps, electronic data interchange (EDI), web content management, and an IoT platform to connect the company's film printers. Bruce tried to anticipate the foundational IT that would be needed to support the transformation to a new digital business model.

In 2016, the Carestream leadership team and board of directors strategically changed the focus from cost savings to monetizing the Carestream assets it had acquired. At the same time, it sold its Digital Dental business.

To plan for the transformation, the CIO and CEO invited key stakeholders across the Film industry to each join in one of a series of two-day workshops. Each workshop had six to nine participants who helped explore the Film processes in depth. Present at each workshop were business decision makers, a consultant, an IT person who was assigned to take notes, Carestream's Director of Design from the Marketing Department (Peter Lautenslager), and Leidal. Together the participants described and documented the current processes with all of their complexities, as well as discussed the preferred way to execute the work. The consultant in each workshop cut short unproductive debates about best practices and made recommendations based on the discussions. The IT person documented the process using Visio, which helped in visualizing the processes by creating flowcharts and diagrams that could be employed in the subsequent systems development efforts. Lautenslager used the information and documentation from the workshops to build storyboards, which offered a visual representation to nail down the steps in the future process and make the process tangible. The storyboards of the future state scenarios were integrated into two high-level stories, electronic ordering (eOrdering) and a customer connection initiative.

A proposal for the new program (i.e., eOrdering and customer connection) was costed out and refined to reflect necessary organizational redesign based on information garnered at meetings with global functional groups such as HR and finance. The storyboards, processes, and new organizational design related to eOrdering and Connected Customer were presented to the Executive Leaders Team and approved in May 2017.

The transformation involved and impacted numerous Carestream departments (e.g., logistics, pricing, sales, legal, product development, field service, and shared service centers). A large program team was assembled with five major leaders: a program manager who was responsible for delivering the overall program, a business program manager who worked with business stakeholders and was responsible for the business side of the program, a project manager who assisted the program manager on project management activities, a technical lead who was responsible for all software and architecture, and an outsourcing manager who communicated with the offshore developer. The first four eOrdering components of the large program were developed (i.e., Shop Carestream, remote management services, customer registration and activation, and managed print services and self-serve kiosks) using agile development methods. These first components of eOrdering were ready for roll-out in 2017.

The initial adoption and use of Shop Carestream was disappointing. Its adoption rate stalled at 20%. After Hobart set a goal of 100% participation, massive efforts were undertaken to understand

Case Study 5-2 **(Continued)**

the reasons behind the low adoption rate. It was learned that ordering and processing requirements varied in different countries and regions of the world. Local adaptation to eOrdering was implemented and metrics were created to assess progress of Shop Carestream adoptions and to track business (e.g., number and percentage of manual orders, number and percentage of Shop Carestream orders, number and percentage of EDI orders) and customer benefits.

The operations of the eOrdering platform were turned over to business owners in Summer 2018. The adoption rate of Shop Carestream has hovered around 85% and customer satisfaction and costs derived from eOrdering have kept improving, thus placing Carestream in a "position of competitive advantage" according to Andy Mathews, Carestream's Director of Film Business Planning and Strategy. CEO Hobart is "generally very happy" and noted cost savings, a reduced headcount from attrition and staff who were doing work that added more value.

Discussion Questions

1. Would you describe this as a digital transformation or a radical change? Why?
2. What do you think is meant by a "single instance of SAP running across the entire company and several horizontal processes such as HR, ordering, supply chain, and purchasing." Which would likely be in place at Carestream: a functional perspective or a business process perspective? Please explain.
3. Why do you think emphasis was placed on developing metrics to measure the adoption and benefits of Shop Carestream?
4. In a complex, global business, do you think that a digital transformation can ever be "one-size-fits-all"? Please explain.
5. CIO Leidal reflected "If I had to do it over again I'd have started the business change earlier. This was a much bigger change for our business than just building an e-commerce engine." Why do you think he said this?

Sources: Adapted from H. A. Smith and R. T. Watson, "Restructuring Information Systems Following the Divestiture of Carestream Health," *MIS Quarterly Executive* 12, no. 3 (2013); https://www.cio.com/article/2374555/careers-staffing/new-cios-at-carestream-health--alere-medical-and-more.html (accessed March 16, 2019); Carestream Corporate Leadership, https://www.carestream.com/en/in/corporate/leadership (accessed March 16, 2019); and e-mail from Heather Smith, March 23, 2019.

Architecture and Infrastructure

6

This chapter provides managers with an overview of IT architecture and infrastructure issues and designs. It begins by translating a business strategy into IT architecture and then from the architecture into infrastructure. The framework used to describe the basic components of architecture and infrastructure, introduced in Chapter 1, is revisited here, providing a language and structure for describing platform, app, network, and data considerations. Common architectures are then presented, including centralized, decentralized, and web-based service-oriented architecture (SOA). Architectural principles are covered, followed by a discussion of enterprise architecture. Virtualization and cloud computing, two current architectural considerations, are reviewed. The chapter concludes with a discussion of current and future managerial considerations that apply to any architecture.

In the early 2000s, LEGO was threatened with extinction due to competition and excessive diversification into video games, parks, clothing, and other ventures. There was a lack of focus on the customer and inadequate information flows within the company. Fortunately, in the first decade of the new millennium, LEGO adopted an enterprise resource planning (ERP) tool and began to set the stage for saving the company.[1]

In the 2010s, the LEGO Group formulated a corporate strategy to create the organization of the future,[2] designed to serve the firm until the year 2032, which will be LEGO's 100th anniversary. With a vision peering so far into the future, it is not surprising that leveraging digital opportunities is a crucial part of that strategy. The LEGO Group decided against creating a separate business unit on digital products, but instead integrated digital into all its activities. They decided to fuse their business strategy and their digital strategy, enabling new business models that integrate physical and digital domains and create new types of digital connections both inside and outside of LEGO. LEGO attacked their new task in three areas: (1) Product design and community building, (2) Marketing, and (3) Enterprise platforms.

Product design and community building: After their experience with the hacking of their proprietary operating system, MindStorms® robotics platform, they found that the hackers were devout LEGO fans who wanted greater control, and LEGO decided to open up their previously closed systems. They teamed up with the hackers, leading to LEGO Fusion in 2013, providing features that would enable new tools customers wanted. LEGO Group also launched a number of digital platforms that allow communities of their customers to share ideas for new products. A review board considers ideas earning over 10,000 "likes" as worthy of attention and potential adoption. Communities for children and teenagers have also been built to allow fans to connect with one another and share their creations. Over 220 user community groups have representatives in LEGO's Ambassador Network.

[1] This opening case is based largely on El Sawy, O. A., Kræmmergaard, P., Amsinck, H., and Vinther, A. L., "How LEGO built the foundations and enterprise capabilities for digital leadership," in *Strategic Information Management*, (Routledge, 2020), 174–201. An earlier version is "How LEGO Built the Foundations and Enterprise Capabilities for Digital Leadership," *MIS Quarterly Executive* 15, no. 2 (2016): 5, 141–66 https://doi.org/10.4324/9780429286797-8.

[2] Törmer, Robert Lorenz and Henningsson, Stefan, "Dynamic Capability Building in The Lego Group – Prospective Activities Vs. Reflective Learning in Preparation for a Turbulent Digital Future." In *Proceedings of the 27th European Conference on Information Systems* (ECIS), Stockholm & Uppsala, Sweden, June 8–14, 2019.

Marketing: LEGO considers customers (retailers), shoppers (buyers), consumers (builders), and fans (devoted followers) as separate constituencies to be addressed in different ways. An omnichannel plan addresses these different groups. For instance, an augmented reality mobile application was developed for those needing animated video help in product assembly.[3] A new plan for the fifth release of an animated LEGO film promised a "complete reinvention of the franchise."[4] Also, extensive marketing data helps them monitor the effectiveness of their efforts. Finally, they are translating content into multiple languages to expand their markets globally.

Enterprise Platforms: Their digital transformation philosophy led to a complete rethinking of its enterprise architecture (EA), to include enterprise platforms providing greater responsiveness to business demands. This was accomplished by adopting a practice of always involving users before developing applications, leading to higher adoption, user excitement, user proficiency without training or change management, fewer change requests, and lower needs for technical support. Two platforms were created, one rather static one called the "transaction platform" that is focused primarily inside the firm (for the digital workforce) and another that rapidly changes on an ongoing basis called the "engagement platform" that is focused primarily outside the firm for consumers, shoppers, and customers.

LEGO's ERP that had been in place wasn't particularly user-friendly and was picked primarily based on cost, followed by quality, reliability, and speed. But the new focus on digital platforms reversed the priorities for the EA: speed (delivering functionality quickly for competitive advantage); reliability, quality, and usability; then cost as a distant last. A system landscape document guided infrastructure decisions.[5] The two platforms needed to be loosely coupled, which was accomplished by using SaaS (software as a service) and APIs (application program interfaces), the latter of which standardized how data could be shared and modified, in spite of changes in the engagement platform.

What were LEGO's business impacts from digital transformation? Moving from pending disaster 20 years before, LEGO and its ecosystem are now alive and healthy, with growing revenues and profits. LEGO was named the most powerful brand globally. El Sawy et al.[6] credited the digital transformation for benefits of the enterprise and engagement platforms, including highly effective governance, dynamic adaptive application development, a high-quality user experience, and agility and resilience in responding to needs of customers, partners, and employees.

One key characteristic in LEGO's journey was their focus on dynamic capabilities, which would be continuously flexible and adaptive to new needs in the future. Over time, the organization learned to focus beyond current needs towards building capabilities for the future, improving what they called LEGO's "technical fitness" (pg. 11) for future uses of technology. Thus, one of the most important guiding principles is to sacrifice the ability to obtain value immediately from the architecture to pave the way for future capabilities.

Not all firms base their entire operations on a cloud platform that permits integration with other organizations. But LEGO's experiences can clearly be named "cutting edge." The LEGO story illustrates how infrastructure decisions can enable the strategic objectives of a firm. However, building such an infrastructure cannot come first. Firms must begin by developing their strategic vision, determining the IS architecture needed to fulfill that vision, and then making it all tangible by putting together an IS infrastructure. In LEGO's case, leaders had a vision to move boldly into becoming a firm that partners when there is a need to expand competencies, and to focus on constructing systems that are flexible and adaptable, providing APIs that simplify connections between systems.

Technology decisions can impact managers' options for business strategy and operations. This chapter therefore examines the mechanisms by which business strategy is transformed into tangible IS architecture and infrastructure. The terms *architecture* and *infrastructure* are often mistakenly used interchangeably in

---

[3] El Sawy, "How LEGO built the foundations and enterprise capabilities for digital leadership," 174–204.

[4] Brail, Nathaniel. 2022 "LEGO Movie Producer Teases Next Film Will Be a Reinvention," Comicbook, https://comicbook.com/movies/news/lego-movie-producer-teases-next-film-will-be-a-reinvention/ retrieved February 12, 2023—para 1.

[5] Törmer, Robert Lorenz and Henningsson, Stefan, "Dynamic Capability Building in The Lego Group – Prospective Activities Vs. Reflective Learning in Preparation for a Turbulent Digital Future." In *Proceedings of the 27th European Conference on Information Systems* (ECIS), Stockholm & Uppsala, Sweden, June 8–14, 2019.

[6] El Sawy, "How LEGO built the foundations and enterprise capabilities for digital leadership," 174–204.

the context of IS. This chapter discusses how the two differ and the important role each plays in realizing a business strategy. Then this chapter examines some common architectural components for IS today.

From Vision to Implementation

As shown in Figure 6.1, architecture translates strategy into infrastructure. Building a house is similar: The owner has a vision of how the final product should look and function. The owner must decide on a strategy about where to live and the type of dwelling, such as in an urban apartment or in a suburban house. The owner's strategy also includes deciding the important attributes for the design such as taking advantage of a beautiful view, having an open floor plan, or planning for special interests by designing areas such as a patio, game room, study, music room, or other amenities. The architect develops plans based on this vision. These plans, or blueprints, provide a guide—unchangeable in some areas but subject to interpretation in others—for the carpenters, plumbers, and electricians who actually construct the house. Guided by experience and by industry standards, these builders select the materials and construction techniques best suited to the plan. The plan helps them determine where to put the plumbing and wiring, important parts of the home's infrastructure. When the process works, the completed house fulfills its owner's vision, even though he or she did not participate in the actual construction.

An IT **architecture** provides a blueprint for translating business strategy into a plan for IS. An IT **infrastructure** is everything that supports the flow and processing of information in an organization, including platforms, apps, data, and network components. Outside partners can take part in any of those four elements, when management makes sourcing decisions.[7] Interestingly, the very successful Australian startup Judo Bank decided upon its debut in 2019 to avoid owning any information technology whatsoever, in favor of using "everything as a service" (EaaS) through outside partners that, like LEGO, use APIs to accomplish all information storage, processing, and retrieval.

At one extreme, an EaaS structure requires finding and assembling many services that would, for a fee, provide the needed functionality, requiring Judo to coordinate them all.[8] Judo secured subscriptions for computer equipment needed by employees, paid for processing transactions only when necessary, and paid for cloud storage only as needed. All these costs scale up and down as business ebbs and flows, rather than the traditional method of buying equipment and then hiring a large staff to build and implement the necessary technologies. A personal metaphor would be purchasing a $40,000 car mainly to secure a job where you might need to travel infrequently around town. Driving would increase when sales increase, and decrease when sales decrease, but the cost of the car remains the same. Using an Uber for $15 per trip would require less of an outlay up front and would only involve intermittent payments, with

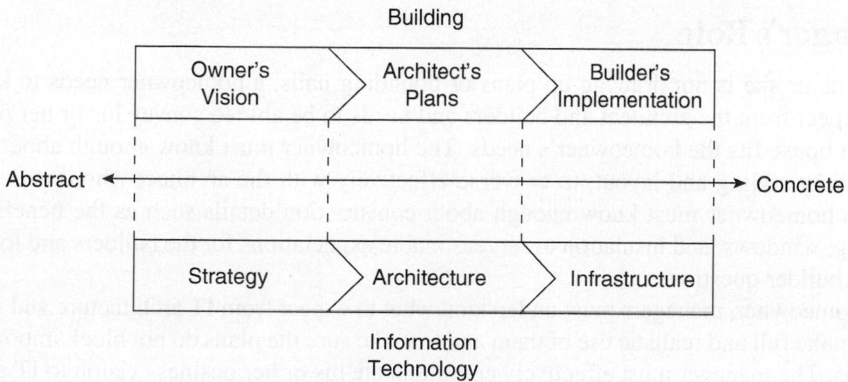

FIGURE 6.1 From the abstract to the concrete—building versus IT.

[7] Sourcing is covered in Chapter 10.

[8] Christoph F. Breidbach, Amol M. Joshi, Paul P. Maglio, Frederik von Briel, Alex Twigg, Graham Dickens, and Nancy V. Wünderlich, "How Everything-as-a-Service Enabled Judo to Become a Billion-Dollar Bank Without Owning IT," *MIS Quarterly Executive* 21, no. 3 (2022), Article 3, https://doi.org/10.17705/2msqe.

no maintenance and repair costs. If sales are light, with one trip per week, then the cost over a five-year period is less than $4,000. If there are five trips per week, the cost rises to almost $20,000 over that period.

Judo makes use of Salesforce.com's cloud-based software as a service (SaaS) to take care of customer relationship management, zero trust networking (ZTN) for authentication as a service (AaaS), and function as a service (FaaS) for back office duties such as processing loan settlements and loan applications. Judo created an architecture with "over 50 individual systems . . . without owning a single physical server or employing any software developers."[9] Just like the Uber example above, all those systems can scale up and down as needed.

In spite of this complexity, Judo keeps the technology invisible for employees to access any of those 50 different systems. Many banks require logging in and re-entering data several times just to complete one loan transaction. Judo mandated one sign-in process with extremely high reliability, availability, and resistance to disasters without data loss. Judo chose external providers that use "open standards" (as opposed to secret mechanisms or languages to couple them), making sure the services work together, and enabling them to replace any of the services if needed.

Many long-established companies purchase, configure, and implement hardware and software, sometimes expanding on their "legacy" (from the past) configurations. Both Judo and LEGO provide examples of how information systems decisions can bypass having to wrestle with hardware (computer equipment) and software (programs that run on the hardware) in configuring how the functions needed in an organization can be provided. Judo Bank has arrived at the extreme, orchestrating[10] rather than acquiring equipment and constructing systems. But in spite of avoiding construction, there is still a need to design an architecture where outside parties do their own wrestling with their own infrastructures to deliver services on an "as needed" and "as much as needed" basis.

Assembling the services means that the architect designs a plan to bind the services together to form an ecosystem. Each component in the orchestra interacts with other components as needed. A Platform as a Service provider can help design the architecture and each service handles its own infrastructure. Platforms will be defined and described later in this chapter, but for now, consider it to be a mechanism that ties together and controls **apps** (applications).

What is the infrastructure? It consists of components, chosen and assembled in a manner that best suits the plan and therefore best enables the overarching business strategy. Infrastructure in an organization is similar to the beams, plumbing, and wiring in a house; In a traditional organization that owns, designs, and builds its own information systems, all processing makes use of hardware, software, networks, and data. But in an organization like Judo Bank, an architect would define the functions that services need to perform, and an infrastructure expert would design how to assemble and configure the platform, apps, network, and data. The components are taken care of by the outside organizations offering the services.

The Manager's Role

Even though he or she is not drawing up plans or pounding nails, a homeowner needs to know what to reasonably expect from the architect and builders and needs to be able to convey his or her preferences to make sure the house fits the homeowner's needs. The homeowner must know enough about architecture, specifically about styling and layout, to converse effectively with the architect who draws up the plans. Similarly, the homeowner must know enough about construction details such as the benefits of various types of siding, windows, and insulation to set reasonable expectations for the builders and to have context to respond to builder questions.

Like the homeowner, managers must understand what to expect from IT architecture and infrastructure to be able to make full and realistic use of them and to make sure the plans do not block important business considerations. The manager must effectively communicate his or her business vision to IT architects and implementers and, if necessary, modify the business plans if IT cannot realistically or financially create or support those plans. Without the involvement of the business manager, IT architects could inadvertently make decisions that limit the manager's business options in the future.

[9] Breidbach et al., Ibid., pg. 199.

[10] Breidbach et al., Ibid.

For example, a sales manager for a large distribution company using its own platforms and apps did not want to partake in discussions about providing sales force automation systems for his group. He felt that a standard package offered by a well-known vendor would work fine. After all, it worked for many other companies, he rationalized, so it would be fine for his company. No architecture was designed, and no long-range thought was given to how the application might support or inhibit the sales group. After implementation, it became clear that the application had limitations and did not support the sales processes at this company. He approached the IT department for help, and in the discussions that ensued, he learned that earlier infrastructure decisions now made it prohibitively expensive to implement the capabilities he wanted.

Earlier involvement with decision-making and the ability to convey his vision of what the sales group wanted to do might have resulted in an IT infrastructure that provided a platform for the changes the manager now wanted to make. Instead, the infrastructure lacked an architecture that met the business objectives of the sales and marketing departments.

In a more modern, service-oriented environment similar to that of LEGO, an ecosystem must be carefully designed so that the parts would work together in the aforementioned orchestra of services. A platform would need to be designed. Decisions would need to be made about which apps would be needed to perform the needed business services, data needs of each app would have to be sketched out, and networking decisions would need to be chosen. The resulting design would represent the architecture, and the companies providing the services via their apps would then be evaluated for forming the physical infrastructure.

Finally, a strategic roadmap recently outlined five levels reached in a progression of making use of open-source components to win the ecosystem "game." First is adopting, resulting in cost savings, quicker deployment of applications, and reduced dependence on vendors. The second level is contributing, which allows you to enhance the standards for all. Third is steering, which involves increasing your leverage as a "player" and an influential force in the ecosystem. Fourth is mobilizing, which involves gaining a competitive advantage over other firms. Last is projecting, where you gain leverage across layers and domains of use, presumably to "win" the game.[11]

The Leap from Strategy to Architecture to Infrastructure

The huge number of IT choices available coupled with the incredible pace of technological change makes the manager's task of designing an IT infrastructure seem nearly impossible. Fortunately, managers have IT professionals to help, but the manager must be a knowledgeable participant in these discussions. In this chapter, the discussion is broken down into two major steps: first, translating strategy into architecture and second, translating architecture into infrastructure. This chapter describes a simple framework to help managers sort through IT issues. This framework stresses the need to consider business strategy when defining an organization's IT building blocks. Although this framework may not cover every possible architectural issue, it does highlight major issues associated with effectively defining IT architecture and infrastructure.

From Strategy to Architecture

The manager must start out with a business strategy and then use the strategy to develop more specific goals as shown in Figure 6.2. Then detailed business requirements are derived from each goal. In the LEGO case, the business strategy was to integrate digital into everything it does. LEGO introduced new products and services with digital and physical components that were developed in collaboration with partners in its ecosystem. LEGO's business requirements were based on goals related to product design, community building, marketing, and digital platforms. By outlining the overarching business strategy and then fleshing out the business requirements associated with each goal, the manager can provide the architect with a clear picture of what IS must accomplish and the governance arrangements needed to ensure their

[11] Hervé Legenvre, Erkko Autio, and Ari-Pekka Hameri, "How to Harness Open Technologies for Digital Platform Advantage," *MIS Quarterly Executive* 21, no. 1 (2022), Article 6 https://doi.org/10.17705/2msqe.00058.

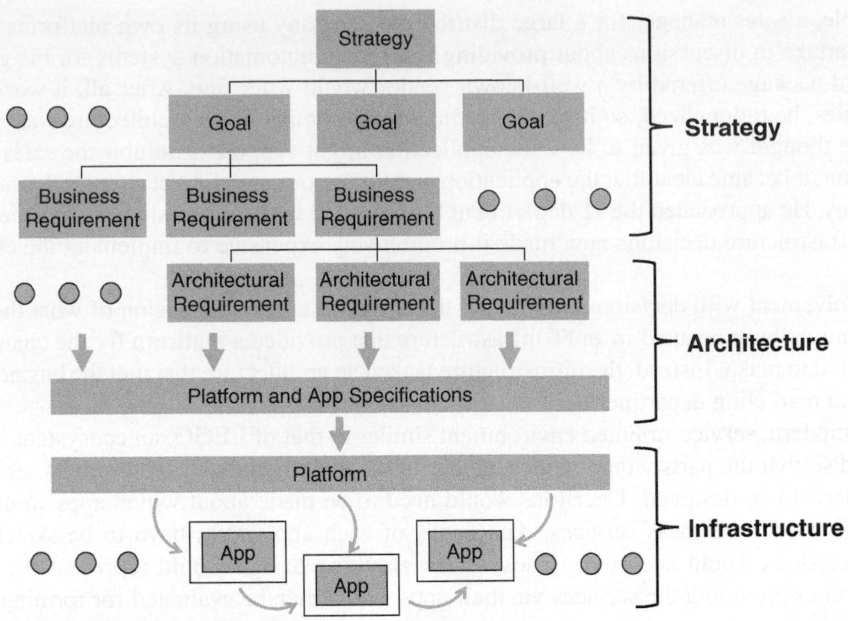

FIGURE 6.2 From strategy to architecture to infrastructure.

smooth development, implementation, and use. The governance arrangements specify who in the company (or externally on the platform) retains control of and responsibility for the IS.

Of course, the manager's job is not finished here. Continuing with Figure 6.2, the manager must work with the IT architect to translate these business requirements into a more detailed view of the system's requirements, standards, and processes that shape an IT architecture. This more detailed view, the architectural requirements, includes consideration of such things as data and process demands as well as security objectives. At LEGO and Judo, the user experience drove the architectural requirements such as consumer-grade-friendly interfaces on the enterprise platform and 24/7 availability and apps that could be added quickly on the engagement platform. The IT architect then takes the architectural requirements and designs the IT architecture.

From Architecture to Infrastructure

A key element in LEGO's fused business strategy is its Enterprise Architecture. After determining the architecture, it then needed to translate the architecture into infrastructure. This task entails adding yet more detail to the architectural plan that emerged in the previous phase. Now the detail comprises actual platforms, apps, networking, and data. Details extend to platforms to consider, applications to build or buy, location of data and access procedures, location of firewalls, link specifications, interconnection design, and so on. This phase is also illustrated in Figure 6.2 where the architecture is translated into functional specifications. The functional specifications can be broken down into platform and app specifications, then the platforms and apps themselves. Then decisions are made about how to implement these specifications, starting with what supplier's platform(s), and which apps to use. Finally, the data and networks (represented by the arrows at the bottom of Figure 6.2) need to be identified for use by the apps.

When we speak about infrastructure, we are referring to more than the components. Plumbing, electrical wiring, walls, and a roof do not make a house. Rather, these components must be assembled according to the blueprint to create a structure in which people can live comfortably. Similarly, platforms, apps, data, and networks must be combined in a coherent pattern to have a viable infrastructure. This infrastructure can be viewed from several levels. At the most global level, the term may be focused on the enterprise and refer to the infrastructure for the entire organization. The term may also focus on the interorganizational level by laying the foundation for communicating with customers, suppliers, or other stakeholders across organizational boundaries. Sometimes *infrastructure* refers to those components needed for an individual application. When considering the structure of a particular application, it is important to consider where the data will be stored, who is responsible for it, how it will work, and how it is going to be made secure.

Framework for the Infrastructure and Architecture Analysis

Information systems of the past were described as having hardware, software, networking, and data. But today, most information systems used by businesses are based on platforms, applications that run on those platforms, networks that can connect applications and platforms, and data. When developing a framework for transforming business strategy into architecture and then into infrastructure, these four basic components make up the information system:

- *Platforms:* The foundation that allow apps (applications) to run. Examples are the PC running Windows, the Mac running MacOS, the iPhone running iOS, and the Samsung phone running Android. Those operating systems are also platforms, enabling the installation of apps that are built to run on any one of those pieces of hardware. Another example is an app such as Chrome or Edge, that supports websites. And interestingly, while there must be separate Windows and Mac versions of Chrome, websites developed for Chrome will work the same on each operating system.
- *Applications:* The apps, or components that generally work on a particular platform, and request data for recording or reporting. They also transform data by performing calculations and making updates as needed. A good example of an app would be one that you can load to your smartphone or PC for banking, email, or obtaining driving directions. Sometimes an app is only available on a particular platform (such as Windows or MacOS) and not on other ones. Some platforms have a growing library of apps that will work on them.
- *Network:* The components for local or long-distance networking. Local networking components include switches, hubs, and routers; long-distance networking components include cable, fiber, and microwave paths for communication and data sharing. All work according to a common protocol, most often Internet protocol (IP). Some networks are private, requiring credentials to connect. Others, like the Internet, are public. The Internet is so flexible that many firms create virtual private networks (VPNs) within that public network by encrypting it so outsiders cannot read it.
- *Data:* The electronic representation of the numbers and text. Here, the main concern is the quantity and format of data and how often it must be transferred from one app to another or translated from one format to another.

Platforms and apps form the basis of information systems decisions today. Seldom do managers choose hardware and software. Instead, managers choose a platform (e.g., MacOS, Windows, Android, or iOS) and the apps they want to use to run the processes and activities necessary to support the business.

How Platforms and Apps Work Together

Platforms are part of the way most organizations design and implement their information systems today. In the section above, a platform is described as the foundation or the orchestrator of the information system, and the apps are the part of the systems that perform the specific function/activities needed.

Judo Bank and LEGO each formulated a **platform** as a service from an outside firm to serve as an orchestrator of multiple apps that can exchange information among themselves or through the platform. For instance, in Judo, the platform could engage many apps that handle the loan. There might be separate apps for calculating loan payments, sending a paper or e-bill, creating late notices, and recording customer payments.

Some or all of these apps can be built by a firm, but recently companies have found that ready-built apps are available as services from outside vendors, as both Judo and LEGO have done. And LEGO has integrated home-built systems with apps available from outside.

Many firms do some internal development. A hotel, for instance, might create a website in-house, using a platform such as Joomla!. The site can serve as a hotel's platform for pulling in paid services such as room availability from data stored in Salesforce.com, allowing a customer to select and pay for a room using IBM Websphere, and an interactive map can show customers how to get to the hotel using a plugin from Google Maps. Building all of this from scratch is seldom done any longer, given that many of these tools are mature and dependable.

The term "platform" has been used in a variety of ways: to identify the hardware and operating system of a computing device. You likely use the iOS or Android platform daily with a host of apps that turn your phone into one of too many devices than we could list here. But an app for your iPhone will not work on the Amazon Echo platform, as the Echo's platform has its own series of apps that enable you to make video calls, play music, play games, watch news reports, open and close your garage door, turn on lights, and many, many others. Both your iPhone and your Echo even have apps that allow you to find other apps!

A platform can also refer to a firm's collection of cloud-based, modular tools as the example from LEGO illustrated. Such platforms use open standards for easy "plugging-in" of components, enabling "mashing-up" of a variety of resources at once. When the hotel uses Google Maps on its website, it is an excellent example of an open, standardized resource that can be accessed by any platform that provides properly formatted requests, determined by the app's design, and the specifications to make them work together are published openly.

Companies use platforms to compete. A platform strategy forms the basis for digital innovation and competition.[12] Some companies have created platforms that have a large influence and have even caught the attention of governments, leading to laws that change how privacy, antitrust, and other regulations are managed by these companies. For example, Meta's Facebook came under government scrutiny after a report highlighted the broad reach of the platform (in this case half of the world's population), the algorithm that promoted misinformation, and the negative health effects on children.[13] Dominant players in the platform business such as Amazon, Apple, Microsoft, Meta, and Google, shape the global economy, the way work is done, and the geo-political issues faced by just about every country in the world.[14]

Apps Can Also Be Platforms

Interestingly, the dividing line between what is an app and what is a platform is not so crisp. Windows is like an app to the Intel or AMD chips in the platform of the computer. Roblox is an app that runs on the Windows platform. And finally, a teen's obstacle course game is an app on the platform of Roblox. As a result, it is quite important to be clear in any communications about platforms and apps.

Some apps can serve as major platforms themselves, as Facebook has long demonstrated by having developers offer games and other functions that run on the Facebook platform.[15] Integration of Meta's flagship apps, including Facebook, Facebook Messenger, Instagram, and WhatsApp, appears to be in their future. In 2019, Mark Zuckerberg first announced an initiative to integrate those core messaging apps.[16] In August 2022, antitrust movements across the technology industry are hastening those plans, as they would make it more difficult to break up Meta.[17]

Two other examples are emerging. WeChat started as a messaging app but has evolved by providing the functionality of Facebook, Uber, Apple Pay, Snapchat, Amazon, Skype, Tinder, and others.[18] At a billion users and growing, this application/platform has become mainstream in China.[19] Integrating all

[12] Michael Cusumano, Annabelle Gawer, and David Yoffie, *The Business of Platforms: Strategy in the Age of Digital Competition, Innovation and Power* (Harper Business Books, 2019).

[13] Lauren Jackson, "How Should we Limit Facebook's Power?" January 15, 2022, https://www.nytimes.com/2021/10/08/podcasts/facebook-regulation.html (accessed April 24, 2023).

[14] Cusumano, Ibid.

[15] Ian Schafer, "What Facebook Critics Don't Understand: It's a Platform, Not a Publisher," Ad Age, May 4, 2012, https://adage.com/article/digitalnext/facebook-s-critics-understand-a-platform-a-publisher/234570 (accessed June 17, 2019).

[16] Mike Isaac, "Zuckerberg Plans to Integrate WhatsApp, Instagram and Facebook Messenger," *New York Times*, January 5, 2019, https://www.nytimes.com/2019/01/25/technology/facebook-instagram-whatsapp-messenger.html (accessed June 15, 2019).

[17] Reuters, "Zuckerberg to Integrate WhatsApp, Instagram, and Facebook Messenger: Report" August 20, 2022, https://tech.hindustantimes.com/tech/news/zuckerberg-to-integrate-whatsapp-instagram-and-facebook-messenger-report-story-4EXJahPp5SLXqJUCJIb0lO.html (accessed February 24, 2023).

[18] Kaitlin Zhang, "Who Uses WeChat and Why Is WeChat So Popular in China?" Medium, October 2, 2018, https://medium.com/@KaitlinZhang/who-uses-wechat-and-why-is-wechat-so-popular-in-china-c8df11577489 (accessed June 16, 2019).

[19] Cyrus Lee, "Daily Active Users for WeChat Exceeds 1 Billion," *ZdNet*, January 9, 2019, https://www.zdnet.com/article/daily-active-user-of-messaging-app-wechat-exceeds-1-billion/ (accessed June 16, 2019).

of those functions enables users to stay within the single app to serve many of their needs. Roblox has 202 million monthly active users and 13.4 billion engagement hours in Quarter 3 of 2022,[20] and is valued with a market capital in February 2023 of $22.7 billion.[21] Roblox is a massively multiplayer online gaming app platform targeted to children, allowing them to both develop and play games on the platform.[22] The merging of the concepts of platforms and apps are in the early stages, and the distinctions between them will fade over the coming years.

Framework for Understanding the Four Components

The IS strategy matrix framework (Figure 1.5) in Chapter 1 is simplified to make the point that initially understanding an organization's infrastructure is not difficult. Understanding the technology behind each component of the infrastructure and the technical requirements of the architecture is a much more complex task. The main point is that the general manager must begin with an overview that is complete and that addresses what the firm needs.

This framework asks three types of questions that must be answered for each infrastructure component: what, who, and where. Most commonly asked are the "what" questions that identify the specific type of technology. The "who" questions seek to understand what individuals, groups, and departments are involved. In most cases, the individual user is not the owner of the system or even the person who maintains it. In many cases, the systems are leased, not owned, by the company, making the owner a party completely outside the organization. In understanding the infrastructure, it is important to get a picture of the people involved. The third set of questions addresses "where" issues. With the proliferation of networks, many IS are designed and built with components in multiple locations, often even crossing oceans. Learning about infrastructure means understanding where everything is located.

We can expand the use of this framework to also understand architecture. To illustrate the connections between strategy and systems, the table in Figure 6.3 has been populated with questions that exemplify those addressing architecture and infrastructure issues associated with each component.

The questions shown in Figure 6.3 are only representative of many to be addressed; the specific questions depend on the business strategy the organizations are following. However, this framework can help IT staff and managers translate business strategy into architecture and ultimately into infrastructure in their organizations. The answers from IT architects and implementers provide a robust picture of the IT environment. That means that the IT architecture includes plans for the data and information, the technology (the standards to be followed and the infrastructure that provides the foundation), and the applications to be accessed via the company's IT system.

There are several different ways in which components can be arranged, with a firm's own equipment and software, or with services that are used. With an older firm that made use of **mainframe** computers, the existing systems that were in place before organizations begin organizational transformation to expand their digitalization plans, can be used in concert with the more modern platforms and apps that are created over time. Those older systems are called *legacy systems*.

Those **legacy systems** can be found in two major forms. Organizations sometimes like the idea of a **centralized architecture** with everything purchased, supported, and managed centrally, usually in a **data center**, to eliminate the difficulties of managing a distributed infrastructure. However, a more common configuration today is a **decentralized architecture**, where the components are arranged in a way that the processing and functionality are distributed between multiple small computers, servers, and devices, with a network that connects them. Typically, a decentralized architecture uses numerous servers, often located in different physical locations, at the backbone of the infrastructure, called a **server-based architecture**.

Another even more decentralized approach is to use a **service-oriented architecture (SOA)**, the architecture that Judo Bank decided to use. Also, LEGO opted to expand on their previous architecture, offering new functionality using an SOA, sometimes in conjunction with their legacy systems. The computing

[20] Daniel Ruby, "Roblox Statistics – How Many People Play Roblox (2023)," DemandSage, https://www.demandsage.com/how-many-people-play-roblox/ (accessed February 23, 2023).

[21] From Yahoo Finance. https://finance.yahoo.com/quote/RBLX/ (accessed February 23, 2023).

[22] Anthony Ha, "Kids' Gaming Platform Roblox Raises $150M," crunchbase, September 5, 2018, https://techcrunch.com/2018/09/05/roblox-series-f/ (accessed June 15, 2019).

Component	What		Who		Where	
	Architecture	Infrastructure	Architecture	Infrastructure	Architecture	Infrastructure
Platform	What type of platform will tie together all the potential apps?	What size hard drives do we equip our laptops with?	Who knows the most about servers in our organization?	Who will operate the platform? Our company, a vendor, or another firm?	Does our architecture work with simple servers or edge servers?	What specific platforms will be needed across the organization, worldwide?
App	Does fulfillment of our strategy require an e-commerce app?	Shall we go with Salesforce or IBM Websphere?	Who is affected by a move to Salesforce?	Who will need Salesforce training?	Should the apps be on a private or a public cloud?	Can we use a cloud instance of Oracle for our data?
Network	How should the network be structured to fulfill our strategy?	Will a particular Cisco switch be fast enough for what we need?	Who needs a connection to the network?	Who provides our wireless network?	Will we let each user's phone be a hotspot?	Shall we lease a cable or use satellite?
Data	What data do we need for our sales management system?	What format will we store our data in?	Who needs access to sensitive data?	How will authorized users identify themselves?	Will backups be stored on-site or off-site?	Will data be in the cloud or in our data center?

FIGURE 6.3 **Infrastructure and architecture analysis framework with sample questions.**

power in an SOA resides in the services offered and are accessed by the applications used by the organization. Please refer to the Judo case, earlier in this chapter, that described how a loan application triggers other information requests by cooperating apps. Recall that the type of software used in an SOA architecture is **software-as-a-service**, or SaaS. Another term for these applications when delivered over the Internet is **web services**. Often this type of architecture is referred to as "**in the cloud**," which means that the processing, applications, and data are all hosted by a provider such as Amazon, Google, or other cloud services provider, and not residing at a location owned by the manager's company.

Another type of configuration is one that can allocate or remove resources automatically based on traffic or other indicators of utilization, referred to as a **software-defined architecture**.[23] Sometimes software-defined architectures can even change the architecture on the fly. For example, many fast-food restaurants and coffee shops that offer free Wi-Fi to customers require more than one connection to the Internet in very busy locations, as well as a separate, secure connection to record sales transactions and inventory updates from individual restaurant and shop operations. One actual very large firm choosing to stay anonymous configures a software-defined architecture for just that purpose. When the retail shop's operations connection fails, a software-defined network automatically reconfigures to convert one of the customer connections to become a substitute operations connection. Customers might find their Wi-Fi connections to be a little slower until the situation returns to normal, but the automatic reconfiguration prevents the shop from having to close or revert to a very clumsy manual system. Even without a catastrophe, customer traffic on the Wi-Fi system and the need for operations capacity can fluctuate. After closing, the Wi-Fi system for customers is not needed, but during busy times, it might be saturated. When software updates are performed or large volumes of transactions are transmitted, the operations connection might become overwhelmed. Shifting resources automatically from one separate architectural component to another is a powerful way to reduce costs.

A manager must be aware of the trade-offs when considering architectural decisions. For example, decentralized architectures are more modular than centralized architectures, allowing other servers to be added with relative ease and provide increased flexibility for adding clients with specific functionality for specific users. Decentralized organizational governance, such as that associated with a networked organization structure,[24] is consistent with decentralized architectures. In contrast, a centralized architecture is

[23] K. Pearlson, "Software Defined Future: Instant Provisioning of IT Services," Connect-Converge (Fall 2014). http://file.connect-converge.com/issues/2014_fall/ (accessed February 24, 2019).

[24] Organization structures are discussed in Chapter 3.

easier to manage in some ways because all functionality is centralized instead of distributed throughout all the devices and servers. A centralized architecture tends to be a better match in companies with highly centralized governance, for example, those with hierarchical organization structures. SOA is increasingly popular because the design enables building large units of functionality almost entirely from existing software service components. SOA is useful for building applications quickly because it offers managers a modular and componentized design and, therefore, a more easily modifiable approach to building applications. **Software-defined architectures** are even easier to manage because they self-manage many of their features. However, each feature must be imagined and designed to be self-managing; the systems are not autonomous beyond those features.

Technological advances such as peer-to-peer architecture and wireless or mobile infrastructure make possible a wide variety of additional options. These designs can either augment a firm's existing way of operating or become its main focus. For example, a **peer-to-peer** architecture allows networked computers to share resources without needing a central server to play a dominant role. ThePirateBay.org is an infamous example of a peer-to-peer architecture. It is a website for illegally sharing music, movies, games, and more, with other users, and any copying is strictly done from one user to another. Zoom has many features of peer-to-peer architecture but requires some outside resources when there are more than two people on a conversation.[25]

Wireless (mobile) infrastructures allow communication from remote locations using a variety of wireless technologies (e.g., fixed microwave links; wireless LANs; data over cellular networks; wireless WANs; satellite links; digital dispatch networks; one-way and two-way paging networks; diffuse infrared, laser-based communications; keyless car entry; and global positioning systems).

Web-based architecture and **cloud architecture** locate significant hardware, software, and possibly even data elements on the Internet. Web-based architectures offer great flexibility when used as a source for **capacity-on-demand**, or the availability of additional processing capability for a fee. IT managers like the concept of capacity on demand to help manage peak processing periods when additional capacity is needed. It allows them to use the web-available capacity as needed, rather than purchasing additional computers to handle the larger loads.

With the proliferation of smartphones and tablets, enterprises increasingly have employees who want to bring their own devices and connect to enterprise systems. Some call this **Bring Your Own Device (BYOD)**, and it raises some important managerial considerations. When employees connect their own devices to the corporate network, issues such as capacity, security, and compatibility arise. For example, many corporate applications are not designed to function on the small screen of a smartphone. Redesigning them for personal devices may require significant investment to accommodate the smartphone platform. And not all smartphone platforms are the same. Designing for an iPhone is different than for an Android phone. Even if a system were redesigned for these two platforms, the resources required to maintain the system increase because each platform evolves at a different rate and the applications need to appear similar on each device.

IT consumerization is a growing phenomenon. Not only do employees want to use their own devices to access corporate systems but also customers increasingly expect to access company systems from their mobile devices. Companies are responding by providing mobile device apps as well as by putting into place new governance systems (see Chapter 9). Making applications robust yet simple enough for customers to use from virtually any mobile device over the web is a challenge for many information systems departments. Many modern websites are designed with the philosophy of "responsive design," permitting them to take the greatest advantage of screens of any size. One example can be found at most banks. Banking can be done on small mobile devices such as smart phones, on larger screen mobile devices such as tablets, and on larger more powerful devices such as laptops and desktop systems. Customers want to be able to access their accounts on the device they commonly use, rather than be told they can only use certain devices.

Architectural Principles

Any good architecture is based on a set of principles or fundamental beliefs about how the architecture should function. Architectural principles must be consistent with both the values of the enterprise and the technology used in the infrastructure. The principles are designed by considering the key objectives

[25] Cressler, Cosette, "A Study of Zoom's Video Conferencing Architecture & System Design," CometChat, October 26, 2021. https://www.cometchat.com/blog/zoom-video-technology-architecture (accessed April 24, 2023).

of the organization, and then translated into principles to apply to the design of the IT architecture. The number of principles varies widely, and there is no set list of what must be included in a set of architectural principles. However, a guideline for developing architectural principles is to make sure they are directly related to the operating model of the enterprise and IS organization. Principles should define the desirable behaviors of the IT systems and the role of the organization(s) that support them. Which principles are prioritized depends on the purpose of the architecture. In the LEGO example covered earlier, the order of preference when evaluating potential ERP systems was reversed when they realized later that speed was the most important consideration. A sample of architectural principles is shown in Figure 6.4.

Enterprise Architecture

Many companies apply a comprehensive framework or methodology, called an **enterprise architecture** (EA), to create the "blueprint" for all IS and their interrelationships in the firm. The basis of EA is business strategy. EA specifies how information technologies support business processes, align with business needs, and produce business outcomes. EA also includes the standard technical capabilities and activities for all parts of the enterprise and guidelines for making choices. As Ross, Weill, and Robertson describe in their book, *Enterprise Architecture as Strategy*,[26]

> *Top-performing companies define how they will do business (an operating model) and design the processes and infrastructure critical to their current and future operations (enterprise architecture). . . . Then these smart companies exploit their foundation, embedding new initiatives and using it as a competitive weapon to seize new business opportunities." (pp. viii—ix)*

The components of an enterprise architecture typically include four key and interconnected layers: the business layer (e.g., business strategies, functions, and models); Applications (e.g., apps supporting business processes and linking apps); Information (e.g., physical storage and data access); and Technology (platform and app infrastructure).[27]

Principle	Description of What the Architecture Should Promote
Ease of use	Ease of use in building and supporting the architecture and solutions based on the architecture
Single point of view	A consistent, integrated view of the business regardless of how it is accessed
Buy rather than build	Purchase of applications, components, and enabling frameworks unless there is a competitive reason to develop them internally
Speed	Acceleration of time to market for solutions
Cost	Costs of the necessary components and labor called for by the architecture. With high complexity, labor costs increase
Quality	The level of excellence of the architecture and its components
Flexibility and agility	Flexibility to support changing business needs while enabling evolution of the architecture and the solutions built on it
Innovation	Incorporation of new technologies, facilitating innovation
Data and system security	Data protection from unauthorized use and disclosure, systems protection from access and modification by unauthorized intruders
Common data vocabulary	Consistent definitions of data throughout the enterprise, which are understandable and available to all users
Data asset	Management of data like other valuable assets

FIGURE 6.4 Sample architectural principles.

Source: Adapted from examples of IT architecture from IBM, The Open Group Architecture Framework, the U.S. Government, and the State of Wisconsin.

[26] Jeanne W. Ross, Peter Weill, and David C. Robertson, *Enterprise Architecture as Strategy* (Boston, MA: Harvard Business School Press, 2006).

[27] Q. N. Bui, "Evaluating Enterprise Architecture Frameworks Using Essential Elements," *Communications of the Association for Information Systems* 41 no. 1, (2017): 121–149, https://doi.org/10.17705/1CAIS.04106.

Architecture	Description	High-level Overview
TOGAF (the open group architecture framework)	A process for creating an enterprise architecture	Four architectures: • business architecture, • application architecture, • data architecture, and • technical architecture
Zachman	A taxonomy for the artifacts of an enterprise architecture	Six descriptive foci for the architecture (data, function, network, people, time, and motivation) and six key player perspectives (planner, owner, designer, builder, subcontractor, and enterprise)
Federal enterprise architecture (FEA)	Models, taxonomy, and processes originally created to build an enterprise architecture for the U.S. Government	Five reference models: • business, • service, • components, • technical, and • data
Gartner	An active process for creating an enterprise architecture bringing together business owners, technology implementers, and information specialists	Uses an ongoing process of creating, maintaining, and revisiting the EA to keep it current and vital to the organization focused on the business strategy of where the business wants to go and how it will get there

FIGURE 6.5 Common enterprise architectures.

There are numerous EAs used by organizations. Most experts agree that these frameworks and methodologies offer structure for aligning IT with business priorities, but each one has inherent weaknesses. Technology managers often start with one of the common approaches and modify it to fit their specific organizational needs. These four frameworks are representative of the most prevalent EAs (and Figure 6.5 compares them)[28]:

Because enterprise architecture is more about how the company operates than how the technology is designed, building an EA is a joint exercise to be done with business leaders and IT leaders. IT leaders cannot and should not do this alone. Because virtually all business processes today involve some component of IT, the idea of trying to align IT with business processes would merely automate or update processes already in place. Instead, business processes are designed concurrently with IT systems. Both the LEGO Group and Judo Bank cases at the beginning of this chapter illustrate this very well. For LEGO, simply continuing its existing business processes or making them faster with newer technology would perpetuate its decline in profitability. The company was able to reverse this trend only by redesigning or redirecting its business processes, an effort that was enabled by IT. The positive results of the decisions made by both LEGO and Judo were undoubtedly attributable to their vision for business processes rather than only on IT processes.

As both firms found, building an enterprise architecture is more than just linking the business processes to IT. It starts with organizational clarity of vision and strategy and places a high value on consistency in approach as a means of optimal effectiveness. The consistency manifests itself as some level of standardization—standardization of processes, deliverables, roles, and/or data. Every EA has elements of all these types of standardization; however, the degree and proportion of each vary with organizational needs, making it dynamic. A good enterprise architect understands this and looks for the right blend for each activity the business undertakes. It means that because organizational groups and individuals are resources for business processes, the organizational design decisions should be part of the enterprise architecture.

[28] For more information on these methodologies, see Roger Sessions, "A Comparison of the Top Four Enterprise-Architecture Methodologies," http://www3.cis.gsu.edu/dtruex/courses/CIS8090/2013Articles/A%20Comparison%20of%20the%20Top%20Four%20Enterprise-Architecture%20Methodologies.html (accessed February 20, 2019); Q. N. Bui, "Evaluate Enterprise Architecture Frameworks Using Essential Elements," *Communications of the Association for Information Systems* 41 (2017): 121–49, https://doi.org/ 10.17705/1CAIS.04106; and T. Magoulas, A. Hadzic, T. Saarikko, and K. Pessi, "Alignment in Enterprise Architecture: A Comparative Analysis of Four Architectural Approaches," *The Electronic Journal Information Systems Evaluation* 15, no. 1 (2012): 88–101, http://www.ejise.com/issue/download.html?idArticle=821.

Despite its many benefits, this is a sophisticated approach, and enterprise architects often have sought to put more rigid standards in place and did not attempt to tackle the more complex organizational design issues. More recently, EA is considered to include organizational design components including organizational structure, incentive systems, and culture, as well as a focus on business processes.[29]

The EA documentation is difficult to prepare and maintain within the complex organizational environment. Sometimes the EA practice is poorly accepted because it is poorly integrated into normal organizational processes. Studies report dismal failure rate ranging from 40% to 90%.[30] Clearly, EA needs to be carefully planned and implemented to be successful.

Multi-Homing, Virtualization, and Cloud Computing

One common practice to increase the reliability of a server's connection to the Internet is to use **multi-homing**, which enables firms or consumers to adopt competing technologies at the same time. On a simple scale, installing and using both Uber and Lyft apps on your smartphone is an example of multi-homing.[31] Also, a computer allowing use of both Windows and Mac OS is another simple example of multi-homing.[32] Some argue that multihoming reduces the business the larger market-share app would have enjoyed if you used single-homing (having only one installed).[33]

In networks, multi-homing allows a firm to have multiple connections to the Internet, using two different Internet service providers. A multi-homed network that connects to two different Internet service providers simultaneously can switch between them if one fails.[34] Researchers have been experimenting for some time to speed up the switching in multi-homing so that consumers, employees, and partners would not even notice any lag.

Some multi-homing applications are largely based on the concept of *virtualization* or *virtual infrastructure*. Physical corporate data centers are rapidly being replaced by **virtual infrastructure**, which originally meant that a "virtual machine" or a "virtual desktop system" was accessible to provide computing power. In this case, software was used to mimic some, or all, of the functions previously provided by hardware. In most virtual architectures, the five core components available virtually are servers, storage, backup, network, and disaster recovery.

Virtualizing the desktop is a common practice. In a virtualized desktop, the user's device locally uses desktop software from a remote server, essentially separating the operating system from the applications. For example, Chromebooks operate this way. The devices are a platform, with a very small amount of software installed on them, and they are designed to access all apps and software from the Google website. The app does not reside on the device, rather it is in the cloud. **Virtualization** is a useful way to design architecture because it enables resources to be shared and allocated as needed by the user and makes maintenance easier because resources are centralized.

Cloud computing describes an architecture based on services (such as apps and storage) provided over the Internet. Cloud computing has increased in importance dramatically over the last decade as the apps and service providers have matured. A 2022 study placed cloud computing at #5 in a list of technologies that should receive more investment.[35] The flexibility of cloud computing has enabled firms such as LEGO and Judo Bank to thrive.

Cloud computing is based on the concept of a virtual infrastructure. Entire computing infrastructures are available "in the cloud." Using the cloud to provide infrastructure means that the cloud is essentially a large cluster of virtual servers or storage devices. This is called *infrastructure as a service* (IaaS).

[29] Törmer and Henningsson, "Dynamic Capabilities in the LEGO Group," 2019, Ibid.

[30] S. Kotusev, "Critical Questions in Enterprise Architecture Research," *International Journal of Enterprise Information Systems (IJEIS)* 13, no. 2 (2017): 50–62, https://doi.org/10.4018/IJEIS.2017040104.

[31] Feng Zhu and Marco Iansiti, "Why Some Platforms Thrive and Others Don't," *Harvard Business Review*, 97 no. 1 (2019), 118–25.

[32] Anitesh Barua and Rajiv Mukherjee, "Multi-Homing Revisited: Level of Adoption and Competitive Strategies," *MIS Quarterly* 45, no. 2 (2021): 897–924, https://doi.org/10.25300/MISQ/2021/15416.

[33] Ibid.

[34] Salma Ibnalfakih, Essaïd Sabir, and Mohammed Sadik, "Multi-homing as an Enabler for 5G Networks: Survey and Open Challenges," in *Advances in Ubiquitous Networking 2: Proceedings of the UNet'16* 2 (Springer Singapore, 2017), 347–56.

[35] Vess Johnson, Russell Torres, Chris Maurer, Smriti Srivastava, Katia Guerra, and Hossein Mohit, "A Preview of the 2022 SIM IT Trends Study," *MIS Quarterly Executive* 21, no. 4 (2022), Article 3. Available at: https://aisel.aisnet.org/misqe/vol21/iss4/3

In addition to IaaS, many other services are found in cloud computing. Software as a service (SaaS) and platform as a service (PaaS) are common examples. Using the cloud for a platform means that the manager will use an environment with the basic platform and app software available, such as web software, applications, database, and collaboration tools.[36] Like Judo Bank, inventive entrepreneurs have created many unique offerings of "aaS" items such as payment processing as a service (PPaaS), device as a service (DaaS), disaster recovery as a service (DRaaS), login recovery as a service (LRaaS), and of course, the logical extreme, everything as a service (EaaS). Using the cloud for an entire application generally means that the software is custom designed, or custom configured for the business but resides in the cloud.

Figure 6.6 illustrates a hierarchy of six rather common "as a service" variants with examples of products offering that service. Some have already been described, but for your convenience, the complete list of the first (capitalized) letters are Software (SaaS), Functions (FaaS), Data (DaaS), Platform (PaaS), STorage (STaaS), and Infrastructure (IaaS).

Consumers of cloud computing purchase capacity on demand and are not generally concerned with the underlying technologies. It's the next step in **utility computing**, or purchasing any part of the consumers' storage or processing infrastructure on demand. Much like the distribution of electricity, the vision of utility computing is that computing infrastructure would be available when needed in as much quantity as needed. Ultimately, the customer is billed only for what is used. In utility computing, a company uses a third-party infrastructure to do its processing or transactions and pay only for what it uses. As in the case of the electrical utility, the economies of scale enjoyed by the computing utility enable very attractive financial models for their customers. As the cost of connectivity falls, new models of cloud computing emerge.

Salesforce.com, Instagram, TikTok, Facebook, Gmail, Windows Azure, Apple iTunes, and LinkedIn are but some examples of applications in the cloud. Some of these apps connect to other apps, making it possible to perform functions without having to retype information from one place to another. For instance, SAP Concur, a travel planning and expense tracking system, allows the user to make a flight reservation, and simultaneously update his or her calendar to include the trip. LinkedIn provides useful services beyond building a network of other business professionals, such as linking a user's blog to her or his profile, sharing and storing documents among the group's members, and accessing applications such as Goodreads to see what network peers are reading and Tripit to learn about their travel plans.

Benefits of virtualization and cloud computing are many. Businesses that embrace a virtual infrastructure can consolidate physical servers and possibly eliminate many of them, greatly reducing the physical costs of the data center. Fees can be based on transaction volumes rather than large up-front investments. There is no separate cost for upgrade, maintenance, and electricity. Nor is there a need to devote physical

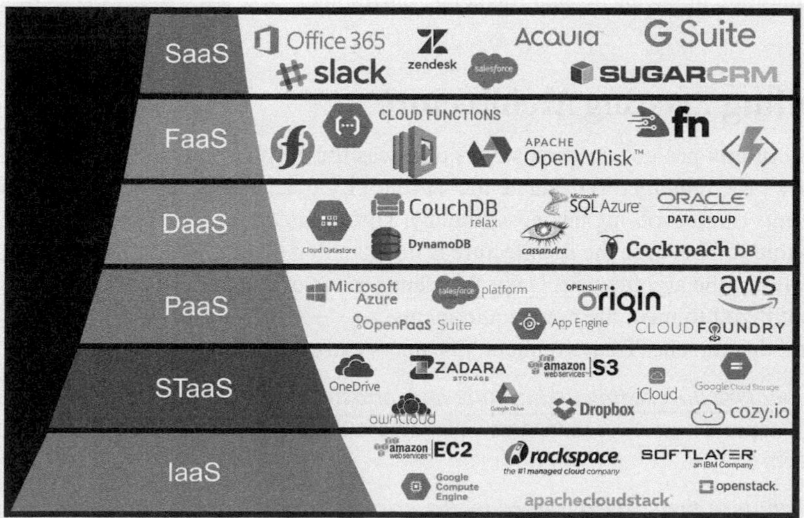

FIGURE 6.6 Hierarchy of "as a Service" offerings and firms.

Source: Ivan Melgrati, "Cloud services delivery models. Which can help your business?" IMELGRAT.ME / https://imelgrat.me/cloud/cloud-services-models-help-business/ last accessed under June 05, 2023.

[36] This is described more fully in Chapter 10.

space or to guess how many storage servers are required. Typically, the network is much simpler, too, because the virtual infrastructure mainly requires Internet connections for all applications and devices. But the biggest benefit of virtualization and cloud computing is the speed at which additional capacity, or provisioning, can be done. In a traditional data center, additional capacity is often a matter of purchasing additional hardware, waiting for its delivery, physically installing it, and ensuring its compatibility with the existing systems. In a virtual infrastructure, the nature of the architecture is dynamic by design, making adding capacity measured in minutes instead of weeks.

For example, *The New York Times* decided to make all 11 million public domain articles from 1851 to 1922 available on the Internet using PDF files of all the articles scanned from the original papers in its archives. This was estimated to be a mountain of work and required significant computing power and space to store them. The manager of this project had an idea to use the cloud. He selected Amazon's EC2 (Elastic Compute Cloud), wrote some code to test the project he envisioned on the Amazon servers. The setup and conversion would have taken at least a month to do if he used the few servers available to him at work. Instead he was able to use a virtual server cluster of 100 servers at Amazon.[37]

But managers considering virtualization and cloud computing must also understand the risks. First is the dependence on the third-party supplier. Building applications that work in the cloud may mean retooling existing applications for the cloud's infrastructure. In terms of market share, as of the writing of this text, the dominant virtualization vendor is VMware, a company that offers software for workstations, virtual desktop infrastructures, and servers.[38] However, applications running on one vendor's infrastructure may not port easily to another vendor's environment.

Architectures are increasingly providing virtualization, multi-homing, and cloud computing as alternatives to in-house old-fashioned infrastructures. As coordination costs drop and new platforms in the cloud are introduced, more of these technologies will increase in their utilization.

Other Managerial Considerations

The infrastructure and architecture framework shown in Figure 6.3 guides the manager toward the design and implementation of an appropriate infrastructure. Defining an IT architecture that fulfills an organization's needs today is relatively simple; the problem is that by the time it is installed, those needs can change. The primary reason to base an architecture on an organization's strategic goals is to allow for inevitable future changes—changes in the business environment, organization, IT requirements, and technology itself. Considering future impacts should include analyzing the existing architecture, the strategic time frame, technological advances, and financial constraints.

Understanding Existing Architecture

At the beginning of any project, the first step is to assess the current situation. Understanding existing IT architecture allows the manager to evaluate the current IT capacity and capabilities and compare them to the IT requirements of an evolving business strategy. The architecture, rather than the infrastructure, is the basis for this evaluation because the architecture is the plan that supports the business strategy whereas the infrastructure follows the architecture. Next, the manager can evaluate the infrastructure and the degree to which it can be utilized to meet the new requirements.

To understand the current IT environment, managers can start with three steps:

1. *Objectively analyze the existing architecture and infrastructure:* Remember that architecture and infrastructure are separate entities; managers must assess the capability, capacity, reliability, and expandability of each.

2. *Objectively analyze the strategy served by the existing architecture:* What were the strategic goals it was designed to attain? To what extent do those goals align with current strategic goals?

[37] Galen Gruman, "Early Experiments in Cloud Computing," *InfoWorld*, April 7, 2008, https://www.infoworld.com/article/2649759/early-experiments-in-cloud-computing.html (accessed May 26, 2023).

[38] Statista, "Market Share of Leading Virtualization Technologies Worldwide as of November 2022," November 2022, https://www.statista.com/statistics/1252355/top-virtualization-technologies-by-domain/ (accessed April 24, 2023).

3. *Objectively analyze the ability of the existing architecture and infrastructure to further the current strategic goals:* In what areas is alignment present? What parts of the existing architecture or infrastructure must be modified? Replaced?

Starting with a clean slate to develop a new architecture allows the most flexibility in determining how to best serve a new business strategy. However, seldom is that the situation. More often, managers must deal in some way with an existing IT environment. Whether managers are facing a fresh start or an existing architecture, they must ensure that the architecture will satisfy their strategic requirements and that the associated infrastructure is modern and efficient. The following sections describe evaluation criteria including strategic time frame, technical issues (adaptability, scalability, standardization, maintainability), and financial issues.

Assessing Strategic Timeframe

Understanding the life span of an IT infrastructure and architecture is critical. How far into the future does the strategy extend? How long can the architecture and its associated infrastructure fulfill strategic goals? What issues could arise and change these assumptions?

Answers to these questions vary widely from industry to industry. Strategic time frames depend on industry-wide factors such as level of commitment to fixed resources, maturity of the industry, cyclicality, and barriers to entry. The competitive environment has increased the pace of change to the point that requires any strategic decision be viewed as temporary.

Architectural longevity depends not only on the strategic planning horizon, but also on the nature of a manager's reliance on IT and on the specific rate of advances affecting the information technologies on which he or she depends. Today's architectures must be designed with maximum flexibility and scalability to ensure they can handle imminent business changes. Imagine the planning horizon for an analytics company in an industry in which Internet technologies and applications are changing daily, if not more often. You might remember the importance of flexibility and agility to LEGO's new business strategy and that the firm's IT architecture was created to support it.

Assessing Technical Issues: Adaptability

With the rapid pace of business, it is no longer possible to build a static information system to support businesses. Instead, adaptability is a core design principle of every IT architecture and one reason why cloud computing and virtualization are increasingly popular.

At a minimum, **adaptability** means that the architecture should be able to handle expected technological advances, such as innovations in storage capacity, end-user devices, and computing power. An exceptional architecture also has the capacity to absorb unexpected technological leaps. Both platforms and apps should be considered when promoting adaptability. For example, new apps that may benefit the corporation emerge daily. The architecture must be able to employ these apps without violating the architecture principles or significantly disrupting business operations.

Note that requirements concerning reliability may conflict with the need for technological adaptability under certain circumstances. If the architecture requires high reliability, a manager seldom is tempted by brand-new or **bleeding-edge** technologies. The competitive advantage offered by bleeding-edge technologies can be eroded by downtime and other problems resulting from untested situations, immature code, and other pioneering efforts with the technology.

Assessing Technical Issues: Scalability and Standardization

A large number of other technical issues should also be considered when selecting an architecture or infrastructure. **Scalability** refers to how well an infrastructure component can adapt to increased, or in some cases decreased, demands. A scalable network system, for instance, could start with just a few connected devices but could easily be expanded to include thousands. Scalability is an important technical feature because it means that an infrastructure or architecture will grow or shrink easily as the needs of the firm change.

What is the company's projected growth? What must the architecture do to support it? How will it respond if the company greatly exceeds its growth goals? What if the projected growth never materializes? These questions help define scalability needs.

Similar to the value of a scalable infrastructure is one that employs *standardization*, which is the implementation of standards. **Standards** are technical specifications that are expected to be followed throughout the infrastructure. Platforms and apps that use a common standard as opposed to a proprietary approach are, as Judo Bank predicted, easier to plug into an existing or future infrastructure or architecture because interfaces often accommodate the standard. For example, many companies use Microsoft Office software, making it an almost de facto standard. Therefore, a number of additional packages come with translators to the systems in the Office suite to make it easy to move data between systems.

Assessing Technical Issues: Maintainability

Maintainability, or the ease and speed with which a system can be made to run correctly again after a failure occurs, is an aspect of infrastructure and architecture that can greatly affect overall lifetime costs of the IT. How easy is the infrastructure to maintain? Are replacement parts available? Is service available? Maintainability is a key technical consideration because the complexity of these systems increases the number of things that can go wrong, need fixing, or simply need replacing. In addition to availability of parts and service people, maintenance considerations include issues such as the length of time the system might be out of commission for maintenance, how expensive and how available the parts are, and obsolescence. Should a technology become obsolete, costs for parts and expertise skyrocket.

Assessing Technical Issues: Security

Securing assets, the data and the systems themselves, is an important, but often neglected, component of architectures and infrastructures. An entire chapter has been devoted to managerial considerations for system security (see Chapter 7), but it is raised here, too. Security is a matter of protecting every end point in a system: the access to the servers, the access to the network, and the access to every end-user device. Security plans look different for different architectures; a centralized or decentralized architecture has security plans that secure all the components in the firm's infrastructure. A web-based SOA architecture that utilizes SaaS and capacity on demand raises an entirely different set of security issues. Because the data and applications reside on servers in the various vendor systems around the web, managers need to be sure they understand how each vendor in the architecture ensures security. Sometimes that means the firm itself has to invest in additional security on top of the vendor's security to achieve the level needed. Chapter 7 describes the multifaceted area of security in more detail.

Assessing Technical Issues: We Are on the Path to Quantum Computing

In the lives of the three coauthors of this book, computers have evolved in exciting and sometimes mystifying ways. Scientists discovered that encoding letters and numbers into binary digits (zeroes and ones only) would enable machines to process them. Those researchers invented vacuum tubes, resembling little lightbulbs, that were able to compare, reverse, and switch stored bits very rapidly and then read the results. With enough of those vacuum tubes, and circuitry to translate binary bits to our letters and numbers, you could calculate much more quickly than a human with ten fingers or a pad and paper.

These hot vacuum tubes, that did not last very long and suffered short lives, were replaced by smaller and cooler components called "transistors" that did not "conduct" but "semi-conducted" depending on the current applied to them. These transistors were much cooler than vacuum tubes, so they were pushed to greater and greater speeds until they also became hot. Scientists then found a way to miniaturize the transistors on to wafers of silicon, and the much smaller size allowed the electrons to flow in shorter distances, reducing the heat and allowing faster speeds. But they became hot when the systems were sped up, which led to "speed limits" for the chips. If you exceed those limits, rather than a citation, you will have a meltdown. No matter how pure a metal wire is made, there is still a little heat resistance from electrons flowing on the wire. And even tiny wires that connect all of the components become hot when pushed to high speeds to process all of those bits (remember, they represent only zeroes and ones).

Heat is the issue that has led us to **quantum computing**. Scientists found that very cold temperatures, near absolute zero (−273 °C) can enable current to flow with almost no resistance.[39] Laser beams or microwaves can temporarily heat selected, so-called qubits, and make them work like bits but they do not have to be either a zero or a one, but a value that is, say, "70% zero and 30% one. Photos from IBM show them looking like eerie upside-down wedding cakes, strikingly resembling chandeliers.[40]

Today, quantum computers have many advantages over classical (today's) computers, but also practical problems. They are especially good at factoring numbers, which makes them efficient at encryption and decryption of secret messages. They are also very good at very difficult problems such as exploring what would happen when combining molecules in millions of combinations, machine learning (see Chapter 12), optimization problems, and physics and algebra problems. However, they are not very good at simple problems, making the most sense when used in conjunction with traditional classical computers. Also, they might endanger encrypted information of today (see Chapter 7), being able to crack passwords and encryption codes quickly, enabling a nefarious character to decode stolen encrypted data in minutes rather than centuries. And don't think you can just plug one in and use it immediately; so far, they require two full days to reach their coldest point.[41] Also, they are very expensive, and the bits are rather unstable, in case of temperature instability and even cosmic rays.[42] They require redundancy so that many Qubits can work together and check each other.

Quantum computers are still in their infancy, and firms are exploring ways in which they can be used. One thing stands out: their fast speed can be an incredible step forward for those difficult problems. One scientist characterized it as follows: "It's not 'whoopee I can do this in two hours instead of two days,' it's 'whoopie I can do this in two hours instead of nine million years.'"[43] This is not an exaggeration because a quantum computer can operate 158 million times faster than today's fastest supercomputers. While IBM has made quantum computers available today, in the cloud, to developers worldwide,[44] applications of quantum computing are currently being explored.

The expectation is that in the decades to come, important quantum applications will come to light. Many predict advancements in medicine and commerce we cannot imagine yet. But with a bit more development of today's quantum technology, you should be able to quickly solve that optimization problem your computer struggles with. You will likely solve that difficult problem of allocating delivery routes among hundreds of vehicles; that nasty supply chain conundrum with many suppliers that involve different costs, risks, and delays; and that confusing portfolio optimization task for hundreds of clients. Those would lead to the proverbial "whoopee" described above because they take long to solve today.

Assessing Financial and Managerial Issues

Like any business investment, IT infrastructure components should be evaluated based on their expected financial value. Unfortunately, payback from IT investments is often difficult to quantify; it can come in the form of increased productivity, increased interoperability with business partners, improved service for customers, or yet more abstract benefits such as capacity or scalability. This suggests focusing on how IT investments enable business objectives rather than on their quantitative returns. Chapter 8 dives deeper into the ways to evaluate IT investments.

Still, some effort can and should be made to quantify the return on infrastructure investments. This effort can be simplified if a manager works through the following steps with the IT staff.

Quantify costs: The easy part is costing out the proposed infrastructure components and estimating the total investment necessary. Work with the IT staff to identify cost trends in the equipment the company proposes to acquire. Don't forget to include installation and training costs in the total.

[39] Neil Savage, "Quantum Computers Compete for 'Supremacy,'" Scientific American, July 5, 2017, https://www.scientificamerican.com/article/quantum-computers-compete-for-supremacy/ (accessed May 26, 2023).

[40] Charlotte Hu, "In photos: Journey to the center of a quantum computer," *Popular Science,* September 7, 2022, https://www.popsci.com/technology/in-photos-journey-to-the-center-of-a-quantum-computer/ (accessed May 26, 2023).

[41] Ibid.

[42] Benard Marr, "Quantum computing now and in the future: Explanation, Applications, and Problems," *Forbes,* August 26, 2022, https://www.forbes.com/sites/bernardmarr/2022/08/26/quantum-computing-now-and-in-the-future-explanation-applications-and-problems/ (accessed May 26, 2023).

[43] Ibid.

[44] IBM, "What is quantum computing?" undated, https://www.ibm.com/topics/quantum-computing (accessed May 26, 2023).

Determine the anticipated life cycles of system components: Experienced IT staff or consultants can help establish life cycle trends for both a company and an industry to estimate the useful life of various systems.

Quantify benefits: The hard part is obtaining input from all affected user groups as well as the IT group, which presumably knows most about the equipment's capabilities. If possible, form a team with representatives from each of these groups and work together to identify all potential areas in which the new IT system may bring value.

Quantify risks: Assess any risk that might be attributable to delaying acquisition as opposed to paying more to get the latest technology now.

Consider ongoing dollar costs and benefits: Examine how the new equipment affects maintenance and upgrade costs associated with the current infrastructure.

Once this analysis is complete, the manager can employ the company's preferred capital budgeting models, such as ROI, payback period, or discounted cash flow.[45]

SUMMARY

- Strategy drives architecture, which drives infrastructure. Strategic business goals dictate IT architecture requirements. These requirements provide an extensible blueprint suggesting which infrastructure components will best facilitate the realization of the strategic goals.
- Enterprise architecture is the broad design that includes both the information systems architecture and the interrelationships in the enterprise. Often this plan specifies the logic for the entire organization. It identifies core processes, how they work together, how IT systems will support them, and the capabilities necessary to create, execute, and manage them. Four common EAs are TOGAF, Zachman, FEA, and Gartner.
- Four configurations for IT architecture are centralized, decentralized, SOA (or web-based), and software-defined architectures. Applications are increasingly being offered as services, reducing the cost and maintenance requirements for clients. Virtualization, multi-homing, and cloud computing provide architectures for flexible, web-based delivery of services.
- The manager's role is to understand how to plan IT to realize business goals. With this knowledge, the manager can work with his or her technology team to translate business goals to IT architecture and identify appropriate infrastructure components.
- Frameworks guide the translation from business strategy to IS design. This translation can be simplified by categorizing components into broad classes (platforms, apps, network, data), which make up both IT architecture and infrastructure.
- Firm leaders increasingly have requests for new devices that employees want to connect to the corporate network. IT consumerization describes the trend to redesign corporate systems for smartphones, tablets, and other consumer-oriented devices.
- While translating strategy into architecture and then infrastructure, it is important to know the state of any existing architecture and infrastructure, to weigh current against future architectural requirements and strategic time frame, and to analyze the financial consequences of the various systems options under consideration. Systems performance should be monitored on an ongoing basis.
- New technologies such as AI and quantum computing are not only likely to change infrastructure, but also architecture, and potentially strategy as well. We are already seeing this today.

KEY TERMS

adaptability, 145
apps, 132
architecture, 131
bleeding-edge, 145
bring your own device (BYOD), 139
capacity-on-demand, 139
centralized architecture, 137
cloud architecture, 139
cloud computing, 142
data center, 137
decentralized architecture, 137

[45] Evaluating IT investments is discussed in Chapter 8.

FOUNDATIONAL READINGS

Erl, T., Puttini, R., & Mahmood, Z. (2013). *Cloud computing: concepts, technology & architecture*. Pearson Education.

Inmon, W. H. H., Linstedt, D., & Levins, M. (2019). *Data Architecture: A Primer for the Data Scientist: A Primer for the Data Scientist*. Academic Press.

Woland, A.T., and Heary, J., *Cisco ISE for BYOD and secure unified access: (2013)*. (Indianapolis, IN: Pearson Education).

Ross, Jeanne W., Weill, Peter, and Robertson, David C. Enterprise Architecture: *Enterprise Architecture as Strategy* (Boston, MA: Harvard Business School Press, 2006).

DISCUSSION QUESTIONS

1. Think about a company you know well. How would you describe the IT architecture at that company? Please share an example of a component that would be part of their IT infrastructure.
2. What, in your opinion, is the difference between a decentralized architecture and a centralized architecture? What is an example of a business decision that would be affected by the choice of the architecture?
3. From your personal experience, what is an example of software as a service? Of BYOD?
4. Each of the following companies would benefit from either software-defined architecture or conventional, owned platform and apps. State which you would advise each of the following organizations to adopt and explain why.

   (a) StableCo is a firm that sells industrial paper shredders. Its business has remained steady for two decades and it has a strong and diverse customer base.

   (b) DynamicCo is a fast-growing six-year-old firm that has relied on three to five key wholesale customers for its entire existence. However, the list of key customers changes every year, and during two of the years, sales declined sharply.

   (c) Plastics3000 is an old, stable plastics manufacturing firm that has kept its sales steady in the face of competitors as the result of an active research and development team that uses advanced software to analyze large amounts of data to develop new compounds. Once or twice a week, office personnel complain of the network becoming very slow.

   (d) A downtown Las Vegas casino monitors each slot machine continuously for early detection of malfunctions such as winnings or losses trending beyond their threshold limits.

   (e) CallPerfect provides call center services to pharmacies. Phone calls are routed to the company after hours and messages are delivered to the pharmacy manager the next morning.

   (f) At the IRS, tax forms are available online for citizens to complete and file with the IRS electronically by April 15. A call center routes calls to agents who answer taxpayers' questions.

   (g) At LittlePeople, Inc., a day care center, parents are called using software on the administrator's computer when there is a weather emergency. The school has averaged 120 families for many years.

Case Study 6-1 Enterprise Architecture at Chubb Industries

Enterprise architecture (EA) at Chubb was the framework the organization used to align IT and the business. EA provided a target architecture for business leaders and IT professionals to use to collaborate and to enable the company to adapt and prosper. "Our EA is the glue that brings Business and IT together," claimed Chubb CIO, Jim Knight.

Chubb Industries, which now operates in 54 countries and territories, is the largest publicly traded property and casualty insurance company in the world and the largest commercial insurer in the United States. Having been founded in North America in 1792, it may well be one of the oldest underwriting companies.

CIO Knight had put in place a decentralized (federated) EA in place to support Chubb's seven lines of business (LOB). However, after six years he realized that tweaks to the decentralized EA were not able to deal with problems that surfaced over time. In particular, standards weren't being followed closely enough and the business units were focusing on their own unit's goals but suboptimizing on the organizational goals. The decentralized approach inhibited agility because it misaligned IT and the enterprise business strategy, created duplication, and impeded coordination across the LOBs. Knight decided to consolidate the LOB architects into a centralized enterprise IT organization with a broader scope.

CIO Knight reorganized Chubb's IT group to have a Chief Architect/Architecture Practice Lead who reported to the Chief Development Officer who, in turn, reported to Knight himself. A Manager in charge of Development also reported to the Chief Development Officer. The Manager in charge of Infrastructure reported directly to Knight. The new IT organization was designed to deliver integrated solutions to the business.

One of the first things Knight did was create a target architecture with four major components: *Architecture Principles* (i.e., general rules and guidelines including "Be business oriented with a business-driven design," "Promote consistent architecture," etc.); *Architecture Governance* (i.e., practices to manage at the enterprise-wide level including controls, compliance obligations, processes, etc.); *Conceptual Reference Architectures* (i.e., target architecture support domains including business, application, information and technical architectures, policy administration, advanced analytics, i.e., content management); and, *Emerging Technology* (processes to promote innovation and explore emerging technologies). The target architecture used 50 architecture compliance rules derived from the TOGAF framework.

All new projects were issued a "building permit" by the Architecture Governance Board and were assigned one or more architects from the five EA domains (i.e., Business, Application, Information, Technical, and Security) to ensure that the target architecture was being adhered to. The architects submitted artifacts and design documents for review and formal approval. Any deviations from the architecture rules must be corrected or remediated. The architects worked closely with the project leader.

One of the projects that earned a "building permit" was Worldview®, a proprietary risk management platform, which provides U.S. and multinational clients and their brokers instant access to Chubb. When the platform premiered in 2011 it received the Business Insurance Innovation award. After the platform underwent a major revision, it again won the Innovation award in 2020. The major redesign and upgrades were driven by customer feedback and led to features such as drill-down and filtering capabilities on personalized interactive charts and graphs, predictive model outputs to support data-driven decisions in underwriting and claims management, an app to translate policies written in a nation's local language into English, and an intuitive, easy-to-navigate home screen. Worldview® supports digitized workflows for a range of activities issuing policies, electronically delivering program documents, handling claims, account servicing, preparing invoices, and moving money.

It was believed by the IT executives that the new EA model delivered value to the business, helped determine the new technologies that offered the greatest potential benefits, and provided better access to IT intellectual capital. The LOBs get the resources that are most appropriate for meeting their needs. But it wasn't only the IT people who thought the EA added value. Dan Paccico, the Senior Vice President and Controller, said: "Chubb now has better long-term and strategic planning reflecting an enterprise point of view."

Case Study 6-1 (Continued)

Source: Adapted from H. A. Smith and R. T. Watson, "The Jewel in the Crown—Enterprise Architecture at Chubb," *MIS Quarterly Executive*, 14, no. 4 (2015), 195–209; https://www.chubb.com/us-en/about-chubb/who-we-are.aspx (accessed March 9, 2019); see also S. Kotusev, "Critical Questions in Enterprise Architecture Research," *International Journal of Enterprise Information Systems (IJEIS)*, 13, no. 2 (2017), 50–62; https://news.na.chubb.com/2020-08-20-Chubb-Wins-Business-Insurance-2020-Innovation-Award (accessed March 1, 2023); https://www.chubb.com/us-en/worldview.html (accessed March 1, 2023).

Discussion Questions

1. What are the key components of the architecture Chubb has created?
2. Why was it important to standardize so much of the architecture? What are the advantages and disadvantages of a standard EA for Chubb?
3. Describe how the new architecture supports the goals and strategy of Chubb.
4. Compare and contrast the advantages and disadvantages of the centralized and decentralized EAs at Chubb.
5. Why was it important to get customer feedback on the redesign of Worldview®?
6. What is your vision of how the target architecture might work in the future? If you were advising Jim Knight, the CIO of Chubb, what challenges would you suggest his group prepare for?

Case Study 6-2 Mohawk Paper

Mohawk, a paper mill established in 1931 in upstate New York, provided an early example of modern information systems architecture. Contrary to a common assumption that information technology was not critical to traditional manufacturing industry players facing a declining market, the firm embraced cloud computing since it enabled the business to strategically transform itself in three ways: (1) moving from a primary focus on manufacturing to providing service, (2) shifting from a self-sufficient model to one of collaboration with a network of partners, and (3) ensuring that the partner network was flexible and its capabilities were tightly integrated with those of Mohawk. Mohawk accomplished this flexibility by using service-oriented architecture (SOA) tools, which enabled the firm to scale technology services (and expenses) up and down instantaneously according to its needs.[1] Also, applications under SOA were added or subtracted as needed, helping to manage costs while increasing flexibility and capacity throughout the transformation.

Mohawk's new envelope manufacturing facility served as a vivid example to illustrate the benefits of flexibility. Along the way, the company learned of the anticipated bankruptcy of the largest envelope manufacturing firm in the United States and saw an opportunity for new business. Managers developed a list of six outsourced firms to turn its premium papers into envelopes. After six months of using those suppliers and investing in building its own in-house envelope manufacturing capabilities, Mohawk was able to shift to an insourcing model for 90% of its volume. Using cloud services avoided the information systems difficulties usually inherent in such a large-scale strategic transformation.

Mohawk realized additional benefits from their ability to more easily manage capacity needs. As processing volumes increased and decreased, sometimes on a seasonal basis and sometimes due to new or discontinued lines of business, Mohawk experienced corresponding increases and decreases in its requirements for information systems capacity such as space, servers, and processing. Its cloud approach allowed the company to set up or dismantle servers quickly and at a fraction of the cost of purchasing them outright.

Mohawk's experience shows that cloud computing is not just a mechanism to avoid or reduce costs or to gain operational benefits. The cloud and associated services can support a transformation of the business itself. Mohawk's mission changed from "making paper" to "making connections," which enabled them to sell consumers five times the number of products sold previously to just a few

***Case Study 6-2* (Continued)**

large distributors. While partners offered many of Mohawk's products, the system provided capabilities to sell from Mohawk's own inventory or from the partners in a seamless way directly to many thousands of small businesses and consumers via its website.

Mohawk was able to make the changes it believed were necessary by shifting to an enhanced web services platform that enabled other organizations and customers to request information, inquire about freight charges and pricing, place orders, and pay for their orders through connections with banks. The platform enabled designers to "mash up" (combine) applications as needed on websites that could be built rather quickly. Each feature "plugs in" using tools that made it easy to connect the websites to existing databases.

Mohawk has also adopted a targeted view of BYOD to remotely monitor and control the firm's processes and operations. Paul Stamas, Mohawk's former vice president of Information Technology at Mohawk, says, "Our view of BYOD seeks to ensure that a specific enterprise footprint is provided on a personally owned or a company-provided device, with. . . either limited to certain applications and data. In our case, that's manufacturing applications and data." It uses an app from a third party to get real-time display and trending data and SQL code generated in-house to obtain non-process manufacturing data from Mohawk's ERP system.[2]

Business benefits to Mohawk included the following:

- Sharply reducing the previous pattern of pre-cloud annual earnings decreases, then tripling its earnings in two years
- Automating its transaction processes, saving $1 million to $2 million annually in staff costs
- Increasing its product variety fivefold
- Increasing its customer base from 10–15 distributors to 100 business partners and many thousands of direct customers
- Allowing it to provide designers, brand-owners and printers in more than 60 countries with carefully crafted papers on which to print in a digital world.[3]

Not all firms base their entire operations on a cloud platform that permits integration with other organizations. But Mohawk's experiences can be considered "cutting edge." The Mohawk story illustrates how infrastructure decisions can enable the strategic objectives of a firm. However, building such an infrastructure cannot come first. Firms must begin by determining their strategic vision, determining the IS architecture needed to fulfill that vision, and then making it all tangible by putting together an IS infrastructure. In Mohawk's case, leaders had a vision to move boldly into the consumer space, and information systems enabled them to do that efficiently.

Sources: Adapted from Paul J. Stamas, Michelle L. Kaarst-Brown, and Scott A. Bernard, "The Business Transformation Payoffs of Cloud Services at Mohawk," MIS Quarterly Executive *13, no. 4 (2014).*

[1] Lheureux, Benoit, "Case study: Mohawk fine papers uses a CSB to ease adoption of cloud computing," Gartner, case study 1747717, January 3, 2023. https://www.gartner.com/document/1747717?ref=solrAll&refval=367747885 (accessed May 27, 2023).

[2] Hebert, Dan, "Mohawk buys into BYOD." May 7, 2014. Control Design.com. https://www.controldesign.com/home/article/11333559/manufacturing-industries-mohawk-buys-into-byod (accessed May 27, 2023).

[3] Paul J. Stamas, Michelle L. Kaarst-Brown, and Scott A. Bernard, "The Business Transformation Payoffs of Cloud Services at Mohawk," *MIS Quarterly Executive* 13, no. 4 (2014).

Discussion Questions

1. Given the different "as a service" types, which types are employed by Mohawk?
2. What other "as a service" options seem most promising for Mohawk?
3. After reading the experiences of Mohawk, along with LEGO and Judo Bank, what issues seem to push firms into using outside services?
4. If you were advising a company trying to make a decision about using cloud computing for key business applications, what would you advise and why?
5. What are the advantages of BYOD? What kind of challenges do you think Mohawk experienced with BYOD? Why do you think they only adopted a limited, targeted approach to BYOD?

Cybersecurity

7

Cybersecurity is one of the top risks faced by businesses. Malicious actors hack systems, steal data and intellectual property, and disrupt businesses, which can put a company out of business or cause physical damage to critical infrastructure. General managers must be knowledgeable participants in information security discussions to ensure their organizations are resilient, even if there is a cyber incident. This chapter explores basic concepts for managing cybersecurity including security planning, governance, culture, and metrics. Lessons from some of the largest and most well-known breaches are covered as well as how they occurred, according to security experts. The chapter also discusses common tools that aim to secure access, data storage, and data transmission to prevent these breaches and their advantages and disadvantages. Winding up the chapter is a discussion of how to answer the question "How do we know how secure we are?"

Colonial pipeline is the largest pipeline system for refined oil products in the U.S. Running 5,500 miles long. Carrying up to 3 million barrels of fuel per day between Texas and New York, it fuels most of the East Coast of the United States (see Figure 7.1). In 2021, a ransomware attack forced Colonial Pipeline to stop delivering fuel, impacting consumer gas stations, airline transportation, and other industries dependent on their fuel across the eastern seaboard.

On May 8, 2021, Colonial Pipeline announced that they were the victim of a ransomware cyberattack and proactively shut down operations to minimize further risks to the operational technology (OT) that controlled the pipeline. The operations team developed a plan to restart their systems, and worked with cybersecurity experts, law enforcement, and other federal agencies. Operations were restored on May 13, one week after the initial incident.

What happened at Colonial Pipeline? A hacker group, DarkSide, exploited an old, unpatched vulnerability in the Colonial Pipeline business system. DarkSide was a ransomware-as-a-service group that offered malware to customers, who were mostly malicious actors, on a subscription basis. Their malware, once deployed, encrypted systems, stole data, and deleted copies it found in the system. A phishing email fooled an employee into clicking on a link that gave the hackers access to the business system, and credentials purchased on the dark web provided a way for the hackers to infiltrate the company's network. Colonial Pipeline executives proactively took operational systems offline and halted all pipeline operations as a preemptive measure once their business systems were locked up. They did not want to risk damage, or worse, a catastrophic accident, should the hackers gain access to the actual pipeline.

Over 100 GB of corporate data was exfiltrated from the company's internal systems, and the company paid 75 Bitcoins in ransom, worth about $5M at the time, to have the files "returned." After paying the ransom, they were given the key to decrypt their systems. Fortunately, when the FBI went after the funds paid as ransom, they recovered about $2.3M using money flow analysis and other techniques to hack into Bitcoin. By doing so, the limits of the anonymity offered by cryptocurrencies were exposed, the criminals were identified, and funds were recovered. However, the legal means to recover illegally gained payments, seize assets, and prosecute potential criminals, also pierced the anonymity of the cryptocurrency.

At the same time, this cyberattack sent a wake-up call to other critical infrastructure organizations. Subsequently, The Department of Homeland Security (DHS) issued new regulations to owners and operators of critical pipelines designed to increase security. The Department of Energy also set up new initiatives to

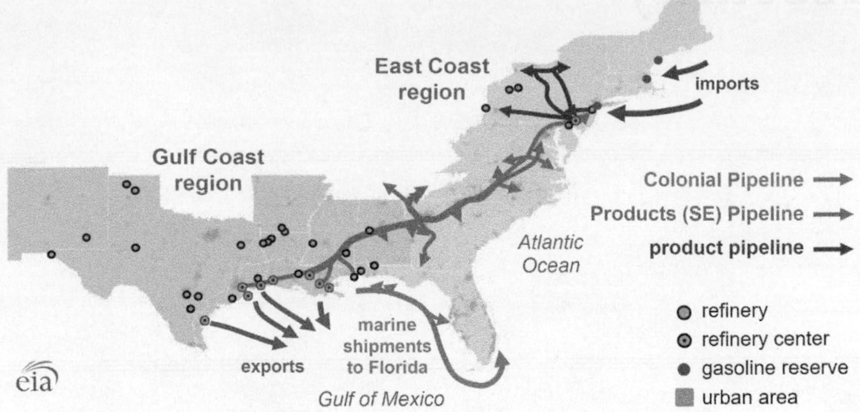

FIGURE 7.1 Scope of the colonial pipeline.
Source: US Energy Information Administration, https://www.eia.gov/todayinenergy/detail.php?id=47917 (retrieved June 8, 2023).

strengthen cybersecurity of critical infrastructure, and CISA (the White House's Cybersecurity and Infrastructure Security Agency) created several initiatives, including a simplified way for organizations to receive ransomware alerts and guidance, a task force to facilitate collaboration across the government, and the Joint Cyber Defense Collaborative (JCDC) to bring in experts to share insights and information in real time.

Cybersecurity is more than just protecting the leakage or exfiltration of information. While many other firms have been victimized, and hundreds of millions of records filled with personal information have been stolen, increasingly malicious actors breach companies to do mischief, disrupt business, or damage operations. It has been estimated that 97% of all firms have been breached at some level.[1] Managers must understand that breaches occur to clarify the picture of what is going on, to understand their organization's vulnerabilities, and to protect their own company from damages caused by successful cyberattacks. Only when threats are more fully understood can management begin to formulate and implement effective security plans and build cyber resilience.

NIST Cybersecurity Framework

The prevailing framework for managing cybersecurity comes from the U.S. National Institute of Standards and Technology (**NIST**). The cybersecurity framework (**CSF**) was designed to protect the country's essential services and critical infrastructure by providing a framework for organizing cybersecurity activities and identifying controls to put in place. It is so widely adopted that it became a de facto standard for organizing cybersecurity activities for many organizations. While the motivation to create the CSF arose from a concern about critical national infrastructure, the resulting framework is used to help leaders plan their organization's cybersecurity strategy.

The NIST CSF (shown in Figure 7.2) consists of five high-level functions that, together, create a robust plan for protecting organizational assets and reducing negative impacts of a cybersecurity attack. The document describing these five functions goes into much more detail, but at the top level, leaders must create plans to *identify, protect, detect, respond, and recover* (Figure 7.3 provides definitions). A sixth function, *govern*, was added in 2023 to provide guidance on implementing and managing cybersecurity within an organization. It is the business leaders' responsibility to make sure plans are in place for all five of these activities to prepare the organization in the event of a breach, to ensure that operations will continue in the event of a cyberattack. It is the cybersecurity leader's responsibility to create the plan and implement it. According to the NIST reports,

> *"These five functions were selected because they represent the five primary pillars for a successful and holistic cybersecurity program. They aid organizations in easily expressing their management of cybersecurity risk at a high level and enabling risk management decisions."*[2]

[1] Bill Whitaker, "What Happens When You Swipe Your Card?" 60 Minutes, November 30, 2014, transcript, http://www.cbsnews.com/news/swiping-your-credit-card-and-hacking-and-cybercrime/ (accessed May 24, 2023).

[2] https://www.nist.gov/cyberframework/online-learning/five-functions (accessed May 31, 2023).

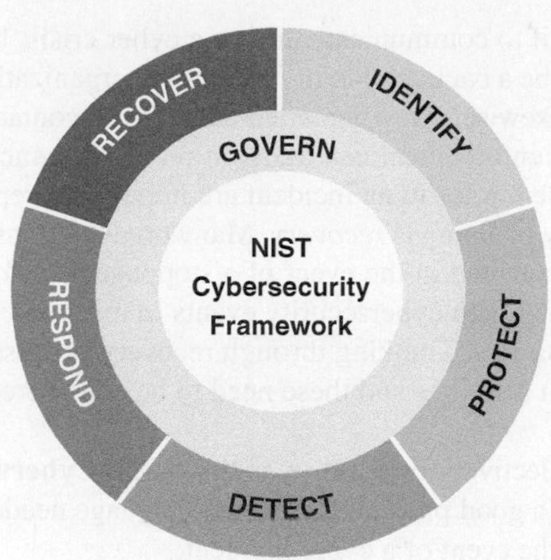

FIGURE 7.2 NIST CSF framework.

Functions	Definitions	Example Activities
Identify	An organizational understanding to manage cybersecurity risk to systems, people, assets, data, and capabilities	Asset management, business environment, risk and vulnerabilities
Protect	Safeguards to ensure delivery of critical infrastructure services	Access control, awareness and training, data security, information protection, maintenance, protective technology
Detect	Activities to identify the occurrence of a cybersecurity event	Continuous monitoring, anomalies and events, detection processes
Respond	Activities to take action regarding a detected cybersecurity incident	Response planning, communication planning, analysis, mitigation, improvement
Recover	Activities to maintain plans for **resilience** and to restore any capabilities or services that were impaired due to a cybersecurity incident	Business recovery planning, improvements, communication planning
Govern	Activities that guide implementation and management of cybersecurity	Risk management, establishing policies and procedures, clarifying roles and responsibilities

FIGURE 7.3 NIST CSF functions and their definitions.

For example, organization leaders concerned about cybersecurity would start by *identifying* the crown jewels, the key valuable assets that must be protected. Leaders would need to also understand the risks and vulnerabilities their organization faces. Plans should include the asset management activities, risk assessment activities, and ongoing updates to keep a current idea of what needs to be protected. Next, leaders would design and implement actions and technologies to *protect* assets and organizations from security events. There are technologies such as identity management systems and asset control systems that help create protections. Processes such as locking up assets (physically and electronically), training team members to identify anomalies, and regular maintenance and updating systems are also part of the protection plans. And building a strong culture of data protection (as discussed later in this chapter) creates another layer of protection.

A plan for *detecting* events is the third set of activities in this framework. Some events are observable, e.g., when a computer screen displays a ransomware notice or a system stops working properly. But in other cases, it's not so obvious. Google's Mandiant, a cybersecurity company, reported in its annual study of cybersecurity trends that in 2022, the dwell time—the time between when a cyberattack happens and the victim detects it—is 21 days. While this is a much shorter time than what was reported in previous years, a hacker only needs a few days to cause severe damage. This suggests that leaders need to create a strong, robust program to detect anomalies in their systems as quickly as possible.

Once an incident occurs, leaders must react and *respond*. Rather than wait until there is an actual event to decide what the reaction should be, a more appropriate scenario is to have a plan for the organization to execute should something occur. One important component is the communication plan. For example, if the plan is for everyone to use e-mail to communicate during a cyber crisis, but e-mail is also compromised during a cyberattack, there must be a backup plan in place or the organization risks not being able to communicate with key personnel. Likewise, knowing when and who to contact in law enforcement is part of this plan. Some agencies of law enforcement can assist in recovery, hence knowing who can assist, and developing a relationship with them prior to an incident are important preparatory actions.

The final area of cybersecurity planning is *recovery*. Many organizations have business continuity plans in place. These are plans to be executed in the event of a stoppage of some sort. But business continuity plans often have not been designed with cybersecurity events in mind, such as wide area power loss, senior leadership loss, or natural disasters. Thinking through recovery processes that assume a cybersecurity event might lead to very different activities and these need to be considered long before an actual event is in motion.

Together these five areas, collectively referred to as the **NIST Cybersecurity Framework** (or NIST CSF) give leaders and managers a good place to start and a language needed to create the necessary plans to protect their organizations in the event of a cyber incident.

IT Security Governance Framework

The first step on the road to an effective security plan is for management to adopt a broad view of security using a framework such as the NIST model described above. This can be done by establishing an information security strategy and then putting the processes, infrastructure (tools), and policies (tactics) in place that can help the organization realize its strategy. To round out the picture, everyone in an organization must understand enough about potential vulnerabilities and their role in protecting company assets, and leaders must make important decisions about trade-offs between security investments and the impact of failures on business processes. The whole security picture can be reflected in five key information security decisions. Understanding these decisions and who is responsible for them (that is, who has the decision rights for them) is presented in Figure 7.4. More detail on each of these components is discussed later in this chapter. We introduced decision rights in Chapter 3, and we use the concept to illustrate appropriate roles of business and IT managers in making a company's security decisions.

1. *Information security strategy:* A company's information security strategy is based on such IT principles as protecting the confidentiality of customer information, strict compliance with regulations, and maintaining a security baseline that is above the industry benchmark. Security strategy is not a technical decision, as it should reflect the company's mission, overall strategy, business model, and business environment. Developing a security strategy requires decision makers who are knowledgeable about the company's strategy and management systems, along with technical input from information systems management.
2. *Information security infrastructure:* Information security infrastructure decisions involve selecting and configuring the right tools. Common objectives are to achieve consistency in protection, economies of scale, and synergy among the components. Top business executives typically lack the experience or expertise to make these decisions. For these reasons, corporate IT typically is responsible for managing the dedicated security mechanisms and general IT infrastructure, such as enterprise network devices. Thus, corporate IT should take the lead and make sure that the technology tools in the infrastructure are correctly specified and configured.
3. *Information security policy:* Security policies provide guidelines for the organization's activities, both technical and organizational, to increase cyber resilience. Following best practices, they broadly define the scope of and overall expectations for the company's information security program. One of the most basic best practices is **cybersecurity hygiene** or applying the basic system updates and patches offered from the vendors of systems, since these updates usually fix known bugs and vulnerabilities. From these security policies, lower-level tactics are developed to control specific security areas (e.g., Internet use, access control) and/or individual applications (e.g., payroll systems, telecom systems). Policies must reflect the delicate balance between the enhanced information security gained from following them versus productivity losses and user inconvenience. For example, some productivity of users is often sacrificed when they have to come up with new passwords every month or when they have to

Information Security Decisions	Who Is Responsible	Rationale	Major Symptoms of Improper Decision Rights Allocation
Security Strategy	Business leaders	Business leaders have deep knowledge of the company's strategies on which security strategy should be based. No detailed technical knowledge is required.	Security is an afterthought and patched on to processes and products.
Infrastructure	IT leaders (CISO)	In-depth technical knowledge and expertise are needed.	There is a misspecification of security and network typologies or a misconfiguration of infrastructure. Technical security control is ineffective.
Security Policy	Shared: IT and business leaders	Technical and security implications of behaviors and processes must be analyzed, and trade-offs made, between security and productivity. The firm's IT infrastructure needs to be understood.	Security policies are written based on theory and generic templates. They are unenforceable due to a misfit with the company's specific IT and users.
Cybersecurity Culture	Shared: IT and business leaders	Business buy-in and understanding are needed to design programs. Technical expertise and knowledge of critical security issues are needed to build them.	User behaviors are not consistent with security needs. Users bypass security measures, fail to recognize threats, or do not know how to react properly when security breaches occur.
Investments	Shared: IT and business leaders	They require financial (quantitative) and qualitative evaluation of business impacts of security investments. A business case must be presented for competing projects. Infrastructure impacts need to be evaluated.	Under- or overinvestment in information security occurs. The human or technical security resources are insufficient or wasted.

FIGURE 7.4 **Key information security decisions for governance.**

Sources: Adapted from Yu Wu, "*What Color Is Your Archetype? Governance Patterns for Information Security*" (Ph.D. Dissertation, University of Central Florida, 2007) and Yu Wu and Carol Saunders, "Governing Information Security: Governance Domains and Decision Rights Allocation Patterns," *Information Resources Management Journal* 24, no. 1 (January–March 2011): 28–45.

spend time judging the legitimacy of dozens of e-mails each day. Both IT and business perspectives are important in setting policies. Business users must be involved in prioritizing what to protect, in identifying how they expect the security function to support their business activities, and in evaluating the trade-off between user convenience and security. On the other hand, IT leaders can help avoid setting unrealistic goals and analyze the technical and security implications of user behaviors and business processes resulting from policy decisions. If either users or IT leaders are not consulted, unenforceable policies will probably result.

4. *Cybersecurity culture:* Employees in an organization perform behaviors that they understand are important to the success of the business. Striving for cybersecure behaviors should not be different; creating that understanding is a function of managerial practices, such as performance rewards and punishments, and the values, attitudes, and beliefs the employees hold about the importance of cybersecurity. It is very important to make business users aware of security policies and practices and to provide information on security education, training, and awareness (SETA). Training and awareness programs provide team members with guidelines and sample behaviors to keep the organization secure. IT and business managers have an additional role to model cybersecure behaviors and to emphasize the importance of cybersecurity.

5. *Information security investments:* The fear, uncertainty, and doubt ("FUD") factor once was all that was needed to get top management to invest in information security. But it is impossible to be 100% secure considering that as new technologies are invented, new ways to breach the systems are also invented. It can be difficult to show how important security is until there has been a breach—and even then, it is hard to put a dollar amount on the value of security. Both IT and business leaders need to participate in investment and prioritization decisions. Answering the question "How much do we need to invest to be safe enough?" is often what leadership wants to know and there is no quick and easy

way to answer this. These decisions about the appropriate level of investment must be made jointly with the security expertise of the IT security managers and with the business priorities expertise of the business managers.

Cyberattacks and How They Occurred

Cyberattacks happen in many ways; malicious actors are as creative as they are ambitious and find new, innovative ways to breach systems every day. These criminals infiltrate systems by obtaining credentials through activities such as phishing, guessing passwords, using third parties for access, launching malware, and many other approaches. Those conducting cyberattacks range from the individual who just wants to see if they can get into someone's system, to the enterprising businessperson with bad ethics wanting to make money through ransomware, to state actors hired by governments to infiltrate systems and steal IP, obtain data, or disrupt business.

Today, attacks happen so frequently that unless the approach is unique, the damage is extensive, or the target is very well-known, they are ignored by readers, or worse, go unreported by the popular press. See Figure 7.5 for the magnitude and cause of some of the more well-known breaches.

Breaches

Breaches occur when unauthorized actors gain access to systems, passwords, data, or other assets. Often this happens because someone accidentally gave a malicious actor access to a system or password that was subsequently used to compromise a system and steal valuable data or plant malware inside a system to disrupt operations. As the following stories indicate, trusting and trustworthy users might have no idea they are opening a security vulnerability by clicking on an attachment, using public Wi-Fi, or following a link to an authentic-looking site.

Statistics show that 80% of breaches are conducted by stealing login credentials such as a password.[3] There are many ways to steal a person's password. One common method is to conduct a successful **phishing attack**, where a person receives a counterfeit e-mail that looks like it is from a known entity. The e-mail includes either a virus-laden attachment or a link that when clicked, opens a back door on the user's system to install malware. Some well-known examples are e-mails from supposedly foreign dignitaries or newly wealthy individuals seeking help to get assets out of their country. More clever versions mimic a well-known company and threaten account closure if the users do not respond.

Malicious actors have advanced from just sending an email to texting, posting on social media, and even seeking victims in chat rooms. Emails, images, video, and even screen rendering have been known to be infused with malware that gives the hacker access to systems or locks up a system. For example, one clever hacker was able to add an image of a piece of lint to the screen of a victim, superimposed on top of a link. When the user went to brush away the lint on their touchscreen, it opened a file that downloaded malware. Other variations of phishing, often called **spear phishing**, target a specific individual and mimic a situation or relationship highly familiar to the target. For example, an unsuspecting user might receive a fake e-mail from a charity the user supports, asking the user to click on a link to make a donation. In another example, a malicious actor obtained the name of the CEO of a company and sent a phishing e-mail to his subordinates pretending to be the executive and asking the CFO to click on a link, which opened a vulnerability and enabled the hacker to steal bank account information. Would you like to hear more examples of spear phishing? Just search the web, since there are unfortunately many stories about this insidious way hackers gain access to systems.

There are many ways to gain access to a system, but the most common is to collect someone's password. The only limit is the malicious actors's imagination to create a scenario that would motivate a user to click on a link or share their password. One common way this works is when the attachment or link in a phishing message initiates a **key logger**, or software that traps keystrokes and stores them for hackers to inspect later. The malicious actor then collects the file with all the keystrokes, searches for a user login that reveals a username and password.

[3] 2022 Verizon Data Breach Report, https://www.verizon.com/business/resources/reports/dbir/ (accessed on May 13, 2023).

Date Detected	Company	Magnitude of Damage	Description of Attack
December 2013	Target	40 million debit and credit card account numbers[a]	Contractor's opening of an e-mail attachment containing a virus, revealing a password[b]
May 2014	eBay #1	145 million user names, e-mails, physical addresses, phone numbers, birth dates, encrypted passwords[c]	Obtaining an employee's password[d]
September 2014	Home Depot	56 million credit card numbers and 53 million e-mail addresses	Obtaining a vendor's password and exploiting an operating system's vulnerability[e]
January 2015	Anthem Blue Cross	80 million names, birthdays, e-mails, social security numbers, addresses, and employment data (including income)[f]	Obtaining passwords of at least five high-level employees[g]
July 2016 (but started August 2013)	Yahoo (largest breach of all time)	For all 3 billion accounts: name, birthdate, answers to security questions, phone number, encrypted password, etc.[h]	An intruder forged cookies to fool Yahoo into thinking the password was already provided
July 2017	Equifax	147 million records of personal information including social security numbers, names, birthdates, addresses, and credit information[i]	Hackers found vulnerability in an Equifax server that should have been fixed and used it to extract data for 76 days before being discovered
March 2018	Facebook	87 million Facebook users profile information, friend information, private messages[j]	Cambridge Analytica illegally harvested users' information without their permission for political motivations to influence the 2016 political campaign
September 2018	Marriott/Starwood	500 million hotel guests' names, addresses, passport numbers, account information, birthdates, hashed credit card information[k]	In 2017: A cybersecurity contractor downloaded a malware sample for analysis, but mistakenly executed it. In 2014, an SQL injection bug was planted[l]
December 2020	Solarwinds	Nation-state gained access to networks, systems, and data from more than 30,000 SolarWinds customers and their customers	First known supply chain attack where malicious code was inserted into the updating patch to the Orion software which created a back door the hackers could access[m]
March 2021	Microsoft	Unauthorized access to emails at over 60,000 businesses and governments worldwide	Hackers exploited vulnerabilities in Microsoft email servers[n]
November 2021	Log4J	Since Log4J is used in so many systems, the scope of impact is still unknown. Hackers who exploited this vulnerability gained admin access to victim's system	Log4J, found in the Apache Log4j2 library, is commonly used in most systems written in Java code. Hackers found a vulnerability they exploited, and the first four patches introduced new vulnerabilities that were exploited[o]

[a] Brian Krebs, "Target Hackers Broke in via HVAC Company," Krebs on Security, February 14, 2014, http://krebsonsecurity.com/2014/02/target-hackers-broke-in-via-hvac-company/ (accessed June 22, 2015).

[b] Brian Krebs, "Home Depot: Hackers Stole 53M Email Addresses," Krebs on Security, November 14, 2014, http://krebsonsecurity.com/2014/11/home-depot-hackers-stole-53m-email-addreses/ (accessed June 28, 2015).

[c] Andy Greenberg, "eBay Demonstrates How Not to Respond to a Huge Data Breach," *Wired*, May 23, 2014, http://www.wired.com/2014/05/ebay-demonstrates-how-not-to-respond-to-a-huge-data-breach/ (accessed June 22, 2015).

[d] Bill Whitaker, "What Happens When You Swipe Your Card?" *60 Minutes*, November 30, 2014, transcript, http://www.cbsnews.com/news/swiping-your-credit-card-and-hacking-and-cybercrime/ (accessed June 24, 2015).

[e] Ashley Carman, "Windows Vulnerability Identified as Root Cause in Home Depot Breach," *SC Magazine*, November 10, 2014, http://www.scmagazine.com/home-depot-breach-caused-by-windows-vulnerability/article/382450/ (accessed June 28, 2015).

[f] Michael Hiltzik, "Anthem Is Warning Consumers About Its Huge Data Breach. Here's a Translation," *LA Times*, March 6, 2015, http://www.latimes.com/business/hiltzik/la-fi-mh-anthem-is-warning-consumers-20150306-column.html#page=1 (accessed June 28, 2015).

[g] Hiltzik, 2015.

[h] Yahoo, undated. Yahoo 2013 Account Security Update FAQs, https://help.yahoo.com/kb/account/SLN28451.html (accessed March 16, 2019).

[i] https://www.cnet.com/news/equifaxs-hack-one-year-later-a-look-back-at-how-it-happened-and-whats-changed/ (accessed February 14, 2019).

[j] https://blog.avast.com/biggest-data-breaches (accessed February 14, 2019).

[k] https://www.npr.org/2018/12/12/675983642/chinese-hackers-are-responsible-for-marriott-data-breach-reports-say (accessed February 14, 2019).

[l] Thomas Brewster, "Revealed: Marriott's 500 Million Hack Came After a String of Security Breaches," *Forbes*, December 3, 2018, https://www.forbes.com/sites/thomasbrewster/2018/12/03/revealed-marriotts-500-million-hack-came-after-a-string-of-security-breaches/?sh=41fa2b44546f (accessed June 8, 2023).

[m] Saheed Oladimeji and Sean Michael Kerner, "SolarWinds Hack Explained," TechTarget, https://www.techtarget.com/whatis/feature/SolarWinds-hack-explained-Everything-you-need-to-know (accessed May 1, 2023).

[n] Edward Kost, "Critical Microsoft Exchange Flaw: What is CVE-2021-26855?" Upguard.com, April 6, 2023. (https://www.upguard.com/blog/cve-2021-26855 (accessed June 8, 2023.)

[o] https://www.wallarm.com/what/log4j-vulnerability-all-that-you-must-know-about-it and https://www.cisa.gov/news-events/news/apache-log4j-vulnerability-guidance (accessed on May 13, 2023).

FIGURE 7.5 Well-known breaches, what was stolen, and how.

Date Detected	Company	Magnitude of Damage	Description of Attack
May 2021	Colonial Pipeline	Ransomware attack forced closure of pipeline, affecting 1,000s of customers (gas stations and other fueling	Single password was found on the dark web giving hackers access to Colonial Pipeline's business systems. Ransomware notice cause concern about potential physical damage to fuel pipeline. Leaders temporarily closed pipeline, disrupting delivery of fuel to entire eastern USA[p]
February 2023	LastPass	Perpetrators downloaded encrypted passwords plus any plain text stored (including web addresses for the sites) by users	Three previous breaches of its development environment over seven years, likely revealed cloud file locations and then a developer's stolen password from old software on a home device enabled them to download the file[q]

[p] https://www.cisa.gov/news-events/news/attack-colonial-pipeline-what-weve-learned-what-weve-done-over-past-two-years and https://www.techtarget.com/whatis/feature/Colonial-Pipeline-hack-explained-Everything-you-need-to-know?Offer=abVidRegWall_gate and https://www.energy.gov/ceser/colonial-pipeline-cyber-incident (accessed on May 13, 2023).

[q] Matt Kapko, "LastPass Breach Timeline: How a Monthslong Cyberattack Unraveled," March 3, 2023, Cybersecurity Dive, https://www.cybersecuritydive.com/news/lastpass-cyberattack-timeline/643958/, (accessed June 8, 2023).

FIGURE 7.5 (continued)

Another way to obtain a password is simply to guess it. Experts warn that large breaches can be caused by using a **weak password**, such as "123456," "qwerty," or "password," which, incredibly, continued to be three of the most common passwords.[4] Users tend to select passwords they can remember, and hackers know that. On the other hand, creating a strong password that cannot be guessed can result in a hard-to-remember string of nonsense characters. The name of a hometown, a team, an employer, or a family member would be among the first guesses of a hacker. Also, even if it is difficult to guess, many people use the same password for multiple purposes, and if one account is breached, all of their other accounts are then wide open. This is a significant issue that might warrant a policy that employees should (or must) not use a password that they also use elsewhere.

Given that the average person has over 70 passwords to remember,[5] it is challenging to keep track of difficult passwords that are different for every account. Tools such as Bitwarden and 1Password can generate long passwords that look like nonsense, encrypt them, then allow access with one master password across multiple platforms. Another option is to use a passphrase, a longer password of several words that the user can easily remember, with a rule of substituting (e.g., zero for "o" and 3 for "e"). Longer passwords are more difficult to guess and harder for automated programs to figure out, but hackers know that, too, and have developed tools to help crack them. Don't use a popular phrase like "ToBeOrNotToBe," even if you disguise it as "T0B30rN0ttT0B3" (the same password but with substitution). Even TBONTB (the same password but as an acronym) is risky.

Yet another way to open a firm to a large breach is for employees to use an unsecured network at a coffee shop, hotel, or airport. Many users do not realize that, even if the network's name matches the coffee shop's name, someone in the shop might have set up a so-called **evil twin**[6] Wi-Fi connection and that all incoming and outgoing Internet traffic becomes routed through the perpetrator's system. Once connected, the unwitting users' keystrokes, including their usernames and passwords, can be captured as they shop online, do Internet banking, or log into their company's intranet site. One solution might be for companies to establish policies forbidding their employees to use public Wi-Fi and use their smartphones as a hotspot to serve as their Internet connection.

Other Attack Approaches

Cross-Site Scripting

A second eBay breach was discovered by an astute user who nagged eBay to fix the problem for over a year.[7] He even created a YouTube video to show how it worked.[8] But management did not respond.

[4] Paulisu Masilauskas, Most Common Passwords: Latest 2023 Statistics, April 20, 2023, https://cybernews.com/best-password-managers/most-common-passwords/ (accessed May 13, 2023).

[5] Attila Tomaschek, "Best Password Manager in 2023," May 1, 2023. CNET, https://www.cnet.com/tech/services-and-software/best-password-manager/ (accessed June 8, 2023).

[6] Ray Walsh, "What Is an Evil Twin Attack?" Comparitech, November 11, 2022, https://www.comparitech.com/blog/information-security/what-is-evil-twin-attack/ (accessed June 8, 2023).

[7] Chris Brook, "A Year Later, XSS Vulnerability Still Exists in eBay," Threatpost, April 29, 2015, https://threatpost.com/a-year-later-xss-vulnerability-still-exists-in-ebay/112493 (accessed June 8, 2023).

The method of the eBay **cross-site scripting (XSS)** attack was a product photo with a hidden trap built in. The photo was a hot-link that led users to a fraudulent, but realistic looking site that required users to enter their eBay login. The log-in ID and password were captured by the hacker. eBay permitted users (at extra cost) to install some computer code in their small, sponsored listings to add animation to make their items in eBay search results grab shoppers' attention. In this attack, malicious code altered the listing's address to point to the fake log-in screen. Users assumed they needed to log-in once again for security purposes, but in reality, everyone who "logged-in" the second time provided the crooks with usernames and passwords.

Third Parties and Supply Chain

Breaches that originate with suppliers or other third parties are increasingly common. The Target attackers broke into the network using credentials stolen from a heating, ventilation, and air conditioning (HVAC) contractor and installed malware on the retail sales system. The malware captured and copied the magnetic stripe card data right from the computer's memory before the system could encrypt and store it. Why would an HVAC contractor have access? Security expert and blogger Brian Krebs reported that it is common for large retailers to install temperature- and energy-monitoring software provided by contractors. HVAC companies update and maintain their customer's software and need access to the customer's systems to do so in a timely manner. In this case, access to the retailing system enabled the malware to spread to a majority of Target's cash registers, collecting information from debit and credit cards and sending it to various drop points in Miami and Brazil to be picked up later by hackers in Eastern Europe and Russia.[9]

Home Depot's story a year later echoed that of Target. Logon credentials were stolen from a vendor that had access to Home Depot's system, and the same malware was unleashed to cash registers. Target's story motivated Home Depot to update its system but the attack occurred before the company could complete all of the improvements.[10]

An attack at Anthem Blue Cross demonstrates that stealing high-level usernames and passwords can provide quick access to large and important files. Target and Home Depot hackers had to wait until transactions were recorded to gain valuable information, which took several days. But at Anthem, being able to download important employment and identity information from 80 million people at one pass was easy with the high-level passwords. Log-in credentials of lower-level employees would involve transaction-by-transaction data collection or further spear phishing attempts targeting higher-level employees. Therefore, log-in accounts of executives need special attention, and their activities should be monitored regularly.

Solarwinds suffered a different kind of attack.[11] Solarwinds provided system management tools and other technical services to thousands of customers. One of their products, Orion, was a monitoring system and that meant it had privileged access to customer systems (which it needed to collect the systems performance information it uses in its product). Hackers, believed to be from a nation-state, inserted malicious code called Sunburst into an Orion update after it had been cleared to send to customers. More than 18,000 customers installed the infected update, giving hackers access to these victims' systems and the data and networks of their customers and partners. Victims included government departments, private companies, and many more. Forensics found that hackers obtained access to SolarWinds in September 2019, installed their malicious code about March 2020, but that was not discovered until December 2020.

The Costs of Breaches

The financial cost of a breach is often significant, but the overall costs can extend far beyond direct recovery costs. When a breach disrupts operations, a company may find itself in violation of contractual arrangements with their customers. Reputations can be impacted, and trust eroded. Jobs can be impacted,

[8] Paul Kerr, "eBay Hacked Proof!" September 16, 2014, https://www.youtube.com/watch?v=WT5TG_LvZz4&feature=youtu.be (accessed June 22, 2015).

[9] Brian Krebs, "Target Hackers Broke in via HVAC Company," KrebsonSecurity, February 5, 2014 https://krebsonsecurity.com/2014/02/target-hackers-broke-in-via-hvac-company/ (accessed June 8, 2023).

[10] Shelly Banjo, "Home Depot Hackers Exposed 53 Million Email Addresses," The Wall Street Journal, November 6, 2014, https://www.wsj.com/articles/home-depot-hackers-used-password-stolen-from-vendor-1415309282 (accessed June 8, 2023).

[11] Saheed Oladimeji and Sean Michael Kerner, "SolarWinds Hack Explained," TechTarget, https://www.techtarget.com/whatis/feature/SolarWinds-hack-explained-Everything-you-need-to-know (accessed May 1, 2023).

with employee firings or executive resignations, for wittingly or unwittingly (through negligence) facilitating the hacker's efforts. Insurance costs might increase if the company is found to be a cybersecurity risk, and expensive litigation can result when a breach occurs.

A Ponemon study[12] sponsored by IBM found that the cost of data breaches continues to rise and varies by industry. For example, healthcare industry breaches cost an average of $10M, while in the financial industry they average $5.97M and in the pharmaceutical industry they average $5.01M. Many firms facing such costs would find themselves in serious jeopardy. The Target breach cost $61 million in its first two months, and it was estimated to have cost $291 million overall.[13] The CIO resigned, the profit for that quarter fell 46%, and revenue for that quarter declined 5.3%.[14] In 2021, the Home Depot breach was estimated to have cost over $200 million.[15] And Home Depot's stock price fell 2.1% the day after the breach was announced.[16]

The Impossibility of 100% Security

It is not possible to completely secure an organization. Consider what it would take to do so. A first step would be to list all of the key assets of the organization, the vulnerabilities, and the potential threats (and this is impossible as the bad guys are coming up with new approaches all the time). The second step would be to obtain tools, design processes, and install protections that would prevent all of them. The challenge would be overwhelming, if even possible. New technologies such as AI and quantum computing hold the promise of new protection mechanisms, but once these become mainstream, malicious attackers will find ways around them, too, likely using the same technology. For example, while quantum computing is expected to introduce radical new ways to protect digital assets, at the same time, it is expected to be able to crack the encryption algorithms widely used today, rendering them useless in the fight to protect digital assets. A conventional computer trying to crack a password protected with 2,048-bit (extremely long) encryption would take 300 trillion years to keep trying keys at random, but a quantum computer powered by 4,099 qubits would need just 10 seconds.[17] Obviously, current password technology will no longer suffice, and new types of protections will be needed by then.

Management must accept some level of risk when designing a cybersecurity strategy; the risk will never be zero. L. Dain Gary, former manager of the U.S. Computer Emergency Response Team (CERT) in Pittsburgh, appeared on an episode of *60 Minutes* in 1995 and let the public in on an unpleasant fact with a sobering statement: "You cannot make a computer secure. You can reduce the risk, but you can't guarantee security."[18]

Because of the futility of seeking 100% security, many companies take out insurance policies to mitigate the financial impacts of a breach. But often the fine print in these policies make it difficult if not impossible to collect when damages occur. Regardless of the low probability of financial recovery, those insurance policies for cybersecurity protection are still popular, even if it is just because it is required by their customers, their corporate policies, or perhaps the regulations governing their business.

Some managers rely on Poulsen's Law, which states that information is secure when it costs more to get it than it's worth.[19] The role of management might be to work with the IT function to make it more costly

---

[12] Ponemon Institute, "IBM Study: Costs of a Data Breach Report 2022" IBM, https://www.ibm.com/reports/data-breach (accessed May 28, 2023).

[13] Woodrow Hartzog and Daniel J. Solove, "We Still Haven't Learned the Major Lesson of the 2013 Target Hack," Slate. April 13, 2022. https://slate.com/technology/2022/04/breached-excerpt-hartzog-solove-target.html (accessed June 8, 2023).

[14] Associated Press, "Target's Tech Boss Resigns as Retailer Overhauls Security in Wake of Massive Payment Card Breach," *Financial Post*, March 5, 2014, https://financialpost.com/technology/cio/target-cio-resigns (accessed June 8, 2023).

[15] ArcTitan, "Case Study: Home Depot Data Breah Cost $179 Million," August 20, 2021, ArcTitan.com, https://www.arctitan.com/blog/case-study-data-breach-cost-home-depot-179-million/ (accessed June 8, 2023).

[16] Hiroko Tabuchi, "Home Depot Posts a Strong 3rd Quarter Despite a Data Breach Disclosure," *The New York Times*, November 18, 2014, https://www.nytimes.com/2014/11/19/business/home-depot-reports-strong-third-quarter-growth-despite-data-breach-disclosure.html (accessed June 8, 2023).

[17] Stephen Shankland, "Quantum Computers Could Crack Today's Encrypted Messages. That's a Problem," CNET.com, https://www.cnet.com/tech/computing/quantum-computers-could-crack-todays-encrypted-messages-thats-a-problem/ (accessed June 8, 2023), paragraph 22.

[18] *60 Minutes*, "E-Systems," February 26, 1995.

[19] "Anything Made by a Man Can Be Hacked," *DSL Reports*, March 6, 2006, http://www.dslreports.com/forum/remark,15623829 (accessed September 15, 2015).

to break in than the value of the assets that could be stolen. This is not the best approach since malicious actors may be breaking in for other reasons than financial gain from stolen assets. They might be nation-state sponsored, looking to disrupt a business or industry or simply steal IP for their sponsors. Further, malicious actors might earn very little from each victim of a single ransomware attack, but they make it up on volume, especially when it takes very little effort to send 1,000s of phishing emails or use automated bots to locate vulnerabilities in systems connected to the Internet.

Stolen information can be worth a lot when sold on the dark web. Credit card numbers and accompanying information and PayPal accounts are most popular. Credit card prices vary according to the balance on the card and the availability of other details such as CVV, type of card, etc. A security expert reported that in 2023, stolen credit card details for cards with a limit of $5,000 was for sale for $110, but one with a balance of $1,000 was $70.[20] Batches of credit cards varied in price and could be found for as low as $1 per credit card. Those prices are much lower than in previous years. Of the 40 million Target credit card numbers stolen, about 2 million (5%) were sold, fetching an average price of $20, and yielding $4 million to the hackers. A member of a street gang who bought one of those credit cards for $20 was likely to yield $400 in purchases of gift cards and electronics.[21] Stolen PayPal account details were for sale for $10 per account.

Bank account information is much more valuable. *Privacy Affairs* reported in 2023 that stolen online banking logins ranged from $40 for general banks, to over $4,000 for verified account information on an ING or HSBC bank account and $500 for Chase Bank logins.[22] Presumably the price is based on supply, demand, and data accuracy. Many other accounts, from social media to Gmail to Netflix logins, are available for a price.

Further, a complete identity-theft "kit" containing not only a credit card but social security number and medical information costs far more—between $100 and $1,000 each.[23] The purchase price is high because identity-theft kits can be used to steal someone's identity to open multiple new credit cards and create false identity documents.

The hackers do not keep stolen credit cards or identity-theft information for their own use, given the staggering volume they acquire. They quickly sell them online to others all over the world who use them before they are reported as stolen. Those cards even come with a return policy in case they are declined, because the black-market shops need to maintain their reputations. However, the guarantees come with a warning that they run out after only a few hours.[24]

One final discouraging thought is important. No longer does the attacker need to be a hacker on the fringe of society. Instead, cybercriminals are businesspeople with poor ethics who pull together services necessary to launch a cyberattack. The intruders' tools are available on the dark web[25] and are sophisticated and user-friendly. One study from MIT researchers documented dozens of "as-a-service" offerings in a cybercriminal service ecosystem that not only provide tools and technologies but also the accompanying services and help-desk activities to assist criminals in using the tools.[26,27] Many of these tools are not designed just for illegal purposes, but when combined with other tools and a hacker motive, the result can be a successful cyberattack. For example, there are tools that can scan for vulnerable systems to repair

[20] Miklos Zoltan, "Dark Web Price Index 2023," Privacy Affairs, April 23, 2023, https://www.privacyaffairs.com/dark-web-price-index-2023/ (accessed May 31, 2023).

[21] Bill Whitaker, "What Happens When You Swipe Your Card?" 60 Minutes, November 30, 2014, https://www.cbsnews.com/news/swiping-your-credit-card-and-hacking-and-cybercrime/ (accessed June 8, 2023).

[22] Miklos Zoltan; Whitaker, 2014.

[23] Ryan Smith, "Revealed: How Much is Personal Information Worth on the Dark Web?," Insurance News, May 1, 2023, https://www.insurancebusinessmag.com/us/news/breaking-news/revealed--how-much-is-personal-information-worth-on-the-dark-web-444453.aspx (accessed May 31, 2023).

[24] Aaron Sankin, "Inside the Black Markets for Your Stolen Credit Cards," *The Kernel*, September 28, 2014, http://kernelmag.dailydot.com/issue-sections/features-issue-sections/10362/inside-the-black-markets-for-your-stolen-credit-cards/ (accessed August 27, 2015).

[25] The web on the Internet actually contains what experts call the surface web and the deep web. The **surface web** is anything that can be indexed by a search engine like Google. The **deep web** is anything that is not found by general search engines. Content on the deep web includes material found on websites such as government databases and library databases that are accessible outside of a search engine. A small part of the deep web, called the **dark web**, is that part of the deep web that is intentionally hidden from the surface web. Special software, such as the Tor browser, is necessary to access the dark web.

[26] Keman Huang, Michael Siegel, Keri Pearlson and Stuart Madnick, "Casting the Dark Web in a New Light," **Sloan Management Review**, Fall 2019, pp. 2–9.

[27] Howard F. Lipson, "Tracking and Tracing Cyber-Attacks: Technical Challenges and Global Policy Issues," Special Report CMU/SEI-2002-SR-009, http://www.sei.cmu.edu/reports/02sr009.pdf (accessed August 27, 2015).

(also useful for finding systems to attack) and send out e-mails (which can be phishing emails). There are also tools for just about any type of illegal activity the attacker wants, such as, laundering money from ransomware attacks, exploiting weaknesses uncovered by system scans, and generating viruses. And with the exploding opportunities to utilize AI technology, we expect new and more innovative attacks in the future.

What Should Management Do?

General managers have a role to play in creating a cybersecurity strategy, since this strategy is more about management actions than technology decisions. Managers need to make sure that cybersecurity policies and practices support, rather than hinder, the goals of the organization. Building on the model described above, non-cybersecurity managers must have a basic understanding of the five elements described earlier in this chapter: security strategy, infrastructure, policies, culture, and investments. Combining these mechanisms is often done to create a defense-in-depth approach to cybersecurity. Since decisions made to secure systems can impact the business opportunities of the organization, non-cyber managers will want to understand the impacts.

Defense in Depth

Security leaders use **defense in depth**, the concept of having multiple layers of different security technologies, policies, and practices, to increase the security and decrease the risk of a cyber breach. The basic idea is that should one layer fail to stop a perpetrator, another layer might be more effective. For example, even if a hacker can get past a firewall, not having the right fingerprint or password might stop the attack. Typical defense in depth plans have physical, technical, and administrative barriers. Figure 7.6 has an example of what multiple layers might look like.

The concept of defense in depth comes from the medieval times when castles had multiple layers of defense. First the castle had very high stone walls making direct attacks difficult. Next, guards were placed on the top of the castle with weapons that they could use to ward off attackers. Castles were often located in a physical location that was difficult to reach, such as on top of a hill. Sometimes there were moats around the castle and access required a bridge to cross the moat. The bridge could be lifted to keep out

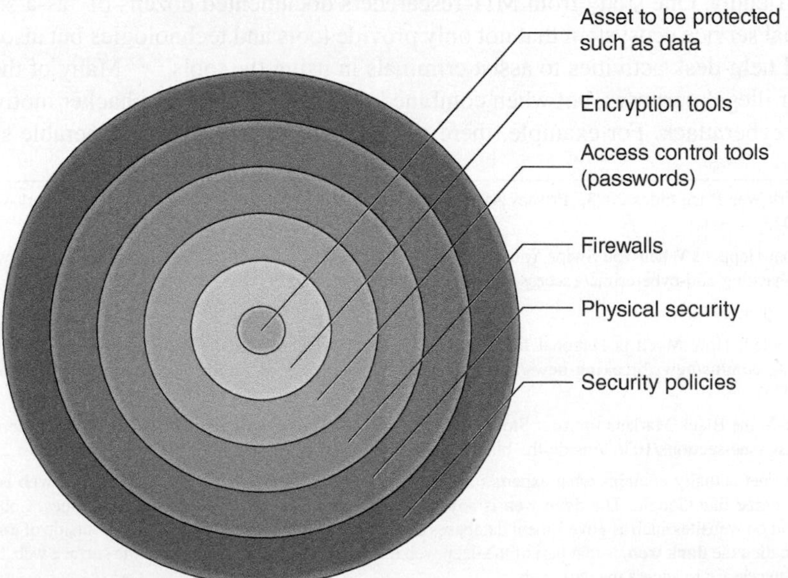

FIGURE 7.6 Example of defense in depth layers.

unwanted visitors. Castles located near towns had the added benefit of the townspeople providing their own defense to invaders, which would protect the castle nearby. Should invaders get into the castle, there were often distractions and decoys to keep attackers from finding the crown jewels or other valuables. In short, there were multiple levels of defense. This is the same concept that has been ported over to cybersecurity strategy. Each layer protects differently so a successful attack must penetrate all layers to do the damage or steal the valuables targeted.

Cybersecurity Infrastructure

Managers must use a combination of technologies, policies, organizational mechanisms, and specialists to reduce risk and increase security. The cybersecurity infrastructure are the people, processes, and tools specifically devoted to securing the organization's digital assets.

The cybersecurity team starts with a senior leader who "owns" the strategy, creates the vision, and designs the processes to keep the organization secure. Many firms employ a chief information security officer (CISO) to lead cybersecurity team, manage activities and processes, keep abreast of new threats that emerge, and manage the policies and education necessary to reduce risk. In other firms, this responsibility falls to the CIO, an outsourced resource, or simply the facilities security staff. Non-cyber managers need to have a high-level understanding of the cybersecurity plans in their organization to communicate effectively with their cybersecurity colleagues to understand how business operations are impacted by security activities.

Using the NIST model described above, tools can be divided into two categories: those that protect the organization from an intrusion (see Figure 7.7), and those that detect (and possibly respond to) an intrusion (see Figure 7.8).

Some tools provide protection from access by undesired intruders and others provide protection for storage and transmission. Protecting access is most commonly done with passwords even though they have proven to be the entry point of most breaches. Some security specialists claim that passwords are obsolete and should be discontinued because of their vulnerabilities and the false sense of security created when users think a password is all they need to be secure.[28] But, like many access protection tools, passwords have the disadvantage of requiring an additional access method if it fails. For instance, because users often forget a password, firms need to make additional investments to create an automated resetting mechanism through an alternate method, such as an e-mail to a known address or a text message to a mobile phone, to provide users with a recovery mechanism.

Access Tool	Concept
Physical locks	Physically protect computing resources
Passwords	Invent a set of characters known only by the user
Biometrics	Scan a body characteristic, such as fingerprint, voice, iris, head, or hand geometry
Challenge questions	Prompt with a follow-up question such as "model of first car"
Token	Use small electronic device that generates a new supplementary passkey at frequent intervals
Text message	Send a text message with a passkey
Multifactor authentication	Couple two or more access techniques, for instance • Passwords and phone call to phone number on file • Biometrics and follow-up questions • Passwords and text messaging

FIGURE 7.7 Common system access security tools.

[28] SecureAuth, "The Password's Pulse Beats On. Hackers Still One Step Away from Your Information," SecureAuth, March 18, 2015, https://www.secureauth.com/newsroom/the-passwords-pulse-beats-on-hackers-still-one-step-away-from-your-information/ (accessed June 8, 2023).

Storage and/or Transmission Tool	Concept
Antivirus/antispyware	Software scans incoming data and evaluates the periodic state of the whole system to detect threats of secret software that can either destroy data or inform a server of your activity
Firewall	Software and sometimes hardware-based filter prevent or allow outside traffic from accessing the network
System logs	They keep track of system activity, such as successful or failed login attempts, file alterations, file copying, file deletion, or software installation
System alerts	System sends a warning when it detects unusual activity in the logs such as multiple failed login attempts or large files being transferred out
Encryption	System follows a complex formula, using a unique **key** (set of characters) to convert plain text into what looks like unreadable nonsense and then to decode back to plain text when presented with the decoding key
WEP/WPA (wired equivalent privacy and wireless protected access)	Encryption is used in a wireless network
VPN (virtual private network)	Software provides a trusted, encrypted connection between your site and a particular server

Vinod Khosia, "Behavioral Analysis Could Have Prevented the Anthem Breach," Forbes, February 24, 2015, http://www.forbes.com/sites/frontline/2015/02/24/behavioral-analysis-could-have-prevented-the-anthem-breach/ (accessed June 28, 2015).

FIGURE 7.8 Common storage and transmission security tools.

There is a general trend toward **multifactor authentication** (MFA), or the use of two or more authorization methods to gain access.[29] There are three types of factors that are popular to use for MFA[30]:

Knowledge—something a user knows (e.g., password, challenge question/answer).
Ownership—something the user has (e.g., cellphone, token, and smartcard).
Biometric—something the user is (e.g., fingerprint, retinal scan).

MFA combines two or more of these factors. One common example of this security technique is when a password is followed by text message to your cellphone with a code to be entered into the system or just requiring approval, using a smartphone or smartwatch app such as Duo, to simply click for system entry.

However, online merchants do not tend to make MFA a requirement for their customers, perhaps due to fear of making site access less convenient. Security and convenience have long been thought of as at odds with each other,[31] and users complain about signing onto MFA multiple times a day. SecureAuth reports the average user signs on with MFA an average of 16 times per day,[32] but a new approach called **passwordless continuous authentication** (also called **universal authentication**) is on the horizon. That technology simply makes use of recognizing the device, your location, your IP address, your network carrier, your behavior, and other commonsense factors, which makes it much more convenient for the user.

Not only are access controls important, but also the form in which information is stored and transmitted requires security tools. Some examples of these types of protection are antivirus software, firewalls, encryption, and VPNs (Virtual Private Networks).

Detection tools provide the cybersecurity team with insight into systems and networks, identifying anomalies. System logs and system alerts let the operations center know when abnormal behavior takes place. For example, data being exfiltrated to an unusual IP address, port, or even phone number might

[29] Ryan A. Higgins, "The Importance of Multifactor Authentication," CIO, October 26, 2022, https://www.cio.gov/2022-10-26-importance-multifactor-authentication/ (accessed June 8, 2023).

[30] A. Ometov, S. Bezzateev, et al., "Multi-Factor Authentication: A Survey" January 5, 2018, https://www.mdpi.com/2410-387X/2/1/1/pdf (accessed February 14, 2019).

[31] David Jeffers, "Why Convenience Is the Enemy of Security," PC World, June 18, 2012, http://www.pcworld.com/article/257793/why_convenience:is_the_enemy_of_security.html (accessed June 25, 2015).

[32] SecureAuth, "MFA Fatigue," https://secureauthcorp.wpenginepowered.com/wp-content/uploads/2022/12/1-FINAL_MFA_Fatigue_2FrontWar_Nov2022.pdf

indicate access by a malicious actor. A system alert would highlight and call attention to the unusual behavior. For example, multiple failed login attempts might trigger an alert, since it might indicate a hacker trying to gain access to a system.

Security Policy

Tools alone are just one component of a cybersecurity plan. Managers also need organizational mechanisms as a layer of their cyber defense. Management's approach to security reveals to the rest of the organization the importance of cybersecurity measures and instructs users on acceptable behaviors. It creates incentives and encourages a cybersecurity culture in the organization. Without sound management policy, technologies can be rendered useless. For example, if employees write their passwords on sticky notes and put them near their workstations, password protection technologies will be ineffective from the start. Figure 7.9 provides sample management policy tactics to prevent security weaknesses.

Staying ahead of hackers with smart policies can require outside assistance. For example, some managed security services provider (MSSP) firms offer the services of **white hat hackers**, hired to try to break into systems to help the client firm uncover weaknesses. White hat hackers lie in sharp contrast to **black hat hackers**, who break in for their own gain or to wreak havoc on a firm. **Grey hat hackers** test organizational systems without any authorization and notify a company when they find a weakness. Although they can be helpful, what they do is nevertheless illegal. Further, some companies create *bug bounty programs* that offer rewards to anyone reporting a vulnerability. These programs are popular ways for technical experts to earn money, and for companies to crowdsource the process of vulnerability identification.

Cybersecurity Culture

Users' behavior is a critical step in keeping organizations secure. Estimates of the exact percent of breaches caused by insider threats, that is, from the people within the organization, vary but it's clear that most cyber breaches begin because insiders do something to let malicious code or actors into their system.[33] Not all insider threats are deliberate, however. They can be caused by poor user behaviors such as not following policies,[34] or just not being aware of how their actions create vulnerabilities.

Managers can shape user behavior by creating a culture of cybersecurity. Culture is defined as the values, beliefs, and attitudes held by members of the organization.[35] Culture is a set of unwritten rules that

Policy	Concept
Perform security updates promptly	Make sure all security updates are applied as soon as possible
Manage access of systems closely	Remove former employees' credentials upon departure of the company
Keep passwords secret	Forbid users from sharing passwords
Perform mobile device management	Provide a BYOD (bring your own device) policy on permitted products and required connection methods
Data disposal policies	Require complete and secure disposal of documents after their usefulness ends (*deleting* data is not "enough")
Test systems regularly for vulnerabilities	Consultants or internal experts perform penetration tests to find vulnerabilities that need to be fixed or patched.

FIGURE 7.9 Commonly used management security policies.

[33] Christos Flessas, "Biggest Insider Threats of 2022" March 31, 2023, https://www.computer.org/publications/tech-news/trends/key-takeaways-from-2022-cyberthreatseaways-for-2023 (accessed May 31, 2023).

[34] John D'Arcy, Anat Hovav, and Dennis Galletta, "Awareness of Security Countermeasures and Its Impact on Information Systems Misuse: A Deterrence Approach," *Information Systems Research* 20, no. 1 (March 2009): 79–98.

[35] Keman Huang and Keri Pearlson, *For What Technology Can't Fix: Building a Model of Organizational Cybersecurity Culture*, HICSS Proceedings (January 8, 2019_, http://hdl.handle.net/10125/60074.

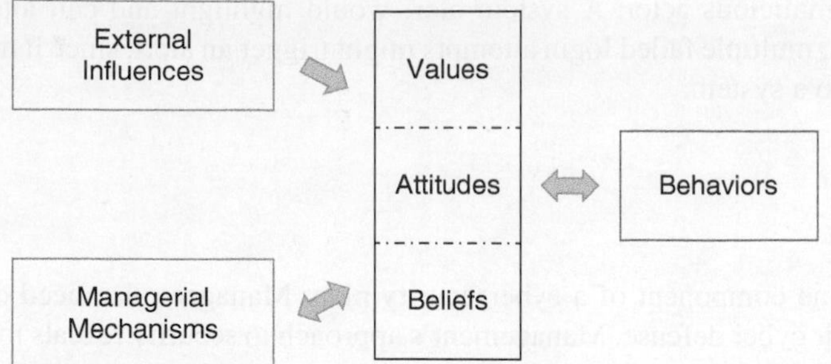

FIGURE 7.10 A model of organizational cybersecurity culture.
Source: Keman Huang and Keri Pearlson, *For What Technology Can't Fix: Building a Model of Organizational Cybersecurity Culture*, HICSS Proceedings (January 8, 2019), http://hdl.handle.net/10125/60074.

users follow even if they are not stated directly. Creating a cybersecurity culture is accomplished through management actions combined with environmental factors that managers do not control. Figure 7.10 summarizes the framework for driving cybersecure behaviors in organizations.

Managers want to encourage cybersecurity behaviors (and curtail bad behaviors). Behaviors are driven by values, attitudes, and beliefs. Employees do what they value, what they believe is important, and what they know are good for their organization. Those are influenced by external factors such as regulations, activities of peer organizations, and the industry of the organization. Financial services and health care organizations, for example, have regulations they must follow for protecting and managing data, creating a different set of attitudes around security than other industries. For example, no one will do business with a bank they don't trust. Values, attitudes, and beliefs are also influenced by managerial mechanisms such as performance review criteria, training programs, communication campaigns, and other management activities. For example, when an executive talks about his/her own experience with a phishing email, it communicates the importance of vigilance to the rest of the team, establishing an attitude that drives a team member's behaviors to not click on phishing emails.

Security Education, Training, and Awareness (SETA)

A key managerial mechanism to communicate cybersecurity policies and encourage values, attitudes, and beliefs is an organization's **security education, training, and awareness (SETA)** program. Most organizations have some type of SETA in place for cybersecurity, but it is usually a module completed during orientation to a company at the beginning of one's employment, or once a year for compliance (which often means it's not given full attention; it's done just to be completed). Education, the E in SETA, provides frameworks, reveals concepts, and builds understanding, while training covers procedures to follow and practice in following them. Awareness, the A in SETA, is usually an ongoing communication campaign with reminders of values, attitudes, and beliefs. Managers who want to create cybersecure behaviors know that a training course or awareness campaign is just not enough to change behaviors.[36]

See Figure 7.11 for a sample list of areas for education and training along with possible activities for each.

A common application for SETA is to help individuals recognize and avoid the consequences of phishing. Most people know that a Nigerian Prince is not leaving them millions of dollars, but there are several other "classic" phishing messages such as:

- An e-mail or bank account is closed, and the user needs to click to log-in and reactivate it.
- An e-mail inbox is too full, and the user is asked to click to increase storage.
- The user just won a contest or lottery and is asked to click to claim the prize.
- A product delivery failed, and the user needs to click to retry.
- An odd or unexpected web address shows up when hovering a mouse pointer over a link in an e-mail.

[36] Mandiant, "M-Trends 2015: A View from the Front Lines," https://www.bankinfosecurity.com/whitepapers.php?wp_id=1390 (accessed June 24, 2023).

Subject	Sample Educational Activities	Sample Training Activities
Access tools	Advantages and limitations of passwords Why passwords should be complex and long How often passwords should be changed Strengths of multifactor authentication	How to choose a password How to change your password How to use multifactor authentication How to use a password manager
Bringing your own devices (BYOD)	Why there are rules What the rules are	How to follow the rules What to do if something goes wrong
Social media	Why there are rules Examples of issues that have occurred in the past How those issues could have been avoided	What to do in particular situations on social media What to do if you need help or clarification on an issue
Vigilance	What signals you might see under certain situations (warning messages; phishing e-mails; customer complaints) What physical intrusions look like What the signals mean Which pieces of equipment have ports (USB, Ethernet)	Where and how to look for warning signs What to do when you see the various signals (for instance, a number to call or way to shut down) How to protect your laptop when traveling

FIGURE 7.11 Major areas for education and training, with examples.

- A familiar name in the "from" box is followed by an odd e-mail address.
- Poor grammar and spelling are in a note that purports to be from a large company.
- Goods or services are offered at an impossibly low price.
- An attachment is executable, often with an extension such of ZIP, EXE, or BAT.

As described above, phishing e-mails are the most common way for outsiders to gain access to company systems. Malicious actors have continued to invent new and even more innovative phish that are difficult to detect. Some security experts recommend only clicking on a link if you know the sender. This is incomplete and potentially dangerous advice. Even if the signals are not present, we recommend not to click on any link or open any attachment in an e-mail unless it was requested and expected from a known source. An unexpected e-mail, even from a known source, could breed viruses because of any one of the following: (1) The e-mail might not really be from the known source, because someone is **spoofing** (counterfeiting) the address. (2) The e-mail might be from a known source's computer, but the e-mail was secretly generated by a virus without knowledge of the owner, and it contains a copy of the virus. (3) The e-mail might have been sent from a familiar person who doesn't know that a virus is attached. Opening the attachment or clicking the link would likely infect the recipient's computer and continue the spread of the virus to her or his own contacts. Users must understand that opening a virus-laden web page or file leads to "catching" the virus. SETA programs are one way to help the organization identify and avoid phishing.

How Do We Measure How Secure We Are?

The big question for most managers is to know how secure their organization actually is. While many have come up with metrics and frequently collect them to help answer this question, there is no universal approach. Instead, the best approach is a type of balanced scorecard with several dimensions. Each measure, by itself, gives some information about how secure an organization is, but each fall short by not measuring enough of the areas of vulnerability faced by an organization. Figure 7.12 illustrates the balanced scorecard categories.[37]

Technology risk measures	People/organizational risk measures
Supply chain risk measures	Financial risk measures

FIGURE 7.12 Cybersecurity balanced scorecard.

[37] Keri Pearlson, *A Tool to Help Boards Measure Cyber Resilience*, Harvard Business Review, October 4, 2023, accessable at https://hbr.org.

In this scorecard, there are four categories of measures: Technology Risk, People Risk, Supply Chain Risk, and Financial Risk. Technology measures indicate the number of technical vulnerabilities in the organization's systems. Many vendors offer tools to "calculate" this metric. These tools go through the network and hardware of the organization and identify open ends, forgotten devices, and other potentially vulnerable points of entry for hackers. For example, an organization might have long-forgotten printers connected to a network in an unused office, or a link to an outside network that they no longer use. A metric might be the percent of systems on the network that are incorrectly configured, or the percent of systems without the most recent updates.

While there is no agreed upon set of standard metrics for reporting cybersecurity, there are many options. The US government's CISA and NIST coordinated efforts to create a cross-sector set of cybersecurity performance goals (CPGs).[38] Products like RedSeal's digital resilience score, BitSight's security rating, and SecurityScorecard's security platform have comprehensive measures that give an overall score to the entire information system. Comparing these scores to competitors, or over time for the same company, provides information about how secure the systems are, and whether trends are promising or alarming. Another might be found in logs (as discussed above), which keep track of successful and unsuccessful intruders into the network.

People measures are critical for understanding the security of a company. One common practice is to conduct phishing exercises and report on results with the goal of reducing the number of employees who click on suspicious e-mails and increasing the number of employees who report them to the security team. Phishing exercises are not always effective in increasing the security of the organization, however, because employees begin to recognize these "fake e-mails," and hackers are always finding new ways to trick users. Other measures might include the number of training hours employees have endured, the number of communication campaigns conducted to raise awareness, and the percent of employees who have reported suspicious activities. But managers are still seeking better ways to measure the security profile and behaviors of their users.

An organization itself may have good security for its technology and people, but could be vulnerable because of its suppliers, so having measures of the security of a supply chain are part of the scorecard. In the Colonial Pipeline case, described in the introduction of this chapter, the impact of shutting down the pipeline was felt not just at the pipeline company, but throughout the northeast US at gas stations, transportation companies, and more. As supply chains increase the connectedness between buyers and suppliers, the vulnerabilities for cyber incidents increase. One study found that 62% of organizations who have experienced a breach found it was caused by a supplier.[39] Some cybersecurity metrics vendors have addressed this with measures that examine suppliers and the linkages to buyers and calculate a score of how secure these linkages are. Independent vendor ratings are increasingly being used by managers as part of their vendor evaluation process. For a company's scorecard, the measure might be an average of BitSight scores of all vendors or the range of scores all vendors have.

Financial risk measures are the next category of the scorecard. When leaders understand the risks associated with their cybersecurity plans and profile, they have a better understanding of the chances and potential costs of a breach. Executives and Boards of Directors often focus on this part of security management, wanting to know the company's risk profile or the risk that they are taking on from the different alternative decisions they might make. Cyber insurance is one way companies manage risk, as it transfers that risk. Managers purchase insurance for a fraction of the cost they would incur should a breach happen, and if a breach does cause damage, they have a source to cover some, if not all, of the cost (although as mentioned above, cyber insurance might not be a reliable source for recovering costs). Another approach to managing risk is to invest in protection tools or to invest in recovery/mitigation plans. Measures of the risk profile might include how likely it is that there would be damage from a breach, what the cost of a breach might be, and how the risk is managed.

Organizational leaders and hackers are two opposing parties in an ever-escalating battle, and each side is arming itself with more and more sophisticated tools as time passes. It is important that managers keep improving their understanding of security problems and prospects to keep directing significant efforts and

[38] For more detail about the CISA CPGs, please visit https://www.cisa.gov/cross-sector-cybersecurity-performance-goals (accessed May 31, 2023).

[39] Kevin Townsend, "Cyber Insights 2023: Supply Chain Security," Security Week, February 2, 2023, https://www.securityweek.com/cyber-insights-2023-supply-chain-security/ (accessed June 8, 2023).

resources to prevent falling behind in the war against cybercriminals. The stakes are too high to become complacent or to let others make all the decisions about the business's cyber resiliency.

Resiliency or Protection?

Since it seems impossible to be 100% secure from cyber threats, managers have pivoted to a new mindset of becoming resilient to cyber incidents. A **cyber-resilient** company is one that absorbs the shock of a cyber incident, quickly recovers and rapidly regains its ability to operate.[40] Companies who focus on cyber resilience build processes to anticipate, absorb, respond, and reimagine. Anticipation is built on the idea that if something can go wrong it eventually will. Cyber-resilient companies focus on ways to respond and recover from known and not-yet-invented cyberthreats. How do they do that? Consider a sports analogy. Teams have a playbook, but by practicing over and over, they develop skills to adapt instantly to changing conditions on the field or court. In a similar way, cyber resilient organizations regularly practice responding to cyber incidents so when a real one occurs, they are able to adapt.

Cyber resilient organizations create ways to absorb the impact of a cyber event by thinking differently about their systems. By thinking about ways in which their technology, business, and organizational systems might be disrupted, and proactively building redundant, diverse, and modular systems, and by involving their entire ecosystem in the preparations, they can minimize the impact and the duration of down time in the event of an attack.

Finally, cyber resilient companies regularly invest in ways to be further resilient. They conduct postmortems should an event occur so they can become better, focusing on lessons learned and additional ways to be resilient.

Cyber resilience is a different mindset than traditional cybersecurity thinking, which focuses on protection and keeping the attacks from happening. Cyber resilience assumes that something will happen (because statistics bear out the fact that likely it will) and prepares for responding and recovering. A company with a more traditional mindset will primarily make cyber investments in technology and processes to protect and detect, while one focused on resilience will still invest in protection and detection, but primarily focus on recovery so they can be back in operation more quickly.

SUMMARY

- The NIST Cybersecurity Framework highlights five areas of cybersecurity management: Identify, Protect, Detect, Respond, and Recover.
- Five key IT security decisions focus on security strategy, infrastructure, policies, culture, and investments.
- Perpetrators (hackers) most often work from a great distance, over long periods of time, and not by accessing data center buildings in person in a feverish hurry.
- Of breaches, stolen passwords are the most common entry point. Those passwords are obtained from phishing messages, cross-site scripting, weak passwords, key loggers, and evil twin connections. Weak security in the supply chain or third party partners are another way passwords might be stolen.
- The statistics are staggering: It takes 21 days for the average breach to be detected, and the longest breach recorded took 11 years to detect. The message is that hackers have plenty of time to figure out how to steal files. Also, 97% of all firms have been hacked, and the average cost of a data breach can be in the millions of dollars. Many breaches involve tens of millions of records.
- Complete, 100% security of data and digital assets is not possible. However, there are best practices for reducing risks by using tools, implementing tactics (policies), and providing training (and education).
- Infrastructure technologies can limit access to authorized people and protect data storage and transmission, but they, alone, do not provide a high level of cyber resilience. A program of defense in depth can increase resilience.

[40] Michael Coden, Martin Reeves, Keri Pearlson, Stuart Madnick, and Cheryl Berriman, "An Action Plan for Cyber Resilience," *Sloan Management Review*, January 2023. https://sloanreview.mit.edu/article/an-action-plan-for-cyber-resilience/.

- Resilience is one approach managers can take to reduce the impact (cost, duration, and disruption of operations) of a cyber incident. Resilience includes anticipation, absorption, response, and recovery.
- A culture of cybersecurity includes managerial decisions and activities that build values, attitudes, and beliefs of the importance of protecting data and securing the organization's systems. Security education, training, and awareness (SETA) refers to security education, training, and awareness, each of which has a specialized purpose.
- Answering the question "How secure are we?" requires a multidimensional approach including technical, people, supply chain, and financial risk measures.

KEY TERMS

antivirus/antispyware, 166
biometrics, 165
black hat hackers, 167
challenge questions, 165
cross-site scripting (XSS), 161
cybersecurity hygiene, 156
dark web, 163
deep web, 163
defense in depth, 164
encryption, 166
evil twin, 160
firewall, 166
grey hat hackers, 167
key, 166
key logger, 158
multifactor authentication, 165
NIST Cybersecurity Framework, 156
phishing attack, 158
resilience, 155
security education, training, and awareness (SETA), 168
spear phishing, 158
spoofing, 169
surface web, 163
passwordless continuous authentication, 166
universal authentication, 166
token, 165
weak password, 160
white hat hackers, 167

DISCUSSION QUESTIONS

1. Did you change your shopping habits after hearing of the widespread breaches at Target, Home Depot, and dozens of other stores? Why or why not? Would you continue banking with an institution that had a major breach? Why or why not?
2. Evaluate your password habits and describe a plan for new ones. Explain why you chose the new habits in your new plan, and how they reduce the risk of compromising your system's security.
3. Across all access tools listed in Figure 7.7 which have the most compelling advantages? What are the most concerning weaknesses? Provide support for your choices.
4. What is an evil twin Wi-Fi connection? What should you do to increase your security in a coffee shop the next time you want to connect?
5. Why are technological defenses not enough to protect an organization? Why do managers also need policies and SETA?
6. Name three commonly used management security policy areas and describe an example policy for each area.
7. Have you experienced multifactor authentication? How has your experience been? Estimate how many times per day you need to use it beyond your password. Do you have it turned on when it is not required?
8. Create an outline for a training session to help your team avoid phishing and spear phishing. What would you include in that training session? What are some typical signs that an e-mail might be fraudulent?
9. Your CEO has asked you "How secure are we?" Design your approach to how you would answer this question. What metrics would you present? Where would you get this information?
10. What is the difference in cyber protection versus cyber resilience? Explain this difference using an example from an industry you know well.

11. How do you think generative AI tools such as ChatGPT will impact cyber security? Please give an example and discuss what impact you imagine.

12. In July 2023, the United States Security and Exchange Commission (SEC) adopted new rules on cybersecurity risk management and governance. These new rules require, among other things, disclosure of cyber incidents on Form 8-K and periodic disclosure of cybersecurity risk management, strategy, and governance in annual reports. Why do you think the SEC adopted these new rules? What will be the impact for companies who must follow the SEC rules (i.e., public companies)? What is the potential impact for other companies who are not public companies?

Case Study 7-1 City of Baltimore

A ransomware attack, using a relatively new strain of ransomware called Robbinhood, took down the City of Baltimore, Maryland in 2019. It was the second time that year that this ransomware was used on a major US city, having infected Greenville, North Carolina a month earlier, and the city of Atlanta was a victim of another type of ransomware the year earlier. RobbinHood was an aggressive ransomware program that infected almost all of Baltimore's computer systems. Hackers locked up about 10,000 government computers and demanded 3 bitcoins for each system to be unlocked, which added up to 13 bitcoins, which at the time was about $75,000. If the ransom was not paid within 4 days, the price increased, and after 10 days, the city was told all data would be permanently lost. The ransom note said,

> "We won't talk more, all we know is MONEY! Hurry up! Tik Tak, Tik Tak, Tik Tak!"

The city leaders did not pay the ransom and many systems were affected. The city's card payment system, debt checking applications, employee email systems, and other systems were impacted and unusable. Real estate transactions, including home sales, were delayed since the city's lien system was not available. Text alerts about clusters of drug overdoses from the Baltimore City Health Department were down. The system for permits and final inspections for vendors was impacted, delaying the opening of completed construction projects. Employees had to set up individual Gmail accounts as a workaround. Agencies impacted included the Baltimore City Council, the Police Department, Department of Transportation, Department of Public Works, Department of Finance, Recreation and Parks, and several others. Recovery took months. Citizens felt the impact. For example, when water bills were finally sent out, the bill included four months of charges and a rate hike that went into effect during the outage. The IT director was put on unpaid leave and eventually replaced. Estimates were that the incident cost the city $18 million.

Why did this happen in Baltimore? Experts said that its IT practices were at fault. They pointed their finger at the decentralized technology budget, making it unclear who should have invested in increased security, pointed at the fact that an earlier risk assessment report identified security gaps to be closed which were left unpatched, and pointed at not purchasing cyberattack insurance, which was requested but not funded by the budget.

Discussion Questions

1. Using the NIST model, evaluate the Baltimore ransomware incident. What would you advise officials in Baltimore to do to be sure they are not victims again.
2. Would you have paid the ransom? Why or why not?
3. What in your opinion is different when the ransom attack is on a city versus a corporation? Should city leaders do something different than corporate leaders? please explain.

Sources: https://www.baltimoresun.com/maryland/baltimore-county/bs-md-co-ransomware-sewer-bills-20190617-story.html; See also https://technical.ly/civic-news/baltimore-cyberattacks-timeline/; https://technical.ly/civic-news/water-bills-are-being-issued-in-baltimore-for-the-first-time-since-the-may-ransomware-attack/; https://www.vox.com/recode/2019/5/21/18634505/baltimore-ransom-robbinhood-mayor-jack-young-hackers; https://mayor.baltimorecity.gov/news/press-releases/2019-05-20-city-provides-update-baltimore-ransomware-attack; https://heimdalsecurity.com/blog/baltimore-ransomware/.

Case Study 7-2 Airline Industry Frequent Flyer Info Data Breach

In early 2021, 11 airlines were affected by a cyberattack targeting frequent flyer data. This attack was actually done to SITA, a third-party system provider for the airlines. SITA's Passenger Service Systems (PSS) help process communications and passenger information for many carriers. Some of the airlines were not "customers" of SITA, but their passenger's frequent flyer information was part of the SITA database to enable verification of membership tier status and facilitate access to other benefits to customers. SITA explained to their customers that, while itineraries, reservations, tickets, passwords, and credit card information were not stolen, frequent flyer account numbers, member names, and status levels were stolen.

More than 2 million travelers were estimated to have been impacted. Passengers from the One World Alliance and the Star Alliance airline groups, including United Airlines, American Airlines, Cathay Pacific, Finnair, Japan Airlines, Jeju Air of Korea, Lufthansa, Malaysia Airlines, SAS, and Singapore Airlines, were victims of this breach.

SITA offers a number of services to airlines, including infrastructure maintenance, fare management information, and operational communications systems for airlines, airports, air navigation providers, governments, and others in the air travel ecosystem. Their products automate and facilitate passenger travel including secure check-in and boarding. While it's not clear that this breach affected any other SITA systems other than the PSS system, it did raise concerns about the breadth of potential impact from third-party vendors on air transportation.

Discussion Questions

1. Why do you think airlines are targets of hackers? What information do they have that is of value to malicious actors?
2. How might a phishing email have led to this kind of breach?
3. What can managers do to reduce the threat of third-party (supply chain) vulnerabilities?

Sources: https://thepointsguy.com/news/airline-industry-data-breach/; See also https://www.sita.aero/pressroom/news-releases/sita-statement-about-security-incident/; https://www.windows-active-directory.com/multiple-airlines-suffer-data-breach-due-to-supply-chain-cyberattack-frequent-flyer-list-compromised.html; https://techcrunch.com/2021/03/04/sita-airline-passenger-breach/; https://www.cpomagazine.com/cyber-security/american-airlines-data-breach-linked-to-a-phishing-campaign-exposed-sensitive-customer-and-employee-personal-information/; https://www.securityweek.com/researchers-attribute-sita-cyberattack-chinese-hackers/; https://www.cpomagazine.com/cyber-security/aviation-it-giant-sita-breached-in-extensive-supply-chain-attack-frequent-flier-programs-of-major-airlines-compromised/; https://www.sita.aero/pressroom/news-releases/sita-statement-about-security-incident/.

The Business of Information Technology

8

This chapter explores the business of information technology (IT) and the customers it serves. Beginning with the introduction of a maturity model to understand the balancing act between the supply and business demand for information systems (IS), the chapter describes key IT organization activities and relates them to one of three maturity levels. The chapter continues with a discussion about the work done by the IT organization and how the leadership within the IT organization ensures that activities are conducted efficiently and effectively, both domestically and globally. We then examine business processes within the IT department, including building a business case, managing the IT portfolio, and valuing and monitoring IT investments. The remainder of the chapter focuses on funding models and total cost of ownership.

After several months in the job of chief information officer (CIO) of Alcoa's Industrial Chemicals Business, Kevin Horner received a wake-up call from the president of the business[1]:

> *"We chose you because you were the best of the IT group, and you are doing a great job completing IT projects and managing the IT organization. But I am afraid that you don't know the business of your business. You haven't thoroughly answered my repeated questions about how much IT costs the business! Furthermore, you can't communicate with the people running the business in words they understand!"*

As a high-achieving math major in college with minors in computer science and business, Horner was quite savvy about his craft and did not expect to hear these remarks. When he protested that the structure of the financial information in European and Asian subsidiaries made it really difficult to find the answer, his boss's response surprised him: "If it wasn't a hard problem, I wouldn't need you here!"

Interpreting this unpleasant meeting as his being "under review" for possible ouster, Horner saw this as a wake-up call to the true meaning of being a C-level executive. He had found some answers about cost issues, but many of the financial numbers were "buried"—inextricably intertwined in general categories of financial statements in Europe and Asia. He had some early results, but managing the IT group took most of his time and effort.

Further, his early presentations were heavy with technical details and were often met with glazed eyes and yawns. Horner reported that he began to realize that this audience did not want to hear about the technology. "They certainly wanted me to handle technology issues, but they wanted me to communicate with them in words they understood . . . people, time, money and the possibilities technology created for them in their businesses. Most importantly they wanted me to help them to use IT to grow the business at either the top line (sales) or bottom line (net income)." Horner embarked on a re-energized mission to answer all of the president's concerns in a more complete way, and that mission ultimately paid handsome dividends both to him and Alcoa.

If success can be measured by promotions, he went far beyond redeeming himself. After five years as CIO of Alcoa Chemical, he had many promotions until he ultimately became CIO of Alcoa Global. Later he moved into and out of retirement, and now serves as an operating partner at 3 Rivers Capital. He won

[1] This story and all the quotes are based on a personal interview with Kevin Horner and one of our authors, March 23, 2015.

several awards in his career, including his listing among 100 Most Influential People by Staffing Industry Analysts. His success was likely informed by many of the lessons he learned at Alcoa.

How did he achieve such resounding success? The first thing he did was to partner with the CFO to understand the financials of the business. The CFO was able to determine how to peel back the layers of accounting numbers and truly wrestle the IT costs from the general accounting categorizations where they comfortably hid. Within 60 days, the president and his management team had their answers.

But Horner did not stop at a good, solid set of internal cost numbers, a remarkable achievement in and of itself. Rather than only gaze inside the firm, he found it most helpful to use the Hackett Group, an external benchmarking consulting firm, to compare his costs against those of similar firms. This analysis was most helpful for the leadership of the business because after finding that the company was high on some key IT costs, the leaders all saw the writing on the wall for the next mission: Find ways to reduce costs but continue to provide improved services.

Two key examples of how Horner addressed those needs will help explain his early success. He accompanied salespeople on actual sales calls to see exactly how the overall supply chain process worked. Then with that information as a base, he was able to have the business provide reliable product information to customers, accelerating delivery of the products customers needed without creating excessive inventory buffers.

Horner also worked with procurement officials to renegotiate contracts for the highest-cost elements within the company's IT spending. For example, two very costly areas included telecommunications costs (including cell phones) and PCs. He found two important cost-savings opportunities: eliminate unnecessary services and negotiate many small separate contracts as a larger unit, raising the business's bargaining power. As contracts would come up for renewal, a joint team from IT and procurement spearheaded an intense process to streamline costs, focusing on the highest cost elements first. These contract negotiations led to another benefit: standardization, which enabled further savings by simplifying items such as interconnectivity between segments of the business and PC and mobile phone support.

The lessons Horner learned in his CIO role in the chemicals business transferred easily into his next role as CIO of Alcoa Europe, which was a collection of historical Alcoa businesses and locations along with several newly acquired companies representing what Horner called "kind of a $3B 'start-up' company." He knew immediately that he had to get a clear picture of the IT business in Europe from several perspectives—technology, applications, people, vendors, cost, and "quick wins," which solved problems for his business leadership colleagues. This time Horner didn't need the questions from the business president to guide him: He had to quickly assess talent in his team, determine total IT cost in the business, assist the management team to move to Europe from a structure focusing on legal entity driven reporting and reporting finances in a new structure that aligned with corporate Alcoa and unified pan-European business units. As a result of his business-focused thrusts, within 24 months, the entire unified structure was created and implemented; legal entity fiscal reporting was maintained; a shared service function for finance, accounting, HR, and procurement plus the technology to operate it was implemented; Y2K remediation was completed; and European IT costs were reduced by 25%.

What does this experience demonstrate? It shows that there are common denominators that every business leader understands: people, time, and money. When a business leader wants to invest capital to produce more products or a new product, that investment is scrutinized for cost and benefit. Horner says that a CIO should make sure IT is not the exception to that rule. "Don't talk about ERP or mobile apps, talk about what is going to happen to the business . . . [and] to people, time, and money when you have the ERP or the mobile app," he says. "Getting the cost side of the IT organization in order represents table stakes for the CIO," implying that you would wear out your welcome by focusing inward. Rather than focusing only on managing the technologies and IT people and describing new investments and initiatives by using "techy" jargon, a CIO should take a business viewpoint. If you follow that advice, you will not only be welcome at the table but also will thrive. This demonstrates the Business of Information Technology, the title of this chapter.

In this chapter, issues related to the business side of IT are explored. We begin by looking at the key activities that managers can expect of their IT organization and, probably just as importantly, what the IT organization does not provide. The chapter continues with a discussion of key business processes within the IT organization, such as building a business case, managing an IT portfolio, and valuing and monitoring IT investments. This is followed by a discussion of ways of funding the IT department and an exploration of several ways to calculate the cost of IT investments, including total cost of ownership and activity-based costing. These topics are critical for the IT manager to understand, but a general manager must also understand how the business of IT works to successfully propose, plan, manage, and use information systems.

Organizing to Respond to Business: A Maturity Model

The Alcoa situation just discussed reveals that IT leaders must make sure they have the right resources and organization to respond to business needs. It is not enough to focus inward on managing personnel, software, and equipment, which can seem like a full-time responsibility. IT managers must go beyond internal matters and partner with their business colleagues and ecosystem partners (often those providing "as a service" functionality). Such co-creators can add value through either enhancing revenue or cutting costs for the business, all while improving product and service offerings. Responding to business demands adds substantially to IT managers' responsibilities because it requires them not only to manage the complexity within the IT function but also to go well beyond what seem to be the boundaries of IT and understand intricacies of their business partners.

To create his **business-IT maturity model**, researcher Vaughan Merlyn studied 35 global IT organizations over three years. The model is shown in Figure 8.1. His model provides characteristics of how engaged the IT function can be with the rest of the organization at three unique levels of maturity. At Level 1, representing an immature IT organization, IT managers maintain an inward focus. They merely react to specific needs that are brought to their attention, often in an environment that emphasizes efficiency. As the IT organization matures to Level 2, the focus shifts to business processes, and IT personnel search for solutions to business problems. This level emphasizes business effectiveness. Level 3 represents IT managers as business partners who search for ideas that provide value to the organization and value relationships both inside and outside not only the IT organization but also the firm. They seek ideas that provide not only new revenue but also help identify new opportunities that redefine, or transform, the business. The LEGO and Judo Bank examples from Chapter 6 illustrate how business can be enhanced, enabled, or transformed by outside ecosystem partners as co-creators of added value.

This model illustrates that for IT to provide the most value to the business, IT managers and business managers must recognize their mutual dependency and ensure that business capability has the technology support needed for success. This model does not comment on the type of technology used but on the way the business organization approaches its use of IT. For example, in Level 3, business leaders see IT's

Maturity Levels	Nature of the Levels	Engagement Characteristics
Level 3: Business transformation	IT as business partner	• Proactive • Outside-in • Relationship centric • Focused on business growth • Framed on a context of business value and value co-creation
Level 2: Business effectiveness	IT as solutions provider	• Active • Process centric • Focused on solutions • Framed in a context of projects
Level 1: Business efficiency	IT as order taker	• Reactive • Inside-out • Technology centric • Framed in a context of cost

FIGURE 8.1 Business-IT maturity model.

Source: Adapted from Vaughan Merlyn, *Business Relationship Management for the Digital Enterprise: Strategies for managing IT to meet the digital challenges facing enterprises now and in the future.* Merlyngroup, LLC, 2019.

role as a business partner that they can include in high-level meetings that explore new lines of business. Compare this approach with lower levels of maturity. At Level 2, the focus would instead be on creating an effective business process, which has a much more limited scope and impact. At Level 1, where the business demand for IT is primarily all about cost savings and foundation systems, the IT function might be seen more as a necessary evil that needs to be pushed into a corner rather than expanded to flex organizational muscles. When the maturity of the IT organization rises to Level 3, it is able not only to keep up with business demands but also to enhance the business in ways that were not envisioned before.

Understanding the IT Organization

Consider the analogy of a ship to help explain the purpose of an IT organization and how it functions. A ship transports people and cargo to a particular destination in much the same way that an IT organization directs itself toward the strategic goals set by the larger enterprise. All ships navigate waters, but different ships have different structures, giving them unique capabilities such as transporting people vs. cargo. Even among similar categories, ships have different features, such as those configured to transport a cargo of finished products vs. one configured to transport a cargo of oil. All IT organizations provide services to their businesses, but based on the skills and capabilities of their people, the organizational focus of their management, and their state of maturity, they, too, differ in what they can do and how they work with the businesses. Sometimes the IT organization must navigate perilous waters or storms to reach port. For both the IT organization and the ship, the key is to perform more capably than any competitors. It means doing the right things at the right time and in the right way to propel the enterprise through the rough waters of business.

Different firms need to do different things when it comes to IT. Because firms have different goals, they need to act in different ways and as a result, there are differences in the IT activities that are provided. But even if two firms have similar goals, the firms' size, organization structure, and level of maturity might affect what the IT organization in each firm is expected to do.

What a Manager Can Expect from the IT Organization

We look at the IT organization from the perspective of the customer of the IT organization, the general manager, or "user," of the systems. What can a manager expect from the IT organization? Just as IT leaders benefit from understanding their business partners, a general manager benefits from understanding what the IT organization does.

Managers must learn what to expect from the IT organization so they can plan and implement business strategy accordingly. Although the nature of the activities may vary in each IT organization depending upon its overall goal, a manager typically can expect some level of support in 15 core activities,[2] which are briefly described in Figure 8.2.

Although the activities could be found at any maturity level, we indicate in Figure 8.2 the level where they are especially important. Recall that Level 1 focuses on efficiency; Level 2 examines effectiveness; and Level 3 focuses on business strategy. This progression implies that the scope of activities in the IT organization expands with increased IT maturity.

The IT organization can be expected to be responsible for most, if not all, of the activities listed in Figure 8.2. However, instead of actually performing the activities, the IT organization increasingly identifies and then works with vendors who provide them. More traditional activities such as data center operations, network management, and system development and maintenance (including application design, development, and maintenance) have been outsourced to vendors for decades. More recently, enterprises use outsourcing providers to perform more newly acquired IT activities such as process management (alternatively called *business process outsourcing*). In our increasingly flat world, many companies are successfully drawing from labor supplies in other parts of the world to meet the business demand that they

[2] Eight activities are described by John F. Rockart, Michael J. Earl, and Jeanne W. Ross, "Eight Imperatives for the New IT Organization," *Sloan Management Review* (Fall 1996): 52–53. Seven activities have been added to their eight imperatives.

Activities	Descriptions	Maturity Levels
Developing and maintaining systems	• Together with business users, analyze needs, design, write, and test the software • Identify, acquire, and install outside software packages and app libraries to fill business needs • Correct system errors or enhance the system to respond to changing business/legal environments	1
Managing supplier and platform-related relationships	• Maximize the benefit of relationships to the enterprise and pre-empt problems that might occur	1
Managing data, information, and knowledge	• Collect and store data created and captured by the enterprise (Level 1) • Manage enterprise information and knowledge (Level 2)	1, 2
Managing Internet and network systems	• Develop and maintain Internet access and capabilities • Manage private networks, telephone systems, and wireless technologies • Design, build, and maintain the network architecture and infrastructure	1, 2 (depending on nature of network)
Managing human resources	• Hire, train, and maintain good staff performers; fire poor performers • Work with enterprise HR personnel to learn up-to-date regulations and practices	1
Operating the data center	• Operate and maintain large mainframe computers, rows of servers, or other hardware on which the company's systems are built • Provide connections between the firm's systems and cloud services	1
Providing general support	• Manage diverse help desk activities • Collect and record support information • Assign appropriate personnel to support cases • Follow up with vendors as needed • Follow up with business contacts with updates or solutions	1
Planning for business discontinuities	• Develop and implement business continuity plan • Make preparations to counter physical or electronic attacks, hacking attempts, weather disasters, and other events that could cripple the enterprise	1
Innovating current processes	• Work with managers to innovate processes that can benefit from technological solutions • Explore modifications that can reduce costs, improve service, or connect with customers • Design systems that facilitate new ways of doing business	2
Establishing architecture platforms and standards	• Develop, maintain, and communicate standards • Maintain consistency and integrity of the firm's data • Develop and implement platform governance	2
Promoting enterprise cybersecurity	• Maintain the integrity of the enterprise infrastructure • Develop and implement enterprise information security policies, strategy, and controls • Identify, prioritize, and guard against threats to the enterprise's information assets • Work with business units to enhance security of operational practices • Train employees to raise awareness and understanding of information security risks • Participate in discussions about cybersecurity investments	2
Anticipating new technologies	• Scout new technology trends and help the business integrate them into planning and operations • Assess the costs and benefits of new technologies for the enterprise • With business and platform partners, prioritize the most promising opportunities on strategic and operational grounds. • Limit investments in technologies incompatible with current or planned systems or that quickly become obsolete	3
Participating in setting and implementing strategic goals	• Enable business managers to achieve strategic goals by acting as educators or consultants • Advise managers on best practices within IT • Work with managers to develop IT-enhanced solutions to business problems • Serve as partners in moving the enterprise forward • Support digital innovation and transformation	3
Co-creating with ecosystem and platform partners	• Support digital innovation • Support service transformation • Develop and implement platform governance	3
Integrating the use of social IT	• Leverage the use of social IT to transform the business • Encourage engagement, collaboration, and innovation in customer-, supplier-, platform-, and employee-directed applications • Manage and analyze the data resulting from social IT to provide business insights	3

FIGURE 8.2 IT organization activities and related level of maturity.

can't handle internally in their own IT organization. Managing the sourcing relationships and global labor supply is so important that a whole chapter (i.e., Chapter 10) is devoted to discussing these sourcing issues in greater depth.

What the IT Organization Does Not Do

This chapter presents core activities for which the IT organization is typically responsible. It is enlightening to examine tasks that should *not* be performed by the organization. Clear examples include core business functions, such as selling, manufacturing, and accounting, and few functional managers would attempt to delegate these tasks to IT professionals. However, some functional managers inadvertently delegate key operational decisions to the IT organization. For example, when general managers ask the IT professional to build an information system for their organization and do not become active partners in the design of that system, they are in effect turning over control of their business operations. Likewise, asking an IT professional to select and implement a software package or app without first partnering with that professional to ensure that the service meets both current and future needs is also ceding control.

Partnerships between the general managers and IT professionals are also important for a number of other decisions. For instance, IT professionals should not have the sole responsibility for deciding which business projects receive IT dollars. Giving carte blanche to the IT professional would mean that the IT organization decides what is important to the business units. If IT professionals try to respond to every request from their business counterparts, they would likely face a backlog of delayed initiatives and become overwhelmed. Business partners participate in prioritizing IT projects to ensure that resources are applied appropriately. Similarly, IT professionals should not solely decide the acceptable level of IT services or security. Because senior managers run the business, they are the ones who must decide on the level of service and security that should be delivered by the IT organization.[3] These are examples of decisions that should be made jointly with business counterparts. Perfection comes at a price that many business leaders may be unwilling to pay. Not every system needs to have gold-plated functionality, and not every system needs to be fortified from every conceivable danger.

As discussed in Chapter 2, the senior management team, including the CIO, sets business strategy. However, in many organizations, the general manager delegates critical technology decisions to the IT professional alone, and this can lead to technology decisions that might hinder business opportunities. Strategy formulation is a joint process including business and IT professionals. The role for the IT professional in the discussion of strategy includes things such as suggesting technologies and applications that enable it, identifying limits to the technologies and applications under consideration, reporting on best practices and new technologies that might enhance opportunities of the firm, and consulting all those involved with setting the strategic direction to make sure they properly consider the role and impact of IT on the decisions they make. The IT organization does not set business strategy. It does, however, participate in the discussions and partner with the business to ensure that IT can provide the infrastructure, applications, and support necessary for the successful implementation of the business strategy. The IT organization can also provide ideas of new business capabilities afforded by new technologies and can enable business transformation. In that sense, IT leaders must be part of key business strategy discussions.

Chief Information Officer

If an IT organization is like a ship, the chief information officer is like the captain. The **chief information officer (CIO)** is the most senior executive in the enterprise responsible for technology vision and leadership for designing, developing, implementing, and managing IT initiatives for the enterprise to operate effectively in a constantly changing and intensely competitive marketplace. The CIO is an executive, a business leader, and therefore a member of the "C-Suite," the major executive team that sets strategy for

[3] J. W. Ross and P. Weill, "Six IT Decisions Your IT People Shouldn't Make," *Harvard Business Review* 80, no. 11 (November 2002): 84–95, 1–8.

the organization as a whole. The CIO has a unique dual-focus role, with a strong voice in both enabling and implementing enterprise strategy, as well as leadership responsibility in developing and implementing IT strategy.

CIOs are a unique breed. They have a strong understanding of the business and of the technology. In many organizations, they take on roles that span both of these areas, as a **business technology strategist**, the strategic business leader who uses technology as the core tool in creating competitive advantage and aligning business and IT strategies.[4] The title *CIO* signals to both the organization and to outside observers that this executive is a strategic IT thinker and is responsible for linking IS strategy with the business strategy. The CIO must understand the business vision to leverage and manage technology investments to support and bring strategic advantage to the business. This means that CIOs need the technical ability to plan, conceive, build, and implement multiple IT projects on time and within budget, as well as the ability to realize the benefits and manage the costs and risks associated with IT, to articulate and advocate for a management vision of IT, to encourage digital innovation and business transformation where appropriate, and to work well with the other executives. In some companies, digital innovation is so important that CIOs have assumed an additional title as Chief Digital Officer, though in other companies this title is held by someone in a separate department that complements the IT department.[5]

Just as the chief financial officer (CFO) is involved in operational management of the financial activities of the organization, the CIO is involved with operational issues related to IT. More often than not, CIOs are asked to perform both strategic tasks and operational tasks during a typical day. Some of their operational activities include identifying and managing the introduction of new technologies into the firm, negotiating partnership relationships with key suppliers and platform partners, setting partner policies, and managing the overall IT budget. Actual day-to-day management of the data center, IT infrastructure, application development projects, vendor portfolio, and other more specific operational issues are typically not handled directly by the CIO but by one of the managers in the IT organization. Ultimately, whether they directly function as operational managers or as leaders with oversight of other operational managers, the CIO must assume responsibility for all the activities described in Figure 8.2 that the IT organization is charged to perform.

Where the CIO fits within an enterprise is often a source of discussion. In the early days of the CIO position, when the role was predominantly responsible for controlling IT costs (Level 1), the position reported to the CFO. Because the CIO was rarely involved in enterprise governance or in discussions of business strategy, this reporting structure worked. However, as IT became a source for competitive advantage and digital innovation in the marketplace, reporting to the CFO proved too limiting. Conflicts arose because the CFO misunderstood the vision for IT or saw only the costs of technology. They also arose because management still saw the CIO's primary responsibility as providing services whose costs had to be controlled. More recently, CIOs most often report directly to the CEO, president, or other executive manager. The 2022 survey of the Society for Information Management reveals that almost half report to the CEO/President, and most of the rest report to the CFO or Chief Operating Officer, in that order. This elevated reporting relationship not only signals that the role of IT is critical to the enterprise and indicates Level 3 maturity but also makes it easier to implement strategic IT initiatives.

Regardless of the importance of technology issues in modern firms, there has been some worry among CIOs of their credibility/perception from the perspective of other business leaders. This is evident in the Kevin Horner story that started this chapter. From 2015 to 2022, the aforementioned SIM survey revealed that the issue of credibility was the sixth or higher most important/worrisome issue for IT leaders. The situation appears to have improved somewhat in 2022, however, because in the previous seven-year survey, that issue came in fourth most important or higher. Other strongly important worries, most often in the top three, were cybersecurity, alignment with business, and a shortage of personnel with IT Skills.[6] The information systems function in modern organizations clearly has the greater organization in mind when taking inventory of their concerns.

[4] M. Carter, V. Grover, and J. B. Thatcher, "The Emerging CIO Role of Business Technology Strategist," *MIS Quarterly Executive* 10, no. 1 (2011): 19–29.

[5] S. Tumbas, N. Berente, and J. vom Brocke, "Three Types of Chief Digital Officers and the Reasons Organizations Adopt the Role," *MIS Quarterly Executive* 16, no. 2 (2017).

[6] Vess Johnson, Russell Torres, Chris Maurer, Katia Guerra, Smriti Srivastava, and Hossein Mohit, "The 2022 SIM IT Issues and Trends Study," *MIS Quarterly Executive* 22, no. 1 (2023): Article 6. Available at: https://aisel.aisnet.org/misqe/vol22/iss1/6.

Their worries are justified, as some organizations choose not to have a CIO. These organizations do not consider that the role of CIO is necessary, in part because technology is highly integrated into virtually every aspect of the business and no single officer need provide oversight. These firms typically hire an individual to be responsible for running the computer systems and possibly to manage many of the activities described later in this chapter. But they signal that this person is not a strategist by giving him or her the title of data processing manager, director of information systems, or some other name that clearly differentiates this person from other top officers in the company. Using the words *chief* and *officer* usually implies a strategic focus, and some organizations that do not see the value of having an IT person on their executive team choose not to use these words.

Although the CIO's role is to guide the enterprise toward the future, this responsibility is frequently too great to accomplish alone. Many organizations recognize that certain strategic areas of the IT organization require more focused guidance. This recognition led to the creation of new positions, such as the chief technology officer (CTO), chief knowledge officer (CKO), chief data officer (CDO), chief digital officer (another CDO), chief analytics officer (CAO), chief information security officer (CISO), and others. The list seems to grow over time, and each organization can create various specializations as needed. With the occasional exception of the CTO, each typically is subordinate to the CIO. Zetlin and Olavsrud[7] observed that many of these have very blurry lines separating their duties. Together, these officers form a management team that leads the IT organization.

Many large corporations take the concept of CIO one step further and identify the CIO of a business unit. This is someone who has responsibilities similar to those of a corporate CIO, but the scope is the business unit and there is not as much concern about defining corporate standards and policies to ensure consistency across the business units. The business unit CIO is responsible for aligning the IT investment portfolio with the business unit's strategy. Typically, the business unit CIO has dual reporting responsibility to both the corporate CIO and the president of the business unit. At IBM, the CIO is a manager from a business unit who serves a two- to three-year term.[8]

Building a Business Case

In order to meet demand, the IT organization is often charged with providing solutions. Businesses managers often turn to IT for good solutions, but IT projects end up competing with those of other managers in tight economic times when there clearly aren't enough budget resources to cover them all. After all, there is often no shortage of other needed business investments such as new production machinery for higher product quality, and lower costs or funding for product research and development on product innovations. Thus, managers need to show that the solution they want would be not only a good IT investment but also a good business investment.

To gain support and a "go-ahead" decision, every manager must often create a business case. Similar to a legal case, a **business case** is a structured document that lays out all the relevant information needed to make a go/no-go decision. The business case for an IT project is also an opportunity to establish priorities for investing in different projects, identify how IT and the business can deliver new benefits, gain commitment from business managers, and create a basis for monitoring the investment.[9]

The components of a business case vary from corporation to corporation, depending on the priorities and decision-making environment. However, there are several primary elements of any business case (see Figure 8.3). Critical to the business case is the identification of costs and benefits, both in financial and nonfinancial terms.

It is particularly important for the business case to describe the benefits to be gained with the acceptance of the project. A useful framework for identifying and describing both financial and nonfinancial

[7] Minda Zetlin and Thor Olavsrud, "What is a chief digital officer? A digital strategist and evangelist in chief," *CIO Magazine,* March 24, 2022.

[8] Ann Majchrzak, Luba Cherbakov, and Blake Ives, "Harnessing the Power of the Crowds with Corporate Social Networking Tools: How IBM Does It," *MIS Quarterly Executive* 8, no. 2 (2009): 103–8.

[9] John Ward, Elizabeth Daniel, and Joe Peppard, "Building Better Business Cases for IT Investments," *MIS Quarterly Executive* 7, no. 1 (March 2008): 1–15.

Sections or Components	Descriptions
Executive summary	One- or two-page description of the overall business case document summarizing key points
Overview and introduction	Brief business background, the current business situation, a clear statement of the business problem or opportunity, and a recommended solution at a high level
Assumptions and rationale	Issues driving the proposal (e.g., operational, human resources, environmental, competitive, industry or market trends, or financial)
Project summary	High-level and detailed descriptions of the project: scope, objectives, contacts, resource plan, key metrics, implementation plan, and key success factors
Financial discussion and analysis	Overall summary followed by projected costs/revenues/benefits, financial metrics, financial model, cash flow statement, underlying assumptions, and total cost of ownership (TCO) analysis
Benefits and business impacts	Summary of business impacts followed by details on nonfinancial matters such as new business, transformation, innovations, competitive responses, organizational, supply chain, and human resource impacts
Schedule and milestones	Entire schedule for the project with milestones and expected metrics at each stage; if appropriate, can include a marketing plan and schedule
Risk and contingency analysis	Analysis of risks and ways to manage those risks, sensitivity analysis of scenarios, and interdependencies and the impact they will have on potential outcomes
Conclusion and recommendation	Primary recommendation and conclusions
Appendices	Backup materials not directly provided in the body of the document, such as detailed financial investment analysis, marketing materials, and competitors' literature.

FIGURE 8.3 Components of a business case.

benefits was created by Ward, Daniel, and Peppard.[10] The first step in this framework is to identify each benefit as an innovation (allowing the organization to do new things), improvement (allowing the organization to do things better), or cessation (stopping unnecessary, counterproductive, or wasteful things). Then the benefits can be classified by degree of explicitness or the ability to assign a value to the benefit. As shown in Figure 8.4, benefits fall into one of these categories, from most to least explicit:

- *Financial:* There is a way to express the benefit in financial terms. These are the metrics that are most easily used to judge the go/no-go decision because financial terms are universal across all business decisions. Examples include sales and profit increases as well as cost decreases by replacing manual systems with automated ones.

	Innovation: Using analytics for planning advertising programs	**Improvement:** Interactive customer support via peer-to-peer support community	**Cessation:** Remove phone support as first tier, replacing it with an AI chatbot
Financial benefits (most explicit)	Higher sales after better matching of ads to locations	Fewer returns; higher sales	Smaller payroll due to fewer phone support personnel
Quantifiable benefits	More frequent reorders in larger quantities	Increase in repeat customers	Shorter wait time; the only calls are for tier 2
Measurable benefits	Fewer personnel asking for overtime pay when staying late to finish up shipments due to inadequate analytical tools.	Fewer registered complaints and returns due to self-help	Positive customer comments about well-written documentation the AI provides
Observable benefits (least explicit)	Less idle time in the shipping department	Number of postings to the forum	Fewer phone calls because the chatbot handles the easy ones

FIGURE 8.4 Benefit examples for a business case.

[10] Ward et al., 2008.

- *Quantifiable:* There is a way to measure the size or magnitude of the benefit, but financial benefits are not directly determinable. For example, a firm might expect a 20% increase in customer retention, but to determine the financial benefit of resulting increased sales, it would require an analysis of what items they would buy. Most business cases revolve around quantifiable benefits, so it is important to ensure the collection of a comprehensive list of quantifiable benefits and any associated costs. Another example is a reduction in head count (the number of employees without analyzing any financial impacts).
- *Measurable:* There is a way to measure the benefit, but it is not necessarily connectable to any organizational outcome. Management must ensure alignment with the business strategy. For example, many organizations collect satisfaction or web engagement data and track changes over time.
- *Observable:* These can be detected only by opinion or judgment. These are the subjective, intangible, soft, or qualitative benefits. Things seem better but no measures are available. For example, customers might be expected to be happier or less argumentative.

Consider the example of a small manufacturing firm that hopes to differentiate itself with excellent customer service but has a lack of tools to analyze its operations, customers who return goods in high numbers due to confusion or defects, a customer support department plagued by long customer wait time, and growing dissatisfaction. The firm identified potential improvements when using analytical tools, creating an interactive customer support community, and using an artificial intelligence (AI) chatbot to serve as the first tier of support. See Figure 8.4 for examples from a potential benefit analysis for this three-pronged project.

Of course, the benefit analysis is only part of the story because costs and risks need to be considered as well. Projected costs would include paying for apps, consulting help, internal costs, training costs, and other new expenditures. There would also be technical risks, financial risks, security risks, and organizational risks. Security risks are covered in Chapter 7, and neglecting any one protective mechanism could open up the entire organization to the risk of a breach or cyber damage. Organizational risks would include inadequate monitoring of the new functionality or inability to recruit knowledgeable monitors for the chat function, support forum, and social media page.

IT Portfolio Management

Managing the set of systems and programs in an IT organization is similar to managing resources in a financial organization. There are different types of IT investments or projects, and together they form the business's IT portfolio. **IT portfolio management** refers to "evaluating new and existing applications collectively on an ongoing basis to determine which applications provide value to the business in order to support decisions to replace, retire, or further invest in applications across the enterprise."[11] This process requires thinking about IT systems as a cohesive set of core assets, not as a discontinuous stream of one-off (one-time only), targeted investments as often has been the case in the past. IT portfolio management involves continually deciding on the right mix of investments from funding, management, and staffing perspectives. The overall goal of IT portfolio management is for the company to fund and invest in the most valuable initiatives that, taken together as a whole, generate maximum benefits.

Four asset classes of IT investments that typically make up a company's IT portfolio have been described by Professor Peter Weill and colleagues at MIT's Center for Information Systems Research (CISR)[12]: In the Business Maturity Model, the first exemplifies level 1, the middle two exemplify level 2, and the last exemplifies level 3.

- *Transactional systems:* Streamlining or cutting costs
- *Infrastructure systems:* Provide a base foundation of IT services such as networks.

[11] James D. McKeen and Heather A. Smith, "Developments in Practice XXXIV: Application Portfolio Management," *Communications of the Association for Information Systems* 26, no. 9 (2010), http://aisel.aisnet.org/cais/vol26/iss1/9 (accessed September 4, 2015).

[12] Peter Weill and Marianne Broadbent, *Leveraging the New Infrastructure: How Market Leaders Capitalize on Information Technology* (Cambridge, MA: Harvard Business School Press, June 1998). © MIT Sloan Center for Information Systems Research 2005–12. Used with permission. For more information, see http://cisr.mit.edu.

- *Informational systems:* Provide information for decision making
- *Strategic systems:* Gaining competitive advantage

In analyzing the composition of any single company's IT portfolio, one can find a profile of the relative investment made in each IT asset class. Weill's study found that firms in diverse industries and with different strategies allocate their IT resources differently.[13] For example, cost-focused firms focused more heavily on transactional systems while agility-focused firms focused more heavily on infrastructure investments. LEGO from Chapter 6 provides an excellent example of an agility-focused firm investing heavily in infrastructure. Infrastructure investments can lead to a platform to be used to more quickly and nimbly create solutions needed by the business, whereas the transactional systems might lock in the current processes and take more effort and time to change.

From the portfolio management perspective, potential new systems are evaluated on their own merits and compared against other systems in the prospective portfolio. Often applications can't stand alone and require integration with other applications, some of which would need to be acquired or developed. A complete picture is required for a fair comparison of portfolio alternatives. Portfolio management helps prioritize IT investments across multiple decision criteria, including value to the business, urgency, and financial return. Just like an individual or company's investment portfolio is aligned with its objectives, the IT portfolio must be aligned with the business strategy.

Valuing IT Investments

New IT investments are often justified by the business managers proposing them in terms of monetary costs and benefits. The monetary costs and benefits are important but are not the only considerations in making IT investments. Soft benefits, such as the ability to make future decisions, are often part of the business case for IT investments, making the measurement of the investment's payback (length of time to recoup the cost) difficult.

Several unique factors of the IT organization make it very challenging to determine the value that can be received from IT investments. First, the systems are complex, and calculating the costs is an art, not a science. Second, because many IT investments are for infrastructure, calculating a **payback period** may be more complex than other types of capital investments. Third, in many situations the payback cannot be calculated because the investment is a necessity rather than a choice without any tangible payback. For example, upgrading to a newer version of an app and/or smartphone operating system may be required because the older version simply is no longer supported. Many of us have experienced this on our phones or tablets, and it is interesting to realize that this is a perennial problem in an IT organization as well, albeit on a much grander scale. Many managers do not want to have to upgrade just because the vendor insists that an upgrade is necessary. In the end, the investment would likely add no incremental value. These factors and more fuel a long-running debate about the value of IT investments. IT managers need to express benefits in a businesslike manner such as **return on investment (ROI)**, which assesses, in percent terms, the extent to which the expected financial benefits exceed the costs of an investment. For instance, if a $1 million investment in a website is expected to save $1.2 million in real estate and labor costs from closing a physical store, the ROI would be 20%. A measurable businesslike outcome would be increased customer satisfaction scores, which can be expressed in terms of improvement on a scale. For instance, a website satisfaction score could improve from 3 stars to 4 stars after extensive revamping.

IT managers, like the business managers who propose IT projects, are expected to understand, and even try to calculate the financial return on these projects. Measuring this return is difficult, however. To illustrate, consider the relative ease with which a manager might analyze whether the enterprise should build a new plant. The first step would be to estimate the costs of construction. The plant capacity dictates project production levels. Demand might vary, and construction costs overrun, but estimates can serve as sufficient information for deciding whether to build. Most often, the benefits of investing in IT are less

[13] Weill and Broadbent, 1998.

tangible than those of building a plant because the IT cannot be felt and touched like a physical building. Such benefits might include tighter systems integration, faster response time, more accurate data, greater innovation potential, and more leverage to adopt future technologies, among others. How can a manager quantify these intangibles? He or she should also consider many indirect, or downstream, benefits and costs, such as changes in how people behave, where staff report, and how tasks are assigned. In fact, it may be impossible to pinpoint who will benefit from an IT investment when making the decision.[14]

Despite the difficulty, the task of evaluating IT investments is necessary. Knowing which approaches to use and when to use them are important first steps. A number of financial valuation approaches are summarized in Figure 8.5. Managers should choose based on the attributes of the project. For example, ROI or payback analysis can be used when detailed analysis is not required, such as when a project is short lived, with clear but short-term costs and benefits. When the project and/or its impacts last long enough that the time value of money becomes a factor, **net present value (NPV)** and **economic value added (EVA)** are better approaches. EVA is particularly appropriate for capital-intensive projects.

Both IT and business managers may encounter a number of pitfalls when analyzing return on investment. First, some situations are heavy in soft benefits and light in projected financial benefits. For example, increased customer satisfaction might or might not result in actual financial inflows. Second, it is difficult to reconcile projects of diverse sizes, benefits, and timing in light of a fixed budget available for new projects. The budget might contain enough funding for only one large project with moderate but quick return, and then there is no room for other smaller projects with higher but slower return. Third, circumstances may alter the way managers make estimates. For instance, in a complex implementation with many moving parts, if experience shows that it usually takes 20% longer than budgeted to build a system, managers might begin to routinely add 20% to future estimates when preparing schedules and budgets to account for the uncertainty. Fourth, managers can fall into "analysis paralysis." Reaching a precise valuation may take longer than is reasonable to make an investment decision. Because a single right valuation may not exist, "close enough" usually suffices. Experience and an eye to the risks of an incorrect valuation help decide when to stop analyzing.

Finally, even when the numbers say a project is not worthwhile, the investment may be necessary to remain competitive. For example, UPS faced little choice but to invest heavily in IT because FedEx had made IT a competitive advantage and, at that time, was winning the overnight delivery war. More recently, companies have needed to invest in analytics and machine learning to keep up with their competitors, while they might be unsure of receiving any payoff at all from using those technologies, particularly if those technologies are not used properly. Nevertheless, a Society of Information Management survey

Valuation Methods	Descriptions
Return on investment (ROI)	Excess of return over the investment is calculated as ROI = (revenue − investment)/investment.
Net present value (NPV)	Accounting for the time value of money, the NPV discounts cash flows from future periods as being worth less than immediate cash flows. Discounting is performed by using a present value factor, which is $1/(1 + \text{discount rate})^{\text{years}}$.
Economic value added (EVA)	The amount of benefit of an investment that exceeds the costs of the capital used for investments. It is sometimes implemented **firmwide** as net operating profit after taxes (capital × cost of capital).
Payback period	This is a simple and popular method that computes how long a firm estimates it must wait until all costs are finally recouped.
Internal rate of return (IRR)	Like an interest rate, IRR represents the rate that is earned on an investment. The rate is compared to a target that is determined by corporate policy.
Weighted scoring methods	Costs and revenues are weighted based on their strategic importance, level of accuracy or confidence, and comparable investment opportunities.

FIGURE 8.5 Financial valuation methods.

[14] John C. Ford, "Evaluating Investment in IT," *Australian Accountant* (December 1994), 3.

shows that in 2022 (and in eight of the ten previous years), the #1 information technology investment named was in analytics and business intelligence.[15]

Monitoring IT Investments

An old adage says: "If you can't measure it, you can't manage it." Management's role is to ensure that the money spent on IT results in value for the organization. Therefore, a common and accepted set of metrics must be created to assess the important business impacts of IT, monitored to make visible the success of the investment, and communicated to senior management and customers to ensure alignment with the business. These metrics are often financial in nature (i.e., ROI, NPV). But financial measurement is only one category of measures used to manage IT investments. Other IT metrics include logs of errors encountered by users, end-user surveys, user turnaround time, logs of computer and communication up-/downtime, system response time, and percentage of projects completed on time and/or within budget. An example of a business-focused method is the extent to which the technology innovation improves the number of contacts with external customers, increasing sales revenue, and generating new business leads.

The Balanced Scorecard

Deciding on appropriate measures is half of the equation for effective IT organizations. The other half of the equation is ensuring that those measures are accurately communicated to the business. Two methods for communicating these metrics are scorecards and dashboards.

Financial measures may be the language of stockholders, but managers understand that such measures can be misleading if used as the sole means of making management decisions. One methodology that is very commonly used to solve this problem today is the **balanced scorecard**, which focuses attention on the organization's value drivers (which include, but are not limited to, financial performance).[16] Companies use this scorecard to assess the full impact of their corporate strategies on their customers and work force as well as their financial performance.

The balanced scorecard methodology allows managers to look at the business from four perspectives: customer, internal business, innovation/learning, and financial. For each perspective, the goals and measures are designed to answer these basic questions:

- Customer: How do customers see us?
- Internal: At what must we excel in carrying out our work?
- Learning: Can we continue to innovate, improve, and create value?
- Financial: How do we look to shareholders?

Figure 8.6 graphically shows the relationships between these perspectives.

Many people have modified or adapted the balanced scorecard technique to apply to their particular organization. Managers of information technology find the concept of a scorecard useful in managing and communicating the value of the IT department.

Applying the categories of the balanced scorecard to IT might mean interpreting them more broadly than originally conceived by Kaplan and Norton. For example, the original scorecard speaks of the customer perspective, but for the IT scorecard, the customer might be a user within the company, not an external customer of the company. The questions asked when using this methodology within the IT department are summarized in Figure 8.7.

Another consideration is that while the balanced scorecard concept has been used widely for 30 years, a 2023 study by Tawse and Tabesh could not find clear evidence of a positive impact of the technique on

[15] Vess Johnson, Russell Torres, Chris Maurer, Katia Guerra, Smriti Srivastava, and Hossein Mohit, "The 2022 SIM IT Issues and Trends Study," *MIS Quarterly Executive* 22, no. 1 (2023): Article 6. Available at: https://aisel.aisnet.org/misqe/vol22/iss1/6 (accessed August 7, 2023).

[16] For more details, see R. Kaplan and D. Norton, "The Balanced Scorecard—Measures That Drive Performance," *Harvard Business Review*, Vol. 70, no. 1 (January–February 1992): 71–79.

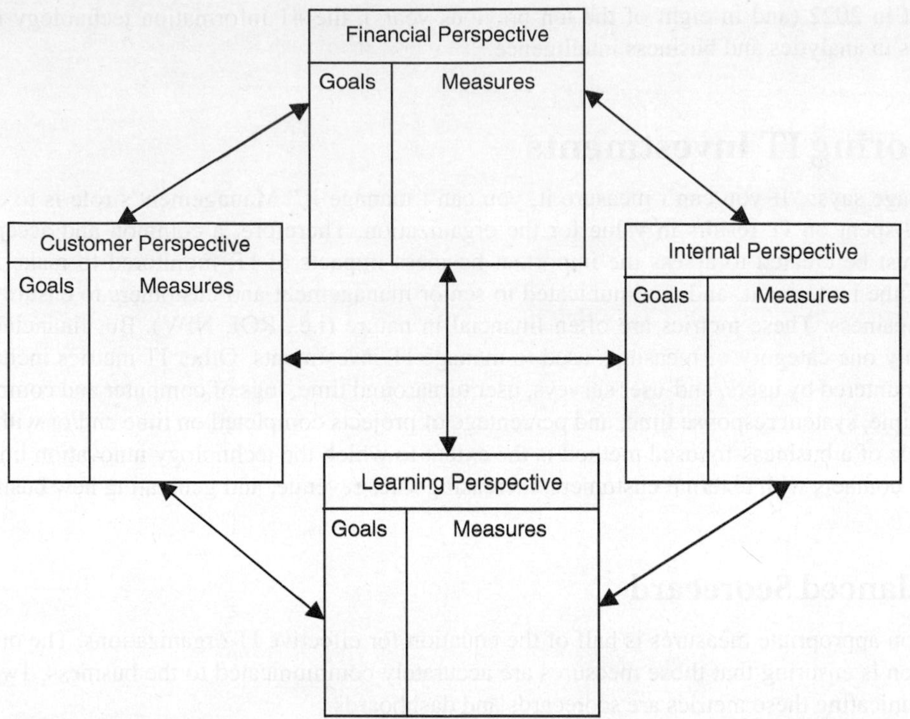

FIGURE 8.6 The balanced scorecard perspectives.
Source: Based on R. Kaplan and D. Norton, "The Balanced Scorecard—Measures That Drive Performance," *Harvard Business Review* (January–February 1992), 72.

Dimensions	Descriptions	Example of IT Measures
Customer perspective	*How do customers see us?* Measures that reflect factors that really matter to customers	Impact of IT projects on users, impact of IT's reputation among users, and user-defined operational metrics
Internal perspective	*What must we excel at?* Measures of what the company must do internally to meet customer expectations	IT process metrics, project completion rates, and system operational performance metrics
Learning perspective	*Can we continue to improve, innovate and create value?* Measures of the company's ability to innovative, improve, and learn	IT R&D, new technology introduction success rate, training metrics
Financial perspective	*How do we look to shareholders?* Measures to indicate contribution of activities to the bottom line	IT project ROI, NPV, IRR, cost/benefit, TCO, ABC

FIGURE 8.7 Balanced scorecard applied to IT departments.
Source: Adapted from R. Kaplan and D. Norton, "The Balanced Scorecard—Measures That Drive Performance," *Harvard Business Review* (January–February 1992), 72.

financial performance of firms.[17] It is possible that the technique is not always deployed in the best way. The authors recommend developing a strategy for using the technique, securing top management support for its adoption, and encouraging participation in the development with frequent communication across the organization. Those 2023 recommendations are in line with the advice from David Norton, who said in a 2002 interview to start with strategy and help others understand it through clear communications.[18] The newer findings provide additional enlightenment about the need for strong buy-in and participation.

A scorecard used within the IT organization helps senior IT managers understand their organization's performance and measure it in a way that supports its business strategy. The IT scorecard is linked to

[17] Alex Tawse and Pooya Tabesh, "Thirty years with the balanced scorecard: What we have learned?" *Business Horizons,* 66, no. 1 (January–February 2023) 123–132.

[18] "Ask the Source: Interview with David Norton," CIO.com, July 25, 2002.

the corporate scorecard and ensures that the measures used by IT are those that support corporate goals. At DuPont Engineering, the balanced scorecard methodology forces every action to be linked to a corporate goal, which helps promote alignment and eliminate projects with little potential impact. The conversations between IT and the business focus on strategic goals, the merits of the project at hand, and the actual impact rather than on technology and capabilities.[19]

IT Dashboards

Scorecards provide summary information gathered over a period of time. Another common IT management monitoring tool is the IT **dashboard**, which provides a snapshot of metrics at any given point in time. There are several ways to differentiate a dashboard from a scorecard. Dashboards address short-term operational goals while scorecards address long-term strategic goals. Dashboards address real-time performance metrics while scorecards address periodic updates, indicating progress towards a target.[20]

Much like a car dashboard, the IT dashboard summarizes key metrics for senior managers in a manner that provides quick identification of the status of projects in the organization. Like scorecards, dashboards are useful outside the IT department and are often found in executive offices as a tool for keeping current on critical measures of the organization. The contents of a dashboard depend on what is important to management, but in most cases graphical representations provide quick, at-a-glance results. Figure 8.8 illustrates an executive dashboard.

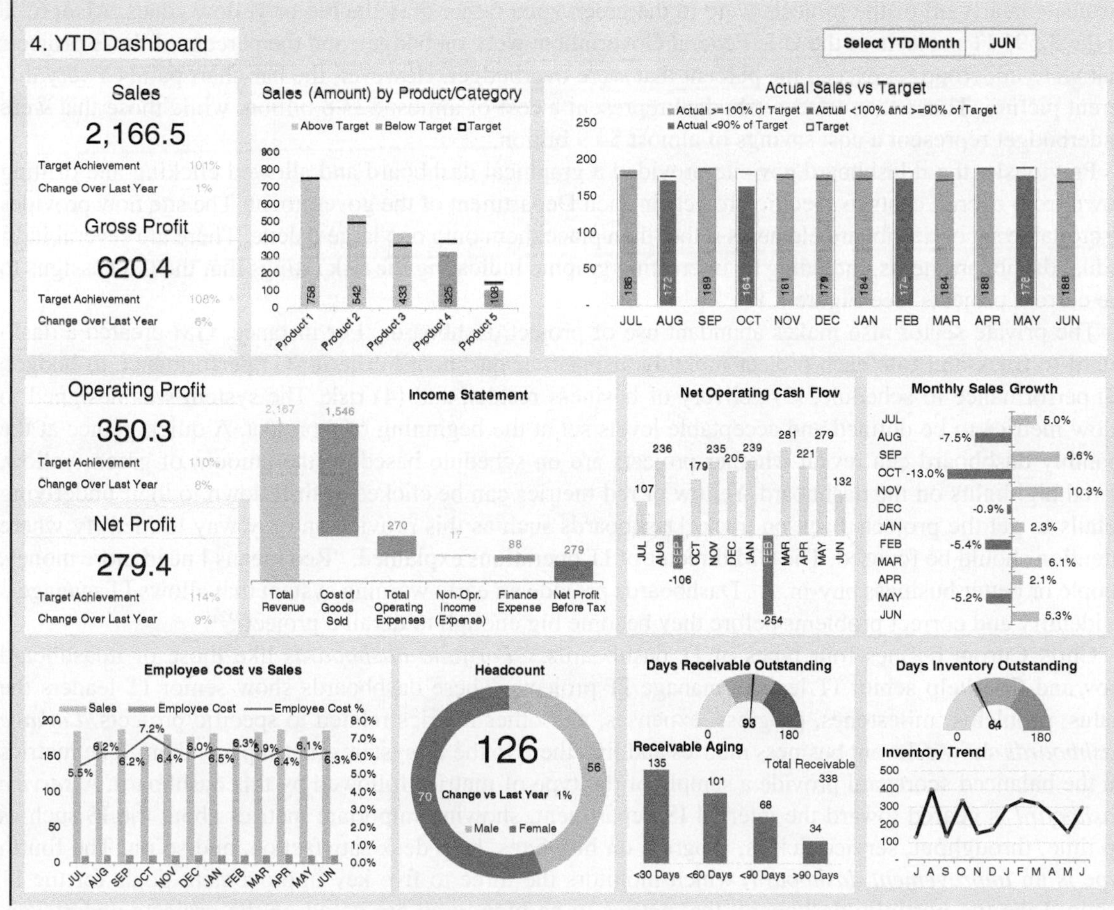

FIGURE 8.8 Example of an executive dashboard.
Source: https://www.bizinfograph.com/dashboard-templates/CEO-Dashboard

[19] Adapted from Eric Berkman, "How to Use the Balanced Scorecard," *CIO Magazine* 15, no. 15 (May 15, 2002): 1–4.

[20] Diana Ramos: "The Ultimate IT Dashboard: Experts Answer," Smartsheet.com, July 15, 2016. https://www.smartsheet.com/ultimate-it-dashboard-experts-answer (accessed August 7, 2023).

Dashboards are useful for tracking nearly everything analytical in an organization, and each product has a unique layout and functionality. Some dashboards are add-ons for Excel, while others are stand-alone products.[21]

The varieties of domains for tracking are endless. Many provide executives with project analytics, as shown in Figure 8.9. However, a few examples of domains to analyze would include advertising expenditures by segment, month, and/or format; employee performance by division, level, and/or geographic region; and projects, by completion status, cost, and/or personnel needs. In this discussion we will focus on the use of these tools within the IT department.

IT dashboards provide frequently updated information on areas of interest such as the status of projects of various sizes or operational systems of various types. For example, a dashboard used by the U.S. Government, available at http://itdashboard.gov, provides data for monitoring IT projects. Because senior officials start by questioning the overall health of a project rather than the details, the dashboard provides exact numbers and dates, but also indications of "red," "yellow," or "green" for each project, for rapid comprehension. A green highlight means that the project is progressing as planned and performance is within acceptable limits. A yellow highlight means at least one key target has been missed. A red highlight means the project is significantly behind and needs some attention or resources to get back on track.

Data downloaded from the U.S. Government's itdashboard can be examined in detail or placed into a graphical dashboard format. Figure 8.9 illustrates a graphical dashboard we created from the government data as of March 2023, using Excel™. Note that many firms offer templates of graphical dashboards that can be customized to the preferences of management. Our simple dashboard illustrates that several measures can be depicted, and many complement each other very well to prevent misinterpretation. For instance, nearly all of the projects were in the green zone rather than the red or yellow zones. Also, 67% of the 3,591 IT projects of the U.S. Federal Government were on budget, and the percent of those projects that were underbudget exceed the percent that were overbudget. However, the bar chart paints a very different picture. Those that were overbudget represent a cost of almost $23.8 billion, while those that were underbudget represent a cost savings of almost $4.9 billion.

Previously, the itdashboard.gov site provided a graphical dashboard and allowed clicking and drilling down from overall costs to specific projects in each Department of the government. The site now provides a scrollable set of dashboard elements rather than place them onto one large palette. There are several individual dashboard items, including an interesting graphic indicating the risk ratings that the CIO assigns to the current projects (see Figure 8.10).

The private sector also makes abundant use of project dashboards. For instance, GM created a dashboard to track and rate each project monthly, using four dashboard criteria: (1) performance to budget, (2) performance to schedule, (3) delivery of business results, and (4) risk. The system was designed to allow metrics to be defined and acceptable levels set at the beginning of a project. A quick glance at the monthly dashboard can reveal whether projects are on schedule based on the amount of green, yellow, or red highlights on the dashboard. Yellow or red metrics can be clicked to drill down to their underlying details to get the projects back on track. Dashboards such as this provide an easy way to identify where attention should be focused. The GM director of IT operations explained: "Red means I need more money, people or better business buy-in. . . . Dashboards provide an early warning system that allows IT managers to identify and correct problems before they become big enough to derail a project."[22]

Chris Curran defines four types of IT dashboards.[23] *Portfolio dashboards* like those of itdashboard .gov and GM help senior IT leaders manage IT projects. These dashboards show senior IT leaders the status, problems, milestones, progress, expenses, and other metrics related to specific projects. *Linkage dashboards* show relevant business metrics and link them to the IT systems that support them. The metrics on the balanced scorecard provide a sample of the type of metrics followed by this dashboard. A *service dashboard* is geared toward the internal IS department, showing important metrics about the IS such as up time, throughput, service tickets, progress on bug fixes, help desk satisfaction, and so on. The fourth type is an *improvement dashboard*, which monitors the three to five key improvement goals for the IT group. Like the portfolio dashboard, the metrics to be monitored are based on the projects undertaken,

[21] Emma Crockett "10 Best Dashboard Software and Tools for 2023," Datamation.com, January 25, 2023, https://www.datamation.com/big-data/best-dashboard-software-and-tools-2020/ (retrieved March 18, 2023).

[22] Tracy Mayor, "Red Light, Green Light," *CIO Magazine* 15, no. 1 (October 1, 2001): 108.

[23] In Diana Ramos; Mayor, 2001.

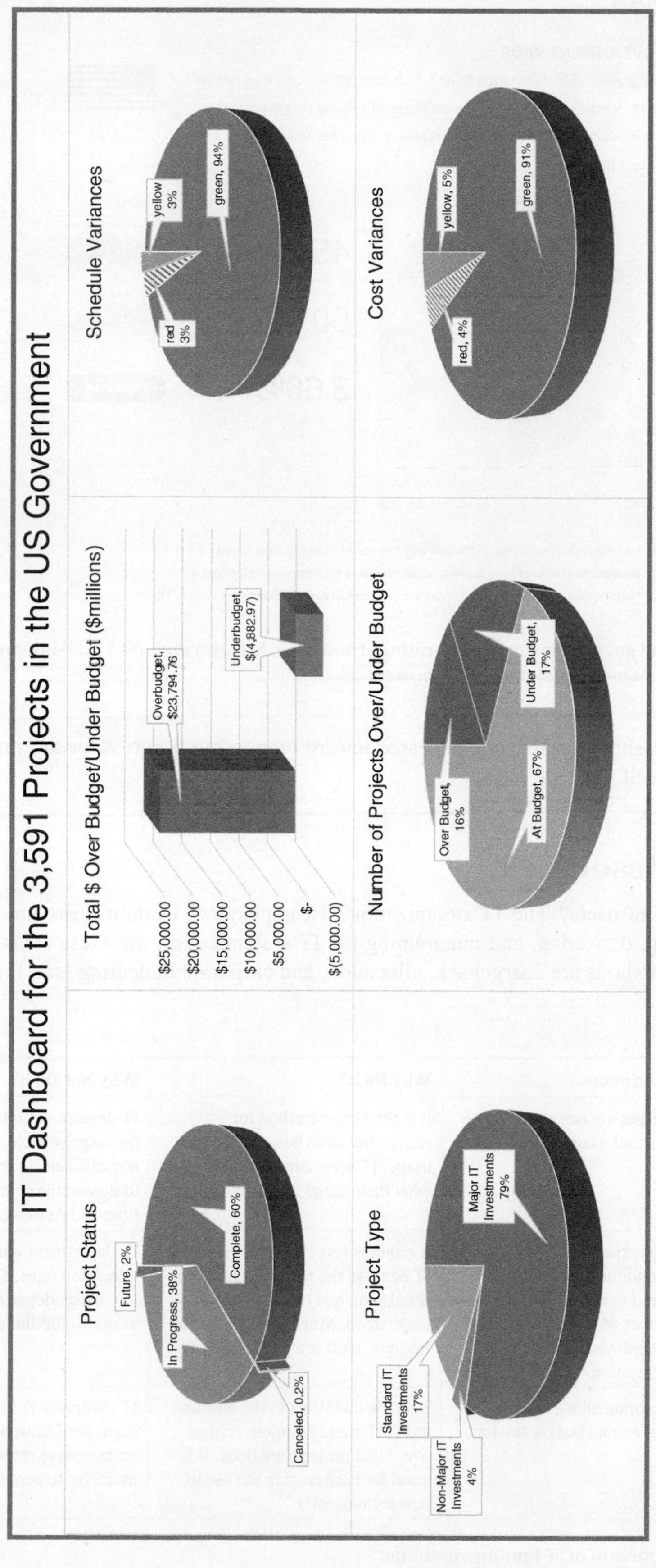

FIGURE 8.9 A Dashboard-style view of the data available on the U.S. Government's itdashboard.gov.

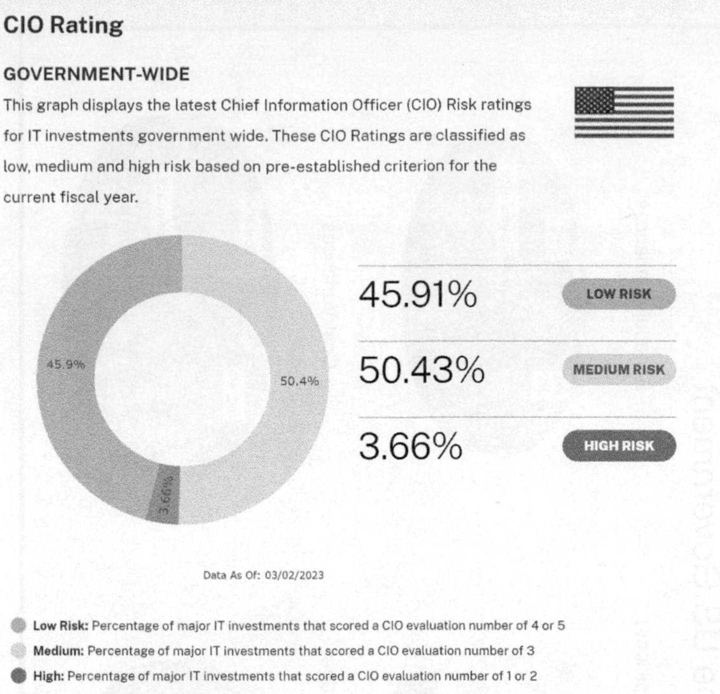

FIGURE 8.10 Overall government-wide risk ratings from the U.S. Government's IT dashboard.
Source: https://www.itdashboard.gov/itportfoliodashboard (accessed March 2, 2023).

but unlike the other dashboards, this one is geared toward monitoring progress toward important goals of the IT organization itself.

Funding IT Resources

Who pays for IT? The users? The IT organization? Headquarters? Certain costs are associated with designing, developing, delivering, and maintaining the IT systems. How are these costs recovered? The three main funding methods are chargeback, allocation, and corporate budgeting (see Figure 8.11). Both

Funding Methods	Descriptions	Why Do it?	Why Not Do it?
Chargeback	Charges are calculated based on actual usage.	It is the fairest method for recovering costs based on actual usage. IT users can see exactly what their usage costs are.	IT department must collect details on usage, which can be expensive and difficult. IT must be prepared to defend the charges, which takes time and resources.
Allocation	Total expected IT expenditures are divided by agreed upon basis such as number of login IDs, number of employees, or number of workstations.	It requires less bookkeeping for IT because the rate is set once per fiscal year, and the basis is well understood. Monthly costs for the business units are predictable.	IT department must defend allocation rates; IT may charge a low-usage department more than its usage would indicate is fair.
Corporate budget	Corporate allocates funds to IT at annual budget session.	There is no billing to the business units. IT exercises more control over what projects are done. It is good for encouraging the use of new technologies.	IT competes with all other budgeted items for funds; users might draw on excessive resources, lacking any incentive to economize.

FIGURE 8.11 Comparison of IT funding methods.

chargeback and allocation methods distribute IT costs back to the businesses, departments, or individuals within the company. This distribution of costs is used so that managers can understand the costs associated with running their organization or for tax reasons when the costs associated with each business must be paid for by the appropriate business unit. Corporate budgeting, on the other hand, is a completely different funding method in which IT costs are not linked directly with any specific user or business unit; costs are recovered using corporate coffers.

Chargeback

With a **chargeback funding method**, IT costs are recovered by charging individuals, departments, or business units based on actual usage and cost. The IT organization collects usage data on each system it runs. Rates for usage are calculated based on the actual cost to the IT group to run the system and billed out on a regular basis. For example, a PC might be billed at the cost of maintaining the system, software license fees, e-mail, network access, a usage fee for the help desk, special consulting fees, and other related services. Each department receives a monthly bill showing the units it has, such as PCs, printers, or servers, multiplied by the charge for each unit.

Chargeback systems are popular because they are viewed as the most equitable way to recover IT costs. Costs are distributed based on usage or consumption of resources, ensuring that the largest portion of the costs is paid for by the group or individual who consumes the most. Chargeback systems can also provide managers with a basis for making decisions about managing and controlling their IT costs, by moving to less expensive devices or removing some software. Because the departments get a regular bill, they know exactly what their costs are.

Creating and managing a chargeback system, however, is itself a costly endeavor. IT organizations must build systems to collect details that might not be needed for anything other than the bills they generate.

Allocation

To simplify the cost recovery process, an allocation system can be used. An **allocation funding method** recovers costs based on something other than usage, such as revenues, log-in accounts, or head count (number of employees) in each business unit or department. For example, suppose the total spending for IT for a year is $1 million for a company with 10,000 employees. A business unit with 1,000 employees might be responsible for 10% ($100,000), of the total IT costs. Of course, with this type of allocation system, it does not matter whether these employees even use the IT; the department is still charged the same amount.

The allocation mechanism is simpler than the chargeback method to implement and apply each month. Actual usage does not need to be captured. The rate charged is often fixed at the beginning of the year. Allocation offers two main advantages. First, the level of detail required to calculate the allocations is much less, which greatly reduces record-keeping expenses. Second, the charges from the IT organization are predictable and can reduce the number of arguments that might arise from the business units. Negotiation takes place only once at the beginning of the year when rates and allocation bases are set, and then less discussion occurs each month because the managers understand and expect the bill.

Two major complaints are made about allocation systems. First is the free-rider problem: An extensive user of IT services pays the same amount as a nonuser when the charges are not based on usage. Second, deciding the basis for allocating the costs is an issue. Choosing headcount over the number of desktops or other basis is a management decision, and whichever basis is chosen, someone will likely pay more than his or her actual usage would imply. Allocation mechanisms work well when required by a corporate directive and when the units agree on the basis for dividing the costs.

Often when an allocation process is used, a follow-up process is needed at the end of the fiscal year to compare the total IT expenses against the total IT funds recovered from the business units, and any extra funds are given back to the business. Sometimes this exercise is called a "true-up" process because true expenses are balanced against payments made. In some cases, additional funds are needed; however, IT managers try to avoid asking for funds to make up for shortfalls in their budget. The true-up process is needed because the actual cost of the information system is difficult to predict at the beginning of the year, due to cost increases or decreases over the year. Often costs are reduced because IT managers, like all managers, work constantly on improving efficiency and productivity. Business managers often prefer the predictability of their monthly IT bills along with a true-up process over the relative unpredictability of being charged actual costs each month.

Corporate Budget

An entirely different way to pay for IT costs is to simply consider them all to be corporate overhead and pay for them directly out of the corporate budget. With the **corporate budget funding method**, the costs fall to the corporate bottom line, rather than levying charges on specific users or business units.

Corporate budgeting is a relatively simple method for funding IT costs. It requires no calculation of prices of the IT systems. And because bills are not generated on a regular cycle to departments, concerns are raised less often by the unit managers. IT managers control the entire budget, giving them control of the use of those funds and, ultimately, more input into what systems are created, how they are managed, and when they are retired. This funding method also encourages the use of new technologies because learners and experimenters are not charged for exploration and potentially inefficient system use.

As with the other methods, certain drawbacks come with using the corporate budget. First, all IT expenditures are subjected to the same process as all other corporate expenditures, namely, the budgeting process. In many companies, this process is one of the most stressful events of the year: Everyone has projects to be done, and everyone is competing for scarce funds. If the business units are not billed in some way for their usage, many companies find that the units do not control their usage. Getting a bill for services motivates the individual business manager to reconsider his or her usage of those services. Finally, if the business units are not footing the bill, the IT group may feel less accountable to them, which may result in an IT organization that is less end-user or customer oriented.

How Much Does IT Cost?

The three major IT funding approaches in the preceding discussion are designed to recover the costs of building and maintaining the information systems in an enterprise. The goal is to simply cover the costs, not to generate a profit (although some IT organizations are profit centers for their corporation). The most basic method for calculating the costs of a system is to add the costs of all the components, including equipment, vendor fees, networking, and the people involved. IT organizations calculate the initial costs and ongoing maintenance costs in just this way.

Activity-Based Costing

Another method for calculating costs is known as **activity-based costing (ABC)**. Traditional accounting methods account for direct and indirect costs. Direct costs are those that can be clearly linked to a particular process or product, such as the components used to manufacture the product and the assembler's wages for time spent building the product. Indirect costs are the overhead costs, which include everything from the electric bill, the salary of administrative managers, and administrative function expenses to the wages of the supervisor overseeing the assembler, the cost of running the factory, and the maintenance of machinery used for multiple products. Further, depending on the funding method used by the enterprise, indirect costs are allocated or absorbed elsewhere in the pricing model. The allocation process can be cumbersome and complex and often is a source of trouble for many organizations. The alternative to the traditional approach is ABC.

Activity-based costing calculates costs by counting the actual activities that go into making a specific product or delivering a specific service. *Activities* are processes, functions, or tasks that occur over time and produce recognized results. They consume assigned resources to produce products and services. Activities are useful in costing because they are the common denominator between business process improvement and information improvement across departments.

Rather than allocate the total indirect cost of a system across a range of services according to an allocation formula, ABC calculates the amount of time that the system supported a particular activity and allocates only that cost to that activity. For example, an accountant would look at the enterprise resource planning (ERP) system and divide its cost over the activities it supports by calculating how much of the system is used by each activity. Product A might take up one-twelfth of an ERP system's capacity to control the manufacturing activities needed to make it, so it would be allocated one-twelfth of the system's costs. The help desk might take up a whole server, so the entire server's cost would be allocated to that activity. In the end, the costs are put in buckets that reflect the products and services of the business rather than the organization structure or the processes of any given department. In effect, ABC is the process of charging all costs to "profit centers" instead of to "cost centers."

Jonathan Bush, CEO of management services company Athenahealth, performed activity-based costing for Children's Hospital in Boston. When he found that it cost the hospital about $120 to admit a patient, he recommended a solution of using the information received from the primary care doctor. He argues, "Your primary-care doctor has already created 90% of that information to see you for your regular visit. Why wouldn't the hospital give the doctor $100 if it was costing them $120 to do it themselves?"[24] The ABC approach allowed the hospital to realize the cost of running the hospital systems to perform the activity and to compare it with the cost of an alternative source that turned out to be cheaper. But until the thorny issues of electronic medical records are sorted out, the doctors and the hospitals will likely continue to create their own records.

Total Cost of Ownership

When a system is proposed and a business case is created to justify the investment, summing up the initial outlay and the maintenance cost does not provide an entirely accurate total system cost. In fact, if only the initial and maintenance costs are considered, the decision is often made on incomplete information. Other costs are involved, and the time value of money affects the total cost. One technique used to calculate a more accurate cost that includes all associated costs is **total cost of ownership (TCO)**. It has become the industry standard. Gartner Group introduced TCO in the late 1980s when PC-based IT infrastructures began gaining popularity.[25] Other IT experts have since modified the concept.

TCO looks beyond initial capital investments to include costs associated with technical support, administration, training, and system retirement. Often, the initial cost is an inadequate predictor of the additional costs necessary to successfully implement the system. TCO techniques estimate annual costs per user for each potential infrastructure choice; these costs are then totaled. Careful estimates of TCO provide the best investment numbers to compare with financial return numbers when analyzing the net returns on various IT options. The alternative, an analysis without TCO, can result in an "apples and oranges" comparison. Consider a decision about printers. The initial cost of a refillable ink-tank printer is generally higher than that of a budget inkjet printer that uses cartridges, but per-page costs are generally lower for the ink-tank printer because of the very high cost of ink cartridges. When comparing the cost of ink refills to ink cartridges over the expected lifetime of the printers, the total cost of ownership of the more expensive refillable printer ends up being lower. Extending this type of analysis to larger IT systems will reveal similar opportunities to save by TCO's "bigger picture" comparisons.

Infrastructure represents a major IT investment. Computer hardware such as printers, computers, and tablets provide infrastructure for those items owned by the organization. Licenses for software must also be purchased. When these costs are tallied up, they often fall short of the actual costs of IT. For instance, there are also "invisible" significant items such as technical support, administration, training, and disposal costs, which can easily be overlooked. "Soft" data costs can include removable media such as thumb drives or portable hard drives, as well as on-site and off-site storage.

Even if managers can't get a completely accurate figure of costs, estimates can be made based on previous experience with purchases. Some firms outsource many or most of these costs, so those service costs

[24] David Lidsky, "#43 Athenahealth," fastcompany.com, July 12, 2012, http://www.fastcompany.com/mic/2010/profile/athenahealth (accessed August 7, 2023).

[25] M. Gartenberg, "Beyond the Numbers: Common TCO Myths Revealed," Gartner Group Research Note: Technology, March 2, 1998.

are sometimes contractual. For instance, when Judo Bank (discussed in Chapter 6) outsourced all their IT services, most of the equipment costs were specified in their contracts. However, general managers often question areas where costs can be cut with varying IT infrastructures. Alcoa's Kevin Horner benchmarked costs and renegotiated contracts to aggressively pursue cost decreases. The concept of TCO also takes into account costs that are not in any contracts, which are described below.

TCO Component Breakdown

TCO is sometimes difficult for managers to fully comprehend. To clarify how the TCO framework is used, this section examines some examples of costs that are not included in the price tags of purchases, whether it is equipment or services purchased. Two extreme examples are provided, covering a "no services" firm that purchases and manages its own equipment, as well as the other extreme, a "services only" firm like Judo Bank, that relies on an ecosystem of platforms and apps that are governed by contracts and relationships. The initial concept of TCO was created before the concept of platform and app ecosystems emerged, but some of the issues persist today.

The sharpest contrast is that of equipment and software. For shared components, such as servers and printers, TCO estimates should be computed per component and then divided among all users who access them.

Soft costs, such as technical support, administration, and training are never described in hardware vendors' offers for sale but can be significant. For example, technical support costs include areas such as phone support, troubleshooting, hot swaps, and repairs. Often, paid service contracts include technical support and some "train the trainer" sessions, but costs such as end-user training and errors, and reduced productivity when adapting to a new system or platform, are seldom included. Sometimes errors are introduced when the new trainers, who might have just undergone their own training literally "yesterday," do not deeply enough understand the systems to provide the most efficient usage patterns or to be able to troubleshoot issues not included in their own training. Sometimes end-users sitting side-by-side with new employees end up providing informal support. Their limited understanding might propagate inefficiencies and troubleshooting errors more broadly throughout an organization.

Another soft cost, informal support, may be harder to determine, but it is important, nonetheless. Informal support comprises the sometimes highly complex networks that develop among coworkers through which many problems are fixed, and much training takes place, without the involvement of any official support staff. In many circumstances, these activities can prove more efficient and effective than working through official channels. Still, managers want to analyze the costs of informal support for two reasons:

1. The costs—both in salary and in opportunity—of a nonsupport employee providing informal support may prove significantly higher than analogous costs for a formal support employee. For example, it costs much more in both dollars per hour and forgone management activity for a midlevel manager to try to help a line employee troubleshoot an e-mail problem than it would for a formal support employee to provide the same service.

2. The quantity of informal support activity in an organization provides an indirect measure of the efficiency of its IT support organization. The formal support organization should respond with sufficient promptness and thoroughness to discourage all but the briefest informal support transactions.

While a "services only" firm might have most of the costs included under the specified contract, it is important to consider them when accepting a contract, and to estimate any additional costs involved. Those not covered by a contract are summed and divided by the number of devices to derive an amount per unit, which is then added to the initial cost of a device, reflecting a truer sense of total cost of ownership, or TCO.

TCO as a Management Tool

This discussion focused on TCO as a tool for evaluating which infrastructure components to choose, but TCO also can help managers understand how infrastructure costs break down. Research has consistently shown that the labor costs associated with an IT infrastructure far outweigh the actual capital investment costs. TCO provides the fullest picture of where managers spend their IT funds. Like other benchmarks, TCO results can be evaluated over time against industry standards (much TCO target data for various IT infrastructure choices are available from industry research firms). Even without comparison data, the numbers that emerge from TCO studies assist in making decisions about budgeting, resource allocation, and organizational structure.

However, like the ABC approach, the cost of implementing TCO can be a detriment to the program's overall success. Both ABC and TCO are complex approaches that may require significant effort to determine the costs to use in the calculations. Managers must weigh the benefits of following these approaches against the costs of obtaining reliable data necessary to make their use successful.

SUMMARY

- IT organizations can be expected to anticipate new technologies, participate in setting and implementing strategic goals, innovate current processes, develop and maintain information systems, manage supplier and platform relationships, establish architecture platforms and standards, promote enterprise security, plan for business discontinuities, manage data/information/knowledge, manage Internet and network services, manage human resources, operate the data center, provide general support, co-create with ecosystem and platform partners, and integrate social IT.
- IT activities can reveal the group's level of maturity. The most mature IT organizations are proactive and partner with business executives.
- The chief information officer (CIO) is a high-level IS officer who oversees many important organizational activities. The CIO must display both technical and business skills. The role requires both strategic and operational skills.
- A business case is a tool used to support a decision or a proposal of a new investment. It is a document containing a project description, financial analysis, marketing analysis, and all other relevant documentation to assist managers in making a go/no-go decision.
- Benefits articulated in a business case can be categorized as observable, measurable, quantifiable, and financial. These benefits are often for innovations, improvements, or cessation.
- The portfolio of IT investments must be carefully evaluated and managed.
- The investments may be valued using methods such as return on investment (ROI), net present value (NPV), economic value added (EVA), payback period, internal rate of return (IRR), and weighted scoring.
- Benefits derived from IT investments are sometimes difficult to quantify and to observe or are long range in scope.
- Monitoring and communicating the status and benefits of IT is often done through the use of balanced scorecards and IT dashboards.
- IT is funded using one of three methods: chargeback, allocation, or corporate budget.
- Chargeback systems are viewed as the most equitable method of IT cost recovery because costs are distributed based on usage, yet it is time-consuming and is not always worth the trouble.
- Allocation systems provide a simpler method to recover costs because they do not involve recording system usage to allocate costs. However, they could penalize groups with low usage.
- The corporate budget method does not allocate costs at all. Instead, the CIO seeks and receives a budget from the corporate overhead account. It is easy to administer but is likely to be abused if the users perceive IT to be "free."
- Activity-based costing (ABC) is another technique to group costs into meaningful buckets, based on the activity, product, or service they support. ABC is useful for allocating large overhead expenses.
- Total cost of ownership (TCO) is a technique used to recognize all the costs beyond the initial investments associated with owning and operating an information system. It is most useful as a tool to help make good decisions in developing the IT portfolio, and to prepare for the actual costs of systems.

KEY TERMS

activity-based costing (ABC), 194
allocation funding method, 193
balanced scorecard, 187
business case, 182
business technology strategist, 181
business-IT maturity model, 177
chargeback funding method, 193
chief information officer (CIO), 180
corporate budget funding method, 194
dashboard, 189
economic value added (EVA), 186
firmwide, 186
IT portfolio management, 184
net present value (NPV), 186
payback period, 185
return on investment (ROI), 185
total cost of ownership (TCO), 195

DISCUSSION QUESTIONS

1. Using an organization with which you are familiar, describe the role of the most senior IS professional. Is that person a strategist or an operational manager?

2. What advantages does a CIO bring to a business? What might be the disadvantages of having a CIO?

3. Under what conditions would you recommend using each of these funding methods to pay for information systems expenses: allocation, chargeback, and corporate budget?

4. Describe the conditions under which ROI, payback period, NPV, and EVA are most appropriately applied to information systems investments.

5. A new inventory management system for ABC Company could be developed at a cost of $260,000. The estimated net operating costs and estimated net benefits over six years of operation would be:

Year	Estimated net operating costs	Estimated net benefits
0	$350,000	$0
1	9,000	60,000
2	15,250	98,000
3	17,000	105,000
4	22,500	121,000
5	18,000	115,000
6	32,000	190,000

(a) What would the payback period be for this investment? Would it be a good or bad investment? Why?

(b) What is the ROI for this investment?

(c) Assuming a 9% discount rate, what is this investment's NPV?

6. Compare and contrast the IT balanced scorecard and dashboard approaches. Which, if either, would be most useful to you as a general manager? Please explain.

7. TCO is one way to account for costs associated with a specific infrastructure. This method does not include additional costs such as the costs of disposing of the system when it is no longer in use. What other additional costs might be important for making total cost calculations?

8. Check out the U.S. government IT dashboard site at http://itdashboard.gov. Click the icon for "IT Portfolio." Click the drop-down box for "Filter by Agency" and you will see the long list of various governmental departments. Then review all the categories of information on the site, and answer the following questions:

(a) Describe the size of the IT portfolio for the Department of Commerce in terms of total spending and spending on major investments.

(b) Do any investments appear to be risky in the Department of Commerce?

(c) If you hover over the "CIO Rating" donut chart (pie chart with a hole in the middle), you will see additional information. Based on that additional detail, does the portfolio considered most risky seem to be larger than the portfolio considered less risky?

(d) In terms of Schedule and cost variances, how does the portfolio seem to perform? Does the schedule look better than the budget, or vice versa?

(e) At the bottom of the Department of Commerce page you will find a list of major projects. Click on any one project and make sure to choose an agency of interest. Then click on the investment name drop-down. Pick any one investment and describe the (1) risk assessment, (2) schedule, and (3) cost performance of that investment.

(f) Is there any additional information that you think a manager would like to see about the status of the projects?

Case Study 8-1 Blockchain Adoption Barriers in the Healthcare Industry in Iran

Many barriers have been identified in the literature that hinder the adoption of blockchain technology in organizations. Among the most commonly mentioned are the absence of a blockchain infrastructure, uncertain governmental policies, absence of expertise, financial constraints, security concerns, challenges of integrating blockchain technologies into existing systems, an absence of awareness, coordination problems, and an absence of standardization.

Approaching the problem from the standpoint of the Balanced Scorecard enables a focus on the issues from multiple points of view specifically in the healthcare sector. Consider the findings from the study of one hospital in Tehran, which employed 64 physicians and 386 nurses. Results from a survey involving physicians, IT managers, and healthcare industry consultants identified the classic four balanced scorecard perspectives (Financial, Customer, Internal Processes, and Learning and Growth), each including 3–6 barriers.

The barriers identified by the participants were as follows, with the ranking of the 20 barriers shown in parentheses. The rankings were derived by weighting the barriers using respondents' opinions of importance and strength of each barrier.[26]

- Financial:
  - Financial constraints (1) (high costs and low rate of return)
  - Absence of external stakeholders (6) (government, shareholders, and investors were reluctant to participate)
  - Absence of trust (10) (between hospitals, third parties, and patients)
- Customer:
  - Competition and uncertainty (9) (time consuming distraction from competing with other hospitals)
  - Absence of awareness (5) (and unclear understanding)
  - Security issues (2)
  - Information disclosure issues (13) (some parties have diverse privacy needs)
- Internal Process:
  - Absence of management support and commitment (7)
  - Resistance of organization members (12)
  - Problems in communication/coordination/collaboration (12) (different parties have varied objectives, incentives, and priorities)
  - Challenges in integrating blockchain into existing systems (12)
  - Lack of organizational culture for change (14)
  - Absence of standardization (11) (record size, format, and retrieval policies)
- Learning and Growth:
  - Immutability (15) (records cannot be modified or retrieved)
  - Absence of expertise (3) (both for users and implementers)
  - Uncertain governmental policies (4)
  - Scalability issues (8)
  - Absence of blockchain infrastructure (4) (limited access to infrastructure facilities for healthcare)
  - Technology immaturity (16)

As a very recent first study, there is little corroboration of these findings in other industries or locations on the globe. However, the lessons might be important to help those looking to implement any technologies using the Balanced Scorecard, and taking into consideration importance and strength measures.

Sources: Adapted from Kannan Govindan, Arash Khalili Nasr, Mohammad Saeed Heidary, Saeede Nosrati-Abarghooee & Hassan Mina (2022) "Prioritizing adoption barriers of platforms based on blockchain technology from balanced scorecard perspectives in healthcare industry: a structural approach," *International Journal of Production Research,* DOI: 10.1080/00207543.2021.2013560.

[26] The authors did not skip succeeding ranks when there were ties.

Case Study 8-1 **(Continued)**

Discussion Questions

1. Are strength and importance the best measures for weighting the potential barriers? Why or why not? If not, what would seem to be a better way to weigh the measures?
2. Point out at least 3 measures that would likely rank differently for a manufacturing firm? For a retailer? Why?
3. Assess the pros and cons of using blockchain in health care in today's situation.
4. Assess the pros and cons of using blockchain in health care with only these improvements: familiarity/expertise, cost reductions, infrastructure improvements, and policy changes.
5. Do you think the Balanced Scorecard would be useful for identifying barriers to adoption of any IT innovation? Please explain your response.
6. Provide a list of emerging technologies that can be analyzed in this way.
7. Choose one of the technologies you pinpointed in your list in the previous question, and list three of the twenty Balanced Scorecard factors that you would predict would be important barriers for that technology.

Case Study 8-2 Air France/KLM Airlines

Air France/KLM Airlines, headquartered in the Netherlands, is one of the world's leading international airlines. As of December 31, 2022, they reported that during the previous fiscal year they carried 93 million passengers, marking steep increases over 2020 and 2021, as the airline followed the heels of the pandemic. The conglomerate employed over 74,600 individuals.[27] The challenging business environment since the 9/11 terrorist attacks in 2001 and the COVID-19 pandemic from 2020–2023 has caused many airlines to transform their operations, and Air France/KLM's story of repeated transformation is quite revealing.

In 2004, after KLM's merger with Air France, the CEO appointed Boet Kreiken as the new CIO. The CEO decided to make a structural break from the past in hiring Kreiken, who was from the operations area, clearly outside of IT. Three priorities included examining outsourcing IT, creating a board of business and IT representatives, and fashioning a process for governance of IT that is shared between the IT function and business units.

The result of the ensuing efforts over several years was to create four levels of committee governance: An executive committee kept an eye on matching the business strategy with IT strategies; A business/IT board, which was composed of the CEO, CIO, and all business unit executive vice presidents, was formed to manage the portfolio and budget; an IT management team worked on tactical planning for the business/IT board; and finally, the CIO/information services management team planned and managed IT operations. Air France/KLM also established a set of key principles and practices and developed a standard business case template that had to be used whenever requesting an investment greater than 150,000 euros.

Air France/KLM experienced five benefits attributed to the governance structure: reduced IT costs per kilometer flown, increased capacity for IT innovation, better alignment of investments to business goals, increased trust between functional units and the IT organization, and a mind-set of the value of IT. In 2017, Kreiken moved on to become Executive VP of Customer Experience at KLM.[28]

In 2012, Jean-Christophe Lalanne (now a senior advisor to the Air France/KLM IT group), took over as CIO of Air France/KLM. Lalanne appears to have had some influence from Kreiken's interest in customer experience, as he tries relentlessly to promote customer intimacy. The watchword is

[27] AirFrance/KLM, "AirFrance: Results 2022," https://www.airfranceklm.com/sites/default/files/2023-02/AFKLM_FY_2022_Results_Presentation_1.pdf (accessed March 19, 2023).

[28] KLM Newsroom, "Boet Kreiken Responsible for Customer Experience at KLM," April 10, 2017, https://news.klm.com/boet-kreiken-responsible-for-customer-experience-klm/ (accessed March 2, 2019).

***Case Study 8-2* (Continued)**

"digital transformation," which Lalanne says will help "manage the customer journey from door to door." Digitization began receiving the highest priority from the executive board.[29]

Lalanne provided surprising detail about business case drivers, costs, and benefits in Air France/KLM's 400 million euro bid for digital transformation. For instance, providing 40,000 tablets for cabin crew and ground staff has a cost of 12 million euros, with projected benefits totaling more than 39 million euros. Benefits include revenue increases of over 35 million euros from sales of ancillary goods and services and paid upgrades. The tablets are projected to provide an employee reduction of 280 full-time equivalent personnel as well as cost decreases of 4 million euros. Those cost decreases include providing online manuals and making lounge access and flight changes more efficient. Other projects include adopting new Human Resources (HR) self-service software and moving toward paperless and real-time cargo processes, costing another 17 million euros but resulting in over 29 million euros of advantage.[30]

Those projects demonstrate how business cases for IT investments can show significant returns, in spite of the size of those investments. By undertaking a three-step process, Lalanne is showing movement toward extending KLM's business model, to complement its products and services to great advantage. The goals are to understand customers better, to provide greater value over their lifetimes, to optimize their journeys, and to reach customers everywhere. To accomplish that vision, KLM sees IT as central to the firm's mission.

The newest CIO on January 1, 2023 became Pierre-Olivier Bandet. Bandet vows to continue Lalanne's initiatives, by including Lalanne in the team designing and implementing the transformation. Bandet stated an intention to "continue to invest and innovate in high performance Information Systems, Data, artificial intelligence, and cyber risk prevention."[31]

Sources: Adapted from Steven De Haes, Dirk Gemke, John Thorp, and Wim Van Grembergen, "KLM's Enterprise Governance of IT Journey: From Managing IT Costs to Managing Business Value," *MIS Quarterly Executive* 10, no. 3 (2011): 109–20; See also "Analyzing IT Value Management at KLM through the Lens of Val IT," https://www.isaca.org/resources/isaca-journal/past-issues/2011/analyzing-it-value-management-at-klm-through-the-lens-of-val-it (accessed May 30, 2015); and "KLM Company Profile," https://www.klm.com/information/corporate/company-profile (accessed March 2, 2019).

Discussion Questions

1. What is likely to have led to increased trust for the IT organization?
2. What might explain an item that is seemingly quite unrelated to IT (costs per kilometer flown) decreased as a result of the new CIO structure?
3. What business/IT maturity level did KLM appear to exhibit (a) in 2000 and (b) in 2017? Why?
4. Why do you think that KLM requires its employees to use a standard business case template when they want to make an investment?
5. Describe how an executive board might react to a proposal to purchase 40,000 tablet devices for nearly all of a firm's employees. What kind of presentation would be necessary to head off a fierce board protest?
6. Do you think passengers might be likely to spend more on food items on a flight when a tablet is used by the flight attendant? Why or why not?

---

[29] Samuels, Mark, "Air France-KLM's CIO on the Impact of the Airline's Digital Transformation," HotTopics.HT, Tata Communications, 2019, https://www.hottopics.ht/29954/air-france-klms-cio-on-the-impact-of-their-digital-transformation/ (accessed August 15, 2019).

[30] Air France/KLM, "Investor Day," May 12, 2017, https://www.airfranceklm.com/sites/default/files/id_2017_afkl_def.pdf (accessed March 2, 2019).

[31] Air France, "Pierre-Olivier Bandet appointed EVP Information Systems – Air France-KLM," October 27, 2022. https://www.airfranceklm.com/en/newsroom/pierre-olivier-bandet-appointed-evp-information-systems-air-france-klm (accessed March 19, 2023).

Information Technology Governance

9

Governance structures define the way decisions are made in an organization and across organizations. This chapter explores three major types of governance: structural governance based on the location of decision making in organization structure (centralized, decentralized, and federated) and based on decision rights; financial control governance; and platform governance. Examples and governance mechanisms are also discussed.

Intel is a leader in process technology development, a major manufacturer of semiconductors and a leading provider of silicon.[1] It is heavily committed to research focused on new semiconductor technologies and products—and plans to move from 100 billion transistors on a package in 2023 to a trillion in 2030. Since the global semiconductor industry over the past three decades has witnessed a change from 80% of semiconductors produced in the west (including the United States and Europe) to 80% produced in Asia, Intel, not surprisingly, diversified its product lines. It now offers products ranging from edge computing and 5G networks to the cloud and AI. It has transformed itself from a PC-centric company to one that is meeting the needs of a data-centric world.

Intel boasts that it has generated savings in excess of USD 5.9 billion, from 2010 to 2021, primarily through a reduction in unit costs from increased efficiencies in energy consumption and operations.[2] Yet, its budget has remained relatively flat, partly because it reduced the number of its data centers from 91 in 2010 to 54 in 2022 while adding two ultrahigh efficiency data centers for centralized batch computing, among other things.

How did Intel accomplish these and other laudable goals? Its approach was the result of 25 years of evolution of its strategy that began by creating a centralized IT organization in 1992 that was in control of decisions about IT.[3] Intel has come a long way from its original governance structure, which was centered on mainframes and wide-area networks. Later, in 2003, Intel initiated its "Protect Era" in response to two alarming events: the then-new Sarbanes–Oxley legislation and a virus that had infected Intel's internal networks through an employee's home-based network connection. The company's "Protect Era," spearheaded by IT, locked down resources to such an extent that employees had to devise risky policy workarounds to be able to complete some of their tasks. Data could be used only within a particular functional area, not shared among areas.

Intel's "Protect to Enable Era" in IT governance began in 2009 after managers found that its overly restrictive policies on Bring Your Own Device (BYOD) had frustrated its employees who saw those policies as both expensive and detrimental to innovation over the long run. This led Intel to discover that consumerization is a powerful force. That six-syllable mouthful, consumerization, describes the increasingly powerful tools available in the consumer space that can impact the corporate space. **IT consumerization** is "the process whereby the changing practices and expectation of consumers, shaped by the wide adoption

[1] Intel website, "Intel Shapes the Future of Technology," Intel Shapes the Future of Technology (accessed May 17, 2023).

[2] Intel IT Authors, "IT@Intel: Data Center Strategy Leading Intel's Business Transformation," Intel white paper, November 2022.

[3] Intel, Inc. "Accelerating Business Growth Through IT: 2012–2013 Intel IT Annual Performance Report," http://www.intel.com/content/dam/www/public/us/en/documents/reports/2012-2013-intel-it-performance-report.pdf (accessed September 1, 2015).

of digital technologies in everyday life, will influence the IT-related activities of workers and managers in organizations."[4] The consumers in this case are not only customers (i.e., consumer-customers) but also workers in organizations (i.e., consumer-workers) whose work practices are shaped by their experiences with the digital technologies that they use in their daily lives.

Intel found that cloud services, desktop applications, social networking, mobile devices, and the management policies surrounding them had changed the business of IT. BYOD forced IT leaders at Intel and many other firms to re-evaluate how IT services are offered. Intel's traditional command and control mentality—with IT leaders making all technology decisions—no longer could work. The consumerization of technology changed Intel's management approach[5] from "How do we stop it?" to "How do we work with this?"

Intel's "Protect Era" governance structure also resulted in a lost opportunity to exploit data and analytics. Because information was restricted to the department in which it was generated, Intel could not explore connections between manufacturing decisions and consumer reactions or between social media trends and product design decisions. A new approach to governance was clearly needed and Protect to Enable addressed that need.

Since 2013, Intel has centralized the management of its high-frequency servers and resources. More recently, Intel extended the reach of its IT governance to support IT innovation in transforming business value. An example is its disaggregated server architecture. Intel also improved time to market for new platforms and designs by adopting machine learning and smart analytics.

How does a governance framework support innovation? Intel now uses information governance boards that include representatives from a variety of its functions, including marketing, manufacturing, product design, human resources (HR), legal, business development, internal audit, and IT. Sharing the governance with business units is credited as one of Intel's five "key success factors." Intel reports that they have moved beyond categorizing challenges as IT problems or business problems. They assert that only integrated solutions work to "disrupt instead of being disrupted."[6]

As for its view of where IT governance is going in the future, Intel's website proclaims: "We saw the industry move from central to decentral to centralized computing with cloud, and we believe that the pendulum of computing's next swing to the edge is now underway."[7] Edge computing, simply put, is a distributed IT architecture that moves some portion of storage and computing resources out of the central datacenter to a client closer to the source of the data itself.

Although each information systems (IS) organization is unique in many ways, all have elements in common. The focus of this chapter is to introduce managers to issues related to the way decisions about IT are made both in the organization and, increasingly, outside the organization but in the organization's digital ecosystem. These issues should reflect the typical activities of an IS organization that were discussed in Chapter 8. The current chapter examines governance of the IS function as it relates to decisions about IT issues and the accountability for them.

IT Governance

Expectations (or more specifically, what managers should and should not expect from the IS organization) are at the heart of IT governance. **Governance** in the context of business enterprises is all about making decisions that define expectations, grant authority, or ensure performance. In other words, governance is about aligning behavior with business goals through empowerment and monitoring. Empowerment comes from granting the right to make decisions and to decide how these decisions will be implemented and controlled. A decision right is an important organizational design variable because it indicates who in the organization has the responsibility to initiate, supply information for, approve, implement, and control various types of decisions.[8]

[4] R. W. Gregory, E. Kaganer, O. Henfridsson, and T. J. Ruch, "IT Consumerization and the Transformation of IT Governance," *MIS Quarterly* 42, no. 4 (2018): 1225–53, page 1228, https://doi.org/10.25300/MISQ/2018/13703.

[5] Paul P. Tallon, James E. Short, and Malcolm Harkins, "The Evolution of Information Governance at Intel," *MIS Quarterly Executive* 12, no. 4 (2013): 189–98.

[6] Intel, Inc., "IT at Intel: Insight for Business Growth," http://www.intel.com/content/www/us/en/it-management/intel-it-best-practices/intel-it-annual-performance-report-2014-15-paper.html, 20 (accessed September 3, 2015).

[7] *Intel Shapes the Future of Technology*, Our Beliefs; Intel, Inc., n.d. (accessed August 4, 2023)

[8] See Chapter 3.

Governance Frameworks	Main Concepts	Possible Best Practices
Structural		
Centralization–decentralization	Decisions can be made by a central authority or by autonomous individuals or groups in an organization.	Use a hybrid, federated approach.
Decision rights and archetypes	Patterns based upon allocating decision rights and accountability are specified.	Tailor the archetype to the situation.
Financial control	Frameworks for defining responsibility for financial control decisions and warding off accounting fiascos or financial loss.	Implement governance tools like COBIT or ITIL.
Platform	Platform ecosystem participants contribute their strengths, giving the whole ecosystem a complete set of governance mechanisms for generativity and control that can impact decision making and operations; IT consumerization results in cross-functional teams that have direct, unmediated access to IT using platforms that promote combinations of assorted digital technologies and resources.	Build generativity, and control mechanisms into governance.

FIGURE 9.1 Governance frameworks.

Three major perspectives of IT governance are described in this chapter and Figure 9.1. The first deals with structural mechanisms related to IT issues and describes two approaches. The most traditional approach to structural IT governance focuses on how decision rights can be distributed to facilitate centralized, decentralized, or hybrid (federated) modes of decision making. In this view of governance, the organization structure plays a major role. The second decision-making approach focuses on the interaction between accountability and allocation of decision rights to executives, business unit leaders, or IT leaders. A second major approach focuses on financial control and includes control governance frameworks developed in response to important legislation. The third perspective, **platform governance**, shifts the focus from well-bounded organizational contexts to contexts beyond organizational or industry boundaries to leverage digital ecosystems and IT consumerization. The platform governance approach considers both structural governance mechanisms focusing on decision making authority and control mechanisms.[9]

Centralized versus Decentralized Organizational Structures

Companies' organizational strategies exist along a continuum from centralization to decentralization. At one end of the continuum, **centralized IS organizations** bring together all staff, hardware, applications, data, and processing into a single location. Decisions about these resources are made by the central (e.g., corporate headquarters) IS organization. **Decentralized IS organizations** scatter these components across different locations to address local business needs. Decisions about these resources are made by the business units or divisional IS groups. These two approaches do not refer to IT architectures but to decision-making frameworks. A hybrid of the two is called federalism, found somewhere in the middle (see Figure 9.2). Enterprises of all shapes and sizes can be found at any point along the continuum. Over time, however, each enterprise may gravitate toward one end of the continuum or the other, and often reorganization is a change toward one end or the other.

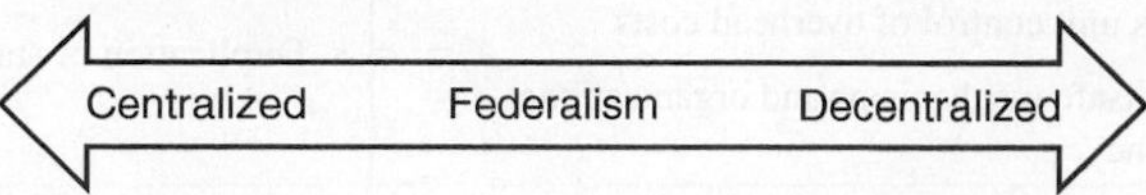

FIGURE 9.2 Organizational continuum.

[9] Carol Saunders, Alexander Benlian, Ola Henfridsson, and Martin Wiener, "IS Control and Governance," *MIS Quarterly Research Curations* (2020): pp. 1–14.

Centralization and decentralization trends have evolved through the seven eras of information usage.[10] In the 1960s, mainframes dictated a centralized approach to IS because the mainframe resided in one physical location and represented a considerable investment. Centralized decision making, purchasing, maintenance, and staff kept these early computing behemoths running. The 1970s remained centralized due in part to the constraints of mainframe computing, although minicomputers planted early seeds for decentralizing. In the 1980s, the advent of the personal computer (PC), which allowed computing power to spread beyond the raised-floor, super-cooled rooms of mainframes, provided further fuel for decentralization. Users especially liked the shift to decentralization because it put them more in control and increased their agility. However, the pressures for secure networks and massive corporate databases in the 1990s caused the pendulum to swing back as some organizations shifted to a more centralized approach. Yet, the increasingly global nature of many businesses makes complete centralization impossible.

What are the most important considerations in deciding how much to centralize or decentralize? Figure 9.3 shows some advantages and disadvantages of each approach.

Consider two competing parcel delivery companies, UPS and FedEx, in the year that they both reported spending about $1 billion on IT as described by Ross and Weill. UPS's IT strategy focused on delivering efficiencies to meet the business demands of consistency and reliability. UPS's centralized, standardized IT environment supported dependable customer service at a relatively low price. In contrast, FedEx chose a decentralized IT strategy that allowed it to focus on flexibility in meeting business demands generated from targeting various customer segments. The higher costs of the decentralized approach to IT management were offset by the benefits of localized innovation and customer responsiveness.

Fast forward to the COVID-19 pandemic. A recent study of U.S. institutions of higher learning found that those that made the best transition to emergency remote teaching during the COVID-19 pandemic

Approach	Advantages	Disadvantages
Centralized	• Global standards; common data • "One voice" for negotiating supplier contracts • Faster decision making because fewer people are involved • Greater leverage in deploying strategic IT initiatives • Economies of scale and a shared cost structure • Access to large capacity • Improved recruitment and training of IT professionals • Improved control of security and databases • Better sharing of enterprise resources (i.e., ERP, CRM)	• Technology not as unsuitable for local needs • Slow support for strategic initiatives • Schism between business and IT organization • "Us versus them" mentality when technology problems occur • Lack of business unit control over overhead costs
Decentralized	• Technology customized to local business needs • Close partnership between IT and business units • Greater flexibility and agility • Reduced telecommunication costs • Consistency with decentralized enterprise structure • Business unit control of overhead costs • More failsafe mechanisms and organizational redundancy	• Difficulty in maintaining global standards and consistent data • Higher infrastructure costs • Difficulty in negotiating preferential supplier agreements • Loss of control • Duplication of staff and data

[a] Adapted from J. W. Ross and P. Weill, "Six IT Decisions Your IT People Shouldn't Make," *Harvard Business Review* (November 2002): 1–8.

FIGURE 9.3 Advantages and disadvantages of organizational approaches.

[10] See Chapter 2, Figure 2.1.

(as measured by satisfied students) were those that had centralized IT governance.[11] The researchers offered several explanations related to the advantages of centralized IT governance: institution-wide standards that were easier to implement quickly and enforce; ability to better identify priorities, communicate and coordinate across organizational units and allocate resources to high-priority areas; and, ability to easily reallocate IT resources and personnel, especially to areas needed for service operations. That is, centralized IT governance provided global standards and greater leverage in deploying strategic, high-priority IT resources and personnel.

Companies adopt a strategy based on lessons learned from earlier years of centralization and decentralization. Most companies want to achieve the advantages derived from both organizational structures. This desire leads to **federalism**,[12] a hybrid federated structuring approach that distributes power, hardware, apps, data, and personnel between a central IS group and IS in business units. For example, federated (hybrid) IT governance might be especially appropriate for organizations seeking to leverage nontraditional data resources because data scientists can be embedded within business units. In that way, they can interact with their business counterparts and understand how the analysis of data can be used to solve business problems. At the same time, a central IT group can ensure a standardized approach to data management and better handle the recruitment and management of scarce technical talent.[13]

A hybrid, federated model is more frequently appearing on the scene to take advantage of the technical agility and tools offered by cloud providers. Centralized governance is still important for organizations with enterprise-wide systems like CRM. However, SaaS, PaaS, and IaaS now make it possible for companies, especially smaller ones, to have IT solutions readily available to them without going through a central IT group. Decentralized governance works best in allowing the business units to respond to local business needs and innovation initiatives using cloud tools and capabilities.[14]

Many companies that adopt a form of federated (hybrid) IT governance (i.e., federalism) still count themselves as either decentralized or centralized, depending on their position on the continuum. Organizations such as Home Depot and the U.S. Department of Veteran Affairs recognize the advantages of a hybrid approach and actively seek to benefit from adopting federated governance. See Figure 9.4 for the interrelationship of these approaches.

Decision Rights and Governance

Sometimes the centralized/decentralized/federated approaches to governance are not fine-tuned enough to help managers deal with complexity and the many contingencies facing today's organizations. This issue is addressed by a framework upon which this section is based—a framework published by Peter Weill and Jeanne Ross in their book, *IT Governance*. They define **IT governance** as "specifying the decision rights and accountability framework to encourage desirable behavior in using IT." IT governance is not about what decisions are actually made but rather about who is making them (i.e., who holds the decision rights) and how the decision makers are held accountable for them.

It is important to match the manager's decision rights with his or her accountability for a decision. Figure 9.5 indicates what happens when there is a mismatch. Where the CIO has a high level of decision rights and accountability, the firm is likely to be at maturity Level 3.[15] Where both the decision rights and accountability are low, the company is likely to be at Level 1. Mismatches result in either an oversupply of IT resources or the inability of IT to meet business demand.

Good IT governance provides a structure to make good decisions. It can also limit the negative impact of organizational politics in IT-related decisions. IT governance has two major components: (1) assignment

[11] Park, Jiyong, Yoonseock Son, and Corey M. Angst, "The Value of Centralized IT in Building Resilience During Crises: Evidence From Us Higher Education's Transition to Emergency Remote Teaching," *MIS Quarterly* 47, no. 1 (2023), https://doi.org/10.25300/MISQ/2022/17265.

[12] John F. Rockart, Michael J. Earl, and Jeanne W. Ross, "Eight Imperatives for the New IT Organization," *Sloan Management Review* (Fall 1996): 52–53.

[13] Anil Gupta, Jon Norberg, Evan Schnidman, and Kai Wu, "Harnessing Alternative Data for Competitive Advantage," *California Management Review*, Insight, (November 7, 2022): 1–9.

[14] Jay Chapel, "How Cloud has affected the Centralization vs. Decentralization of IT", Dataversity, August 9, 2021, *How Cloud Has Affected the Centralization vs. Decentralization of IT – DATAVERSITY*.

[15] Introduced in Chapter 8.

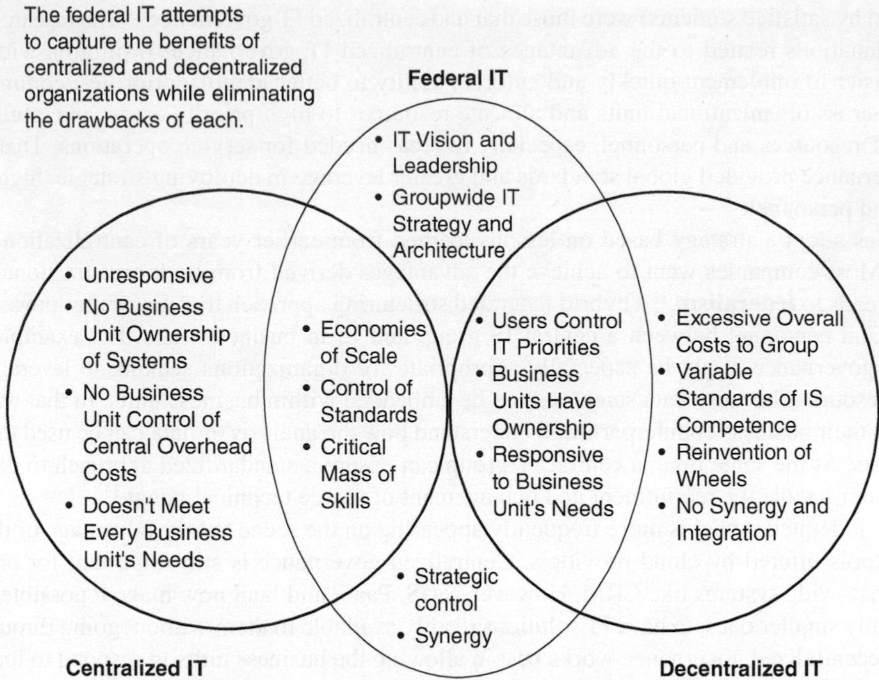

FIGURE 9.4 Benefits of centralized, federated (federalism) and decentralized IT.
Source: Michael J. Earl, "Information Management: The Organizational Dimension," *The Role of the Corporate IT Function in the Federal IT Organization*, ed. S. L. Hodgkinson (New York: Oxford University Press, 1996), Figure 12.1. By permission of Oxford University Press, Inc.

		Accountability	
		Low	**High**
Decision Rights	**High**	**Technocentric Gap** • There is danger of overspending on IT, creating an oversupply • IT assets may not be utilized to meet business demand • Business group might become frustrated with IT group	**Strategic Norm (Level 3 Balance)** • IT is viewed as competent • IT is viewed as strategic to business
	Low	**Support Norm (Level 1 Balance)** • It works for organizations where IT is viewed as a support function • Its focus is on business efficiency	**Business Gap** • Cost considerations dominate IT decision • IT assets may not utilize internal competencies to meet business demand • IT group might frustrate the business group

FIGURE 9.5 IS decision rights accountability gap.
Source: Adapted from V. Grover, R. M. Henry, and J. B. Thatcher, "Fix IT-Business Relationships through Better Decision Rights," *Communications of the ACM* 50, no. 12 (December 2007), 82, Figure 1.

of decision-making authority and responsibility and (2) decision-making mechanisms (e.g., steering committees, review boards, policies). When it comes specifically to IT governance, Weill and his colleagues proposed five generally applicable categories of IT decisions: IT principles, IT architecture, IT infrastructure strategies, business application needs, and IT investment and prioritization. A description of these decision categories with an example of major IS activities affected by them is provided in Figure 9.6.

Archetypes of Accountability and Decision Rights

Weill and Ross's study of 256 enterprises shows that a defining trait of high-performing companies is the use of proper decision right allocation patterns for each of the five major categories of IT decisions. They

Category	Description	Examples of Affected IS Activities
IT principles	How to determine IT assets that are needed	Participating in setting strategic direction
IT architecture	How to structure IT assets	Establishing architecture and standards
IT infrastructure strategies	How to build IT assets	Managing Internet and network services, data, human resources, cloud and mobile computing
Business application needs	How to acquire, implement, and maintain IT (insource or outsource)	Developing and maintaining information systems
IT investment and prioritization	How much to invest and where to invest in IT assets	Anticipating new technologies

FIGURE 9.6 Five major categories of IT decisions.
Source: Adapted from P. Weill, "Don't Just Lead, Govern: How Top-performing Firms Govern IT," *MIS Quarterly Executive* 3, no. 1 (2004), 4, Figure 2.

use six political archetypes with highly descriptive names (business monarchy, IT monarchy, feudal, federal, IT duopoly, and anarchy) to label the combinations of people who either input information or have decision rights for the key IT decisions. An **archetype** is a pattern resulting from allocation of decision rights. Decisions can be made at several levels in the organization: top executives, IT executives, or business unit executives. Figure 9.7 summarizes the level and function for the allocation of decision rights in each archetype.

For each decision category, the organization adopts an archetype as the means to obtain inputs for decisions and to assign accountability for them. Although there is little variation in the selection of archetypes regarding who provides information for decision making, there is significant variation across organizations in terms of archetypes selected for decision right allocation. For instance, the duopoly is used by the largest portion (36%) of organizations for IT principles decisions whereas the IT monarchy is the most popular for IT architecture and infrastructure decisions (i.e., 73% and 59%, respectively).

There is no one best arrangement for the allocation of decision rights. Rather, the most appropriate arrangement depends on several factors, including the type of performance indicator in use. Some common performance indicators are asset utilization, profit, or growth.

Decision rights or inputs rights for a particular IT decision are held by:		CxO Level Execs	Corp. IT and/ or Business Unit IT	Business Unit Leaders or Process Owners
Business Monarchy	A group of, or individual, business executives (i.e., CxOs). Includes committees comprised of senior business executives (may include CIO). Excludes IT executives acting independently	✓		
IT Monarchy	Individuals or groups of IT executives		✓	
Feudal	Business unit leaders, key process owners or their delegates			✓
Federal	C-level executives and at least one other business group (e.g., CxO and BU leaders)—IT executives may be an additional participant. Equivalent to a country and its states working together	✓	✓	✓
IT Duopoly	IT executives and one other group (e.g., CxO or BU leaders)	✓	✓	
Anarchy	Each individual user			

FIGURE 9.7 IT governance archetypes.
Source: P. Weill, "Don't Just Lead, Govern: How Top-Performing Firms Govern IT," *MIS Quarterly Executive* 3, no. 1 (2004), 5, Figure 3.

Decision-Making Mechanisms

Many different types of mechanisms can be created to ensure good IT governance. Policies are a very popular governance mechanism. They are useful for defining the process of decision making under certain situations. However, when the environment is complex, policies are often too rigid. A second method, a **review board**, or committee that is formally designated to approve, monitor, and review specific topics, can be an effective governance mechanism in complex environments. For example, the CIO of Deutsche Bahn, Bernd Rattey, restructured the company's CIO and CDO review boards.[16] He now has representatives from his core IT team matched with a business unit CIO on the boards. Rattey claims, "I expect the two to act as a team, so IT and business pull together instead of raising concerns about each other." That said, he recognizes that digitization must occur across the entire DB.

A third mechanism that is used very frequently for IT decisions is the IT **steering committee**, also called an IT governance council. Such a committee is composed of key stakeholders or experts who provide guidance on important IT issues. Steering committees work especially well with the federal archetype, which calls for joint participation of IT and business leaders in the decision-making process. Steering committees can be geared toward different levels of decision making. Steering committees at the highest level report to the board of directors or the CEO and are often composed of top-level executives and the CIO. At this level, the steering committee provides strategic direction and funding authority for major IT projects and ensures that adequate resources be allocated to the IS organization for achieving strategic goals. They are vital in ensuring that IT is aligned with the business, especially when digital transformation is the goal.

Committees with lower-level players typically are involved with allocating scarce resources effectively and efficiently. Lower-level steering committees provide a forum for business leaders to present their IT needs and to offer input and direction about the support they receive from IT operations.

Either level may have working groups to help increase the steering committee's effectiveness and to measure the performance of the IS organization. The assessment of performance differs for each group. For example, the lower-level committee likely would include more details and would focus on the progress of the various projects and adherence to the budget. The higher-level committee would focus on the performance of the CIO and the ability of the IS organization to contribute to the company's achievement of its strategic goals.

Although an organization may have both levels of steering committees, it is more likely to have one or the other. If the IS organization is viewed as being critical for the organization to achieve its strategic goals, the firm's C-level executives are likely to be on the committee. Otherwise, the steering committee tends to be larger so that it can have widespread representation from the various business units. In this case, the steering committee is an excellent mechanism for helping the business units realize the competing benefits of proposed IT and other business unit projects and develop an approach for allocating among the project requests.

Governance Frameworks for Financial Control Decisions

As can be seen from various discussions throughout the book, control can be viewed from various perspectives. Managerial control[17] adopts a cybernetic or thermostat view of control in which standards are set according to organizational goals. When deviations are detected, often by various IT monitoring systems, various corrective actions are taken, often using IS applications. The focus of the thermostat managerial control perspective is at the organizational level. Behavioral and outcome controls are important for managing remote workers and virtual teams at the individual and team levels.[18] Another perspective of control has focused on ensuring quality control, supporting accounting guidelines, and auditing software systems

[16] Jens Dose, "*Deutsche Bahn CIO on Track to Decentralize IT*," CIO.com, April 19, 2023, Deutsche Bahn CIO on track to decentralize IT | CIO (accessed May 16, 2023).

[17] See Chapter 3.

[18] See Chapter 4.

and system-based data processing that support managerial control.[19] Several governance frameworks have been employed specifically to define responsibility for financial control decisions and ward off accounting fiascos. These frameworks focus on processes defined by legislation and describe risks associated with them.

Sarbanes–Oxley Act of 2002

In response to rogue accounting activity by major global corporations such as Enron and WorldCom, the **Sarbanes–Oxley Act (SoX)** was enacted in the United States in 2002 to increase regulatory visibility and accountability of public companies and their financial health. All corporations that fall under the jurisdiction of the U.S. Securities and Exchange Commission are subject to SoX requirements. This includes not only U.S. and foreign companies that are traded on U.S. exchanges but also those entities that make up a significant part of a U.S. company's financial reporting.

According to SoX, CFOs and CEOs must personally certify and be accountable for their firms' financial records and accounting; auditors must certify the underlying controls and processes that are used to compile the financial results of a company; and, companies must provide real-time disclosures of any events that may affect their stock price or financial performance within a 48-hour period. Penalties for failing to comply range from monetary fines to a 20-year jail term.

Although SoX's focus is on financial controls that did not originally apply to IT departments, it soon became clear that IT played a major role in raising the accuracy of financial data. Many auditors encouraged (forced) IT managers to extend their focus to organizational controls and risks in business processes. This means that IT managers must assess the level of controls needed to mitigate potential risks in organizational business processes and work continuously to improve IS process maturity.

Frameworks for Implementing SoX

COBIT (originally the acronym for Control Objectives for Information and Related Technology) is a well-known governance tool for ensuring that IT provides the systematic rigor needed for strong internal controls and SoX compliance. The most current framework is COBIT 2019, which is a dynamic, end-to-end framework for achieving enterprise objectives.[20] COBIT 2019 provides a framework for linking IT processes, IT resources, and information to a company's management objectives and governance objectives. As a governance framework, it provides guidelines about who in the organization should make decisions about these processes, resources, and information. When implementing a COBIT 2019 framework, a company determines the processes that are the most susceptible to the risks that it judiciously chooses to manage. There are far too many risks for a company to try to manage all of them.

One advantage of COBIT 2019 is that it is well suited to organizations focused on risk management and mitigation. Another advantage is that it is very detailed. However, this high level of detail unfortunately can serve as a disadvantage in the sense that it makes COBIT 2019 very costly and time consuming to implement. Yet, despite the costs, companies can realize benefits from its implementation. As a governance framework, it designates clear ownership and responsibility for key organizational processes in such a way that is understood by all organizational stakeholders. COBIT 2019 can be viewed as a formal framework for aligning IS strategy with the business strategy or even guiding a digital business transformation. COBIT 2019 helps align IS and business strategy by using a governance framework that focuses on three governance functions: *evaluating* organizational needs and objectives, *directing* through prioritization and making decisions according to these priorities, and *monitoring* performance in light of enterprise objectives. COBIT 2019 may provide direction related to how a digital transformation can be delivered using IT.[21]

---

[19] Carol Saunders et al. (2020), "IS Control and Governance."

[20] Kumaragunta Harisaiprasad, "COBIT 2019 and COBIT 5 Comparison," ISACA, April 27, 2020, https://www.isaca.org/resources/news-and-trends/industry-news/2020/cobit-2019-and-cobit-5-comparison (accessed May 20, 2023).

[21] Oluwaseyi Ojo, "Achieving Digital Business Transformation using COBIT 2019," ISACA, August 19, 2019, https://www.isaca.org/resources/news-and-trends/industry-news/2019/achieving-digital-business-transformation-using-cobit-2019 (accessed May 30, 2023).

Although COBIT 2019 is the most common set of IT control guidelines for SoX, it is by no means the only control framework. Others include those provided by the International Standards Organization (ISO), as well as the **Information Technology Infrastructure Library (ITIL)**. ITIL, developed in the United Kingdom, is a set of concepts and techniques for managing IT infrastructure, development, and operations. It is a widely recognized framework for IT service management and operations management that has been adopted around the globe. ITIL encourages fewer silos and more collaboration and communication across the entire business, making it easier to align IT services with the needs of the business.

Platform Governance

New consumer technologies challenge "top-down" IT governance approaches for making all decisions in a planned and methodical manner. These "top-down" approaches focus on the IT function and assume that applications will be developed by IT professionals with specialized expertise and that the firm can fully control its IT assets. However, these approaches don't always work in a world in which firms are increasingly relying on digital platforms to leverage the contribution of third-party developers and other important players in their digital ecosystem. It also doesn't work in a world with IT consumerization, where consumer-workers and consumer-customers expect systems provided by organizations to be as good as the technologies they use daily on their own devices.[22] Emerging digital technologies demand flexible and agile governance approaches that allow ecosystems, societies, and businesses to react to and leverage them.

The technology at the heart of digital ecosystems and, to a great extent, IT consumerization, is the digital platform. The digital platform has technical elements such as digital infrastructures and apps, as well as associated processes, standards, and control arrangements. More formally, a **digital platform** is "a layered architecture of digital technology combined with a governance model."[23] The governance model affects the growth of the ecosystem and the success of the platform.

Digital Ecosystems

There are many freely available and widely used apps, websites, social networks, smartphones, and other IT assets; it would be foolish to try to invent something identical in-house, so firms often exploit them. Using a variety of such assets implies that platform governance might need to be more flexible and follow patterns of adaptation much like biological ecosystems, forming an interrelated set of interacting species.[24] Just as a species cannot ignore predators, prey, and complementary species, an information systems department cannot ignore new technologies and information assets that emerge suddenly and unexpectedly as digital ecosystems.

From a technical standpoint, a digital ecosystem can be defined as an assembly of complementary apps available on a core technical platform. Organizationally it could be firms collaborating over a technical platform to co-create value. One interesting definition of **digital ecosystem** regards those systems as self-interested, self-organizing, and autonomous digital entities.[25] In essence, this means that a digital ecosystem is nourished by the significant impacts of the large variety of resources available from individuals, organizational units, and outside services.

In recent years, social media and increasingly intelligent mobile phones have indeed presented new, unexpected challenges and opportunities as digital ecosystems. For example, social media platform ecosystems consist of users who are connected with one another on a platform such as Facebook and who

[22] S. Baller, S. Dutta, and B. Lanvin, "The Global Information Technology Report 2016: Innovating in the Digital Economy," *World Economic Forum and Insead*, 2016, http://online.wsj.com/public/resources/documents/GITR2016.pdf (accessed February 27, 2019).

[23] G. Parker, M. Van Alstyne, and X. Jiang, "Platform Ecosystems: How Developers Invert the Firm," *MIS Quarterly*, 41, no.4 (2017), page 256.

[24] Maja Hadzic and Elizabeth Chang, "Application of Digital Ecosystem Design Methodology Within the Health Domain," *IEEE Transactions on Systems, Man and Cybernetics, Part A: Systems and Humans* 40, no. 4 (2010): 779–88.

[25] Rahnuma Kazi and Ralph Deters, "Mobile Event-Oriented Digital Ecosystem," *Digital Ecosystems Technologies (DEST), 2012 6th IEEE International Conference* (2012).

benefit from complementors who provide services on the platform for them.[26] Operating systems of mobile phone platforms for iOS and Android make it possible for mobile users to access almost unlimited apps posted by app developers to the phone platforms. Digital ecosystems in the sharing economy include people who want rides connecting with people who have cars to give them rides using a company's digital platform (e.g., Uber, Lyft) or people who have homes, condos, or apartments in desirable places connecting with people who want to rent them for a relatively short time using a company's digital platforms (e.g., Airbnb, VRBO). New digital ecosystem opportunities are made possible with technologies such as cloud computing, blockchains, the IoT and edge computing. *Edge computing* is the most recent development, which represents an Industrial "Internet of Things" approach to collecting, aggregating, and transmitting big data (to the cloud), while also using local processing to detect and solve problems right where they are occurring (at the edge).[27]

A more detailed example can be useful in understanding the various participants of a digital ecosystem. Intel IT's collaboration with the Michael J. Fox Foundation (MJFF) resulted in an edge-to-cloud artificial intelligence platform designed to remotely monitor patients with Parkinson's disease (PD) using wearable sensors that collect high-quality data about heart rate, glucose levels, physical activity, and much more. These data are used to help patients assess their own health and treat their symptoms more efficiently. The platform's machine-learning algorithms generate objective measures to gauge the impact of various therapies, and thereby accelerate clinical trials and the drug-approval process while lowering drug development costs.[28]

Since that first foray of MJFF with Intel in sponsoring and creating the platform, a number of other partners have contributed to the digital platform and extended its digital ecosystem: Teva Pharmaceuticals licensed the platform and its services in a phase-2 clinical trial for a new drug for Huntington's disease; and 23andMe, a genetic testing company, is augmenting patient-reported data with genetic data; scientists funded by MJFF and in partnership with Google research have published their findings on deep learning methods for cellular profiling; Verily Life Sciences LLC, an Alphabet company, and MJFF are collaborating in a scientific study using data gathered from Verily's wearable watches and clinic-based data and biospecimens.[29] This PD wearables digital ecosystem has grown considerably since its creation in 2014, and it now reflects a layering of industries/communities (e.g., chip manufacturers, health foundations, pharmaceuticals, researchers, and device manufacturers).

In this example, the PD wearables digital ecosystem has two major **platform owners (or sponsors)**, or in this case the organizations initially establishing the digital platform, Intel and MJFF. Platform owners typically own, make platform policy, and administer the platform, like Apple or Facebook. We are using the term platform sponsor when there are multiple organizations involved in the governance of the platform. In this PD case there are two organizational sponsors, but for other platforms there may be many more. Sponsors may be called by different names such as owners or providers. In this case, Intel provided the technical infrastructure, an edge-to-cloud artificial intelligence platform, and MJFF helped in establishing the platform ecosystem and administering the platform. The *users*, those individuals (or possibly organizations) who receive a service of value from the platform, initially were people with Parkinson's disease. Their wearable sensor devices monitor their health and at the same time provide high-quality training data to refine the platform's machine-learning algorithms. The **platform complementors**, or those participants who contribute to value co-creation of the platform, include Teva Pharmaceuticals, 23andMe, and Verily Life Sciences LLC. Platform complementors can be competitors or collaborators; they can have the same or widely different interests in or goals for the digital platform—not all of which are aligned with the platform's objectives.

Because of differing, if not conflicting goals and interests of the various digital ecosystem participants, establishing and enacting digital platform governance may be a delicate task. Platform owners (sponsors)

[26] De Reuver, Mark, Carsten Sørensen, and Rahul C. Basole, "The Digital Platform: A Research Agenda," *Journal of Information Technology* 33, no. 2 (2018): 124–35, https://doi.org/10.1057/s41265-016-0033-3.

[27] General Electric Digital blog, "Edge Computing and Cloud Give Intelligent Machines a Balanced Load," May 30, 2023, https://www.ge.com/digital/blog/edge-computing-and-cloud-give-intelligent-machines-balanced-load (accessed May 30, 2023).

[28] Intel Corporation, "2016–2017 Intel IT Annual Performance Report," https://www.intel.com/content/www/us/en/it-management/intel-it-best-practices/intel-it-annual-performance-report-2016-17-paper.html?wapkw=it+performance+report (accessed February 5, 2019).

[29] Michael J. Fox Foundation, "Collaboration with Verily Aims Deepen Parkinson's Understanding through Digital Health Tools," Foxfeed Blog, May 9, 2018, https://www.michaeljfox.org/news/collaboration-verily-aims-deepen-parkinsons-understanding-through-digital-health-tools (accessed May 30, 2023).

need to mindfully design governance mechanisms that will enable them to attract, coordinate, and control diverse groups of platform participants over time. Sometimes these governance mechanisms are designed by a single owner or multiple sponsors or owners. However, the symbiotic multifirm and adaptive situations occurring more frequently in digital ecosystems typically cannot be completely planned or orchestrated by a single owner. Much decision making exists outside the firm, and, therefore, complete plans can no longer be made in a single boardroom. Consequently, platform participants often find themselves moving in directions that could not be predicted.

Platform Governance Mechanisms

Platform sponsors want to make the platform as flexible and adaptable as possible. They typically embrace reusable and malleable code, multilayered architecture, flexible combinations of assorted digital technologies, modular technologies, and loosely defined boundaries that accommodate layered industries. A fancy term, often used to describe digital platforms, is **generativity**, or "the ability of any self-contained system to create, generate, or produce a new output, structure, or behavior without any input from the originator of the system."[30] Generativity plays an important part in the governance of digital ecosystems because it helps the platform grow and be innovative. And control is also important. Control is needed to ensure that there is adequate stability about how the participants interact to co-create value and to coordinate their activities and contributions. Control sometimes needs to be exerted to resolve conflicts among the participants.

Platform owners try to leverage the expertise and resources of third-party participants by getting them to become complementors on their platforms. However, because of conflicting goals, platform owners may need to use controls to get them to act in desired ways and interact with other platform participants effectively. They often have to align the interests of the diverse set of stakeholders to entice them to contribute to the platform. A tension is created between encouraging growth and innovation (generativity) and keeping the interactions structured effectively without conflict (control). To do so, they have to orchestrate the mechanisms to balance the tensions of generativity and control.

Figure 9.8 provides some examples of governance mechanisms being applied simultaneously to address these tensions. Let's expand on some of these examples. In terms of *interfaces*, it has been found that platform owners can provide application programming interfaces (APIs) that make it easier for app developers (i.e., complementors) to add their apps onto the core platform—thereby enhancing the likelihood of platform growth (generativity).[31] Owner-provided APIs also can make it easier for complementor apps to access and retrieve data and connect to smart devices or other external data sources. To control the data interfaces, the platform owner can provide design rules and standards for data exchange that the app developers need to follow.

Another governance mechanism example relying on *relational control* was recently demonstrated in the US state of Virginia's response to COVID-19.[32] The state built a government platform to make it possible for state agencies and private entities (e.g., emergency equipment suppliers, hospitals, utility companies) to share detailed, accurate and timely data. State agencies had started working with one another during the earlier (and continuing) opioid crisis, and in the process they had started building trust in one another and a spirit of collaboration (relational control) that served the state well when COVID-19 reared its ugly head. Early on, the Office of Data Governance (ODG), the central entity sponsoring the platform, hired the platform vendor to build a platform similar to the one it had built to generate an opioid dashboard. The ODG's Chief Data Officer worked to develop shared goals among the state agency administrators. A key step in building and reenforcing trust was to ensure that the data was kept secure and accessible only to those with a need to know. Other governance mechanisms were also employed such as establishing an independent data commission that provided oversight by evaluating data sharing proposals, as well as implementing transparent, straightforward processes for agreement modifications and data access.

[30] D. Tilson, K. Lyytinen, and C. Sørensen, "Research Commentary—Digital Infrastructures: The Missing IS Research Agenda," *Information Systems Research* 21, no. 4 (2010): 748–59, https://doi.org/10.1287/isre.1100.0318. page 751, citing Wikipedia, 2010.

[31] Staub, Nicola, Kazem Haki, Stephan Aier, Robert Winter, and Adolfo Magan, "Acquisition of Complementors as a Strategy for Evolving Digital Platform Ecosystems," *MIS Quarterly Executive* 20, no. 4 (2021): 237–58, https://doi.org/ 10.17705/2msqe.00052.

[32] Tremblay, Monica Chiarini, Rajiv Kohli, and Carlos Rivero, "Data Is The New Protein: How the Commonwealth of Virginia Built Digital Resilience Muscle and Rebounded from Opioid and Covid Shocks," *MIS Quarterly* 47, no. 1 (2023): 423–450.

Mechanism	Generativity	Control
Interfaces—connect and integrate complementors' add-ons to core platforms	Standardize access and connection	Retain fine-grained control over complementor activities
Programming resources—platform owner provided resources to help complementors develop add-ons	Support complementors with the provision of tools and knowledge	Facilitate tight control over development quality through software tools and regulations
Gatekeeping—"bouncer rights" or input control	Increase the diversity in offered apps and functionalities	Restrict access to ensure quality and attractiveness for complementors and users
Decision Rights—who decides about platform objectives and their implementation	Ensure decision-making autonomy of complementors to increase their innovation output	Define the complementors' amount of freedom (e.g., regarding their goals and task types)
Intellectual Property Sharing—licensing or open-source projects	Attract more complementors by expanding their intellectual property rights	Increase control through agreements with different complementor groups
Relational control—informal "soft" control	Increase complementor motivation and commitment through community building	Align platform and complementor strategy

FIGURE 9.8 Governance mechanisms for generativity and control.
Source: Adapted from Staub, N., Haki, K., Aier, S. and Winter, R. "Governance Mechanisms in Digital Platform Ecosystems: Addressing the Generativity-Control Tension," *Communications of the Association for Information Systems* 51, no. 43 (2022), page 913. Table 1.

When building platform governance, it is especially important for digital platform owners to decide how open their platforms should be. Open platforms have less stringent gatekeeping requirements, making it easier for app developers to add their apps onto the core platform. For example, Apple's iOS platform is relatively closed: iOS applications built by third-party developers must pass rigorous quality reviews and Apple controls the distribution channel. In contrast, Google's Android platform, at least initially, was relatively open: Google released the platform under an open-source license and encouraged the participation of hardware manufacturers by publishing reference designs to reduce the cost of building Android handsets. Which governance model is best? It's hard to say at this point. The closed Apple platform generates higher margins by charging higher prices for the core platform. But, the more open Google platform, while generating less revenues from its core platform, has generated far more "apps," is on many more smartphones, and has a larger digital ecosystem.[33] That said, even Google now has started exerting more control over apps developed for its Android platform.

Staub and colleagues[34] who write about governance tensions note that mechanisms don't need to simultaneously promote generativity and control. For example, pricing and revenue sharing strategies may focus primarily on generativity by not charging consumers for access in the early life of a platform or by establishing revenue sharing agreements that are attractive to complementors.

IT Consumerization

In addition to digital ecosystems, platform governance plays an important role in IT consumerization. In an intriguing article by Gregory, Kaganer, Henfridsson, and Ruch, IT consumerization is based on the concept of "everyone's IT" and characterized by the individualization of IT and the democratization of IT access.[35] The authors argue that IT consumerization is such a powerful force that it is transforming traditional IT governance that focuses on a single organization's assets into a platform governance that

[33] G. Parker, M. Van Alstyne, and X. Jiang, "Platform Ecosystems: How Developers Invert the Firm."

[34] Staub et al., "Acquisition of Complementors as a Strategy for Evolving Digital Platform Ecosystems."

[35] R. W. Gregory, E. Kaganer, O. Henfridsson, and T. J. Ruch, "IT Consumerization and the Transformation of IT Governance," *MIS Quarterly* 42, no. 4 (2018): 1225–53.

capitalizes on resources from the external environment. The scope of platform governance is on autonomous cross-functional teams that can develop applications without the aid of IT professionals.

Gregory and colleagues described how a large global bank tried to force-fit "everyone's IT" into a governance model that assumed the IT function would develop all systems. The bank's IT function could not avoid the deluge of requests for BYOD-type applications. When BYOD practices ran amok, the IT managers developed standards that satisfied neither the consumer-customers nor emergent consumer-workers. In the end, the IT governance model was transformed into a platform-based one. Cross-functional teams were created to develop their own applications and the consumer-workers worked in harmony with the consumer-customers in their firm.

SUMMARY

- Alternative approaches to governance of an IS organization are possible. We focus on three types: Structural based on decision making, financial control, and platform.
- One structural approach is based on where IS decisions are made in the organization's structure. Centralized IS organizations place IT staff, hardware, apps, and data in one location and have control of the decision making about these resources. At the other end of the continuum, decentralized IS organizations with distributed resources disperse control of IS decision making throughout the organization in such a way as to best meet the needs of local users. Federalism (federated) in IS organizations is a hybrid approach on the centralization/decentralization continuum.
- A second structural governance approach involves decision rights and archetypes. In this approach, IT governance specifies how to allocate decision rights in such a way as to encourage desirable behavior in the use of IT. The allocation of decision rights can be broken down into six archetypes (business monarchy, IT monarchy, feudal, federal, IT duopoly, and anarchy). High-performing companies use the proper decision rights allocation patterns for each of the five major categories of IT decisions.
- Another governance approach is based on financial controls. The Sarbanes–Oxley Act (2002) was enacted to improve organizations' internal controls. COBIT-19 and ITIL are IT governance frameworks based on control that can be used to promote IT-related internal controls and Sarbanes–Oxley compliance.
- An emergent governance approach is platform governance. The platform governance approach recognizes the power of combining complementary technologies on digital platforms in ways that were not predicted or controlled by an organization. This so-called digital ecosystem represents formal recognition of a firm's healthy adaption to and synergistic adoption of new hardware, applications, and connections with customers, employees, and other firms.
- IT consumerization of technology which highlights "everyone's IT" belief has the power to transform earlier approaches into a platform approach, especially in large organizations.
- There are governance mechanisms related to the two major characteristics of platform governance: generativity and control.

KEY TERMS

archetype, 209
centralized IS organizations, 205
COBIT 2019, 211
decentralized IS organizations, 205
digital ecosystem, 212
digital platform, 212
federalism (federated) governance, 207
generativity, 214
governance, 204
Information Technology Infrastructure Library (ITIL), 212
IT consumerization, 203
IT governance, 207
platform complementor, 213
platform governance, 205
platform owner (sponsor), 213
review board, 210
Sarbanes–Oxley Act (SoX), 211
steering committee, 210

FOUNDATIONAL READING

Decision Rights and Governance: Peter Weill and Jeanne W. Ross, *IT Governance: How Top Performers Manage IT Decision Rights for Superior Results* (Cambridge, MA: Harvard Business School Press, 2004) The definition is on page 3; Peter Weill, "Don't Just Lead, Govern: How Top-Performing Firms Govern IT," *MIS Quarterly Executive* 3, no. 1 (2004), 1–17.

DISCUSSION QUESTIONS

1. The debate about centralization and decentralization is heating up again with the advent of BYOD and the increasing use of the cloud. Why does the Internet make this debate topical?
2. Why is the discussion of decision rights among managers in a firm important?
3. Why can an IT governance archetype be good for one type of IS decision but not for another?
4. In platform governance, why are both generativity and control important?

Case Study 9-1 Governance to Keep Deutsche Bahn on Track

The DB Group, of which Deutsche Bahn is a part, is a global leader in mobility and logistic services. The DB Group, based in Germany, is involved in designing and operating transportation networks. Using multiple modes of transportation, it moves people and goods over its highly integrated traffic and railway infrastructure. Of its over 330,000 DB Group employes globally, 15,000–20,000 Deutsche Bahn employees work on digital issues.

The DB Group's complex and diverse IT needs have been handled by a subsidiary company called DB Systel. Claudia Plattner, the CIO of DB Systel, explained, "Success for us is when users do not need a centralized IT department that takes care of [technology products] for them." The new CIO of Deutsche Bahn (DB), Bernd Rattey, agrees: "The organizational solution at Deutsche Bahn can't be to centralize all digital projects." DB projects are so tightly integrated that digital solutions are likely to create the greatest impact in the business areas.

Rattey has since taken steps to get rid of silo thinking and cumbersome governance processes at DB. Governance is now leaner and less reliant on rules and guidelines. For example, Rattey allows the individual business areas to design certain aspects of the IT system since they are most familiar with the details. The business areas often act as IT islands by using different systems tailored for their individual needs such as personnel planning. Apart from cybersecurity and systems for the railway system consortium (which includes various DB business areas and non-DB transport companies), the business areas can pick which comprehensive IT services they will use. All business projects are managed by a person from the business area, as well as a person with a technical IT background.

However, some operating processes that run across multiple companies must be supported equally by IT. He said, "it's our job to bring these things to the group level. In this way we ensure that such network processes work across the board." To make this a reality, IT has a large SAP R/3 to take care of maintenance across DB Group companies. It also provides a centralized office communications service. Recently SAP S4/HANA was installed to transform business processes across the groups.

Sources: Primarily adapted from "Deutsche Bahn CIO on track to decentralize IT" by Jens Dose, CIO, April 19, 2023 https://www.cio.com/article/473071/deutsche-bahn-cio-on-track-to-decentralize-it.html; See also, DB website, "Facts and Figures 2022," https://www.deutschebahn.com/en/group/ataglance/facts_figures-10467662 (accessed May 16, 2023) and "Deutsche Bahn Systel uses ServiceNow to put the power of IT in the hands of users," by Derke du Preez, Diginomica, October 6, 2020, https://diginomica.com/deutsche-bahn-systel-uses-servicenow-put-power-it-hands-users#:~:text=DB%20Systel%20has%20been%20rethinking,a%20central%20function%20to%20dictate (accessed May 16, 2023).

Discussion Questions

1. Describe the advantages and disadvantages of centralization, decentralization, and federalism.
2. Based on the description above, which of these three governance approaches (i.e., centralization, decentralization, and federalism) most closely describes governance at Deutsche Bahn). Explain your response.
3. What challenges do you see down the road for Rattey with the current governance system?
4. Of the different types of governance systems discussed in this chapter, which is most appropriate for a company undergoing a digital transformation? Explain your response.

Case Study 9-2 The "MyJohnDeere" Platform

"The customer is in control of the data and can share with dealers, crop consultants, and anyone in their network of trusted advisers; securely, from any internet enabled device," says Chris Batdorf, a marketing manager at John Deere.[1] The MyJohnDeere project was designed with the realization that there was synergy in linking together disparate sources of information into this "platform."[2]

Who would be interested in using this application? You might expect that John Deere customers and employees would be the only parties. But according to Accenture, a multinational management consulting, technology services, and outsourcing company, John Deere realized that there was value in opening access to its system to farmers, ranchers, landowners, banks, and government workers. The platform is useful for all those people because it integrates information about equipment, production data, and farm operations and helps users improve their profitability.[3]

Case Study 9-2 **(Continued)**

A farmer described how the John Deere Operations Center allowed him to upload a treasure trove of data about planting, spraying, fertilizing, and harvesting. He said that he accessed that information later not only to diagnose problems about the equipment but also to make decisions about the use of land and personnel. He said that he can send that information to consultants for real-time recommendations on what to change even while he was harvesting.[4] The data that the farmer provided via sensors on the John Deere equipment are being added to data provided by other farmers, as well as historical items such as weather, soil conditions, and crop characteristics. Analytic software can then provide information via smartphones, tablets, and laptops to help the farmers to manage their fleets and operations more efficiently.

A platform such as MyJohnDeere makes it possible to introduce new capabilities that can provide strategic value to customers, other firms, and, of course, its host. According to Accenture, the platform integrates the IoT with social, mobile, analytics, and cloud technology. The combination encourages the development of new applications over time and represented a recent pivotal technology trend. Some of the new applications on the platform are even being created by third-party developers. Hence, the platform provides reusable components that can evolve over time.[5]

The newest platform in the evolution includes the application JDLinkT, which allows farmers to view real-time information about their farm operations, field locations, and important equipment performance data. The newest platform also offers products and services to help them improve their machine uptime, logistics management, and agronomic decisions.[6]

Sources: Adapted from John Deere press release, "The MyJohnDeere Operations Center—New Tools to Manage Data," August 21, 2014, https://www.deere.com/en_US/corporate/our_company/news_and_media/press_releases/2014/agriculture/2014aug21_mjd_operations_center.page (accessed September 4, 2015); See also Cindy Zimmerman, "MyJohnDeere Operations Center Connectivity," March 2, 2015; http://precision.agwired.com/2015/03/02/myjohndeere-operations-center-connectivity/ (accessed September 4, 2015); Accenture.com, "Proliferating digital ecosystems through the platform," January 26, 2015; and C. Perlman, "Product to Platform: John Deere Revolutionizes Farming," HBS Digital Initiatives, February 26, 2019, https://digit.hbs.org/submission/from-product-to-platform-john-deere-revolutionizes-farming/ (accessed February 7, 2019).

[1] https://www.deere.com/en_US/corporate/our_company/news_and_media/press_releases/2014/agriculture/2014aug21_mjd_operations_center.page (accessed September 4, 2015).

[2] Accenture.com, "Proliferating digital ecosystems through the platform," January 26, 2015.

[3] Accenture.com, "Proliferating digital ecosystems through the platform," January 26, 2015.

[4] http://precision.agwired.com/2015/03/02/myjohndeere-operations-center-connectivity/ (accessed September 4, 2015).

[5] http://www.accenture.com (accessed September 4, 2015).

[6] https://www.trigreenequipment.com/new-equipment/agricultural-equipment/precision-farming-solutions/information-management/myjohndeere-com/ (accessed May 20, 2023).

Discussion Questions

1. What governance approach did John Deere appear to have adopted? Did it fit the profile of an "old" heavy industry player?
2. What difficulties do you think an "old" heavy industry player such as John Deere encountered internally when proposing to develop the MyJohnDeere platform?
3. What difficulties do you believe John Deere faced externally among the proposed users?
4. How do you think John Deere might have overcome those internal and external difficulties?
5. What are the advantages and disadvantages of having third-party developers develop applications for the platform? What governance mechanisms should be implemented to leverage third-party developer contributions?
6. What other parties might be interested in obtaining the information in John Deere's cloud? What might they do with it?
7. What platform governance mechanisms likely encouraged generativity? What type of control mechanisms might have been put in place?

10 Information Technology Sourcing

How IT services are provided to a firm has become an important strategic, as well as tactical, discussion. This chapter is organized around myriad decisions in the Sourcing Decision Cycle. The first question regarding information systems (IS) in the cycle relates to the decision to *make* (insource) or *buy* (outsource) them. This chapter's focus is on issues related to outsourcing, whereas issues related to insourcing are discussed elsewhere in this book. Discussed are the critical decisions in the Sourcing Decision Cycle: *how* and *where* (cloud computing, crowdsourcing, onshoring, offshoring). When the choice is offshoring, the next decision is *where abroad* (farshoring, nearshoring, or Global In-house Centers). Explored next in this chapter is the final decision in the cycle, *happy with arrangement as is or need change* in which case the current arrangements are assessed and modifications are made to the outsourcing arrangement, a new outsourcing provider is selected, or the operations and services are backsourced or brought back in-house. Then a new cycle begins. Risks and strategies to mitigate risks are discussed at each stage of the cycle.

Kellwood Company, an American apparel maker, specializes in clothing for women, juniors, and girls. It produces its own privately-owned brands (e.g., Jolt, reCreation, Missy) that are sold in stores like Target, Nordstrom's, and Cracker Barrel, as well as private-label clothing for department stores (e.g., Kohl's, JC Penney).[1]

Though Kellwood espouses the value of global sourcing, it ended its 13-year, multi-million dollar, soups-to-nuts IT outsourcing arrangement with EDS. The primary focus of the original outsourcing contract was to integrate 12 individually acquired units with different systems into one system. Kellwood had been satisfied enough with EDS's performance to twice renegotiate the contract over a six-year period. Yet, at each renegotiation point, Kellwood had considered bringing the IS operations back in-house (i.e., backsourcing). The second contract iteration resulted in a more flexible \$105 million contract that EDS estimated would save Kellwood \$2 million in the first year and \$9 million over the remaining contract years. But the situation at Kellwood had changed drastically.

When Kellwood was purchased by Sun Capital Partners and taken private, the chief operating officer (COO) found himself facing a mountain of debt and even Kellwood's possible bankruptcy. He thought the best way to avoid bankruptcy and reduce costs was to consolidate and backsource the IT operations. Kellwood was suffering from a lack of IT standardization as a result of its many acquisitions. The chief information officer (CIO) recognized the importance of IT standardization and costs, but she was concerned that the transition from outsourcing to insourcing would cause serious disruption to IT service levels and project deadlines if it went poorly.

Kellwood hired a third-party consultant to help it explore the issues and decided that backsourcing would save money and respond to changes caused by both the market and internal forces. Kellwood decided to backsource and started the process late the next year. It carefully planned for the transition,

[1] Kellwood Company, https://www.kellwood.com (accessed January 31, 2023).

and the implementation went smoothly. By streamlining operations in-house, it reported an impressive $3.6 million savings, or about 17% of annual IS expenses after the first year.[2]

When Kellwood was purchased yet again seven years later, the new owners decided to close the data center and move the insourced operations to the cloud. The Chief Technologist and Director of Enterprise Infrastructure were tasked with finding a cloud-based solution and migrating the data center to the cloud within 90 days. Working with a consultant, they decided on the Microsoft Azure Cloud platform. A migration plan was designed, and the transition was made efficiently and seamlessly with Kellwood and the consultant's employees. As part of the 90-day migration, Kellwood's IT team developed a digital purge routine to delete data from the on-premises database after transferring it to the cloud and built a platform that compartmentalized company data as needed.[3] The cloud provider allows Kellwood high scalability—to be able to adjust its IT costs upward and downward according to its monthly needs. As the clothing industry has high seasonal fluctuation, that flexibility can increase management's ability to control spending.[4]

Kellwood's decisions to outsource IT operations, then to bring them back in-house, and finally move them to the cloud were based on a series of factors. These factors, similar to those used by many companies in their sourcing decisions, are discussed later in this chapter.

Companies of all sizes pursue outsourcing arrangements, and many multimillion-dollar deals have been widely publicized. As more companies adopt outsourcing as a means of controlling IS costs and acquiring "best-of-breed" capabilities, managing these supplier relationships has become increasingly important. IT departments must maximize the benefits derived from these relationships to the enterprise and preempt problems that might occur. Failure in this regard could result in deteriorating service quality, loss of competitive advantage, costly contract disputes, low morale, and loss of key personnel.

How IT services are provided to a firm has become an important strategic, as well as tactical, discussion. There are numerous alternatives to sourcing computing power, applications, and infrastructure. This chapter examines the sourcing cycle to consider the full range of decisions related to who should perform the organization's IT work. The cycle begins with a decision to make or buy information services and products. Once the decision to make or buy has been finalized, a series of questions must be answered about where and how these services should be delivered or products developed. The discussion in this chapter is built around the Sourcing Decision Cycle framework discussed in the next section. For each type of sourcing decision, the risks, or likelihood of something negative occurring because of the decision, are discussed, and some steps that can be taken to manage the risks are proposed.

Sourcing Decision Cycle Framework

As noted above, sourcing does not really involve just one decision. A system has many components and separate decisions need to be made about most of these components. Thus, sourcing involves many decisions. The rest of this chapter is built around the critical sourcing decisions shown in Figure 10.1. Many chapter headings are tied to key decisions in Figure 10.1. Although the Sourcing Decision Cycle can start anywhere, we choose to start with the initial make-or-buy decision. If an organization decides to "*make*," that means that it plans to provide its own services and create and run its applications on its own computers, or on rented systems from an outsourcing provider, possibly in the cloud. "*Buy*," on the other hand, means the organization plans to obtain its applications and services from an outside provider or providers. When the "buy" option is selected, the organization becomes a client company that must then decide on "*how*" and "*where*" to outsource.

The answers to the "how" question include the scope of the outsourcing and the steps that should be taken to ensure its success. The answers to the "where" question focus on whether the client company should work with an outsourcing provider (i.e., vendor) in its own country, offshore, on a platform supporting a "crowd," or in the cloud. If the client company decides to go offshore because labor is cheaper or needed skills are more readily available, it must make another decision: It must decide whether it wants the work done in a

[2] For more information, see Stephanie Overby, "Company Saves Millions by Ending Outsourcing Deal," *Computerworld*, https://www.computerworld.com/article/2420418/outsourcing/company-saves-millions-by-ending-it-outsourcing-deal.amp.html (accessed May 27, 2023) and B. Bacheldor, "Kellwood Stayed on Top of Its Outsourcing All the Way to the End," CIO, https://www.cio.com/article/295006/it-organization-kellwood-stayed-on-top-of-its-outsourcing-all-the-way-to-the-end.html (accessed May 27, 2023).

[3] Valorem Reply, "Kellwood Company," https://www.valoremreply.com/work/kellwood-company (accessed May 27, 2023).

[4] Valorem Reply, "How Kellwood Migrated to the Cloud with Azure and Valorem," kellwood-company-story.pdf available at https://www.valoremreply.com/work/kellwood-company (accessed August 6, 2023).

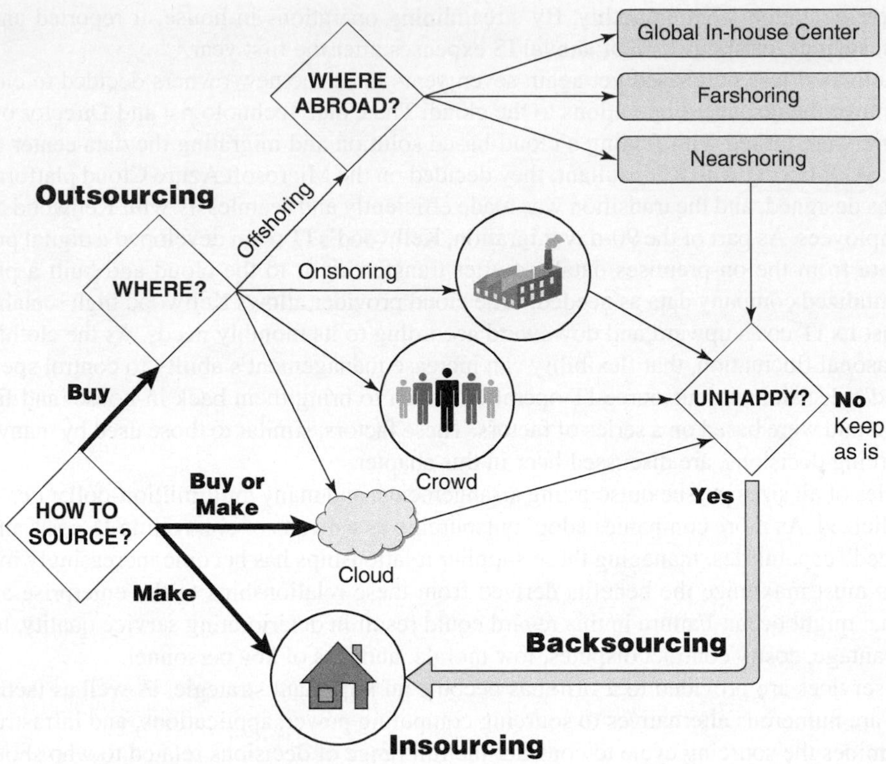

FIGURE 10.1 Sourcing decision cycle framework.

country that is relatively nearby or in a country that is quite distant. Finally, the client company chooses an outsourcing provider (or decides to do its own IT work).

After a while, the client company faces another decision. It must periodically evaluate the sourcing arrangement and see whether a change is in order because it is *unhappy with the arrangement*. If the in-house work is unsatisfactory or opportunities that are preferable to the current arrangement become available, then the client company may turn to outsourcing. If, on the other hand, the outsourcing arrangement is unsatisfactory, the client company has several options to consider: to correct any existing problems and continue outsourcing with its current provider, to outsource with another provider, or to backsource. If the company decides to make a change in its sourcing arrangements at this point, the Sourcing Decision Cycle starts over again.

Starting the Cycle: The Make-or-Buy Sourcing Decision

Managers decide whether to make or buy IS products and services. IS products include an application or a system, and services can range from help-desk support, telecommunications, running data centers, cloud migration, technology modernization, and advising on digital transformation. To a lesser extent, some outsourcing is focused on implementing and operating business processes as in business process outsourcing (BPO). A simple "make" decision often involves insourcing some or all of the business's IT infrastructure, and a simple "buy" decision often involves outsourcing, although it could also include purchasing packaged software. In its simplest form, the make-or-buy decision hinges on whether to insource ("make") or outsource ("buy").

Insourcing

The most traditional approach to sourcing is **insourcing** or providing IT services and products or developing them in the company's own in-house IT organization and/or in its local cloud. Several "yes" answers to the questions posed in Figure 10.2 favor the decision to insource. Probably the most common reason is to keep core competencies in-house. Managers are concerned that if they outsource a core competency, they risk losing control over it or losing contact with providers who can help them remain innovative in relation

Make or Buy Questions	Suggests Insourcing	Suggests Outsourcing	Examples of Associated Risk in Worst-case Scenarios
Does it involve a core competency?	Yes	No	*If outsourced*: Loss of control over strategic initiatives; loss of strategic focus or competitive advantage
Does it involve confidential or sensitive IS services or software development?	Yes	No	*If outsourced*: Competitive secrets leaked; competitive advantage lost
Is there enough time available to complete software development projects in-house?	Yes	No	*If insourced*: Project not completed on time
Do the in-house IS professionals have adequate training, experience, or skills to provide the service or develop the software?	Yes	No	*If outsourced*: Technological innovations limited to what provider offers; overreliance on provider's skills
Are there reliable outsourcing providers who are likely to stay in business for the duration of the contract?	No	Yes	*If outsourced*: Project not completed or, if completed, project over budget and late when another provider takes it over
Is there an outsourcing provider that has a culture and practices that are compatible with the client?	No	Yes	*If outsourced*: Conflict between client and provider personnel
Does the provider have economies of scale that make it cheaper to provide the service or develop the software than in-house?	Most likely no	Most likely yes	*If outsourced*: Excessive costs of project or operations because of the way the contract is written
Does it offer a better ability to handle peaks?	Most likely no	Most likely yes	*If insourced*: Loss of business
Does it involve consolidating data centers?	Most likely no	Most likely yes	*If insourced*: Inefficient operations

FIGURE 10.2 Make or buy? Questions and risks.

to that competency. Failing to control the competency or stay innovative is a sure way to forfeit a company's competitive advantage. On the other hand, by outsourcing commodity work, a firm can concentrate on its core competencies or other value-added work. Other factors that weigh in favor of insourcing are having an IS service or product that requires considerable security, confidentiality, or adequate resources in-house (e.g., time to complete the project with current staffing or IS professionals with the needed skills and training).

In some companies, the IT function is underappreciated by top management. Southwest Airlines' meltdown over the holiday season is a sad illustration with negative consequences.[5] As long as everything is running somewhat smoothly, top managers may not notice the work done or services provided by the IT organization. Often in organizations that insource IT, the IT department has a hard time competing for resources. An insourcing risk is that running IT in-house might require management attention and resources that would better serve the company if focused on other value-added activities.

Outsourcing

Outsourcing means purchasing a good or service from an outside provider(s). In the early days of outsourcing, outside providers often took over entire IT departments, including people, equipment, and management responsibility. Reducing costs was the primary motivation for outsourcing. Also, many firms sold data center equipment and buildings to the outsourcing provider, which resulted in a large one-time cash inflow.

This classic approach prevailed through most of the 1970s and 1980s but then began to experience a decline in popularity. In 1989, Eastman Kodak Company's multivendor approach to meeting its IT needs created the "Kodak effect." Kodak outsourced its data center operations to IBM, its network to Digital Equipment Company, and its desktop supply and support operations to Businessland. Kodak managed these relationships through strategic alliances. It retained a skeleton IS staff to manage the relationships with outsourcing providers. Its approach to supplier management became a model emulated by Continental Bank, General Dynamics, Continental Airlines, National Car Rental, and many more.

Kodak's groundbreaking outsourcing arrangement ushered in new practices that put all IT activities up for grabs, including those providing competitive advantage. As relationships with outsourcing providers became more sophisticated, companies realized that even such essential functions as customer service are

[5] See introductory case in Chapter 1.

sometimes better managed by experts on the outside. Over the years, motives for outsourcing broadened beyond cost control. The next section examines factors and risks to be considered in making the outsourcing decision. The sourcing strategy suggested by the answers to the key "how to source?" question and associated risks are listed in Figure 10.2.

Factors in the Outsourcing Decision

Under what conditions would an organization decide to outsource? There are three primary factors that are likely to favor the decision to seek to buy the services or products of an outsourcing provider: lower costs due to economies of scale, ability to handle processing peaks, and the client company's need to access people with IT skills, training, and experience. These and other factors are listed in Figure 10.2.

Traditionally, one of the most common reasons given for outsourcing is the desire to reduce costs. Outsourcing providers derive savings from economies of scale that client companies often cannot realize. Outsourcing providers achieve these economies through centralized (often "greener") data centers, preferential contracts with providers, and large pools of technical expertise. Most often, enterprises lack such resources on a sufficient scale within their own IT departments. For example, a single company may only need 300 licenses for a particular software application, but an outsourcing provider might negotiate a contract for 1,000 to spread over many clients and at a much lower cost per license.

Second, the outsourcing provider's larger pool of IT resources than the client company's allows the provider leeway in assigning available capacity to its clients on demand. For instance, cloud computing can easily accommodate a company's expanding and contracting server capacity needs. Using cloud computing, Sysco, a global food distributor, was able to purchase additional server capacity the Thursday before Mother's Day (its busiest day of the year) and dial it back on the following Monday.[6]

Third, if an organization does not have enough employees with the training, experience, or skills in-house to successfully implement new technologies, it should consider outsourcing. This is because outsourcing providers generally have larger pools of talent with more current knowledge of emerging technologies and best practices. For example, many outsourcing providers gain broad experience solving cybersecurity problems, whereas IS staff within a single company would have only limited experience, if any. That is why client companies turn to outsourcing providers to help them implement such technologies as cybersecurity, Industry 5.0, Web 3.0 tools, cloud computing, and business analytics. Outsourcing providers may also have a large enough pool of employees to draw from to complete projects that the client is not adequately staffed to complete by important deadlines.

Acquiring and retaining IS talent is becoming more difficult than ever in today's "digitally transforming world."[7] Outsourcing providers face that same competitive IS labor market, but they have an added advantage: Their extensive experience in dealing with IS professionals helps them to understand how to hire and manage IS staff effectively. Often, they can offer IS personnel a more diverse and motivating professional environment than a typical company. Outsourcing providers are proficient at finding, training, and retaining highly marketable IS talent. Outsourcing can relieve a client of costly investments in continuous training and the headaches of hiring and retaining highly skilled staff.

Outsourcing Risks

Opponents of outsourcing cite a considerable number of risks with it (see Figure 10.2). However, each risk can be mitigated with effective planning and ongoing management.

First, outsourcing requires that a client company *surrender some control* over potentially critical aspects of the enterprise, such as: project control, scope creep, technologies employed, costs, financial controls, accuracy, and clarity of financial reports, and even the company's IS direction. By turning over data center operations, for example, a company puts itself at the mercy of an outsourcing provider's ability to manage

[6] Clint Boulton, "Sysco Modernizes IT and ERP for the Cloud," *CIO Magazine*, October 12, 2018, www.cio.com.

[7] Deloitte 2022 Global Outsourcing Survey, Global Outsourcing Survey 2022 | Deloitte United States (includes pdf of report available at website) https://www2.deloitte.com/us/en/pages/operations/articles/global-outsourcing-survey.html?gclid=EAIaIQobChMIjaS43djIgQMVQ0pHAR1JoQ0jEAAYASAAEgL3yfD_BwE (accessed February 8, 2023).

this function effectively. A manager must choose an outsourcing provider carefully and negotiate terms that encourage an effective working relationship.

Second, client companies may not adequately anticipate new technological capabilities when negotiating outsourcing contracts, which can *result in a loss of IT flexibility*. Outsourcing providers may not recommend so-called bleeding-edge technologies for fear of losing money in the process of implementation and support, even if their implementation would best serve the client company. For example, some outsourcing providers were slow to adopt social technologies for their clients because they feared that the benefits would not be as tangible as the costs of entering the market. This reluctance impinged on clients' ability to realize social business strategies. To avoid this problem, an outsourcing client should have a chief technology officer (CTO) or technology group that is charged with learning about and assessing emerging technologies that can be used to support its company's business strategy.

Third, by surrendering IT functions, a client company *risks the potential loss of competitive advantage*, in two different ways. First, technology developed for one client might be used by the outsourcing firm when helping another client. Second, knowledge about existing competitive secrets could be leaked inadvertently (or otherwise) to another client. With both of these risks, managers might justifiably be concerned that they can no longer keep their databases secure if they outsource. The outsourcing agreement should be sophisticated enough to include measures that minimize these risks. Security in an IT firm is often more sophisticated than it is in a client firm, which is helpful. But how can the other technology sharing issues be prevented? Some firms develop a partnering arrangement whereby competitive advantage is developed in tandem with the outsourcing company. Outsourcing contracts should be scrutinized carefully by client firms, because under some circumstances, the outsourcing provider becomes the primary owner of any technological solutions that it develops for the client, allowing the outsourcing provider to leverage the knowledge to benefit other clients, possibly even competitors of the initial client company.

Fourth, contract terms may leave clients *highly dependent on their outsourcing provider*. More troublesome is that clients may be locked into an arrangement that they no longer want. It may be too expensive to switch to another outsourcing provider should the contract turn sour. Despite doing due diligence and background checks, the outsourcing provider may be unreliable or go out of business before the end of the contract. The risk of overreliance for any number of reasons typically increases as the size of the outsourcing contract increases.

Fifth, the *outsourcing provider's culture or operations may be incompatible* with that of the client company, making the delivery of the contracted service or system difficult. Conflicts between the client's staff and the outsourcing provider's staff may delay progress or harm the quality of the service or product delivered by the outsourcing provider.

Finally, although many companies turn to outsourcing because of perceived cost savings, these *savings may never be realized*. Typically, the cost savings are premised on the old way that the company performed the processes. However, new technologies may usher in new processes, and the anticipated savings over the old processes become moot. Further, the outsourcing client is, to some extent, at the mercy of the outsourcing provider. Increased volumes due to unspecified growth, software upgrades, or new technologies not anticipated in the contract may end up costing a firm considerably more than it anticipated when it signed the contract. Also, some savings, although real, may be hard to measure.

Decisions about How to Outsource Successfully

Clearly, the decision about whether to outsource must be made with adequate care and deliberation. It must be followed by numerous other decisions about how to mitigate outsourcing risks and make the outsourcing arrangement work. Three major decision areas are selection, contracting, and scope.

Selection decisions focus on finding compatible outsourcing providers whose capabilities, managers, internal operations, technologies, and culture complement those of the client. This means that compatibility and cultural fit might trump price, especially when long-term partnerships are envisioned. Selection factors are discussed more fully in the "where" and "where abroad" decisions.

Many "how" decisions center around outsourcing *contracting*. The 10-year contracts that were so popular in the early 1990s are being replaced with more flexible contracts of shorter duration lasting 3 to 5 years and full life-cycle service contracts that are broken up into stages. Deal size also has declined this millennium.[8] Often client companies and outsourcing providers contract for formal outsourcing arrangements, called *service level agreements (SLAs)* that define the level of service to be provided. SLAs focus on dyadic (bilateral) governance mechanisms between the client and provider and, thus, often describe the contracted delivery time, expected service performance, and actions to be taken in the event of a deterioration in service quality or noncompliance with the SLA.

Given their complexity, it is a good idea for the client company to develop contract management skills and to hire both outsourcing and legal experts. Unfortunately, a tight contract does not offer much solace to a client company when the service/product provided does not meet the business' goals or when an outsourcing provider goes out of business. It also does not replace having a good relationship with the outsourcing provider that allows the client to work out problems together when something unanticipated occurs. Tight contracts are not advised when the client wants to encourage innovation and experimentation on the provider's part.[9]

Most enterprises outsource at least some IT functions. This is where *scope* questions come into play. Defining the scope of outsourcing means that the client must decide whether to pursue outsourcing fully or selectively with one (single sourcing) or more providers (multisourcing). See Figure 10.3 for a description of types and issues related to scope of outsourcing.

Adidas, a multinational footwear and sports apparel company, adopted a multisourcing strategy, which carefully pitted three IT providers against each other at the same time that they were working cooperatively together.[10] Adidas split virtually all of its huge IT budget allocated for outsourcing among three providers: a large Indian outsourcing company with which it had worked for a decade and two "hungry" smaller firms. Adidas selected the three firms in such a way that at least two providers, and sometimes all three, could perform key services. The large Indian outsourcing provider had become complacent, and the competition

	Description	Why Do It	Disadvantages
Full Outsourcing	Client outsources all its IT functions	• IT does not offer a strategic advantage. • Resources are freed up for activities that add greater value. • Providers' economies of scale reduce costs.	• Client may never develop internal knowledge and skills to do IT. • Client may become unable to separate from provider.
Selective Outsourcing (Strategic Sourcing)	Some IT capabilities are provided in-house and others are given to one or more providers.	• Client gets "best of breed" for each service it outsources. • Client is less dependent on just one supplier. • Client has greater flexibility and gets better service.	• Effort required to manage each provider may be significant.
Multisourcing	IT projects and services are delegated to multiple providers who must work together to meet clients' business objectives.	• Client limits risk of working with just one provider. • Quality improves with best of breed services. • Client enhances ability to adapt to changing market conditions. • Client has easier access to specialized expertise.	• Multiple providers require more coordination. • Providers may "point fingers" at each other when a problem occurs. • Client requires a collective approach to supplier governance. • Unexpected competition among providers may hurt client if not managed well.

FIGURE 10.3 Types of outsourcing related to scope.

[8] Rachel King, "Outsourcing Contract Deals are Getting Smaller," *Wall Street Journal*, May 23, 2016, https://blogs.wsj.com/cio/2016/05/23/outsourcing-contract-deals-are-getting-smaller/ (accessed January 29, 2019).

[9] Gambal, Marfri-Jay, Aleksandre Asatiani, and Julia Kotlarsky, "Strategic Innovation Through Outsourcing—A Theoretical Review," *The Journal of Strategic Information Systems* 31, no. 2 (2022): 101718, https://doi.org/10.1016/j.jsis.2022.101718.

[10] Martin Wiener and Carol Saunders, "Forced Coopetition in IT Multi-Sourcing," *The Journal of Strategic Information System* 23, no. 3 (2014): 210–25, https://doi.org/10.1016/j.jsis.2014.08.001.

spurred it to provide better IT services at a lower price. In addition, all three providers were charged to be more innovative. Through careful management, Adidas orchestrated the delicate balance between provider cooperation and competition among the providers, a situation known as *forced coopetition*. Careful management of a multisourcing arrangement requires a collective approach to governance that focuses on achieving joint performance outcomes.[11] Conflict resolution mechanisms such as regular meetings where all providers air concerns and resolve issues have been found to help improve joint performance.

Deciding Where—In the Cloud, Crowd, Onshoring, or Offshoring?

Until recently, outsourcing options were limited to using services either onshore (work performed in the same country as the client) or offshore (work performed in another country). More recently, a new sourcing option has become very popular: cloud computing. Cloud computing is one of the fastest-growing technologies globally and COVID-19 only served to dramatically spur its growth. Cloud services are viewed by many as an indispensable catalyst for enacting digital transformation. Another "where" sourcing option that has appeared fairly recently is getting a "crowd" that is available on a platform to help out with various needs. For IT outsourcing needs, that means crowdsourcing (in particular, crowdworking). Next, we describe four "where" sourcing options as well as some pointers on "how" to make these arrangements successful.

Sourcing in the Cloud

Outsourcing in the cloud or **cloud computing**[12] is the dynamic provisioning of third-party-provided IT services over the Internet using the concept of shared services and resources. Companies offering cloud computing make anything from just one server to multiple data centers' worth of servers, networking devices, systems management, security, storage, and other infrastructure available to their clients. In that way, their clients can buy the exact amount of storage, computing power, security, or other IT functions that they need, when they need it, and pay only for what they use. Thus, the client company can realize cost savings by sharing the provider's resources with other clients. Cloud providers also offer 24/7 access using multiple mobile devices and high availability for large backup data storage. Apps, platforms, and other services are also available in the cloud.

Cloud computing's many advantages make it quite popular with executives. The total global cloud computing market is expected to increase from $480 billion in 2022 to $1,712 billion in 2029.[13] This growth was originally fueled by small- to medium-size businesses that lacked large IT functions or internal capabilities. More recently, larger companies have been signing up for cloud services to take advantage of the cloud's many benefits and promote strategic initiatives such as digital transformation projects. Other drivers of cloud computing market growth are widespread adoption of Big Data, Artificial Intelligence, and Machine Learning.

Advantages and Risks/Challenges of Cloud Computing Cloud computing offers numerous advantages. Because resources can be shared, costs for IT infrastructure and services can be slashed. There are no up-front investment costs, and ongoing costs are variable according to the firm's needs, especially for those with multinational units in large countries.[14] Flexibility is enhanced because infrastructure needs that vary over time can be met dynamically. For many companies, cloud computing means "pay-as-you-go." Further, cloud computing is scalable, which means that more providers can be added if requirements increase, or they theoretically can be taken out of play if the needs decrease. This allows business units to focus on their core competencies. Kellwood, the company discussed at the beginning of the chapter, turned to the cloud because of its scalability and flexibility in controlling spending.

As with any sourcing decision, organizations considering cloud computing must weigh its benefits against its risks and challenges. Executives worry about the same types of risks that are found with other types of

[11] Krancher, Oliver, Ilan Oshri, Julia Kotlarsky, and Jens Dibbern, "Bilateral, Collective, or Both? Formal Governance and Performance in Multisourcing," *The University of Auckland Business School Research Paper Series, Journal of Association for Information Systems* 23, no. 5 (2022), https://doi.org/10.17705/1jais.00751, 2022.

[12] See Chapter 6.

[13] Fortune Business Insights, "IT Hardware and Services/Cloud Computing Market," (2023) https://www.fortunebusinessinsights.com/cloud-computing-market-102697 (accessed February 1, 2023).

[14] Till Winkler, Alexander Benlian, Marc Piper, and Henry Hirsch, "Bayer HealthCare Delivers a Dose of Reality for Cloud Payoff Mantras in Multinationals," *MIS Quarterly Executive* 13, no. 4 (2014): 193–207. We rely on this article for a number of insights in this section.

outsourcing: technical lock in, decreased ability to tailor service-level requirements, long-term business commitments, and lost IT capabilities, which ultimately could lead to overdependence on the outsourcing provider. IT executives are particularly concerned that they might lose control over the IT environment for which they bear responsibility. Another big concern with cloud computing has been security, specifically with external threats from remote hackers and security breaches as the data travel to and from the cloud. Tied to the concerns about security are concerns about data privacy and, for multinationals, *data sovereignty*, which means that data are subject to the laws of the country in which they are located. The Commonwealth Bank of Australia has excluded some application providers because the core data needed to remain in Australia.[15]

Finally, executives need to be aware that cloud migration initiatives can be both costly and lengthy. Mike Albritton, C-Data's Senior Vice President of Cloud, confirms that even IT companies can find the migration daunting: "Despite being a business built to solve the challenges of digital transformation, we also face the typical challenges surrounding cloud migration and adoption."[16]

Cloud Computing Options Cloud computing comes in several different forms. Options include on-premise or private clouds, community clouds, hybrid clouds, multi-clouds, and public clouds. In a **private cloud**, data are managed by the organization and remain within its existing infrastructure, or it is managed offsite by a third party for the organization (client company) in the third party's private cloud. Intel's significant investments in its private cloud for hosting its data center workloads ultimately generated billions of U.S. dollars in savings compared to what it would have spent for comparable services on a public cloud.[17]

In a **community cloud**, the cloud infrastructure is shared by several organizations and supports the shared concerns of a specific community. An example of a community cloud is Norway's BankID community whose members include Norwegian banks, the Norwegian government, the Norwegian Banking Federation, students, students' landlords, and merchants. BankID relies on a cloud infrastructure to enable electronic identification, authentication, and signing.[18]

A **hybrid cloud** is a combination of two or more other clouds, either public and/or private clouds, where their services are integrated. Sometimes a hybrid cloud refers to a combination of mainframe and cloud platforms. Mohawk, a U.S. manufacturer of premium paper products, has a hybrid cloud. It is part of a computing environment with on-premises ERP and manufacturing systems, a secure suite of private cloud services to send and receive data files among on-premises databases and integrated with its business partners, and a suite of public cloud applications integrated with internal applications and business processes.[19] Alibaba Group Holding Limited recently announced a hybrid cloud solution to provide better security, compliance, dependability, and scalability.[20]

A **multi-cloud** includes multiple clouds under centralized management. In multi-clouds, there is no distinction between private and public clouds, and none of the clouds need to work in combination.[21] For example, a company with multi-cloud could be operating on public clouds offered by Amazon's AWS and Microsoft's Azure.

In a **public cloud**,[22] data are stored outside of the corporate data centers in the cloud provider's environment. Often, managers access services in a public cloud through "as a service" or (aaS) offerings. For example:

- *Infrastructure as a service (IaaS):* Provides infrastructure through grids or clusters or virtualized servers, networks, storage, and systems software designed to augment or replace the functions of an entire

[15] Daniel Schlagwein, Alan Thorogood, and Leslie Willcocks, "How Commonwealth Bank of Australia Gained Benefits Using a Standards-Based, Multiprovider Cloud Model," *MIS Quarterly Executive* 13, no. 4 (2014): 209–22. We rely on this article for a number of insights in this section.

[16] Paul Hetzel, "Top 9 Challenges IT Leaders Will Face in 2023," CIO, January 9, 2023, https://www.cio.com/article/416550/top-9-challenges-it-leaders-will-face-in-2023.html (accessed February 2, 2023).

[17] Intel IT Authors, "IT@Intel: Data Center Strategy Leading Intel's Business Transformation," Intel white paper, November 2022.

[18] Ben Eaton, Hanne Kristine Hallingby, Per-Jonny Nesse, and Ole Hanset, "Achieving Payoffs from an Industry Cloud Ecosystem at BankID," *MIS Quarterly Executive* 13, no. 4 (December 2014): 51–60.

[19] Paul J. Stamas, Michelle L. Kaarst-Brown, and Scott A. Bernard, "The Business Transformation Payoffs of Cloud Services at Mohawk," *MIS Quarterly Executive* 13, no. 4 (December 2014): 177–92.

[20] Fortune Business Insights, "IT Hardware and Services/Cloud Computing Market," 2023.

[21] Scott Lowe, "Multi-Cloud vs. Hybrid Cloud: Assessing the Pros and Cons," TechTarget, June 2018, https://searchstorage.techtarget.com/feature/Multi-cloud-vs-hybrid-cloud-Assessing-the-pros-and-cons (accessed January 30, 2019).

[22] See Chapter 6.

data center. This is the fastest growing segment of the public cloud services market.[23] The earlier Sysco and Kellwood examples illustrate the IaaS cloud option.

- *Software as a service (SaaS):* Provides software application functionality through a web browser. Examples are CRMs and Salesforce.com. This is the most widely known and used form of cloud computing.
- *Platform as a service (PaaS):* Provides services using virtualized servers on which clients can run existing applications or develop new ones without having to worry about maintaining the operating systems, server hardware, load balancing, or computing capacity; the cloud provider manages the hardware and underlying operating system. During COVID-19, the Dutch Railways used the Mendix platform, along with platform apps and features, to build a seat and bike reservation system in just 4 weeks.[24] Often, organizations purchasing public cloud IaaS do so from an integrated IaaS and PaaS provider.

Crowdsourcing

Crowdsourcing is "the act of a company or institution taking a function once performed by employees and outsourcing it to an undefined (and generally large) network of people in the form of an open call."[25] Crowdsourcing can occur when individuals use a platform to collectively create a common document or solution such as Wikipedia or bug bounty where hackers identify cybersecurity vulnerabilities—typically without being paid. Crowdsourcing can also occur when a company or individual uses a platform to solicit and collect independent solutions from a potentially large number of individuals but selects just one or a few to "win" financial or nonfinancial rewards for their contributions. Most contributors are paid nothing for their efforts.

A particular form of crowdsourcing that focuses on paid work only has acquired a special name—crowdworking. **Crowdworking** is typically performed by workers outside the provider's organization and refers to "all types of paid work organized via online labor."[26] Crowdworking is especially good for microwork and online freelancing. Microwork involves well-defined and highly targeted tasks, especially those that can be decomposed into small activities or microtasks. Organizations and individuals can outsource microtasks on platforms such as Amazon's Mechanical Turk or Upwork and pay a small fee for each microtask completed.

Platforms for online freelancing promote contract-based crowdworking for knowledge work, development projects and skilled tasks, as well as flat fee services performed by members. Consider 99designs (99designs.com), which is the largest online graphic design marketplace where people or firms can go to get affordable designs for things such as logos, labels, business cards, and websites. Over 100 million designs have been created on 99designs, about one every two seconds. Businesses can source graphic design work by launching design contests to the 99design community, contracting individually with designers who are members of the community, or purchasing design templates from 99designs' ready-made logo store.[27]

From the perspective of the firm or person doing the hiring, the task or project needs to be carefully designed, the appropriate incentives in getting the crowd or freelancer to contribute need to be carefully determined, and the value of their contributions needs to be assessed. From the perspective of the crowd, individuals need to decide their motivation for participating (i.e., monetary rewards, skill development for future employability, pleasure, work autonomy, etc.) and learn over time how to contribute effectively to the crowdsourced task or project.[28]

---

[23] Gartner, "Gartner Forecasts Worldwide Public Cloud End-User Spending to Reach Nearly $600 Billion in 2023," Gartner Forecasts Worldwide Public Cloud End-User Spending to Reach Nearly $600 Billion in 2023 (accessed February 1, 2023).

[24] See Case 11.2 to find out more about the Dutch Railway development project. https://www.mendix.com/videos/digitalizing-customer-experience-in-4-weeks-with-dutch-railways/ (accessed May 24, 2023).

[25] Nevo, Dorit, and Julia Kotlarsky, "Crowdsourcing as a Strategic IS Sourcing Phenomenon: Critical Review and Insights for Future research," *The Journal of Strategic Information Systems* 29, no. 4 (2020): 101593, https://doi.org/10.1016/j.jsis.2020.101593.

[26] Gol, E. S., Stein, M. K., and Avital, M., "Crowdwork Platform Governance Toward Organizational Value Creation," *The Journal of Strategic Information Systems* 28, no. 2 (2019): 175–95, https://doi.org/10.1016/j.jsis.2019.01.001 Get rights and content.

[27] I. Blohm, J. M. Leimeister, and H. Krcmar, "Crowdsourcing: How to Benefit from (too) Many Great Ideas," *MIS Quarterly Executive*, 12, no. 4 (2013), 199–211 and About 99designs, http://99designs.com/about (accessed May 26, 2023).

[28] Nevo, Dorit and Kotlarsky, Julia (2020), 'Crowdsourcing as a Strategic IS Sourcing Phenomenon".

Onshoring and Offshoring

Outsourcing does not necessarily mean that IT services and software development are shipped abroad. **Onshoring**, also called *inshoring*, means performing outsourcing work domestically (i.e., in the same country).

An onshoring option in the United States is *rural sourcing*, which is hiring outsourcing providers with operations in rural parts of the country. Rural sourcing firms can take advantage of lower salaries and living costs, unlike firms in many domestic metropolitan areas. Further, rural companies can have advantages in terms of fewer time zone differences, similar culture, and fewer hassles compared with foreign outsourcing providers. However, the rural sourcing firms are usually too small to handle large-scale projects. Also, they may not have the most technologically advanced employees, although this may be less of an issue with more people working remotely. Rural sourcing is often viewed as more politically correct than offshoring.[29]

Offshoring (which is short for *offshore sourcing*), on the other hand, occurs when the IS organization uses contractor services, or even its own center in a distant land. Offshoring may be considered the "opposite" of onshoring. Offshoring is most often done because programmer salaries can be a fraction of those in the home country due to a lower cost of living in the distant country. However, these savings come at a price because other costs might increase. Additional costs include technology, telecommunications, travel, process changes, and management overhead for those who relocate to supervise overseas operations.

Even though the labor savings are often very attractive, companies sometimes turn to offshoring for other reasons. The employees in many offshore companies are typically well-educated (often holding master's degrees) and proud to work for an international company. The offshore service providers are often "profit centers" that have established Six Sigma, ISO 9001, Capability Maturity Model Integration (CMMI),[30] or another certification program. These offshore providers usually are more willing to "throw more brainpower at a problem" to meet their performance goals than many companies in the United States or Western Europe. In offshore economies, technology know-how is a relatively inexpensive commodity in ample supply.

Offshoring raises the fundamental question of what to send offshore and what to keep within the enterprise IS organization when implementing the selective outsourcing model. Because communications are made difficult by differences in culture, time zones, and possibly language, outsourced tasks are usually those that can be well specified. They typically, but not always, are basic non-core transactional systems that require the users or customers to have little in-depth knowledge. In contrast, early-stage prototypes and pilot development are often kept in-house because this work is very dynamic and requires familiarity with the firm's business processes. Keeping the work at home allows CIOs to offer learning opportunities to in-house staff. In summary, the cost savings that lure many companies to turn to offshoring need to be assessed in relation to the increased risks and communication problems in working with offshore workers and relying on them to handle major projects.

Deciding Where Abroad—Farshoring, Nearshoring, or Global In-house Centers?

Offshoring can be either in a distant land (farshoring) or relatively proximate (nearshoring). It could also be in a client-owned Global In-house Center. Each of these offshore options is described below and shown with other domestic and nondomestic sourcing options in Figure 10.4. In some cases, the distinction is hard to make because some cloud computing can be considered as insourcing if it is a local private cloud or local community cloud or one of the hybrid forms. However, in most cases, cloud computing tends to be a form of outsourcing either domestically or non-domestically.

Far, Near, or Everywhere

Farshoring is a form of offshoring that involves sourcing service work to a foreign, lower-wage country that is relatively far away in distance or time zone (or both). For countries such as the United States and United Kingdom that outsource large amounts of work, India and China are the most popular farshoring

[29] Bob Violino, "Rural Outsourcing on the Rise in the U.S.," March 7, 2011, http://www.computerworld.com/s/article/353556/Lure_of_the_Countryside?taxonomyId=14&pageNumber=1 (accessed September 22, 2011).

[30] Previously CMMI was referred to as Capability Maturity Model (CMM).

	Insourcing	Outsourcing
Domestic (local)	Situation in which a firm provides IS services or develops IS products in its own in-house organization and/or in its local private cloud or, possibly, local community cloud	Purchase of an IS good or service that is provided by an outside domestic outsourcing provider (i.e., onshoring), or by a rural or local cloud provider
Nondomestic	Situation in which a firm uses an offshore Global In-house Center (GIC)	Situation when the IS organization uses contractor services in a distant land or in the ether; may include nearshoring, farshoring, cloud computing, or crowdsourcing

FIGURE 10.4 Different types of sourcing based on location.
Source: Adapted from http://www.dbresearch.com/PROD/DBR_INTERNET_EN-PROD/PROD0000000000179790/Offshoring%3A+Globalisation+wave+reaches+services+se.PDF (accessed May 22, 2015).

destinations. Ironically, companies in India and China are now themselves farshoring to countries with lower labor costs.

Nearshoring, on the other hand, uses providers in foreign, lower-wage countries that are relatively close in terms of distance, time zones or even cultural, linguistic, economic, political, or historic linkages. Nearshoring basically challenges the assumption on which farshoring is premised: Distance doesn't matter. Erran Carmel and other advocates of nearshoring argue that distance really does matter, and when closer on one or more of these dimensions, the client faces fewer challenges in terms of communication, control, supervision, coordination, or social bonding. For example, language makes a difference in explaining why Latin American nearshoring destinations are growing in popularity in North America,[31] especially in the U.S. Southwest border states where there is a large Spanish-speaking population, and why French-speaking North African nations are appealing to France.

Global In-house Centers (GICs), first known as captives, are service delivery operations which are owned and operated by the client company to retain oversight on work quality, productivity, and efficiency. GICs typically are launched in less expensive locations, usually away from the company's headquarters or major operating units.

Selecting an Offshore Destination: Answering the "Where Abroad?" Question

A difficult decision that many companies face is selecting an offshoring destination. To answer the *where abroad* question, client companies must consider attractiveness, level of development, and cultural differences.

Attractiveness Over 150 countries are now exporting software services and products. For various reasons, some countries are more attractive than others as hosts of offshoring business because of the firm's geographic orientation. With English as the predominant language of outsourcing countries (i.e., United States and United Kingdom), countries with a high English proficiency are more attractive than those where different languages are spoken. Geopolitical risk is another factor that affects the use of offshore firms in a country. Countries on the verge of war, with high rates of crime, and with hostile relationships with the client's home country are typically not suitable candidates for this business. Other factors including regulatory restrictions, trade issues, data security, and intellectual property also affect a country's attractiveness for an offshoring arrangement. Hiring legal experts who know the laws of the outsourcing provider's country can mitigate legal risks. Nonetheless, some countries are more attractive than others because of their legal systems. The level of technical infrastructure available in some countries also can add to or detract from a country's attractiveness. Although a company may decide that a certain country is attractive overall for offshoring, it still must assess city differences when selecting an offshore outsourcing provider. For example, Chennai is a better location in India for finance and accounting, but Delhi has better call center capabilities.

Some countries have created an entire industry of providing IT services through offshoring. India, for example, took an early mover advantage in the industry. With a large, low-cost English-speaking labor pool, many entrepreneurs set up programming factories that produce high-quality software to meet even

[31] Deloitte 2022 Global Sourcing Survey, pg 12.

the toughest standards. One measure of the level of proficiency of the development process within an IS organization is the Software Engineering Institute's CMMI. Its Level 1 means that the software development processes are immature, bordering on chaotic. Few processes are formally defined, and output is highly inconsistent. At the other end of the model is Level 5 in which processes are predictable, repeatable, and highly refined. Level 5 companies are consistently innovating, growing, and incorporating feedback. The software factories in many Indian enterprises are well known for their CMMI Level 5 software development processes, making them extremely reliable, and, thus, desirable as providers. However, if the client is not at the same CMMI level as the provider, it may want to specify which CMMI processes it will pay for to avoid wasting money. Further, it may seek to elevate its own CMMI certification to close the process gap between what it can do and what the outsourcing provider can do.

The consulting firm Kearney has produced a Global Services Location Index (GSLI) to help companies explore potential offshoring locations. The GSLI has four components: financial attractiveness, people skills and availability, business environment, and digital resonance.[32] See Figure 10.5 for details. In 2021, the top four GSLI rankings went to India, China, Malaysia, and Indonesia, while Asia Pacific countries of Vietnam, the Philippines and Thailand were also in the top 10. Brazil, the United States, and the United Kingdom rounded out the top 10 list.

Cultural Differences Often misunderstandings arise because of differences in culture and, sometimes, language. For example, U.S. programmers have a greater tendency to speak up and offer suggestions whereas Indian programmers might think something does not make sense, but they go ahead and do what they were asked, assuming that this is what the client wants. Thus, a project, such as creating an automation system for consumer credit cards that is common sense for a U.S. worker, may be harder to understand and take longer when undertaken by an offshore worker. The result may be a more expensive system that responds poorly to situations unanticipated by its offshore developers. It is important to be aware of and to manage the risks due to cultural differences.

Sometimes cultural and other differences are so great that companies take back in-house operations that were previously outsourced offshore. Carmel and Tjia outline some examples of communication failures with offshore developers due to differences in language, culture, and perceptions about time.

Re-evaluation—Unhappy with Sourcing Arrangement Decision

The final decision in the Sourcing Decision Cycle requires an assessment as to whether the sourcing arrangement is working as it should be. If everything is basically satisfactory, then the arrangement can continue as is. Otherwise, if the firm is unhappy with the arrangement, it may need to be adjusted. If the arrangement is very unsatisfactory, another outsourcing provider may be selected or backsourcing may occur. According to Hirschheim, **backsourcing** is a business practice in which a company takes back in-house assets, activities, and skills that are part of its information systems operations and were previously outsourced to one or more outside IS providers. Kellwood often evaluated its sourcing arrangements: In the beginning it insourced. Then it outsourced, backsourced, and eventually moved to the cloud.

Component	Metrics Used for Each GSLI Component	% of GSLI
Financial Attractiveness	Compensation costs, infrastructure costs, and tax/regulatory costs	35%
People Skills & Availability	ITO/BPO experience and skills, labor force availability, education, and language skills	25%
Business Environment	Country environment, country infrastructure, cultural adaptiveness, Intellectual Property security	25%
Digital Resonance	Digital skills, legal adaptability, corporate activity, outputs	15%

FIGURE 10.5 Components of Global Sourcing Location Index (GSLI).

[32] Kearney, Toward a Global Network of Hubs: The 2021 Kearney Global Services Location Index, April 12, 2021, https://www.kearney.com/digital/article/-/insights/the-2021-kearney-global-services-location-index (accessed February 2, 2023).

Backsourcing may involve partial or complete reversal of an outsourcing contract. A growing number of companies around the globe have brought their outsourced IS functions back in-house after terminating, renegotiating, or letting their contracts expire. Some companies, such as Continental Airlines, Cable and Wireless, Halifax Building Society, Dell, Farmers Group, Sears, and Xerox, have backsourced contracts worth a billion dollars or more.

The most expensive contract that was backsourced to date was the one that JP Morgan Chase signed with IBM for a whopping $5 billion dollars.[33] JP Morgan Chase terminated its contract and brought IT operations back in-house only 21 months into a seven-year mega-contract. The CIO of JP Morgan Chase, Austin Adams, stated at that time: "We believe managing our own technology infrastructure is best for the long-term growth and success of our company, as well as our shareholders. Our new capabilities will give us competitive advantages, accelerate innovation, and enable us to become more streamlined and efficient." Several factors appear to have played a role in the decision to bring the IS operations back in-house. Outsourcing appeared to stagnate IT at JP Morgan Chase under the outsourcing arrangement. Another factor is that the company had undergone a major change with its July 2004 merger with Bank One, which had gained a reputation for consolidating data centers and eliminating thousands of computer applications. And the man who had played a big role in the consolidation was Bank One's CIO, Austin Adams. In his new role at JP Morgan Chase, Adams managed the switch from IBM to self-sufficiency by taking advantage of the cost-cutting know-how he had gained at Bank One. Thus, the underperforming JP Morgan Chase learned much from the efficient Bank One.

It is not only large companies that are backsourcing. Small- to medium-size firms also report having negative outsourcing experiences, and many of these have backsourced or are considering backsourcing. Given the difficulties of delivering high-quality information services and products, backsourcing is likely to remain an important option to be considered by many client companies.

Ironically, the reasons given for backsourcing often mirror the reasons for outsourcing in the first place. That is, companies often claim that they backsource to reduce costs and become more efficient. Based on reports in the popular press, the most common reasons given for backsourcing are a change in the way IS are perceived by the organization, the need to regain control over critical activities that had been outsourced, a change in the executive team (where the new executives favor backsourcing), higher than expected costs, and poor service. The studies found that backsourcing was not always due to problems. Sometimes companies saw opportunities, such as mergers, acquisitions, or new roles for IS, that required backsourcing to be realized.

Outsourcing decisions can be difficult and expensive to reverse because outsourcing requires the enterprise to reacquire the necessary infrastructure and staff. Unless experienced IS staff from elsewhere in the firm can contribute, outsourcing major IT functions means losing staff to either the outsourcing provider or other companies. When the IT staff members get news that their company is considering outsourcing, they often seek work elsewhere. Even when employees are hired by the outsourcing provider to handle the account, they may find some or all of their time to be transferred to other accounts, taking with them critical knowledge. Although backsourcing represents the final decision in one Sourcing Decision Cycle, it is invariably followed by another cycle of decisions as the company seeks to respond to its dynamic environment, as demonstrated in the introductory Kellwood case.

Outsourcing in the Broader Context

The outsourcing industry is maturing, and this has implications for both provider and client firms. To stay competitive, provider firms need to deliver customized, often innovative, solutions that cannot easily be copied by their competitors. This often involves combining and reshaping several of their "best practice" solutions into new systems that suit a client's specific business context. Such customized solutions command higher project revenues and promote greater customer lock-in. On the other hand, client firms are looking for these innovative solutions that create value for them—even if they come with higher price tags.[34]

[33] For a backstory on backsourcing, see Foundational Readings at end of chapter; Also see foundational backsourcing studies of reasons for backsourcing.

[34] Gambal, Marfri-Jay, Aleksandre Asatiani, and Julia Kotlarsky, "Strategic Innovation Through Outsourcing—A Theoretical Review," *The Journal of Strategic Information Systems* 31, no. 2 (2022): 101718, https://doi.org/10.1016/j.jsis.2022.101718.

Most of our discussion about outsourcing has focused on the dyadic relationship between a client and its outsourcing provider(s) based on traditional cost-based assumptions. However, as business becomes more complex and strategic innovation from outsourcing arrangements becomes more expected, it is becoming crucial to consider outsourcing in a broader context that includes strategic networks and business ecosystems.

Strategic Networks

Typically, outsourcing relationships are couched in terms of an outsourcing provider and a client—just as we have done in this chapter. A different approach to viewing outsourcing arrangements is the **strategic network**, which is defined by Jarillo (pg 7) as a long-term, purposeful "arrangement by which companies set up a web of close relationships that form a veritable system geared to providing product or services in a coordinated way." The client becomes a hub and its providers, including its outsourcing providers, are part of its network. A strategic network that has worked well is a Japanese *keiretsu* which has a hub company that encourages specialization within the network and many different types of providers. A variation on the hub-type strategic network is when parent or multinational organization is the hub and a number of its subsidiaries are nodes in the network. Often, one subsidiary performs outsourcing services for another subsidiary in the network. The advantage of the hub-type strategic network is that it can result in increased efficiency and flexibility for the client.

Another type of strategic network is a decentralized value network where firms join forces for innovation and value co-creation. In today's mature outsourcing world, clients are increasingly looking for innovation and often expect their providers to be valuable network nodes.[35] In value networks, they may also collaborate with other firms in the same or complementary industries.

Business Ecosystems

Digital ecosystems are discussed in Chapter 9. Another type of ecosystem is the **business ecosystem**, which we define as an economic community in which the members interact and coevolve their capabilities as well as the collective value around an innovation. This economic community is comprised of customers, providers, lead producers, competitors, outsourcing providers, and other stakeholders. Over time, the community members' investments, capabilities, and roles become aligned as they all move toward a shared vision.

In Norway, a business ecosystem was created by two major Norwegian banks using the BankID cloud community discussed earlier in the chapter.[36] Eventually, other Norwegian banks, the Federation of Norwegian Banking, and the government joined in as core members to subsidize and nurture the ecosystem. Merchants were brought into the ecosystem to grow the community and its offerings. Students and landlords were brought in when BankID was expanded to allow students to pay for their housing online. The BankID ecosystem also includes the main cloud infrastructure providers as core members and equipment vendors and the outsourcing companies as peripheral members. Business ecosystems such as BankID are becoming more and more common.

Over the last 20 years, the IT industry has been leading the charge for another type of ecosystem based on an integrated view of service delivery: the ecosystem of IT providers.[37] This ecosystem is a type of multisourcing arrangement that consists of many IT providers (and GICs), each with their own areas of expertise. Clients need to carefully select and coordinate the services of the many providers that they hire, and then leverage them so as to support and align their highly integrated business strategy with their IT strategy.

The ecosystem of IT providers may explain the recent increase in the number of smaller outsourcing deals (i.e., less than $10 million). It appears that clients are using the ecosystem of IT providers on deals for smaller, more agile projects. The clients are also adopting an "a la carte" approach when they employ a larger number of specialized ecosystem providers on a single project.[38] Of course, managing a configurable sourcing strategy is both challenging and time-consuming.

[35] Gambal et al. (2020), "Strategic Innovation Through Outsourcing - A Theoretical Review."

[36] Eaton et al., "Achieving Payoffs From an Industry Cloud Ecosystem at BankID," 51–60.

[37] Deloitte 2022 Global Sourcing Survey, 7–8.

[38] Tom Seal, "Two Forces Driving Down IT Services Deal Sizes," July 13, 2020, https://blog-idceurope.com/the-two-forces-driving-down-it-services-deal-size/ (accessed January 31, 2023).

SUMMARY

- Sourcing starts with the organization's critical decision to "*Make*" (i.e., provide its own services and create and run its own applications) or "*Buy*" (i.e., obtain its applications and services from an outside provider or providers.)
- A system has many components and separate decisions need to be made about most of these components. Thus, sourcing involves many decisions. The Sourcing Decision Cycle framework highlights decisions about where the work will be performed. Decisions include insourcing vs. outsourcing; onshoring vs. cloud computing vs. crowdsourcing vs. offshoring; and selecting among offshoring options (nearshoring vs. farshoring vs. Global In-house Center). The cycle involves an assessment of the adequacy of the IS service/product delivery. The assessment can trigger a new cycle.
- Cost savings and filling the gaps in the client company's IT skills are powerful reasons for outsourcing. Other reasons include the ability of the company to adopt a more strategic focus, manage IS staff better, better handle peaks, or consolidate data centers. The numerous risks involved in outsourcing arrangements must be carefully assessed by IS and general managers alike.
- Full or selective outsourcing offers client companies an alternative to keeping top-performing IS services in-house. These firms can meet their outsourcing needs by using single-vendor or multiple-vendor models (multisourcing).
- Cloud computing allows client firms to buy the exact amount of storage, computing power, security, or other IT functions that they need, when they need it. It includes infrastructure as a service (IaaS), platforms as a service (PaaS), and software as a service (SaaS).
- Offshoring may be performed in a country that is proximate along one or several dimensions (nearshoring) or that is distant (farshoring). It may also be performed in Global In-House Centers. Offshoring must be managed carefully.
- As business becomes more complex, outsourcing should be considered in the broader context of strategic networks and business ecosystems.

KEY TERMS

backsourcing, 232
business ecosystem, 234
community cloud, 228
crowdsourcing, 229
crowdworking, 229
farshoring, 230
full outsourcing, 226
Global In-house Center (GIC), 231
hybrid cloud, 228
insourcing, 222
multisourcing, 226
multi-cloud, 228
nearshoring, 231
offshoring, 230
onshoring, 230
outsourcing, 223
private cloud, 228
public cloud, 228
selective outsourcing, 226
strategic network, 234

FOUNDATIONAL READINGS

Backsourcing: Rudy Hirschheim, "Backsourcing: An Emerging Trend" (1998) and Mary C. Lacity and Leslie P. Willcocks, "Relationships in IT Outsourcing: A Stakeholder's Perspective," *Framing the Domains of IT Management. Projecting the Future . . . through the Past*, ed. Robert W. Zmud (Cincinnati, OH: Pinnaflex Education Resources, 2000), 355–384; N. Veltri, C. Saunders, and C. B. Kavan, "Information Systems Backsourcing: Correcting Problems and Responding to Opportunities" (2008); and Dwayne Whitten and Dorothy Leidner, "Bringing IT Back: An Analysis of the Decision to Backsource or Switch Providers," *Decision Sciences* 37, no. 4 (2006), 605–621.

For the backstory on the JP Morgan backsourcing deal, please see: Stephanie Overby, "Outsourcing—and Backsourcing—at JP Morgan Chase," CIO, 2005, https://www.cio.com/article/252676/outsourcing-outsourcing-and-backsourcing-at-jpmorgan-chase.html (accessed September 15, 2023).

Business Ecosystem: Our definition of a business ecosystem relies heavily on the pioneering work of James Moore - James F. Moore, "Predators and Prey: A New Ecology of Competition," *Harvard Business Review* 71, no. 3 (May/June 1993), 75–83;

James F. Moore, *The Death of Competition: Leadership & Strategy in the Age of Business Ecosystems.* (New York: *Harper Business, 1996*). ISBN 0-88730-850-3.

Offshoring: Erran Carmel and Paul Tjia, *Offshoring Information Technology* (Cambridge, UK: Cambridge University Press, 2005). See Chapter 3 for further information related to these differences; Erran Carmel and Pamela Abbott, "Why 'Nearshore' Means That Distance Matters," *Communications of the ACM* 50, no. 10 (October 2007), 40–46.

Strategic Networks: J.C. Jarillo, *Strategic Networks: Creating the Borderless Organization* (Oxford, UK: Butterworth-Heinemann, 1993).

DISCUSSION QUESTIONS

1. The make-vs.-buy decision is important every time a new application is requested of the IS group. What, in your opinion, are the key reasons an IS organization should make its own systems? What are the key reasons it should buy an application?
2. Is offshoring a problem in your country? To the global economy? Please explain.
3. When does cloud computing make sense for a large corporation that already has an IS organization? Give an example of cloud computing that might make sense for a start-up company.
4. Does a Global In-house Center resolve the concerns managers have about outsourcing to a third-party vendor? Why or why not?
5. Design a crowdworked offer for a microtask. What is an example of a problem or request you might ask a crowd to solve? How would you "reward" the contributions offered?

Case Study 10-1 Delta: Landing in the Cloud

Delta Airlines is one of the largest airlines in America. The Atlanta-based carrier is the second largest in terms of the flights and seats flown. Delta has transported over 200 million travelers to 275 destinations; It has 4,000 departures daily. IT plays an important role in supporting all these flights and in keeping all these travelers satisfied. As indicators of its ability to keep its customers satisfied, Delta is doing something right; it repeatedly has been named as Fortune's most admired airline and has taken the top place in Business Travel News Annual Airline Survey. Delta also has been recognized as one of Fortune's top 50 most admired companies and Fast Company's most innovative companies worldwide.

Because the dependability of its IT support is so essential, Delta relies on a mainframe to keep its mission-critical reservation and crew scheduling systems up and running 24/7. The airline also has its traditional backend workloads on the mainframe such as its CRM system and FAA maintenance documentation. When its mainframe was down for just five hours in 2016 due to a power outage at its data center, it cost Delta $150 million.

At his 2020 Consumers Electronics Show keynote, Delta's CEO Ed Bastian, laid out a bold plan that mapped out Delta's digital transformation. He explained that Delta had studied what aspects of travelers' air journeys were especially stressful with the intent of mitigating the stressors and transforming the air travel experience. To make that happen he said: "We see technology as a tool to further our mission of connecting people and creating opportunities."

The technology he was talking about was not the mainframe platform. Delta had a number of ambitious projects that had either been initiated or planned. They included a: *digital travel concierge*: a mobile app available on Fly Delta to help Delta customers receive suggestions about getting to the airport, flight notifications, recommendations about faster security checkpoints, and reminders of key times such as when their group is boarding using AI; *parallel reality*: an airport display which allows up to 100 customers looking at it to see a personalized message about their travel using Augmented Reality/Virtual Reality; *wireless in-flight wifi*: a service that allows travelers access to a dedicated channel for viewing TV shows or movies that meet the Reframe Stamp standard; and, *proprietary AI-driven platform*: to aid Delta personnel in making better operational decisions.

These projects are steps in Delta's journey to streamline its processes and modernize its core technology. "We're not just transforming our IT Backbone—we're rallying our entire organization to use leading technology to improve our customers' travel experience in a meaningful way," says Rahul Samant, Delta's Executive Vice President and Chief Information Officer. In essence, Delta is in the midst of a digital transformation.

Delta's digital transformation journey calls for IT apps and data that can be stored in multiple places and a platform that provides high agility and availability. The IT must be able to support the heavy-duty processing needs of analytical workloads, AI and machine learning, as well as offer integrated AI tool sets. This all points to migrating front-end and distributed apps, as well as app development to the public cloud. For that reason, Delta adopted a hybrid cloud architecture.

For its digital transformation, Delta teamed up with three partners. IBM provided support for the mainframe, helps modernize existing solutions, co-creates new solutions, and even trains Delta's IT staff on using the hybrid cloud infrastructure. Red Hat OpenShift offers a family of software products that make it possible for its customers to build, deploy, and manage their own apps. Delta's mainframe infrastructure is now provided by Kyndrl, which is a spin off of IBM's infrastructure services since 2021. Kyndryl is the largest infrastructure services provider in the world.

In 2022, Delta signed a multiyear contract with AWS (Amazon's Web Service) for a portfolio of cloud technologies and solutions. AWS is providing Delta with a secure infrastructure for its Customer Engagement Center, as well as its cloud-based omnichannel contact center service, Amazon Connect, to support Delta customers online or by text.

One especially well-received app released in 2023 is the wifi portal that Delta developed in partnership with T-Mobile. With the app, Delta's travelers on approximately 550 Delta airplanes can run any content on their devices—not just the content on the backseat screens. Matt Cincera, Delta's Senior Vice President of Software Engineering, said "The speed of the cloud allowed us to move from concept to installation and provisioning within six months."

***Case Study 10-1* (Continued)**

Truly, Delta's digital transformation has taken off on the back of its hybrid cloud architecture–– and with the assistance of its skilled personnel and visionary leadership.

Video: See Ed Bastian's Keynote recap (5.25 min) Delta CEO lays out vision for the future of travel at CES in Las Vegas | Delta News Hub.

Sources: Olivia Mayes, "Delta CEO Lays Out Vision for the Future of Travel at CES in Las Vegas," Delta, January 7, 2020, Delta CEO lays out vision for the future of travel at CES in Las Vegas | Delta News Hub (accessed March 30, 2020); Caroline Donnelly, "Delta Airlines Signs Multi-year Cloud Deal with AWS as Customer Experience Revamp Gathers Pace," ComputerWeekly.com, July 13, 2022, Delta Airlines signs multi-year cloud deal with AWS as customer experience revamp gathers pace | Computer Weekly (accessed March 30, 2022); Wylie Wong, "Delta is Departing its Own Data Centers to Land in the Cloud," Data Center Knowledge, March 15, 2021, Delta Is Departing Its Own Data Centers to Land in the Cloud (datacenterknowledge.com) (accessed March 31, 2023); Paula Rooney, "Delta Takes Off with a Modernized Blend of Mainframes and Cloud," CIO, March 13, 2023, Delta takes off with modernized blend of mainframes and cloud | CIO (accessed March 31, 2023).

Discussion Questions

1. What role, if any, did the vision of Delta CEO Ed Bastian play in its architecture decisions?
2. Explain why Delta turned to the cloud as a part of its digital transformation?
3. Why do you think that Delta chose to use a public cloud rather than a private cloud or community cloud?
4. Based on your reading of the case, what type(s) of As.a.Service is Delta using? Please explain your response.

Case Study 10-2 O2 and RPA

O2 started in 1985 as Cellnet and has now grown to become the telecom provider with the broadest coverage in the United Kingdom. It was bought in 2005 by Spain's Telefonica. Its back-office transformation began in 2004 when it engaged an Indian Business Process Outsourcing (BPO) provider to realize back-office cost savings. As the volume of offshore transactions rose, so did the number of FTEs in India—from 200 in 2005 to 375 five years later. At the same time, the provider's headcount in the United Kingdom dropped from 98 to 50 as the provider sought to cut back on its most expensive labor costs. In another cost-cutting purge, O2 eliminated nonvalue adding processing and optimized its 60 core back-office processes. O2 started looking for a better way to get a handle on its back-office processes. Robotic Process Automation offered some promise here.

Robotic Process Automation (RPA) "refers to configuring the software to do the work previously done by people." If it is in the cloud, it may be referred to as Robot-as-a-Service (R.a.a.S.). Typically, RPA tasks are "swivel chair" meaning that they are performed at a workstation and involve electronic inputs (e.g., e-mails, faxes, spreadsheets), deterministic outcomes, and rule-based, highly standardized processes that may access data from one or more systems and then input the completed work to other systems. An RPA is relatively easy to configure in the sense that developers do not need to have programming skills and it accesses other systems through a presentation layer that doesn't disturb underlying computer systems. The precipitous 50% drop in the value of BPO contracts in the first half of 2022 over a year earlier could partially be attributed to RPA since RPA allows companies to automate their back-office work with relative ease.

In 2010, the head of O2's back-office services, Wayne Butterfield, started a two-year proof-of-concept initiative with two pilot tests of RPA using Blue Prism software. The first pilot swapped a customer's existing SIM with a new one while keeping the same phone number. The second process applied a precalculated credit to a customer's account. Both pilots were configured by Blue Prism consultants on site and were completed in two weeks. They both worked seamlessly with O2's systems. In fact, one worked so well that Butterfield was called in to answer to O2's Security and Fraud division to explain why so many transactions were being completed in such a short period of time.

Case Study 10-2 **(Continued)**

Butterfield purposely had not told the Security and Fraud division about the two pilots. He also had not communicated with the IT department because he was concerned that they would object to acquiring additional software (Blue Prism). In fact, the IT department had already developed negative feelings about RPA. Feathers were smoothed when the IT department was asked to build identical systems using BPM as proof-of-concept. The IT developers and scrum teams built the pilots in three weeks each, but at substantially greater cost because of IT labor. Using the results of the two pilot tests, Butterfield built three-year business cases for RPA: Using BPM and the IT department, there would be an estimated zero net financial benefit while with RPA there would be a million £ ($1.4 million) benefit. O2 selected RPA for automating routine back-office processes.

O2 issued a Request for Proposal to initiate a formal RPA vendor search and the IT department verified that Blue Prism offered the best proposal. O2 asked its India-based BPO to take on the RPA work. Recognizing that the BPO made its money on headcount—and that its headcount would be drastically reduced—O2 tried to sweeten the offer. However, after a six-month review by the BPO, the BPO declined the offer without any official reason. (The BPO continues to deliver O2's nonautomated back-office processes, e-mail, and web chat services with a total of approximately 900 FTEs in 2015.) O2 sent its back-office staff to Blue Prism. Using only four people, O2 has now deployed over 160 software bots, which process between 400,000 and 500,000 transactions each month. This translates into a three-year return on investment of over 650% with a payback period of 12 months.

Sources: Adapted from Mary Lacity, Leslie P. Willcocks, and Andrew Craig, "Robotic Process Automation at Telefonica O2," *MISQ Executive* (2015) (15:1): 21–35; The quote is page 22; M. C. Lacity and L. P. Willcocks, "A New Approach to Automating Services," *MIT Sloan Management Review* (2017); Ashleigh Macro, "The Best Phone Network in UK," *Tech Advisor*, January 3, 2019, https://www.techadvisor.co.uk/test-centre/broadband/best-phone-network-uk-3681692/ (accessed February 2, 2019); Irving Wladawsky-Berger, "RPA Provides a Lightweight, Agile Approach to Automation," April 10, 2018, https://blogs.wsj.com/cio/2018/08/10/rpa-provides-a-lightweight-agile-approach-to-automation/ (accessed February 2, 2019); Laura Bergerson, "IDC Worldwide Services Contracts Reached $48 Billion in 1H 2022 with Strong Growth in Average Deal Size," September 10, 2022; Asatiani, Aleksandre, Olli Copeland, and Esko Penttinen, "Deciding on the Robotic Process Automation Operating Model: A Checklist for RPA Managers," *Business Horizons* 66, no. 1 (2023): 109–121 (accessed on March 1, 2023).

Discussion Questions

1. Discuss why O2 turned to offshoring. Do you think these reasons still apply for O2 as it continues its sourcing arrangement with the Indian BPO?
2. Why do you think the Indian BPO provider decided not to work with O2 on its RPA initiative? Do you think this was a good decision for the BPO provider?
3. Describe the approach Wayne Butterfield adopted to study the benefits of RPA? What are the strengths and weaknesses of this approach?
4. Do you think that other companies could achieve results from RPA similar to O2? Why or why not?

11 Managing IT Projects

A major function of the information systems (IS) organization has always been to build and implement systems. This chapter begins by defining a project and a program and identifying key players. It then follows up with a description of how information technology (IT) projects are managed. Various system development methodologies and approaches are introduced and compared. The chapter concludes with a discussion of two critical management areas for project success: risk management and change management.

The Rural Payments Agency (RPA), an agency responsible for administering agricultural subsidies to farmers in the United Kingdom (U.K.), was charged with implementing a European Union (EU) Single Payment Scheme designed to simplify subsidy payments by decoupling them from production. The complex system for administering the scheme was developed and implemented in 2005 by the Government Digital Services (GDS). At the time, it was heralded as a "digital exemplar."[1] But, the Single Payments system soon proved incapable of paying out £1.5 billion of EU subsidies.[2] By the end of 2006, only 15% of the subsidies had been paid to farmers and many farmers who hadn't received their subsidies faced bankruptcy. The delays in subsidy payments were blamed on poor planning and lack of testing of its IT system. Attempts were made to correct the Single Payment system, but in early 2012, RPA's CEO concluded that the agency still had many deep-rooted problems including inaccurate data sources of scheme claims, a lack of standard processes and controls, aging systems, unsuitable technology, and an organizational structure and associated corporate services that didn't fit well with the RPA's purpose.[3] When continued system revival efforts failed, the plug was finally pulled on the Single Payment system in 2015. It had cost £350 million, which is considerably more than the original estimated cost of £75.5 million. An additional £304 million was spent on staff costs to respond to the early payment fiascos.[4]

But the story does not end there. In response to new agreements in the EU, the RPA announced a new system, the Basic Payment Scheme, which collected richer property and payment data. That system was intended to be 100% online and required farmers to verify their identity and accurately measure and map their properties, including certain surface features of the property such as terrain and vegetation.[5]

In January 2015, the identity verification process proved to be a barrier for many farmers because it was difficult to use by farmers who had lower digital literacy levels than the general population and who lived in rural areas with poor broadband coverage.[6] A telephone assistance service was quickly overloaded and

[1] Kat Hall, "GDS Gets It in the Neck from MPs over Rural Payments Agency Farce," The Register, March 2, 2016, https://www.theregister.co.uk/2016/03/02/government_digital_service:criticised_commons_public_accounts_rural_payments_agency/ (accessed January 15, 2019).

[2] At that time, that amount represented about U.S.$2.77 billion when the exchange rate was £1.7 to U.S.$1.00. By spring, 2015, the exchange rate had dropped to £1.52 to U.S.$1.00.

[3] Warmwell postings, February 26, 2012, http://www.warmwell.com/rpa.html (accessed April 10, 2012).

[4] Bryan Glick, "What Went Wrong with Defra's Rural Payment Scheme?" *Computer Weekly*, March 20, 2015, http://www.computerweekly.com/news/2240242763/What-went-wrong-with-Defras-rural-payments-system (accessed September 1, 2015).

[5] Warmwell postings, June 2014, http://www.warmwell.com/rpa.html (accessed September 1, 2015).

[6] Kat Hall, "GDS Gets It in the Neck from MPs over Rural Payments Agency Farce."

became difficult or impossible to reach.[7] Also, even with only a few farmers online, the servers operated at 100% capacity, and the system became intolerably slow. In March, the CEO announced that "all farmers are now being offered the opportunity to complete applications on paper," using forms that were "tried and tested" in the past.[8] By December 1, 2015, only 38% of the farmers had signed up for the Basic Payment Scheme.[9] There was improvement by the end of December 2017 when the target of 90.6% payments to farmers through the Basic Payment Scheme eventually was achieved, as were other targets.[10]

An independent watchdog group investigated the situation and learned that system implementation began before final specifications and regulations were agreed on by the European Commission (the EU's executive body). The RPA then had to make many substantial changes to the system after implementation. Further, the investigation found that testing did not take into account the real environment, and a lot of unanticipated work was spent populating the database with what is now known to be largely inaccurate data. And as if there were a shortage of problems, a turf war between GDS and RPA civil servants further contributed to a "mega IT [mess]-up."[11] Four separate governmental reviews have all been deeply critical of the system and its implementers.[12]

Despite receiving three "red" warnings from the Office of Government Commerce during reviews, the implementation continued. Time was not built into the schedule for testing the whole system as well as the individual components. The components were not compatible with the business processes they were supposed to support.[13]

The RPA's Single Payment Scheme clearly was a failure, and its story highlights the possible financial and social consequences of a failed IS project. Unfortunately, such complete failures occur at an astonishing rate. The Standish Group, a technology research firm, found that only 31% of all software projects succeed and 19% are complete failures.[14]

But could the replacement system, the Basic Payment Scheme, be considered a success? In 2015, it had cost £154 million and had accumulated minimally £600 million more in EU fines.[15] It clearly exceeded its budget and was not working well. However, if we fast forward to 2022, we learn that RPA had logged steady improvement in the targeted Basic Payments Scheme percentages from 2018 to 2021 and it had reached a high of 98.3% of over 83,000 claims paid by December 31, 2021; In the 2021–2022, RPA reported[16] that it had received fewer complaints and it had made faster and more reliable broadband services available to rural communities. It took a while, but RPA evolved and worked out the kinks in its Basic Payments Scheme. Yet, RPA (and the UK government) was patient to an extent that few organizations can be—which is why so many systems don't survive.

To survive in today's frenetic, dynamic environment, businesses must initiate business projects to adjust to or even leverage change. Business projects, especially the more frequently occurring strategic transformation projects, increasingly rely on IS to attain their objectives. A strategic transformation project makes it possible to adjust to shifting organizational goals. It does so by leveraging organizational capabilities and resources, notably IS, to match strategy with operations. A report by CEB, now a part of Gartner, studied 400 strategic transformation projects in various global corporations and found that only about a third were successful.[17]

---

[7] Warmwell postings, January 2015, http://www.warmwell.com/rpa.html (accessed September 1, 2015).

[8] Warmwell postings, March 20, 2015, http://www.warmwell.com/rpa.html (accessed September 1, 2015).

[9] Kat Hall, "GDS Gets It in the Neck from MPs over Rural Payments Agency Farce."

[10] Rural Payments Agency, "Rural Payments Agency Annual Report and Account 2017–2018," July 12, 2018, https://assets.publishing.service.gov.uk/government/uploads/system/uploads/attachment_data/file/725226/Rural_Payments_Agency_annual_report_and_accounts_2017_to_2018.pdf (accessed January 15, 2019).

[11] Kat Hall, "GDS Gets It in the Neck from MPs over Rural Payments Agency Farce."

[12] Nick Ismail, "Why IT Projects Continue to Fail at an Alarming Rate," *Information Age*, February 16, 2018, https://www.information-age.com/projects-continue-fail-alarming-rate-9611/ (accessed January 16, 2019).

[13] "Review Calls for Rationalisation of the Rural Payments Agency's IT Systems," *Computing*, July 21, 2010.

[14] The information from the Standish Group CHAOS Report for 2020 was quoted in Henry Portman, "Review Standish Group – CHAOS 2020: Beyond Infinity," January 6, 2021, Review Standish Group – CHAOS 2020: Beyond Infinity | Henny Portman's Blog (wordpress.com) https://hennyportman.wordpress.com/2021/01/06/review-standish-group-chaos-2020-beyond-infinity/

[15] Parliamentary business report, March 24, 2015, http://www.publications.parliament.uk/pa/cm201415/cmselect/cmenvfru/942/94203.htm (accessed September 1, 2015); also, Glick, "What Went Wrong with Defra's Rural Payment Scheme?"

[16] Rural Payments Agency, Successful and Sustainable Futures: Annual Report and Accounts 2021–2022, HC448, www.gov.uk/rpa (downloaded January 12, 2023).

[17] James Jiang, Gary Klein and Wayne Huang, *Projects, Programs, and Portfolios in Strategic Organizational Transformation* (New York, NY: Business Expert Press, 2020), 8–9.

To ensure project success, a general manager must be both a project manager, a risk manager, and a team player with IT managers. It is through the adroit application of project management techniques and the leveraging of managerial skills that strategic transformations are more likely to be successful in organizations.

Successful business strategy requires executive management to decide which objectives can be met through normal daily operations and which require a specialized project. Rapidly changing business situations make it difficult to keep IT projects aligned with dynamic business strategy. Furthermore, the complexity of IT-intensive projects has increased over the years, magnifying the risk that the finished product will no longer satisfy the needs of the business originally targeted to benefit from the project in the first place. Thus, learning to manage projects successfully, especially their IT component, is a crucial competency for every manager. Executives acknowledge skilled IT project management as fundamental to business success.

This chapter provides an overview of what a project is and how to manage one. It begins with a general discussion of program and project management and then continues with aspects of IT-intensive projects that make them uniquely challenging. It identifies the issues that shape the role of the general manager in such projects and helps them to manage risk. Finally, the chapter considers what it means to successfully complete IT projects.

What Defines a Project?

In varying degrees, organizations combine two types of work—projects and operations—to transform resources into profits. Both types are performed by people and require a flow of limited resources. Both are planned, executed, and controlled. The flight of an airplane from its point of departure to its destination is an operation that requires a pilot and crew, the use of an airplane, and fuel. The operation is repetitive: After the plane is refueled and maintained, it takes new passengers to another destination. The continuous operation the plane creates is a transportation service. However, developing the design for such a plane is a project that may require years of work by many people. When the design is completed, the work ends. Figure 11.1 compares characteristics of both project and operational work. The last two characteristics are distinctive and form the basis for the following formal definition:

> *"[A]* ***project*** *is a temporary endeavor undertaken to create a unique product, service, or result. Temporary means that every project has a definite beginning and a definite end."*[18]

All projects have stakeholders. **Project stakeholders** are the individuals and organizations that either are involved in the project or whose interests may be affected as a result of the project. The most obvious project stakeholders are the project manager and project team. But other stakeholders include the project sponsor who typically is a general manager providing the resources for the project and often *expecting* to use the project deliverables. Customers, also stakeholders, are individuals or organizations who use the project output. Multiple layers of customers may be involved. For example, the customers for a new pharmaceutical product may include the doctors who prescribe the medications, the patients who take them, and the insurers who pay for them. Finally, employees in the organization undertaking the project are stakeholders with varying degrees of involvement.

Characteristics	Operations	Projects
Purpose	To sustain the enterprise	To reach a specific goal or accomplish a task
Trigger to change	Operation no longer allows an enterprise to meet its objectives	Project goal is reached, or task is completed
Quality control	Formal	Informal
Product or service	Repetitive	Unique
Duration	Ongoing	Temporary

FIGURE 11.1 Characteristics of operational and project work.

[18] Project Management Institute, *A Guide to the Project Management Body of Knowledge*, 3rd ed. (Newtown Square, PA: Project Management Institute, 2004), 5.

To organize the work of a project team, the project manager may break a project into subprojects. He or she then organizes these subprojects around distinct activities, such as quality control testing. This organization method allows the project manager to contract certain kinds of work externally to limit costs or other drains on crucial project resources. At the macro level, a general manager may choose to organize various projects as elements of a larger program if doing so creates efficiencies. A **program** is a temporary organization "established to coordinate, command, and monitor a group of related projects, where the goal is to produce outcomes and benefits consistent with organizational strategic goals."[19] For example, total quality management (TQM) and workplace safety are *programs*, and each might involve several IT (and non-IT) *projects*. TQM might require projects to develop defect databases, deploy online training programs, and implement measurement systems to track improvements. Others include the SpaceX Iridium Satellites program or Dutch Railways Information Display Program[20] (see Case Study 11.1). Such programs provide a framework from which to manage competing resource requirements and assign priorities among a set of projects.

Programs typically arise in change efforts designed to effect a digital transformation. Such strategic transformations tend to be very complex to the extent that the stakeholders hold different goals in terms of the change, the scope of the change is quite broad, and the environment is very dynamic and loaded with interdependencies. Involved managers come to realize the transformation actually involves a collection of projects that can be better managed in combination. Doing so creates synergies from interactions among the projects and increases the organizational benefits derived from the change.[21]

In order to better understand how to complete projects, we next describe what is meant by project management as well as the role of the Project Management Office (PMO). We also distinguish between projects and programs.

What Is Project Management?

Project management is the "application of knowledge, skills, tools, and techniques to project activities in order to meet project requirements."[22] Project management always involves continual trade-offs, and it is the manager's job to manage them. Even the tragic sinking of the *Titanic* has been attributed, in part, to project trade-offs. The company that built the *Titanic*, Harland and Wolff of Belfast, Northern Ireland, had difficulty finding the millions of rivets it needed for the three ships it was building at the same time. Under time and cost pressures to build these ships, the company managers decided to sacrifice quality by purchasing low-grade rivets for some parts of the *Titanic*. When making the trade-offs, it was unlikely that the company's management knew that they were purchasing something so substandard that their ship would sink if it hit an iceberg. Nonetheless, the trade-off proved disastrous.[23]

Three well-known trade-offs are depicted in the project triangle (see Figure 11.2), which highlights the importance of balancing scope, time, and cost for project quality. *Scope* may be subdivided into that of the

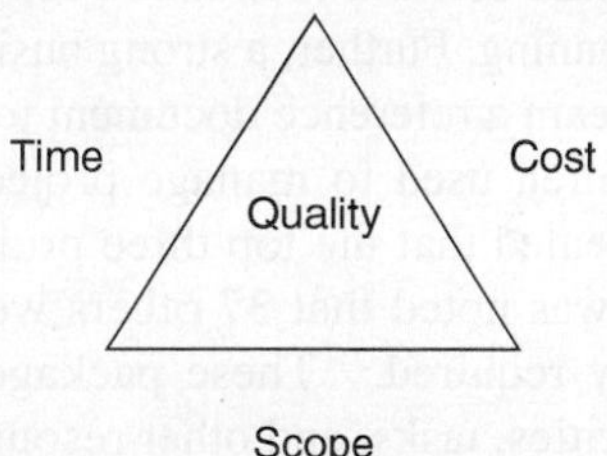

FIGURE 11.2 Project triangle.

[19] James Jiang, Gary Klein and Wayne Huang, *Projects, Programs, and Portfolios in Strategic Organizational Transformation* (New York, NY: Business Expert Press, 2020), 74.

[20] An earlier MTS is described in the Dutch railways in which MTS system helped in Operational Control Central Rail to help resolve railway network calamities in G. F. Goodwin, P. J. M. D. Essens, and D. Smith, "Multiteam Systems in the Public Sector," *Multiteam Systems: An Organization Form for Dynamic and Complex Environments* (2012), 53–78.

[21] James Jiang et al. (2020).

[22] Dan Friedmann, "Program vs. Project Management," http://www.proj-mgt.com/PMC_Program_vs_Project.htm (accessed September 1, 2015); Good summary of differences; quote from page 8.

[23] This research was described in J. H. McCarty and T. Foecke, *What Really Sank the Titanic* (New York: Citadel Press, 2008) and is based on J. H. McCarty, PhD Thesis, The Johns Hopkins University (2003).

product (the detailed description of the system's quality, features, and functions) and of the project itself (the work required to deliver a product or service with the intended product scope). *Time* refers to the time required to complete the project, whereas *cost* encompasses all the resources required to carry out the project. In the tragic case of the *Titanic*, the managers were willing to trade off *quality* for lower-*cost* rivets that allowed them to build all three ships (*scope*) in a timelier fashion (*time*). In contrast, a successful balance of scope, time, and cost yields a high-quality project—one in which the needs and expectations of the users are met.

The tricky part of project management is successfully juggling these three elements. Changes in any one side of the triangle affect one or both of the other sides. For example, if the project scope increases, more time and/or more resources (cost) are needed to do the additional work. This increase in scope after a project has begun is aptly called *scope creep*.

In most projects, only two of these elements can be optimized, and the third must be adjusted to maintain balance. A project can be finished in a specific amount of time for a specific budget, but then the scope must be adjusted accordingly. Or if the project is needed quickly and with a specific scope, then the cost must be adjusted accordingly. It is usually not possible to complete a project cheaply, quickly, and with a large scope. To do so usually means introducing errors and completion at a quality level that is too low for acceptance testing. The reasoning is that many cutting-edge technologies can be acquired, but they are often proprietary and unique, requiring steep fees or specialized "rock star" developers to adapt or install them. The final choice is to attempt to build an excellent system cheaply; however, it will take a long time if the firm waits for competing vendors to offer less expensive alternatives. Sometimes a firm might hire college interns with up-to-date, excellent skills at a very low rate, but their availability is often limited because of classes, homework, or exams. If a firm waits several years, it might find technologies available at no cost from an open-source provider.

It is important that the project stakeholders decide on the overriding "key success factor" (i.e., time, cost, or scope) although the project manager has the important responsibility of demonstrating to the stakeholders the impact on the project of selecting any of these. In the RPA case at the beginning of this chapter, scope was a key success factor that was managed inappropriately, ultimately resulting in a much longer time and much higher cost.

But the key success factor is only one metric to use when managing a project. Stakeholders are concerned about all facets of the project. Measuring and tracking progress is often done by tracking time (How are we doing compared to the schedule?), cost (How are we doing compared to the budget?), scope (Are we on track to provide the intended functionality?), resources (How much of our resources have we consumed so far?), quality (Is the quality of the output/deliverables at the level required for success?), and risks (How are we doing managing the risk associated with this project?).

A successful business project often begins with a well-written business case that spells out the components of the project. The business case clearly articulates project details and argues for resources for it. (The components of a business case and common financial metrics are discussed in Chapter 8.) The process used to develop the business case sets the foundation for the project itself. The business case is useful for detailed and contingency planning. Further, a strong business plan developed from the business case gives all members of the project team a reference document to help guide decisions and activities.

Project management software is often used to manage projects and keep track of key metrics. A recent ranking by Forbes Advisor revealed that the top three project management systems are monday .com, ClickUp, and Wrike though it was noted that 37 others were assessed and may be more appropriate depending on the functionality required.[24] These packages can keep track of team members, deliverables, schedules, budgets, priorities, tasks, and other resources. Most provide a dashboard of key metrics to help project managers quickly identify areas of concern or potentially critical issues that need attention. Some packages have "moved to the cloud" and enable employees to access status reports and plans anywhere.

Organizing for Project Management

Although managing projects is not a new set of activities for management, it is a struggle for many to bring a project in on time, on budget, and within scope. Some organizations create a **project management office (PMO)**, which is a department responsible for boosting efficiency, gathering expertise, and improving

[24] Alana Rudder, "Best Project Management Software in 2023," Forbes Advisor, January 9, 2023 (accessed January 10, 2023).

project delivery. A PMO operates at the project level and often is tasked with accomplishing goals defined in various organizational programs. Although companies may not immediately realize the financial benefits, the increased efficiencies and project discipline from a PMO should eventually lead to cost savings.

The responsibilities of a PMO range widely based on the preferences of the chief information officer (CIO) under which the management of the PMO typically falls. Sometimes the PMO is simply a clearinghouse for best practices in project management, and other times it is the organization that more formally manages all major projects.

Project Elements

Project work requires in-depth situational analyses and the organization of complex activities into often coincident sequences of discrete tasks. The outcomes of each activity must be tested and integrated into the larger process to produce the desired result. The number of variables affecting the performance of such work is potentially enormous.

Four elements essential for any project include (1) project management, (2) a project team, (3) a project plan, and (4) a common project vocabulary. Project management includes the *project sponsor* who initiates the project and a **project manager** who makes sure that the entire project is executed appropriately and coordinated properly—often without the authority typical of the line manager. A good project manager defines the project scope realistically, and then manages the project so that it can be completed on time and within budget. The *project team* has members who work together to ensure that all parts of the project come together correctly and efficiently. The plan represents the methodology, budget, and schedule to be used by the team to execute the project. Finally, a common project vocabulary allows all those involved with the project to understand the project and communicate effectively.

It is essential to understand the interrelationships among these elements and with the project itself. Both a commitment to working together as a team and a common project vocabulary must permeate the management of a project throughout its life. The project plan consists of the sequential steps of organizing and tracking the team's work. Finally, the project manager ensures the completion of work by team members at each step of the project plan (see later discussion) and as situational elements evolve throughout the project cycle.

Project Management

Two key players in project management are the sponsor and the manager. The project sponsor liaises between the project team and the other stakeholders. The sponsor is the project champion and works with the project manager in providing the leadership to accomplish project objectives. Often the sponsor is a very senior-level executive in the firm, someone who has influence with the key stakeholders and other senior-level executives. The project sponsor secures the financial resources for the project.

The project manager is central to the project. It is the project manager who is responsible for producing a deliverable to meet specifications on budget and on time. The project manager role is not an easy one because it requires a range of management skills to make the project successful. These skills include most notably providing project leadership, but also identifying requirements of the systems to be delivered, structuring the project, assigning team members to work on the project, managing risks, leveraging opportunities, and keeping the project on track.[25]

Project leadership guides the other skills. Lack of leadership can result in unmotivated or confused people doing the wrong things and ultimately derailing the project. Strong project leaders skillfully manage team composition, reward systems, and other techniques to focus, align, and motivate team members. Figure 11.3 reflects the inverse relationship between the magnitude of the project leader's role and the experience and commitment of the team. In organizations with strong processes for project management and professionals trained for this activity, the need for aggressive project leadership is reduced.

[25] Adapted from K. Forsberg, H. Mooz, and H. Cotterman, *Visualizing Project Management* (Hoboken, NJ: John Wiley, 1996).

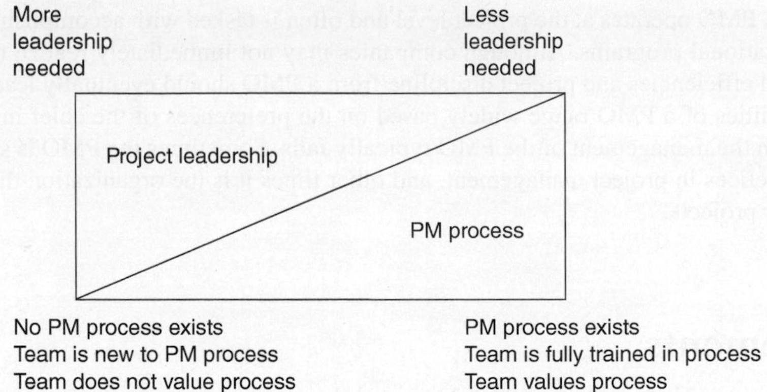

FIGURE 11.3 Project leadership vs. project management (PM) process.

Project Team

The project team consists of those people who work together to complete the project. Teamwork begins by clearly defining the team's objectives and each member's role in achieving these objectives. Teams need to have norms about conduct, shared rewards, a shared understanding of roles, and team spirit. Project managers should leverage team member skills, knowledge, experiences, and capabilities when assigning them to complete specific activities on an as-needed basis. In addition to completing their team activities, team members also represent their departments and transmit information about their department to other team members. Such information sharing constitutes the first step toward building consensus on critical project issues that affect the entire organization. Thus, effective project managers use teamwork both to organize and apply human resources, to motivate an acceptance of change, and to collect and share information throughout the organization.

Project Plan

The **project plan** takes into account the project's scope, time, and cost. Using the project plan, the time and resources (e.g., financial, IT, and human) needed to complete the work based on the project's scope are identified, and tasks are assigned to team members. The project plan is based on estimates, of which the most commonly presented are cost and schedule.[26] Two different surveys report that the most common way to prepare estimates is to compare the project to similar past projects using either personal memory or documented facts. However, a surprising number of respondents admit to just guessing. That being said, the respondents tend to find the estimation of IT projects to be moderately or very important. Estimation is important because it is used to staff and schedule projects, control or monitor project implementation, and evaluate project success. Most estimates are made at the start of the project, but often they are adjusted because of changes in requirements or scope, overlooked tasks popping up, or a better understanding of what is involved in the project.

The **project schedule** is a time management tool that organizes discrete project activities and sequences them in steps along a timeline so that the project fulfills the requirements of customers and stakeholders. It identifies critical beginning and end dates and breaks the work spanning these dates into phases. General managers track the phases to coordinate the eventual transition from project to operational status, a process that culminates in the "go-live" date. Project managers use the phases to control work progress. They may establish "control gates" or "mileposts" at various points along the way to verify that project work to date has met key requirements regarding cost, quality, and features. If it has not met these requirements, they might need to make changes, which could also delay the project plan's "go-live" date.

[26] Nelson R. Ryan and Michael G. Morris, "IT Project Estimation: Contemporary Practices and Management Guidelines," *MIS Quarterly Executive* 13, no. 1 (2014).

Study Period		Implementation Period	Operations Period	
Initiating	Planning	Executing	Monitoring and controlling	Closing

FIGURE 11.4 Project Management Institute Project Life Cycle by Period.

The project schedule can be developed using various approaches and software tools. Project management software products typically offer specialized automated scheduling tools. Some schedules are generated using network diagrams such as those used in project evaluation and review technique (PERT) and the critical path method (CPM) which take into account the time requirements, sequencing, and interdependencies of tasks. Gantt charts, or bar charts, are commonly used as visual tools for displaying time relationships of project tasks in a more linear fashion and for monitoring the progress toward project completion. Kanban software visually represents project workflow, task placement within the workflow, and project status in terms of progress.

The *project budget* is a project cost management tool that indicates how much should be spent on completing the various tasks. Unfortunately, the tendency is to underestimate these costs.

Even though most project life cycles in practice have unique phases, all can loosely be described by three major periods (shown at the top of the diagram): study, implementation, and operations. Figure 11.4 relates the five phases of the Project Management Institute's project life cycle to the three major periods. Figure 11.6 relates the Generic System Development Life Cycle stages to the three major periods.[27]

Projects are all about change. They bring new products, services, or systems into organizations or make them available for the organization's customers. These project deliverables need to be integrated into the organization's (or its customers') operations. Not surprisingly, the three major periods in the project life cycle in Figure 11.4 (study, implementation, and operations) correspond respectively to Lewin's classic change model introduced in Chapter 4: unfreezing, changing, and refreezing. First, according to Lewin, people need to be given a motivation for change in the unfreezing stage. People don't want to change unless they see some reason for doing so. This is what happens in the study period when it is determined what needs to be changed and why. The project sponsor is often a key mover in providing answers to these questions. Then in the changing stage, when the system is built (or purchased) and installed, people in the organization are made aware of what the change is and receive training about how to take advantage of it. It is not possible for people to fully understand the change until the implementation period, after the service, product, or system has been designed or built, and they are then trained to use it. Those on the project team can better understand what the project deliverable is and why it was designed the way it was. Finally, the refreezing stage occurs when the organization helps the employees integrate the change into their normal way of working. This occurs in the operations period.

Common Project Vocabulary

Typical project teams include members from different backgrounds and parts of the organization (e.g., consultants, technical specialists, and business members). Each area of expertise represented by team members uses a different technical vocabulary. For example, an accountant in a manufacturing firm might consider the "end of year" to be June 30, the end of the company's fiscal year, but a sales representative might consider the "end of year" as December 31 when the frantic sales activity ends for a while. When used together in the team context, these different vocabularies make it difficult to carry on conversations, meetings, and correspondence.

To avoid misunderstandings, project team members need to commit to a consistent meaning for terms used on their project, and then record and explain them in its own common project vocabulary. The common project vocabulary includes many terms and meanings that are unfamiliar to the general manager and the team's other business members. To improve their communications with general managers, users, and other nontechnical people, technical people should limit their use of acronyms and cryptic words and should strive to place only the most critical ones in the common project vocabulary. Good management of

[27] K. Forsberg, H. Mooz, and H. Cotterman, *Visualizing Project Management,* 3rd ed. (Hoboken, NJ: John Wiley, 2005).

the common project vocabulary, project management, project team, and project life cycle are all essential to project success.

IT Projects

While many business projects involving IT, there continue to be some aspects of managing the IT in projects that require special focus. Sometimes managing the IT component of a project is referred to separately as an IT project—not only for simplicity's sake but also because the business world perceives that managing an IT project is somehow different from managing any other type of project. The IT project's leader is typically an IT person who works together with the business project owner. However, the more complex the IT aspect of the project is, the higher the risk of project failure. This makes IT projects worthy of special consideration.

The time and costs of IT projects are difficult to estimate despite the increasing amount of attention given to mastering this task. Like the case of the RPA's Single Payment system, most software projects fail to meet their schedules and budgets. Managers attribute that failure to poor estimating techniques, poorly monitored progress protocols, and the misinformed idea that schedule slippage can be solved by simply adding more people to the team. In *The Mythical Man Month*, Brooks point out the fallacy which assumes that people and months are interchangeable. In truth, if the project is off schedule, it may be that it was incorrectly designed in the first place, and putting additional people on the project just hastens the process to an inappropriate end.

The size of many more traditional IT projects is measured in terms of **function points**, or the functional requirements of the software product, which can be estimated earlier than total lines of code. Others are measured in "man-months," the most common unit for discussing the size of a project. For example, a project that takes 100 man-months means that it will take one person 100 months to do the work, or 10 people can do it in 10 months.

Managing projects using the man-months metric has been linked to more underperforming projects than those using any other metric of size (i.e., budget, duration, team size). Man-months may be a poor metric for project management because some projects cannot be sped up with additional people. An analogy is that of pregnancy. It takes one woman nine months to carry a baby, and putting nine people on the job for one month cannot speed that process. Software systems often involve highly interconnected, interdependent, and complex sets of tasks that rely on each other to complete a system. Further, adding people means that more communication is needed to coordinate all the team members' activities. In sum, additional people can speed the process in some cases, but most projects cannot be made more efficient simply by adding talent. Often, adding people to a late project only makes the project even later.

A now common way of speeding up the process of developing systems in IT projects is to use a range of tools including application development platforms (such as Mendix, mentioned in the Dutch Rail case—Case 11.2) and application programming interfaces (APIs) which are formally specified and well-understood ways in which apps can communicate with one another. Further, the cloud can be used in building scalable, portable applications with relative ease and/or for training and testing in AI applications. Some development platforms allow applications to be deployed to public, private, or hybrid clouds with as little as one click.

Projects vs. Programs

Program management is concerned with the integration of multiple project deliverables to maximize program-related organizational opportunities.[28] Many of the elements of program management are similar to those of project management (i.e., managers, sponsors, teams, plan, common vocabulary). However, there are differences. For example, for the program, having multiple sponsors in a project requires a lot more coordination and a reconciliation of different project goals than is typical when there is only one

[28] James Jiang et al. (2020).

sponsor. And, instead of one project team, multi-team systems (MTS) are now the norm. **Multi-team systems** involve two or more teams that work interdependently and directly interface with one another within a system designed to pursue at least one common superordinate goal (such as a program goal).[29] Further, the program plan, notably scheduling, becomes more complex because of pacing considerations and manifold interdependencies among the stakeholders.

There are other differences as well between projects and programs. The outcome of a program is often defined as anticipated business benefits, whereas project outcomes are clear deliverables. Success in programs is measured by the extent to which benefits are achieved vs. the assessments of project cost, time, and scope that often are used in assessing the success of a project. Further, programs have more flexible boundaries which makes it possible for them to capitalize on change whereas a project's narrower focus on meeting the budget and deadlines makes it more resistant to changes.

IT Project Development Methodologies and Approaches

The choice of development methodologies and managerial influences also distinguishes IT projects from other projects. The general manager needs to understand the issues specific to the IT aspects of projects to select the right management tools for the particular challenges presented in such projects. A very popular development approach is **agile software development**.[30] It is an iterative, incremental approach that allows development teams to respond to the unpredictability of building and implementing software. (See Figure 11.5 for a depiction of the iterative approach.) Its four core values and 12 principles are laid out in the Agile Manifesto.[31] Another iterative approach that is designed to give quick, high-level results is prototyping. We next introduce these two approaches. In addition, we provide an overview of a more traditional tool for developing IS or for implementing software developed by an outsourcing provider or software developer: the *Systems Development Life Cycle (SDLC)*. Many steps in the SDLC are used by other methodologies, although not to the same extent. For example, most other methodologies try to determine user needs and test the new system, even though these other methodologies do not perform all other steps in the SDLC.

Agile Software Development

One big danger developers face is expecting a predictable development process when in reality it's not predictable at all. The development process needs to respond to challenges created by dynamic customer demands and complex software requirements. In response to these challenges, agile software development methodologies are being increasingly championed. In a recent survey, 97% of the respondents said that agile was practiced somewhere in their organization.[32]

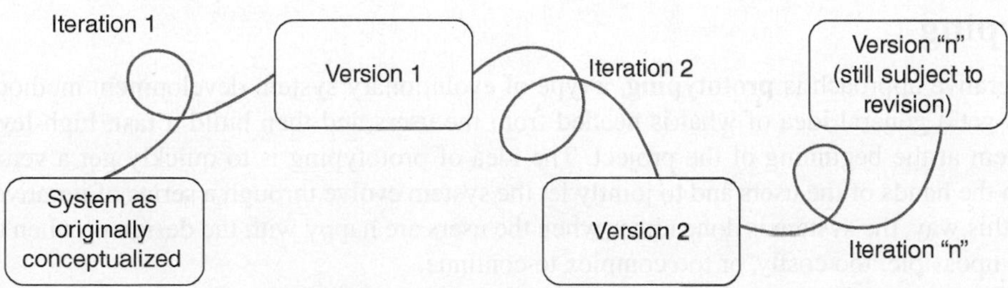

FIGURE 11.5 Iterative approach to systems development.

[29] S. J. Zaccaro, M. A. Marks, and L. A. DeChurch, *Multiteam Systems* (Routledge, 2012), 5.

[30] Henry Portman, "Review Standish Group – CHAOS 2020: Beyond Infinity.

[31] Manifesto for Agile Software Development, http://agilemanifesto.org/ (accessed August 11, 2023).

[32] Rashina Hoda, Norsaremah Salleh, and John Grundy, "The Rise and Evolution of Agile Software Development," *IEEE Software* 35, no. 5 (2018): 58–63, https://doi.org/10.1109/MS.2018.290111318.

To deal with unpredictability, agile methodologies tend to be people- rather than process-oriented. They adapt to changing requirements by iteratively developing systems in small stages and then testing the new code extensively. The mantra for agile programming is "Code a little; test a little." Agile methodologies are also characterized by more interactions with customers and frequent redesign to accommodate modifications emerging from the changing user requirements. They focus on speed and flexibility in development.

Multiple agile software development methodologies are in use, often in combination with one another. These include Scrum, Extreme Programming (XP), Kanban, Scrumban, Crystal, Lean, Rapid Applications Development, and Dynamic System Development Method (DSDM). The most popular is Scrum. In Scrum, software is delivered by cross-functional teams in increments called "sprints." Each sprint is usually performed in two to four-week iterations; it starts with planning, ends with a review, and includes every other system development life cycle phase in between. Part of the planning is done in a "time-boxed" sprint meeting which could last up to four hours. Other typical scrum meetings are sprint review meetings with project stakeholders and retrospective meetings to assess the teamwork in completed sprints. Scrum is especially known for its short daily meetings, say 15 minutes, in which team members communicate what they did the preceding day, what they are going to do that day, and what barriers they need to overcome that day. Scrum deliverables include product backlogs (requirements for the software product), sprint backlogs (tasks to be performed by the development team during the next sprint), and burn-down charts (cumulative work remaining).

Rapid Application Development (RAD) is often considered to be a form of agile development methodology since it is an interactive process that incorporates tools to drastically speed up the development process. RAD typically employs tools for developing the user interface. The user interface is often a **graphical user interface (GUI)**, which is a term used to refer to the use of icons, windows, menus, and pointing devices to interact with a computer. These tools make it easy for the developer to build a library of standard sets of code (sometimes call *objects*) that can easily be used (and reused) in multiple applications. Similarly, RAD systems typically allow developers to simply "drag and drop" many objects such as buttons, tables, menus, and drop-down lists into the design, and they automatically generate some or all of the code necessary to achieve the desired functionality. Finally, RAD includes a set of tools to create, test, and debug the programs written in the pure programming language and is thus useful for rewriting legacy applications. However, one must remember that "a fool with a tool is still a fool," and testing of designs with actual users will help flesh out problems with the design. Testing is crucial because designers do not always understand well enough the user's context or level of understanding of terminology peppered across screens in the system.

Although it allows speedy development and creates happy customers, there are some downsides to agile development. For large projects, it is difficult to estimate the effort that will be required. Further, in the rush to get the project completed, designing and documentation might be underemphasized. Also, an agile development project can easily get off track if the customer representatives are not clear about what final outcome they want.

Prototyping

Another iterative approach is **prototyping**, a type of evolutionary system development method in which developers get a general idea of what is needed from the users and then build a fast, high-level version of the system at the beginning of the project. The idea of prototyping is to quickly get a version of the software in the hands of the users and to jointly let the system evolve through a series of iterative cycles of design. In this way, the system is done either when the users are happy with the design or when the system is proven impossible, too costly, or too complex to continue.

Some IS groups use prototyping as a methodology by itself so that users can see the day-to-day growth of the system and contribute frequently to the development process. In other cases, prototyping is used as a phase in the SDLC or as part of Rapid Application Development to capture project requirements. Through this iterative process, the system requirements usually are made clear. Prototyping can also be used to assess project feasibility, such as when Bosch was considering the development of a platform that would inform drivers about potentially dangerous situations. Bosch built a lightweight platform with basic functionalities (e.g., showing how a wrong-way driver is detected and a collision is prevented) using agile principles. The prototype was able to demonstrate that the business model was viable, the opportunities associated with the business model were realistic, and potential users were willing to pay for the platform.[33]

There are several drawbacks to prototyping. First, documentation may be more difficult to write as the system evolves because of frequent changes over time. Second, users often do not understand that a final prototype may not be scalable to an operational version of the system without additional costs and organizational commitments. Once users see a working model, they typically assume that the work is also almost done, which is not usually the case. An operational version of the system needs to be developed using enterprise-level tools rather than desktop tools. In many cases, a system built with desktop tools can serve only one or a few users at a time. An enterprise-ready system can often serve hundreds or thousands of users simultaneously. Third, a seemingly operational version may be difficult to complete because users are unwilling to give up a system that is up and running, and they often have unrealistic expectations about the amount of work involved in creating an enterprise-ready version. This reluctance leads to the fourth drawback. Because it may be nearly impossible to definitively say when the prototype is complete, the prototyping development process may be difficult to manage.

A fifth problem with prototyping is caused by the difficulty of integrating across a broad range of requirements; this approach is best suited for "quick-and-dirty" types of systems. Developers should rely on a more structured approach such as the SDLC for extremely large and complex systems. Finally, because of the speed of development and reliance on a small number of people for quick (perhaps hasty) feedback, there may be flaws in the system's design.

Systems Development Life Cycle

The **Systems Development Life Cycle (SDLC)**, often called the *Waterfall Method*, is the set of activities used to create an IS, a process in which the phases of the project are well documented, milestones are clearly identified, and all individuals involved in the project fully understand what exactly the project consists of and when deliverables are to be made. The SDLC typically refers to the process of designing and delivering the entire system and typically is used in one of two distinct ways. On the one hand, it is the general project plan of all the activities that must take place for the entire system to be put into operation, including the analysis and feasibility study, development or acquisition of components, implementation activities, maintenance activities, and retirement activities. On the other hand, the term *SDLC* can refer to a highly structured, disciplined, and formal process for design and development of system software. In either view, the SDLC is grounded in the systems approach and allows the developer to focus on system goals and trade-offs. Documentation is provided throughout the SDLC.

The SDLC approach is a process-oriented approach that is much more structured than other development approaches, such as agile software development or prototyping. However, despite being a highly structured approach, no single well-accepted SDLC process exists. For any specific organization, and for a specific project, the actual tasks under each phase may vary. In addition, the checkpoints, metrics, and documentation may vary somewhat. That said, the SDLC typically consists of seven phases (see Figure 11.6).

Note that system construction or acquisition cannot begin until the requirements are specified, and the functional and technical designs are completed. After the new system is built or bought, it is tested, and users must approve it before the implementation phase can begin. The implementation phase is where the new system is put into operation, all links are established, users are trained, and users are trained and sign off on deliverables.

Also, note that implementation is not the final stage. The final stage is the maintenance and review stage in which periodic evaluations are conducted to ensure that the project continues to meet the needs for which it was designed. The system development project is evaluated using post-project feedback (sometimes called *postimplementation audit*) from all involved in the project. Post-project feedback brings closure to the project by identifying what went right and what could be done better next time. Maintenance is conducted on the system and enhancements are made until it is decided that a new system should be

[33] Hodapp, Daniel, Florian Hawlitschek, Felix Wortmann, Marco Lang, and Oliver Gassmann, "Key Lessons from Bosch for Incumbent Firms Entering the Platform Economy," *MIS Quarterly Executive* 21, no. 2 (2022), 3.

Period	Phase	Description	Sample Activities
STUDY	Initiation and feasibility	Project is begun with a formal initiation and overall project is understood by IS and user/customers.	• Document project objectives, scope, benefits, assumptions, constraints, estimated costs and schedule, and user commitment mechanisms • Plan for human resources, communication, risk management, and quality
	Requirements definition	The system specifications are identified and documented.	• Define business functionality; review existing systems • Identify current problems and issues, potential solutions • Identify and prioritize user requirements
	Functional design	The system is designed.	• Complete a detailed analysis of new system • Define security needs; revise system architecture • Identify standards • Freeze design
IMPLEMENTATION	Technical design and construction	The system is built, or a purchased system is customized and implemented.	• Finalize architecture, technical issues, standards, and data needs • Complete technical definition of data access, programming flows, interfaces, inter-system processing, conversion strategy, and test plans • Construct system • Monitor and control the development process • Revise scope, schedule, and costs, as necessary
	Verification	The system is reviewed and tested to make sure it meets specifications and requirements.	• Finalize all system testing, error-handling procedures, acceptance testing • Review all deliverables to user
	Implementation	The system is brought up for use.	• Put system into production environment • Establish security procedures • Deliver user documentation • Execute training and complete monitoring of system
OPERATIONS	Maintenance and review	The system is maintained and repaired as needed throughout its lifetime.	• Run system • Conduct reviews and evaluations • Fix errors and add new features

FIGURE 11.6 Systems development life cycle (SDLC) phases.

developed and the SDLC begins anew. The maintenance and review phase is typically the longest phase of the life cycle.

Several problems arise with using traditional SDLC methodology for newer IT projects. First, many systems projects fail to meet objectives even with the structure of the SDLC. The second and related reason is often because the skills needed to estimate costs and schedules are difficult to obtain, and each project is often unique so that previous experience may not provide the skills needed for the current one. Third, even though objectives that were specified for the system were met, those objectives may reflect a scope that is too broad or too narrow or has changed since the project was initiated. Thus, the problem that the system was designed to solve may or may not still exist, or the opportunity that it was to capitalize on may not be appropriately leveraged. Fourth, organizations need to respond quickly because of the dynamic nature of the business environment. Not enough time is available to adequately complete each step of the SDLC

Methodology	Advantages	Disadvantages
Agile development	• Good for adapting to changing requirements • Good for understanding and responding to changing user requirements • Allows face-to-face communication and continuous inputs from users • Speeds up the development process • People-oriented and liked by users	• Hard to estimate system deliverables at start of project • Underemphasizes designing and documentation • Easy to get project off track if user is unclear about what the final outcome should be
Prototyping	• Improves user communications • Liked by users • Speeds up the development process • Good for eliciting system requirements • Provides a tangible model to serve as basis for production version	• Often under-documented • Not designed to be an operational version • Often creates unrealistic expectations • Difficult-to-manage development process • Often difficult to integrate system components • More subject to design flaws than in SDLC
SDLC	• Structured approach with milestones and approvals for each phase • Uses a system approach • Process-oriented • Focuses on goals and trade-offs • Emphasizes documentation • Requires user sign-offs	• Often fails to meet objectives • Needs skills that are often difficult to obtain • Project scope may be defined too broadly or too narrowly • Very time consuming

FIGURE 11.7 Comparison of IT development methodologies.

for each IT project. The advantages and disadvantages of the agile development, prototyping, and SLDC approaches are summarized in Figure 11.7.

Other Development Methodologies and Approaches

A variety of other methodologies and approaches exist. These include user-centered design; object-oriented analysis, design, and development; and open sourcing.

User-Centered Design

User-centered design uses tools for RAD, JAD, agile software development, and prototyping to ensure that users' needs will be met. Early in the process, users are involved on the project team and are asked to: evaluate impacts on system utility, usability, organizational/social/cultural impact, and the holistic human experience. The goals of user-centered design are to improve efficiency and reduce effort; reduce or prevent errors; strive for a fit between the user's task, the information provided, and the format of the information provided; enable an enjoyable, engaging, and satisfying interaction experience; promote trust; and keep the design simple.[34]

The U.S. government maintains the website usability.gov, which provides about 200 design guidelines, such as "do not require users to remember information from place to place on a Web site" and "avoid jargon." Each guideline provides an assessment of importance and the strength of evidence that supports it.[35] Although it might be difficult to remember and follow hundreds of recommendations, heeding them will likely reduce frustration and confusion and perhaps save millions of dollars by reducing the amount of maintenance that could be needed.

However, the guidelines do not cover all possible ways in which to simplify design and engage users. Some of the most popular technologies from Apple, Microsoft, and Google demonstrate that incorporating usability into the design has great commercial value in the marketplace. Sometimes technological designs fail

[34] Dov Te'eni, Jane Carey, and Ping Zhang, *HCI: Developing Effective Organizational Information System* (New York: John Wiley, 2006).

[35] Usability.Gov. Research Based Web Design and Usability Guidelines, Department of Health and Human Services and General Services Administration, http://www.usability.gov/sites/default/files/documents/guidelines_book.pdf (accessed August 11, 2023).

at first but form the basis of very successful products as time goes on. For example, Apple's Newton boasted ground-breaking mobile device features but relied on hardware of its time—the early 1990s—and users found it slow with a dim screen and short-lived batteries. Twenty years later, better screens, processors, and batteries became available, and Apple tried again with an unprecedented successor to the Newton that also served as a phone, music player, and camera: the iPhone. It is obvious that when it was introduced the iPhone revolutionized not only the product category and the entire company, but also the entire electronics industry.

Research on usability and the user experience (UX) has been conducted for decades, but even today many systems are not very usable. For instance, websites sometimes use language in their links that is unfamiliar to users, and it is difficult to understand precisely where to click next. Search functions sometimes fail to unearth the desired results unless users know exactly what terms to use in their search. Artificial intelligence offers a new approach to better usability since systems can "learn" how users actually use the systems and adapt to preferences.

Object-Oriented Development

Object-oriented development is a way of avoiding the pitfalls of procedural methodologies. Object-oriented development, unlike more traditional development using the SDLC, builds on the concept of objects. An **object** encapsulates both the data stored about an entity and the operations that manipulate that data. A program developed using object orientation is basically a collection of objects. The object orientation makes it easier for developers to think in terms of modular, reusable components. Using existing components can save programming time. Such component-based development, however, assumes that the components have been saved in a repository or library and can be retrieved when needed and assumes that the components in the programs in newly developed information systems (IS) can communicate with one another.

Open-Sourcing Approach

Linux, the brainchild of Linus Torvalds, is a world-class operating system created from part-time hacking by several thousand developers scattered all over the planet and connected only by the Internet. This system was built using a development approach called open sourcing or building and improving "free" software by an Internet community. The brilliance of Linux is that Torvalds took a very powerful but proprietary operating system, Unix, and rewrote it to make it available as an open-source product. In fact, the kernel of Linux contains the statement, "Linux is a Unix clone written from scratch by Linus Torvalds with assistance from a loosely knit team of hackers across the Net."[36] Torvalds managed the development process by releasing early and often, delegating as much as possible, being open to new ideas, and archiving and managing the various versions of the software.

Eric Raymond, the author of *The Cathedral and the Bazaar*, suggests that the Linux community resembles a great bazaar of differing agendas and approaches (with submissions from *anyone*) out of which a coherent and stable system emerged. This development approach is in contrast to cathedrals in which software is carefully crafted by company employees working in isolation. The most frequently cited example of a cathedral is Microsoft, a company known, if not ridiculed, for espousing a proprietary approach to software development. However, Microsoft has now endorsed a movement toward open-source code in many of its projects. One example is the adoption of open XML file formats to replace the proprietary and secret formats in previous versions of Word, PowerPoint, and Excel files.[37]

Open-source software (OSS) is released under a license approved by the Open Source Initiative (OSI). The most widely used OSI license is the GNU general public license (GPL), which is premised on the concept of free software. *Free software* offers the following freedoms for the software users:

- To run the program for any reason you want
- To study how the program works and to adapt it to your needs and wishes, assuming you have access to the source code
- To distribute copies so that you can help others

[36] Vivek Gite, "Difference Between Linux and UNIX," June 7, 2021 https://www.cyberciti.biz/faq/what-is-the-difference-between-linux-and-unix/ (accessed September 29, 2023).

[37] Microsoft, "Overview of the XML File Formats in Office 2010," https://technet.microsoft.com/en-us/library/cc179190.aspx (accessed August 11, 2023).

- To improve and release your improvements to the public so that the whole community benefits, assuming you have access to the source code[38]

A user who modifies the software must observe the rule of *copyleft*, which stipulates that the user cannot add restrictions to deny other people their central freedoms regarding the free software.

Open sourcing is a movement that offers a speedy way to develop software. Further, because it is made available to a whole community, testing is widespread. Finally, in its most idealistic form, its price is always right—it is free. However, a number of managerial issues are associated with its use in a business organization.

- *Preservation of intellectual property:* The software is open to the whole community. It cannot be sold, and its use cannot be restricted. Thus, the community is the owner of the code. But how are the contributions of individuals recognized?
- *Updating and maintaining open-source code:* A strength of the open-source movement is that it is open to the manipulation of members of an entire community. That very strength makes it difficult to channel the updating and maintenance of code.
- *Competitive advantage:* Because the code is available to all, a company would not want to open-source a system that it hopes can give it a competitive advantage.
- *Tech support:* The code may be free, but technical support usually isn't. Users of an open-source system must still be trained and supported.
- *Standards:* Standards are open. Yet, in a technical world that is filled with incompatible standards, open sourcing may take a very long time to provide a viable strategy for its many organizations.

Applications written following the open-source standards were initially rejected by corporate IT organizations. Executives wondered how code that was free, open, and available to all could be counted on to support critical business applications. However, executives began to see the benefits of open-source code after OSI created a series of examples and case studies that highlighted the benefits. In addition to Linux, Android (Google's smartphone operating system), Mozilla (a popular web browser core), Apache (the most well-known web server), NGINX (the most widely-used web server), PERL (web scripting language), TensorFlow (for tasks with heavy numerical computations as in machine learning and deep neural networks), and PNG (graphics file format) are examples of very popular software that are based on open-source efforts. Advances in the applications available on the Internet are open sourced. Corporations are learning to manage the open-source process by more clearly stating their requirements and interfacing with developers on what typically begin as their noncore or least critical systems (those that, if copied, do not endanger the firm). Some companies are even paying programmers to work on open-source projects. Recent research found that paying programmers resulted in greater productivity in the short-term. However, continued contributions in the long-term were more often obtained from unpaid programmers who believed in the importance of contributing for altruistic reasons.

Many good references are available for systems development, but further detail is beyond the scope of this text. The interested general manager is referred to a more detailed systems development text for a deeper understanding of this critical IS process.

Managing IT Project Risk

IT projects are often distinguished from many non-IT projects on the basis of their high levels of risk. Although every manager has an innate understanding of what risk is, there is little consensus as to its definition. **Risk** is perceived as the possibility of additional cost or loss due to the choice of an alternative. Some alternatives have a lower associated risk than others. Risk can be quantified by assigning a probability of occurrence and a financial consequence to each alternative. Based heavily on the work

[38] GNU Project—Free Software Foundation, "What is Free Software?" https://www.gnu.org/philosophy/free-sw.en.html (accessed August 11, 2023).

of Applegate, McFarlane and McKenney, we consider project risk to be a function of complexity, clarity, and size.

Complexity

The first determinant of risk on an IT project is its *complexity level*, or the extent of difficulty and number of interdependent components. Several factors contribute to increased complexity in IT projects. The first is the sheer pace of technological change. The increasing numbers of products and technologies affecting the marketplace cause rapidly changing views of any firm's future business situation. Such uncertainty makes it difficult for project team members to identify and agree on common goals. Technical complexity increases in projects when it is decided to use new technologies or techniques in the development process that have not previously been used by the organization. An example is the introduction of AI into the development of an insurance claims management system by ELIS Innovation Hub described in the end-of-the-chapter case (Case 11.1). A dynamic external environment also creates uncertainties that make it hard for project teams to respond to unanticipated changes. Relatedly, the fast rate of change creates new vocabularies to learn as technologies are implemented, which can undermine effective communication.

The development of more complex technologies accelerates the trend toward increased specialization among project team members and multiplies the number of interdependencies that must be tracked in project management. Team members must be trained to work on the new technologies. More subprojects must be managed, which, in turn, means developing a corresponding number of interfaces to integrate the pieces (i.e., subprojects) back into a whole. In short, increased interdependencies, specialization, stakeholders, and subprojects make the project more complex.

Clarity

A project is risky if it is hard to define. *Clarity* is concerned with the ability to define the requirements of a system. A project has low clarity if the users cannot easily state their needs or define what they want from the system. A project also has low clarity if user demands for the system or regulations that guide its structure change considerably over the life of the project, or if there are no common goals, or even conflicting goals, across different project stakeholders.

A project with high clarity is one in which the system's requirements do not change and can be easily documented. A payroll package that calculates gross pay and deductions and then automatically deposits net pay into predetermined bank accounts is an example of a high-clarity project for most firms; each firm could likely use exactly the same package with minimal tailoring. In contrast, a project with low clarity would be one using AI to develop a chatbot which allows users to carry on a text-based conversation with reasonable facsimiles of natural conversations with a range of people from William Shakespeare to Elon Musk. Such software would have to navigate the anomalies of conversation in varying contexts and with often ambiguous meanings.

Size

Size also plays a big role in project risk. All other things being equal, big projects are riskier than small ones. A project can be considered big if it has the following characteristics:

- Large budget relative to other budgets in the organization
- Large number of team members (and, hence, a large number of man-months)
- Large number of organizational units involved in the project
- Large number of programs/components
- Large number of function points
- Large number of source lines of code (i.e., the number of lines of code in the software product's source file)

The relative size of a company also impacts on the available project budget. At a small company with an average project budget of $30,000, $90,000 would be a large project. However, to a major corporation that just spent $5 million implementing an ERP, a $90,000 budget would be peanuts.

Managing Project Risk Level

Risk management is usually a two-stage process: First the risk is assessed and then actions are taken to control it. The project's complexity, clarity, and size determine the level of risk. Varying levels of these three determinants differentially affect the amount of project risk. At one extreme, large, highly complex projects that are low in clarity are extremely risky. In contrast, small projects that are low in complexity and high in clarity have low risk. Everything else is somewhere in between.

The level of risk determines how formal the project management system and how detailed the planning should be. When it is difficult to estimate how long or how much a project will cost because it is so complex or what should be done because its clarity is so low, using extremely formal management practices or planning is inappropriate. A high level of planning makes it almost impossible in these circumstances because of the uncertainty surrounding the project and makes it difficult to adapt to external changes that are bound to occur. On the other hand, formal planning tools may be useful in low-risk projects because they can help structure the sequence of tasks and provide realistic cost and time targets.

Managing the Complexity Aspects of Project Risk

The more complex the project, the greater is its risk. A project is complex when there are a lot of functions or interconnected components involved. Rapid and unexpected changes in the project environment make for more complex projects, too. Additionally, the increasing dependence on IT in all aspects of business translates to greater risk, especially when untried, state-of-the art, or advanced technologies and techniques are embedded into business processes and systems. Managing the risk level of complex projects is critical to a general manager's job. Many companies now rely entirely on IT for their revenue-generating processes. For example, airlines depend on IT for generating reservations and ultimately sales. If the reservation system goes down, that is, if it fails, agents simply cannot sell tickets. In addition, even though the airplanes technically can fly if the reservation system fails, the airline cannot manage seat assignments, baggage, or passenger loads without the reservation system. In short, the airline would have to stop doing business should its reservation system fail. That type of dependence on IT raises the risk levels associated with adding or changing the system—or retaining hopelessly obsolete ones. A manager may adopt several strategies in dealing with complexity, including leveraging the technical skills of the team, relying on consultants to help deal with project complexity, and a host of internal integration strategies.

Leveraging the Technical Skills of the Team When a project is complex, it is helpful to have a project manager with experience in similar situations or who can translate experiences in many different situations to a new complex one. For projects high in complexity, it also helps to have team members with significant work experience, especially if it is related to similar technologies.

Relying on Consultants and Vendors Few organizations develop or maintain the in-house capabilities they need to complete complex IT projects. Risk-averse managers want people who possess crucial IT knowledge and skills. Often that skill set can be attained only from previous experience on similar IT projects. Such people are easier to find at consulting firms because consultants' work is primarily project-based. Consulting firms rely on processes that develop the knowledge and experience of their professionals. Thus, managers often choose to "lease" effective IT team skills rather than try to build them with their own people. However, the project manager must balance the benefits achieved from bringing in outsiders at the cost of not developing in-house the skill set that the outsiders have. When the project is over and the consultants leave, will the organization be able to manage without them? Having too many outsiders on a team also increases the difficulty of alignment. Outsiders may have different objectives, such as selling more business or learning new skills, which might conflict with the project manager's goal for the project.

Integrating Within the Organization Highly complex projects require good communication among the team members, which helps them to operate as an integrated unit. Ways of increasing internal integration include holding frequent team meetings and informal discussions, documenting critical project decisions, and conducting regular technical status reviews. These approaches ensure that all team members are "on the same page" and are aware of project requirements and milestones.

Managing Clarity Aspects of Project Risk

When a project has low clarity, there typically is ambiguity regarding goals and/or multiple interpretations about the goals among stakeholders. A project's low clarity may be the result of its multiple stakeholders' conflicting needs and expectations for the system. In such cases of low clarity, project managers need to rely more heavily on the users to define system requirements. It means managing project stakeholders and sustaining commitment to projects.

Managing Project Stakeholders To manage project stakeholders, the project manager must balance the goals of the various project stakeholders to achieve desired project outcomes. The project manager also must identify all project stakeholders, which is not always a simple task. They may be employees, managers, users, other departments, or even customers. Failure to manage these stakeholders can lead to costly mistakes later in the project if a particular group does not support the project.

Managing stakeholders' expectations and needs often involves both the project manager and the general manager. Project sponsors are especially critical of IT projects with organizational change components. Sponsors use their power and influence to remove project barriers by gathering support from various social and political groups both inside and outside the organization. They also prove to be valuable when participating in communication efforts to build the visibility of the project.

Sustaining Commitment to Projects An important way to increase the likelihood of project success is to gain commitment from stakeholders and to sustain that commitment throughout the life of the project. Research indicates five primary determinants of project commitment: project (e.g., a project with large potential payoff), psychological (e.g., a project associated with a previous history of success), social (e.g., stakeholders believe the project will be successful), organizational (e.g., executives strongly support the project), and cultural (e.g., project's organization has a culture of teamwork).[39] Project teams often focus on only the project factors, ignoring the other four because of their complexity.

By identifying how these factors manifest in an organizational project, managers can use tactics to ensure a sustained commitment. For example, to maintain commitment, a project team might continually remind stakeholders of the benefits to be gained from completion of this project. Likewise, assigning the right project champion the task of selling the project to all levels of the organization can maintain commitment. Other strategies encourage stakeholders, especially users, to buy-in so that they can help clarify project requirements. Examples include making a user or the project sponsor the project team leader; encouraging the project sponsor to provide public support for the project; placing key stakeholders on the project team; placing key stakeholders in charge of the change process, training, or system installation; and formally involving stakeholders in the specification approval process. Being involved in the project makes stakeholders more aware of the trade-offs that inevitably occur during a system implementation and perhaps more willing to accept the consequences of the trade-offs. In addition, being involved in the project allows stakeholders who are users to better understand how the system works and thus may make it easier for them to use it.

Pulling the Plug

The risk management strategies described here are designed to turn potentially troubled projects into successful ones. Often projects in trouble (like the Single Payments system described at the beginning of this chapter) persist long after they should be abandoned. Interestingly, this would be a case of sustaining too much commitment to a project. Research shows that the amount of money already spent on a project biases managers toward continuing to fund the project even if its prospects for success are questionable.

[39] See, for example, Mark Keil, "Pulling the Plug: Software Project Management and the Problem of Project Escalation," *MIS Quarterly* 19, no. 4 (December 1995), 421–47 and Michael Newman and Rajiv Sabherwal, "Determinants of Commitment to Information Systems Development: A Longitudinal Investigation," *MIS Quarterly* 20, no. 1 (March 1996), 23–54.

Other factors can also enter into the decision to keep projects too long. For example, when the penalties for failure within an organization are high, project teams are often willing to go to great lengths to ensure that their project persists even if that means extending resources. Also, a propensity for taking risks or an emotional attachment to the project by powerful individuals within the organization can contribute to the continuation of a troubled project well beyond reasonable time limits.

To ensure a timely demise to projects, metrics to identify problem projects should be established. For example, Bosch used platform engagement metrics for deciding whether or not to make big investments in a platform designed for users to book rides. Using various metrics, they found that although a goodly number of users registered, the platform engagement was low, and users seldom used the platform more than once. The former CEO[40] said: "We were able to show that there was no organic traction." Based on "concrete metrics" about letting go of projects, the decision was made to shut down the platform.

Gauging Success

How does a manager know when a project has been a success? At its start, the general manager who built the business case would have considered several aspects based on achieving the business goals. It is important that the goals be measurable so that they can be used throughout the project to provide the project manager with real-time feedback. The general manager probably also wants to know whether the system meets the specifications and project requirements set in the project scope, but measuring this is complex. Metrics may be derived specifically from the requirements and business needs that generated the project to determine whether the system meets expectations. Such metrics need to be based on the specific system, such as automating the order entry process or building an AI-based system to detect fraud in insurance claims.

Four dimensions that are useful in determining whether a project is successful are shown in Figure 11.8. The dimensions are defined as follows:

- *Resource constraints:* Does the project meet the established time and budget criteria? Was there a *schedule slip* (i.e., the current scheduled time divided by the original scheduled time)? Most projects set some measure of short-term success along this dimension that is easy to measure.
- *Impact on customers:* How much benefit does the customer receive from this project? Although some IT projects are transparent to the organization's end customer, every project can be measured on the benefit to the immediate customer of the IS. This dimension includes performance and technical specification measurements.
- *Business success:* How high are the profits and how long do they last? Did the project meet its return on investment (ROI) goals? This dimension must be aligned with the organization's business strategy.

Success Dimension	**Low Tech**	**Medium Tech**	**High Tech**
	Existing technologies with new features	*Most technologies new but available before the project*	*New, untested technologies*
Resource constraint	On time and on schedule	Overruns acceptable	Overruns most likely
Impact on customers	Added value	Significantly improved capabilities	Quantum leap in effectiveness and value
Business success	Profit; return on investment; payback period	High profits; market share	High profits and market share but may come much later; market leader
Prepare the future	Gain of additional capabilities	New market; new service	Leadership core and future technologies

FIGURE 11.8 Success dimensions for various project types.

Source: Adapted from Aaron Shenhar, Dov Dvir, Ofer Levy, and Alan C. Maltz, "Project Success: A Multidimensional Strategic Concept," *Long Range Planning* 34, no. 6 (2001): 699–725.

[40] Daniel Hodapp et al. (2022), 122.

- *Prepare the future:* Has the project altered the organization's infrastructure so that its future business success and positive customer impact are likely? The overall success of this strategy is measurable only in the future, although projects underway now can be evaluated on how well they prepare the business for future opportunities.

What other considerations should be made when defining the success of an IS? Is it enough just to complete a project? Is it necessary to finish on time and on budget? If other dimensions are important, what are they? The type of project can greatly influence how critical each of these dimensions is in determining overall success. It is the responsibility of the general manager to coordinate the company's comprehensive business strategy with the project type and the project success measurements. In this way, the necessary organizational changes can be coordinated to support the new information system. After the project is completed, post-project feedback should be elicited to ensure that the system meets its requirements, and its development process is a good one.

SUMMARY

- A general manager fulfills an important role in project management. As a project sponsor, the general manager may be called on to select the project manager, provide resources to the project manager, and give direction to and support for the project.
- The business case provides the foundation for a well-managed project by specifying its objectives, required resources, critical elements, and stakeholders.
- Project management involves continual trade-offs. The project triangle highlights the need to delicately balance cost, time, and scope to achieve the specified level of quality in a project.
- The four important project elements are project management, project team, project plan, and common project vocabulary.
- Many digital transformations are so complex that they require multiple projects being combined into a program. A *program* is a temporary organization "established to coordinate, command, and monitor a group of related projects, where the goal is to produce outcomes and benefits consistent with organizational strategic goals."
- The Project Management Office (PMO) brings focus and efficiency to project management activities.
- Understanding the complexity of the project, the environment in which it is developed, and the dimensions used to measure its success allows the general manager to balance the trade-offs necessary for using resources effectively and to keep the project's direction aligned with the company's business strategy.
- Agile programming is a very popular information technology (IT) project development methodology. Prototyping, and the Systems Development Life Cycle (SDLC) are more traditional methodologies, and new ones are constantly emerging. Each of these methodologies offers both advantages and drawbacks.
- In increasingly dynamic environments, it is important to manage project risk, which is a function of project size, clarity, and level of complexity. For low-clarity projects, interfacing with users and gaining their commitment in the project are important. Projects that are highly complex require leveraging the technical skills of the team members, bringing in consultants when necessary, and using other strategies to promote internal integration.
- Projects are here to stay, and every general manager must be a project manager at some point in his or her career. In that capacity, the general manager is expected to lead the daily activities of the project. This chapter offers insight into the necessary skills, processes, and roles that project management requires.

KEY TERMS

agile software development, 249
function points, 248
graphical user interface (GUI), 250
multi-team systems, 249
object, 254
open-source software (OSS), 254
open sourcing, 255
program, 243
program management, 248
project, 242
project management, 243
project management office (PMO), 244
project manager, 245
project plan, 246
project schedule, 246
project stakeholders, 242
prototyping, 250
rapid applications development (RAD), 250
risk, 255
systems development life cycle (SDLC), 251
user-centered design, 253

FOUNDATIONAL READINGS

L. Applegate, F. W. McFarlan, and J. L. McKenney, *Corporate Information Systems Management: Text and Cases*, 5th ed. (Homewood, IL: Irwin/McGraw-Hill, 1999). The ideas about Project Risk Management were derived from this source, but we used different names and expanded the application. We also used R. Schmidt, K. Lyytinen, M. Keil, and P. Cule, "Identifying Software Project Risks: An International Delphi Study," *Journal of Management Information Systems* 17, no. 4 (Spring 2001), 5–36 and H. Barki, S. Rivard, and J. Talbot, "An Integrative Contingency Model of Software Project Risk Management," *Journal of Management Information Systems* 17, no. 4 (Spring 2001), 37–69.

Frederick Brooks, *The Mythical Man-Month: Essays on Software Engineering* (Reading, MA: Addison-Wesley, 1982).

The GNU Operating Systems, What is Free Software? - GNU Project - Free Software Foundation (accessed August 11, 2023)

Kurt Lewin, "Frontiers in Group Dynamics II. Channels of Group Life; Social Planning and Action Research," *Human Relations* 1, no. 2 (1947), 143–53.

Eric S. Raymond, *The Cathedral and the Bazaar: Musings on Linux and Open Source by an Accidental Revolutionary,* 1st Edition (January 15, 2001) O'Reilly Media, Inc., oreilly.com

DISCUSSION QUESTIONS

1. What are the trade-offs between cost, quality, and time designing a project plan? What criteria should managers use to manage this trade-off?
2. Why does it often take a long time before troubled projects are abandoned or brought under control?
3. What are the critical success factors for a project manager? What skills should managers look for when hiring someone who would be successful in this job?
4. Since agile practices are based on a philosophy of close, frequent, and co-located collaborations, do you think that software development by global teams can ever be agile? Explain. If you think they can, what adjustments need to be made to the agile approach?
5. What determines the level of technical risk associated with a project? What determines the level of organizational risk? How can a general manager assist in minimizing these risk components?
6. Lego's Mindstorms Robotics Invention System was designed for 12-year-olds. But after more than a decade of development at the MIT Media Lab using the latest advances in artificial intelligence, the toy created an enormous buzz among grown-up hackers. Despite its stiff $199 price tag, Mindstorms sold so quickly that store shelves were emptied two weeks before its first Christmas. In its first year, a staggering 100,000 kits were sold, far beyond the 12,000 units the company had projected. Of Mindstorms' early customers, 70% were old enough to vote. These customers bought the software with the intention of hacking it. They wanted to make the software more flexible and powerful. They deciphered Mindstorms' proprietary code, posted it on the Internet, began writing new advanced software, and even wrote a new operating system for their robots. To date, Lego has done nothing to stop this open-source movement even though thousands of Lego's customers now operate their robots with software the company didn't produce or endorse and can't support. In fact, Lego actively supports the open-source

movement by providing source code on its site.[1] There is said to be some danger: software that others develop may end up damaging the robot's expensive infrared sensors and motors.[2]

(a) What are the advantages of Lego's approach to open sourcing?

(b) What are the disadvantages of Lego's approach to open sourcing?

(c) How should Lego manage the open-source movement?

Sources:

[1] John Baichtal, "Lego Mindstorms EV3 Source Code Available," *Makezine Blog*, August 2, 2013, http://makezine.com/2013/08/02/lego-mindstorms-ev3-source-code-available/ (accessed September 2, 2015).

[2] Lego, http://www.lego.com/en-us/mindstorms/downloads (accessed September 2, 2015) and Paul Keegan, "Intellectual Property Is Not a Toy," *Business 2.0* 2, no. 8 (October 2001), 90.

Case Study 11-1 Digital Transformation of Insurance Claim Management

Recently, forward-looking insurance companies have been digitalizing as many steps of the claims management process as possible. A major impetus has been cost reduction, often through increased efficiency and accuracy in processing claims and in reducing settlement timelines. In response to clients in its insurance market, ELIS Innovation Hub initiated an Artificial Intelligence (AI) project to explore the viability of anonymizing sensitive information on insurance claims. The ELIS Innovation Hub, which is a business unit of the Italian consulting company, CONSEL, has over 60 client companies and is committed to innovation, consulting, and training.

The AI project was viewed as the first step in an end-to-end digital transformation of the insurance claim management process to make operations more streamlined and personnel allocation more efficient. Other goals were to make the claim management process more effective in terms of time and accuracy, as well as more satisfying to customers because of its personalized and more secure services. Digitally transforming the insurance claims management process is especially complex when its intent is to have the customer take an active part in it and when AI deep learning technology is involved.

This particular project was designed to build a lightweight, scalable prototype (called a use case) that detects and removes sensitive data from claim images. The data needed to be anonymized to comply with the European Union General Data Protection Regulation (GDPR) and the process needed to be automated. Automating the process could shrink the average time to process claims from days to hours. The prototype was built using open-source software and an "over-the-top" cloud platform. It applied a deep-learning-based, six-step workflow developed by ELIS Innovation Hub:

1. *Problem setting:* The problem to be solved needed to be clearly defined from both a business and a technical point of view. The major problem was identifying sensitive objects in insurance claim forms. This involved the subtasks of figuring out which items were sensitive and specifying their location through a coordinate system. Sensitive data were defined to be license plates, people's faces and shapes, and vehicle identification numbers (VINs). Using the coordinates provided through localization, a box could be drawn around the sensitive data—which could then be blurred or removed from the image.
2. *Functional model analysis, selection, and evaluation:* This step focused on identifying algorithmic models for solving the problem and then selecting the one that best meets business objectives. The most appropriate functional architecture and relevant performance evaluation metrics needed to be identified and selected as well. The RetinaNet architecture was selected on the basis of performance accuracy, ease of implementing with Python TensorFlow and high-performance cloud platforms, and ability to handle class imbalance with the available data set through the "focal loss function." The focal loss function makes it possible to concentrate the algorithm design on learning from "real" data. The training and validation losses were selected as the in-process performance indicators, whereas post-process indicators included Recall and Precision. It was especially important to maximize Recall, to minimize false negatives (FN), and to reduce the need for humans in the process.
3. *Data preparation:* Data preparation involved Data Collection and Analysis, Data Annotation, and Data Organization. In Data Collection and Analysis, the data (i.e., 14,000 claim images from business units in several European countries) to be used in training and validating the deep learning model were already collected and available to the developers. The claim image data were analyzed to understand the distribution of classes within the dataset. In Data Annotation, the claim images were labeled for subsequent AI training and learning phases. The labeled data were entered into the Analytical Base Table for a detector model to process them during training. Annotations were done manually using an open-source software called LabelImg. During Data Organization, the data set was partitioned into separate training, validation, and testing sets that were fed to the deep learning architectures. Specifically, of the 6500 claim images with sensitive data, 70% were used for training, 25% for validation and 5% for testing. The training set was composed in such a way that the model could generalize image content and simultaneously be able to learn specific features for the sensitive objects to be recognized. The Data Annotation and Organization

Case Study 11-1 **(Continued)**

were carried out incrementally in batches until all collected image data were used. The manual annotation of the training and validation sets was the most time-consuming aspect of the project.

4. *Model set-up:* In the model set-up step, the underlying model was implemented and refined. In this AI case, a machine-learning algorithm to detect sensitive data in images was used. In particular, the convolutional neural network, designed according to the RetinaNet architectural framework, was trained on several samples of images, and its algorithm was fine-tuned.
5. *Model training, validation, and testing:* In this step, training, validation, and testing were repeated three times until the measured value for the most relevant performance metrics satisfied the insurance company requirements. The training sets were expanded with each interaction. The deep neural network architecture (ResNet-50) was used to extract sensitive features from the claim images for each class (e.g., person faces, VIN). To do so, weights were obtained from the API reference of Keras library that it could set up a statistical sample with a feature distribution that was representative of reality. Also, using the OpenCV Python library made it possible to blur (anonymize) the sensitive data.
6. *Model Deployment:* This step involved the creation of a proof of concept (PoC) for a visual web application that claimants could use. The web application employed a user interface that allows the claimants to upload their claim images. The web application relies on high-performing cloud platforms (e.g., Microsoft Azure, Google Cloud, or Amazon We Services) to deal with scalability, as well as model training issues.

After three training iterations, the prototype (use case) proved to be very sensitive and had an average Recall of 94%. This means that the prototype identified 94% of the actual positive (sensitive data) correctly. The average Precision over the various classes (mAP) was 83%, which was deemed satisfactory by the insurance company. Other metrics were also good. The prototype results were deemed good enough to demonstrate the viability of a digital transformation of the claim management process. It was concluded that the prototype might be a viable first step in digitalizing the entire claim management process.

Sources: Primarily adapted from Alessandra Andreozzi, Lorenzo Ricciardi Celsi, and Antonella Martini, "Enabling the Digitalization of Claim Management in the Insurance Value Chain Through AI-Based Prototypes: The ELIS Innovation Hub Approach," in *Digitalization Cases Vol. 2: Mastering Digital Transformation for Global Business*, edited by N. Urbach, M. Roeglinger, K. Kaurz, R. Alinda Alias, C. Saunders, and M. Wiener (Springer Nature Switzerland AG, Cham, Switzerland, 2021); See also Allesandra Andreozzi, R. Celsi, and A. Martini (2019). "Leveraging Deep Learning for Automated Image Anonymization in the Insurance Domain," R&D Management Conference, Paris; J. Kremer and P. Peddanagari. "How Insurers Can Optimize Claims," Ernst & Young, March 2, 2021, How insurers can optimize claims: Automation and humans in the loop | EY - US (accessed January 15, 2023); ELIS Innovation Hub, https://www.elis.org/eih/ (accessed January 14, 2023).

Discussion Questions

1. Compare and contrast the development methodology developed by the ELIS deep-learning-based, six-step workflow with the waterfall (Systems Development Life Cycle) methodology.
2. Was ELIS deep-learning-based, six-step workflow approach a good approach for this project? Provide a rationale for your response.
3. Discuss the advantages and disadvantages of developing a prototype in this case.
4. Assess the IT project risks in the prototype project described in this case. Were they managed well? Please explain.
5. Evaluate the prototyping project's measures of success.
6. Claims are often submitted by customers who have just undergone an emotionally stressful experience—an automobile accident. What could be done to enhance the customer experience when using the system? To what extent might end-to-end automation without any human in the loop on the side of the insurance company affect the customer experience?
7. What needs to be done now to achieve a digital transformation in an insurance company?

Case Study 11-2 A Tale of Two Scrum Projects at Dutch Railways (Nederlandse Spoorwegen)

Each day, 750,000 passengers complete their train journeys on Dutch Railways (Nederlandse Spoorwegen)—down from 1.3 million in 2019. It is important that these passengers have the most current information about train arrivals, departures, and connections in the network. That was the reason that Dutch Railways, which prides itself on 94.4% (2021) of its trains running on time, decided to build a system to provide travel information to its passengers in all Dutch train stations. Train departure times were stored centrally and updated with information entered manually or by sensors in the infrastructure. Dutch Railways decided to outsource the contract for building the system to an Indian company. The requirements for the new system (called PUB for publishing) were handed over to the outsourcing vendor that was expected to use the waterfall method with little customer involvement. This approach didn't work and after three years, the contract was cancelled because of vendor's inability to deliver a working system. Dutch Railways decided to outsource again—but this time to Xebia, a vendor that would use Scrum to build the system in close cooperation with Dutch Railway personnel. The PUB project was part of a program that involved many other related software projects tobuild and implement the displays in all stations across the Netherlands.

Given the problems that Dutch Railways had previously experienced with outsourcing, Xebia decided to have a three-week kick-off with a project manager, system architect, and Scrum Master to make sure that everything was set up correctly before the sprints started. But the problem of identifying a Product Owner became immediately apparent. Ideally, the Product Owner should be someone who has the necessary time, business knowledge, and authority to prioritize requirements. Lacking such a person, two Product Owners were appointed—business analysts who had been involved in the earlier attempt to build PUB. Unfortunately, the Product Owners did not know how to write user stories, so the Scrum Master helped them produce the initial product backlog with user stories to get started.

One seven-person Scrum team in the Netherlands started the project by agreeing on norms for working together and providing rough estimates for how long it would take to complete the required functions—estimates that would be used to communicate progress on the release burn-down chart. The project estimates were especially important because the project needed to meet program deadlines. Two Indian developers joined the Scrum team in the Netherlands on its third iteration (as soon as immigration and logistical constraints allowed them to do so) since it was known that Indian scrum teams soon would be added to the PUB project. The team in the Netherlands worked in two-week iterations called sprints. The early iterations allowed the teams to build, test, and demonstrate user stories at the core of the system, greatly pleasing the client, Dutch Railways.

After the fifth iteration, the two Indian developers returned to India and were joined by engineers to form two full Scrum teams. Eventually, there were three distributed Scrum teams, each with their own tester and with both Dutch and Indian teammates. The teams used daily Skype sessions, regularly scheduled travel, a project news gazette after every iteration, and informal updates by the Product Owner to communicate with one another and share knowledge. Their tools included ScrumWorks to manage the product backlog and sprint backlog electronically, burn-down graphs posted daily to a wall of the team rooms, and a computerized whiteboard. Pair programming was performed only with co-located pairs. A local Dutch Scrum team was created to deal with team barriers and perform specific customer facing compliance activities such as writing documentation in Dutch that was compliant with the waterfall (SDLC) documentation approach that Dutch Railways wanted to maintain and discussing requirements with technical stakeholders.

The Scrum Master had to modify the typical two-part Sprint planning meeting because the Product Owners wanted to speak Dutch. So, in the modified first part, the Product Owner clarified the user stories and set the priorities without the Indian team members being present. Then the second part was conducted in English over Skype without the Product Owners. The information from the first part was communicated to the Indian teammates in the second part and tasks to complete the user stories were identified and estimated.

Case Study 11-2 **(Continued)**

Dutch Railways was pleased with PUB when it was delivered: 100,000 Lines of Code reflecting 20 man-years of effort over a period of eleven months. Unfortunately, the nationwide deployment was hindered by other projects in the program that were not completed as planned. However, by 2023 electronic information displays had been installed on the platforms to tell passengers about the next train's destination and intermediary stops, delays (in 5-minute increments), and service cancellation if applicable.

It is hard to say that the PUB project was delivered "on time" and "on budget" since required functionality, deadlines, and budget shifted during the project. However, during these shifts, project success factors were discussed with the client. An external audit company concluded: "The maintainability of the systems is very good; The quality of the source code is very high."

A second Scrum project initiated during the COVID-19 pandemic was very different. In April of 2020, the Netherlands had just entered its first Covid lockdown and Dutch Railway's ridership had decreased precipitously to 10% of what it had been before the lockdown. Before the pandemic, railway cars were considered crowded if people were standing due to the unavailability of seats. But in April of 2020, passengers, concerned about COVID-19, found having more than four occupied seats meant that the car was too crowded to board. Drastic measures were needed. . . . And Dutch Railways decided to build a seat and bike spot reservation system in a short time period—about four weeks. It had to be a high-performing mobile app that was available on a 24/7 basis and capable of scaling up to be used by one million daily travelers. Other requirements were that it needed to be flexible to be able to respond to rapidly changing (biweekly) government measures, GDPR-compliant, and accessible to blind people and English speakers.

It was decided that the system would be built using the Mendix lo-code application development platform using a planner API (with available data about ridership) and a capacity management software in the Dutch Railway library. It was a complex project that required input from and collaboration among many different departments at Dutch Railway. Representatives from these departments met in a large room that allowed for social distancing. They participated in an intense design sprint over a two-day period to flesh out the specifications. The agile development (Scrum) started on day 3. Two Scrum sessions were held each day (instead of the typical daily one). Transparency in development progress was facilitated with a Scrum board that displayed both development tasks and alignment tasks. Usability (UX) and User interface (UI) experts at Dutch Railway were consulted and an external group of testers tested the software. Mendix's Application Performance Diagnostics was also used.

A pilot test with 8,000 participants was conducted to find bugs/bottlenecks and users were surveyed to get suggestions for improvement. Then the size of the user group was enlarged to include 500 daily bicycle spot reservations. Next, more users were reached through newspapers, TV, and radio outlets. An accessibility step provided an English version with a Mendix platform feature, application of web content accessibility guidelines (i.e., usability guidelines), and support for the visually impaired. The final step was a promotion campaign using digital advertisement, radio advertisements, and social media to get more users. And all of this was done in just four weeks!

Video: If you want more details about the project, view this 20-minute video—https://www.mendix.com/videos/digitalizing-customer-experience-in-4-weeks-with-dutch-railways/.

Sources: Adapted from Marco Mulder, "Case Study: Distributed Scrum Project for Dutch Railways," Infoq, August 12, 2008, https://www.infoq.com/articles/dutch-railway-scrum (accessed February 16, 2019); J. Sutherland, G. Schoonheim, and M. Rijk, "Fully Distributed Scrum: Replicating Local Productivity and Quality with Offshore Teams" in *2009 42nd Hawaii International Conference on System Sciences*, pp. 1–8. IEEE, January 2009; NS Annual Report 2017, pg 19, https://2018.nsjaarverslag.nl/FbContent.ashx/pub_1001/downloads/v180419111054/NS_annualreport_2017.pdf (accessed February 16, 2019); Scrum Case Studies, Dutch Railways, February 1, 2014, http://www.scrumcasestudies.com/dutch-railways/ (accessed February 16, 2019); Dutch Railways Guide | Rail Network Netherlands NS Trains Travel (amsterdamtips.com) (accessed January 24, 2023); Mendix. Digitalizing Customer Experience in four weeks with Dutch Railways. https://www.mendix.com/videos/digitalizing-customer-experience-in-4-weeks-with-dutch-railways/ (accessed January 13, 2023).

Case Study 11-2 **(Continued)**

Discussion Questions

1. Compare the development methodology employed by the Xebia PUB project with the waterfall (Systems Development Life Cycle) methodology. Was the Xebia PUB project approach a good approach? Provide a rationale for your response.
2. Describe some possible reasons that Dutch Railways selected Xebia as the outsourcing vendor to build PUB. (See Chapter 10 on outsourcing.)
3. Describe the challenges of using distributed Scrum teams. How effective do you think were the changes made to typical Scrum practices in the PUB project in addressing these challenges?
4. Compare and contrast the Scrum approach used in the PUB project with that used in the passenger and bike reservation mobile app project. Explain why they are different.
5. Discuss how program management differs from project management using both the development of the electronic information display system and the passenger and bike reservation mobile app as examples. Which is more difficult? Provide a rationale for your response.
6. Assess the PUB system that Xebia developed and the Scrum passenger and bike reservation mobile app project using the four dimensions of project success. How successful do you think each project is?

12 Business Intelligence, Artificial Intelligence, Knowledge Management, and Analytics

Business intelligence, artificial intelligence and analytics have become a source of strategic advantage for those firms who understand and develop skills to manage big data. Those skills are at the heart of digital business because of the importance of mining the abundant digital assets for value. We begin by understanding how to build capabilities in knowledge management, business intelligence, and analytics. Knowledge (both tacit and explicit) is then defined and discussed because it is the foundation of making better decisions. The four main processes of managing knowledge are then covered. Next, the chapter covers business analytics and big data amassed in data warehouses. Finally, the chapter takes a more technical turn, addressing the rapidly-developing areas of artificial intelligence, machine learning, and deep learning.

While Emily and John didn't know each other, both were young product managers at fiercely competing software firms in downtown San Francisco. Both also faced an overload of duties and tasks at work. They felt they were approaching crises from work–life imbalances, because their post-COVID firms had each suffered with diminished production after many retirements and layoffs took place. Their to-do lists only grew after long workdays that seemed to stretch far beyond eight hours, resulting in some late nights and missed events. They both looked for ways to increase their efficiency so they could reunite with their families.

Both had heard news reports about the use of chatbots, which were described as artificial intelligence (AI) "robots" that would answer questions, write essays and emails, detect trends, and even code computer programs. They were amused and intrigued by the news reports, as the second capability didn't even seem possible, and if chatbots could do a good job, they would be extremely helpful. But they shrugged off chatbots and resumed suffering in silence.

Both were required to write occasionally in their jobs, but thankfully not too frequently; each lacked confidence in their grammar and spelling abilities, and even more importantly, struggled with structuring a convincing and logical set of arguments. And in spite of their fears, both suddenly faced a troublesome task. On a Friday, just before an exciting family-oriented weekend, each had to write a report for a shareholder meeting about current technologies with future promise, requiring extensive research. The conflict between their important personal time, their striving for a promotion at work, and their writing issues were overwhelming. The notion of using a chatbot to write the report came right to mind.

They had never used AI before, but they decided to "play around" with it a little to see what it might suggest. A web search quickly revealed where to go and what to do, and after they typed a sentence or two with the report's requirements, they were stunned by the authoritative, well-written, and persuasive report that was generated. They each made a small number of edits and looked forward to a wonderful family weekend. They were thrilled with how much time and energy the chatbot saved them. They felt they had found the perfect solution to their overwhelming workloads.

Their bosses were equally pleased with the end products, as they expected extensive editing would again be needed, as before. However, the reports were so polished, there was no need for editing. And furthermore, the content was so time sensitive that both bosses had the reports posted on their company websites.

After a few happy weeks, the nightmare began. A social media comment proclaimed that the two reports were nearly identical. The writer called it plagiarism. Both Emily and John were promptly called into a meeting together with both CEOs, in an attempt to have one of them confess in front of the other. Unexpectedly, each stated nearly simultaneously that they used a chatbot to help write the reports. An IT technician verified their statements by using GPTZero, an AI detector created by Edward Tian, a college student at Princeton.[1]

Both Emily and John were warned to never again pass off a chatbot's work as their own. They were both passed over for a promotion, but given the newness of chatbot technologies, and the lack of rules preventing their use, they kept their jobs without any other sanctions. Their lesson: While chatbots can be helpful tools, they should be used with caution.

At this point, we need to disclose that a previous version of Mary's story was generated by ChatGPT using OpenAI.com,[2] and a previous version of John's story was generated by GPT4 using Bing Chat.[3] We asked both chatbots the following question: "Write a fictional story about a person at work who used a chatbot and then got into trouble for plagiarizing. The story should be about 2 pages long, double-spaced, and must include some surprises." We extensively re-wrote and combined the two stories, and added our own flair, but the chatbots got us started to provide an illustration of how these bots can work. We also guarantee that a chatbot was not used to generate any other content in this book!

Decades ago, technologies were used mainly to assist organizations to understand a firm's historical performance. More recently, technologies were found to make accurate predictions. For instance, Netflix used advanced analytics to "test" ideas for shows such as *Orange Is the New Black, The Queen's Gambit,* and *Umbrella Academy* even before they were filmed.[4] They also followed that model for testing *Stranger Things* and *Squid Games*.[5] And now, firms can use AI to *generate* ideas.

Enterprises have long sought a way to access the value locked inside the extensive data they collect and store about customers, markets, competitors, products, people, and processes. In today's business environment, external data sources and real-time data flows add opportunities for insight that might otherwise be missed. Algorithms and analytics programs are the way this value is unlocked and used to describe, predict, and prescribe future activity. Managers use these insights to make better decisions in virtually every corner of their business from marketing and customer management to supply chains, risk management, hiring practices, and research and development activities. New applications keep appearing as technologies improve, and there is no end in sight. The amount of data available to analyze will continue to explode, especially with the growth of the Internet of Things (IoT), fueled by rapid growth of smart devices connected to the web. By consulting large amounts of data on the Internet, chatbots can come up with ideas for firms and individuals alike. This chapter describes how organizations compete with analytics, then addresses basic concepts of knowledge management and AI. It also reviews the current thinking about business intelligence, artificial intelligence, business analytics, big data, and intellectual property.

Knowledge Management

Before the terms "big data," "analytics," and "AI" were all the rage, managers talked about knowledge management as a way to make better decisions. Managing knowledge is not a new concept,[6] but it has been invigorated by new technologies for collaborative systems, the emergence of the Internet and

[1] Bowman, Emma, "A College Student Created An App that Can Tell Whether AI Wrote An Essay," National Public Radio, January 9, 2023, https://www.npr.org/2023/01/09/1147549845/gptzero-ai-chatgpt-edward-tian-plagiarism (accessed May 6, 2023).

[2] Ortiz, Sabrina, "What Is ChatGPT and Why Does It Matter? Here Is What You Need to Know. ZDNet, April 18, 2023, https://www.zdnet.com/article/what-is-chatgpt-and-why-does-it-matter-heres-everything-you-need-to-know/ (accessed May 6, 2023).

[3] Truly, Alan, "Bing Chat: How to Use Microsoft's Own Version of ChatGPT, March 22, 2023. https://www.digitaltrends.com/computing/how-to-use-microsoft-chatgpt-bing-edge/ (accessed May 6, 2023).

[4] Mixson, Elizabeth, "Data Science at Netflix: How Advanced Data & Analytics Helps Netflix Generate Billions," March 30, 2021, https://www.aidataanalytics.network/data-science-ai/articles/data-science-at-netflix-how-advanced-data-analytics-helped-netflix-generate-billions, (accessed May 6, 2023).

[5] Engati Team, "Netflix Predictive Analytics: Journey to 220Mn+ subscribers, April 13, 2023, https://www.engati.com/blog/predictive-analytics (accessed May 12, 2023).

[6] The cuneiform texts found at the ancient city Ebla (Tall Mardikh) in Syria are more than 4,000 years old, representing some of the earliest known attempts to record and organize information.

intranets—which in themselves act as a large, geographically distributed knowledge repository—and the well-publicized successes of companies like Netflix that use business analytics. The discipline draws from many established sources, including anthropology, cognitive psychology, management, sociology, artificial intelligence, statistics, information technology (IT), and library science.

Knowledge management was the term used for many years to describe the processes necessary to generate, capture, codify, integrate, and transfer knowledge across the organization to achieve competitive advantage. Individuals are the ultimate source of organizational knowledge. The organization gains only limited benefit from knowledge isolated within individuals or among workgroups; to obtain the full value of knowledge, it must be captured and transferred across the organization.

Business intelligence can be considered a component of knowledge management. **Business intelligence** (BI) is the term used to describe the set of technologies and processes that use data to understand and analyze business performance.[7] It is the management strategy used to create a more structured approach to decision making based on facts discovered by analyzing information collected in company databases. While knowledge management includes the processes necessary to capture, codify, integrate, and make sense of all types of knowledge as described earlier, business intelligence is more specifically about extracting knowledge from data. Davenport and Harris suggest that **business analytics** is the term used to refer to the use of quantitative and predictive models, algorithms, and evidence-based management to drive decisions.[8] By this definition, business analytics is a subset of BI. Some, however, use the terms BI and analytics interchangeably.

Data, Information, and Knowledge

The terms *data*, *information*, and *knowledge* represent three levels of the hierarchy provided in the Introduction of this book are often used interchangeably but have significant and discrete meanings within the knowledge management domain (see Figure 12.1). **Data** are specific, objective facts, or observations, such as "distributor ABC bought 600 of our sweaters." Standing alone, such facts have limited intrinsic meaning. But key features of data are that it can be easily captured, transmitted, and stored electronically.

Information is defined by Peter Drucker as "data endowed with relevance and purpose."[9] People turn data into information in different ways. One way is by organizing them into some unit of analysis (e.g., dollars, dates, or customers), which helps interpret the data by giving it context. Another way is by combining related data to create relevance. For example, a customer's data such as name or address become information when combined with the average order size as well as orders from that customer over time because at that point, the combined facts give a different meaning than the individual facts alone. Extending the ABC example from above, knowing that an average distributor buys 800 sweaters annually provides context and adds meaning to the data about ABC's purchase of 600 this year. Also, knowing that

	Data	Information	Knowledge
Definition	Simple observations of the state of the world	Data endowed with relevance and purpose	Information from the human mind (includes reflection, synthesis, context)
Characteristics	• Easily structured • Easily captured on machines • Often quantified • Easily transferred • Mere facts presented	• Unit of analysis required • Data that have been processed • Human mediation necessary	• Hard to structure • Difficult to capture on machines • Often tacit • Hard to transfer

FIGURE 12.1 The relationships between data, information, and knowledge.
Source: Adapted from Thomas Davenport, *Information Ecology* (New York: Oxford University Press, 1997).

[7] Davenport and Harris, Competing on Analytics, p. 7.

[8] Davenport and Harris.

[9] Peter F. Drucker, "The Coming of The New Organization" (January–February 1988), 45–53.

ABC bought 400 sweaters last year and 200 sweaters the year before provides additional relevance and gives new purpose to knowing that the purchase was 600 this year.

Knowledge is a mix of contextual information, experiences, rules, and values. It is richer and deeper than information, and more valuable because someone has thought deeply about that information and added their own unique experience, judgment, and wisdom.[10] Continuing with the sweater example, the sales manager might know more about distributor ABC and therefore have some additional information or experiences that add value. The manager knows that this is a new distributor, one with a strategy to add additional retail outlets each year. Then the information put in a richer context indicates something very different than just the sales numbers alone. The sales manager knows that his or her company has an opportunity to grow as the distributor grows.

As we described in the Introduction to this book, wisdom is even more difficult to capture and process, as that begins to exceed our current technological capabilities, even with Artificial Intelligence.

The amount of human contribution increases along the continuum from data to information to knowledge. Computers work well for managing data but are less efficient at managing information. The more complex and ill-defined elements of knowledge (e.g., "tacit" knowledge described in the next section) are difficult if not impossible to capture electronically.

Types of Knowledge

Organizations possess large amounts of knowledge, but it is not always easily accessed. That knowledge exists in many different forms, places, and availability. Some of it is well-organized into stockpiles that can be searched from a keyboard, and some of it is disjointed and disorganized. Some of it exists in very high volume, called "big data" (discussed later in this chapter), and some of it is powerful but compact (like a secret formula for a soft drink). Some of it results from creative processes (like that secret formula), some of it comes from research (like best practices), and some of it is common knowledge (like chemical properties). It is important to be able to recognize the vast resources that are available, figure out how to organize them, and learn how to use them.

Tacit vs. Explicit Knowledge

Knowledge can be further classified into two types: tacit and explicit. **Tacit knowledge** was first described by philosopher Michael Polanyi with the classic assertion that "We can know more than we can tell."[11] For example, try writing, or explaining verbally, how to swim or ride a bicycle. Describe the color aqua to someone who cannot see, or the sound made by a piano to someone who has never heard one. Tacit knowledge is personal, context specific, and hard to formalize and communicate. It consists of experiences, beliefs, and skills. It is entirely subjective and is often acquired through physically practicing a skill or activity.

Information systems have traditionally focused on **explicit knowledge**, that is, knowledge that can be easily collected, organized, and transferred through digital means, such as a memorandum or financial report. Individuals, however, possess both tacit and explicit knowledge. Explicit knowledge, such as the knowledge gained from reading this textbook, is objective, theoretical, and codified for transmission in a formal, systematic method using grammar, syntax, figures, and the printed word. Figure 12.2 summarizes these differences.

Knowledge conversion strategies are often of interest in the business environment. Companies often want to take an expert's tacit knowledge and make it explicit or to take explicit, book-learning to their new hires and make it tacit. In their book *The Knowledge Creating Company*, Ikujiro Nonaka and Hirotaka Takeuchi describe four different modes of *knowledge conversion* (see Figure 12.3). The modes are (1) from tacit knowledge to tacit knowledge, called socialization, (2) from tacit knowledge to explicit knowledge, called **externalization**, (3) from explicit knowledge to explicit knowledge, called **combination**, and (4) from explicit knowledge to tacit knowledge, called **internalization**.[12] **Socialization** is the

[10] See a discussion about wisdom in the Introduction.

[11] Michael Polanyi, *The Tacit Dimension* (Chicago, IL: University of Chicago Press, 1966), 4.

[12] Ikujiro Nonaka and Hirotaka Takeuchi, *The Knowledge-Creating Company* (New York: Oxford University Press, 1995), 62–70.

Tacit Knowledge	Explicit Knowledge
• Knowing how to identify the key issues necessary to solve a problem	• Procedures listed in a manual
• Applying similar experiences from past situations	• Books and articles
• Estimating work required based on intuition and experience	• News reports and financial statements
• Deciding on an appropriate course of action	• Information left over from past projects

FIGURE 12.2 Examples of explicit and tacit knowledge.

From \ To	Tacit Knowledge	Explicit Knowledge
Tacit Knowledge	**SOCIALIZATION** Transferring tacit knowledge through shared experiences, apprenticeships, mentoring relationships, on-the-job training, "talking at the water cooler"	**EXTERNALIZATION** Articulating and thereby capturing tacit knowledge through use of metaphors, analogies, and models
Explicit Knowledge	**INTERNALIZATION** Converting explicit knowledge into tacit knowledge; learning by doing; studying previously captured explicit knowledge (manuals, documentation) to gain technical know-how	**COMBINATION** Combining existing explicit knowledge through exchange and synthesis into new explicit knowledge

FIGURE 12.3 The four modes of knowledge conversion.

Source: Ikujiro Nonaka and Hirotaka Takeuchi, *The Knowledge-Creating Company: How Japanese Companies Create the Dynamics of Innovation* (New York: Oxford University Press, 1995), 62.

process of sharing experiences; it occurs through observation, imitation, and practice. Common examples of socialization are sharing war stories, apprenticeships, conferences, and casual, unstructured discussions in the office or "at the water cooler."

Knowledge Management Processes

Knowledge management involves four main processes: the generation, capture, codification, and transfer of knowledge. **Knowledge generation** includes all activities that discover "new" knowledge, whether such knowledge is new to an individual, a firm, or an entire discipline. **Knowledge capture** involves continuous processes of scanning, organizing, and packaging knowledge after it has been generated. **Knowledge codification** is the representation of knowledge in a manner that can be easily accessed and transferred. **Knowledge transfer** involves transmitting knowledge from one person or group to another and the absorption of that knowledge. Without absorption, a transfer of knowledge does not occur. Generation, codification, and transfer generally take place constantly without management's intervention. Knowledge management systems seek to enhance the efficiency and effectiveness of these activities and leverage their value for the firm as well as the individual. But with the increasing introduction of new and more robust systems for managing and using knowledge, knowledge management processes are dynamic and continuously evolving.

Knowledge management processes can make use of external, robust search tools such as Google or Bing. Whereas traditional knowledge management systems had well-defined processes for generation, capture, codification, and transfer, technologies such as large data warehouses, ubiquitous websites, search tools, and **tagging** made it possible to capture and find information without those formal processes. Search engines, aided by machine learning (ML), AI, and natural language processing tools, have changed the way information is accessed, making it possible to quickly find virtually anything on any system connected to the Internet. Many reporters have spoken of replacing search engines with social networks, in the general population[13] as well as the corporate world.[14] These technologies have replaced traditional knowledge management systems and have given individuals the ability to find information traditionally locked within structures that had to be designed, managed, and then taught to users.

Value of Knowledge Management

Managing knowledge provides value to organizations in several ways as described in Figure 12.4. Organizations discovered how wasteful it was to approach the same problem over and over again with different personnel who had to "reinvent the wheel" time and time again.

Intellectual Capital and Intellectual Property

Valuable knowledge that has been captured and used by people within an organization becomes **intellectual capital**, an asset that can provide competitive advantage. That knowledge can address processes within an organization, secret recipes or formulas, or even expertise. Because it can provide competitive advantage, sometimes the knowledge that is captured can be of value to those in other organizations. Those parties might try to acquire it in some way, such as buying it, stealing it, or reverse engineering it (by studying it closely to discover how a product was made or how a service is performed). Intellectual capital is often considered the property of the organization, and when it is explicit, it is sometimes called **Intellectual Property** (IP), the term used to describe these creative and innovative information-based outputs.

Because intellectual property is information based, it differs from physical property in two important ways. First, information-based property is nonexclusive to the extent that when one person uses it, another

Value	Sources of Value
Sharing of best practices	• Avoid reinventing the wheel • Build on valuable work and expertise
Sustaining competitive advantage	• Shorten the life cycle of innovation • Impact bottom-line returns
Managing overload	• Filter data to highlight relevant knowledge • Organize and store data for easier retrieval
Rapid change	• Build on previous work to build agility • Streamline processes/build dynamic processes • Sense and respond to changes more quickly • Customize preexisting solutions for unique customer needs
Embedded knowledge from products	• Use smart products to gather product usage information automatically, enabling improvements through upgrades and fixes • Add value through intangibles such as fixing systems before customers know they're broken
Globalization	• Decrease cycle times for global processes because information moves faster than physical process components • Manage global competitive pressures • Provide global access to knowledge • Adapt to local conditions
Insurance for downsizing	• Prevent loss of knowledge when workers leave • Provide portability to enable workers to move between roles • Reduce time for knowledge acquisition

FIGURE 12.4 The value of managing knowledge.

[13] Kelly Huang, "For Gen Z, TikTok is the New Search Engine," September 16, 2022, https://www.nytimes.com/2022/09/16/technology/gen-z-tiktok-search-engine.html (accessed August 9, 2023).

[14] Stacey McLachlan and Christina Newberry, "22 Benefits of Social Media for Business," June 29, 2021, Available at https://blog.hootsuite.com/social-media-for-business/ (accessed August 9, 2023).

		Types of Protections[15]			
		Patents	**Trademarks**	**Design Registration (UK and EU only)[16]**	**Copyrights**
Strategies[17]	Defensive	Protect inventions	Protect brand identity	Protect product appearance	Protect artistic and literary material
	Collaborative	Develop an ecosystem	Identify and protect the partners	Make design improvements together	Subdivide credit clearly to the source of the art
	Impromptu	Failure to prevent unexpected copies	Failure to prevent counterfeit products	Failure to prevent knockoffs	Failure to secure artistic and literary material

FIGURE 12.5 Intellectual property types and strategies.

Sources: Adapted from Intellectual Property Office, U.K., "Types and Uses of Intellectual Property: Detailed Information," https://www.gov.uk/topic/intellectual-property/intellectual-property-types (accessed May 12, 2023); see also Grimaldi, M., Greco, M., and Cricelli, L., "A Framework of Intellectual Property Protection Strategies and Open Innovation." *Journal of Business Research*, 123, (2021): 156–64, https://doi.org/10.1016/j.jbusres.2020.09.043.

person can use it without degradation or loss of quality. Consider an MP3 music file that can easily be copied and shared with another without losing the original property. Second, unlike the cost structure of physical property, the marginal cost of producing additional copies of information-based property is negligible compared with the cost of original production. These factors create differences in the ethical treatment of physical and information-based intellectual property. The economics of information vs. the economics of physical property is further explored in the Introduction of this text.

The protections available for intellectual property make it possible for owners to be rewarded for the use of their ideas and it allows them to have a say in how their ideas are used. To protect their ideas, owners typically apply for and are granted intellectual property rights. In some cases, as soon as a record is made of what has been created, the owner can expect some protection automatically. An owner only needs to declare ownership and mark the ideas appropriately.

A framework we created by combining two models can be helpful to understand intellectual property protection (Figure 12.5). We plotted the types of protections against three strategies to follow, so management can be aware of the combinations of these concepts and then act accordingly.

The U.S. Congress continues to propose and discuss ways to protect intellectual property, particularly from piracy of online materials by sites and companies outside of U.S. jurisdiction. The U.S. government also has additional organizations to monitor and manage these issues. The Executive Office of the President of the United States oversees the Office of the U.S. Trade Representative, which annually reviews the state of intellectual property rights protection and enforcement with global trading partners. It publishes the "Special 301" report annually to share the status of intellectual property management around the world.[18]

But management of intellectual property is a concern not only to the U.S. government. On May 25, 2018, the EU implemented the General Data Protection Regulation (GDPR). The GDPR sets up laws on data protection and privacy for all individuals within the European Union, including its residents who travel outside the EU. Large penalties are specified for those organizations who violate the regulations, and every business with even a single customer in the EU must make changes to accommodate this regulation. GDPR and its wide-ranging global impact are described further in Chapter 13. In 2014, the United Kingdom passed the Intellectual Property Act of 2014,[19] introducing criminal liability and penalties for infringing on registered designs and specifying processes for determining ownership in some situations.

[15] Intellectual Property Office, U.K., "Types and Uses of Intellectual Property: Detailed Information," https://www.gov.uk/topic/intellectual-property/intellectual-property-types (accessed May 12, 2023).

[16] In the USA, designs are protected by patents.

[17] Grimaldi, M., Greco, M., & Cricelli, L., "A framework of intellectual property protection strategies and open innovation," *Journal of Business Research*, 123, (2021): 156–64, https://doi.org/10.1016/j.jbusres.2020.09.043.

[18] For more information on intellectual property and the Special 301 report for 2023, see Office of the U.S. Trade Representative, https://ustr.gov/sites/default/files/2023-04/2023%20Special%20301%20Report.pdf (accessed May 23, 2023).

[19] http://www.legislation.gov.uk/ukpga/2014/18/contents/enacted (accessed May 23, 2023).

The Australian Parliament passed a similar bill, the Intellectual Property Laws Amendment Bill 2014, which also clarified earlier IP and patent protection laws.[20] The World Intellectual Property Organization (WIPO), an agency of the United Nations, has 193 member states and works with governments to "lead the development of a balanced and effective international intellectual property system that enables innovation and creativity for the benefit of all."[21]

Business Analytics and Business Intelligence

Knowledge management can serve as a foundation for more than simply making knowledge more visible or available. Yes, it is important to find and share the knowledge internally, but sometimes managers have trouble making sense of what could be vast storehouses of knowledge. Business analytics and business intelligence can make knowledge more vivid and understandable, at least inside the enterprise, so it can be analyzed and acted upon to meet business objectives.

Business Analytics

Tools used for business analytics use data to identify trends and environmental changes and then create predictions that inform business strategy and long-term goal setting. The tools can provide tables, charts, and graphs that allow the user to see details, trends, and comparisons at multiple levels of detail. An analyst can examine results of the company as a whole, a particular division (such as food products), a particular product line (such as frozen vegetables), or a particular product (such as broccoli florets). Also, the analyst can see changes over a requested time period, and measure impacts of ad programs, temporary discounts, or coupons.

Measuring impacts of those events requires statistical tools to see how the events rise above the typical unsystematic, random variation over time. The tools also can perform statistical analysis that makes predictions for the future given a combination of ads and discounts, in light of seasonal and demographic fluctuations that have been recorded.

Examples are provided in the section of this chapter called "Competing with Business Analytics."

Business Intelligence

In the past, traditional BI meant providing real-time, easy-to-use dashboards and reports to assist managers in monitoring key performance metrics. Common elements of BI systems included reporting, querying, dashboards, and scorecards. Dashboards, described in Chapter 8, tend to be simple, online displays of key metrics, often graphically displayed in pie charts, bar charts, red-yellow-green coded data, and other images that easily convey both the value of the metric and, with color coding, indicating whether the metric is within acceptable parameters. Traditional BI was useful for strategic, tactical, and operational decisions, but they were limited by requiring heavily processed and summarized data. Also, if the designers of the system did not anticipate some of the questions that a manager might ask, the system would need to be rewritten or changed, imposing long delays on providing answers to each question.

More modern BI systems of today still provide those features, but also tend to incorporate several additional characteristics and capabilities. Some function as a service in the cloud. Others are event driven, offer instant access to real-time information, and provide dynamically created reports that "mash up" or combine streaming data, internal data sources, and external data sources. It is also common to find systems that enable mobile/ubiquitous access.

These and other newer technologies have enabled BI to move to a new level with robust user interfaces and powerful visualization and analytics tools. Algorithms are much more sophisticated than ever before,

[20] http://www.aph.gov.au/Parliamentary_Business/Bills_Legislation/Bills_Search_Results/Result?bId=r5192 (accessed May 23, 2023) and https://consultation.ipaustralia.gov.au/policy/streamlining-bill/ (accessed May 23, 2023).

[21] WIPO - World Intellectual Property Organization, https://www.wipo.int/portal/en/index.html (accessed August 9, 2023).

giving managers more accurate, timely, and helpful insights. Crowdsourcing allows creation of data structures and report designs by a community rather than by a single designer. Data and reports are infused with narratives from the users to provide richer context. Dynamic capabilities in the BI system allow for exceptions, alerts, and notifications that change based on what the system learns from the data, which is enabled by AI and machine learning (ML) tools. Those applications predict more realistic and more reliable outcomes than static information charts. A manager who sees something in the data that requires an intervention is able not only to perform it but also to tag it and link it with the data so that the collective knowledge grows over time.

Competing with Business Analytics

In recent years, many companies have found success competing through better use of analytics. Companies have used analytics to improve on their otherwise lackluster business results to become industry leaders, such as when Netflix used a very reliable, complex "recommendation algorithm" for judging the qualities of movies, even before they are filmed. Caesars Entertainment, the largest gaming company in the world by multiple measures, found a way to more than double revenues by collecting and analyzing customer data. The casinos have information on customer preferences down to how long one plays a slot machine, what time they like to visit the buffet, and how much they spend at the Blackjack table. This information enables the company to customize offers that appeal to customers and increase the bottom line. Their analytics capabilities were valued at a billion dollars for Caesars Entertainment.[22]

Sports teams have propelled themselves to league success through business analytics. The systematic use of factual data in proprietary models is credited with helping the Oakland As and the Boston Red Sox. As seen in the movie, *Moneyball*, Billy Beane was one of the first general managers in Major League Baseball to build his organization, the Oakland As, around analytics. Although this industry collected data extensively, it was mostly used to manage the game in process. The Oakland As used data on things that it could measure such as the on-base percentage (the number of times a player gets on base) instead of softer criteria such as estimating the effort the player is willing to put in. The Oakland As used analytics in its recruiting efforts to predict which young players had the best chances of becoming major league players and hired players that other teams overlooked at salaries that were much more affordable. This strategy paid off, consistently carrying the Oakland As to the playoffs despite a budget for player's salaries that was a fraction of what some of its competitors had.

An interesting website offered by Tableau allows anyone to learn how all of the major teams performed over a 15-year period.[23] The site allows you to visualize how the payroll relates to the number of wins and to see how many titles were won across the years or in any specific year. Bar charts, axis plots, and color coding can provide easy-to-use entertainment and useful research for a baseball fan. The site shows that only the Oakland As consistently won more than average while spending less than average. This is persuasive evidence for competing through analytics and the evidence for this assertion can ironically only be detected through proper analytical tools. Otherwise, the amount of manual computation that would be required would be too time-consuming and confusing.

At least two media firms have found competitive advantage using analytics. Pandora created an early stir when they created a new way to understand music, which they trademarked as their "Music Genome project,"[24] launched back in 2000. The project developed hundreds of different characteristics found in music, such as what instruments are used, the tempo of the music, and how a singer's voice sounds.[25] They also assess the joyfulness of the lyrics, dominance of the vocals, gospel influence, and many other items. Spotify was unable to precisely mimic this approach, resulting in much repetition when streaming music.[26]

One reason for the rise in companies competing on analytics is that numerous companies in many industries offer similar products and use comparable technologies. Therefore, business processes are among the

[22] Bernard Marr, "Big Data at Caesars Entertainment – A One Billion Dollar Asset?" *Forbes,* May 18, 2015, https://www.forbes.com/sites/bernardmarr/2015/05/18/when-big-data-becomes-your-most-valuable-asset/?sh=112f8b651eef (accessed May 23, 2023).

[23] https://public.tableau.com/app/profile/walter.allen/viz/15YearsofMoneyball/Story1 (accessed May 8, 2023).

[24] https://www.pandora.com/about/mgp (accessed August 9, 2023).

[25] Amanda Modell, "Mapping the Music Genome: Imaginative Geography in Pandora Internet Radio and the Genographic Project," *Media Fields Journal, 10* (2015).

[26] Pelle Snickars, "More of the Same – On Spotify Radio," *Culture Unbound: Journal of Current Cultural Research,* 9, no. 2 (2017): 184–211, https://doi.org/10.3384/cu.2000.1525.1792184. 184–211.

last remaining points of differentiation, and analytic competitors are wringing every last drop of value from those processes.[27] Business analytics fuel fact-based decision making. For example, a company may use simple inventory reports to figure out what products are selling quickly and which are moving slowly, but a company that uses analytics also knows who buys them, what price each customer pays, how many items the customer will likely purchase in a lifetime, what motivates each customer to purchase, and which incentives to offer to increase the revenue from each sale.

According to a study by consulting firm McKinsey and Company, there are five ways big data and analytics can help an organization[28]:

- Making information more transparent and usable at a frequency that outpaces the competition.
- Exposing variability and boosting performance by collecting and analyzing more transactional and performance data.
- More precisely tailoring products and services using better-designed segmentation and large data samples.
- Improving decision making through experiments, forecasting and feedback, and just-in-time analysis.
- Developing the next generation of products and services more quickly using sensor data to collect after-sales information on product usage, performance, and other valuable issues.

Components of Business Analytics

To successfully build business analytics capabilities in the enterprise, companies make a significant investment in their technologies, their people, and their strategic decision-making processes. Four components are needed (see Figure 12.6).

Data Sources

In the past, data used in the analytical processes originated from various sources and were stored in corporate databases, usually as tables of data in a very structured format. A customer database contains several pieces of data such as name, account number, and address. These pieces can help create a coherent picture of business conditions at a single point in time. Much of the data used by the organization are generated internally and capture operational and financial information. Other data can be gathered from external sources, such as a competitor's public activities, weather patterns, and economic trends. Because the information in these data sources is clear and easily categorized into databases, it is called **structured data**.

Component	Definition	Example
Data sources	Data streams and repositories	Data warehouses; weather data
Software tools	Applications and processes for statistical analysis, forecasting, predictive modeling, and optimization	Data-mining process; forecasting software package
Data-driven environment	Organizational environment that creates and sustains the use of analytics tools	Reward system that encourages the use of the analytics tools; willingness to test or experiment
Skilled workforce	Workforce that has the training, experience, and capability to use the analytics tools	Data scientists, chief data officers, chief analytics officers, analysts, etc.

FIGURE 12.6 Components of successful business analytics programs.

[27] Pelle, 2017.

[28] James Manyika et al., "Big Data: The Next Frontier for Innovation, Competition, and Productivity," May 2011, https://www.mckinsey.com/capabilities/mckinsey-digital/our-insights/big-data-the-next-frontier-for-innovation (accessed September 5, 2015).

Other data, such as conversations, posts on Twitter/X, and videos, are considered **unstructured data**. These data sources have information embedded in them, but work needs to be done to extract the useful information. Other examples of unstructured data are the data in blogs, e-mails, documents, photos, audio files, presentations, web pages, and other similar files. A single unstructured data file might contain multiple items of interest. When data are taken out of the context of the original file, they lose some of their meaning. The common characteristic of these data sources is that the data are not easily put into a tabular or other structured format and therefore do not fit neatly into a database.

Data warehouses, or collections of data designed to support management decision making, sometimes serve as repositories of a collection of an organization's databases. The warehouses are centralized so all the organization's departments can access the data and store new data in formats that are easily used by others. Data warehouses traditionally have held structured data, but today, there are multiple examples of data warehouses that manage large collections of unstructured data. Another type of data storage is the **data lake**, which refers to a storage technology that doesn't attempt to organize data, but rather just stores it in "raw" form for future analysis or other use.

Real-time data sources are another type of data stream that companies use in their analytics program. Many people have seen stock prices flow across a screen for financial traders. This is a type of real-time data. A recent trend is to make use of IoT data sources, which employ sensors to detect physical data such as GPS location, traffic congestion, vehicle speed, weather conditions, or a patient's heart rate, and transmit the data to an information system that automatically and continuously stores and analyzes them. As the information can change dramatically from minute to minute, systems, as discussed below, can assess the situation in real time and recommend action, or even respond automatically, to prevent problems or take advantage of opportunities. Modern analytics programs use real-time data streams in their algorithms.

Software Tools

At the core of business analytics are the tools. An approach used to extract information from data sources is **data mining**, which is the process of analyzing data warehouses and other sources for "gems" that can be used in management decision making. The term typically refers to the process of combing through massive amounts of customer data to understand buying habits and to identify new products, features, and enhancements. It also identifies previously unknown relationships among data. The analysis may help a business better understand its customers by answering such questions as these: Which customers prefer to contact us via a chat app instead of through a call center? How are customers in Location X likely to react to the new product that we will introduce next month?

Using data mining to answer such questions helps a business reinforce its successful practices and anticipate future customer preferences. For example, *The New York Times* reported that by using data mining, Walmart uncovered the surprising fact that when a hurricane is predicted, its Florida customers stocked up on beer and strawberry pop tarts. It now initiates quick shipments to its stores when hurricanes are on the horizon so that plenty of these two items are stocked should the hurricane become a more tangible threat.[29]

Four categories of tools are typically included under the business analytics umbrella.[30] They include the following:

1. *Statistical analysis:* Descriptive analysis which answers questions such as "What is happening?"
2. *Forecasting/Extrapolation:* Prescriptive analysis, which answers questions such as "What should we do if these trends continue?"
3. *Predictive modeling:* Predictive analysis, which answers questions such as "What will happen next?"
4. *Optimization:* Answers questions such as "What is the best that can happen?"

These tools are used with the data in the data warehouse to gain insights and support decision making.

[29] Constance Hays, "What Walmart Knows about Customers' Habits," *The New York Times*, November 14, 2004, https://www.nytimes.com/2004/11/14/business/yourmoney/what-walmart-knows-about-customers-habits.html (accessed August 9, 2023).

[30] Davenport and Harris; Hays, 2004.

Data-Driven Environment

A **data-driven culture**, an environment that supports and requires analytics, is a critical factor for success. Frequently now the data-driven business strategy and IS strategy are one and the same, and the organizational strategy must be aligned with them. Executives demand that staff provide not only a decision or recommendation but also the data to support it. Gone are the days of just evaluating results at the end of a financial period. In a data-driven culture, staff use data streams to continually evaluate and make corrections in midcourse.

To achieve a data-driven organization, there must be alignment of the corporate culture, the incentive systems, the metrics used to measure success of initiatives, and the processes for using analytics with the objective of building a competitive advantage through analytics. As an example of aligning organizational strategy with a business strategy promoting the use of analytics to gain competitive advantage, one financial services firm encouraged the use of analytics by changing its appraisal system. Employees demonstrating skills in applying analytics reaped rewards in their paychecks.

Those companies who gain competitive advantage from analytics use these capabilities in mainstream decision making and strategy formulation, as well as an integral component of their business. Companies such as GE, Procter and Gamble, Walmart, Chevron, and HP routinely expect data-driven decision making and have built strong analytics capabilities into their teams to expand the use of data in decision making.

Leadership plays a big role in creating a strong analytics environment. Leaders must move the company's culture toward an **evidence-based management** approach in which evidence and facts are analyzed as the first step in decision making. Those in this type of culture are encouraged to challenge others by asking for data support, and when no data are available, to experiment and learn how to generate facts. Use of evidence-based management encourages decisions based on data and analysis rather than on only experience and intuition.

Skilled Workforce

It's clear that to be successful with analytics, data and technology must be used. But experts point out that even with the best data and the most sophisticated analytics, people must be involved. Managers must be able to leverage their knowledge of analytics to improve decision making and ask the right questions, so the analytics performed give the best answers. Leaders must set examples for the organization by using analytics and requiring that decisions made by others use that process. Perhaps the most important role is sponsorship. Davenport and Harris point out that it was the CEO-level sponsorship and the corresponding passion for analytics that enabled firms such as Caesars Entertainment[31] and Netflix[32] to achieve the successes they enjoyed.

Although leadership is important and general management and staff must be data driven, the staff must also have analytics experts. A key role for a successful analytics program is the **data scientist**, a professional who can skillfully blend art and science. The art is the use of judgment to recognize how data can be used to solve a business problem. The science is how properly visualizing the data and using statistical testing to examine the data rigorously can extract the appropriate information for making a decision.

Leading the analytics program is often a chief analytics officer (CAO) and chief data officer (CDO). As the name implies, the **chief analytics officer (CAO)** is the individual at the helm of the analytics activities of an organization. Organizations typically create a center of excellence for analytics capabilities that operates as a shared service of expertise. The CAO would be the leader of this center. Increasingly more popular is a **chief data officer (CDO)**, the lead executive responsible for the data assets owned and used by the organization. The CDO has the responsibility for the data warehouse, organizational databases, relationships with vendors who supply external data sources, and sometimes the algorithms that use these data sources. The CDO has responsibility for all aspects of the data from collection or generation to storage, usage, and disposal.

---

[31] Bernard Marr, "Big Data at Caesars Entertainment – A One Billion Dollar Asset?" *Forbes,* May 18, 2015, https://www.forbes.com/sites/bernardmarr/2015/05/18/when-big-data-becomes-your-most-valuable-asset/?sh=112f8b651eef (accessed May 23, 2023).

[32] Davenport and Harris, Competing on Analytics.

Levels of Analytical Capabilities

All businesses collect data, but some do a better job than others at capturing and using it, creating a potent source of competitive advantage. Companies tend to fall into one of five levels of analytical capabilities, with each level adding to the lower levels. Understanding the different levels can help organizations envision how to improve their capabilities to gain additional advantages. Figure 12.7 summarizes these levels.

Social Media Analytics

Managers have seen a rise in interest in using social IT that can be attributed to the increase in the number and ease of ways to mine the rich data sets using a class of tools called **social media analytics**. The goal of social media analytics is to measure the impact of social IT investments on a business. At issue, however, is how to analyze conversations, tweets, blogs, and other unstructured social IT data to create meaningful, actionable information from statements of preferences and emotions. For example, it might be relatively easy to measure the number of *hits* on a website or the number of *click-throughs* from a link. But what does that information really tell a manager? What action would the manager consider taking based on these types of data? *Hits* and *click-throughs* are meaningful only in context and with other data that indicate whether business value was achieved. That is, they become information only when they are processed to become relevant and purposeful.

Sentiment analysis uses algorithms to analyze text to extract subjective information such as emotional statements, preferences, likes/dislikes, and so on, found in blogs, Tweets, social media posts, and other unstructured files. Sometimes these items can grow into big business problems. Managers seeking to understand what is being said in social media use sentiment analysis. This type of process helps answer questions such as the following:

1. What do our customers think about our position on this issue?
2. How well received is our latest marketing campaign?
3. What is our customer's experience with this problem?

A useful platform or app does this analysis in real time to allow dynamic changes in the way business is done. Some customizing is also necessary; asthma researchers in Arizona needed to create their own

Level	Description	Source of Business Value
Level 1: Reporting	Answers "**What** happened?" by creating batch and ad hoc reports that summarize historical data; sometimes at this level data is received from across functions and is inconsistent or poorly integrated	Reduction in costs of report generation and printing
Level 2: Analysis	Answers "**Why** did it happen?" by using ad hoc, real-time reports, and business intelligence tools to understand root causes	Understanding root causes
Level 3: Descriptive	Answers "**What** is happening now?" by linking business intelligence tools with operational systems to provide instantaneous views and updated status; data integrated, clean, and reliable	Real-time understanding of action/ reaction and course correction instantly to improve operations
Level 4: Predictive	Answers "**What** will happen?" by using predictive models that extrapolate from current data to enable possible scenarios for the future; may be used to see potential for strategic advantage to business	Ability to take action on predictions to help the business
Level 5: Prescriptive	Answers "**How** should we respond?" by automatically linking analytics with other systems, creating continuous updates from business intelligence tools that automatically are understood by operational tools and trigger events as needed	Automated reactions based on real-time data stream; value from dynamic process that "learns and corrects" automatically

FIGURE 12.7 Analytical capabilities levels.

Sources: Adapted from conversations with Farzad Shirzad, leader of Teradata's Center for Excellence in Analytics in 2011 and Jeff Bertolucci, "Big Data Analytics: Descriptive vs. Predictive vs. Prescriptive," *Information Week*, December 31, 2013.

algorithms to analyze the context of each tweet to make sure it was indeed of concern. For example, a tweet describing how a person's breath was taken away after watching a concert video with a new teen sensation needed to be differentiated from a tweet describing how a person had trouble catching her or his breath after a run.[33]

Vendors such as Google Analytics and Salesforce.com offer platforms with social media analytics tools. A platform includes tools that enable:

1. *Listening to the community:* Identifying and monitoring all conversations in the social web on a particular topic or brand.
2. *Learning who is in the community:* Identifying customer demographics such as age, gender, location, and other trends to foster closer relationships with the community.
3. *Engaging people in the community:* Communicating directly with customers on social platforms such as Facebook, Threads, YouTube, LinkedIn, and Twitter/X using a single app.
4. *Tracking what is being said:* Measuring and tracking demographics, conversations, sentiment, status, and customer voice using a dashboard and other reporting tools.
5. *Building an audience:* Using algorithms to analyze data from internal and external sources to understand customer attributes, behaviors, and profiles and to then find new similar customers.

UPS, Pizza Hut, Pepsi, AMD, JetBlue, and Dell Computers are examples of companies with well-known case studies about their use of social analytics and monitoring tools for engaging and encouraging collaboration among their customers. For example, JetBlue used its social media analysis capabilities to connect with a bridesmaid who had been asked by the future bride to relinquish her role as a bridesmaid. The jilted bridesmaid had asked JetBlue for a refund on social media, and they responded with both the refund and a free flight to help the friends patch things up. When the story unfolded on social media, it not only helped out the customer but also was picked up by many other media outlets and the Twitter community, giving lots of attention, and good will, to JetBlue.[34]

Google Analytics, on the other hand, is a set of analytics tools that enable organizations to analyze traffic coming and going on their website. The Google Analytics suite thoroughly analyzes many aspects of the key words used by visitors to reach a website and provides statistics to help managers understand the searches potential customers use. Some of its features are as follows:

1. *Website testing and optimizing:* Understanding traffic to websites and optimizing a site's content and design for increasing traffic.
2. *Search optimization:* Understanding how Google sees an organization's website, how other sites link to the organization's site, and how specific search queries drive traffic to the organization's site.
3. *Search term interest and insights:* Understanding interests in particular search terms globally and regionally, top searches for similar terms, and popularity over time.
4. *Advertising support and management:* Identifying the best ways to spend advertising resources for online media.

Several firms have enjoyed benefits from Google Analytics tools. For instance, Watchfinder, a reseller of used watches in the United Kingdom, was able to generate almost two dozen remarketing lists focused on the location of potential buyers, their stage in the buying process, and interest in particular brands. The firm reported a return on investment of 1300%, with average order values that increased by 13%. Other firms have also benefited from Google Analytics tools, such as Airbnb, Fairmont Hotels, PBS, and GoPro.[35]

---

[33] Ram et al., "Predicting Asthma-Related Emergency Department Visits Using Big Data."

[34] Caitlin O'Kane, "Bridesmaid Begs JetBlue for Refund After Bride Asks Her to Relinquish Her Role via Email," CBSnews, July 30, 2018, https://www.cbsnews.com/news/bridesmaid-begs-jetblue-for-refund-after-bride-asks-her-to-relinquish-title-in-email/ (accessed August 10, 2023) and Alex Horton, "A Bridesmaid Was Asked to Relinquish Her Duties. JetBlue Helped Soften the Blow," Washington Post, July 30, 2018, https://www.washingtonpost.com/news/dr-gridlock/wp/2018/07/30/a-bridesmaid-was-asked-to-relinquish-her-duties-jetblue-helped-soften-the-blow/ (accessed August 10, 2023).

[35] Bawa, Priya, "Top 10 Google Analytics Case Studies in 2023," undated, https://www.safalta.com/online-digital-marketing/google-analytics-case-studies (accessed May 23, 2023).

Big Data and the Internet of Things

One impact of our information-based economy is the very large amount of data amassing in databases both inside companies and out in the environment. Consider, for a moment the vast amount of data Google must process every time it is queried. Google tells the inquirer how many results are found and how fast the search process found them. For instance, searching Google in August 2023 for the two words "big data" produced, in about a half second, over 570 million results with quotation marks and 12.6 trillion results without quotation marks. Google creates indexes on billions of websites for its search algorithm, and the indexes are searched quickly.

Big data is the term used to describe techniques and technologies that make it possible to deal with very large data sets at the extreme end of the scale. The size of some of these data sets is staggering. While you might purchase a 16-terabyte hard drive for $250, and consider it virtually unlimited, some huge datasets far exceed your capability for storing them. A terabyte is 10^{12} bytes while some files holding big data are measured in exabytes (10^{18} bytes and zettabytes (10^{21} bytes). A zettabyte-sized file cannot fit into any hard drive you can purchase for your home, which dwarfs your sparkling new hard drive, requiring over 3 million of those drives to fit the entire file.

Extreme data sets grow to be so large so quickly because volumes of information are continuously created, usually automatically, and stored for analysis. Having large data sets is desirable because of the potential trends and analytics that can be extracted, but when the sets are so large, managers need to plan for the use of specialized computers and tools to mine the data.

One reason for the explosion of data is that firms now store not only transaction data, but also information surrounding a transaction. Consider Netflix, which tracks not only what movie or show is watched but also what was in the user's search results but not chosen, when the user stopped watching and at what point in the program this occurred, and other events that occur before, during, and after the actual transaction.

Social media channels are another source of big data. Conversations contain words that get their meaning from the other words in the sentence, and companies want to know that meaning. They want to analyze the conversation, not just keywords or tags associated with it. For example, if consumers discuss on social media political statements by a certain company, it is important to determine the context of those statements to determine if they are positive or negative. For instance, "That's ridiculous" could be positive or negative,[36] depending on the next few words of the posting. For example, "It's ridiculous how great that dress looks!" would be positive and "It's ridiculous to say something so cruel!" would be negative. For that reason, social media data often is captured in its entirety so analysis can be done as needed later. However, conversations are large, unstructured clusters of words, and the resulting database is considered big data.

An important practical application of big data can illustrate how analytics of social media data can be useful. Researchers at the University of Arizona found that they could predict the number of asthma-related emergency room visits with 70% accuracy by tracking real-time pollution data and the incidence of words such as *wheezing, sneezing*, and *inhaler* found in tweets and Google searches. Although only about 1% of tweets reported those words out of 464.8 million tweets in a two-and-a-half-month period, that proportion represented about 15,000 tweets per day globally. The researchers plotted the trends on a map and alerted hospitals that an outbreak was likely in areas with larger numbers of asthma tweets and search queries. The hospitals then could schedule more staff in their emergency rooms.[37]

Big data has enabled advances in traditionally low-tech industries using sensors, processing power, and large data sets. Smart services and products combine traditional functionality with new information-based features and can transform work. For example, farmers recognized that weeds infest farms to such an extent that they make up 5% to 10% of a field. Smart farming uses cameras on machines that have a water tank, a chemical tank with herbicides that kill harmful weeds, and a nutrient tank that feeds valuable vegetable plants. The machine rolls along the fields, with a camera attached to the front, and sprayers on the back. Rather than merely capturing the data to assess what should be done later, the machines can recognize which are weeds and which are vegetable plants, and then make real-time decisions to spray herbicides or nutrients exactly where needed. The technology even recognizes the species of weed so that

[36] https://english.stackexchange.com/questions/557190/ridiculous-what-an-ambiguous-word-please-help-to-understand (accessed August 10, 2023).

[37] Sudha Ram, Wenli Zhang, Max Williams, and Yolande Pengetnze, "Predicting Asthma-Related Emergency Department Visits Using Big Data," *IEEE Journal of Biomedical and Health Informatics* 19, no. 4 (July 2015): 1216–23, https://doi.org/10.1109/JBHI.2015.2404829.

the right dilution of herbicide is used. As the machine rolls along, by the time the sprayers are lined up with the weed, it is doused with just the right amount of herbicide, and the vegetable plants are fed with the nutrients.[38]

Internet of Things

The **Internet of Things (IoT)** generates massive amounts of data. IoT technology embedded in devices stream sensor data from those devices to create rich databases of operational data. Sensors and devices produce large quantities of data enabling new uses of robots and artificial intelligence in a wide variety of industries. Applications span operational and management processes such as regulating temperature in assembly lines to recording location, speed, traffic, and obstacles in a feature-rich modern vehicle, to recording biological measures in smart watches, such as pulse rate and skin temperature. In the case of a smart watch, the measures can serve to warn a very active person to take a break, or for a desk worker to start moving. Recently, the third author was congratulated by his smartwatch after several hours of sitting and writing this chapter, when he took a break and started walking to the refrigerator. In contrast, on a recent very brisk walk from Grand Central Station on the way to a Broadway play, he was warned in real time by his watch of his excessive heart rate and needed to slow the pace.

Several sensors on a car result in big data in a hurry. Many car manufacturers provide options to help the driver avoid collisions or sudden lane changes. The third author drives a car with a "safety package," which includes active cruise control, lane-keeping assistance, and autonomous parking, requiring 17 sensors for all those functions. A single fully self-driving car would be expected to have 32 sensors, generating 19 terabytes per hour.[39] That fancy 16 Terabyte home hard drive of yours cannot even store data from your one-hour self-driving commute to work!

Other devices such as elevators, refrigerators, industrial equipment, pacemakers, and more are all equipped with sensors that capture relevant operational information such as floors of buildings visited; food stored; forklifts in use; time of day; heart health including blood flow; and sensor-maintenance information such as the health of the device, time between failures, and battery level. Advanced sensors also interact with other sensors, sending and receiving signals that guide the operations of the device. As these technologies proliferate, the information generated grows exponentially.

Database warehouse vendors, such as Teradata, IBM, and Oracle, have tailored tools for customers with big data problems. To integrate with business applications and provide appropriate accessibility, backup and security, data warehouses must be *scalable* to allow capture and storage of all the data; *agile* to accommodate changing requirements, mixed types of work, and quick turnaround of queries and reports; and *compatible* with the enterprise infrastructure.

The Dark Side of Big Data

There is a "dark side" to big data. The intense number crunching is likely to yield several "false discoveries." Managers should question all results before applying them. Extensive analysis might yield a correlation and lead to a statistical inference that is unfair or discriminatory. When a statistician says that the confidence of the result of an analysis is 95%, that typically means that there is 95% confidence that the results are generalizable to a larger sample (than the one used in the analysis). General managers must question not only the results but also the confidence level of the results.

Also, some false conclusions could be reached if a hidden causal factor is omitted. A famous illustration is based on the fact that drownings are statistically related to ice-cream sales. The conclusion that some might reach would be that eating ice cream causes drownings, where the missing factor is the weather. When temperatures rise, more people eat ice cream, and also, more people swim.[40] Big data might offer a

[38] Miller, Dan, "Smart Sprayer Technology," February 9, 2022, Progressive Farmer. https://www.dtnpf.com/agriculture/web/ag/news/article/2022/02/10/smarter-sprayers (accessed August 10, 2023).

[39] Götz, Florian, "The Data Deluge: What Do We Do With The Data Generated by AVs?" January 22, 2021, from Siemens.com. https://blogs.sw.siemens.com/polarion/the-data-deluge-what-do-we-do-with-the-data-generated-by-avs/ (accessed August 10, 2023).

[40] John Higgins, "Ice Cream Doesn't Cause Drowning and Other Warnings about Misinterpreting Data," December 4, 2013, http://blogs.seattletimes.com/educationlab/2013/12/04/ice-cream-doesnt-cause-drowning-and-other-warnings-about-interpreting-data/ (accessed March 16, 2019).

FIGURE 12.8 Tweet from Netflix.

high-tech twist to the old practice of "I know what the facts are—now let's find the ones we want." Here again, care must be applied when using powerful tools.[41]

But the biggest recent concern is what some consumers consider an invasion of privacy. Companies now can use analytics to paint a far more accurate picture of a customer than he or she might like. For example, Netflix tweeted about a show that their data highlighted was binge watched by 53 people. The tweet is shown in Figure 12.8. Netflix Twitter followers found this tweet creepy because it made them aware of how much personal data the company has, and the kind of inferences they can make.[42]

Personalization and Time Data Streams

Similar to the experience of the pregnant teen girl who was a Target customer, big data combined with savvy analytics and large computing power can yield accurate insights about anyone. While companies use personalization as a convenience, sometimes it can feel like a violation. Consider this scenario: you search Google for couches, read about them, but decide not to purchase. Then for several days, you are shown advertisements for couches and other furniture. Somehow the system knows that you were shopping for couches and makes some leaps about other items you might like. It seems like the system knows you; in fact, it does, but perhaps not how you might think.

In this case, a cookie, a small data element, has been deposited into a folder on your computer or smartphone by a third-party ad provider partnering with many site owners. That cookie is accessed by the same third-party ad provider when you navigate to other sites, and the third-party provides ads that correspond to your browsing behavior, attempting to stimulate future purchases thus personalizing the information delivered to you. Third-party cookies, which so far have outlived their intended existence, are described in more detail in Chapter 13.

Another way to personalize the information seen by a user is to draw inferences from the Internet Protocol (IP) address of the user. When you access the Internet, your connection has a unique IP address. Geolocation systems can connect the IP address with your approximate location with a high degree of accuracy. Coupling this with other demographic information provides enough clues about the user to predict her or his likes and dislikes and ultimately personalize the message delivered by the website. For example, a large hotel chain uses the IP address of visitors to their website to customize their home page with offers that correspond to the location the visitor is viewing.

Conversations are another source of personalization. Real-time data streams are fertile ground for clues about users. Systems "monitor" the public data streams, and analytics find patterns and trends. Managers place great value on the inferences they can draw from real-time data streams, and executives can make more impactful decisions. For example, suppose a sporting event's half-time show is not well received by the public. Twitter/X and other social media sites will begin to buzz with comments. Systems designed to monitor and notice these remarks will alert managers of a possible situation that may need action, damage control, or other decision.

As algorithms, analytics, and other data management hardware and software increase in sophistication, we can expect to see increasingly more accurate predictions and more personalized interaction.

[41] Davenport and Harris, Competing on Analytics.

[42] Twitter.com; https://medium.com/@laurapoulos/this-is-the-line-between-creepy-and-creative-bd8ca9730f82 (accessed March 23, 2019); and https://www.adweek.com/creativity/where-do-we-draw-the-line-between-creepy-and-creative-in-advertising/ (accessed March 23, 2019).

Artificial Intelligence, Machine Learning, and Deep Learning

The area of artificial intelligence has reached a tipping point where applications are more routinely deployed, and value more regularly realized from investments. The tipping point has come about because of the ability to collect, manage, store, and process data in very large quantities. Artificial Intelligence (AI) has been around for decades, but it wasn't until recently that the combination of data and technologies aligned properly for AI to really take off. A recent report on a survey in MIT Technology Review[43] reveals that 94% of the firms represented by the Chief Information Officers reported some use of AI and machine learning (ML) in 2022 in many of the firms' functions, but more than 50% are merely pilots or limited in scope. By 2025, however, those tools are expected to be deployed much more widely, with more than 50% in "widescale" adoption or as a "critical part of the [firms'] function[s]."[44] For example, Adobe is using AI and ML to enhance customer support, provide "self-healing" of its platform, and even provide powerful new capabilities in its flagship products such as PhotoShop and Illustrator.[45]

Artificial Intelligence (AI) usually refers to the broader field of development of computer science where systems perform tasks that are naturally performed by humans. Examples are visual perception, speech recognition, and decision making. When AI was first imagined by Alan Turing, he suggested that a system would have artificial intelligence if it behaved in a way that was indistinguishable from a human.[46] In the early days, AI software was simple and contained a list of responses to possible text statements from the user. For instance, one of the earliest demonstrations of AI to the public was a 1966 "chatterbot" (now called "**chatbot**")[47] called "Eliza," which identified itself as a psychological therapist and was "rudimentary but effective."[48] That chatbot enabled a person to hold a chat conversation and provided human-like responses. Eliza would even probe further with its own follow-up questions. [49] But in reality, the software merely looked for, and responded in predefined ways to, certain words and phrases. For instance, if you typed the word "mother" in any phrase, the software would respond "tell me more about your family," even if you had merely stated that "necessity is the mother of invention." When this occurred, the primitive nature of Eliza was revealed in 1981, at least to one of the authors of this book who quickly turned from being mystified to becoming slightly disappointed.

Over the years, the bar has risen for what people think is AI (behavior indistinguishable from a human), and AI has progressed enough to impress us once again. There have been many exciting innovations. Another example is OpenAI, which can generate images or text. Just one example of an image generator is Dall-E 2, which can actually paint photo-realistic images by request.[50] On the OpenAI website, one interesting example is a sunflower wearing sunglasses on a sunny day in a field which it created.[51] That resulting image never existed before that request was made, yet it looks like a photograph.

More recently, as many students well know, a chatbot can go beyond images to words. For instance, a chatbot such as **ChatGPT** can handle general tasks. A **GPT**[52] takes as input questions (for instance, from a college course) for solving a problem, and then the software will answer it. It can even structure an answer in the form of a letter or essay. The secret to a chatbot is that it has a library of curated answers[53] to small segments of problems. For instance, if you are looking for a consulting job and are required to write a

---

[43] MIT Technology Review Insights, "The great acceleration: CIO perspectives on generative AI," July 18, 2023, https://www.technologyreview.com/2023/07/18/1076423/the-great-acceleration-cio-perspectives-on-generative-ai/ (accessed August 10, 2023).

[44] MIT Technology Review, p. 8.

[45] MIT Technology Review.

[46] Anyoha, Rockwell. "The History of Artificial Intelligence, August 28, 2017, Harvard Special Edition on Artificial Intelligence. https://sitn.hms.harvard.edu/flash/2017/history-artificial-intelligence/ (accessed May 11, 2023).

[47] Ronkowitz, Kenneth, "ELIZA: A Very Basic Rogerian Psychotherapist Chatbot, Undated https://web.njit.edu/~ronkowit/eliza.html (accessed May 11, 2023).

[48] Rossen, Jake, " 'Please tell me about your problem': Remembering ELIZA, the pioneering '60s chatbot," Mentalfloss.com, Feb. 14, 2023. https://www.mentalfloss.com/posts/eliza-chatbot-history (accessed May 11, 2023).

[49] Ronkowitz, Kenneth; Jake, 2023.

[50] Guinness, Harry, "How to Use Dall-E 2 to Create AI Images, Zapier.com, March 16, 2023, https://zapier.com/blog/how-to-use-dall-e-2/ (accessed May 11, 2023).

[51] https://labs.openai.com/ (accessed May 11, 2023).

[52] The acronym stands for "Generative Pre-Trained Transformer."

[53] Livingston, Christine, "ChatGPT, The Rise of Generative AI," *CIO Magazine,* April 25, 2023. https://www.cio.com/article/474809/chatgpt-the-rise-of-generative-ai.html#:~:text=GPT%20stands%20for%20generative%20pre,powerful%20models%20such%20as%20ChatGPT (accessed May 12, 2023).

cover letter for your resume packet, you might stare at a blank page for a while, not knowing quite how to start. If you ask ChatGPT to "write a letter for a consulting job at Deloitte in Pittsburgh," you will find a nicely phrased, grammatically correct letter in a few seconds. You will likely find that it begins with "Dear Hiring Manager," using a common template structure. Some of the letters are completely made up, such as stating qualifications that may or may not be true. Like the sunflower picture, the letter is built by components that were collected over time from humans, and we can thank ML for this capability.[54]

Machine learning (ML) is a specific kind of AI where the system "learns" from large amounts of data that provides examples, or trains, the system. For example, ML might analyze millions of credit card records, and instead of a programmer creating steps for analyzing anomalies, the system would "learn" what an anomaly would look like by understanding many parameters of what "normal" looks like. When an anomaly occurs, like a strange charge for tickets to Cancun, when the credit card owner never travels, the system can recognize it and sound an alert.

ChatGPT assembled the letter from a large sample of cover letter components. The key is that patterns in millions of sample letters emerge, such as greeting the reader, trying to be impressive, and expressing keen interest in the job. Cover letters available on websites highlight particular skills, providing additional content for the letter, even if they do not apply to the current candidate! This is why most educators consider the use of chatbots as plagiarism, and this is also why there are detectors such as GPTZero[55] that will flag the use of a chatbot in "your" essay; it is really not yours, and its components have been published many, many times before.

Other shortcomings of chatbots are numerous. The components used to build your answer might not fit together very well. Also, the content might be limited and obsolete; In 2023, the content of ChatGPT was limited to 2021 and before. Many of these problems have been addressed in newer chatbots, such as ChatGPT4, but time marches on and the content of any chatbot will likely be biased towards old entries in the early days of use. Because the components come from products provided by humans, it will likely have human errors in grammar, facts, mathematics, biases, and reasoning.[56]

Note again that these systems require a learning phase followed by a feedback phase to determine if the system's learning phase was effective. Some systems have physical consequences, such as a robot vacuum cleaner that bumps into objects it fails to detect, so it can use the feedback by detecting the consequences of their actions directly. Other systems, such as those that categorize photos, must have their learning validated by humans.

SAS describes four types of ML: supervised, semi-supervised, unsupervised, and reinforcement learning.[57] Supervised learning algorithms are provided with large data sets of examples, such as the sunflower photos (in different sizes, from different angles, in different lighting, and even in pieces) that are identified by labels. The algorithm then matches patterns to judge whether previously unseen photos contain sunflowers or not. Such systems can perform classification, correlational, and forecasting tasks.

Semi-supervised ML throws in unlabeled data in the first step so that the algorithm can label unlabeled data. Unsupervised learning tries to identify patterns without any concept of what is correct or incorrect. The algorithm tries to group data in some way, attempting to find order in the chaos of large data sets. Data can be clustered or organized into smaller sets. Finally, reinforcement learning provides "reward" and "punishment" feedback as the algorithm learns. For example, the robotic vacuum cleaner can develop a map of your entire floor without any human intervention, then use the map to do its work.

Deep learning is a third term often discussed in the context of AI. **Deep learning** is a type of ML used for unstructured data. Using a number of images that are broken up into small bits, the deep learning system would come up with a probability of what a new image might be. For example, Google ran a challenge to enable a system to recognize 8,000 categories of plants, animals, and fungi.[58] This is such a resource-intensive process that it wasn't even possible until breakthroughs in processing power were achieved.

---

[54] See Chapter 13 for a discussion of concerns about Chatbot ethical issues and misinformation.

[55] Emma Bowman, "A College Student Created an App that Can Tell Whether AI Wrote An Essay," NPR.org, January 9, 2023, https://www.npr.org/2023/01/09/1147549845/gptzero-ai-chatgpt-edward-tian-plagiarism (accessed May 12, 2023).

[56] Tegan George, "What Are The Limitations of ChatGPT?" Scribbr.com, April 20, 2023, https://www.scribbr.com/ai-tools/chatgpt-limitations (accessed May 12, 2023).

[57] Katrina Wakefield, "A Guide to The Types of Machine Learning Algorithms and Their Applications, Undated. https://www.sas.com/en_gb/insights/articles/analytics/machine-learning-algorithms.html (accessed May 24, 2023).

[58] Yang Song, "Introducing the iNaturalist 2018 Challenge," March 9, 2018, https://ai.googleblog.com/2018/03/introducing-inaturalist-2018-challenge.html (accessed March 16, 2019).

Bias

Firms might use ML to save time and maximize results from decisions to be made, but they struggle to remove bias. If they are based on previous decisions that reached optimality, they exhibit the previous human biases. By changing them, the departure from optimality has been termed "less accurate." That is, there is a "trade-off between accuracy and good behavior."[59] Human bias is likely to creep back into the mix.[60] For instance, characteristics of people applying for loans can be statistically linked to loan defaults. Examples of characteristics can include income, credit rating, and zip code. Some demographics such as zip code can cause unfair generalizations that bias loan success on protected demographic classes such as race or age. Recent work has revealed that political policies must be adopted carefully and tested mathematically because some policies aimed at removing social inequity, such as removing from consideration any of those protected characteristics, unfortunately "can make everyone worse off, including the very class they aim to protect."[61] There is not yet a clear answer to how both fairness and accuracy can be put into balance, but researchers are working hard to find how to carefully design the algorithms and regulations.[62]

Paul et al. (2022) have outlined four major steps to mitigate bias in Human-AI interaction[63]:

- Identify the bias that unfairly disadvantages a person or category of people.
- Draw attention to the bias by making it transparent.
- Allow users to provide feedback about the bias.
- Remedy the bias.

An important observation after considering all of the analytical tools from the past, present, and future is that people lie at the heart of knowledge management and business intelligence. Establishing and nurturing a culture that values evidence-based decision making and learning and sharing of knowledge will enable effective and efficient use of tools such as analytics, business intelligence, artificial intelligence, and knowledge management. These practices must be valued by all employees for their maximum effectiveness. A personal and organizational willingness to learn will be a key principle for success.

SUMMARY

- Knowledge management includes the processes necessary to generate, capture, codify, and transfer knowledge across organizations. *Business intelligence* (BI) is the set of technologies and practices used to analyze and understand data and to use it in making decisions about future actions. Business analytics is the set of quantitative and predictive models used to drive decisions.
- Data, information, and knowledge should not be viewed as interchangeable. Knowledge is more valuable than information, which is more valuable than data because of the human contributions involved.
- The two kinds of knowledge are tacit and explicit. *Tacit knowledge* is personal, context specific, and hard to formalize and communicate. *Explicit knowledge* is easily collected, organized, and transferred through digital means.
- The four main types of intellectual property are patents, trademarks, designs, and copyrights.
- In the past, traditional business intelligence periodically provided updated dashboards to monitor key performance metrics. The current generation of BI is event driven, offers instant access, and can dynamically update dashboards in real time from streaming data, ubiquitous access, and user configurability.

[59] Michael Kerns and Aaron Roth, *The Ethical Algorithm,* New York: Oxford University Press, 2020 (p. 19).

[60] Andreas Fuster, Paul Goldsmith-Pinkham, Tarun Ramadorai, and Ansgar Walther, "Predictably unequal? The effects of machine learning on credit markets." *The Journal of Finance*, 77, no. 1 (2022): 5–47, https://doi.org/10.1111/jofi.13090.

[61] Runshan Fu, Manmohan Aseri, Param Vir Singh, and Kannan Srinivasan, "Un"Fair Machine Learning Algorithms," *Management Science*, 68, no. 6 (2022): 4173–4195, https://doi.org/10.1287/mnsc.2021.4065. The quote is taken from p. 4173.

[62] Fu et al., 2022.

[63] Souren Paul, Lingyao Yuan, Hemant Jain, Lionel Robert, Jim Spohrer, and Hila Lifshitz-Assaf, "Intelligence Augmentation: Human Factors in AI and Future of Work." *AIS Transactions on Human-Computer Interaction* 14, no. 3 (2022): 426–445, https://doi.org/10.17705/1thci.00174.

- Competing with analytics is done by building analytics capabilities that give insights to a new way to operate a business. Decisions can be made much more quickly, and the use of different business models or better information can be facilitated.
- The five levels of analytics capabilities are reporting, analyzing, describing, predicting, and prescribing.
- Social media analytics provide companies with the tools to monitor and engage their communities, and to evaluate the success of their investment in social IT. Sentiment analysis is used to extract insights from conversations and social media data streams.
- The term *big data* refers to very large data repositories often found in environments where volumes of information are generated at a high velocity. Much big data is unstructured, requiring different algorithms to mine for insights than those used with structured data.
- The Internet of Things (IoT) is the term used for the connection of physical devices to the Internet using sensors and creating large, real-time data streams.
- Artificial intelligence has reached the tipping point where applications are routinely deployed, and value is realized from the investment. *Machine learning* (ML) is a specific type of AI where the system is trained by large amounts of data. *Deep learning* is a type of ML useful for unstructured data.
- Chatbots provide much promise but also many cautions as to their use, with richly deserved concerns about accuracy, fairness, and bias.

KEY TERMS

artificial intelligence (AI), 285
big data, 282
business analytics, 270
business intelligence, 270
chatbot, 285
ChatGPT, 285
chief analytics officer (CAO), 279
chief data officer (CDO), 279
combination, 271
data, 270
data-driven culture, 279
data lake, 278
data mining, 278
data scientist, 279
data warehouses, 278
deep learning, 286
evidence-based management, 279
explicit knowledge, 271
externalization, 271
GPT, 285
information, 270
intellectual capital, 273
intellectual property (IP), 273
internalization, 271
Internet of Things (IoT), 283
knowledge, 271
knowledge capture, 272
knowledge codification, 272
knowledge generation, 272
knowledge management, 270
knowledge transfer, 272
machine learning, 286
real-time data sources, 278
sentiment analysis, 280
social media analytics, 280
socialization, 271
structured data, 277
tacit knowledge, 271
tagging, 272
unstructured data, 278

FOUNDATIONAL READINGS

Davenport, Thomas, and Jeanne Harris. *Competing on Analytics: Updated, with a New Introduction: The New Science of Winning* (Harvard Business Press, 2017).

Davis, Gordon B. and Margrethe H. Olson. *Management Information Systems: Conceptual Foundations, Structure, and Development*, 2nd edition, 1985, New York: McGraw-Hill.

Gorry, G. A., & Morton, M. S. (1989). A framework for management information systems. *Sloan Management Review*, 30(3), 49–61.

Nonaka, Ikujiro and Hirotaka Takeuchi. *The Knowledge-Creating Company* (New York: Oxford University Press, 1995), 62–70.

Polanyi, Michael. *The Tacit Dimension* (Chicago, IL: University of Chicago Press, 1966).

DISCUSSION QUESTIONS

1. What does it take to be a successful competitor using business analytics? What is the role of information technology (IT) in helping build this competence for the enterprise?

2. The terms *data*, *information*, and *knowledge* are often used interchangeably. But as this chapter discussed, they can be seen as three points on a continuum. In your opinion, what could be next on this continuum after knowledge?

3. What is the difference between tacit and explicit knowledge? From your own experience, describe an example of each. How might an organization manage tacit knowledge?

4. How might the Internet of Things change the way managers make decisions? Give an example of a data stream from sensor data that you would like to monitor. Please explain why this would be beneficial to you.

5. How do social media analytics aid an organization? Give an example of a social media data stream and the type of insight that might be drawn from it.

6. Why is it so difficult to protect intellectual property? Do you think that the GDPR is the type of legislation that should be enacted to protect privacy? Why or why not?

7. Test a chatbot of your choice (such as ChatGPT (from https://openai.com/) or Bing (https://www.bing.com/new)), by asking it to create a cover letter for three job positions. Use the following structure "Write a cover letter for a _<occupation>_ position at _<Company>_ in _<city>_." Describe the similarities and differences in the letters.

(a) A consulting position at Deloitte in Pittsburgh.

(b) An advertising position at the Rock N Roll Hall of Fame in Cleveland.

(c) Another position at a company and location of your choice.

8. Test a chatbot of your choice more intensively, by doing the following:

(a) Come up with a question such as "how has the internet of things impacted e-commerce so far, and how might things change in the near future?" Answer that question yourself in a couple of paragraphs.

(b) Ask the chatbot the same question and record the answer.

(c) Ask the chatbot to evaluate your answer. In ChatGPT, this can be done as follows: *Evaluate my answer to the question "how has the internet of things changed e-commerce so far, and how might things change in the near future?" The answer is as follows: "<paste in your answer here in its entirety in quotes>"*

(d) Ask the chatbot to improve your answer by asking the same question in (c) above but replace the word "Evaluate" to "Improve." You will likely see a combination of your answer and its answer.

(e) Then ask the chatbot to evaluate the new answer using the same format as in (c) above.

(f) To see a sample of such a chat, please see https://sites.pitt.edu/~galletta/SundayAfternoonWithChatGPT.htm

Case Study 12-1 Netflix: Analytics Now, AI Later?

Netflix knew the series *The Queen's Gambit* and *Umbrella Academy* would be blockbusters before they aired the first episodes, using advanced analytics to "test" those ideas even before they were filmed.[64] Using data from its millions of customers worldwide, Netflix data scientists had their own internal data source of viewing customer preferences, and analysis of a number of parameters showed patterns that indicated the shows would be a success. By "running the numbers," execs knew these new shows would appeal to a very large group of people and that they would become hits before filming even started. You might think this was just a lucky guess, but Netflix used this process earlier to bring the hit *Orange Is the New Black*, and others, to its audiences. The first time Netflix used this strategy, paid subscriptions increased by almost 25%. Research shows that 90% of Netflix subscribers at the time interacted with their blockbusters.[2]

Netflix has a competitive advantage because of its big data and analytics investment—the company knows not only what is watched on its site by all its customers but also much more. For example, the company knows when someone pauses, rewinds, or fast forwards; what is being searched for and what is chosen from the search results; what device is used to watch the program; and when the viewer leaves the content and whether he or she ever comes back. Analytics can provide valuable insights from this data. Analytics results differed significantly from the results obtained by convening focus groups, and it turned out the analytics algorithms give better direction for a more successful outcome. Netflix's data-driven culture extends not only to decisions about original content but also to many other major decisions such as what films to license, what shows to recommend to customers, and what colors and images to use on their site.

Today, firms can use AI to *generate* ideas using tools like chatbots. AI can detect patterns in data, finding what appears to be causal links, and then predict future outcomes from strategic decisions. What if Netflix began using AI to write scripts? After all, using a human for writing does not scale up very well. It takes one person several weeks to write one script for a mini-series, but a chatbot might be able to write multiple scripts per day.

Going one more step, with future technological development, Netflix might be able to use the technology of "deep fakes" to actually produce the episodes that were written overnight. When the technology can work more quickly, it is also possible that each show can be customized to the individual family or each individual viewer. Do you favor a happy ending? Done. Choose your rating: G, PG, PG-13, or R. Just want to trim down the bad language? Done. Prefer to see and hear Matt Damon instead of Ben Affleck? Done.

Using their current, mature AI tools that use viewer data to make suggestions of what to watch, the marketing of these targeted, tailored episodes can be served on a real-time basis. In the future, there might not even be a notion of viewers watching mass-marketed products. The name of a movie might lose its meaning if it is heavily customized. Actors and writers could lose their jobs or suffer sharply reduced pay for their work. In 2023, AI tools caused labor disputes between studios and actors for these potentialities.[65]

Sources: Adapted from "Giving Viewers What They Want," *The New York Times* (February 24, 2013), http://www.nytimes.com/2013/02/25/business/media/for-house-of-cards-using-big-data-to-guarantee-its-popularity.html (accessed September 5, 2015); "Big Data Lessons from Netflix" (March 11, 2014), http://www.wired.com/2014/03/big-data-lessons-netflix/ (accessed September 5, 2015); "What Netflix's 'House of Cards' Means for the Future of TV" (March 4, 2013), http://www.forbes.com/sites/gregsatell/2013/03/04/what-netflixs-house-of-cards-means-for-the-future-of-tv/ (accessed September 5, 2015); Bernard Marr, *Big Data in Practice: How 45 Successful Companies Used Big Data Analytics to Deliver Extraordinary Results* (New York: Wiley and Sons, 2016); Mixson, Elizabeth, "Data Science at Netflix: How Advanced Data & Analytics Helps Netflix Generate Billions," March 30, 2021. (https://www.aidataanalytics.network/data-science-ai/articles/data-science-at-netflix-how-advanced-data-analytics-helped-netflix-generate-billions, retrieved May 6, 2023); Engati Team, "Netflix predictive analytics: Journey to 220Mn+ subscribers, April 13, 2023. (https://www.engati.com/blog/predictive-analytics, accessed May 12, 2023).

---

[64] Mixson, Elizabeth, "Data Science at Netflix: How Advanced Data & Analytics Helps Netflix Generate Billions," March 30, 2021, https://www.aidataanalytics.network/data-science-ai/articles/data-science-at-netflix-how-advanced-data-analytics-helped-netflix-generate-billions (accessed May 6, 2023).

[65] Jasmin Pfefferkorn, "Computer-written scripts & deepfakes: AI is part of the Hollywood strikes," August 1, 2023, https://www.thefashionlaw.com/computer-written-scripts-deepfakes-ai-is-part-of-the-hollywood-strikes/ (accessed August 10, 2023).

Case Study 12-1 **(Continued)**

Discussion Questions

1. When using a movie streaming service, what is your reaction to seeing suggestions for movies displayed on the screen, based on your viewing history? Explain your reaction.
2. Do you think that engineering production based on data models is generally beneficial or detrimental to the industry and to creative work?
3. In your opinion, what are some of the potential future ideas above that are likely? Unlikely? Why?
4. Would you like to "dial in" your own favorite characteristics in a customized movie? Explain your reaction.
5. Think of a movie you've seen that had some unpleasant characteristics. How would you customize it if you had the chance?

Case Study 12-2 Nest and the Internet of Things (IoT)

Nest and its parent company Google are at the forefront of the smart homes trend. Nest began as a smart thermostat that learned how users liked to keep their homes heated or cooled. While it was designed to be very simple to use, the machine learning technology embedded in the device makes this Internet of Things device one of the most well-known success stories, and in some circles, the device leading the smart home transformation.

Nest smart thermostats can be controlled by physically touching the device, or by using an app on the customer's personal smartphone. But over time, the device learns the preferences of its users and dynamically changes the temperature in the home, building a schedule based on the data collected from the user's behaviors. The schedule adapts as the user's preferences change and as the seasons change. It also knows when users are away from home, using sensors and the location of the smartphone connected to the device. According to the Nest website, not only does the device keep customers comfortable in their homes, but the device pays for itself with its dynamic features, saving users an average of 10–12% on heating bills and 15% on cooling bills.

But Google Home, the parent organization of Nest, has invested in smart home technologies that expand the capabilities into other devices. Nest offers smart thermostats, cameras, doorbells, alarm systems, locks, smoke detectors and CO alarms. All are controllable from a Google Home Hub or from a smartphone app. To take the smart home to the next level, Nest has built connections to smart appliances such as refrigerators, washing machines, sprinkler systems and ovens. The website clarifies their vision, "With Nest and Google Products, you'll always know what's happening at home. You'll have some help around the house. And you'll make sure everyone is safe and sound."

Sources: https://nest.com (accessed August 10, 2023) and Bernard Marr, "The Amazing Ways Google Uses AI and Satellite Data to Prevent Illegal Fishing," *Forbes.com*, April 9, 2018, https://www.forbes.com/sites/bernardmarr/2018/04/09/the-amazing-ways-google-uses-artificial-intelligence-and-satellite-data-to-prevent-illegal-fishing/?sh=7d01a7761c14 (accessed August 10, 2023).

Discussion Questions

1. Why would someone want a smart home? What are the advantages of having everything connected? What is an example of something in your home that you would not want to see become a smart device? Why?
2. Reflect on the change in the number of smart (connected) "things" in your home or apartment today compared with five years ago. Has your life become easier or more complicated because of such objects?
3. What connected "things" would you still want to connect in your home or apartment? How would having these devices connected make things easier or more complicated for you?
4. Smart devices collect a lot of data about the use of the device and the habits of the user. What concerns do you have knowing that smart home devices are listening and learning your habits?

13 Privacy, Ethical, and Societal Considerations for Information Management

Information technology (IT) has created a unique set of ethical issues related to the use and control of information. This chapter addresses those issues from various perspectives using three normative theories (stockholder, stakeholder, and social contract) to understand the responsible use and control of information by business organizations. Social contract theory is extended to the evolving issue of responsiveness to foreign governments when ethical tensions emerge. At the individual and corporate levels, Mason's privacy, accuracy, property, accessibility (PAPA) framework is applied to information/data control. Subsequently, the chapter covers the ethical role of managers in today's dynamic world of social business, artificial intelligence, and security controls to keep information safe and accurate. The chapter concludes with a discussion of green computing.

This is a "tale of two Ubers," one from 2022 and one from 2016. Learning how the firm reacted to two distinct cybersecurity incidents, six years apart, is valuable in highlighting ethical decision-making.

On September 15, 2022, Uber tweeted that an attacker claimed to have full administrative control over its data.[1] The hacker alerted Uber on its Slack account on that same date, which made the claim relatively credible. A day later,[2] it was found that an Uber employee's password was purchased from a dark web marketplace by an 18-year-old hacker, who initially failed to log on to the employee's account due to multifactor authentication (MFA). The hacker simply notified the user to approve the MFA again and again, resulting in so many notifications that the employee finally approved the request. The hacker merely wanted the thrill and fame of breaking into Uber's system and quit before accessing customer information.[3]

Uber's same-day notification was an improvement over what happened almost six years earlier, when names, email addresses, and phone numbers of 57 million drivers and app users were stolen by hackers who demanded $100,000 to delete the information.[4] The hack occurred in October 2016, and Uber found out about it on November 14, 2016, 10 days after J. Sullivan, Uber's Chief Security Officer, had testified to the Federal Trade Commission (FTC) about an unrelated 2014 breach that resulted in the theft of 50,000 names and driver's license numbers. Sullivan paid the $100,000 ransom the following month with the condition that the hackers would delete the stolen data and would sign a nondisclosure agreement. A year later, Uber determined the hackers' identities and Sullivan required them to sign new nondisclosure agreements using their true names. The FTC determined that Sullivan knew that the hackers were actively stealing data from other companies and lied

[1] Faiz Siddiqui and Joseph Menn, "Uber Suffers Computer System Breach, Alerts Authorities," *Washington Post*, September 16, 2022, https://www.washingtonpost.com/technology/2022/09/15/uber-hack/ (accessed June 2, 2023).

[2] Corben Leo, tweet thread "Uber Was Hacked," September 15-16, 2022, https://twitter.com/hacker_/status/1570582547415068672 (accessed June 2, 2023).

[3] Edward Kost, "What Caused the Uber Data Breach in 2022?" March 2, 2023, Upguard.com https://www.upguard.com/blog/what-caused-the-uber-data-breach (accessed June 2, 2023).

[4] Corinne Reichert, "Uber's Former Head of Security Convicted Over Concealing 2016 Data Breach," CNET.com, October 5, 2022, https://www.cnet.com/tech/services-and-software/ubers-former-head-of-security-convicted-over-concealing-2016-data-breach/ (accessed June 2, 2023).

to Uber's management and attorneys about the ransom payment.[5] The hack was finally disclosed to the FTC in November 2017, and Sullivan was convicted in October 2022 of obstructing justice by hiding the breach from the FTC and hiding the felony by authorizing the payment to the hackers.[6] Uber reached a settlement agreement with the 50 US states and the District of Columbia with a fine of $148 million for delaying to report the hack.

It might be tempting to conclude that the reason for shrinking Uber's delay in disclosing to law enforcement breaches from a year to just a few moments is simply that Uber learned a lesson. However, delays in reporting breaches across many firms have shortened in recent years.[7] Even though the USA has 50 different laws about delays in breach notifications, there are shorter notification windows for certain types of transactions, customers, and companies operating in the USA.

Breaches involving personal health records must be reported within 60 days, and breaches involving critical infrastructure must be reported within 72 hours of their discovery. Also, many larger firms do business in Europe, and the European Union's General Data Protection Regulation (GDPR) requires any firm having EU customers to report a breach within 72 hours. Finally, as of July 2023, the Securities and Exchange Commission (SEC) adopted rules requiring publicly traded firms to notify the SEC of a significant breach within four business days.[8]

These laws are still evolving, and one might question why a breach would ever have been hidden for over a year. Uber customers in 2016 could have taken some easy actions immediately, such as changing their passwords or turning on MFA to protect their accounts and their identities. The reasoning in the earlier days for a firm to delay or suppress news of breaches was to protect the firm's reputation. This ethical dilemma has resulted in governments in many countries tightening laws surrounding breach announcements. It is logical to see ethical failures such as these leading to tightening of laws.

Managers in organizations today are increasingly faced with many other types of ethical issues. This chapter will describe an important framework to use in understanding, and making decisions about, ethical management and use of information systems.

What Is Expected of Management?

Because many of these IT-related dilemmas do not yet have laws to dictate behavior, managers are left with little direction as they face difficult decisions. Without guaranteed solutions, managers could easily become perplexed with their charge to manage both technically and ethically. They must manage the information generated and contained within their systems for the benefit not only of the corporation but also of society as a whole. The predominant issue concerns the just and ethical use of the information that companies collect in the course of everyday operations. Without official guidelines and codes of conduct, who decides how to use this information? More and more, this challenge falls on corporate managers. They must understand societal needs and expectations to determine what they ethically can and cannot do in their quest to learn about their customers, suppliers, and employees and to provide greater service and business growth.

In a society whose legal standards are continually challenged, managers must serve as guardians of the public and private interest, although many may have no formal legal training and, thus, no firm basis for judgment. This chapter addresses many such concerns. It begins by expanding on the definition of ethical behavior and introduces several heuristics that managers can employ to help them make better decisions. Then the chapter elaborates on the most important issues behind the ethical treatment of data and information and some newly emerging controversies that will surely test society's resolve concerning the increasing presence of IS in every aspect of life.

[5] Justice Department Press Release, October 5, 2022, "Former Chief Security Officer Of Uber Convicted Of Federal Charges for Covering up Data Breach Involving Millions Of Uber User Records" https://www.justice.gov/usao-ndca/pr/former-chief-security-officer-uber-convicted-federal-charges-covering-data-breach (accessed June 2, 2023).

[6] Corinne Reichert, "Uber's Former Head of Security Convicted Over Concealing 2016 Data Breach," CNET.com, October 5, 2022, https://www.cnet.com/tech/services-and-software/ubers-former-head-of-security-convicted-over-concealing-2016-data-breach/ (accessed June 2, 2023).

[7] Tony Burgess, "Understanding Breach Notification Delays," Blog, December 20, 2022, https://blog.barracuda.com/2022/12/20/breach-notification-delays/ (accessed June 2, 2023).

[8] Andrew Harnik, "New SEC rule requires public companies to disclose cybersecurity breaches in 4 days," US News & World Report, July 26, 2023, https://www.usnews.com/news/business/articles/2023-07-26/new-sec-rule-requires-public-companies-to-disclose-cybersecurity-breaches-in-4-days.

This chapter takes a high-level view of ethical issues facing managers in today's environment. It focuses primarily on providing a set of frameworks the manager can apply to a wide variety of ethical issues. Outside the scope of this chapter are several important issues such as the digital divide (the impact of computer technology on the poor or "have-nots," racial minorities, and third world nations), cyberwar (politically motivated hacking to conduct sabotage and espionage), or cyberbullying. Given today's politics, such problems have no easy answers, and researchers are just beginning to define and understand them, a necessary step in finding future solutions. Although these are interesting and important areas for concern, the objective in this chapter is to provide managers with a way to think about the issues of information ethics and corporate responsibility.

Responsible Computing

The technological landscape is changing daily. Increasingly, however, technological advances come about in a business domain lacking ethical clarity. Because of its newness and complexity, this area of IT often lacks accepted norms of behavior or universally accepted decision-making criteria. Companies daily encounter ethical dilemmas as they try to use their IS to create and exploit competitive advantages. These ethical dilemmas arise when a decision or an action reflects competing moral values that may impair or enhance the well-being of an individual or a group of people. These dilemmas arise when there is no one clear way to benefit all in dealing with the ethical issue.

Managers must assess current information initiatives with particular attention to possible ethical issues. Collecting customer information in an uncontrolled manner can lead to unintended consequences, such as the increasing number of breaches that are occurring and invasion of privacy. There are indeed benefits for both buyers and sellers in storing and using detailed information, making purchases more convenient and presenting products that are truly interesting to customers. Using high volumes of data that are stored about customers can raise the relevance of ads they see, in turn improving the efficiency of the browsing and shopping experience. However, managers need to also consider **information ethics**, or the "ethical issues associated with the development and application of information technologies."[9] Stated more directly, just because we *can* do something does not mean we *should*.

It is useful to consider three theories of ethical behavior in the corporate environment that managers can develop and apply to the particular challenges they face. They are "normative" in that they prescribe behavior, specifying what people should do. These theories—stockholder theory, stakeholder theory, and social contract theory—are widely applied in traditional business situations. Smith and Hasnas also refer to them as "intermediate-level" principles that can be understood by ordinary businesspeople and that can be applied to the "concrete moral quandaries of the business domain."[10] Following is a description of each theory accompanied by an illustration of its application using the Uber example outlined at the beginning of this chapter.

Stockholder Theory

According to **stockholder theory**, stockholders provide funding for a firm and expect its managers to act as agents in furthering the stockholders' goals.[11] The nature of this contract binds managers to act in the interest of the shareholders (i.e., to maximize shareholder value). As Milton Friedman wrote, "There is one and only one social responsibility of business: to use its resources and engage in activities designed to increase its profits so long as it stays within the rules of the game, which is to say, engages in open and free competition, without deception or fraud."[12]

When a breach is discovered, management is likely caught in an emotional quagmire because people have an instinct to freeze and delay and hope an event "blows over" like a temporary storm. Perhaps they

[9] M. G. Martinsons and D. Ma, "Subcultural Differences in Information Ethics Across China: Focus on Chinese Management Generation Gaps," *Journal of AIS* 10 (Special Issue) (2009).

[10] H. Jeff Smith and John Hasnas, "Ethics and Information Systems: The Corporate Domain," *MIS Quarterly* (March 1999), 112.

[11] Smith and Hasnas, 1999.

[12] M. Friedman, *Capitalism and Freedom* (Chicago, IL: University of Chicago Press, 1962), 133.

hope that new evidence will arrive that shows the breach that was detected is smaller or even nonexistent. However, delay usually makes things worse over the long term, as the Uber case illustrated.

So, what is their obligation, according to stockholder theory? Stockholder theory qualifies the manager's duty in two salient ways. First, managers are bound to employ legal, nonfraudulent means. Second, managers must take the long-term view of shareholder interest (i.e., they are obliged to forgo short-term gains if doing so will maximize value over the long term). The stipulation under stockholder theory that the pursuit of profits must be legal and nonfraudulent meant that Sullivan—and Uber—should have reported the breach to the FTC in the "most expedient time possible" under California law at that time.[13] The subsequent legal decision may have hurt Uber's reputation, and ultimately, its stock price in the long term. Paying the bribe was not the legal path, and Sullivan took a giant gamble, assuming that the hackers would discard the data and keep silent about it. In hindsight, the gamble was foolish because logical events followed: A new CEO entered the picture, examined records, and asked Sullivan about the breach. Sullivan lied about it, but the true facts were later discovered.

In the end, while Sullivan wanted the stockholders to benefit from his covert actions, they were actually harmed by the $148 million fine in the end when the real facts were revealed to the FTC.

Stakeholder Theory

Stakeholder theory holds that managers, although bound by their relation to stockholders, are entrusted also with a responsibility, fiduciary, or otherwise, to all those who hold a stake in or a claim on the firm.[14] The word *stakeholder* is currently taken to mean any group that vitally affects the survival and success of the corporation or whose interests the corporation vitally affects. Such groups normally include stockholders, customers, employees, suppliers, the local community, and, possibly, many other groups who may hold a stake in the firm. At its most basic level, stakeholder theory states that management must balance the rights of all stakeholders without impinging on the rights of any one particular stakeholder.

Stakeholder theory diverges most consequentially from stockholder theory in affirming that the interests of parties other than the stockholders also play a legitimate role in a firm's governance and management. As a practical matter, it is often difficult, if not impossible, to figure out what is in the best interest of each stakeholder group and then balance any conflicting interests.

When stakeholders feel that their interests haven't been considered adequately by the managers making the decisions, their only recourse may be to stop participating in the corporation: Customers can stop buying the company's products, stockholders can sell their stock, and so forth. But some stakeholders are not in a position to stop participating in the corporation. In particular, employees may need to continue working for the corporation for financial reasons even though they dislike practices of their employers or experience considerable stress due to their jobs.

Viewed in light of stakeholder theory, the ethical issue facing Uber presented a more complex dilemma. John Philip Coghlan, CEO of Visa USA noted: "A data breach can put an executive in an exceedingly complex situation, where he must negotiate the often-divergent interests of multiple stakeholders."[15] Uber's shareholders stand to gain in the short term by delaying or permanently suppressing an announcement of the breach and of the payment, but what would be the effects on other stakeholders? Two stakeholder groups, the drivers and app users (customers), definitely could benefit from knowing about the breach and its severity as soon as possible because they could take steps to protect themselves. Uber could offer information hotlines, free credit-monitoring, and compensation for those who are injured. Research has shown that customers who receive adequate compensation after making a complaint are actually more loyal than those without complaints.[16] On the other hand, if the breach were not announced, fewer hackers might be attracted to the situation or inspired to be a "copycat" and break into Uber's systems and ask for a ransom. Nonetheless, it probably could be shown that the costs to the drivers and customers outweighed the benefits within the larger stakeholder group.

[13] IT Governance, "Data Breach Notification by State," https://www.itgovernanceusa.com/data-breach-notification-laws, accessed August 10, 2023.

[14] Smith and Hasnas, "Ethics and Information Systems," 115.

[15] McNulty, "Boss I Think Someone Stole Our Customer Data."

[16] McNulty.

Social Contract Theory

Social contract theory places responsibility on corporate managers to consider the needs of the society (societies) in which the corporation is embedded. Social contract theorists assert that a corporation is permitted legally to form to create more value to society than it consumes. Thus, society gives legal recognition to the organization and charges it with enhancing society's welfare by satisfying particular interests of consumers and workers.[17] The social contract comprises two distinct components: social welfare and justice. *Social welfare* addresses the issue of providing benefits exceeding their associated costs, and the need for *justice* addresses the need for corporations to pursue profits legally without fraud or deception and avoid activities that injure society. The social contract obliges managers to pursue profits in ways that are compatible with the well-being of society as a whole.

Social contract theory is sometimes criticized because no mechanism exists to actuate it. In the absence of a real contract whose terms subordinate profit maximization to social welfare, most critics find it hard to imagine that corporations are willing to lose profitability in the name of altruism. Yet, the strength of the theory lies in its broad assessment of the moral foundations of business activity.

Applied to the Uber case, social contract theory would demand that the manager ask whether the delay in notifying customers about the security breach and paying the hackers a ransom could compromise fundamental tenets of fairness or social justice. If customers were not apprised of the delay as soon as possible, Uber's actions could be seen as unethical because it would not seem fair to delay notifying the customers. Furthermore, by hiding the hackers' identities, Uber made it possible for them to do the same thing to other companies, potentially leading to harm to millions of their customers.

The different perspectives not only have conflicts within each normative theory perspective they also have conflicts between the perspectives. Hence, ethical conflicts can pop up in many complex and perplexing situations. The three normative theories of business ethics possess distinct characteristics, but they are not completely incompatible. All offer useful metrics for defining ethical behavior in profit-seeking enterprises under free market conditions. The theories provide managers with an independent standard by which to judge the ethical nature of superiors' orders as well as their firms' policies and codes of conduct. Upon inspection, the three theories appear to represent concentric circles with stockholder theory at the center and social contract theory at the outer ring. Stockholder theory is narrowest in scope, stakeholder theory encompasses and expands on it, and social contract theory covers the broadest area. Figure 13.1 summarizes these three theories.

Corporate Social Responsibility

Corporate Social Responsibility (CSR) is self-regulated behavior promoting the well-being of communities and society.[18] Application of social contract theory helps companies adopt a broad perspective. In this section, we address a "big picture" by exploring three areas in which CSR is particularly visible with

Theory	Definition	Metrics
Stockholder	Maximize stockholder wealth, in a legal and nonfraudulent manner	Will this action maximize long-term stockholder value? Can goals be accomplished without compromising company standards and without breaking laws?
Stakeholder	Maximize benefits to all stakeholders while weighing costs to competing interests	Does the proposed action maximize collective benefits to the company? Does this action treat one or more of the corporate stakeholders unfairly?
Social contract	Create value for society in a manner that is just and nondiscriminatory	Does this action create a "net" benefit for society? Does the proposed action discriminate against any group in particular, and is its implementation socially just?

FIGURE 13.1 Three normative theories of business ethics.

[17] Smith and Hasnas, "Ethics and Information Systems," 116.

[18] Nadia Reckmann, "What is Corporate Social Responsibility?" *Business News Daily*, February 21, 2023, https://www.businessnewsdaily.com/4679-corporate-social-responsibility.html (accessed June 6, 2023).

regard to managing information systems: responsible use of information, ethical tensions with governments, and green computing.

Responsible Use of Information

Beyond the concerns of data breaches, organizations today are sitting on more data than ever before thought imaginable. Those data enable a company to profile us, estimate our incomes, predict our needs, and tempt us to make purchases. In the past, this activity would strike customers as being a "Big Brother" situation, but the name for this has become "big data," and has become familiar with widespread publicity surrounding the practices of Facebook, Inc.

Facebook users had been very open with their personal details until the Cambridge Analytica scandal, which was not technically a breach, because it did not involve theft of a password and break-in to their servers. The political data firm captured personal data from information stored on Facebook and left public (not made private) by the users themselves. In the end, they had captured information about their preferences, location, and friends, to send political ads to 50 million Facebook users. Publicity about this event has led to scrutiny in Congress, which in turn led to Facebook's banning of scraping that information, and a feature added in 2019 allowed quick and easy ways for users to clear their histories.[19]

But legal precedent about sharing such information is still developing. Firms often disclose, in the fine print of privacy policy statements, that they can sell valuable information about their customers to third parties. Recently, discount prescription app GoodRx was accused of sharing personal information with Facebook and Google about millions of its customers' illnesses and prescriptions so that targeted ads could be provided to these users. The company had promised this would not occur. GoodRx paid a civil penalty of $1.5 million to the FTC for sharing health information. Surprisingly, those details were not covered by any current laws.[20]

Once such data is captured,[21] modern statistical packages provide advanced methods to detect patterns in enormous sets of data such as that obtained by Cambridge Analytica. Large data sets are difficult for people to envision, but the larger the data set, the clearer the picture becomes for detecting and understanding those patterns. The data indicate that many behaviors tend to cluster together; for example, camera purchases tend to be accompanied by photography accessories. Zip Codes in affluent neighborhoods tend to predict purchases of more expensive equipment and more accessories. Those who qualify and who also frequently purchase hiking and sporting goods might be ripe for a new 360-degree action camera or drone complete with accessories. A merchant who passes up the opportunity to advertise products related to past or current behavior or locations to carefully targeted individuals will not be in a good position to compete in today's world. However, there is a downside to these practices.

Target inadvertently revealed a teen's concealed pregnancy to her parents by mailing to her home address ads for maternity clothes and diapers.[22] The mailing was triggered by analysis of purchases of unscented soaps, vitamins, and cotton balls, which matched purchasing patterns of tens of thousands of other pregnant women. Although Target now sprinkles in other ads to be less blatant, the fact that it is aware of such personal facts is a stark illustration of the potential for large retailers to learn an alarming amount of private information by keeping track of purchasers and combining it with other identifying information they receive along the way or from other organizations.

That story becomes more surprising when consumers consider that even data with concealed but uniquely coded account numbers can reveal personal information, as a study in *Science* reported.[23] The researchers found that knowing three facts, such as time and date, location, and approximate amount spent

---

[19] Salvador Rodriguez, "Facebook Says It Will Finally Launch Its Long-Awaited Clear History Feature This Year, and It Could Hurt Ad Targeting," February 26, 2019, https://www.cnbc.com/2019/02/26/facebook-clear-history-coming-in-2019-could-hurt-ad-targeting-wehner.html (accessed March 2, 2019).

[20] Natasha Singer, "GoodRx Leaked User Health Data to Facebook and Google, FTC says," *New York Times Digest,* February 2, 2023, 4.

[21] See Chapter 12 for a discussion of Big Data.

[22] K. Hill, "How Target Figured Out a Teen Girl Was Pregnant Before Her Father Did," *Forbes*, February 16, 2012, https://www.forbes.com/sites/kashmirhill/2012/02/16/how-target-figured-out-a-teen-girl-was-pregnant-before-her-father-did/ (accessed August 10, 2023).

[23] Y. A de Montjoye, L. Radaelli, V. K. Singh, and A. S. Pentland, "Unique in the Shopping Mall: On the Re-Identifiability of Credit Card Metadata," *Science* 347, no. 6221 (January 30, 2015): 536–39.

while visiting a merchant, 90% of individuals can be identified even with an anonymized data set that includes 1.1 million records spread over three months. Knowing when a person visited a particular restaurant or coffee shop can be discerned quickly from matching receipt dates and times to social media entries and pictures that can establish what a person is eating and where. Discovering the person's identity can, of course, reveal all of his or her other credit card transactions throughout the entire data set. The message is quite clear: Be cautious about inadvertently revealing to social media users exactly where you were and exactly when you were there.

The *Science* study might imply feelings of futility are in order; that just when a manager tightens security practices to thwart yesterday's criminals, new threats render those practices inadequate. After all, few would have expected even disguised data to be a threat to customers just a few years ago. Further, many security professionals warn that it is not possible to provide 100% assurance of security in any system.[24]

However, that does not mean that managers should give up. Failures often occur when firms don't take even basic precautions. For example, the 2022 Uber breach described in the chapter opener demonstrates that we still have not learned from the largest retail data breach ever in the United States: the hack of Target, with 40 million credit card numbers stolen in 2013. The hack was perpetrated by data thieves who sent a virus-laden email to personnel from a contractor's heating/air conditioning firm. All it took was one person opening the email and triggering a virus for so many customers to be impacted. These personnel were able to tap into the system using their assigned terminals. There might be two lessons here: Don't provide access to contractors and anticipate that people will make mistakes from time to time. The reason Chapter 7 describes the need for resilience is that most breaches can be prevented, but people do commit errors in judgment from time to time."[25]

Firms have the responsibility to protect data, but if history is our guide, there will be more failures in keeping data private. History shows us that security personnel should be armed with knowledge of best practices, common sense in allowing people access to computer systems, and tools for providing vigilance at points of vulnerability. User training is important, but not all understand or follow accurately the advice they receive during training. Chapter 7 provides specific strategies to try to carry out a firm's responsibility for protecting data.

Ethical Tensions with Governments

For many years, governments and IT personnel acted like cooperative friends. As computers reached the office and systems became more sophisticated over time, governments followed suit, weaning themselves from paper filing cabinets, graduating to electronic storage, and then reengineering themselves to enable individuals and companies to interact electronically. More recently, there have been significant tensions relating to border issues, freedom of expression, and IP protection.

Data Borders

Firms have been able to make use of their previous policies for keeping track of their wholesale and retail customers no matter where they reside. Markets are often global, and many companies operate on different continents. One complication recently is that many nations around the world have created privacy laws, which are designed to help keep private sensitive data on their citizens. Those privacy laws make it difficult to have data flowing from nation to nation, as we now have digital border walls. Some countries have introduced myriad regulations requiring that certain data be prevented from being transported to other countries.

This makes it difficult to do business globally, as either the lowest common denominator must be adopted, or separate systems might need to be built in each country of a firm's operation, impairing the ability of firms like Google, Amazon, and Meta to provide the same services worldwide. While the United States is relatively free and open about data, countries such as China and Russia have erected barriers to

[24] Pringle, M, "Security Expert: All Systems Vulnerable to Cyberattacks," December 23, 2014, https://www.wbaltv.com/article/security-expert-all-systems-vulnerable-to-cyberattacks/7090957# (accessed August 10, 2023).

[25] Woodrow Hartzog and Daniel J. Solove, "We Still Haven't Learned the Major Lesson of the 2013 Target Hack," Slate.com, April 13, 2022, paragraph 2 https://slate.com/technology/2022/04/breached-excerpt-hartzog-solove-target.html (accessed August 10, 2023).

data sharing, and the European Union has strict data privacy regulations in GDPR, described later in this chapter.[26]

The differences between the freewheeling data spigot from the West and the Boundaries and rules elsewhere have not only made it difficult to do business, but it also serves to feed a foundation of conflict between some nations. TikTok provides one example of a successful app that feeds conflict. From the United States' point of view, for example, privacy concerns have been raised over doubts about how TikTok is structured: TikTok is not permitted to hide information about its users from the Chinese government. Congresspersons have provided a possible solution: They want a US company to be in charge of TikTok's data and algorithms, and thus operate under US law. Like Britain, Australia, New Zealand, Canada, France, and the European Union, in February 2023, the United States government banned TikTok apps from being installed on US federal government devices. India has banned TikTok altogether.[27] Also, 33 of the 50 United States have banned TikTok from devices controlled by state employees,[28] and Montana has banned it altogether starting in 2024.[29] There is a bill in Congress to ban TikTok from the United States altogether.[30]

Freedom of Expression and Protection of Intellectual Property (IP)

Ethical behavior is seen differently in different cultures. "Managers may need to adopt much different approaches across nationalities to counter the effects of what they perceive as unethical behaviors."[31] Two important areas often addressed are the freedom of expression and protection of IP. While these two topics could fill entire books, it is important for managers to understand the fundamentals of how some differences can impact business.

First, a product can be made illegal in another country. Restrictions on Google's search engine by the Chinese government compelled Google to unhappily withdraw from the gigantic Chinese market in 2010. Then Google worked on a censored version of their search engine for use in China, Google employees protested, and in 2019, work ended,[32] presumably due to the mounting criticism. The firm weighed their choices on the ethics of permitting censorship or the exciting potential to serve a market that dwarfs that of the United States by a factor of nearly 10.[33] This dilemma is likely to become very common with increased globalization. In this case, the balancing act is at an international level.[34]

Finally, IP laws and norms differ widely worldwide. There are dimensions of culture that could impact the rules from one country to another, but one study[35] found that individualistic cultures (emphasizing individual rights rather than those of groups or society) appear to be more favorable places for fostering IP laws. A collectivist culture would thus view IP more as property for the group rather than the individual. Therefore, copying of patents and software might be deemed perfectly appropriate in a collective society, while it is not permitted in an individualistic society.

---

[26] David McCabe and Adam Satariano, "The Era of Borderless Data Is Ending," *New York Times*, May 23, 2022, https://www.nytimes.com/2022/05/23/technology/data-privacy-laws.html (accessed June 9, 2023).

[27] Sapna Maheshwari and Amanda Holpuch, "Why Countries Are Trying to Ban TikTok," *The New York Times*, May 23, 2023, https://www.nytimes.com/article/tiktok-ban.html (accessed June 3, 2023).

[28] Brian Fung and Christopher Hickey, "TikTok Access From Government Devices now Restricted in More Than Half of US states," CNN Business, January 16, 2023, https://www.cnn.com/2023/01/16/tech/tiktok-state-restrictions/index.html (accessed June 3, 2023).

[29] Adi Robertson, "TikTok Is Now Banned in Montana," The Verge.com, May 17, 2023, https://www.theverge.com/2023/5/17/23686294/montana-tiktok-ban-signed-governor-gianforte-court (accessed June 3, 2023).

[30] Josh Hawley. "Hawley, Buck Introduce New Bill to Ban Tiktok in United States," January 25, 2023, is a https://www.hawley.senate.gov/hawley-buck-introduce-new-bill-ban-tiktok-us#:~:text=The%20No%20TikTok%20on%20United%20States%20Devices%20Act%20would%3A,attempt%20to%20evade%20these%20sanctions (accessed March 11, 2023).

[31] D. Leidner and T. Kayworth, "A Review of Culture in Information Systems Research: Toward a Theory of Information Technology Culture Conflict," *MIS Quarterly* 30, no. 2 (2006): 357–99.

[32] BBC News, "Google's Project Dragonfly 'Terminated' in China,"BBC.com, July 17, 2019, https://www.bbc.com/news/technology-49015516 (accessed June 9, 2023).

[33] Kate Conger and Daisuke Wakabayashi, "Google Employees Protest Secret Work on Censored Search Engine for China," *The New York Times*, August 16, 2018, https://www.nytimes.com/2018/08/16/technology/google-employees-protest-search-censored-china.html?hp&action=click&pgtype=Homepage&clickSource=story-heading&module=first-column-region®ion=top-news&WT.nav=top-news (accessed March 2, 2019).

[34] See a more detailed discussion of Google's Dragonfly Project in Chapter 2.

[35] Tian Zengrui, Guillermo A. Buitrago, and Shoirahon Odilova, "Will a Collectivistic Culture protect your Intellectual Property? Effect of Individualism on Intellectual Property Protection," *International Business Research* 10, no. 11 (2017).

PAPA: Privacy, Accuracy, Property, and Accessibility

In an economy that is rapidly becoming dominated by knowledge workers, the value of information is paramount. And in these days of AI, even raw data, in sufficient quantities, can also be valuable. Those who possess the "best" information and know how to use it will win. The recent trends in cloud computing and big data permit high levels of computational power and storage to be purchased for relatively small amounts of money. Although this trend means that computer-generated or stored information now falls within the reach of a larger percentage of the populace, it also means that collecting and storing information is becoming easier and more cost effective. Although this circumstance can affect businesses and individuals for the better, it also can affect them substantially for the worse.

Almost four decades ago, in a Foundational Reading, visionary researcher Richard Mason proposed a framework with four general areas of information ethics in which the control of information is crucial. He summarized the four areas with the acronym PAPA: privacy, accuracy, property, and accessibility.[36] Recently his framework was reexamined in a *Communications of AIS* special issue. The main article by Sandy Richardson, Stacie Petter, and Michelle Carter suggests that the framework still has value even when considering contemporary issues related to big data analytics.[37] They add that the framework should be changed to PAPAS to take into account societal issues such as when big data analytics (along with AI) are used intentionally or unintentionally to marginalize certain communities of people. Other scholars known for their writings on ethics agreed on the value of the original PAPA framework. Mason's framework has limitations in terms of accommodating the range and complexity of ethical issues encountered in today's information-intensive world, the diverse contexts in which ethical decisions are made, and the conflicting values of the many different parties involved. That said, this popular framework is a good beginning step in trying to understand information ethics.

Mason suggests a number of questions that can be asked by managers (or actually any individual) to gain control over information. We have updated these questions with some additional ones suggested by Richardson, Petter, and Carter in the world of big data (see Figure 13.2). Their questions are stated in terms of data and datasets vs information and files.

Privacy

Many people consider privacy to be the most important area in which their interests need to be safeguarded. **Privacy** has long been considered "the right to be left alone."[38] Although it has been argued that

Area	Critical Questions
Privacy	What data and information must people reveal about themselves to others? Can the data and information that people provide be used for purposes other than those for which the people were told that it would be used? Do people know what data and information is collected about them? Can the data people provide in multiple datasets be aggregated and processed so that they can be identified?
Accuracy	Who is responsible for the reliability, authenticity, and accuracy of data and information? Is there a plan in place to identify errors or biases? What level of inaccuracy is tolerable in a dataset? Who has the right to access IoT sensor data?
Property	Who owns the data, information, and aggregated data sets? Who owns the channels of distribution, and how should they be regulated? What is the fair price of data and information that is exchanged?
Accessibility	What data and information does a person or organization have a right to obtain, with what protection, and under what conditions? Does the person accessing personal data and information "need to know" the information that is being accessed? Will a person be harmed by choosing not to provide data or information to a service or organization?

FIGURE 13.2 Mason's areas of managerial control.

Source: Adapted from Richard O Mason, "Four Ethical Issues of the Information Age," *MIS Quarterly* 10, no. 1 (March 1986), 5 and Richardson, Sandra M., Stacie Petter, and Michelle Carter, "Five Ethical Issues in the Big Data Analytics Age," *Communications of the Association for Information Systems* 1 (2021), 18.

[36] Richard O. Mason, "Four Ethical Issues of the Information Age," *MIS Quarterly* 10, no. 1 (March 1986).

[37] Richardson, S. M., Petter, S., and Carter, M. (2021). Five Ethical Issues in the Big Data Analytics Age. *Communications of the Association for Information Systems*, (49), 18.

[38] Samuel D. Warren and Louis D. Brandeis, "The Right to Privacy," *Harvard Law Review* 4, no. 5 (December 1890): 193–200.

so many different definitions exist that it is hard to satisfactorily define the term,[39] it is "fundamentally about protections from intrusion and information gathering by others."[40] Typically, it has been defined in terms of individuals' ability to personally control information about themselves. But requiring individuals to control their own information would severely limit what is private. In today's information-oriented world, individuals really have little control.

Privacy Paradox

Managers must consider the *privacy paradox*, which trades off convenience, irritation, and even entertainment for privacy. For instance, a company might store credit card numbers of its customers so that they do not have to enter that information every time they visit the firm's website. However, by doing so, there is additional risk of theft of that information. There is also convenience in tailoring advertisements according to a person's unique interests. Rather than suffer with relentless advertisements that have little relevance, ad networks that share information across sites potentially provide less irritation to consumers. Finally, teenagers and adults alike post private information about location, friends, and activities, largely for entertainment purposes in spite of abundant warnings.

Why would people be willing to give up their privacy for convenience? First, by supplying the information to vendors, they can receive personalized services in return. For example, their mobile phone's GPS might alert them that the restaurant that they are just walking by has a special offer on one of their favorite foods—sushi. Second, they might be paid for the information at a price that they believe exceeds what they are giving up. Third, they might see providing information, such as that contained on many Facebook pages, as something that everybody is doing. Some individuals, especially younger ones, share information that would otherwise be considered private simply because they view it as a way to have their friends know them and to get to know their friends. "Digital natives" who have grown up in the Internet age do not know a society without the web. They are comfortable building relationships, and, consequently, sharing information on the web that others might consider private or sensitive. Later, though, they may regret their disclosures.

A research study performed by the third author of this book[41] revealed that users immediately grant even questionable permission requests in the context of a calendar-related app they downloaded. Some of those requests included access to the camera, the microphone, body sensors, and storage. It took several iterations of our materials to not only tell users they could refuse any and all of the nine permissions but also we had to quiz them repeatedly until they answered correctly that the permissions were not required. Many consumers make choices carelessly. Interestingly, the concern about privacy on Internet sites varies across the globe; for example, concern about privacy is greater in Europe than in the United States; and, it is of much less concern in Korea than in the United States or Europe.[42]

Another challenge to privacy is the ease with which data from various sources can be connected and then combined to provide information that individuals don't want to share about themselves and that is anonymized. This was demonstrated in the study reported in *Science,* discussed earlier in this chapter, where the data was matched across multiple data sets.

The Federal Trade Commission (FTC), serving as a privacy watchdog, fined Amazon a USD $25 million civil penalty for violating the Children's Online Privacy Protection Act by keeping information collected from children's conversations with Alexa (Amazon's virtual voice assistant) longer than the parents agreed upon in Amazon's Child Privacy Disclosure. The FTC also advocates for more understandable privacy notices for consumers that will result in more transparency about data provided to firms disclosed only "in the fine print." The Director of the FTC's consumer protection bureau has warned that the agency is "not afraid to take companies to court" for poor data practices.[43]

---

[39] Paul Pavlou, "State of the Inform Privacy Literature: Where Are We Now and Where Should We Go?" *MIS Quarterly* 35, no. 4 (2011): 977–85.

[40] E. F. Stone, D. G. Gardner, H. G. Gueutal, and S. McClure, "A Field Experiment Comparing Information-Privacy Values, Beliefs, and Attitudes across Several Types of Organizations," *Journal of Applied Psychology* 68, no. 3 (August 1983): 459–68.

[41] David Eargle, Dennis Galletta, Shadi Janansefat, Dimitar Kunev, & Shivendu Singh, "The chaos of order: sequence and mindlessness effects in obtaining successive app permissions." December 2017. In Proceedings of the 12th Pre-ICIS Workshop on Information Security and Privacy (Vol. 1).

[42] N. Kshetri, "Big Data's Role in Expanding Access to Financial Services in China," *International Journal of Information Management* 36, no. 3 (2016): 297–308.

[43] Ashley Gold, "Top FTC Official Warns Companies on data." Axios, December 15, 2022, https://www.axios.com/2022/12/15/ftc-official-warns-consumer-protection-data (accessed June 6, 2023).

Managers must avoid ethical blunders while they seek to provide customers convenient and useful opportunities. Managers might benefit by meeting ethical standards about privacy that are even higher than what the law demands.[44] However, given that so much data is collected by sensors that people don't even know is being collected and that hackers are getting even better at accessing data that people do know has been collected, it might be realistic to conclude that we live in a world where true privacy is hard to achieve.

Taking Control

Although total control is difficult in today's digital world, individuals can exert control by making efforts to manage their privacy through *choice*, *consent*, and *correction*. In particular, individuals can *choose* situations that offer the desired level of access to their information ranging from "total privacy to unabashed publicity."[45]

Individuals may also exert control when they manage their privacy through *consent*. When they give their consent, they are granting access to otherwise restricted information and they are specifying the purposes for which it may be used. In granting access, people should recognize that extensive amounts of data that can personally identify them are being collected and stored in databases and that these data can be used in ways that the individuals had not intended. When giving their consent, individuals should try to anticipate how their information might be reused as a result of data mining or aggregation. They should also try to anticipate unauthorized access through security breaches or internal browsing in companies whose security is lax. Finally, individuals should have control in managing their privacy by being able to access their personal information and *correct* it if it is wrong. To protect the integrity of information collected about individuals, federal regulators have recommended allowing consumers limited access to corporate information databases. Consumers thus could update their information and correct errors.

A new **online reputation management** industry has sprung up in recent years, targeting both individuals (such as CEOs and public figures) and firms. For a fee, firms such as Reputation.com continuously search for negative formal or informal reviews about companies or individuals on websites and report results periodically. Experts advise managers to take an active role in protecting their brand by improving the presentation of search results, creating and controlling brand pages on popular social networks, participating actively in blogs, and providing press releases.

For organizations, the tension between the proper use of personal information and information privacy is considered to be one of the most serious ethical debates of the Information Age.[46] One of the main organizational challenges to privacy is surveillance of employees.[47] For example, to ensure that employees are productive, employers can monitor their employees' e-mail and computer utilization while they are at work even though companies have not historically monitored employees' telephone calls.

Disney faced unintended consequences when it displayed a leaderboard with an efficiency report of housekeepers at some of its hotels. The fastest housekeepers found their names displayed in green, and the slowest ones were displayed in red. Disney had wanted to motivate its employees, but instead, the employees felt as if they were being controlled by a machine.[48]

Individuals are also facing privacy challenges from organizations providing them with services. Their actions are being traced with **cookies** that can follow individuals' surfing behaviors. Every time someone uses one of the main search engines or merely visits a site directly, a "cookie," or small coded text message, is created, updated, and retrieved from the user's hard drive. That cookie message is sent back to the host company each time the browser requests a page from the server,[49] enabling these companies to track their surfing habits. Cookies have been ruled to be legal by U.S. courts.[50] *Essential* cookies allow a website to have a shopping cart, allowing the browser to remember what you're doing from page to page. Imagine

[44] Loebbecke, C., & Galliers, R. D. (2021). CAIS Rebuttal for "Five Ethical Issues in the Big Data Analytics Age" by Richardson et al. (2019). Communications of the Association for Information Systems, 49(1), 22, p. 472.

[45] H. T. Tavani and James Moore, "Privacy Protection, Control of Information, and Privacy-Enhancing Technologies," *Computers and Society* (March 2001): 6–11.

[46] Pavlou, "State of the Inform Privacy Literature," 977–85.

[47] B. C. Stahl, "The Impact of UK Human Rights Act 1998 on Privacy Protection in the Workplace," *Computer Security, Privacy, and Politics: Current Issues, Challenges, and Solutions* (Hershey, PA: Idea Group, 2008), 55–68.

[48] A. F. Rutkowski and C. Saunders, *Emotional and Cognitive Overload: The Dark Side of Information Technology* (New York: Routledge, 2018).

[49] Vangie Beal, "Cookie," October 20, 2021, Webopedia, http://www.webopedia.com/TERM/c/cookie.html (accessed June 5, 2023).

[50] Patti Croft and Catherine McNally, "Do I Need a Cookie Policy on My Website?" All about Cookies.org, March 2, 2023, https://allaboutcookies.org/do-i-need-cookie-policy-website (accessed June 11, 2023).

having to furnish your username and password for each new page view in the steps for creating an order! Cookies prevent the need to do that.

You might have noticed that many websites now ask if you are willing to accept the use of cookies on their website. This is a demonstration of the far-reaching effect of the EU's GDPR, which applies not only to EU member states but also to companies in any part of the globe that want to do business with EU members. A similar law has been adopted by voters in California, the **CCPA California Consumer Privacy Act**. GDPR treats cookies as personal data since they can be used to identify individuals. The EU Cookie law doesn't just pertain to essential cookies that are necessary to perform the shopping cart or logging in services desired by site visitors. It especially targets the *nonessential* cookies, also called *third-party cookies (TPCs),* that are from advertisers or third parties, or that are used for analytics.[51]

The TPC was a very creative invention for ad providers. Although a nonessential cookie is accessible only to the server that created it, the server of a third-party service *does* have access by contributing a container for an ad on web pages of hundreds of different firms. The ad provider records the address for a product you examine on a popular website inside their cookie, amassing detailed information about your browsing practices across a wide variety of sites the ad provider partners with. The ad provider then uses it to determine which advertisements to provide or even to sell their databases to other firms. A revealing examination of the 50 most popular US websites determined that more than two-thirds of the 3,000 plus tracking files installed by a total of 131 companies after people visited these websites were used to create rich databases of consumer profiles that could be sold.[52]

These TPC ad providers have so many clients that some customers are surprised when a social network site displays a baseball glove in an ad just after you were looking at that same glove on Amazon.com. Its rich understanding of your interests enable it to sell the proper ads to any of its client websites in real time. The sites do not even need to know your identity because your interests are of primary concern for serving an ad to you.

TPCs have been criticized for invasion of privacy, and in response, Google, Mozilla, and Apple have stated their intentions to discontinue using them. One concern has been raised about how advertisers can reach people who would be interested in their products after TPCs are gone. Well, advertisers can rest easy because on the horizon is a new technology "Zero Party Cookies" (ZPC). The browser will store answers to questions about your interests, and no longer will advertisers have to rely on the TPCs to find out. Rather than lose out on the targeting from TPCs, ZPCs will be more valuable to advertisers because of higher specificity, reliability, and accuracy.[53] Another bonus is that this information is enabled by the user, which is more consistent with the "opt in" requirement of GDPR.

Do customers in the United States have a right to privacy while searching the Internet? So far, courts have decided that the answer is no, but questions have increasingly come up in Congress about strengthening privacy laws. Governments around the world are grappling with privacy legislation. Not surprisingly, they are using diverse approaches for ensuring the privacy of their citizens. The National Security Agency (NSA) computer system administrator Edward Snowden engaged in "whistle-blowing" but revealed many government secrets, violating several laws and perhaps endangering enforcement agents. In the coming years, if he returns to the United States and engages in extensive dialog, history will draw more definitive and perhaps more holistic conclusions than those that are available today.

The United States' the so-called "sectorial" approach relies on a mix of legislation, regulation, and self-regulation. It is based upon a legal tradition with a strong emphasis on free trade. In the United States, privacy laws are enacted in response to specific problems for specific groups of people or specific industries. Examples of the relatively limited privacy legislation in the United States include the 1974 Privacy Act that regulates the US government's collection and use of personal information and the 1998 Children's Online Privacy Protection Act that regulates the online collection and use of children's personal information.

The Gramm–Leach–Bliley Act of 1999 applies to financial institutions. It followed in the wake of banks selling sensitive information, including account information, Social Security numbers, credit card purchase histories, and so forth to telemarketing companies. This US law somewhat mitigates the sharing

[51] CookieYes.com, "Understanding Third-Party Cookies: A Guide," CookieYes, February 21, 2023, https://www.cookieyes.com/blog/third-party-cookies/ (accessed June 11, 2023).

[52] Julia Angwin, "The Web's New Gold Mine: Your Secrets," *The Wall Street Journal*, July 30, 2010, http://online.wsj.com/article/SB10001424052748703940904575395073512989404.html (accessed June 11, 2023).

[53] Vlad Gozman, "The Slow Death of Third Party Cookies," Forbes, September 12, 2022, https://www.forbes.com/sites/theyec/2022/09/12/the-slow-death-of-third-party-cookies/?sh=5c70d9f44026 (accessed May 29, 2023).

of sensitive financial and personal information by allowing customers of financial institutions the limited right to "opt out" of the information sharing by these institutions with nonaffiliated third parties. This means that the financial institution may use the information unless the customer specifically tells the institution that his or her personal information cannot be used or distributed. The Fair Credit Reporting act limits the use of credit reports provided by consumer reporting agencies to "permissible purposes" and grants individuals the right to access their reports and correct errors in them.

The Health Insurance Portability and Accountability Act (HIPAA) of 1996 is designed to safeguard the privacy and security of electronic information in the health-care industry. Its Privacy Rule ensures that patients' health information is properly protected while allowing its necessary flow for providing and promoting health care. HIPAA's Security Rule specifies national standards for protecting electronic health information from unauthorized access, alteration, deletion, and transmission. That said, not every single fact is protected by HIPAA, as the GoodRx situation discussed earlier demonstrated. However, precedents in court may eventually trigger the need for new legislation.

In contrast to the sectorial approach of the United States and its strong encouragement of self-regulation by industry, the European Union relies on omnibus legislation that requires creation of government data protection agencies, registration of databases with those agencies, and, in some cases, prior approval before processing personal data. The legislation is linked with the continental European legal tradition where privacy is a well-established right.[54]

We have talked about the GDPR frequently in this chapter and in this book. **GDPR (General Data Protection Regulation)** is a law that has been adopted by all EU member states and that places even greater emphasis on individual rights. It prohibits the transfer of personal data to non-European Union nations that do not meet the European privacy standards. Individual rights include allowing the data subjects to see what data has been collected and held in an intelligible form and to restrict processing of their data. GDPR applies not only to the companies that collect/control the data but also to the companies that process them. Further, there has to be a contract between the companies that collect/control the data and those that process them. That is why you have been seeing so many requests for your consent to use the cookies generated when you visit websites. If firms do not adhere to GDPR when they transact business in any EU country or with any EU citizen, they face heavy fines. While many US companies originally believed that the GDPR could hamper their ability to engage in many trans-Atlantic transactions, a 2022 report[55] indicates that the actual impact was to have over 100 countries adopt privacy standards.

Some firms made errors in the beginning, such as Amazon in 2021, as they learned only too well. In 2021, Amazon was fined USD $887 million by the EU privacy watchdog, the Luxembourg National Commission for Data Protection, for the processing of personal data in a way that did not comply with the GDPR.[56] As of mid-year 2023, the United States is not included in a very short list of countries with "adequate security" and faces more GDPR restrictions as a result until negotiations are resolved.[57]

As described earlier in this chapter, CCPA is the first similar law in the United States, but it is limited to protecting customers in California.[58] The law applies only to larger firms (greater than $50 million in sales or 50,000 consumers), or firms that derive more than 50% of their revenue from the sale of consumers' personal information. Fines are levied on companies that do not apply unspecified "reasonable care" to how they handle and share data. Unlike GDPR, CCPA does not require "opt in" consent for adults. However, for children under 13, there is a need to explicitly provide permission for selling private information. CCPA also requires firms to make it easier for consumers to manage their personal information, to see what information is collected from them, delete that personal information, and opt out of personal information being sold.

The **CPRA California Privacy Rights Act** is an amendment to CCPA that went into effect in early 2023. CPRA still works from the perspective of "opt out," so firms can sell information until consumers

---

[54] Stahl, "The Impact of UK Human Rights Act 1998 on Privacy Protection in the Workplace," 55–68.

[55] Anthony Jones, "GDPR Three Years Later: What Impact Has it Made?" IS Partners, August 16, 2022, https://www.ispartnersllc.com/blog/gdpr-one-year-later-impact/ (accessed June 5, 2023).

[56] Sam Shead, "Amazon Hit with $887 Million Fine by European Privacy Watchdog," July 30, 2021, CNBC, https://www.cnbc.com/2021/07/30/amazon-hit-with-fine-by-eu-privacy-watchdog-.html (accessed June 6, 2023).

[57] European Parliament, "Texts Adopted" May 11, 2023, https://www.europarl.europa.eu/doceo/document/TA-9-2023-0204_EN.html (accessed June 6, 2023).

[58] Privacy Team, "CPRA vs CCPA vs GDPR: Key Changes & Differences," March 1, 2022, Securiti.com, https://securiti.ai/cpra-vs-ccpa-vs-gdpr/ (accessed May 30, 2023).

make a specific request for keeping their information private. Interestingly, CPRA requires a clearly visible banner on a firm's homepage that says "limit the use of my sensitive personal information," that contains a link to accomplish that action. CCPA also raises the threshold to 100,000 consumers. Also, firms are required to minimize the data that they capture and store.[59]

Accuracy

The **accuracy**, or the correctness, of information assumes real importance for society as computers come to dominate in corporate record-keeping activities. When records are entered incorrectly, who is to blame? Some firms fail to keep accurate records or even fail to bill customers for several years, as several homeowners have discovered, when they fail to account for refinancing, mortgage modifications, or other unusual events. Sometimes lenders sell a second mortgage to other investors with inadequate recordkeeping. For example, one pair of Florida homeowners in 2021 received a notification that their second mortgage was in default, and that they owed $100,000 on the second mortgage that was initially $57,200 in 2006. The first and second mortgages were from the same lender. The billing statements on the second mortgage had stopped, which led them to believe that both mortgages were included in the mortgage modification in 2014.[60] Had the billing continued, it is likely that the subsequent foreclosure in 2022 would not have happened.

Although these incidents may highlight the need for better controls over the banks' internal processes, it also demonstrates the risks that can be attributed to inaccurate information retained in corporate systems. Although they cannot expect to eliminate all mistakes from the online environment, managers must establish controls to prevent situations such as this one.

Over time, it becomes increasingly difficult to maintain the accuracy of some types of information. Although a person's birth date does not typically change (the second author's grandmother's change of her birth year notwithstanding), addresses and phone numbers often change as people relocate, and even their names may change with marriage, divorce, and adoption. The European Union Directive on Data Protection requires accurate and up-to-date data and tries to make sure that data are kept no longer than necessary to fulfill their stated purpose. This is a challenge many companies don't even attempt to meet.

Another challenge is assessing accuracy in an era where big data analytics and AI are becoming ever more prevalent. It's not only the volume of data that poses a challenge is assessing accuracy. It's also the fact that it is harder to assess accuracy when there are multiple datasets and the aggregation might exacerbate inconsistencies. Further, some of the data may be gathered from faulty sensors. For example, faulty sensor data fed into the flight control system of Lion Air 610 falsely indicated that the plane was flying at too steep an upward angle. The flight control system reacted by forcing the plane to fly downward—into the ground.[61]

One method of improving accuracy is to allow the users to see their own records and then to allow them to request changes if inaccuracies are found. One example is seen from Google, which provides a page[62] that enables you to see what it concludes are your characteristics. They can be turned on and off and also altered to make them more accurate if you desire greater accuracy. You can also make them completely inaccurate if you'd like, but ads you receive will be less targeted.

Property

The increase in monitoring leads to the question of **property**, or who owns the data. Now that organizations have the ability to collect vast amounts of data on their clients, do they have a right to share the data with others to create a more accurate profile of an individual? Consider what happens when a consumer

[59] Privacy Team (2022).

[60] Nicole Friedman and Ben Eisen, "Zombie Mortgages Could Force Some Homeowners Into Foreclosure," *Wall Street Journal*, June 4, 2023 https://www.wsj.com/articles/zombie-mortgages-could-force-some-homeowners-into-foreclosure-e615ab2a (accessed June 6, 2023).

[61] Richardson, S. M., Petter, S., & Carter, M. (2021). Five Ethical Issues in the Big Data Analytics Age. *Communications of the Association for Information Systems*, (1), 18.

[62] As of this writing, you can see this at https://myadcenter.google.com/controls (accessed June 5, 2023).

provides information for one use, say a car loan. This information is collected and stored in a data warehouse and then "mined" to create a profile for a completely different use. And if some other company creates such consolidated profiles, who owns that information, which in many cases was not divulged willingly for that purpose?

Also consider what happens when you "like" a product. Your face is displayed on your friend's page when she or he sees an advertisement for that product, which might surprise you. This raises the question of who owns images that are posted in cyberspace. The images are *by* a photographer, *of* you, and *on* Facebook's servers. All can argue ownership to some extent. But when a site sells your data to a third party, where is the ownership at that point? The answer to this question is unclear. Further, with ever more sophisticated methods of computer animation, another question can arise: Can companies use newly "created" images or a character resembling a celebrity in other media without paying royalties? Law practices will have their hands full for years to come in trying to sort out these issues.

The issue of data ownership is becoming ever more salient in this era of big data. Using Kirzner's Finders-Keepers theory, some have argued that if a third party obtained the data in a "just" way, then if that third party mines the data and derives valuable insights, the fruits of that data mining legitimately belong to the third party. Author Marijn Sax disagrees with applying Finders-Keepers theory to big data/analytics and argues that you can't really separate individuals from their data because a person's information and feelings are part of that person's identity. Further, in many cases, the person's data are acquired without adequate informed consent. Also, in many cases, the person lacks the ability to anticipate how the acquisition of the data will impact them when combined with data aggregated from huge databases. This makes it difficult to confirm that the data were acquired in a "just" way—muddying the whole issue of data ownership.[63]

Finally, Mason (page 5) suggests that information, which is costly to produce in the first place, can be easily reproduced and sold without the individual who produced it even knowing what is happening—and certainly not being reimbursed for its use. In talking about this information that is produced, Mason notes:

> *". . . information has the illusive quality of being easy to reproduce and to share with others. Moreover, this replication can take place without destroying the original. This makes information hard to safeguard since, unlike tangible property, it becomes communicable and hard to keep it to one's self."*

Accessibility

In the age of the information worker, **accessibility**, or the ability to obtain the data, becomes increasingly important. Would-be users of information must first gain the physical ability to access online information resources, which broadly means they must access computational systems. Second and more important, they then must gain access to the information itself. In this sense, the issue of access is closely linked to that of property. Looking forward, the major issue facing managers is how to create and maintain access to information for society at large without harming individuals who have provided much, if not all, of the information.

Accessibility is becoming increasingly important with the surge in **identity-theft**, which occurs "when someone uses your personal information, such as your name, Social Security number, or credit card information, without your permission to commit fraud or other illegal activities."[64] The breach at Equifax has made identity-theft a concern for over 140 million Americans. The Equifax breach and the concept of identity-theft is covered in Chapter 7, and you can see an obvious link between accessibility of information and security.

Managers' Role in Ethical Information Control

Managers must work to implement controls over information highlighted by the PAPA principles. Managers should not only deter identity theft by limiting inappropriate access to customer information but also respect their customers' privacy. Three best practices can be adopted to help improve an organization's information control by incorporating moral responsibility.[65]

---

[63] M. Sax, "Big Data: Finders Keepers, Losers Weepers?" *Ethics and Information Technology* 18, no. 1 (2016): 25–31.

[64] Identity Theft Organization, Frequently Asked Questions, http://www.identitytheft.org (accessed June 6, 2023).

[65] Mary J. Culnan and Cynthia Clarke Williams, (2009). "How Ethics Can Enhance Organizational Privacy: Lessons from the Choice Point and TJX Data Breaches." *MIS Quarterly*, 673–87.

- *Create a culture of responsibility:* CEOs and top-level executives should lead in promoting responsibility for protecting both personal information and the organization's information systems. Internet companies should post their policies about how they will use private information in understandable language and make a good case as to why they need the personal data that they gather from customers and clients. Author Mary Culnan noted in *CIO* magazine about customers providing information: "If there are no benefits or if they aren't told why the information is being collected or how it's being used, a lot of people say, "Forget it."[66] The costs of meaningfully securing the information may seem to outweigh the obvious benefits—unless there is a breach. Thus, it is unlikely that an organization can create a culture of integrity and responsibility unless there is a moral commitment from the CEO.
- *Implement governance processes for information control:* In Chapter 9, we discuss the importance of mechanisms to identify the important decisions that need to be made and who would make them. Further, control governance structures, such as Control Objectives for Information and Related Technology (COBIT) and Information Technology Infrastructure Library (ITIL), can help identify risks to the information and behaviors to promote information control. Organizations need governance to make sure that their information control behaviors comply with the law and reflect their risk environment.
- *Avoid decoupling:* Often organizations use complex processes to treat personal privacy issues. Should an apparent conflict appear, managers can decouple the impact of institutional processes and mechanisms on individuals. In that way, managers can shift the responsibility away from themselves and onto the company. It would be much better if the managers were to act as if the customer's information were actually their own. This would mean that in delicate situations involving privacy or other issues of information control, managers would ask themselves "How would I feel if my information were handled in this way?"[67]

AI, Business, and Society

We have covered generative AI earlier,[68] but its implications on business and society are still coming to light. By January 2023, two months after its launch, 100 million users were experimenting with ChatGPT to check it out, discover its capabilities, and even do homework by using it. ChatGPT is known as the fastest growing consumer application in history, with 13 million unique visitors every day in January 2023. Compare that to Instagram, which took 2½ years to reach 100 million users.[69] ChatGPT broadsided schools at all levels, who were not prepared to receive assignments and programming computer code that could have been generated by a machine. Racing in to help teachers and professors, private industry has wasted no time to respond, by enhancing existing plagiarism detectors to check for signs of machine authoring.

The software industry is also responding quickly, incorporating the generative AI tools into products exemplified by Microsoft's Bing for their Edge browser and Google's Search Generative Experience for their Chrome browser (the latter by invitation only from a waitlist).

Other industries have incorporated AI into products such as self-driving cars, chatbots for help lines, digital cameras, and even medical diagnosis. However, generative AI is new to them as well. Many now are setting their sights to figure out the impacts of generative AI on the future of work, and some worry that it might not take long for generative AI to replace workers.

Industry after industry has found progress in technology to replace workers. Supermarkets have eliminated many human cashiers in favor of self-service lines. It was not that long ago that bookkeepers and librarians kept manual records and used large filing cabinets to keep track of transactions. New technologies have certainly made work more efficient, which is defined as getting more output with the same or less input.

[66] "Saving Private Data," *CIO Magazine*, October 1, 1998.

[67] Culnan and Williams, "How Ethics Can Enhance Organizational Privacy," 685.

[68] See Chapter 12.

[69] Krystal Hu, "ChatGPT Sets Record for Fastest-Growing User Base – Analyst Note," Reuters, https://www.reuters.com/technology/chatgpt-sets-record-fastest-growing-user-base-analyst-note-2023-02-01/ (accessed June 4, 2023).

Four months after ChatGPT made its splash, Forbes examined industries most and least likely to be impacted by generative AI.[70] They predict that the jobs most impacted will be in banking/finance, media, marketing, and legal services, because those jobs require analyzing real-time data and reading and writing volumes of text. Least impacted will be jobs in manufacturing, agriculture, and healthcare, largely because the first two have already been revolutionized by robots, and the third requires a sympathetic and sensitive touch to understand and instruct patients.

But, there have been some expressions of worry. In early 2023, a few months after ChatGPT made its "big splash," Many AI researchers began expressing reservations about society's ability to absorb the technology's impact. A petition was started that called for a six-month pause in development of more advanced AI technology to give people a chance to catch up with its concepts, capabilities, and impacts. By May 3, 2023, almost 30,000 people signed the petition, which includes many AI and technology researchers and designers, including Elon Musk.[71]

One of the most insightful points of view is from a founder of an AI company who warns that creators of AI systems do not know what the technology can do. In an interview, he stated that management should realize that AI technology is changing rapidly and it's also unpredictable. He predicts that the future will be "a lot weirder than the present."[72] This suggests an interesting 2 × 2 framework (see Figure 13.3).

The potential for an unpredictable future with AI has made some scientists fearful of the end of civilization, where top people in top firms were "admitting that their own products terrify them."[73] The fears are centered around AI not having a sense of morality, committing crimes to achieve a goal set by the user. Also, because the technology can be used to create disinformation through "deep fake" audio and video messages, which can be created in eight minutes for only a few dollars,[74] eventually we will only be able to trust face-to-face communications. One proposed remedy is to require under penalty of law, "watermarks" on AI-generated materials to identify the content as AI-generated and also to identify the source. Laws have not caught up to technology, so managers should expect some vigorous discussion, and hopefully, action in this regard over the next decade. Otherwise, brands, political candidates, countries, and the human race itself could indeed be threatened. Vice President Kamala Harris told a set of executives that they had a moral obligation to make AI products safe,[75] and it might be helpful for firms to formulate plans in this direction before legislation is created that forces them to do so.

But according to David Autor of MIT, a happy scenario is more likely than a dangerous and depressing one, and managers of today need to be prepared for this.[76] He predicts that people will not any longer need

		Technological Predictability	
		Unpredictable	Predictable
Speed of Technological Change	Slow	Operate with caution and scan the technological horizon	Operate with confidence while innovating strategies and processes
	Fast	Chaos followed by careful study and rethinking	Careful Planning; concentrate on strategy

FIGURE 13.3 Advice for management facing technology unpredictability and fast technological change.

[70] Arianna Johnson, "Which Jobs Will AI Replace? These 4 Industries Will be Heavily Impacted," Forbes.com, March 31, 2023, https://www.forbes.com/sites/ariannajohnson/2023/03/30/which-jobs-will-ai-replace-these-4-industries-will-be-heavily-impacted/ (accessed June 4, 2023).

[71] Bernard Marr, "Should We Stop Developing AI for the Good of Humanity?" Forbes.com, May 3, 2023, https://www.forbes.com/sites/bernardmarr/2023/05/03/should-we-stop-developing-ai-for-the-good-of-humanity/ (accessed June 4, 2023).

[72] NPR Technology, "Artificial Intelligence Can be Found in Many Places. How Safe Is The Technology?" https://www.npr.org/2023/05/10/1175165491/artificial-intelligence-can-be-found-in-many-places-how-safe-is-the-technology (accessed June 4, 2023, para. 12).

[73] Hiawatha Bray, "This Is Civilization-Threatening: Here's Why AI Poses an Existential Threat," The Boston Globe, May 31, 2023. https://www.msn.com/en-us/news/technology/this-is-civilization-threatening-here-s-why-ai-poses-an-existential-risk/ar-AA1bXm34 (accessed June 4, 2023, para. 3).

[74] Shannon Bond, "AI-Generated Deep Fakes Are Moving Fast. Policymakers Can't Keep Up," NPR April 27, 2023, https://www.npr.org/2023/04/27/1172387911/how-can-people-spot-fake-images-created-by-artificial-intelligence (accessed June 5, 2023).

[75] David McCabe, "White House Pushes Tech CEOs to Limit Risks of AI," New York Times, May 4, 2023, https://www.nytimes.com/2023/05/04/technology/us-ai-research-regulation.html (accessed June 10, 2023).

[76] Greg Rosalsky, "What If AI Could Rebuild the Middle Class?" NPR Planet Money, May 9, 2023. https://www.npr.org/sections/money/2023/05/09/1174933574/what-if-ai-could-rebuild-the-middle-class (accessed June 4, 2023).

high skills to perform work, and AI tools could "rebuild the middle class." Those with "fundamental skills" will be able to use AI tools to perform the duties formerly by highly educated workers such as doctors, lawyers, and other professionals. The machines are shown patterns in a lot of data and then they classify, predict, and recommend, but we do not know how they draw inferences. Autor refers to this as Polanyi's Revenge, where computers have tacit knowledge and cannot explain to us how they understand things. Some experiments at MIT show how less-skilled writers using ChatGPT improved their writing skills. So, Autor predicts that jobs currently made only for those with high levels of education could in the future be filled by those only with foundational skills, helped by AI tools. We have skills that computers do not yet have: creativity, adaptive problem-solving, and common sense. A resurgence of the middle class is a more comforting vision for humanity's future than the scenarios provided by the alarmists.

Green Computing

Green computing is concerned with using computing resources efficiently. The need for green computing is becoming more obvious considering the amount of power needed to drive the world's computers and telecommunication parts. It was estimated that the digital economy uses 10% of the world's electricity to run data centers, charge smartphone and tablet batteries, and transmit data globally.[77] Powering just Google's 40,000 searches in one second takes as much energy as a ceiling fan that runs continuously for a month.[78] Google's own disclosure in 2022 revealed that in 2021 it consumed 18.6 terawatt hours,[79] or about 10% more than three counties the size of San Francisco.[80] Today, it is likely to be even higher.

In the not-too-distant past, few households had personal computers, and they were off much of the time. Nowadays, many households run multiple laptop computers, as well as "always on" smartphones, tablets, and smart watches. To serve these products, high-speed Internet connections are used constantly so that users can be alerted immediately about new e-mails, texts, social media posts, and news bulletins.

Some very surprising recent developments have entered the picture as well. In 2018, Bitcoin, for instance, was estimated to consume about the same amount of energy as the country of Ireland (22 terawatt hours annually). The detailed technology of Bitcoin is beyond our scope, but, essentially, Bitcoin needs users to serve as "miners" for new virtual coins. A Bitcoin miner needs a computer to solve a difficult computational puzzle, encrypting chunks of data for storage. After each computation, the computer compares the result to a rare goal, and then if it does not meet the goal, the computer must expand the chunk of data by adding one to a special numerical part of the record and trying again, and again, and again. Once it meets the goal, a new Bitcoin is created and the first "miner" to succeed earns a fraction of the coin plus a flat fee as a reward. The encryption goal becomes more difficult over time and increased competition drives the miners to buy and install faster and faster PC components to provide a continued competitive edge,[81] as well as an exponentially increasing appetite for electric power.

Many firms have developed sustainability plans that extend from manufacturing to executive travel to information systems use. The increased focus on sustainability and the use of more energy-saving technologies have contributed to reduced energy use by many firms, although overall energy use is still substantial.

Sustainability measures taken by firms include replacing older systems with more energy-efficient ones, moving workloads based on energy efficiency, using the most power-inefficient servers only at times of peak usage, improving air flows in data centers, and turning to cloud computing as well as using virtualization. As introduced in Chapter 6, virtualization lets a computer run multiple operating systems or several versions of the same operating system at the same time. SAP used virtualization to become greener.

[77] B. Walsh, "The Surprisingly Large Energy Footprint of the Digital Economy [UPDATE]," *Time*, August 14, 2013, http://science.time.com/2013/08/14/power-drain-the-digital-cloud-is-using-more-energy-than-you-think/ (accessed September 7, 2015).

[78] Direct Energy Business, "Powering a Google Search: The Facts and Figures," November 28, 2017, https://business.directenergy.com/blog/2017/november/powering-a-google-search (accessed March 3, 2019).

[79] Google, 2022 Environmental Report, https://www.gstatic.com/gumdrop/sustainability/google-2022-environmental-report.pdf (accessed June 5, 2023), pg. 13.

[80] Find Energy, "San Francisco County, California Electricity Rates & Statistics," August 4, 2022, https://findenergy.com/ca/san-francisco-county-electricity/ (accessed June 10, 2023).

[81] G. F. "The Economist Explains: Why Bitcoin Uses So Much Energy," *The Economist*, July 9, 2018, https://www.economist.com/the-economist-explains/2018/07/09/why-bitcoin-uses-so-much-energy (accessed March 3, 2019).

SAP noted that green IT "presents some of the greatest opportunities to increase our efficiency, improve our operations and reach our sustainability goals. It is one of the best examples of how creating positive impact also benefits our business. By reducing our total energy consumption, we can be both sustainable and profitable."[82]

Google's high energy needs to power servers has resulted in many ambitious plans to save power. For example, Google implemented a plan to transform a paper mill in Hamina, Finland, into a data center with massive computing facilities. Part of the appeal of the mill was its underground tunnel system that pulls water from the Gulf of Finland. Originally, that frigid Baltic water cooled a steam generation plant at the mill, but Google saw it as a way to cool its servers.[83]

Green programs can have a triple bottom line (TBL or 3BL): economic, environmental, and social. That is, green programs create economic value while being socially responsible and sustaining the environment, or "people, planet, profit."

Not only could technological progress cut down on the high-consumption footprint of technology itself, but it can also assist in efforts for current business to be greener. One German firm responded to the shocking amounts of used food containers discarded, by creating a new no-deposit returnable container with a QR code for tracking the containers along the supply chain and those returned by consumers. Thanks to the participation of thousands of partners all over Germany, 4.7 million disposable containers were prevented from entering landfills.[84]

Green computing can be considered from the social contract theory perspective by considering the first two of these: "people" and "planet." Managers benefit society by conserving global resources when they make green, energy-related decisions about their computer operations. In addition, stockholder theory explains the "profit" side of a firm's actions because energy-efficient computers reduce not only the direct costs of running the computing-related infrastructure, but also the costs of complementary utilities, such as cooling systems for the infrastructure components.

SUMMARY

- Ethics is about maintaining one's own personal perspective about the propriety of business practices. Managers must make systematic, reasoned judgments about right and wrong and take responsibility for them. Ethics is about taking decisive action rooted in principles that express what is right and important and about taking action that is publicly defensible and personally supportable.
- Three important normative theories describing business ethics are (1) stockholder theory (maximizing stockholder wealth), (2) stakeholder theory (maximizing the benefits to all stakeholders while weighing costs to competing interests), and (3) social contract theory (creating value for society that is just and nondiscriminatory).
- Social contract theory offers the broad perspective to display corporate responsibility in areas such as green computing and dealing with ethical issues in tensions with foreign governments about IT and its use.
- PAPA is an acronym for the four areas in which control of information and data is crucial: privacy, accuracy, property, and accessibility.
- To enhance ethical control of information systems, companies should create a culture of responsibility, implement governance processes, and avoid decoupling.
- Green computing is concerned with using computing resources efficiently. One action companies take to promote green computing is to create and implement sustainability plans.
- Green computing can yield a triple bottom line (TBL or 3BL): economic, environmental, and social.

[82] "Total Energy Consumed," SAP Sustainability Report, http://www.sapsustainabilityreport.com/total-energy-consumed (accessed June 11, 2023).

[83] Cade Metz, "Google Reincarnates Dead Paper Mill as Data Center of Future," *Wired*, January 26, 2012, https://www.wired.com/2012/01/google-finland/ (accessed June 11, 2023).

[84] Theresa Bockelmann and Jan Recker, "How One Company Used Data to Create Sustainable Take-Out Food Packaging," *Harvard Business Review*, November 11, 2022.

KEY TERMS

accessibility, 306
accuracy, 305
CCPA (California Consumer Privacy Act), 303
CPRA (California Privacy Rights Act), 304
cookies, 302
GDPR (General Data Protection Regulation), 304
green computing, 309
identity theft, 306
information ethics, 294
online reputation management, 302
privacy, 300
property, 305
social contract theory, 296
stakeholder theory, 295
stockholder theory, 294

FOUNDATIONAL READING

Mason, R. O. (1986). "Four ethical issues of the information age." *MIS Quarterly* 10, no. 1, 5–12.

DISCUSSION QUESTIONS

1. Private corporate data are often encrypted using a key, which is needed to decrypt the information. Who within the corporation should be responsible for maintaining the "keys" to private information collected about consumers? Is that the same person who should have the keys to employee data?
2. Google has planned to remove third party cookies and replace them with ad preferences that would be created when you establish a new Google account. You would answer a questionnaire to build these preferences. You might be surprised to learn that Google has already profiled you. Using your own computer, go to your ad center: https://myadcenter.google.com/controls. How accurate is the picture Google paints about you in your profile? What did you have to correct?
3. Consider arrest records that are mostly computerized and stored locally by law enforcement agencies. They have an accuracy rate of about 50%—about half of them are inaccurate, incomplete, or ambiguous. People other than law enforcement officials use these records often. Approximately 90% of all criminal histories in the United States are available to public and private employers. Use the three normative theories of business ethics to analyze the ethical issues surrounding this situation. How might hiring decisions be influenced inappropriately by this information?
4. The European Community's General Data Protection Regulation (GDPR) is a law that became applicable in May 2018. GDPR strictly limits how database information is used and who has access to it. Some restrictions include registering all databases containing personal information with the countries in which they are operating, collecting data only with the consent of the subjects, and telling subjects of databases the intended and actual use of the databases. What effect might these restrictions have on global companies? Should the United States bring its laws into agreement with the EU's?
5. If you were a famous consultant and were asked to create a global Internet privacy policy, what would you include in it? Create a summary of your recommendations.
6. Do you believe sending targeted advertising information to a computer using third party cookies is objectionable? Why or why not?
7. There have been several letters by tech leaders cautioning about the use of AI, especially generative AI.[1] Do you think those letters will have the desired effect, or not? Do you think we risk global extinction due to AI? Please explain your answers.

Source:

[1] Lucas Mearian, "ChatGPT Creators and Others Plead to Reduce Risk of Global Extinction from their tech," *Computerworld*, May 30, 2023. https://www.computerworld.com/article/3697738/chatgpt-creators-plead-to-reduce-risk-of-global-extinction-from-their-tech.html (accessed June 10, 2023).

Case Study 13-1 A TikTok Challenge . . . To TikTok Itself

The story starts in 2014 in China. TikTok was created from two apps. An app called "musical.ly" became popular in both China and the USA. A large company named ByteDance created a similar app named Douyin in 2016, and then purchased Musical.ly in 2018. The two apps were merged into one, named TikTok, still owned by ByteDance.[1]

At the start of 2023, TikTok showed an incredible rise in five years, and it is ironic that the USA became TikTok's largest market outside of China, with over 113 million users. It has been downloaded 2.3 billion times.[2] There is an extraordinary number of global users after only five years of operations (1.7 billion at the end of 2022 with a forecast of 2.2 billion in 2027) and users in the USA spent, on average, 46 minutes per day using the app.[3] In the US, TikTok was the #1 most downloaded app in both 2021 and 2022, with some of the 150 million users saying they "can't imagine an America without it."[4] A Statista survey puts TikTok 10th in the world's 25 most valuable brands for 2023[5] and #1 in the world's highest valued start-ups.[6]

But in 2023, TikTok faces a major challenge of its own from the United States, Canada, Europe, and India. This is not a "TikTok challenge" that users can post and send out on a viral basis. Harmful content can endanger TikTok's survival.

There is a movement to control content on TikTok and other social media sites in the United States. Several arguments are being used by groups testifying to Congress. First is that the app is addictive. The statistics on daily minutes of use mentioned above serve as initial evidence of that problem. Second, studies have shown that social media is associated with sleep deprivation, fear of missing out, bullying, body shaming, anxiety, depression, and loneliness in 14- to 24-year olds.[7] However, studies do show positive effects as well, such as keeping connected, access to research, conducting financial transactions, online learning, social awareness, and others.[8]

But TikTok in particular has suffered some negative publicity, initiated on the platform by teens, in popular TikTok Challenges. Some examples: Individuals posted challenges to encourage teens to steal certain models of Kia automobiles using a thumb drive, swallow Benadryl to promote hallucinations, hold their breath until they passed out, play "Cha-Cha Slide" while driving and swerve into the left lane of oncoming traffic when the music calls for it, and filing down teeth with a nail file. Some deaths have been caused by such actions.[9]

Like other social media sites, addictive behavior is promoted by design. If a user sees a Challenge TikTok video, and taps a "heart" button, more similar videos will be shown. Thus, those who are most vulnerable will be fed their addiction and shown more of these Challenges. With the autoplay and endless scrolling, this promotes use over longer and longer periods of time.

The promoters of the Kids Online Safety Act (KOSA) bill strongly recommended that social network sites take what they call "reasonable steps" to prevent and mitigate dangers of social media. Two key steps are forcing use of the highest degree of security settings and conducting annual audits to make sure minors are not exposed to risks.[10] Some people have mentioned the role of parents in the mix, but parents might have less recognition of the platforms available, less understanding of the ill effects, and, for some, less concern.[11]

Social media postings are not created by the platforms, yet there is not yet a legal assignment of blame for social media's dangers. There are complex issues and diverse interests from many parties; those opposing free reign of technology firms point out fatalities and injuries, while those opposing government control argue that, similar to guns, the tool doesn't cause the ills; the people do. The users see content that they like, even if it is fake or dangerous, and when they tap or click on that content, they see similar content more often.

In their view, the social networks enjoy a "win-win" situation where platforms win (by promoting continued use), and users win (by enjoying similar content that is pushed to them. This simultaneously boosts traffic and ad revenue; They do not need to create the content, as the visitors have that creative task, exercising their rights to free speech. Many teens demand and enjoy that content to such an extreme extent that they behave as if they are addicted. There is not yet an answer to this ethical dilemma.

Case Study 13-1 **(Continued)**

Sources:

[1] Joe Tidy and Sophia Smith Galer, "TikTok: The Story of a Social Media Giant," BBC News, August 5, 2020, https://www.bbc.com/news/technology-53640724 (accessed June 3, 2023).

[2] L. Ceci, "TikTok – Statistics & Facts," Statista, May 30, 2023, https://www.statista.com/topics/6077/tiktok/#topicOverview (accessed June 3, 2023).

[3] L. Ceci, "TikTok Users Worldwide from 2018 to 2027," Statista, https://www-statista-com.pitt.idm.oclc.org/forecasts/1142687/tiktok-users-worldwide (accessed June 3, 2023).

[4] Aditi Sangal, Brian Fung, and Catherine Thorbecke, "March 23, 2023 – TikTok CEO Shou Chew Testifies Before Congress," CNN Business, https://www.cnn.com/business/live-news/tiktok-ceo-congressional-hearing-shou-chew-03-23-23/index.html (accessed June 3, 2023), paragraph 3.

[5] Julia Faria, "Most Valuable Brands Worldwide 2023," Statista, May 16, 2023. https://www.statista.com/statistics/264875/brand-value-of-the-25-most-valuable-brands/ (accessed June 3, 2023).

[6] Statista Research Department, "Leading Unicorns Worldwide as of April 2023," May 22, 2023. https://www.statista.com/statistics/407888/ranking-of-highest-valued-startup-companies-worldwide/ (accessed June 3, 2023).

[7] The Data Team, "How Heavy Use of Social Media is Linked to Mental Illness," The Economist, May 18, 2018, https://www.economist.com/graphic-detail/2018/05/18/how-heavy-use-of-social-media-is-linked-to-mental-illness (accessed June 3, 2023).

[8] Frances Dalomba, "Pros and Cons of Social Media," Lifespan.org, March 1, 2022, https://www.lifespan.org/lifespan-living/social-media-good-bad-and-ugly (accessed June 3, 2023).

[9] Harry Fletcher, "The Most Dangerous TikTok Trends of All Time," January 21, 2023, Indy100.com, https://www.indy100.com/viral/tiktok-most-dangerous-challenges (accessed May 28, 2023) and Quinn Nguyen, "Don't Let Your Kids Try These 9 Dangerous TikTok Trends!" Cyberpurify.com, https://cyberpurify.com/knowledge/9-dangerous-tiktok-trends/ (accessed May 28, 2023).

[10] Lauren Feiner, "Lawmakers Update Kids Online Safety Act to Address Potential Harms, But Fail to Appease Some Activists, Industry Groups," May 4, 2023, CNBC.com, https://www.cnbc.com/2023/05/02/updated-kids-online-safety-act-aims-to-fix-unintended-consequences.html (accessed May 28, 2023).

[11] Lauren Feiner, "Lawmakers Update Kids Online Safety Act to Address Potential Harms, But Fail to Appease Some Activists, Industry Groups," May 4, 2023, CNBC.com, https://www.cnbc.com/2023/05/02/updated-kids-online-safety-act-aims-to-fix-unintended-consequences.html (accessed May 28, 2023).

Discussion Questions

1. Does the growing trend of governments outside of China to ban TikTok seem to indicate a dim future of the site and app? What do you think will happen in the future? That is, will the app be sold to a company in a different country?
2. Will a general ban on TikTok in your country or state have an impact on your voting for future government offices? What impact would that have?
3. Have you witnessed any signs of some of the ill effects mentioned above in your circle of friends or your family? Do you think social media was the cause?
4. Have you witnessed any positive effects from the use of social media? What are some examples?
5. Have you taken part in any TikTok Challenges? What happened as a result?
6. Do you believe social media companies can effectively prevent or remove messages that promote aggressive and dangerous behaviors? If so, how? If not, why not?
7. Given your experiences, do you think social media provides net positive or net negative results to society? What would be your answer if you considered only teens?
8. What decisions do you think parents should make about how their young children and teens use social media?

Case Study 13-2 Ethical Decision Making

Situation 1

ChatGPT is being used by millions of people, and one attractive feature is for the AI tool to do writing. Chapter 12 describes how generative AI tools could create a realistic looking photo that was never taken with a camera, write a cover letter for a resume, or even create the resume itself based on information that it is given.

At the same time, students have used it to write essays based on questions and specifications that teachers or professors have provided. If you have tried using it, you might find that surprisingly convincing essays come out of it. A caution is that some of the chatbots "hallucinate" and provide bogus references in research papers.

Some have predicted the end of education because of such tools, and others predict that there are valuable insights in our future.

1. Ask ChatGPT to create a one-page essay about a particular topic germane to a class you are taking now.
2. Ask two others to do the same. These can be your classmates, your friends, or your family members.
3. Compare the three essays. Are they identical? If not, describe the differences among them.
4. Importantly, and don't use ChatGPT for an answer, what are your own thoughts about what role these tools have in education?

Situation 2

Rumors of the death of third-party cookies have been greatly exaggerated. Open Chrome on your own personal computer. (If you do not have it, and enter in the URL field https://tiny.cc/lightbeam-chrome-plugin and click the Add to Chrome button and then click the Add Extension button. This extension allows you to see what cookies are active while you browse various sites.

Open the Lightbeam app by clicking on the new small black icon near the top and right of your screen. It looks strangely like a black fountain pen tip aiming diagonally up and to the right, with two little arms. You might recognize it from when you installed that extension.

Open a new Chrome tab and visit Amazon.com. Search for a product and look at its page. Click on one of the search results.

Click back to the Lightbeam tab in Chrome and notice the number of circles and triangles that are in the diagram.

Discussion Questions

1. The circles represent sites that have been visited, and the triangles represent third-party sites with which you have connected in displaying your page. How many sites have you actually connected with by visiting Amazon.com?
2. Open another browser tab and navigate to CNN.Com. Click on an article. Go back to the Lightbeam tab. How many sites have connected with you now after visiting the two sites?
3. Open another tab and navigate to YouTube.com. Watch a video of your choice. Go back to the Lightbeam tab. How many sites do you see now after visiting the three sites?
4. Hover your mouse pointer over each circle and several of the triangles. What do you notice about this? Have you heard of any of the names in the triangles?
5. You have just witnessed how third-party cookies can help firms figure out what ads you want to see, by connecting your browsing experiences over three sites. What is your reaction to this revelation?

Situation 3

Facebook has been cited by the United Nations as enabling genocide in Myanmar. Myanmar did not have any type of telecommunication network when Facebook persuaded the government to reduce the price of cell phones. In return, Facebook provided a basic Internet infrastructure for the people living in Myanmar. Military personnel posted fake stories and propaganda that incited the violence against the Muslim Rohingya minority group. Reports indicated that 1.3 million people followed

Case Study 13-2 **(Continued)**

the accounts created by hundreds of military personnel who posed as fans of rock stars, models, national heroes, and even a beauty queen. Photos of victims of conflicts from other countries were even falsely labeled as a current conflict caused by the Rohingya to fuel anger among the majority. The "fake news" Facebook posts were largely believable because many of the 18 million users in Myanmar believed what they read—they are known to confuse Facebook with the Internet itself. Facebook admitted it was slow to react and to remove those accounts, as the hate speech campaign stretched over "half a decade." The result: in just one year 700,000 Rohingya left the country.[1] One report in December 2018 revealed that Facebook employed two full-time moderators who spoke Burmese in 2011, but in late 2018, Facebook employed over 100 and claimed it was getting better at removing fake and hateful content.[2,3] Roger McNamee claimed in an interview on *1A* on National Public Radio that Facebook sees such unfortunate incidents as a cost of doing business in its virtuous goal of connecting the whole world.

1. Do you think that Facebook was blamed unfairly by the United Nations for the genocide? Please explain.
2. Did Facebook act in an unethical way? If you think it did, why were its actions unethical and what should it have done differently? If you think Facebook did not act in an unethical way, please explain why not.

Sources:

[1] Mozur, Paul (October 15, 2018). "A genocide incited on Facebook, With posts from Myanmar's military," *The New York Times*, https://www.nytimes.com/2018/10/15/technology/myanmar-facebook-genocide.html (accessed June 11, 2023).

[2] Why we keep forgiving Facebook. Interview of Roger McNamee on 1A on NPR Feb 7,2019 https://the1a.org/shows/2019-02-07/why-we-keep-forgiving-facebook (accessed June 11, 2023).

[3] Kurt Wagner (December 18, 2018). "Facebook removed hundreds more accounts linked to the Myanmar military for posting hate speech and attacks against ethnic minorities" https://www.vox.com/2018/12/18/18146967/facebook-myanmar-military-accounts-removed-rohingya-genocide (accessed June 11, 2023).

Situation 4

Kate Essex is the supervisor of the customer service representative group for Enovelty.com, a manufacturer of novelty items. This group spends its workday answering calls from and sometimes placing calls to customers to assist in solving a variety of issues about orders previously placed with the company. The company has a rule that personal phone calls are allowed only during breaks. Essex is assigned to monitor each representative on the phone for 15 minutes a day as part of her regular job tasks. The representatives are aware that Essex will be monitoring them, and customers are immediately informed of this when they begin their calls. Essex begins to monitor James Olsen and finds that he is on a personal call regarding his sick child. Olsen is not on break.

Discussion Questions

1. What should Essex do?
2. What, if any, ethical principles help guide decision making in this situation?
3. What management practices should be in place to ensure proper behavior without violating individual "rights"?
4. Apply the normative theories of business ethics to this situation.

Source: Adapted from short cases suggested by Professor Kay Nelson, Southern Illinois University—Carbondale. The names of people, places, and companies have been made up for these stories. Any similarity to real people, places, or companies is purely coincidental.

Situation 5

Jane Mark is the newest hire in the IS group at We_Sell_More.com, a business on the Internet. The company takes in $30 million in revenue quarterly from web business. Jane reports to Sam Brady, the vice president of IS. Jane is assigned to a project to build a new capability into the company web

Case Study 13-2 **(Continued)**

page that facilitates linking products ordered with future offerings of the company. After weeks of analysis, Jane concluded that the best way to incorporate that capability is to buy a software package from a small start-up company in Silicon Valley, California. She convinces Brady to accept her decision and is authorized to lease the software. The vendor e-mails Jane the software in a ZIP file and instructs her on how to install it. At the initial installation, Jane is asked to acknowledge and electronically sign the license agreement. The installed system does not ask Jane if she wants to make a backup copy of the software, so as a precaution, Jane takes it upon herself to copy the ZIP files that were sent to her onto a thumb drive. She stores the thumb drive in her desk drawer.

A year later, the vendor is bought by another company, and the software is removed from the market to prevent further sale. The new owner believes this software will provide it a competitive advantage that it wants to reserve for itself. The new vendor terminates all lease agreements and revokes all licenses on their expiration. But Jane still has the thumb drive she made as backup.

Discussion Questions

1. Is Jane obligated to stop using her backup copy? Why or why not?
2. If We_Sell_More.com wants to continue to use the system, can it? Why or why not?
3. Would your opinion change if the software is a critical system for We_Sell_More.com? If it is a noncritical system? Explain.

Situation 6

Some of the Internet's biggest companies (i.e., Google, Microsoft, Yahoo, IBM, and Verisign) implemented "single sign-on" systems, including OpenID Connect, and 0-Auth (zero auth). One of these services is available at thousands of websites. It allows the widespread practice that users, who are separately (perhaps in a different window) logged into Facebook or Google, to click either button for an instant login. The benefits are obvious; the system makes it easier for users to sign on to a number of sites without having to remember multiple user IDs, passwords, and registration information. Under these services, the companies share the sign-on information, which can include personal information such as credit card data, billing addresses, and personal preferences for any web user who agrees to participate.

Discussion Questions

1. Discuss any potential and real threats to privacy in this situation. Search for news articles about Facebook to find problematic incidents, if any.
2. Who would own the data? Explain.
3. Who do you think should have access to the data? How should that access be controlled?

Situation 7

Spokeo is a company that gathers online data for employers, the public, or anybody who is willing to pay for its services. Clients include recruiters and women who want to find out whether their boyfriends are cheating on them. Spokeo recruits via ads that urge "HR-Recruiters—Click Here Now."

Discussion Questions

1. Do you think it would be ethical for a business to hire Spokeo to find out about potential employees? If so, under what conditions would it be appropriate? If not, why not?
2. Do you think it is ethical for women to hire Spokeo to see if their boyfriends are cheating on them? Why or why not?

Source: From Lori Andrews, "Facebook Is Using You," *The New York Times*, February 4, 2012, SR7, https://www.nytimes.com/2012/02/05/opinion/sunday/facebook-is-using-you.html (accessed June 11, 2023).

Case Study 13-2 **(Continued)**

Situation 8

In recent years, mountains of online misinformation have been created and pushed into social media. Famously called "Fake News," they often try to persuade the reader about things that are completely fictitious. Sometimes these are for political purposes, but they could also be used to attack a firm or even a manager of a firm if the creator has an axe to grind. Some social media sites use thousands of moderators to guard against obscenity or antisocial language, but a fact-checking task is much more difficult.

The incentives for trying to preserve truth are oriented toward social value theory. But stockholder theory includes strong benefits from the fake news. When these items are clicked, they inform the social media platform of a users' interests, and then they show them more of the same. This feeds the emotions of the people for whom the false messages resonate, and keeps them using the platform, generating more and more ad dollars.

Stakeholders are a more complex issue in fake news. Perhaps some stakeholders are helped by allowing fake news to be propagated, and perhaps others are harmed. Think about the nuances of such a dynamic and answer the following questions:

1. Can you think of any stakeholders who might benefit from propagation of fake news on social media?
2. Can you think of any stakeholders who are harmed by propagation of fake news on social media?
3. Present an argument (a) for and an argument (b) against hiring thousands of content moderators to do fact checking on social media sites.

Source: The material on emotions and fake news is from Christy Galletta Horner, Dennis Galletta, Jennifer Crawford, and Abhijit Shirsat. "Emotions: The unexplored fuel of fake news on social media." *Journal of Management Information Systems*, 38 no. 4 (2021), 1039–66.

Situation 9

Ethics can naturally be expected to vary across countries. An interesting study of 1,100 Chinese managers showed that it can also vary over time in the same country, depending upon subcultures resulting from major events within a country. Maris Martinsons and David Ma studied the responses to PAPA-based ethical situations made by three different Chinese generations: *republican*—people born before the People's Republic of China was established in 1949; *revolution*—people born between 1950 and 1970 under Communist rule during Mao Zedong's Cultural Revolution in 1966 and the Great Leap Forward (1958–1961); and *reform*—people born after 1970 when Deng Xiaoping's government introduced the Open Door and the One Child policies as part of economic and social reforms.

Survey results indicate significant differences in information ethics across generations. The revolution generation experienced a profound event that appears to have increased its ethical acceptance of both inaccurate information and intellectual property violations. Chinese managers from the reform generation are much less accepting of privacy violations than are those from the older generations. They are more conscious of the right to privacy and less inclined to compromise the privacy of others.

Discussion Questions

1. Do you see general differences in what is considered ethical and what is not? What are some examples?
2. Have you experienced differences in privacy preferences among people across generations? Do they avoid purchasing online, social media, or using a voice-based home assistant such as Amazon Alexa or Google Assistant?

Source: Adapted from M. G. Martinsons and D. Ma, "Subcultural Differences in Information Ethics across China: Focus on Chinese Management Generation Gaps," *Journal of AIS 10* (Special Issue) (2009), 816–33.

Case Study 13-2 **(Continued)**

Situation 10

Many firms and researchers have found Amazon's Mechanical Turk (discussed in Chapter 10) (MTurk) to be a valuable platform to create "microtasks," and people can sign up to earn money. Some of those tasks take only a minute and pay a few pennies, but some take several minutes and pay dollars. Firms have used the platform to, for example, recommend alternative product ads, transcribe short documents, or provide opinions of a website. Researchers usually ask participants to fill out questionnaires as part of a research project. Norms are often to pay people for their time at least on the scale of a minimum wage, but tasks vary widely on the hourly rates, and participants vary widely in speed.

Many workers have expressed positive results: they can work from home, enhance their income (especially when workers are from countries with a low wage standard of living), sometimes enjoy the tasks, have autonomy, and can help researchers. But many have expressed that they feel marginalized, from low pay, abuse of scammers, technical constraints, and deskilling.

The third author of this book is a researcher who has used Mturk in the past, attempting to pay a fair amount for the workers' effort. Often the payments are between $1 and $2 for about 15 minutes of work. Some signs of underpayment have been evident, in that some of the workers do not follow instructions and simply insert random text into text boxes in questionnaires and miss attention checks such as "Choose 'strongly agree' for this question." Two of his studies involved disqualifying over a third of the responses.

Another platform named Prolific has started to become popular for researchers. The workers are subjected to more careful screening and tasks are more fairly compensated, as the platform requires a minimum hourly wage, treating the initial offer by the researcher as only an estimate. After workers finish the tasks, the platform computes the average time and requires the researcher to boost the per-subject payment if the payment falls short of the platform's minimum wage.

Discussion Questions

1. Given the positive and negative feelings expressed by those workers, do you believe a researcher should avoid making use of such a platform? Why or why not?
2. Some questionnaires are filled out by workers who use "bots" that answer questions by software, which often leads to detection by the attention check questions. Some workers even use multiple accounts and answer the questions repeatedly when the requirement is only to participate once. How do you think these problems relate to the feelings workers express? Make sure you refer to both positive and negative feelings in your answer.
3. Do you believe the more stringent screening in Prolific biases the results? If so, in which direction (better or worse)? Why?

Source: Based on Zuefei (Nancy) Denb, K.D. Joshi, and Robert Galliers, "The duality of empowerment and marginalization in microtask crowdsourcing: Giving voice to the less powerful through value sensitive design," *MIS Quarterly* 40, No. 2 (2016), 279–302.

GLOSSARY

Accessibility: Area of information control involved with the ability to obtain data; one of the four parts of the information ethics framework, PAPA.

Accuracy: Area of information control dealing with the correctness of information or lack of errors in information; one of the four parts of the information ethics framework, PAPA.

Activity-Based Costing: Costing method that calculates costs by counting the actual activities that go into making a specific product or delivering a specific service.

Adaptability: Architecture that is able to handle expected technological advances, such as innovations in storage capacity, end-user devices, and computing power.

Agile (Business) Processes: Processes designed with the intention of simplifying redesign and reconfiguration by making it possible to make incremental changes in order to easily adapt to the business environment.

Agile Software Development: System development methodologies used to deal with unpredictability. They adapt to changing requirements by iteratively developing systems in small stages and then testing the new code extensively. They include XP (Extreme Programming), Crystal, Scrum, Feature-Driven Development, and Dynamic System Development Method (DSDM).

Algorithmic Control: The use of algorithms to monitor platform worker's behavior and ensure its alignment with the platform organization's goals.

Algorithmic Management: A platform's large scale data collection and use of data to develop and improve learning algorithms that carry out coordination and control functions traditionally performed by managers in a highly automated and data-driven fashion.

Alignment: The situation in which a company's current and emerging business strategy is enabled and supported yet unconstrained by technology; May include the synchronization or convergence among organizational strategy, IS strategy, and business strategy.

Allocation Funding Method: Method for funding IT costs, which recovers costs based on something other than usage, such as revenues, login accounts, or number of employees.

Antivirus/Antispyware: Software that scans incoming data and evaluates the periodic state of the whole system to detect threats of secret software that can either destroy data or inform a server of your activity.

Application (also called app): The components that request data for recording or reporting, and also transform data by performing calculations and making updates as needed; self-contained software program that fulfills a specific purpose and run on a platform.

Archetype: A pattern from decision rights allocation.

Architecture: Provides a blueprint for translating business strategy into a plan for IS.

Artificial Intelligence (AI): Refers to the broader field of development of computer science where systems perform tasks that are naturally performed by humans.

Assumptions: Deepest layer of culture or the fundamental part of every culture that helps discern what is real and important to a group; They are unobservable since they reflect organizational values that have become so taken for granted that they guide organizational behavior without any of the groups thinking about them.

Backsourcing: A business practice in which a company takes back in-house assets, activities, and skills that are part of its information systems operations and development and were previously outsourced to one or more outside IS providers.

Balanced Scorecard: Method that focuses attention on the organization's value drivers (which include, but are not limited to, financial performance). Companies use it to assess the full impact of their corporate strategies on their customers and workforce, as well as their financial performance.

Behavior control: A type of formal control in which specific actions, procedures, and rules for the employees are explicitly prescribed and their implementation is monitored.

Beliefs: Perceptions that people hold about how things are done in their community.

Big Data: Term used to describe techniques and technologies that make it economical to deal with very large datasets at the extreme end of the scale.

Biometrics: Access tool that scans a body characteristic, such as fingerprint, voice, iris, or head or hand geometry.

Black Hat Hackers: Hackers who break in for their own gain or to wreak havoc on a firm.

Blended Workforce: A work arrangement in which some employees in a workforce work remotely all of the time, some work remotely part of the time, and some work at the company office all of the time.

Bring Your Own Device (BYOD): The term used to refer to the scenario when employees bring their own devices to work and connect to enterprise systems. This is commonly used to mean devices such as smart phones, tablets, and laptops.

Business Analytics: The use of data, analysis, and modeling to arrive at business decisions. Some organizations use business analytics to create new innovations or to support the modification of existing products or services.

Business Case: A structured document that lays out all the relevant information needed to make a go/no go decision. It contains an executive summary, overview, assumptions, program summary, financial discussion and analysis, discussion of benefits and business impacts, schedule and milestones, risk and contingency analysis, conclusion, and recommendations.

Business Ecosystem: An economic community in which the members interact and coevolve their capabilities as well as the collective value around an innovation; a number of partners provide important services to each other and jointly create value for customers.

Business Intelligence: This term refers to the broader practice of using technology, applications, and processes to collect and analyze data to support business decisions.

Business-IT Maturity Model: Framework that displays the demands on the business side and the IT offerings on the supply side to help understand differences in capabilities.

Business Model: The blueprint of how a company does business.

Business Process Management (BPM): A well-defined and optimized set of IT processes, tools, and skills used to manage business processes.

Business Process Reengineering (BPR): Radical change approach that occurs over a short amount of time.

Business Strategy: A plan articulating where a business seeks to go and how it expects to get there.

Business Technology Strategist: The strategic business leader who uses technology as the core tool in creating competitive advantage and aligning business and IT strategies.

Capacity-on-demand: The availability of additional processing capability for a fee.

CCPA (California Consumer Privacy Act): California law that protects the privacy of customers in California; applies only to larger companies or firms that derive more than 50% of their revenue from the sale of consumers' personal information; Similar to the GDPR from the European Union.

CCRA (California Privacy Rights Act): An amendment to CCPA that went into effect in early 2023.

Centralized Architecture: Architecture where everything is purchased, supported, and managed centrally, usually in a data center.

Centralized IS Organization: Organization structure that brings together all staff, hardware, software, data, and processing into a single location.

Challenge Question: Access tool that prompts with a follow-up question such as "Model of first car?"

Chargeback Funding Method: Method for funding IT costs in which costs are recovered by charging individuals, departments, or business units based on actual usage and cost.

Chatbot: AI software that enables online conversations with the use of a library of curated answers.

ChatGPT: OpenAI's generative AI software application.

CIO (Chief Information Officer): The senior-most officer responsible for the information systems activities within the organization. The CIO is a strategic thinker, not an operational manager. The CIO is typically a member of the senior management team and is involved in all major business decisions that come before that team, bringing an information systems perspective to the team.

Client: A software program that requests and receives data and sometimes instructions from another software program, usually running on a separate computer.

Cloud Computing: This is a style of infrastructure where capacity, applications, and services (such as development, maintenance, or security) are provided dynamically by a third-party provider over the Internet often on a "fee for use" basis. Customers go to the web for the services they need.

COBIT (previously used as acronym for Control Objectives for Information and Related Technology): IT governance framework for decision controls that is consistent with COSO and that provides systematic rigor needed for the strong internal controls and Sarbanes–Oxley compliance; COBIT 2019 is the latest version of COBIT.

Combination: Mode of knowledge conversion from explicit knowledge to explicit knowledge.

Complementor: One of the players in a co-opetitive environment. It is a company whose product or service is used in conjunction with a particular product or service to make a more useful set for the customer. (See Value Net.)

Co-opetition: A business strategy whereby companies cooperate and compete at the same time with companies in their value net.

Corporate Budget Funding Method: Method for funding IT costs in which the costs fall to the corporate bottom line, rather than being levied to specific users or business units.

Cost Leadership Strategy: A business strategy where the organization aims to be the lowest-cost producer in the marketplace. (See Differentiation Strategy; Focus Strategy.)

Creative Destruction: Competitive practice where companies cannibalize their own products before they are attacked by competitors so as to promote their business in other ways.

CRM (Customer Relationship Management): The management activities performed to obtain, enhance, and retain customers. CRM is a coordinated set of activities revolving around the customer.

Cross-Site-Scripting (XSS): Security breach involving booby traps that appear to lead users to their goal, but in reality, they lead to a fraudulent site that requires a login.

Crowdsourcing: The act of taking a task traditionally performed by an employee or contractor and outsourcing it to an undefined, generally large group of people, in the form of an open call.

Crowdworking: A form of crowdsourcing that focuses on paid work only that is organized and performed on online labor platforms that are typically not in the provider's organization.

Cybersecurity Hygiene: Doing the basic system updates and patches offered from the vendors of systems since these updates usually fix known bugs and vulnerabilities.

Cycle Plan: A project management plan that organizes project activities in relation to time. It identifies critical beginning and end dates and breaks the work spanning these dates into phases. The general manager tracks the phases to coordinate the eventual transition from project to operational status, a process that culminates on the "go live" date.

Culture: A set of shared values and beliefs that a group holds and that determines how the group perceives, thinks about, and appropriately reacts to its various environments; A collective programming of the mind that distinguishes not only societies (or nations), but also industries, professions, and organizations.

Dark Web: A part of the Deep web where data, information, tools, support and applications, often illegal, can be purchased.

Dashboard: Common management monitoring tool, which provides a snapshot of metrics at any given point in time.

Data: Set of specific, objective facts or observations that standing alone have no intrinsic meaning.

Data Center: Place where a firm's computers, servers, and peripherals are housed together, typically to store, process, and distribute large amounts of data.

Data-Driven Culture: Organizational environment that supports and encourages the use of analytics to support decision making.

Data Lake: A storage technology that does not organize data, but rather just stores it in "raw" form for later analysis or other use.

Data Mining: The process of analyzing databases for "gems" that will be useful in management decision making. Typically, data mining is used to refer to the process of combing through massive amounts of customer data to understand buying habits and to identify new products, features, and enhancements.

Data Scientist: A professional who has the skills to use the right analytics with the right data at the right time for the right business problem.

Data Warehouse: A centralized collection of data designed to support management decision-making. They sometimes include all organizational-level databases of the organization.

Database: A collection of data that is formatted and organized to facilitate ease of access, searching, updating, addition, and deletion. A database is typically so large that it must be stored on disk, but sections may be kept in RAM for quicker access. The software program used to manipulate the data in a database is also often referred to as a "database."

DBA (Database Administrator): The person within the information systems department who manages the data and the database. Typically, this person makes sure that all the data that goes into the database is accurate and appropriate and that all applications and individuals who need access have it.

Decentralized Architecture: Architecture in which the platforms, apps, networking, and data are arranged in a way that distributes the processing and functionality between multiple small computers, servers, and devices, and they rely heavily on a network to connect them together.

Decentralized IS Organization: IS organization structure that scatters hardware, software, networks, and data components in different locations to address local business needs.

Decision Models: Information systems-based model used by managers for scenario planning and evaluation. The information system collects and analyzes the information from automated processes and presents them to the manager to aid in decision making.

Decision Rights: Indicate who in the organization has the responsibility to initiate, supply information for, approve, implement, and control various types of decisions.

Deep Learning: A type of machine learning used for unstructured data.

Deep Web: A large part of the web includes unindexed websites that are only accessible by specialized browsers (most common is named "Tor"), which guarantees anonymity and provides access to sites offering both legal and illegal items.

Defense in Depth: The concept of having multiple layers of different security policies and practices so that when one layer fails to stop a perpetrator, another layer might be more effective.

Differentiation Strategy: A business strategy where the organization qualifies its product or service in a way that allows it to appear unique in the marketplace. (See Cost Leadership Strategy; Focus Strategy.)

Digital Business Strategy: A business strategy inspired by the capabilities of powerful, readily accessible digital technologies (like social media, analytics, cloud, and Internet of Things), intent on delivering unique, integrated business capabilities in ways that are responsive to constantly changing market conditions.

Digital Ecosystem: System that consists of self-interested, self-organizing, and autonomous digital entities; System of entities that is nourished by the significant impacts of the large variety of resources available from individuals, organizational units, and outside services.

Digital Immigrant: A person born before the 1990s who was not always around computers when young.

Digital Native: An individual who has grown up completely fluent in the use of personal technologies and the web.

Digital Platform: A layered architecture of digital technology combined with a governance model.

Digital Transformation (also called digitalization): The use of digital technology by an organization to redefine (and not just support) its value proposition and which leads the organization to identify itself in a new way.

Dynamic Business Process (also called agile business process): Agile process that iterates through a constant renewal cycle of design, deliver, evaluate, redesign, and so on.

Dynamic Capabilities: Refers to the firm's ability to create, extend, and alter the firm's resources to respond to its rapidly changing environment. Dynamic capabilities must encompass one or more of these three capacities: Sensing, Seizing, and Transforming.

Economic Value Added (EVA): Valuation method that accounts for opportunity costs of capital to measure true economic profit and revalues historical costs to give an accurate picture of the true market value of assets.

Ecosystem: A collection of interacting participants, including vendors.

Enacted Values: Value and norms that are actually exhibited or displayed in employee behavior.

Encryption: The translation of data into a code or a form that can be read only by the intended receiver. Data is encrypted using a key or alphanumeric code and can be decrypted only by using the same key.

Enterprise Architecture: The term used for a "blueprint" for the corporation that includes the business strategy, the IT architecture, the business processes, and the organization structure and how all these components relate to each other; Often this term is IT-centric, specifying the IT architecture and all the interrelationships with the structure and processes; It specifies how information technologies support business processes, align with business needs, and produce business outcomes.

Enterprise Social Network (ESN): A social networking site that is used within organizations, that is formally sanctioned by management, and that can restrict membership and interactions to the organization's employees.

Enterprise System: A set of information systems tools that many organizations use to enable the information flow within and between processes across the organization; sometimes called Enterprise Information System.

ERP (Enterprise Resource Planning Software): A large, highly complex software program that integrates many business functions under a single application. ERP software can include modules for inventory management, supply chain management, accounting, customer support, order tracking, human resource management, and so forth. ERP software is typically integrated with a database.

Espoused Values: Explicitly stated, preferred organization values.

Evidence-Based Management: An approach in which evidence (data) and facts are analyzed as the first step in decision making.

Evil Twin Connection: A bogus Wi-Fi connection that appears genuine-looking but is actually a counterfeit connection that is set up to deceive people into providing information unwittingly.

Explicit Knowledge: Objective, theoretical, and codified for transmission in a formal, systematic method using grammar, syntax, and the printed word. (See Tacit Knowledge.)

Externalization: Mode of knowledge conversion from tacit knowledge to explicit knowledge.

Extranet: A network based on the Internet standard that connects a business with individuals, customers, suppliers, and other stakeholders outside the organization's boundaries. An extranet typically is similar to the Internet; however, it has limited access to those specifically authorized to be part of it.

Farshoring: Form of offshoring that involves sourcing service work to a foreign lower-wage country that is relatively far away in distance or time zone (or both).

Federalism (federated): Hybrid organization structuring approach that distributes power, as well as platforms, apps, data, and personnel between a central IS group and IS in business units.

Firewall: A security measure that blocks out undesirable requests for entrance into a website and keeps those on the "inside" from reaching outside.

Flat Organization Structure (also called horizontal organization structure): Organization structure with less well-defined chain of command with ill-defined, fluid jobs.

Focus Strategy: A business strategy where the organization limits its scope to a narrower segment of the market and tailors its offerings to that group of customers. This strategy has two variants: cost focus, in which the organization seeks a cost advantage within its segment, and differentiation focus, in which it seeks to distinguish its products or services within the segment. This strategy allows the organization to achieve a local competitive advantage, even if it does not achieve competitive advantage in the marketplace overall. (See Cost Strategy, Differentiation Strategy.)

Full Outsourcing: Situation in which an enterprise outsources all its IS functions from desktop services to software development.

Function Points: The functional requirements of the software product, which can be estimated earlier than total lines of code.

Functional Perspective: Also called silo perspective, the view of an organization based on the functional departments, typically including manufacturing, engineering, logistics, sales, marketing, finance, accounting, and human resources. (See also Process Perspective.)

GDPR (General Data Protection Regulation): Law that has been adopted by all European Union member states and that places even greater emphasis on individual rights; It prohibits the transfer of personal data to non-European Union nations that do not meet the European privacy standards.

Generative Artificial Intelligence (AI): A type of Artificial Intelligence (AI) using machine learning that can produce new content in response to prompts.

Generativity: The ability of any self-contained system to create, generate, or produce a new output, structure, or behavior without any input from the originator of the system.

Global In-house Center (GIC): Service delivery operations which are owned and operated by the client company to retain oversight on work quality, productivity, and efficiency.

Governance (in the context of business enterprises): Making decisions that define expectations, grant power, or verify performance.

Green Computing: An upcoming technology strategy in which companies become more socially responsible by using computing resources efficiently.

Grey Hat Hackers: Hackers who test organizational systems without any authorization and notify the IT staff when they find a weakness.

GUI (Graphical User Interface): The term used to refer to the use of icons, windows, menus, and pointing devices as the means of representing information and links on the screen of a computer. GUIs give the user the ability to control actions by clicking on objects rather than by typing commands to the operating system.

Hierarchical Organization Structure: An organization form or structure based on the concepts of division of labor, specialization, spans of control, and unity of command.

Hybrid Cloud: A combination of two or more other clouds, with a combination of public and private clouds where the services are integrated with one another.

Hybrid Remote Work Arrangement: A work arrangement in which people work at home for up to four days a week and at the office, the remainder of the time.

Hypercompetition: A theory about industries and marketplaces that suggests that the speed and aggressiveness of moves and countermoves in any given market create an environment in which advantages are quickly gained and lost. A hypercompetitive environment is one in which conditions change rapidly.

Identity Theft: The taking of the victim's identity to obtain credit cards from banks and retailers, steal money from the victim's existing accounts, apply for loans, establish accounts with utility companies, rent an apartment, file bankruptcy, or obtain a job using the victim's name.

In the Cloud: Processing, applications, and data are all hosted by a provider such as Amazon, Google, or other cloud services provider, and not residing at a location owned by the manager's company.

Industry 4.0: Pertains to smart factories with advanced technologies such as embedded software, sensors, robotics, and connected machines that are transforming manufacturing; Fourth Industrial Revolution.

Information: Data endowed with relevance and purpose.

Information Ethics: Ethical issues associated with the development and application of information technologies.

Information Integration: Involved with determining information to share, the format of that information, the technological standards they will both use to share it, and the security they will use to ensure that only authorized partners access it.

Information Model: A framework for understanding what information will be crucial to the decision, how to get it, and how to use it.

Information Resource: The available data, technology, people, and processes within an organization to be used by the manager to perform business processes and tasks.

Information System (IS): The combination of technology (the "what"), people (the "who"), and process (the "how") that an organization uses to produce and manage information.

Information Systems (IS) Strategy: The plan an organization uses in providing information services and products.

Information Systems Strategy Triangle: The framework connecting business strategy, information system strategy, and organizational systems strategy.

Information Technology: All forms of technology used to create, store, exchange, and use information.

Infrastructure: Everything that supports the flow and processing of information in an organization, including platforms, apps, data, and network components. It consists of components, chosen and assembled in a manner that best suits the plan and enables the overarching business strategy.

Insourcing: The situation in which a firm provides IS services or develops IS from its own in-house IS organization.

Integrated Supply Chain: An enterprise system that crosses company boundaries and connects vendors and suppliers with organizations to synchronize and streamline planning and deliver products to all members of the supply chain.

Intellectual Capital: The knowledge that has been identified, captured, and leveraged to produce higher-value goods or services or some other competitive advantage for the firm.

Intellectual Property (IP): Term used to describe a creative and innovative information-based output. It is information-based and, unlike physical property, it is nonexclusive and has a negligible marginal cost of producing additional copies.

Intelligent Augmentation: Expanding human knowledge and expertise by combining human strengths with machine-generated analysis, often using large data sets, to assist humans in performing a task or job. Keeps humans "in the loop."

Intelligent Automation: The application of AI technologies to replace human capabilities, particularly those involving cognition such as learning and problem solving, for the execution of work tasks that were previously carried out by a human; Takes humans "out of the loop"—and possibly out of a job.

Internalization: Mode of knowledge conversion from explicit knowledge to tacit knowledge.

Internet: The system of computers and networks that together connect individuals and businesses worldwide. The Internet is a global, interconnected network of millions of individual host computers.

Internet of Things (IoT): Technology embedded in devices stream sensor data from those devices to the Internet to create rich databases of operational data; machines and sensors talking to each other over the Internet.

IS (Information Systems): The technology (platforms, apps, networking, data), people, and processes that an organization uses to manage information.

ISP (Internet Service Provider): A company that sells access to the Internet. Usually, the service includes a direct line or dial-up number and a quantity of time for using the connection. The service often includes space for hosting subscriber web pages and e-mail.

IT (Information Technology): All forms of technology used to create, store, exchange, and use information; the technology component of an information system (platforms, apps, networking, data).

IT Asset: Anything, tangible or intangible, that can be used by a firm in its processes for creating, producing, and/or offering its products (goods or services).

IT Capability: Something that is learned or developed over time for the firm to create, produce, or offer its products.

IT Consumerization: The process whereby the changing practices and expectation of consumers, shaped by the wide adoption of digital technologies in everyday life, will influence the IT-related activities of workers and managers in organizations; Technologies such as social tools, mobile phones, and web applications targeted at individual, personal users are creating pressures for companies.

ITIL (Information Technology Infrastructure Library): Control framework that offers a set of concepts and techniques for managing information technology infrastructure, development, and operations that was developed in United Kingdom.

IT Governance: Specifying the decision rights and accountability framework to encourage desirable behavior in using IT.

IT Portfolio Management: Evaluating new and existing applications collectively on an ongoing basis to determine which applications provide value to the business in order to support decisions to replace, retire, or further invest in applications across the enterprise.

Joint Applications Development (JAD): A version of RAD or prototyping in which users are more integrally involved, as a group, with the entire development process up to and, in some cases, including coding.

Key Loggers: Technique used by hackers that tracks keystrokes either through hardware (an unseen thumb drive on a public computer) or software (i.e., a compromised website).

Knowledge: Information synthesized and contextualized to provide value.

Knowledge Capture: Continuous processes of scanning, organizing, and packaging knowledge after it has been generated.

Knowledge Codification: The representation of knowledge in a manner that can be easily accessed and transferred.

Knowledge Generation: All activities that discover "new" knowledge, whether such knowledge is new to the individual, the firm, or the entire discipline.

Knowledge Management: The processes necessary to capture, codify, and transfer knowledge across the organization to achieve competitive advantage.

Knowledge Repository: A physical or virtual place where documents with knowledge embedded in them, such as memos, reports, or news articles, are stored so they can be retrieved easily.

Knowledge Transfer: Transmitting knowledge from one person or group to another, and the absorption of that knowledge.

Legacy System: Systems in place before organizations transitioned to newer systems; Often used older programming languages such as COBOL.

List Server: A type of e-mail mailing list where users subscribe, and when any user sends a message to the server, a copy of the message is sent to everyone on the list. This allows for restricted-access discussion groups: Only subscribed members can participate in or view the discussions because they are transmitted via e-mail.

Machine Learning: A specific kind of AI where the system "learns" from large amounts of data that provides examples, or trains, the system.

Mainframe: A large, central computer that handles all the functionality of the system.

Maintainability: The ease and speed with which a system can be made to run correctly again after a failure or error occurs.

Managerial Levers: Organizational, control, and cultural variables that are used by decision makers to effect changes in their organizations.

Matrix Organization Structure: An organizational form or structure in which workers are assigned two or more supervisors, each supervising a different aspect of the employee's work, in an effort to make sure multiple dimensions of the business are integrated.

Metaverse: A 3-D enabled digital world that is accessed through technologies such as virtual reality, augmented reality, and other advanced Internet technologies, and where users can interact with others via simulated shared experiences.

Middleware: Software used to connect processes running in one or more computers across a network.

Mission: A clear and compelling statement that unifies an organization's effort and describes what the firm is all about (i.e., its purpose).

Mobile Workers: Individuals who work from wherever they are. (See Remote Workers.)

Multi-cloud: Multiple clouds under centralized management.

Multi-factor Authentication: The use of two or more than one authorization method to gain access.

Multi-homing: Practice that enables firms or consumers to adopt competing technologies at the same time; Increases the reliability of a server's connection to the Internet.

Multisourcing: Type of sourcing in which IT projects and services are allocated to multiple vendors who work together to achieve the client's business objectives.

Multi-team Systems: Two or more teams that work interdependently and directly interface with one another within a system designed to pursue at least one common superordinate goal (such a program goal).

NIST Cybersecurity Framework: National Institute of Standards and Technology (NIST) framework for cybersecurity management, with five key components: Identify, protect, detect, respond, and recover.

Nearshoring: Sourcing service work to a foreign, lower-wage country that is relatively close in distance or time zone (or both).

Net Present Value (NPV): Valuation method that takes into account the time value of money in which cash inflows and outflows are discounted.

Network: Platform and app components for local or long-distance networking.

Network Effect: The value of a network node to a person or organization in the network increases when another joins the network.

Networked Organization Structure: Organization form or structure where rigid hierarchies are replaced by formal and informal communication networks that connect all parts of the company; Organization structure known for its flexibility and adaptiveness.

Object: Encapsulates both the data stored about an entity and the operations that manipulate that data.

Observable Artifacts: Most visible layer of culture that includes physical manifestations such as traditional dress, symbols in art, acronyms, awards, myths and stories about the group, rituals, and ceremonies, etc.

Offshoring (short for outsourcing offshore): Situation in which IS organization uses contractor services, or even builds its own data center, in a distant land.

Omni-Cloud: The use of all clouds simultaneously.

Online Reputation Management: Service provided to a person or company for a fee to find negative formal or informal reviews on websites, and report results periodically.

Onshoring (also called inshoring): Situation in which outsourcing work is performed domestically.

Open Source Software (OSS): Software released under a license approved by the Open Source Initiative (OSI).

Open Sourcing: A development approach called the process of building and improving "free" software by an Internet community.

Operating System (OS): A program that manages all other programs running on, as well as all the resources connected to, a computer. Examples include Microsoft Windows, DOS, and UNIX.

Oracle: A widely used database program.

Organizational Strategy: A plan that answers the question "How will the company organize to achieve its goals and implement its business strategy? includes the organization's design as well as the choices it makes to define, set up, coordinate, and control its work processes.

Organizational Systems: The fundamental elements of a business including people, work processes, structure, and the plan that enables them to work efficiently to achieve business goals.

Outcome Control: Type of formal control in which the controller/manager explicitly defines intermediate and final goals for the employee.

Outsourcing: Purchasing a good or service from an outside provider(s). The business arrangement where third-party providers and vendors manage information systems activities and assets.

Payback Period: Length of time needed to recoup the cost of an investment.

Peer-to-Peer: Infrastructure that allows networked computers to share resources without a central server playing a dominant role.

Phishing Attack: A type of security breach when a person receives a convincing e-mail about a problematic situation with a link to perform some important task to solve it.

Platform: The "orchestrator" that calls into action apps that record, report, or transform data. Examples are the operating system of a computing device or Facebook.

Platform Complementor: Those participants in the platform ecosystem that contribute to value co-creation of the platform.

Platform Governance: Governance type that involves decisions about platforms and establishes rules and policies for running platforms; considers both structural governance mechanisms focusing on decision making authority and control mechanisms; shifts the focus from well-bounded organizational contexts to contexts beyond organizational or industry boundaries to leverage digital ecosystems and IT consumerization.

Platform Owner (Sponsor): Participant in platform ecosystem that typically has control of the platform, makes platform policy and administers the platform, like Apple or Facebook. We are using the term platform sponsor when there are multiple organizations involved in the governance of the platform.

Privacy: Area of information control involved with the right to be left alone; involved with the protections from intrusion and information gathering by others; individuals' ability to personally control information about themselves; one of the four parts of the information ethics framework, PAPA.

Private Cloud: Type of cloud in which data are managed by the organization and remain within its existing infrastructure, or it is managed offsite by a third party for the organization (client company) in the third party's private cloud.

Process: An interrelated, sequential set of activities and tasks that turn inputs into outputs and have a distinct beginning, a clear deliverable at the end, and a set of metrics that are useful to measure performance.

Process Perspective: The "big picture" view of a business from the perspective of the business processes performed. Typically, the view is made up of cross-functional processes that transverse disciplines, departments, functions, and even organizations; Also called Business Process Perspective. (See also Silo Perspective.)

Program: A temporary organization established to coordinate, command, and monitor a group of related projects, where the goal is to produce outcomes and benefits consistent with organizational strategic goals.

Program Management: Application of knowledge, skills, tools, and techniques to integrate multiple project deliverables to maximize program-related organizational opportunities.

Project: A temporary endeavor undertaken to create a unique product, service, or result. Temporary means that every project has a definite beginning and a definite end.

Project Management: Application of knowledge, skills, tools, and techniques to project activities in order to meet project requirements

Project Management Office (PMO): The organizational unit that is responsible for boosting efficiency, gathering expertise, and improving project delivery.

Project Manager: Person who makes sure that the entire project is executed appropriately and coordinated properly; defines project scope realistically and manages project so that it can be completed on time and within budget.

Project Plan: Consists of the sequential steps of organizing and tracking the work of the team.

Project Schedule: Organizes discrete project activities and sequences them in steps along a timeline so that the project fulfills the requirements of customers and stakeholders.

Project Stakeholder: Individual or organization that is actively involved in the project, or whose interests may be affected as a result of project execution or project completion.

Property: Area of information control focused on who owns the data; one of the four parts of the information ethics framework, PAPA.

Protocol: A special, typically standardized, set of rules used by computers to enable communication between them.

Prototyping: An evolutionary development method for building an information system. Developers get the general idea of what is needed by the users, and then build a fast, high-level version of the system as the beginning of the project. The idea of prototyping is to quickly get a version of the software in the hands of the users, and to jointly evolve the system through a series of cycles of design and build, then use and evaluate.

Public Cloud: Type of cloud in which data are stored outside of the corporate data centers in the cloud provider's environment.

RAD (Rapid Application Development): This process is similar to prototyping in that it is an interactive process, where tools are used to speed up development. RAD systems typically have tools for developing the user, reusable code, code generation, and programming language testing and debugging. These tools make it easy for the developer to build a library of a common, standard set of code that can easily be used in multiple applications.

Reengineering: The management process of redesigning business processes in a relatively radical manner. Reengineering traditionally meant taking a "blank piece of paper" and designing (then building) a business process from the beginning. This was intended to help the designers eliminate any blocks or barriers that the current process or environment might provide. This process is sometimes called BPR, Business Process Redesign or Reengineering or Business Reengineering.

Remote Work (Working Remotely): Refers to work performed from home, at a customer site, or from other convenient locations instead of coming into the company office; sometimes called telecommuting or teleworking.

Remote Workers: Refers to employees working from home, at a customer site, or from other convenient locations instead of coming into the employing company office. The broad term encompassing teleworkers, telecommuters, and mobile workers.

Resilience: Ability of an organization to rapidly regain its ability to operate after a cyber-attack.

Resource-Based View (RBV): A theoretical perspective that attaining and sustaining competitive advantage comes from creating value using information and other resources of the firm.

Return on Investment (ROI): Valuation method that calculates the percentage rate that measures the relationship between the amount the business gets back from an investment and the amount invested.

Review Board: Committee that is formally designated to approve, monitor, and review specific topics.

Reuse: Relatively small chunks of functionality are available for many applications.

Risk: Perceived as the possibility of additional cost or loss due to the choice of an alternative.

Robot: A reprogrammable, multifunctional manipulator designed to move material, parts, tools, or specialized devices through variable programmed motions for the performance of tasks.

Robotic Process Automation (RPA): Refers to configuring the software so that software agents (robots) do process-oriented work previously done by people; uses rules to process structured data to produce deterministic outcomes.

RSS or Really Simple Syndication (also called web feeds): Refers to a structured file format for porting data from one platform or information system to another.

SAP: The company that produces the leading ERP software. The software, technically named "SAP R/3," is often simply referred to as SAP.

Sarbanes–Oxley (SoX) Act of 2002: United States Act to increase regulatory visibility and accountability of public companies and their financial health.

Scalability: Refers to how well an infrastructure component can adapt to increased, or in some cases decreased, demands.

SDLC (Systems Development Life Cycle): The process of designing and delivering the entire system. SDLC usually means these seven phases: initiation of the project, requirements definition phase, functional design phase, technical design and construction phase, verification phase, implementation phase, and maintenance and review phase; Sometimes called waterfall approach.

Selective Outsourcing (Strategic Sourcing): The situation when an enterprise chooses which IT capabilities to retain in-house and which to give to an outsider.

Sentiment Analysis: Type of analytics that uses algorithms to analyze text to extract subjective information such as emotional statements, preferences, likes/dislikes.

Server-Based Architecture: A decentralized architecture that uses numerous servers, often located in different physical locations. A server is a software program or computer intended to provide data and/or instructions to another software program or computer. The hardware that a server program runs is often also referred to as "the server."

Service-Level Agreement (or SLA): Formal service contract between clients and outsourcing providers that describes level of service including delivery time and expected service performance.

Service-Oriented Architecture (SOA): This is the term used to describe the architecture where business processes are built using services delivered over a network (typically the Internet). Services are software that are distinct units of business functionality residing on different parts of a network and can be combined and reused to create business applications.

SETA (Security Education/Training/Awareness): Training to make business users aware of security policies and practices and to build a security-conscious culture.

Six Sigma: An incremental data-driven approach to quality management for eliminating defects from a process. The term "Six Sigma" comes from the idea that if the quality of all output from a process were to be mapped on a bell-shaped curve, the tail of the curve, six sigma from the mean, would be where there were less than 3.4 defects per million.

Social Contract Theory: A theory used in business ethics to describe how managers act. The social responsibilities of corporate managers by considering the needs of a society with no corporations or other complex business arrangements. Social contract theorists ask what conditions would have to be met for the members of such a society to agree to allow a corporation to be formed. Thus, society bestows legal recognition on a corporation to allow it to employ social resources toward given ends.

Social Media Analytics: A class of tools to measure the impact of social IT investments (i.e., tweets, blogs, Facebook, etc.) on the business.

Social Media Management: Type of security policy that provides rules about what can be disclosed on social media, such as who can Tweet and how employees can identify themselves.

Social Network (SN): An IT-enabled network that links individuals together in ways that enable them to find experts, get to know colleagues, and see who has relevant experience for projects across traditional organization lines; Also, a network of social interactions and personal relationships.

SMACIT: An acronym for the powerful, readily accessible digital technologies social media, mobile, analytics, cloud, and Internet of Things.

Social Networking Site (SNS): A networked communication platform in which participants (1) have uniquely identifiable profiles that consist of user-supplied content, content provided by other users, and/or system-provided data; (2) can publicly articulate connections that can be viewed and traversed by others; and (3) can consume, produce, and/or interact with streams of user-generated content provided by their connections on the site; Examples are Renren, Facebook, and LinkedIn.

Socialization: Mode of knowledge conversion from tacit knowledge to tacit knowledge using the process of sharing experiences; it occurs through observation, imitation, and practice.

Software-as-a-Service (SaaS): This term is used to describe a model of software deployment that uses the web to deliver applications on an "as-needed" basis. Often when software is delivered as a service, it runs on a computer on the Internet, rather than on the customer's computer, and is accessed through a web browser.

Software-Defined Architecture: Type of configuration that can allocate or remove resources automatically based on traffic or other indicators of utilization.

Spear Phishing: A more advanced version of phishing attacks; highlights the targeted nature of the attack by mimicking a situation or relationship highly familiar to the targeted user.

Spoofing: Security breach in which a hacker counterfeits an Internet address.

Stakeholder Theory: A theory used in business ethics to describe how managers act. This theory suggests that managers, although bound by their relation to stockholders, are entrusted also with a fiduciary responsibility to all those who hold a stake in or a claim on the firm, including employees, customers, vendors, neighbors, and so forth.

Standard: Technical specifications that will be followed throughout the infrastructure. Often standards are agreed on for development processes, technology, methods, practices, and software.

Steering Committee: IT governance mechanism that calls for joint participation of IT and business leaders in making decisions about IT as a group.

Stockholder Theory: A theory used in business ethics to describe how managers act. Stockholders advance capital to corporate managers who act as agents in advancing their ends. The nature of this contract binds managers to act in the interest of the shareholders (i.e., to maximize shareholder value).

Strategic Alliance: An interorganizational relationship that affords one or more companies in the relationship a strategic advantage.

Strategic Network: A long-term, purposeful arrangement by which companies set up a web of close relationships that form a veritable system geared to providing product or services in a coordinated way.

Strategy: A coordinated set of actions to fulfill objectives, purposes, and goals.

Structured Data: Facts that are clear and easily categorized when stored in databases or used.

Supply Chain Management (SCM) System: System that manages the integrated supply chain; processes are linked across companies with a companion process at a customer or supplier.

Synchronized Planning: Partners agree on a joint design of planning, forecasting, replenishment, and what to do with the information.

System Software: Software such as Microsoft Windows, Apple OSX, and Linux that provides instructions to the hardware.

Tacit Knowledge: Personal, context-specific, and hard to formalize and communicate. It consists of experiences, beliefs, and skills. Tacit knowledge is entirely subjective and is often acquired through physically practicing a skill or activity. (See Explicit Knowledge.)

Tagging: Process in which users themselves list key words that codify the information or document at hand, creates an ad-hoc codification system, sometimes referred to as a folksonomy.

Technology-Mediated Control (TMC): The use of technology in managerial control processes.

Telecommuting (also called teleworking): Combining telecommunications with commuting. This term usually means individuals who regularly work from home instead of commuting into an office.

TOGAF (also called The Open Group Architecture Framework): Includes a methodology and set of resources for developing an enterprise architecture based on the idea of an open architecture, an architecture whose specifications are public (as compared to a proprietary architecture, where specifications are not made public).

Token: Small electronic device that generates a new supplementary passkey at frequent intervals.

Total Cost of Ownership (TCO): Costing method that looks beyond initial capital investments to include costs associated with technical support, administration, training, and system retirement and so on.

Total Quality Management (TQM): A management philosophy in which quality metrics drive performance evaluation of people, processes, and decisions. The objective of TQM is to continually, and often incrementally, improve the activities of the business toward the goal of eliminating defects (zero defects) and producing the highest quality outputs possible.

Unified Communications (UC): An evolving communications technology architecture that automates and unifies all forms of human and device communications in context and with a common experience.

Unstructured Data: Facts that are embedded (i.e., in blogs, tweets, conversations) that have to be extracted before they can become useful information; facts are not easily categorized.

User-Centered Design: Development approach that makes use of tools for RAD, JAD, agile development, and prototyping to provide assurance that users' needs are met efficiently and responsively.

Utility Computing: Purchasing entire computing capability on an as-needed basis.

Value: Reflects the community's aspirations about the way things should be done.

Value Architecture: Business model dimension focused on the configuration of core resources and capabilities that a firm needs to create its market offerings.

Value Finance: Business model dimension primarily focused on a firm's revenue model, pricing strategies, and cost structure.

Value Net: The set of players in a co-opetitive environment. It includes a company and its competitors and complementors, as well as their customers and suppliers, and the interactions among all of them. (See Complementor.)

Value Network: Business model dimension that involves interfirm relationships and interactions with key external partners and stakeholders.

Value Proposition: Business model dimension focused on a firm's market offerings and targeted customer group(s).

Video Teleconference (also called videoconference): A set of interactive telecommunication technologies that allow two or more locations to interact via two-way video and audio transmissions simultaneously.

Virtual Private Network (VPN): A private network that uses a public network such as the Internet to connect remote sites or users. It maintains privacy through the use of a tunneling protocol and security procedures.

Virtual Team: Two or more people who (1) work together interdependently with mutual accountability for achieving common goals, (2) do not work in either the same place and/or at the same time, and (3) must use electronic communication technology to communicate, coordinate their activities, and complete their team's tasks.

Virtual World: A computer-based simulated environment intended for its users to inhabit and interact via avatars.

Virtualization: Allows a computer to run multiple operating systems or several versions of the same operating system at the same time; virtual infrastructure where software replaced hardware in a way that a "virtual machine" or a "virtual desktop system" was accessible to provide computing power.

Weak Password: A password such as "123456," which is easy to guess.

Web-Based Architecture: Architecture in which significant hardware, software, and possibly even data elements reside on the Internet.

Web Logs (blogs): Online journals that link together into a very large network of information sharing.

Web Services: The software systems that are offered over the Internet and executed on a third party's hardware. Often web services refer to a more fundamental software that uses XML messages and follow SOAP (simple object access protocol) standards.

White Hat Hackers: Hackers who break into a firm's systems to help them uncover weaknesses.

Wiki: Software that allows users to work collaboratively to create, edit, and link web pages easily.

Wireless (mobile) Infrastructure: Infrastructure that allows communication from remote locations using a variety of wireless technologies (e.g., fixed microwave links, wireless LANs, data over cellular networks, wireless WANs, satellite links, digital dispatch networks, one-way and two-way paging networks, diffuse infrared, laser-based communications, keyless car entry, and global positioning systems).

Wisdom: Knowledge fused with intuition, judgment, insights, and empathy that facilitates decision making, often with a long-term perspective.

Workflow: Describes activities that take place in a business process.

Workflow Diagram: A picture, or map, of the sequence and detail of each process step.

Zachman Framework: Enterprise architecture that determines architectural requirements by providing a broad view that helps guide the analysis of the detailed view.

Zero Day Threat: Brand-new outbreaks of a security problem.

Zero Time Organization: An organization designed around responding instantly to customers, employees, suppliers, and other stakeholder demands.

INDEX

Q

R